D1233528

FROM ALEXANDER
TO CONSTANTINE

Oxford University Press, Amen House, London E.C.4

GLASGOW NEW YORK TORONTO MELBOURNE WELLINGTON
BOMBAY CALCUTTA MADRAS KARACHI CAPE TOWN IBADAN

Geoffrey Cumberlege, Publisher to the University

FROM ALEXANDER
TO CONSTANTINE

Passages and Documents Illustrating
the History of Social and Political Ideas
336 B.C.–A.D. 337

TRANSLATED WITH
INTRODUCTIONS, NOTES, AND ESSAYS

BY

ERNEST BARKER

HONORARY FELLOW OF MERTON COLLEGE, OXFORD
AND OF PETERHOUSE, CAMBRIDGE

OXFORD
AT THE CLARENDON PRESS
1956

PRINTED IN GREAT BRITAIN

PREFACE

Two causes have moved me to attempt this book—one immediate; the other of a more distant origin. The immediate cause is some work which I did, in recent years, as one of the editors of *The European Inheritance*, a general study of European history illustrated in each of its parts by a number of contemporary documents. I was impressed by the documents which were selected by the different contributors to that study, and not least by those selected by Sir W. W. Tarn for the part entitled 'Greece and Rome'. It occurred to me that a useful employment of my old age might be the collection of a series of documents to illustrate the social and political ideas of the six hundred years that lie between the career of Alexander and the conversion of Constantine. When that idea had entered my mind I found encouragement in a sentence at the end of Professor Momigliano's inaugural lecture delivered at University College, London, in 1952: 'A history of Greek political theories after Aristotle . . . is still to be written: the continuity in political . . . thought has often been postulated; it has never been described.' Could I make some contribution to that history, and might I perhaps attempt to illustrate that continuity? Could I build a bridge—or rather lay stepping-stones (for this book is really of the nature of stepping-stones rather than a bridge)—across the six centuries of time between the emergence of the Hellenistic world of great states and solemn kings and the appearance of that Christian world of Church and State in which we still live and have our being?

Here a more distant cause came into operation, and finally impelled me to make the attempt. As long ago as 1899 I had started work on a book which was eventually published in 1906 under the title of *The Political Thought of Plato and Aristotle*. The book went out of print; and in 1918 there was published what was intended to be the first volume of a new edition, under the new title of *Greek Political Theory: Plato and his Predecessors*, with a promise in the preface (or a hope, if not a promise) that it would be followed by a second volume to be entitled *Aristotle and his Successors*. That second volume was never written. Instead of attempting it, I found myself led, by imperceptible steps (after some years of diversion from any scholarly work), to a translation of the *Politics* of Aristotle, with an introduction, notes, and appendixes; and that work was eventually published in 1946. I had thus made my offering to Aristotle—not in a book about his *Politics*, but in a version and explanation of its actual text. But what of 'his Successors'? Would it not be best, I began to wonder, if I followed the same path in dealing with them that I had followed in dealing with Aristotle himself, and if I attempted a series of translations, with introductions and notes, and with some explanatory essays, which might throw light on the development of social and political thought in the general course of ancient history after the time of Aristotle? I answered the question in the affirmative; and thus the result of my wanderings (which were unintended and seemed haphazard, and yet were not, after all, without some sort of a plan which has somehow been always there) is that the second volume projected in 1918 has now become two separate but connected volumes—the 1946 volume on the *Politics* of Aristotle, and this 1956 volume on the period *From Alexander to Constantine*. I have to confess that it has taken me more than half a century to complete the work to which I first set my hand in 1899; and it has been completed in a different way, and by a different method, from what I had originally in mind. But in some sense the work has been done, and the monument (such as it is) built; and I am tempted to say to myself, *Finis coronat opus*. At any rate I may say, *Explicit*.

The present volume is what may be called a *florilegium* or anthology. As I worked on it, it fell naturally (or so I thought) into five parts—a Hellenistic part down to 150 B.C.; a Hellenistic-Jewish part from about 200 B.C. to the middle of the first century A.D.; a Latin part from 100 B.C. to A.D. 100; a Late Greek part covering the period in which Greece and Greek thought were included in the Latin empire of Rome; and a fifth and last part concerned with the development of Christian thought on social and political problems from the middle of the first century A.D.

to the middle of the fourth. The anthology which I have collected[1] is thus mixed and various: it is based on Greek (particularly
Greek) and on Latin, Jewish, and Christian writings; it includes
passages drawn not only from the works of writers on politics,
but also from those of philosophers, poets, historians, lawyers,
and theologians. (Not that I am versed in these fields—I wish I
were—but I could not help peeping over the fences around them,
and even climbing over to pick some flowers, in a spirit of
pardonable curiosity.) I may be criticized, and indeed I have
criticized myself, for gathering so large and varied a flora and
filling my collector's basket so full. Ought I to have dealt at such
length with Stoicism, or to have translated so much of the philosophy of the Pseudo-Aristotelian treatise *De Mundo*, or to have
sought to include in my scope the Neoplatonism of Plotinus?
Were these high themes—and other similar themes such as the
general conceptions of the Roman jurists and the development of
the thought of the Christian Church—germane to my enterprise?
I could not but conclude, when I looked into the matter, that they
were not only germane, but even essential. It is impossible to
understand the social and political ideas of the ancient world apart
from Stoicism, or apart from Roman law, or apart from Christian
thought—or even apart from Neoplatonism; for is not the fact that
Plotinus preferred to think of the flight of the Alone to the Alone,
and had no attention to give to social and political life, itself a fact
of the first importance in the history of social and political ideas?

There is still another sense in which this volume is mixed and
various. It is in part composed of translations and in part of
introductions and essays—not to speak of a number of notes.
Ought I to have intruded my own comments and explanations so
much on the *ipsi dixerunt* of the authors whom I have translated,
and may not the reader be confused between the text and the commentary? I can only reply that besides assembling stones—to
revert to that metaphor—I had also to provide some sort of
mortar (though my readers may tell me that stepping-stones need

[1] Plutarch (*Moralia* 93 D), quoting from a lost play of Euripides, speaks of 'the
nursling of Hypsipyle' as sitting in a meadow and 'culling one after another a
spoil of flowers with a happy heart'. That has been my experience in the course
of collecting this anthology.

no mortar, and I must confess that I am changing my metaphors in mid-stream); in other words, I had to give some sort of continuity to the book and to suggest some sort of a plan for the building I was seeking to erect. Kingship and federalism, for instance, could both be illustrated from ancient writers and from recorded inscriptions; but both of these subjects needed—or so I thought—some general exposition to give the documents cohesion and to establish their connexion. Besides—to make a frank confession—there were things I had learned in a life of reading which I wanted to say, and which, I ventured to hope, would be of some interest and even help to my readers.

I have two acknowledgements which I am anxious to make: one to the scholars whose work or advice has guided me, and one to an institution (the Cambridge University Library) without which this book could never have been begun, far less brought to completion. Among the scholars whose books have been my constant resource I would first of all mention Sir W. W. Tarn, and especially his *Alexander the Great* and his *Hellenistic Civilisation*. He is the doyen of all of us who seek to work in these fields; and I render him my affectionate homage as well as my sincere thanks. I must also mention with gratitude the help I received in the past from the late Sir John Myres (it was he who advised me not to stop, as I had originally intended, at the end of the reign of Marcus Aurelius, but to continue down to the reign of Constantine); and I owe a deep debt, among the living, to Mr. C. H. Roberts of St. John's College, Oxford, and (through him) to Mr. P. M. Fraser of All Souls College, for help and advice about papyri and inscriptions. Professor C. H. Dodd has helped me with advice in Part V; and I also owe a debt to the Rev. H. M. Chadwick, of Queens' College, Cambridge, for help in the section of that part which deals with Origen. In the section of Part I which deals with Greek federalism I have learned much and received generous help from Professor Larsen of the University of Chicago; and Mr. G. T. Griffith, of Gonville and Caius College, Cambridge, has also helped me, in selecting inscriptions and tracing references, in some of the sections of that part. Indeed it is one of the delights of attempting a work of this nature that scholars leap to one's aid; and I have a feeling, as I look back, that not I but a company of scholars (some by their writings and some by their advice) have been its author. Let me add, in conclusion of these acknowledgements, that among the books which have been my guides the volumes of Hans Lietzmann on the history of the Christian Church down to the age of Constantine have been of the greatest service; and I have also learned much, especially in the Latin part, from C. N. Cochrane's book (to which Sir John Myres drew my attention) on *Christianity and Classical Culture.*

So far of my debt to scholars and their books. But I should be ungrateful if I did not also acknowledge my debt to the Cambridge University Library. To have the run of its open shelves, and to be able to borrow and take home for use in my study the various books I have used, has been a privilege of the first order. I have had to consult a large number of texts of ancient authors, several volumes of inscriptions, and many works by modern writers. I have never needed a book which I could not find and borrow in the University Library—unless it were a book on Roman Law which had been transferred to the custody of the departmental Law Library, and even then the book I needed could readily be had for the asking. I have come to feel that I ought to dedicate this volume to the Librarian of the University Library and his assistants, whom I have learned to regard as my friends. It may be a novelty, and perhaps an embarrassment, to dedicate a book to a University Library . . . it will get there anyhow under the Copyright Act . . . but I have ventured to risk the novelty.

Before I end this Preface, which I confess has run to some length (perhaps owing to the garrulity of age), I should like to turn back to a word I used in the beginning—the word 'stepping-stones'. This book is not a bridge: it is a preparation for a bridge. My hope is that it may lead to a stronger and more permanent structure. I dream of a second edition when I am gone. I hope (not in vanity, but rather, I venture to think, in modesty) that somebody may arise from my ashes (*exoriare aliquis nostris ex ossibus auctor*) who will correct and prune, and, it may be, also amplify and extend, the work I have here begun.

And now I say 'Farewell'. As I do so I am tempted to quote some words from the preface to Pennant's *London*, in the edition of 1790: 'I feel within myself a certain monitor, that warns me to hang up my pen in time, before its powers are weakened and visibly impaired. . . . I take leave of a partial public with the truest gratitude for its long endurance.'

E. B.

Cambridge,
November 1954

CONTENTS

PART II

HELLENISTIC-JEWISH THOUGHT 200 B.C.–A.D. 50

PART IV

LATER GREEK THOUGHT: FROM POSIDONIUS
TO THEMISTIUS

PART V

THE SOCIAL AND POLITICAL IDEAS OF THE CHRISTIAN CHURCH DOWN TO THE AGE OF CONSTANTINE

NOTES FOR THE READER

1. The texts followed in the translations are as a rule those of the Oxford Classical Texts, the Loeb Classical Library, the Budé collection, and the Teubner series; and where the text which I have followed is not in one of these collections, the edition used is specified in the index of authors at the end of this volume. Except where it is otherwise stated, I have made my own translations; this has perhaps the benefit of uniformity of style and method. I hope the translations are accurate; I have done my best to make them clear.

2. The use of quotation marks to enclose the passages of translation may help the reader to distinguish between the original texts translated and the translator's own interpretative comments and summaries. (Some few passages have been summarized, and printed without quotation marks, where a translation of the full text was unnecessary or irrelevant but where some indication of the argument of the passage was necessary in order to preserve continuity.)

3. Passages in square brackets represent words inserted in the translation to elucidate the meaning of the original. Words in round brackets are intended either to give the original word (or words) of the text where it seemed important to do so, or to give a date or a reference or some other information of that order.

PART I

THE HELLENISTIC PERIOD
(334–146 B.C.)

INTRODUCTION

THERE is no need for more than a few words of introduction, and explanation, of the documents which follow in this Part. The ideas and ideals of Alexander; the doctrines of Stoicism; Plutarch's story of the careers of the reforming Spartan kings Agis IV and Cleomenes III; the political theories and maxims of Polybius—all these, or most of these, are familiar to English scholars. It is true that the Hellenistic period of history, which extends from the conquests of Alexander (334–323) to the Roman annexation of Greece (146), has left fewer monuments of literature than the Hellenic, or Attic, period by which it was preceded, or the Roman and Latin period by which it was succeeded. But it was none the less a seminal period; and the seeds of thought which it sowed—not least the seed of Stoic philosophy—continued to grow for centuries. The joint influence of Alexander and Zeno, making for the idea of a world-order, is not yet dead; and it will continue to live as long as men continue to dream of the reign of a universal fraternity (or, as Alexander called it, *homonoia*) of which they both were the prophets. The theory of kingship which was developed during the reigns of the successors of Alexander is another influence which still survives; indeed there is a continuous doctrine of monarchy, originally expounded in the many Greek treatises written in successive centuries on the theme 'Of Kingship', which runs through the history of the Roman Empire, survived during the thousand years of the Byzantine Empire of the East, was still vigorously championed by defenders of the cause of monarchy and divine right in the days of the Stuarts, and may even be traced today in theories of the office and function of the modern British sovereign as a magnet of allegiance and a symbol of association for the general body of nations which we call 'the Commonwealth'.

But if a theory of monarchy was thus developed during the Hellenistic period—mainly across the Aegean Sea, in the lands of western Asia and in the Egypt of the Ptolemies—a practice of federalism was also developed on the Greek mainland, mainly by the Achaean League in the south but also by the Aetolian League in the north, which was also destined to a long, though sadly interrupted, history. Submerged after 146 B.C. by the might and majesty of Rome, and disappearing for more than a thousand years, it reappeared during the Middle Ages (in the Lombard League of the twelfth century and the Swiss Confederation of the thirteenth and fourteenth); and from 1787 onwards, with the foundation of the federal constitution of the United States of America and the general growth of federal institutions during the nineteenth and twentieth centuries, it has established itself as a great and permanent element of political life and ideas in every continent. Little if any Greek literature dealing with the nature and practice of federalism has come down to us; but the Greek idea of federation is none the less part of our tradition, and the authors of the *Federalist* appealed to the legacy and precedent of the Achaean League.[1]

Here are many seeds, or, as a Stoic might have called them, *spermatikoi logoi*, 'seminal ideas'. They are all expressed in the Greek language: Latin did not become a language of thought and the expression of thought—or at any rate of thought and the expression of thought which has endured—till the beginning of the first century B.C. The period covered by this part is thus a Greek period. But it is proper to add at once that it is not the only Greek period in the course of the six shifting centuries with which this work is concerned. Latin indeed climbed the throne, and wore the crown, for two of those centuries (100 B.C. to A.D. 100); but at the end of the Latin period, which came with the reign of the Emperor Hadrian, a second Greek period followed, and that period runs from Epictetus and Dio Chrysostom to Plotinus and the great Greek theologians of Alexandria and the East. There is a see-saw between East and West in the development of social and political ideas during these six centuries. But the general tilt

---

[1] Especially in No. xviii, written by Hamilton and Madison.

of the balance inclines on the whole to the East. It inclines all the more when we remember to throw into the balance the Jewish–Hellenistic thought and literature of the period between the composition of the 'visions' of the Book of Daniel (*circa* 165 B.C.) and the conclusion of the voluminous writings of the Alexandrine Jew Philo (A.D. 50). For even during the centuries in which Latin was triumphant, the Greek genius of expression could still combine with the Jewish passion for apocalyptic and allegory to produce new monuments which attest the power and the subtlety of the language of Greece.

§ I. THE IDEAS AND IDEALS OF ALEXANDER

[In all this section I am largely indebted to Sir W. W. Tarn's *Alexander the Great*, vol. ii, and especially to Appendix 25, on 'Brotherhood and Unity', and Appendix 22, on 'Alexander's Deification'.]

Preliminary Note on the Sources for the History of Alexander

Arrian's preface, at the beginning of his *Anabasis Alexandri*, is translated here for its touch of humour (perhaps unconscious) and for the light which it throws on the sources for the history of Alexander. Arrian himself wrote his work about the middle of the second century A.D., nearly five centuries after the death of Alexander. He possibly had at his command material now lost to us, and he was certainly a competent soldier, with an experience of affairs which enabled him to use his sources with judgement. But it illustrates the difficulty of interpreting the career and ideas of Alexander that our chief authority should be a soldier of the Roman Empire who was almost as far removed from Alexander in time as we are today from King Henry V. (Plutarch's Life of Alexander and his treatise *De Fortuna aut Virtute Alexandri* are hardly any earlier than the *Anabasis* of Arrian; and though the ten books of Quintus Curtius' history of Alexander are about a century earlier than Arrian's *Anabasis*, they are of less value.)

'Wherever Ptolemy the son of Lagus [Ptolemy I, a writer of history as well as a king] and Aristobulus [a Greek technician in Alexander's army] have given the same account of the career of Alexander, I record what they say as altogether accurate: where they give different accounts, I have preferred the one which seemed to me the more credible and the more worth recounting. Different writers have given different accounts of Alexander: indeed there is no man whose career has been described by more writers—or by writers more discrepant with one another. In my view Ptolemy and Aristobulus give the more credible accounts: Aristobulus served with King Alexander; Ptolemy not only served with him, but he was also a king himself, and it would have been more disgraceful for him than for anybody else not to tell the truth.[1] Both of them are the more to be trusted as they wrote after the death of Alexander, and were under no necessity or inducement to set down anything otherwise than as it actually happened. But I have also recorded some of the details given by other writers about Alexander—but only as 'hearsay' (*legomena*)—because they seemed to me worth recounting, and not wholly incredible. . . .'

A. *Alexander's Views on Human Concord* (Homonoia)

1. *Arrian's account of the scene at Opis, 324*

In 324 B.C., at Opis on the river Tigris, Alexander had to face an incipient mutiny among his Macedonian soldiers. They had already been made discontented by the policy which he had followed towards the conquered Persians—by his admission of Persian nobles to the *agēma* or infantry 'Guard' round his person; by his enrolment of Asiatics in the two 'crack' regiments of cavalry[2] (the 'Companions', originally drawn from the Macedonian upper classes); and by his wearing of Persian dress. When, in addition, he proposed to send home the Macedonian veterans who were past service, they suspected that this was a move towards further dilution of their ranks, and they countered it by a

---

[1] This remarks seems humorous, and even naïve; but as Mr. Griffith of Caius College suggests to me, it would seem much less curious in those days of solemn treatises 'On Kingship' than it does today.

[2] It is a curious parallel that in the English New Model Army of the Civil Wars Cromwell's 'Ironsides', originally a single regiment of horse, came ultimately to form the two 'crack' cavalry regiments, just as Alexander's 'Companions', originally one body of horsemen, were reorganized in two 'hipparchies' about 330 B.C.

demand that they should *all* be allowed to return to Macedonia.
Alexander, in a passion, bade them all go if they wished; and he
then proceeded to distribute military commands among the
Persians. The Macedonian soldiers, thus taken at their word, fell
into a revulsion of feeling: and there followed a scene of entreaty,
pardon, and reconciliation which is an epoch in the relations of
'Greeks and barbarians' and a landmark of progress in the movement of the age towards human equality and general fraternity.

'The Macedonian troops ran towards the palace; they piled
their arms before the gates, in token of supplication to their king,
and standing there in person they cried aloud for permission to
enter; they were ready, they said, to surrender the authors of the
trouble and those who had begun the outcry; they would not
leave the gates, either by day or by night, until he had mercy upon
them. When Alexander heard of this, he hurried out of the palace;
and seeing the men so humbly disposed, and hearing so many of
them crying aloud with a voice of lamentation, he was moved to
tears himself. He came forward as if to speak: they continued their
entreaties. Then one of them, a man distinguished both by his age
and by his service in one of the cavalry regiments of "the Companions"—Callines by name—said to him, "This, Sire, is what
grieves us Macedonians: you have already made some of the
Persians 'kinsmen' to yourself; there are Persians who are called
'Alexander's kinsmen', and they give you a kiss; but none of us
Macedonians has ever yet tasted this honour." Thereupon
Alexander broke in and said, "But I count *all* of you as my
kinsmen, and from this day forth I shall call you so." When he
had said this, Callines went up to him and gave him a kiss; and so
did any other man who wished. So they shouldered their arms
again, and went back shouting and singing in triumph to their
camp. Thereupon Alexander offered sacrifice to the gods to whom
he was accustomed to sacrifice, and afterwards made a public
feast, sitting himself in person at the table, with all the Macedonians seated round him and the Persians next to them, and after
the Persians men of the other races who were pre-eminent in
reputation or in any other respect. At this feast Alexander and his

fellows dipped their cups in the same bowl of wine and made the same drink-offerings, with the seers of the Greeks and the Magi [of Persia] taking the lead. As they did so, Alexander prayed for blessings, and especially for the blessing of human concord (*Homonoia*) and of fellowship in the realm (*Koinōnia tēs archēs*) between Macedonians and Greeks. The story goes that those who partook of the feast amounted to nine thousand men, and that all of them made the same drink-offering and thereupon sang in triumph [together].' (From Arrian, *Anabasis Alexandri*, book VII, c. xi, §§ 4–9.)

2. *Plutarch's account of the policy and achievement of Alexander*

In the passages which follow Plutarch brings the ideas of Alexander into relation with the teaching of Aristotle and the doctrine of Zeno, the founder of Stoicism. A passage from the writer's introduction to his translation of Aristotle's *Politics* (pp. lix–lx) may throw some light on this relation.

'The Aristotelian theory of man's natural citizenship of the *polis* . . . was a theory which . . . was peculiar to an inner Mediterranean world of "urbanity", and in no way designed for the outer world of the nations (or *ethnē*) immersed in the "rurality" of barbarism. Aristotle would have preserved the distinction of the two worlds: he advised Alexander . . . to distinguish between Greeks and barbarians, dealing with the former as a leader or *hēgemōn*, and with the latter as a master or *despotēs*. Alexander did the opposite. He preferred to act in the spirit of the policy afterwards enunciated by Eratosthenes [an Alexandrian scholar of the next century] who, "refused to agree with those who divided men into Greeks and barbarians and who advised Alexander to treat the former as friends and the latter as foes—holding that it was better to divide men simply into the good and bad". By 330 B.C., while Aristotle was still teaching the theory of the *polis* in the Lyceum, Alexander was already planning an empire in which he should be equally lord of Greeks and Persians, and both should be equally knit together by intermarriage and common military service. This meant a great revolution. It meant the appearance of the *cosmopolis*[1] or world-state in place and instead of the *polis* or city-state. It meant the appearance of the idea of the equality of all men—urban or rural, Greek or barbarian—in that *cosmopolis*. Alexander anticipates in action, as Plutarch long afterwards wrote, what Zeno and the Stoics were soon to be teaching in theory. . . . This conception of the *cosmopolis*, and the cognate conception of the equality and fraternity of all men within its general embrace, are the two fundamental conceptions which inaugurate a new epoch—an epoch which succeeds to that of the *polis*, as it precedes that of the national state: an epoch which covers the eighteen centuries from 300 B.C. to A.D. 1500, . . . and which embraces in its scope the three empires of Macedon, Rome, and Charlemagne. First Stoicism and then Christianity—inheriting and transfiguring the teaching of Stoicism—was the vehicle of these conceptions. If Zeno believed in one city of all men, St. Paul believed in one Church of all Christians . . . and he held that in that Church there was "neither Greek nor Jew, . . . Barbarian, Scythian, bond nor free".'

A question which arises about this 'great revolution', with its new fundamental conceptions, is whether it proceeded from Alexander the man of action or from Zeno the man of theory. In point of time the verdict must go in favour of Alexander: his idea—and his acts—are already there, and fully fledged, by 324 B.C.: Zeno began to teach in Athens in 301 B.C. But Alexander's ideas might not have gone so far or so deep, if similar ideas had not been afterwards adopted by the Stoics and incorporated in their general system of philosophic thought.

(1) 'The much admired polity[2] of Zeno, the founder of the Stoic School, is directed to this one main point, that we should not live in city-states (*poleis*) and their parishes (*dēmoi*), each separated by its peculiar system of justice (*idia dikaia*), but should regard *all* men as fellow-parishioners and fellow-citizens; and there should be one way of life and one system of order (*cosmos*),

[1] The word *cosmopolis* is here used, perhaps loosely, as a shorthand word to denote the great society and the great state—not, indeed, a 'world-state' in point of geography—which henceforth overshadows and proceeds to absorb the *polis*.
[2] By the word 'polity' (*polīteiā*) Plutarch refers not to Zeno's early treatise called by that name, but rather to his general system of political ideas, as it was developed in his later years. See Section II on Stoicism.

as it were of one flock on a common pasture feeding together under a common law (*nomos*).[1] Zeno wrote this as one imagining a dream or mental picture of a system of law and polity based on philosophy: Alexander added act and deed (*ergon*) to the principle (*logos*) of Zeno. He did not, as Aristotle advised him, treat the Greeks in the spirit of a leader and the barbarians in that of a master, or cultivate the Greeks as friends and members of a family and behave to the barbarians as if they were animals or plants, thus filling the days of his leadership with a multitude of wars and exiles and with festering factions: rather he believed that he had a mission from God to harmonize men generally, and to be the reconciler of the world. He drew men together by the appeal of principle (*logos*), and not by force of arms. Bringing them, from every quarter, into a unity, and mixing, as in a loving-cup, their ways of life and their customs, their marriages and their social habits, he bade them all consider the whole of the inhabited world (*oikoumenē*) as their country, to regard the army as their citadel (*acropolis*) and garrison, and look on good men as their kinsmen and the bad as foreigners.' (From Plutarch, *De Alexandri Fortuna aut Virtute*, i, c. 6. 329 A–C.)

(2) 'Alexander did not overrun Asia in the spirit of a brigand, or as if it were a booty and the spoils of war. . . . He wished to show that all things on earth were subject to one principle (*logos*) and included in one polity (*polīteiā*), and that all men were one people; and he demeaned himself accordingly. If the power that sent into the world the soul of Alexander had not quickly recalled it, one law would have governed all men, and they would have turned their gaze to one system of justice as though to a common light. But as it happened, that part of the world which never saw Alexander remained in the dark.

'Thus the underlying idea of his expedition shows Alexander as a philosopher, whose purpose it was to secure for all men concord (*Homonoia*), and to give them peace and communion with one another, but not to gain for himself the means of extravagance and luxury' (ibid. i, c. 8. 330 D–E).

[1] There is here a double play on words in the Greek. 'Cosmos' has the double sense of *order* and *universe*: 'nomos' has equally the double sense of *pasture* and *law*.

B. *Alexander and the Deification of the Ruler*

The deification of the ruler—serving in the issue, if not originally intended, as the cement of a great State, in virtue of its power of holding together in the common 'adoration' of a single king many 'cities' and many 'nations' (*ethnē*)—is a prominent feature in the Hellenistic kingdoms, and after them in the Roman Empire. It has its connexion with Alexander's views on human concord; but in his thought it would seem to have come second to that great and primary aim. The actual deification of Alexander may already be traced among the Ionian Greeks in the beginning of his campaign, before he reached Egypt or Persia; it was a thing natural to the Greeks, who, as they conceived gods in the likeness of men, were ready also to elevate men to the rank of gods. But Egyptian and Persian influences may well have accentuated the trend in the further course of his 'anabasis'. The Egyptian kings were regarded, if not as gods in themselves, at any rate as incarnations or the off-spring of the god Ammon or Re: the Persian kings claimed adora-tion in virtue of the *Hvarenô*, a nimbus 'conceived . . . as emanating from the sun, but also as a token of supernatural grace'.[1] It was in the Hellenistic kingdoms of the East that the deification and adoration of the ruler ultimately became—what it had never been formally made by Alexander himself—an institution of State. Alexander was deified by the first Ptolemy in 305 B.C.: the Ptolemies themselves became the objects of a cult, and were worshipped as 'Gods': the first two Seleucids were canonized only after death, but Antiochus II was already a 'God' during his life.

1. *Arrian's and Plutarch's accounts of Alexander's visit to the Priest of Ammon in the oasis of Siwah (332 B.C.)*

'After this [he had, according to one account, just been crowned Pharaoh in Egypt, and as such had become, in Egyptian belief,

---

[1] H. Stuart Jones, *The Roman Empire*, p. 217. E. R. Goodenough, in a paper in *Yale Classical Studies*, vol. i, p. 78, referring to 'the divine kingly glory made by Mazda [the supreme god Ahura Mazda] which shone upon true kings', quotes a passage from the *Avesta*: 'It clave unto King Vîstâspa, so that he thought accord-ing to the Law, spoke according to the Law, and did according to the Law.' The *Hvarenô*, therefore, does not make the king absolute: it makes him one with the Law.

the offspring of the god Ammon] he was seized by a desire to visit the temple of Ammon in Libya: partly to consult the god, since the oracle of Ammon was said to be unerring, and Perseus and Heracles were said to have consulted it; ... moreover, he was emulous of them, being descended from both, and besides he ascribed some share in his birth[1] to Ammon, just as the myths ascribe the births of Heracles and Perseus to Zeus. With this idea, then, he journeyed to the temple of Ammon, hoping to learn more exactly the facts about himself, or at least to say that he had done so. ... [On his arrival, led, it was said, by divine guidance] he looked at the place with wonder, and consulted the god. He was told, so he said, what he wished in his heart to hear, and so he returned to Egypt' (Arrian, *Anabasis Alexandri*, III, c. iii, §§ 1–2 and c. iv, § 5).

'When he had crossed the desert and reached the place, the priest of Ammon bade him welcome in the name of the god, as being his [divine] father. Alexander then asked whether any of the murderers of his [human] father Philip had escaped his vengeance. The priest in reply bade him hush, for his father was no mortal man. On this Alexander altered his question, and asked whether he had punished all the murderers of Philip: he also asked about his future dominion, and whether it was granted to him to be lord (*kyrios*) of all mankind. The god answered that this was granted, and that full justice had been done to Philip; whereupon Alexander gave rich offerings to the god and made presents to his attendants. This is the account of the answers of the oracle which is given by most writers; but Alexander himself, in a letter to his mother, said only that he had received certain secret answers from the oracle, which he would tell her, and her only, after his return to Macedonia. Some writers say that the priest, wishing to address him in Greek with the friendly greeting "My son" (*O Paidion*), was misled by his use of a foreign tongue into substituting a final *s* for the final *n* and thus addressing Alexander as *O Pai Dios* (O

---

[1] This somewhat mysterious phrase, 'some share in his birth', may be based, as Sir W. W. Tarn suggests, on the fact that in Egyptian belief 'the reigning Pharaoh ... was son of his human father and also son of the god Amon-Re, not mystically but through union of the god with his mother' (*Alexander the Great*, vol. ii, p. 354).

son of Zeus): they add that Alexander was glad at this slip of the tongue, and that the story thus came to be spread abroad of the god having addressed him as the son of Zeus.[1] He is also reported to have listened to a discourse of the philosopher Psammon in Egypt, and to have liked particularly his teaching that all men are governed by a divine kingship, because the ruling and sovereign element in each is divine. He is even more generally reported to have held and expressed the opinion that God is the common father of all men alike [whence, perhaps, his passion for *Homonoia*], but He makes the best among them particularly His own' (Plutarch, *Life of Alexander*, c. xxvii. 680–1).

2. *Alexander's attempt to introduce* proskynēsis, *or 'adoration' of the King, at Bactra in the winter of 329–328.*

Proskynēsis, or prostration before the king with the forehead touching the ground, was common in Persia: indeed it was common in the East generally, and may be traced in the Chinese 'kotow'. Alexander sought at Bactra to make it part of the etiquette of his empire. Here, however, he encountered difficulties, and had to abandon his attempt. To the Persians prostration was only a ceremony; to the Greeks it was an act of worship of the gods, and a form of homage reserved for the gods. In their eyes, therefore, Alexander was 'assuming the god'; and by laughter and open objection they defeated his assumption.

   Why did he make the attempt to introduce *proskynēsis*? Tarn (op. cit. ii, pp. 359–69) urges that he seriously meant to 'assume the god', and to claim deification as the god of his empire; and he suggests that he derived the idea partly from Isocrates, but mainly from the teaching of Aristotle (see book III, c. xiii, § 13 of the *Politics*)—that a man, *or men*, pre-eminent in goodness can no longer be treated as a part of the State, but must be given a superior position, 'for a person of this order may very well be like a god among men'. It is of course possible that Aristotle may

---

[1] In whatever way Alexander may have been addressed—whether as the son of Ammon or as the son of Zeus—the fact is that he never called himself the son of either. He allowed *others* to call him the son of Zeus—but never the son of Ammon (Tarn, op. cit., p. 359). His own idea of himself seems only to have been that he was *ultimately* descended from Zeus, which was the tradition of his family.

have said something of this sort to Alexander when he was his tutor; but it seems unlikely that such an *obiter dictum* could have impressed Alexander so much, or stayed so long in his memory, as to determine his action years afterwards.[1] What seems far more likely is that Alexander, admiring Persian etiquette, sought to introduce one of its forms, perhaps without reflecting what it might mean to the Greeks, and probably, therefore, without any ultimate idea of claiming deification.

The story as told by Arrian. 'The story goes that Alexander wished that men should prostrate themselves before him, having at the bottom of his mind the notion of Ammon being his father rather than Philip, and being by this time an admirer of the habits of the Persians and Medes, as he showed by the change of his dress and the alteration of his general mode of life. . . . Callisthenes of Olynthus, who had attended Aristotle's lectures and was rather boorish in his ways, did not approve of Alexander's design. . . . The following story is told of his opposition to Alexander on this issue of prostration. Alexander had arranged with the "sophists",[2] and with the most distinguished of the Persians and Medes in attendance on him, that mention should be made of the issue in the course of a wine-party.[3] Anaxarchus [one of the "sophists"] first raised the question, saying that it would be far more just to acknowledge Alexander as a god than it was to acknowledge Dionysus and Hercules [who were strangers to Macedonia]; . . . the Macedonians were more justified in doing homage with divine

---

[1] Aristotle never mentions *proskynēsis*, but there *may* be a reference to it in book v, c. xi, § 6 of the *Politics*. Here he notes that a line of policy pursued traditionally by *tyrants* is to require citizens to be always hanging about the palace gates, and to adopt 'other measures of a similar character *common in Persia* and among the barbarians'. W. L. Newman, in his note on this passage, suggests that Aristotle may have had in mind *proskynēsis*. If this be so, Aristotle would have strongly deprecated the policy which Alexander attempted to follow, and have called it 'playing the tyrant' rather than 'assuming the god'. In the *Rhetoric* he classifies *proskynēsis* among *ta barbarika*.

[2] The Greek scholars or 'philosophers' who accompanied his expedition.

[3] It is difficult to disentangle the actual course of events in regard to this issue of *proskynēsis*. The issue may have been raised twice over—theoretically, in a debate (but the story of a debate may be apocryphal); and practically, at a wine-party, during the course of which *proskynēsis* was actually to be done. But there are different accounts, which it seems impossible to fit into one another. See J. P. V. D. Balsdon's article in *Historia*, i (1950), pp. 363 ff.

honours to their own king: there was no doubt that when he was dead they would honour him as a god, and it would be much more just that they should do him honour in his lifetime than that they should do so only after his death, when honours would profit him nothing.

'When Anaxarchus had spoken in this sense, those who were privy to the design applauded his words and were even prepared to proceed at once to the act of prostration. Most of the Macedonians, however, disagreed with the speech, and were silent. At this point Callisthenes took up the matter and made his rejoinder. "Anaxarchus," he said, "I think Alexander worthy of any honour that is appropriate to a man, but a line has been drawn for men between human honours and honours which are reserved for the gods . . . and more especially in respect of this habit of prostration. Where men are concerned, salutation takes the form of a kiss; but deity has its seat in some upper region and may not be so much as touched, and for this reason accordingly it [and it only] is honoured by the act of prostration. . . . It is not proper, therefore, to confuse these things, or to raise men to an excessive state, by exaggerating their honours, and to reduce the gods, in consequence, to unseemly humiliation, by giving them no more honours than men. . . ."

'When Callisthenes spoke in this sense, he gave great annoyance to Alexander, but his speech pleased the Macedonians. Seeing this, Alexander sent word to the Macedonians that they need no longer think of doing prostration before him'.[1]

(From Arrian, *Anabasis Alexandri*, IV, c. ix, § 9; c. x, § 1, §§ 5–7; c. xi, §§ 1–4; c. xii, § 1.)

Plutarch (*Vita Alexandri*, c. lxxiv. 705) tells a somewhat similar story, but he refers the scene to Babylon and to the end of Alexander's life, 323 B.C. Cassander, the son of Antipater (Alexander's regent in Europe), had recently come to the East,

---

[1] It may be added that the leading Persians, as Arrian goes on to narrate, prostrated themselves during the wine-party—though one of the Macedonian 'Companions' mocked at a Persian, who seemed to him clumsy in the act of prostration, for doing such a 'low' thing. But so far as the Macedonians and Greeks were concerned, the idea of prostration, and any idea of deification which may have been connected with it, proved a failure and was dropped.

and 'seeing some "barbarians" prostrating themselves he, like a man who had had a Greek training and had never seen such a sight, burst recklessly into laughter: Alexander was enraged, and seizing him violently by the hair with both hands dashed his head against the wall'. Quintus Curtius also has a similar story of Macedonian laughter at the act of prostration (*Historia Alexandri*, VIII, c. v, §§ 22–24); but here it is Polysperchon who laughs, bidding a Persian knock his head harder against the ground, while Alexander in anger hurls him to the ground and makes him 'prostrate' himself involuntarily.

Note on the supposed decree of 324 B.C. for the recognition in Greece of Alexander's divinity. Sir W. W. Tarn, accepting it as a fact that Alexander requested recognition of his divinity in Greece by a decree issued in 324 B.C., argues that this decree was a purely political measure, intended to solve a particular problem, and to solve it in the one area of Greece. Alexander (he argues) wished to end Greek faction fights and to promote 'Homonoia' in Greece, if only to secure his rear while he was engaged in the East; and he therefore wished to restore to their homes all Greek exiles and their families, in order to stop continual plotting and disturbance. But he could not do this without breaking the Covenant of the League of Corinth[1] (made by his father Philip and renewed by himself), under which the Greek cities retained autonomy and their constitutions were guaranteed. In order to gain a free hand he sought to do as a god what he could not do as a man; and he therefore simultaneously decreed his own deification in Greece and the return of all Greek exiles to their cities. The Greek cities, Tarn concludes, obeyed the decrees, if reluctantly, minding less about the recognition of Alexander's divinity than about the return of the exiles; but when Alexander died next year, there was a general reaction and revolt. On this basis it should be noticed that the scene at Opis, with its note of *Homonoia*, and the assumed deification decree for Greece (with its ultimate purpose of *Homonoia* in Greece), both belong to the same year 324 B.C.

There is no record in any ancient authority of the text of the decree in which Alexander is supposed to have requested recog-

---

[1] On the terms of the League see below, pp. 68 ff.

nition of his divinity. Indeed there is little or no evidence that such a decree was ever actually issued. Diodorus Siculus, it is true, tells us that at the Olympic games of 324 B.C. decrees requesting deification and the restoration of exiles were presented by Alexander's envoys and read aloud by the herald who had come first in the heralds' contest (book XVIII, c. 8). Plutarch (or whoever the compiler of the *Apophthegmata Lacōnica* may have been) records a reply said to have been returned by the Spartans to Alexander's request, 'We agree that Alexander should call himself a god if he wishes.' Arrian (*Anabasis Alexandri*, VII, c. xxiii, § 2) makes a statement which *may* imply some previous request for the recognition of Alexander's divinity: 'Embassies came from Greece [to Babylon], and their members, wearing crowns themselves, approached Alexander and crowned *him* with crowns of gold, as if they had been religious ambassadors [*theōroi*, such as Greek cities sent on sacred missions to present offerings at a shrine] who had come to do honour to a god.' But this is the whole of the evidence, and it does not carry us far. The testimony of Plutarch (if it is his testimony) is late, and it proves little: the passage from Arrian may relate to a spontaneous mission of recognition and congratulation which was not inspired by any request for deification: Diodorus Siculus, though he mentions a decree requesting deification as having been issued along with a decree for the return of exiles, does not give the terms of that decree, as he does the terms of the other. The conclusion of the matter, at the highest reckoning. is a verdict of 'Not Proven'; and it may well be the case that Alexander never issued, or thought of issuing, any request to the cities of Greece for the recognition of his divinity. On the whole issue see J. P. V. D. Balsdon's article in *Historia* i (1950), pp. 363–88.

If there is nothing more to be said about the supposed decree requesting deification, something may well be added about the actual decree commanding the return of exiles. It throws light on Alexander's policy towards the cities of Greece, and shows how he sought to reconcile their liberty with his own *de facto* empire. Diodorus Siculus (loc. cit.) gives the general terms of the decree: 'King Alexander, to the exiles from the Greek cities: We have not been the cause of your exile, but we will be the cause of the restoration of all of you to your own cities, except those who are under a curse [i.e. 'excommunicated' for bloodshed in a temple or the like offence]; and we have written to Antipater [Alexander's regent in Europe] instructing him to compel cities which are reluctant to grant the right of return to their exiles.' This statement seems only to be a brief summary of a decree which in its original form must have been a longer document. Fortunately it can be supplemented and amplified by an earlier decree, of the year 332, in regard to the island of Chios, which is preserved for us in an inscription, and which shows how Alexander had already, in the beginning of his career of conquest, laid down the lines of the policy which he was to follow afterwards in dealing generally with the Greek cities of the League of Corinth.

'The exiles from Chios [who had fled during the oligarchical revolution of 333 B.C.] are all to return, and the constitution in Chios is to be a democracy. Law-commissioners are to be elected who will so record and amend the laws that there shall be nothing in conflict with democracy and the return of the exiles: the amendments or records made are to be referred to Alexander. . . . As regards those who betrayed the city to the Persians [in 333 B.C.], such of them as shall have made their escape are to be banished from all the cities which participate in the peace [the League of Corinth?], and are to be subject to trial according to the judgement of the Greeks [i.e. the members of the League]; such as shall still remain in the city are to be produced before, and tried in, the Council of the League; and if there be any disputes between those who have returned and those who stayed in the city, judgement is to be given before us [i.e. in Alexander's own court]. Until the people of Chios are reconciled to one another, a garrison is to be maintained in the city by King Alexander, sufficient for the purpose, and the people of Chios are to maintain it'.[1] (From Dittenberger, *Sylloge*[3], No. 283: also in Tod, *Selection of Greek Historical Inscriptions*, vol. ii (1948), No. 192.)

[1] An inscription in regard to Tegea (Dittenberger, *Sylloge*[3], No. 306; Tod, op. cit., No. 202) shows how Greek cities sought to follow the instructions of the general decree promulgated by Alexander's representative at the Olympic games of 324. The initial clause gives its general purport: it begins with a reference to

c. *Alexander and the Idea of Empire*

Alexander cannot be said to have established in his lifetime, or bequeathed to his successors, a united *political institution* which can be called an empire. He united personally, as long as he lived, a number of different positions, which were combined in himself on a system of *personal union*; and it needed long years of struggle among the generals of his army, contending for the succession or rather for a share in the succession (and hence called the *Diadochoi* or 'successors'), to sort out, and turn into a system or group of several different organized States, the sum of personal positions which he had accumulated. (1) He had been king of the Macedonians; (2) he had been general or president (*hēgemōn*) of the League of Corinth in Greece, a league of autonomous cities with their constitutions guaranteed against any interference; (3) he had, according to one authority, been crowned Pharaoh in Egypt in 332 B.C.; (4) he had become 'great king' of Persia by right of conquest, but he had not effectively occupied parts of the Persian Empire (especially the north of Asia Minor); (5) he had conquered new territories to the east of the Persian Empire, as far as the valley of the Indus, though he had relinquished some of these conquests before his death. It is true that by a variety of policies, which may be called social rather than political, though some of them were semi-political, he had aimed at fusion between the various peoples subject to his sway, and especially between the Macedonians and the Persians. He had encouraged mixed marriages; he had sought to create a mixed army (*supra*, A. 1); he had founded new cities with a mixed population; and he had given political offices, such as the office of satrap, to a number of Persians. But these were various and mainly personal policies. The only evidence of any larger design or conception comes in a passage of the *Universal History* of Diodorus Siculus, composed nearly three centuries later (*c.* 60–30 B.C.). This evidence cannot be trusted; but the passage is here translated in order to illustrate the

the decree (*diagramma*) of Alexander, and proceeds, 'Let record be made, according to the amendments made by the city, of the matters raised in the decree'. Otherwise the inscription contains only a number of detailed legal arrangements on questions of property, marriage, debts, and the like.

ideas current about Alexander at the time of the foundation of the Roman Empire by Julius Caesar and Augustus.

The 'Successors' found a sort of political testament, which Diodorus describes as 'written injunctions' or 'memoranda'; but they deliberately put the testament aside. 'The most important and memorable of these memoranda was one for the building of a thousand long ships (or men of war) larger than triremes, in Phoenicia, Syria, Cilicia, and Cyprus; for an expedition against Carthage and the maritime peoples of Libya, Iberia, and neighbouring countries on the sea-coast down to Sicily [i.e. round the Gulf of Lyons]; for the making of a road along the shores of Libya, as far as the Straits of Gibraltar; and for the construction of harbours and docks, at suitable points, appropriate to such a force [i.e. the force to be sent by sea or to march along the land-route]. A second memorandum was for the establishment of large cities by the method of "synoecism" [the drawing together into one of a number of different cities or communities]. A third was for a movement of emigration from Asia to Europe, and conversely from Europe to Asia, for the purpose of bringing these two great continents into mutual concord (*Homonoia*), and into the amity of kinship, by means of mixed marriages and the domestic ties (*oikeiōsis*) thus created.' (From Diodorus Siculus, *Bibliotheca Historica*, xviii. 4.)

Note. (1) There is no evidence, or probability, that Alexander ever entertained the idea of a conquest of the Western Mediterranean: he was interested, indeed, in exploration; but that is another matter. The notion that he had such an idea may have arisen later, when Rome was conquering the Eastern Mediterranean, and some Greek may have thought, 'Ah, Alexander would have done that—the other way round—if he had lived.' (2) The method of 'synoecism' *was* actually followed, in some instances, by Alexander's successors: Thessalonica, for example, was a 'synoecism' of some twenty-six communities. (3) There is no evidence for a policy of mass emigration; but the purpose suggested by Diodorus (the creation of *Homonoia*) may be a reminiscence of ideas actually entertained by Alexander (cf. *supra*, A). On the whole, however, it has to be repeated that Alexander did not establish— if only for lack of time—any form of united empire or any single political institution of the nature of an empire; nor is there any good evidence that he planned to do so.

D. *Alexander and Alexarchus*

Sir William Tarn has suggested that we may possibly trace a curious derivative of the ideas and ideals of Alexander in the career and policy (if the word 'policy' may properly be used) of Alexarchus of Uranopolis. Alexarchus, a son of Antipater (one of Alexander's generals), was given by his brother Cassander, the ruler of Macedonia from 316 B.C. onwards, a small territory on the Athos peninsula (which became long afterwards, and still is today, a home of monks of the Greek Church). Here he sought to found a new 'city of heaven', for which he struck a special coinage, and the inhabitants of which he styled *Ouranidai*, or 'sons of heaven'. He is recorded to have called himself 'the Sun' (a style which may remind us of later Hellenistic 'Sun-states', see p. 61 below, or again of the Roman Emperor Aurelian and his view of himself as vicegerent of the Sun); and Tarn suggests that his Uranopolis was 'a little World-State in miniature, a good many years before Zeno appeared'. Alexarchus even created a special language, possibly a would-be world-language, for the citizens of his little would-be world-state. Tarn suggests that the scheme of Alexarchus may well be derived from Alexander himself, and that it thus throws light on Alexander's thoughts and dreams: 'it is as near a proof as one is likely to get ... that Alexander did think of all men as brothers, and did put forward ideas which led Alexarchus, as later they led Zeno, to the idea of a world-state, though Alexander did not think of or desire such a thing himself' (Tarn, *Alexander the Great*, vol. ii, pp. 429–33). But it may be that Alexarchus was a self-taught and fantastic visionary, who played with ideas and language in the solitude of his little peninsula.

§ II. STOICISM FROM ZENO TO CHRYSIPPUS
(The third century B.C.)
Introduction

§ 1. There are no original Stoic texts preserved to us till we come to the *Discourses* and the *Manual* (*Encheiridion*) in which Arrian (who was also the historian of Alexander's campaigns) recorded the teaching of his master Epictetus in the first half of the second century A.D., and to the *Meditations* in which the Emperor Marcus Aurelius recorded the thoughts he addressed 'to himself' somewhere between A.D. 170 and 180. Our knowledge of the history of Stoic thought and Stoic writings for the four centuries before Epictetus, from the beginning of Zeno's teaching about 300 B.C. to the time (about A.D. 100) when the Roman official and soldier Arrian began to take full notes of the 'Discourses' of his master, is drawn from two inadequate and tantalizing sources. One of them is the quotations or paraphrases of passages from Stoic works, now lost, which are to be found in later writers, from the days of Cicero (and even earlier) down to the time of St. Augustine. The other is the accounts of Stoic theory to be found in the writings of compilers who made compendia of the history of the lives and opinions of ancient philosophers: among these the most notable is the ten books of the *Lives and Opinions of Eminent Philosophers*, written by Diogenes Laertius some time after A.D. 200, and containing, in its seventh book, an account of the early Stoics from Zeno to Chrysippus—or, roughly, from 300 to 200 B.C.

§ 2. The Stoics gave to the ancient world, during the whole of the six centuries which lie between Alexander of Macedonia and the Emperor Constantine I, the system of philosophy (both 'natural' and mental), of ethics, and—we may even add—of religion, which was generally current among thinking men. There were of course other schools—the earlier Cynics, with whom the Stoics had many connexions; the Epicureans, on whom Lucretius drew; the Platonists of the Academy, who departed from their master and turned to scepticism; the Peripatetic successors of Aristotle, who continued their master's passion for accurate knowledge and the sober registering of 'histories' of recorded facts. But the fact remains that 'the philosophy of the Hellenistic world was the Stoa and all else was secondary',[1] and that the Hellenistic world transmitted this philosophy to the Romans of the later Republic and the early Empire, with modifications to

[1] W. W. Tarn, *Hellenistic Civilisation*, 3rd edition, p. 325.

suit their genius, and with qualifications, mainly derived from a revived Platonism (but also, in part, from Aristotle), which gave it a more eclectic and comprehensive character. During the six long centuries of its history this dominant Graeco-Roman philosophy of the world and human life went through three main phases or stages: that of the early Stoa, of the third century B.C., which alone is represented in the 'documents' or excerpts that follow; that of the middle Stoa, from Panaetius of Rhodes (185–109 B.C.) to Posidonius, a native of Apamea (a town of Syria) and afterwards a citizen of Rhodes (135–50 B.C.)—during which a close contact was established with Roman statesmen and thinkers, first with the members of the Scipionic circle in the days of Panaetius, and then with Cicero, Caesar, and Pompey in the days of Posidonius; and finally the later Stoa of the second century A.D., which may be said to have been domiciled at Rome from the days of Nero and Seneca to the reign of Marcus Aurelius.

§ 3. Stoicism in its origin was Hellenistic, but it can hardly be called Hellenic. The founders of the school, and many of their successors, came from cities and provinces that lay outside the mainland of Hellas, and even outside the wider world of pre-Alexandrine Hellenic colonization. Zeno himself—that gaunt, tall, and swarthy figure[1]—came from Citium in Cyprus, a Greek town (*polisma*) which included Phoenician settlers among its inhabitants; and we may assume that he had in his veins Semitic blood, or some sort of Semitic tincture. Cleanthes, his successor as head of the Stoic school (*prostatēs*), came from Assus, a town in the north-west of Asia Minor where Aristotle had once lived for a couple of years (347–345 B.C.); but if he was probably a Greek, he was a curious Greek who had once been a boxer, and who worked hard in a garden at Athens for a living—earning the nickname of 'the Second Hercules'—while he learned (and afterwards expounded) the doctrines of his master Zeno. Chrysippus, the third head of the Stoic school, came either from Soli or Tarsus, in the province of Cilicia: Sphaerus, a Stoic who also flourished in the third century, and was associated with the Spartan king Cleomenes III, came from the neighbourhood of the Crimea;

---

[1] Apollonius Tyrius in Diogenes Laertius vii. 1.

Persaeus, who was intimate with Zeno and who served, on his behalf, Antigonus Gonatas the King of Macedonia, was from Zeno's own town of Citium. The same width of recruitment persisted into the second century B.C.: among the disciples and successors of Chrysippus were three who came from Tarsus, one who came from Sidon, one who came from Babylon, and one who came from Seleucia, the city on the Tigris founded by the Seleucid kings.

§ 4. In the ferment and general dispersion which followed the conquests of Alexandria this far-flung range was perhaps natural: but the net of Stoicism was exceptionally wide, and it extended particularly into the East, penetrating into the region of Syria and even into Mesopotamia.[1] The Stoics, by their very origin, brought something of the East into Greek thought; though they also borrowed from earlier Greek thought and depended upon it for their foundations. It was natural that they should add a new note of Eastern 'enthusiasm': it was natural, too, that they should burst the bounds of the Greek city-state, and think of a greater 'city of the world', or *civitas Dei*, which could be entered by barbarians as well as Greeks and by the bond as well as the free. A man such as Meleager of Gadara, a semi-Hellenized town in the north of Palestine, is typical of the world of thought in which Stoicism grew and flourished. Born in Palestine (*circa* 140 B.C.), educated in the Phoenician city of Tyre, and spending his later life in the Greek island of Cos, he was at once something of a philosopher, who wrote lay sermons in the Cynic style, and the original creator of the Greek Anthology; and he mixed with his varied life, and with the versatility of his genius, a temper of what may be called 'syncretism' and an instinct of 'cosmopolitanism' (in the better sense of that word) which are admirably expressed in two epigrams which reveal his feelings. They deserve quotation because they strike a keynote of Stoicism. In one of the epigrams, addressed

[1] The region round the Gulf of Cilicia was particularly productive of Stoic thinkers. Zeno and Persaeus both came from Cyprus; Chrysippus came from the mainland opposite, which also produced, as has been noted in the text, three of his disciples and successors; and a little later Posidonius came from the town of Apamea, on the mainland to the east of Cyprus. It is this same region which also produced St. Paul—the first Christian philosopher, and a thinker not ignorant of Stoicism.

to a stranger whom he imagines as passing his tomb, he ends with the words, 'If thou art a Syrian, say to me *Salam*; if thou art a Phoenician, say *Naidios*: if a Greek, say *Chaire*: they are all the same.' In the other epigram, recounting his career, he writes, 'If I am a Syrian, what wonder is that? We all live in the same country, and that country is the world (cosmos).' That is the very keynote of Stoicism, even if Meleager himself professed Cynicism rather than Stoicism.

§ 5. But Stoicism itself was suckled in Cynicism. Zeno, when he came to Athens about 317 B.C. (some six years after the death of Alexander), attached himself originally to Crates, the pupil and successor of Diogenes—a citizen of Sinope on the Black Sea, nicknamed for his behaviour and teaching 'the dog' (*kuōn*), whence his followers derived their name of Cynics (*kunikoi*). It was while he was attending the lectures of Crates that Zeno is reported to have written his early work, the *Republic*, which, so far as we can judge from surviving fragments, had something of the 'shamelessness'—or frank and brutal realism—professed by the Cynics.[1] But he also attended the lectures of the Platonist Xenocrates (the contemporary head of the Academy) and those of the Megarian Stilpo, the head of another school, from whom he is said to have learned his skill in dialectic. Towards the year 300 B.C. he was already teaching on his own account, and expounding his own system, by lectures delivered in a public 'stoa' or porch which gave its name to his school. He became a notable and influential figure in Athens by virtue of his personality: he was admired by the Athenians for the austerity of his life and the pithy brevity of his speech;[2] they voted him a crown in his life and a public funeral at his death; and Diogenes Laertius records a decree in honour of 'the philosopher and good man' who 'made his own life an example to all, in harmony with the lessons he taught'. He was not only acceptable to the people of Athens: he was the friend and adviser of Antigonus Gonatas of Macedonia, 'the first king whom philosophy could

---

[1] 'Some said in jest', according to Diogenes Laertius (vii. 4), 'that he had written this work on the tail of the dog' (i.e. when he was still holding Cynic opinions).

[2] His rebuke to a young chatterbox became famous: 'The reason why we have two ears and only one mouth is that we may listen the more and talk the less' (Diog. Laert. vii. 23).

claim as her own', who attended his lectures whenever he visited Athens and pressed him more than once to come to his court in Macedonia. Zeno refused to go, but he sent his pupil Persaeus; and indeed it is a notable thing that the Stoics often appear in a close connexion with the statesmen and statesmanship of their day. Not only did the Stoic Sphaerus seek to serve Cleomenes III of Sparta: Panaetius, the head of the Stoic school in the next century, had much to do with the Scipionic circle and the intro-duction of a reformed Stoicism among the governing classes of Rome; and another Stoic, Blossius, was a friend of Tiberius Gracchus and afterwards joined in the movement at Pergamum in 133 B.C., which was in the nature of a social revolution as well as a political revolt against the growing pressure of Roman imperialism. Again and again the Stoics are found in connexion with social movements—at Sparta, at Rome, and in Pergamum.

§ 6. The great achievement of Zeno was the foundation of a school, and it showed itself in the quality and character of the men whom he attracted as his disciples and colleagues. Conspicuous among them is Cleanthes, the hard-working market-gardener whose very life was itself a denial of class and of class-distinction, and whose two poems addressed to Zeus are the most deeply moving of all the utterances of Stoicism. He attained the age of nearly a century (331–232 B.C.); and when Zeno died in 263 he became, and remained for the next thirty years, a successor worthy of the master himself. Little survives of all that he wrote; but the world has not forgotten his great hymn to Zeus, or the prayer, quoted by Epictetus, in which he commits himself to the guidance of Zeus and Destiny. The relics of his successor Chrysippus are more abundant, and they fill two volumes in J. von Arnim's *Stoicorum Veterum Fragmenta*. He was the head of the Stoic school from 232 to 207, and defended and expanded its philosophy in opposition to the scepticism into which the Platonic Academy had fallen. It was in logic and epistemology that he made his contributions to Stoicism: he did not change or develop its ethical and political doctrine. He was mainly a voluminous writer of the scholastic type, and he had not the personality of Zeno or of Cleanthes.

Note. Some reference is made to the Middle Stoa (from Panaetius, *circa* 150 B.C., to Posidonius of Apamea, of the first half of the first century B.C.) in later sections—pp. 205–7 and pp. 281 ff. On the last phase of Stoic teaching, of the second century A.D., the reader is referred to the sections on Epictetus and Marcus Aurelius, pp. 310 ff. and pp. 317 ff. Otherwise, as noted above, it is only the early Stoa, from Zeno to Chrysippus, which is illustrated by the passages translated in this volume.

A. *The Theory of Zeno's* Republic *as recorded or mentioned in ancient authorities*

[The references are to the sections in J. von Arnim's *Stoicorum Veterum Fragmenta*, vol. i.]

1. From Plutarch's *Vita Lycurgi*. 'It was not, at that time, the aim of Lycurgus to leave his city in the enjoyment of a great empire. Rather, he thought that what was true of the life of an individual was also true of the whole of a city: he believed that the happiness of both depended on virtue and internal concord (*homonoia*); and therefore he so arranged, and so bound together, his citizens that they should become free and sufficient to themselves, should learn the art of self-control, and should stay in that condition as long as possible. It was this actual system which was adopted, as the basis of their "Republics", by Plato, Diogenes, Zeno, and all the rest who have attained to fame by what they have said on these subjects, and have left behind them, as their memorial, writings and discourses only [and not, like Lycurgus, acts and enactments]' (*S.V.F.* 263 and 261).

2. From Athenaeus' *Deipnosophistae*. 'Zeno of Citium is said to have held that Love was the god of friendship and freedom, and that he also produced concord (*homonoia*)—but nothing else. Accordingly he wrote in his *Republic*, "Love is a God, being a fellow-worker in bringing about the salvation of a city."' [This may mean that the sentiments and emotions of sex ultimately help to foster civic unity and concord, though they do not produce other good results—such as, for example, the strength and self-sufficiency of the 'wise man'.] (*S.V.F.* 263.)

3. From Diogenes Laertius' *Lives of Eminent Philosophers*. 'Again, in his *Republic*, Zeno represented the good, and the good only, as citizens and friends and kinsmen and free' (ibid. 222).

From Seneca. 'Zeno says: the wise man will go into politics (*accedet ad rempublicam*), unless something stops him from doing so. . . . I follow Zeno and his disciples promptly and readily; but none of them actually went into politics, though none of them failed to send some pupil into politics' (ibid. 271).

4. From Clement of Alexandria, on religion. 'Zeno, the founder of the Stoic school, says in his book the *Republic* that men ought not to erect temples or to make images, since no work of man's hands is worthy of the gods. He does not shrink from pressing his point in these very words: "there will be no need to erect temples: a temple which is not precious and holy must be counted as nothing, and no work of masons and mechanics is precious or holy"' (ibid. 264. Origen also quotes the same passage from Zeno's *Republic*, ibid. 265.)[1]

5. In matters other than religion—such as education, the administration of justice, the use of money, and the institution of marriage—Zeno also sought to make a clean sweep in the theory of his *Republic*.

(*a*) On education, from Diogenes Laertius. 'Some, however, attack Zeno at many points—and first for saying, in the beginning of his *Republic*, that he can prove the uselessness of a general education' (ibid. 259).

(*b*) On the administration of justice, from Diogenes Laertius. 'Zeno held the opinion that neither temples nor courts of justice nor schools should be erected in cities' (ibid. 267). (In the same sense Zeno also said, as reported by Stobaeus, that cities should be adorned by the virtues of their inhabitants, and not by votive offerings, ibid. 266.)

(*c*) On the use of money, from Diogenes Laertius. 'On the theme of currency he wrote thus: "one ought not to think it necessary to institute a currency either for internal exchange or for foreign travel"' (ibid. 268).

(*d*) On the institution of marriage, from Diogenes Laertius. 'The Stoics hold that women should be enjoyed in common among the wise, so that any chance comer may unite himself with

---

[1] On the different views entertained by the Stoics in regard to religion see below, pp. 32–3, p. 45.

any chance-met woman'[1] (ibid. 269). (Diogenes says elsewhere that Zeno's attitude to marriage was like the attitude of Plato; actually Plato's system of temporary State-regulated marriages was wholly different.)

But from Diogenes Laertius (vii. 121) we also learn that 'the wise man will marry, as Zeno says in his *Republic*, and will beget children'. If the word 'marriage' is here used in any strict sense, Zeno was hardly consistent.

(On the relation of the views of his *Republic* (*Politeia*), probably an early work, to the later views of Zeno, see below, pp. 39 ff.)

B. *The General Theology and Cosmology of the Early Stoics,
as reported by Diogenes Laertius* (book VII)

1. *Creation.* 'God, Reason (*Nous*), Destiny, and Zeus are one (135). . . . In the beginning He was by Himself . . . as the seminal principle (*spermatikos logos*) of the Universe. . . . Then He created first the four elements—fire, water, air, and earth. . . . (136) . . . The uppermost element is fire, which is also called ether: in it the sphere of the fixed stars was first created, and then that of the planets: after that came air, then water, and then, as the base and foundation of all, the earth, which is the centre of all' (137).

2. *The Cosmos.* 'The term "cosmos", or universe, is used [by the Stoics] in different senses; but it primarily signifies God Himself as what He is in His nature by virtue of the whole of all being: unbegotten and incorruptible, the artificer of the ordering of things, who at regular periods of time draws into Himself all being and again creates it out of Himself[2] (137). . . . The universe is under the government of thought (*nous*) and forethought (*pronoia* or providence); for reason pervades and penetrates every part of it, as does the soul every part of us. . . . (138) . . . Thus the whole universe is a living being, animate [i.e. endowed with a "soul", the *anima mundi*] and rational, with ether as its ruling principle. . . . Cleanthes [the successor of Zeno] regards the Sun as the ruling

---

[1] Diogenes Laertius also states that Zeno bade men and women to wear the same dress, and to leave no part of the body wholly covered. (*S.V.F.* 257.)
[2] This is the Stoic idea of cycles and cyclical recurrence—each cycle ending in a 'conflagration', or *ekpyrōsis*, to make way for a new cycle.

principle of the universe, but Chrysippus [the successor of Cleanthes] takes a somewhat different line, and conceives the purer part of the ether as the true ruling principle: this his followers hold to be pre-eminently God, and they think that it has come to pervade, as it were by a visible motion, all that is in the air, and all animals and plants, and also the earth itself, as a holding and binding force (139). . . .

'That the universe is a living being, in the sense of an animate substance with the faculty of perception, may be proved in this way:—a living being is better than a being which has no life; but nothing is better than the universe; and therefore the universe is a living being. That the universe is animate (or possessed of a soul) is clear from this fact:— our own individual souls are each a fragment (*apospasma*) derived from it' (143).

3. *God and the Cosmos*. '[Such being the nature of the Cosmos], God [who pervades it] is a living being, immortal, rational, perfect and intelligent in the happiness which He enjoys, susceptible of no evil, taking forethought for the world and all that is in it but not made in the likeness of man. He is the artificer of the cosmos, and as it were the father of all being, both generally [i.e. by virtue of his whole nature] and by virtue of that part of Him which is all-pervading, and which is called by many names according to His various powers.' He is, for example, Zeus as the cause of life (*zēn*), Athena in virtue of the extension of His ruling power through the ether (*aithēr*), and so forth[1] (147).

4. *The place of Nature in the Cosmos*. 'The term nature (*physis*) is sometimes used by the Stoics to mean the binding force which holds the cosmos together, and sometimes to denote the life-force which causes the growth of things on the earth.[2] They define nature as a self-moved force which, acting on seminal principles (*spermatikoi logoi*), brings into being and holds together the offspring that issues from it at the appointed times, and so produces effects corresponding to the origins from which they are derived (148). Nature aims both at utility and at pleasure, as is plain from

---

[1] These etymologies, which connect Zeus with the word *zēn* and Athena with the word *aithēr*, are, of course, fanciful.

[2] In the former of these senses nature seems to be one with the 'purer part of the ether' which is 'pre-eminently God': in the latter it is just the thrust of growth.

the analogy of the creative activity of man (149). . . . Again, in the view of the Stoics, nature is a fire, acting by rules of crafts-manship, and going on its way about the business of creation: that is to say, it is a breath or spirit (*pneuma*), which is in the likeness of fire and acts in the way of a craftsman' (156). (See section C below for a fuller account of the Stoic conception of Nature.)

5. *Predestination and Divination.* 'That all things happen accord-ing to destiny (*Heimarmenē*) is the view of Chrysippus. Destiny is defined as the linked series of causes which brings things to pass, or as the principle (*logos*) according to which the cosmos is admin-istered. Moreover, they hold that divination in all its phases is a reality, and not a sham, if Providence (*pronoiā*, fore-thought or fore-knowledge) be also a reality; and they prove it to be actually an art, or science, by virtue of some of the results it has achieved. This was the view of Zeno and Chrysippus, . . . but Panaetius denies that there is any substance in divination[1] (149).

'The Stoics hold that there are certain spirits (*daimones*) who are in sympathy with men, and have an eye to human affairs. They have, too, a belief in what they call "heroes", meaning by them the souls of the righteous [the good and "wise", the *sapientes*] which remain after the death of the body' (151).

6. *The Mortal and the Immortal.* After reporting the Stoic defini-tion of Nature as a fire, or a *pneuma* which is in the likeness of fire, Diogenes Laertius proceeds to the Stoic view of the human soul. 'The soul is a nature, or form of nature, capable of percep-tion: the Stoics regard it as the spirit (*pneuma*) which is born and congenital with us; they therefore conceive it as a body [i.e. as being physical], but they regard it as surviving after the death [of the material body]. They believe that it is [finally] perishable, though the soul of the universe, of which the souls of living beings are parts, is itself imperishable. . . . Cleanthes held that *all* souls continued to survive until the general conflagration [the *ekpyrōsis*

---

[1] The earlier Stoics thus held that, on the assumption of predestination, you could attain a pre-view of coming events by resort to *mantikē* or divination. This led Stoicism to ally itself with Babylonian astrology (a curse of the ancient world). Panaetius, who introduced Stoicism to the Roman world about 150 B.C., dis-carded astrology and gave Rome a purer philosophy; but Posidonius of Apamea went back to astrology. (Tarn, *Hellenistic Civilisation*, 3rd edition, pp. 348–9.)

which ended one cycle and began the next, cf. *supra*, § 2]; but Chrysippus took the view that it was only the souls of the wise which thus survived' (156–7).

c. *The General Stoic Conception of Nature as reported by Diogenes Laertius* (vii. 85–89)

1. 'The first impulse of animals is towards self-preservation, because Nature endears them to themselves from the beginning of their life; this is what Chrysippus says in his treatise *On Ends*, where he writes that the first thing which attracts every animal is its own constitution and its consciousness of it; for it could not be expected that nature should alienate animals from themselves, or that, having made them, she should simply leave them in a neutral state, neither alienated from nor attracted to their own constitution. The conclusion thus left to us is that nature, when she created animals, implanted in all of them a feeling of attraction towards themselves, which makes them reject what is injurious to them and admit what is proper and advantageous (85).

2. 'There are some, it is true, who declare that the first impulse of animals is towards pleasure [and not towards self-preservation]; but the Stoics repudiate this opinion as false. In their view pleasure, if it is really present, is of the character of a by-product, which comes into existence when, and after, nature has sought and found by her own motion the things that belong to the constitution of each kind of animal: it is in this way, they say, that animals come to be of good cheer and plants to flourish. Nature, they add, has made no difference between animals and plants: plants too, like animals, have their life managed by her, even though they are without motive impulses and sensations; and, conversely, there are things in the being of plant-life which go on in us men. [Yet they acknowledge a difference, after all, between animals and plants, and between men and other animals.] When impulse supervenes in animals over and above [the elements of plant life], and they act on that impulse in moving towards what is proper for them, then, and for them, to follow nature is the same as to act in obedience to *impulse*. But when reason has been given to rational beings, by a further and higher gradation, life in obedience to

reason rightly and properly becomes, for such beings, the life which is in accordance with nature; for here reason enters the scene and brings art to the shaping of impulse (86).

3. 'This is the reason why Zeno, in his treatise *On the Nature of Man*, was the first thinker to define the end of man as "life in conformity with nature", which means the same as the life of virtue, virtue being the goal to which we are led by our nature. . . . It may also be said that the life of virtue is the same as living in accordance with experience of the [whole] course of nature, as Chrysippus says in the first book of his treatise *On Ends*; for our natures are parts of the nature of the whole of the universe. This is why the end of man consists in living agreeably to nature, which means, in effect, a life in accordance both with our own nature and with the nature of the whole universe. Such a life eschews all acts forbidden by the "common law", which is one and the same as "right reason", pervading and penetrating all things, and which is also one with Zeus, the head of the government of all things. What makes the virtue of the happy man, and constitutes the essence of happiness (defined by the Stoics as "the smooth current of life"), is that all actions should be guided by the aim of creating harmony between the genius (*daimōn*) of the individual and the will of the Governor of the universe . . . (88).

4. 'In speaking of the duty of "living agreeably to nature", Chrysippus understands by the term both universal, or common, nature and also, and more particularly, [individual] human nature; but Cleanthes [the contemporary, disciple, and successor of Zeno] admits only universal, or common, nature as the rule which ought to be followed, and does not include the nature of individuals or parts' (89).

D. *The Ethics of Stoicism, or the Wise Man's Conduct of Life*

[Mainly from Diogenes Laertius, vii. 117–30, with some references to von Arnim's *Stoicorum Veterum Fragmenta*, vol. i, Part I, 2 C.]

1. 'They say that the wise man is free from emotion (*apathēs*), because he does not fall into such weakness (117).

'Emotion, or passion (*pathos*), is defined by Zeno as an irrational movement of the soul which goes contrary to nature, or again as impulse running to excess.[1] [On "impulse", as characteristic of animals, and as guiding them to follow nature, and on man's additional gift of "reason", which is *his* guide in the following of nature, see above, C, § 2.] The chief of the emotions, as . . . Zeno states in his treatise *On the Emotions*, come under the four headings of grief, fear, craving, and pleasure (110).

2. 'They say that the wise man is free from conceit (*tȳphos*); for he counts both fame and obscurity as equally indifferent (117).

3. 'They say that all good men [the good and the wise being regarded as identical] are austere and of a dry flavour, because they neither consort with pleasure themselves nor tolerate an appetite for pleasure in others (117).

4. 'They say that the good are genuine [like good money] and sincere, with a vigilant eye to their own improvement by means of a discipline which seeks to set defects in the background and to bring good qualities to the forefront. The good are also natural and unaffected; for they have stripped themselves of all affectation either in accent or in appearance (118).

5. 'The good are the opposite of meddlesome: they decline to do any action which lies outside the path of duty (118).

6. 'They will not abstain from wine, but they will avoid intoxication. They will not fall into delusions; but they may be occasionally visited by strange fancies due to melancholy or mere folly, which are based on no principle of preference but are contrary to nature. The wise man will never feel grief, because grief is an irrational contraction of the soul (118).

7. 'The good are god-like, for they have, as it were, a god who is immanent in themselves: the bad are godless. . . . The good are also pious and god-fearing; for they are acquainted with the rites of divine worship, and piety consists in knowledge of the service of the gods. They will therefore offer sacrifices to the gods; they keep themselves pure and upright, and shun religious offences:

[1] The Stoics regarded 'emotions' as not only 'impulses running to excess', but also as 'judgements'. But these 'judgements' were erroneous judgements, based on falsehoods which produced a perversion of man's intelligence; e.g. the emotion of avarice, a form of 'craving', was based on the false assumption that money was a good (111).

the gods are well pleased in them, because they are devout and just in all their dealings with heaven. The wise alone are priests: for their study has been in sacrifices, in the building of temples, in rites of purification, and in all that is a proper offering to the gods[1] (119).

8. 'It is a doctrine of the Stoics that sins are all equal. For if one truth is not more true than another, or one falsehood falser than another, so, they hold, one deceit is not more so than another, or one sin more of a sin than another. The man who is a hundred furlongs away from Canopus and the man who is only a furlong away are equally not in Canopus; and in the same way the man who sins more and the man who sins less are equally not at the goal of right action. . . . But some of the Stoics assert that sins are not equal (130–1).

9. '[In matters of public and social conduct] the Stoics hold:

(a) that the wise man will take part in politics if nothing hinders him [cf. *supra*, A, § 3] . . . for by doing so he will at once keep vice in check and encourage men to be virtuous (121);

(b) that he will marry and have children, 121 [cf. *supra*, A, 5 (d)];

(c) that he alone is a free man, and the bad are slaves—freedom consisting in the power of independent action, and slavery in the privation of such power; though there is a second form of slavery which consists in simple subordination, and a third which consists in being the property of another as well as in being subordinate to him: . . . this last form is matched by the opposite position of being a master (*despoteia*), which is also evil (121–2);[2]

(d) that the wise are not only free, but also kings: kingship

---

[1] The philosophy of Stoicism is here closely connected with the regular practice of orthodox religion. This contradicts what Zeno himself had said in his *Republic*, *supra*, A, § 4. We may either hold that Zeno himself modified the views of his *Republic* (an early work), or that the later Stoics modified his views, or that in matters of religion—as also of politics—the Stoics held contrary views, sometimes speaking ideally, and sometimes in a more practical and realistic way.

[2] The influence of Stoicism was on the whole directed against slavery, and in favour of the principle of human equality: slaves might be as wise and good as freemen, and that alone counted. On the other hand, the Stoic distinction of the *sapiens* and the *stultus* drew a gulf between wisdom and folly, and provided a justification for the enslavement of the bad and foolish.

being irresponsible rule, which can be exercised permanently only by the wise (122) [here it would appear, at first sight, as if the Stoics were in favour of absolute monarchy, but a little later in his argument (131) Diogenes Laertius notes that they held the mixed constitution to be the best, with its combination of democracy, aristocracy, and kingship];

(e) that the good man will not live in solitude (*erēmiā*), as a hermit, for he is naturally sociable and active; but he will undergo training and discipline (*askēsis*), in order to increase his power of physical endurance (123);

(f) that friendship is possible only among the good and wise, in virtue of their likeness to one another; that it consists in sharing together the means of life, so that we treat our friends as though they were ourselves; that a friend is worth having for his own sake, and an abundance of friends is a blessing (124);

(g) that all things belong to the wise,[1] for the law [? of nature] has given them complete authority over all things; though there is a sense in which some things are said to belong to the bad, just as things acquired by the unjust are said in one sense to belong to those by whom they are enjoyed, if in another sense they are also said to belong to the State' (125).

10. [Apart from these matters of social and public conduct, and in the conduct of their inner life,]

(a) 'The wise commit no sin, because they are free from temptation to sin, and they do no injury, since they do no harm either to others or to themselves; but they show no pity,[2] and they have no forgiveness for any man; they refuse to remit the penalties imposed by the law, because in their view any yielding or pity, or even any show of equity [as distinct from strict justice], is mere infirmity of the soul, which affects an attitude of kindliness when con-

---

[1] Similarly St. Augustine holds that *jure divino . . . cuncta justorum sunt*; though he holds that *jus humanum* has introduced private property as a necessary remedy for sin and the craving that covets everything.

[2] Lactantius, quoted by von Arnim, 213, says of Zeno: 'misericordiam . . . tanquam morbum animi dijudicavit'.

fronted by the task of punishment. Nor do they think penalties too severe (122–3).

(b) 'The wise man refuses to marvel at anything extraordinary (nil admirari) (123).

(c) 'The wise man, if he sees reason for it, will commit suicide [the Stoics called this "making an exit", or exagōgē], either on behalf of his country, or for the sake of his friends, or [for his own sake] if he is suffering from very great pain or some injury or an incurable disease' (130).

11. In handling the abstract theme of the intrinsic nature of goodness, as distinct from the more concrete theme of the visible characteristics of the wise and good man, the Stoics developed the following ideas:

(a) 'All of them [i.e. Zeno and his early disciples] hold in common the view that virtue is a disposition or capacity of the ruling principle of the soul, which has been brought about by reason; or rather they hold that it *is* itself reason—reason agreed, assured, and unchanging. They taught that the emotional and irrational element in man was not distinguished from the rational by a difference in the soul and by the nature of its parts: the same part of the soul was concerned with both; ... and emotion or passion was just bad and undisciplined reasoning, which drew its intensity and strength from poor and erroneous judgement' (Plutarch, in von Arnim, op. cit. 202).

(b) '[On this rationalist basis, they proceed to the conclusion that] the different virtues involve one another, and the possessor of one of them possesses them all, inasmuch as they have all the basis of common principle (Diogenes Laertius, vii. 125). . . . All of them are forms of knowledge or practical wisdom (phronēsis), and they differ only in regard to the subject-matter to which they are applied: so Zeno defined the virtue of justice as practical wisdom in regard to the distribution of things, the virtue of temperance as practical wisdom in regard to the choice of things, and courage as practical wisdom in respect of the endurance of things' (Plutarch in von Arnim, op. cit. 200–1).

(c) 'They hold that there is nothing intermediate between virtue and vice; while the followers of Aristotle believe that moral improvement is something intermediate between the two.[1] The Stoics, on the contrary, hold that just as a piece of timber must be either straight or crooked, so a man must be either just or unjust, and cannot have more or less of justice; and the same is true of the other virtues' (Diogenes Laertius, vii. 127; cf. *supra*, § 8).

(*d*) 'They hold that virtue is worthy of choice for its own intrinsic quality: at all events, they say, we are ashamed of the wrong we do, which implies our knowing that the right is the one and only good. They also hold that virtue is sufficient in itself to ensure happiness, arguing that . . . "if magnanimity, which is only a part of virtue, is sufficient to make men superior to all other considerations, then it must also be true that virtue itself as a whole will despise what appear to be troubles, and will be sufficient to ensure happiness". But Panaetius and Posidonius [who both belonged to the period of the middle Stoa, 150–50 B.C.] held that virtue was not sufficient in itself for happiness: they believed that there was also needed health and strength and an "equipment" of means [such as Aristotle had postulated in his *Ethics*]' (Ibid. 127–8).

(*e*) 'It is also one of their tenets that the exercise of virtue is a continuous activity [i.e. that it is never interrupted by lapses or omissions]. This is the view of Cleanthes and his circle: virtue to them is something that can never be lost, and the good man is always occupied in the exercise of the powers of a soul which is always perfect' (Ibid. 129).

E. *Cleanthes' Invocation to Zeus, the God of the whole universe, who is also the 'Common Law' and one with 'Right Reason'*

(α) *Hymn to Zeus*

'Hail to thee, Zeus, most glorious of immortals, God of many names, almighty for ever, sovereign of nature, who dost govern all things with law at Thy side. Thee all mortal men may invoke; for they are Thy offspring, alone of all creatures that live or

---

[1] Panaetius, head of the Stoic school from 129 to 109 B.C., modified the early strict Stoic doctrine on Aristotelian lines, and recognized an intermediate stage of moral improvement (*prokopē*), which it was the duty of the philosopher to help ordinary men to attain; cf. infra, p. 43 and note 6.

creep on the earth, and to them it is given to have the likeness of echoes of Thee; wherefore with my voice I will hymn Thee and ever sing Thy power. To Thee all this universe, as it revolves round the earth, pays its obedience wheresoever Thou guidest it, and it is willingly ruled by Thee; so mighty is the two-edged thunder-bolt of ever-living fire which Thou holdest in Thy invincible hands to do Thee service. Beneath its blows are all the works of nature accomplished; with it Thou guidest on its course the Common Reason that pervadeth all things[1], mingling itself with both great and small lights; by it Thou art great as Thou art, King in the highest, through all eternity. Without Thee, O God, nothing comes to pass that is done on the earth, or within the divine vault of heaven, or in the sea, save the things that are done by the wicked in their own folly. Thou knowest how to make the odd even, and to turn disorder into order: what is not dear [unto others] is dear unto Thee; and thus Thou hast blended all things harmoniously in one, the good and the bad together, so that there should be one reason from everlasting to everlasting through all things. All mortal men who are evil shun this one reason and pass it by, ill-starred beings that they are; yea, those who are always coveting the possession of things neither see nor hear the common law of God, which, if they but obeyed it with an understanding mind, would bring them to a good life. But instead they go their way in their folly, drawn by their impulses to one evil course after another, some running into a passion for glory that breeds unhappy strife, some turning their minds in disorder to the making of gain, and some bent on enjoyment and the pleasures of the body: . . . they are carried about now here and now there, in spite of all their great longing for the very opposite of such a fate. But do Thou, O Zeus the giver of all gifts, Zeus who hidest Thyself in dark clouds, Zeus who hurlest the flashing thunderbolt, do Thou save men from their sore witlessness; scatter it, O Father, away from their souls; grant that they may attain wisdom, the wisdom in which Thou puttest Thy trust as Thou governest all things with Justice at Thy

---

[1] For the idea here expressed see the previous passage (c. 4 *ad finem*) from Diogenes Laertius vii. 88. I have translated *logos* as 'reason'. What is meant by it is a fiery ether, the subtlest form of matter, which is 'the breath of God' and a 'spirit' as well as matter.

side. So, being honoured by Thee, we shall honour Thee in return, hymning Thy works without ceasing, as befits every mortal man; for neither to men nor to gods is any greater gift given than always to hymn, as is just [literally, "in justice"], the common law.' (From the *Florilegium* of Stobaeus, quoted in von Arnim, op. cit., vol. i. 537.)

(β) *The Prayer of Cleanthes*

'Lead me, O Zeus, and thou too, Destiny, whithersoever I am appointed by you to go; for I will follow you without delay. And if I am unwilling to go, because I have fallen into wrong-doing—I will follow, none the less.' (From Epictetus, quoted in von Arnim, op. cit., vol. i. 527.)

Seneca translated these lines into Latin. His translation, which comes in his *Epistles*, and which is quoted by von Arnim immediately after the Greek, deserves mention. It adds artifice to the original, and it misses the exact sense of the first line: it also adds a line at the end, which is Seneca's own invention, but which became, in time, a common motto:

> Duc, o parens celsique dominator poli,
> quocumque placuit: nulla parendi mora est.
> adsum impiger. fac nolle; comitabor gemens,
> malusque patiar quod pati licuit bono.
> ducunt volentem fata, nolentem trahunt.

F. *The General Theory and Influence of Stoicism*

There are elements in the tradition and record of Stoicism—especially the Early Stoicism of the third century B.C., prior to the Middle Stoicism of the second and first centuries—which seem contradictory to one another. Three of these elements deserve some mention and examination. The first of them, and the least serious, is the apparent discrepancy between Zeno A (if this term may be used)—the early Zeno who wrote a *Republic* on the Platonic model, tracing the lines of a reformed Greek city-state—and Zeno B, the later Zeno who conceived and expounded the theory of a new world-state. A second and larger, and a more obvious, discrepancy is that between the materialistic naturalism which may be traced in some of the accounts of Zeno's teaching and the moral idealism which is the general trend and legacy of the record of the Stoic school. Here again there seem to be two Zenos, or at any rate there would appear to be something of a gulf of division between a period of Zeno's teaching in which he was largely influenced by the realism and naturalism of the Cynics, and a later period in which he had escaped from that influence and ceased to be 'attached to the tail' of the Cynic 'dog'. A third and last element of internal contradiction, still wider in its scope, is the general ambivalence of Stoic theory on a number of issues. The Stoics, for instance, sometimes appear to be monarchists, and sometimes votaries of a mixed constitution: they are sometimes opposed to the institution of marriage, and sometimes the exponents of a higher view of true marriage: they sometimes set their faces against religion and temples, and we sometimes find them preaching that the 'wise man' of their theory will restore the temples and foster the worship of the gods. Are these various elements of contradiction really present in Stoicism? And if they are, how can they be reconciled, or at any rate explained?

1. The discrepancy, or distinction, between the Zeno A of the *Republic* (or *Politeia*) and the Zeno B of a new world-state has been suggested and pressed by Sir W. W. Tarn.[1] He suggests that a great change had intervened between the early and the later period of Zeno's thought, and he argues that this change, which lifted the outlook of his mind from the narrow confines of the Greek city-state to the breadth and scope of the one comprehensive city of Zeus, was due to the influence of Alexander. Not that Alexander had himself ever dreamed of instituting a world-state (see above, pp. 18–19); but he had, by various measures, sought to reconcile and fuse the various peoples who had come under his rule in a common allegiance and a common way of life, and he had been a votary and an apostle of the spirit of a common concord, 'a union of hearts', which he called by the name of *Homonoia*. This (it is argued) was what Zeno learned from Alexander: this was the lesson that changed his theory and his teaching. He adopted Alexander's great idea of a common concord, but in

---

[1] *Alexander the Great*, vol. ii, pp. 417 ff.

adopting it he also changed it; and while Alexander had thought that concord, not yet present among men, ought to be created for them by a king, he preferred to think that concord already had its dwelling in the minds of men, and that they only needed to be led to believe that it actually existed and to act in the strength of that belief.

The argument is attractive. But it is permissible to doubt whether Zeno ever borrowed any of his ideas from Alexander. It is even permissible to doubt whether there was ever a Zeno A distinct from a Zeno B, or a definite change of view from the idea of a reformed Greek city-state to the idea of a new world-state. What is more likely is that Zeno held both ideas suspended in his mind without distinction, and that his followers after him continued to think in the same hazy (and yet intelligible) way as he had done. It is always possible to have one foot in the actual and one in the ideal without any sharp distinction between the two positions. A Stoic might theorize about the value of a mixed constitution, in a city-state modelled on Sparta, with one side of his mind, at the same time that with another side he dreamed of a city of Zeus, a 'megalopolis' as Philo called it, which was somehow already there (just because Zeus was Zeus), but had to be thought and brought into a more actual and concrete existence. Indeed this is the way in which the Stoics would seem to have continued to think as long as their school continued to flourish. There is nothing impossible, or indeed unusual, in such ambivalent or unresolved thought, which can hold together different, and yet somehow allied, ideas in an undifferentiated unity. A Christian thinker today can be a believer in a confessional or national Church, and theorize about its proper constitution (episcopal, or congregational, or a mixture of both), at the same time that he believes in a catholic or universal Church common to all Christians of all confessions. Zeno and his followers had to solve the same problem, and they solved it in the same way. They held together in solution both the local city-state which was and the world-state that ought to be.

2. But there is a deeper difference in the heart of Stoicism than that between the Stoic's idea of the cities of men and his idea of

the city of God. This is the difference between an element, or elements, of materialistic naturalism and an element—a stronger and ultimately victorious element—of moral idealism. The conjunction of the two would seem to be the result of the historical development of the school. It began by being suckled in the creed of the Cynics; or (to alter the metaphor) it came from the egg of the philosophy of the Cynics, with their passion for 'facing the facts' (even if they were nasty, and perhaps especially if they were nasty), and their frank and uninhibited 'realism'. Coming from that egg, Stoicism retained fragments of shell on its wings; and those fragments were a part of the nature of Early Stoicism. Perhaps they never entirely disappeared: even Marcus Aurelius, with all his gravity and nobility, has flashes and phrases of a crude 'realism'. Indeed they were, in a measure, inescapable for a would-be honest thinker in the ancient world; and Stoic thinkers (though perhaps we may except the younger Seneca) strove hard to be honest. It was something more than the lingering influence of Cynicism which made them the 'realists' that they were.

But Cynicism, none the less, had its influence on the theory of Early Stoicism; and we may therefore turn to consider briefly some of the features of Cynicism. Diogenes, its main figure and most influential teacher (*circa* 400–325 B.C.), had come to Athens from the city of Sinope on the Black Sea, exiled—according to tradition—for having joined with his father in the offence of *paracharaxis*, or falsification of the coinage. In Athens he studied in the schools, and becoming a teacher himself he continued the practice of *paracharaxis* (if ever he had been guilty of it in the literal sense) by turning ideas upside down as he was supposed to have done with coins. In a word, he was a thinker of the type of Samuel Butler, the author of *Erewhon*: he stood ideas on their head, and his habit of *paracharaxis* made him a master of paradox. Diogenes Laertius (vi. 71) records that his action, like his instruction, was against the grain of current opinion: 'he really falsified currency, allowing the rules of convention no such authority as he gave to the rules of nature, and professing to lead the same sort of life as Hercules did in preferring liberty to everything else'.

Diogenes is said to have written a treatise called the *Republic*, or 'on Polity', as Zeno did after him; and it was the tradition of antiquity that Zeno drew on the treatise. In the 'Republic' of Diogenes there was to be no coinage (knuckle-bones were to serve in its stead): weapons of war were condemned as useless: marriage was rejected as a folly, and women and children were to be common (he is even said to have defended incest). Along with coinage, armaments, and marriage, the city-state itself was to go: 'the only proper polity was one in' (or of) 'the whole world'. It would be an error to interpret this saying in a positive sense, or to hold that Diogenes meant that there was, or should be, a world-state: it is probably to be understood in no more than a negative sense, and as only meaning that there ought not to be such a thing as a polis or city-state; in other words it is an assertion of the unchartered liberty of a Hercules rather than the proclamation of a city of Zeus. So, too, when he answered the question, 'Where do you come from?' by saying, 'I am a cosmopolitan', he really meant, not that he was a citizen of the world, but rather that he was what may be called an 'a-politan', a disbeliever in the city-state. In the same way, and in the same sort of sense, the Cynic Crates, one of his followers, is reported to have declared that his country—a country which Fortune could never assail—was Obscurity and Penury (Diogenes Laertius vi. 93).

Banishing the city, Diogenes banished with it ranks and degrees, mocking the ideas of nobility of birth and good repute, and similar follies, as mere showy trappings of vice. Property, too, was banished: all things belonged to the wise, and belonged to them in common; and this was proved by a sort of syllogism. 'All things belong to the gods; but the gods are friends of the wise, friends have all things in common, and therefore all things belong to the wise'. This philosophy, if it can be called such, is that of the Shelley of *Prometheus Unbound*: the individual emerges

> Sceptreless, free, uncircumscribed, but man:
> Equal, unclassed, tribeless, and nationless,
> Exempt from awe, worship, degree. . . .

The supreme passion of Diogenes was freedom, and, above all, freedom of speech. 'Asked the question, "What is the finest thing

among men?" he answered, "Freedom of speech" [*parrhēsia*].'
This was the innermost essence of Cynicism.

The gospel of *parrhēsia*, with its accompaniment of a frank
naturalism and a realism which is sometimes repulsive, passed into
the Stoicism of Zeno and his disciples. Zeno too, according to
ancient testimony, could defend incest.[1] He could also defend or
condone the practice of homosexuality, as Plutarch records that
he did in his *Republic*.[2] He could even make a case for the practice
of cannibalism:[3] flesh, after all, was nothing but flesh; what did
it matter how it was used, either in life or in death?[4] Chrysippus,
a disciple of Zeno and the third head of the Stoic school, was ready
to justify the gross indecencies of an ancient and crude mythology:
Diogenes Laertius reports a tradition that his account of the intercourse of Zeus and Hera was regarded as most obscene, and more
appropriate to harlots than deities (vii. 187–8). It is little wonder
that the record of the tenets of Early Stoicism was afterwards
revised and even 'bowdlerized': a Stoic called Athenodorus, in
charge of the library at Pergamum (perhaps in the second century
B.C.), is said to have expurgated 'what was wrongly said' from
the Stoic books in his custody.[5] Indeed it was the work of the
Middle and the Later Stoic School to purify and elevate the teaching of the Stoics of the first generation. Panaetius of Rhodes, the
head of the school at the end of the second century B.C., imported
into it a new moral fervour and a belief in the possibility of moral
progress,[6] which the early Stoics had denied: in touch with Rome
and the Roman aristocracy, he attuned Stoicism to Roman ideas
of *gravitas* and *virtus*. Posidonius of Apamea (and afterwards of
Rhodes), the last prophet of the Middle Stoa, drew elements
from Plato to fortify and ennoble his thought: he knew the sin-
fulness of natural man, pulled downward by the dark horse of
passion, and he could almost have said with St. Paul, 'Who shall

---

[1] J. von Arnim, *Stoicorum Veterum Fragmenta*, i, No. 256.
[2] Ibid., No. 252, cf. 249–251.   [3] Ibid., No. 254.
[4] 'Throw the dead to animals or into the fire, and practise homosexuality without any let or hindrance'; ibid., No. 253.
[5] Diogenes Laertius vii. 34.
[6] Here we may perhaps trace the influence of Aristotle's *Ethics* and its theory
of moral progress from 'natural disposition' through 'habituation' to 'moral
wisdom' (*phronēsis*).

deliver me from the body of this death?' (see below, p. 282, n. 1).
Finally Epictetus, in the days of Later Stoicism, about A.D. 100,
added to the moral fervour which inspired the Middle Stoa a new
passion of religious feeling (see below, p. 312), which also nerved
Marcus Aurelius. In the five hundred years of its long history,
from Zeno's original teaching about 300 B.C. to the *Meditations* of
Marcus Aurelius in the latter half of the second century A.D.,
Stoicism had suffered changes, but it had lived and grown
through the changes which it had suffered.

Yet it would be wrong, at the end of the account, to refuse to
recognize the moral fervour which already stirred in the early
Stoics—Zeno himself and his successor Cleanthes—and which
gave them their hold on the minds of men. Zeno was Semitic as
well as Greek; and with all his naturalism (perhaps an accretion
rather than an inherent attribute) he had something of the quality,
and some of the feeling for righteousness, which are the marks of
the Hebrew prophets. Origen reports one of his sayings which
has a Christian ring: 'A man said to him, "May I perish if I do not
revenge myself on you"; and he replied, "May I perish if I do not
make you my friend." '[1] Plutarch records another saying which
shows that he could see through matter to spirit, and which makes
his materialism appear no more than a transparent veil. Going to
a theatre to hear a harpist, he said to his disciples, 'Let us enter and
learn how gut and string and wood and bone, when they are
made partakers of reason and rhythm and order, can issue in
harmony and find a voice.' But perhaps the best testimony to his
moral teaching and influence is that of the Athenians, who
deposited in his custody the keys of their city walls and honoured
him with a golden crown and a statue. The words of the decree
conferring the crown are a noble compliment, which becomes
all the greater when one reflects that its recipient was a stranger
from distant Cyprus and had non-Greek blood in his veins.
'Whereas Zeno . . . of Citium has for many years been concerned
with philosophy in the city, and whereas he has not only continued
to be a good man in all other ways, but has also inspired to the
highest endeavours the young men who came to him for instruc-

[1] J. von Arnim, *S.V.F.*, vol. i, No. 297.

tion, encouraging them in the path of goodness and temperance, and making his own life a pattern to all by following himself the teaching he gave; it has been resolved by the people—and may good fortune attend their resolve—to render him their praise, and to crown him with a golden crown, according to the law, for his goodness and temperance . . .'.[1]

3. The general elements of internal contradiction in Stoic theory, over and above the discrepancy between the materialistic naturalism and the moral idealism of its early phase, may be explained, in some measure, by the variety of its teachers and the long span of its history. A theory which flourished, with little or no intermission, for the space of four hundred years, and flourished among different teachers of different origins and outlooks, cannot in fairness be judged as if it were a single philosophy developed by a single mind. There were inevitable contradictions in the course of the generations. There was a political contradiction, not only on the higher issue between the city-state and the world-state, but also on the lower ground of debate between the cause of monarchism and the cause of the mixed constitution (see below, p. 47). There was religious contradiction, between thinkers who would have no temples and no houses of the gods built by men's hands, and thinkers who held that it was the wise man's duty to see to the proper upkeep of religious buildings and services. There were, again, contradictions in matters of social policy; if some of the early Stoics decried the institution of marriage, there were Stoics of a later age who inspired a higher conception of the communion of husband and wife; and though the abolition of slavery was not a Stoic tenet, the Stoics generally cherished the idea of human equality—while acknowledging, as Chrysippus drily said, that nothing could prevent some seats in the theatre from being better than others—and we find Stoics more than once concerned in movements for social reform and even for revolution. Finally, there was contradiction on the great and fundamental issue between free will and determinism; between the liberty of man and the predestination of God as written in the stars above. The moral autonomy of the free individual is a keynote of Stoicism; but

---

[1] The decree is quoted in Diogenes Laertius vii. 10–11.

there were Stoics who coquetted with astrology and were the disciples of a blind fate. Zeno himself is said to have been moved by astrology; and a modern scholar has noted that astrology was 'the shadow side of Stoicism', and that 'the man who did most to establish astrology and its kin firmly in Europe' was the Stoic Posidonius.[1]

If we seek, in conclusion, to estimate the general influence of Stoicism on the thought and action of the ancient world, we cannot but conclude that it was, on the whole, an influence making for good. Stoicism stiffened the moral fibre: allied with Rome, as it began to be from the middle of the second century onwards, it encouraged the best of the Roman qualities (*gravitas* and *pietas*); and it helped to refine the Assyrian savagery into which Roman militarism could too easily fall. But already during the third century, and even before it came into contact with Rome, Stoicism had begun its work of amelioration. It has been said that 'the germs of modern international law go back to third-century Stoicism'; and it may be that Stoic preaching, reinforcing a growing practice of inter-State conventions for the peaceful settlement of private disputes between citizens of different cities, helped the development of a *jus gentium* in the Hellenistic world. In the third century, too, as afterwards in the second, we find Stoic philosophers concerned in movements of social reform, and acting with their leaders either in the capacity of advisers or in that of apologists (see below, p. 55). It has already been noted that Stoicism in a later age helped to improve the status of married women, and to inspire the higher conception of marriage which appears in the definition of the Roman jurist Modestinus.[2] It was also a Stoic leaven which fermented in the treatment of slavery by the Roman jurists of the Empire (see below, pp. 267–8); and indeed as early as the third century B.C. we may trace the working of Stoicism in the better treatment of slaves, and in the increase (more especially among the ranks of those who were touched by

---

[1] Tarn, *Hellenistic Civilisation*, 3rd edition, pp. 347, 349. On the other hand, Panaetius, a century before Posidonius, had discarded astrology: ibid., p. 348.

[2] 'Nuptiae sunt . . . consortium omnis vitae, divini et humani juris communicatio.' *Dig.* 23 2. 1.

philosophy) of the manumission of slaves by will on the owner's death.[1]

In the sphere of domestic politics Stoicism is generally associated with monarchy. This was perhaps a matter of opportunism rather than of conviction. Theoretically, at any rate in their early days, the Stoics seem to have been wedded to the idea of the mixed constitution, in which monarchy was but one ingredient, qualified and tempered by the two other elements of aristocracy and democracy. Practically, however, they were ready, and even eager, to ally themselves as advisers and philosophic guides with the ruling powers of the day; and as the ruling powers were generally monarchs, they are generally to be found in alliance with monarchy. There is one exception to this rule—the alliance of the Stoic Panaetius with the aristocratic governing circle gathered round the younger Scipio at Rome in the middle of the second century B.C. But this exception is apparent rather than real: the members of the Scipionic circle were the uncrowned kings of Rome; and here, as elsewhere, the Stoic philosopher sought to play the part of a father confessor, or *éminence grise*, to the powers that were. Plato had thought that philosophers should be kings; the Stoics (following Aristotle rather than Plato) thought that they should be the confidants and advisers of kings. They are thus to be found in the circle which gathered round Antigonus Gonatas in Macedonia, and perhaps they helped to inspire his conception of monarchy as 'a noble servitude': they are also to be found (at any rate in the person of the Stoic Sphaerus) in association with Cleomenes III of Sparta a little later in the same century. There was indeed one period—the second half of the first century A.D.—when the Stoics seemed to be involved in a philosophic *Fronde* against the Roman Empire; and three of the Roman emperors—Nero, Vespasian, and Domitian—took measures against the 'philosophers' (Cynic as well as Stoic) which went to the length of banishment. But the *Fronde* which led to these measures was really based on an aristocratic circle, essentially Roman in spirit, and inspired by memories of the Roman past

[1] Tarn, *Hellenistic Civilisation*, 3rd edition, p. 104. Aristotle, in his will, had already set the example of such manumission.

rather than by Stoic teaching, though members of the circle belonged to the Stoic creed and professed themselves the disciples of philosophic directors.[1] Even during this period the younger Seneca, Stoic though he was, could write a panegyric on monarchy in his *De Clementia* (see below, pp. 236–8); and in the following century, from the accession of Trajan to the death of Marcus Aurelius (A.D. 98–180), the Golden Age of the Roman Empire saw Stoic philosophy seated by the throne, or even (during the reign of Marcus) on the throne. This was what Musonius Rufus (one of the banished philosophers of the previous century, and a teacher of Epictetus) had taught that philosophy ought to do;[2] and this was what it now did.

With its belief in the world-city of Zeus, and its conception of the unity of the world under one rational government, Stoicism served, in its measure, as a basis or cement of the unity of the Roman Empire. But it influenced the development of religion as well as the movement of secular life. It entered, along with Platonism, into the philosophy of Philo Iudaeus; and traces of Stoic philosophy, and even the technical terms of Stoicism, have been detected in the language of the prayers used in Jewish–Hellenistic synagogues.[3] The Book of Wisdom has Stoic elements: St. Paul could use Stoic conceptions and phrases; and the philosophy of some of the Fathers of the Church, both in the East and the West (and notably of Tertullian in the West), was influenced by Stoic ideas. Above all, the Stoic conception of the world-city of God, as it had in its day sustained and cemented the unity of the Roman Empire, served also to prepare a way for the idea of the unity of the Christian Church in the *Civitas Dei* represented on earth by the *ecclesia Catholica*.

Note on other Schools of Philosophy

There were three other main schools of philosophy in the ancient world besides the Stoicism of the Porch. One of them was the Epicurean school ('the Garden'), of which some account is given below (pp. 172–81) in connexion with Lucretius, the great exponent of the tenets and teaching of Epicurus. The Platonic school (the

---

[1] D. R. Dudley, *A History of Cynicism*, pp. 128 ff.
[2] See below, pp. 309–10.   [3] See below, pp. 164–6.

Academy) survived continuously, but with diminished lustre: in the period of the middle Academy it even suffered a temporary eclipse, passing under the influence of scepticism; but it revived to become an ingredient and inspiration in the eclectic Stoicism of Posidonius, and it finally emerged with a splendid independence in the Neoplatonism of Plotinus and his successors (see below, pp. 331 ff.). The Aristotelian school (the Lyceum) had less influence than the others on the development of thought, but it contributed greatly to the increase of knowledge. The theory of Aristotle continued to be taught, and his lecture-notes used (perhaps in a revised and modified form), by the teachers of the Lyceum; and the ethical theory of their master may probably be the source of the new and notable turn which Panaetius gave to the ethics of Stoicism. But the Peripatetics, as the followers of Aristotle were called, devoted themselves mainly, and indeed almost wholly, in the encyclopaedic spirit of their founder, to the collection of data, and to the compilation of what the Greeks called 'histories' (or records of inquiries), in almost every field of knowledge.

Two Aristotelians of the late fourth and early third centuries deserve some notice. The first was Demetrius of Phalerum, a pupil of Aristotle who governed Athens for the Macedonian Cassander from 317 to 307, and who sought to translate into law many of Aristotle's ideas. Expelled from Athens by another Demetrius ('the Besieger'), he ultimately made his way to Egypt, where he may have inspired the foundation of the Museum at Alexandria, by Ptolemy I, to serve as a centre of learned research, and where he is also recorded to have been the head keeper of the library (the greatest library of antiquity) that rose by the side of the museum. (He is also recorded to have advised Ptolemy to read books on kingship; but Ptolemy knew more about kingship than was to be found in books.) The other Aristotelian, a contemporary of Demetrius of Phalerum, was Dicaearchus of Messina, who had also sat at the feet of Aristotle. He spent most of his life in the Peloponnese, where he studied and described Sparta; but he was a great traveller, and he visited and described much of the Greek world. He was a polymath in the style of his master, and his writings were many and various. They are all now lost; but

E

there are several of them which a scholar would be glad indeed to recover.[1] One of them was his 'Circuit of the World', a work of descriptive geography which was the parent of many later Greek (and Arabic) works on geography, and which had an early atlas or *mappa mundi* for its companion. Another, which must have been unique in its day, was his 'Life of Hellas', a study of Greek culture in its general range. It is said to have begun with a study of the primitive life of man in the time of Cronus; to have gone on to a description of the culture of the East and its influence on Greece; and to have ended with an account of Greek cultural life as it stood in his time. The third of his works, which may have been written in Sparta and was apparently based on Sparta, was his *Tripoliticus*, a treatise on the mixed constitution which may have been, at any rate indirectly, the parent of the ideas of the mixed constitution expounded afterwards by Polybius and Cicero. There is a tradition, based on a passage in the Byzantine writer Photius, that the mixed constitution came to be called 'the Dicaearchan type': the tradition may be erroneous (see below, p. 115 n. 1), but there can be no doubt that Dicaearchus—following his master's theory of what is called in the *Politics* by the name of 'the polity'—gave a general vogue to the idea of the mixed constitution. It has been suggested that the Stoic Panaetius of Rhodes (who was in Italy at the same time as Polybius) knew and used the *Tripoliticus*; and it may be through Panaetius that its theory passed to Polybius and subsequently to Cicero. This is why Dicaearchus deserves to be remembered, even if he is now but a voiceless shadow.

§ III. SOCIAL THEORIES AND MOVEMENTS IN THE THIRD
AND SECOND CENTURIES B.C.

Introduction

The end of the Hellenic Age, in the fourth century B.C., had been a period of ideas of social and political reform, as we may see from

---

[1] Cicero (*Epistulae ad Atticum*, XIII. xxxii, § 2) wrote of three of the works of Dicaearchus, *Tris eos libros maxime nunc vellem: apti essent ad id quod cogito*. I echo Cicero's words, though the three works of Dicaearchus which I should most wish to have those mentioned in the text are not the same as what Cicero desired.

the *Republic* and *Laws* of Plato, and from the seventh and eighth books of Aristotle's *Politics*. The beginning of the Hellenistic Age, in the third century B.C., was a period of social movements, as well as of social ideas and theories. The social movements are illustrated in the history of Sparta from the middle of the century onwards: the fear of such movements and the apprehension of social and political unrest in Greek communities during that century are attested by contemporary inscriptions which have been discovered and recorded by modern scholars. The social ideas and theories appear in the poetry of Cercidas of Megalopolis, and in the Utopia painted by Iambulus and reported by Diodorus Siculus.

There is something paradoxical in the Spartan radicalism of the latter half of the third century. Sparta had hitherto stood for the Greeks as the type of a strict discipline and the home of tradition; and the Spartan constitution had been praised as a peculiarly balanced and poised constitution, which mixed in a just and steady equilibrium the three elements of monarchy, aristocracy, and democracy. But from the reign of Agis IV onwards (243–240 B.C.) Sparta became, for nearly half a century, a home of revolution. It was a reduced and humbled Sparta that went through this phase of history. To the far north of Greece Macedonia now towered in supremacy, as she had done since the latter half of the fourth century: in the north of the Peloponnese the Achaean League, under its general Aratus, menaced Sparta with defeat and possible absorption. If Sparta was to make head against these dangers, she had to replenish a depleted civic body: if she was to do that, she had to redivide the land, which had fallen into the hands of a few owners, and to grow a new crop of Spartan citizens with a stake in the country. She was thus driven into social revolution in order to restore her old self; and a battle came to be engaged—paradoxical, but real and bitter—between a new revolutionary Sparta and the traditional bourgeois conservatism of the various cities of the Achaean League. Sparta failed in the battle, and eventually fell before the League, which invoked the intervention of Macedonia; but Rome stood in the background as the residuary legatee of the fruits of Achaean victory.

If there is something of a paradox in the movement of social reform at Sparta in the second half of the third century, there is also a paradox in the social ideas of Cercidas, as they are expressed in a remarkable meliambic poem discovered on a papyrus roll in the present century. We have to guess the identity of the Cercidas who wrote the poem; but there seems to be reason for thinking that he was (like Polybius the historian) a citizen of Megalopolis, and that he flourished some time after 250 B.C. The paradox of his poem is that a citizen of one of the cities of the conservative Achaean League—a man who was a friend of Aratus, and himself a member of the land-owning class—should have been so radical an exponent of the idea of social justice. But the paradox can be explained. Cercidas, if he was a man of means, was also a Cynic thinker, and as such an egalitarian: he may have been attracted (as Plutarch tells us in his life of Cleomenes III of Sparta that many members of the cities of the Achaean League were) by Sparta's attempt to achieve some system of social equality. There is a definite occasion in the history of Megalopolis which may be connected with the plea of Cercidas for social justice. After the destruction of the city in the course of a war with Sparta, and when plans for rebuilding it were being mooted, a proposal was made (which led to disputes) that one-third of the estates of the land-owning class should be divided among new owners.[1] It is possible to conjecture—but it is a pure conjecture—that the poem of Cercidas was connected with this proposal and with the disputes to which it led.

The poem of Cercidas is brief but trenchant. The Hellenistic Utopia painted by Iambulus—possibly about the time when Cercidas wrote his poem—has a larger span. It is a general play of fancy, which peoples Utopia with strange animals, and goes into curious details of vegetation and diet, in addition to suggesting, as it were incidentally, a new system of social life in which there was no jealousy, and under which concord, or *Homonoia*, was regarded as the chief of blessings. Perhaps it should be counted a romance rather than a utopia: it is certainly more like Lucian than Plato. But Iambulus' 'Sun-State', or 'Heliopolis' as he calls it, is

[1] See D. R. Dudley, op. cit., p. 78.

animated by scattered ideas of equal sharing and even-handed social justice which deserve attention, though they are hidden and overshadowed by a wealth of romantic detail.

(On the reforms attempted at Sparta under Agis IV and Cleomenes III the reader is referred to W. W. Tarn's chapter in the *Cambridge Ancient History*, vol. vii, pp. 739–44 and 752–5.)

A. *Attempts at Social Reform in Sparta under Agis IV (c. 243–240 B.C.)
and Cleomenes III (c. 227–222 B.C.)*

1. *Plutarch's Life of Agis IV*

c. 5. '[A century or more before the reign of Agis IV] a Spartan called Epitadeus, a man of influence but also of a self-willed and difficult temper, became one of the ephors. Having had a quarrel with his son, he proposed and carried a measure which made it lawful for any Spartan to alienate freely his house and estate, either by gift in his lifetime or by bequest in his will. [This brought to an end the old Spartan system[1] of inalienable plots of land or *klēroi.*] . . . Henceforward men of position accumulated estates to an unlimited extent, through the exclusion of the next-of-kin from their inheritance. Soon wealth became concentrated in a few hands; the citizen body was impoverished; and the result was that most men had now no time for honourable pursuits, or any freedom from mean occupations, and began to feel envy and hatred for men of property. There were only 700 full Spartan citizens left; and there were only about 100 of these who had land and a plot of their own. The rest were merely a rabble, lounging about the city without any means or position, destitute of energy or spirit to defend their country against a foreign enemy, and always watching for an opportunity for change and revolution at home.

c. 6. 'In this condition of affairs Agis thought it right (as indeed it was) to bring the citizens back again to an equality, and by that means to replenish the city.' The young men rallied to his ideas,

---

[1] The system was based on considerations of military policy, and was thus analogous to the land-system of early medieval feudalism. According to a tradition which dates from the fourth century B.C., the plots had originally been equal as well as inalienable. There is no evidence that they ever were.

but he found himself opposed (1) by the older generation, (2) by many of the wealthy women of Sparta, who feared the loss of their property and influence, and (3) by his co-sovereign in the Spartan dual monarchy, Leonidas II, who spread the rumour that Agis was aiming at absolute power by his policy of transferring property from the rich to the poor, and that he was only proposing a redistribution of land and a cancelling of debts as a way of 'purchasing guards for his person and not of providing citizens for Sparta'.

c. 8. 'Eventually Agis succeeded in securing the election of Lysander (a supporter) as one of the ephors for the year, and by his means he introduced a measure into the Council of Elders, the effect of which was to release debtors from their obligations and to redistribute [the home territories of Sparta] into 4,500 lots, and the further territories [which were controlled by Sparta] into 15,000. The latter were to be divided among the lower ranks of citizens (*perioikoi*) who were capable of bearing arms: the lots in the home territories were to go to full Spartan citizens (*Spartiatiai*). The deficiency in the number of full citizens was to be made good by enfranchising such citizens in the lower ranks and such [alien] residents as had enjoyed a liberal education and were of good physique and in the prime of life. The whole body [of the 4,500 who were given lots in the home territories] was to be divided into 15 messes (*phiditia*), numbering from 400 to 200 each, and living under the traditional diet and discipline of Sparta.'

Such was the attempted policy of social reform—or rather of restoration; for Agis IV and his party were conservatives, or even reactionaries, rather than revolutionaries, though their policy naturally won favour with the poorer classes in Sparta and in the Peloponnese generally. But the policy failed. Agis IV himself, it is true, offered to throw into the common stock his own considerable estate in arable and pastoral land, along with 600 talents in money; and his mother and friends and relatives, who were among the wealthiest people in Sparta, made a similar offer. But a struggle ensued in which both the dual monarchy of Sparta and her social classes were both divided against themselves; and in its course one of the supporters of King Agis gave him the fatal advice, which he followed, that he should have debts cancelled at once (*chreōn apokopē*) but should postpone the redistribution of land (*gēs anadasmos*). Agis was thus left engaged in a struggle with the old owners and their party without the backing which he might otherwise have had from new owners of plots; and distracted at the same time from domestic affairs by his military duties he fell an easy victim to the hostility of the opposition. He was executed by the ephors: his mother, and her mother too, perished with him; and his plans and policy passed, for the moment, into oblivion.

2. *Plutarch's Life of Cleomenes III*

Within a few years, however, the plans of Agis were resuscitated and again attempted by Cleomenes III, who had married the widow of Agis IV and learned from her the nature of his policy and aspirations. He was also a disciple of the Stoic philosopher Sphaerus, whose pupil he had been, just as, a century later, the Roman reformer Tiberius Gracchus found some stimulus in the teaching of the Stoic Blossius.[1]

c. 2–3. 'Cleomenes is said to have been instructed in philosophy during his early years, when Sphaerus, who came from Olbia [a Greek colony in the north of the Black Sea], was a visitor in Sparta and was occupied in discoursing to the young men and boys.[2] This Sphaerus was one of the chief disciples of Zeno, and it would seem that he admired the manly temper of Cleomenes and fanned his ambition. . . . Stoic philosophy has something in it which is risky and hazardous for great and ardent natures; but

[1] Blossius, who came from Cumae, seems to have been a stormy petrel of his time. When Aristonicus of Pergamum revolted against Rome in 133 B.C. and joined forces with a rising of slaves, he found a coadjutor in Blossius; and Sir W. W. Tarn has suggested (in *Hellenistic Civilisation*, 3rd edition, p. 125) that 'the two proposed to set up something resembling Iambulus' Sun-State upon earth'. See below, p. 62.

[2] Sphaerus was not the source of the ideas of Cleomenes (they were derived from his wife and his predecessor Agis IV), but at any rate he was a coadjutor in his schemes. He wrote a treatise on the Spartan constitution for him, which may have presented the history of Sparta as it was understood by Agis IV and his associates. He also wrote a treatise in three books, according to Diogenes Laertius, *On Lycurgus and Socrates*, and another *On Kingship*. There was plenty here for Cleomenes, and 'the young men and boys' of Sparta, to study.

when it is applied to grave and gentle characters it encourages their development towards their proper goal.'

Sparta was at this time involved in a struggle with the Achaean League and its general Aratus. It was a struggle for the control of the Peloponnese; and Cleomenes, ambitious for success in the struggle, decided that he must first attempt a policy of reform in Sparta. If he did so, he would not only be true to the lessons he had learned from his wife and to the teaching of Sphaerus: he would also be strengthening the Spartan army, and thus strengthening himself to defeat Aratus and to secure control of the Peloponnese. He accordingly attacked the conservative college of ephors, put four of the five to death, and announced his programme to a meeting of the Spartan popular assembly.

c. 10, § 6–c. 11. 'He would, he said, throw all the land into a common pool for the benefit of all; he would free debtors from their debts: he would cause the aliens to be sifted and tested, with a view to making the best of them Spartan citizens who would guard the city in arms; "and thus", he concluded, "we shall cease to see our country a prey . . . for want of a force sufficient to defend it".

'Then, as a first step he surrendered his own estate into the common stock—an example followed by his stepfather and all his other friends. All the rest of the citizens did the like, and the land was redivided. Cleomenes even assigned lots to all such as had been driven into exile by his action, promising that they should all be allowed to return when things became quiet. He proceeded to fill up the civic body by enrolling in it the most promising among the lower ranks of citizens (*perioikoi*); and he thus created a force of 4,000 heavy-armed infantry [whom he taught a new drill]. Then he turned his attention to the education of the young and the restoration of the old "discipline" (*agōgē*). Here he was aided in most of the steps which he took by the presence of Sphaerus: the system of gymnasia and of common meals was soon restored to order; and though a few had to be compelled by force, most men came voluntarily under the plain and simple Spartan diet and the Spartan way of life. . . .'

Cleomenes made such headway in the Peloponnese, aided by

his own direct simplicity and absence of state, that Aratus appealed for help to Antigonus Doson, the King of Macedonia, whom he had hitherto sought to keep at arm's length. Thus, in Plutarch's phrase, 'while he sought to escape the Spartan barley-bread and coarse cloak and the policy of abolishing wealth and relieving poverty which was the gravest count in his indictment of Cleomenes, Aratus put himself and the Achaean League under the heel of the Macedonian monarchy, with its crown and purple and its oriental edicts' (c. 16, § 5). The consequence was something of a split in the Achaean League: attracted by the radical policy of Sparta, 'the common people hoped for a distribution of land and abolition of debts' (c. 17, § 5), while even the leading men in many of the cities of the League resented the action of Aratus. For a time Cleomenes, in spite of the odds, made some headway: he even succeeded in capturing the city of Argos: 'men admired his alertness and intelligence, and instead of laughing, as they had done before, at his saying that he followed Solon and Lycurgus in his cancellation of debts and equalization of property, they now began to be fully persuaded that his policy had been the cause of the change in the fortunes of Sparta' (c. 18, § 2). But the pressure of the Macedonian armies was too great: he was forced to retire upon Sparta, where he was met by the news of the death of his wife; as a last desperate fling he enfranchised all the Spartan serfs (the helots) who could pay 500 drachmas for their liberation,[1] and he armed 2,000 of them in the Macedonian style to oppose the 'White Shields' of Antigonus (c. 23, § 1). It was all in vain: he was decisively defeated by the Macedonians at the battle of Sellasia (222 B.C.): Sparta fell to the victors, and Cleomenes, escaping to Egypt, was entangled in a web of intrigue and finally committed suicide.

A final attempt at social reform, or social revolution, was made at Sparta under Nabis (207–192 B.C.). A descendant of one of the two Spartan royal houses, he seized the crown in 207; and with

---

[1] Tarn doubts the story that Cleomenes obtained 500 talents by selling 6,000 helots their liberty, and speaks of his having 'freed and armed a small body' (*C.A.H.* vii, p. 760).

the aid of a mercenary guard, and in alliance with the Cretan pirates he carried out a social policy even more thoroughgoing than that of Cleomenes III. His policy included, like that of his predecessors, the abolition of debts and the redistribution of land; but he went farther than they had done in his confiscation of *personal* property (which he used to attach his mercenary guard and other supporters to his cause) and in his treatment of the helots, many of whom he enfranchised and endowed with estates in land. But the policy of Nabis—again like that of his predecessors—was restoration rather than revolution; he might use revolutionary means, but he used them as means to the restoration of the independence and the power of Sparta. He too failed in the issue; and after being defeated in a struggle with Rome (195 B.C.), he fell a victim to an attack by the Aetolians of northern Greece (192), and Sparta was forced into membership of the Achaean League.

B. *Cercidas on Social Justice*

(The poem, found on a papyrus, is printed in *Collectanea Alexandrina*, edited by J. U. Powell, Oxford, 1925, pp. 203–6. It is translated and discussed in D. R. Dudley's book on *Cynicism*, pp. 79 ff.)

'I blame Zeus because he did not turn that fellow Xenon, who is packed with malice and a mass of incontinence, into a child of poverty, thereby giving *us* a flood of silver that now runs to waste.[1] What was there to prevent the god, if one asked him—it is easy for a god to do everything that comes into his mind— what was there to prevent him [from striking down] either some dirty base usurer and hoarder of dead pelf, or some spendthrift who cannot keep a hold on his money and ruins his property, and then emptying them of the pig's wash of their wealth and endowing the poor man—who just munches the necessaries of life and fills his cup from the common bowl—with the means of meeting the little expenses now beyond him? Surely it cannot be that the

---

[1] I owe this interpretation to Mr. E. A. Barber, the Rector of Exeter College, Oxford, and the author of a chapter on Cercidas in *New Chapters in Greek Literature* (Oxford, 1921). Mr. Barber points out to me that a marginal gloss speaks of Xenon as 'a certain acquaintance (of Cercidas), incontinent and bitter'.

eye of justice is blinded like a mole's; that Phaëthon (the sun) sees crookedly with one eye; and that the brightness of Themis (Justice) has been dimmed. How can gods still be gods when they have neither hearing nor sight?

'And yet the august Compeller of the lightning, who has his seat in mid-Olympus, keeps the balance stretched straight and fair, and never for a moment nods;[1] and Homer in the *Iliad* speaks these words, "The balance sinks when the fated day cometh unto men of renown". [Cercidas, assuming that the sinking of the balance signifies the gift of wealth to such men—whereas Homer meant that it signified the coming of death—now continues his argument on that assumption.] Why, then, has Zeus, being as he is a just officer of weights and measures, never inclined the scales in *my* favour? while as for the Mysians [or, as we might say, the Philistines], who are the very dregs of mankind—ah, I fear to say how much the scale of his balance comes down upon *their* side. To what sort of sovereign, then, or to which of the sons of Heaven, can one turn in order to discover how to get one's desert—when the Son of Cronus, who begat us all and gave us all birth, shows himself a mere stepfather to some and a real father to others? It were better to leave these things to the astrologers; for I expect *they* would not have a whit of trouble in dealing with them.

'But as for us [Cercidas here turns round, and no longer speaks for the poor, but as one of the well-to-do and *to* the well-to-do], let us make Paean the Healer and the goddess Sharing-with-others our guides [i.e. let us help the sick and give to the needy]; for Sharing-with-others is a divinity, and Nemesis [a word which in its original sense means a proper distribution of shares] is still present on earth. ... So while the gods send us a favouring wind, honour *her*, ye short-lived race of men; for if heaven's breeze should change and blow contrary, you will have, I ween, to disgorge from the bottom of your purses your wealth and all that fortune has given you.'[2]

[1] This would seem to be ironical. Zeus is supposed to keep the balance just: does he?

[2] The latter half of this sentence is translated from a highly conjectural restoration of the defective text of the papyrus by J. von Arnim.

c. *The fear of social and political unrest in Greek communities*

1. An inscription from Itani (the modern Palaeokastro) in Crete—not dated, but probably of the Hellenistic period—shows the nature of the social and political apprehensions of Greek communities, and of the movements against which they sought to guard. It is printed in Dittenberger, *Sylloge*³, No. 526.

'This was the oath taken by the people of Itani. I will not betray the city, or its territory, or the islands belonging to the Itanians: I will not bring in enemies or betray the ships of the Itanians: I will not betray any of the citizens, or any of their goods. I will not form a party [*synōmosia*, a political club of members united by oaths sworn to one another] to the detriment of the city or its citizens; nor will I help any man, if he desires to do any of these things; on the contrary I will inform the magistrates. I will not bring about the redistribution (*anadasmos*) of lands or houses or building-plots, or the abolition of debts (*chreōn apokopē*). Nor will I bring a suit for deprivation of his civic rights against any of the citizens, on the ground that he is intriguing or on any pretence whatsoever; but I will act as a citizen in a fair and equal manner, both in things divine and things human, according to the existing laws which we follow in regard to such matters as well as those we are now enacting or any others which we may enact in time to come, whether about things divine or things political; and I will not abandon my citizenship either in peace or war. To those who abide by, and keep, their oaths may there be the blessing of children, and good harvests from the soil, and prosperity among their flocks, and many other blessings; but to those who break their oaths may there be no harvest from the soil, and no blessing of children, or prosperity among their flocks, but may such evil men be evilly destroyed, and their offspring with them.'

2. A similar inscription from Chersonesus Taurica (a Greek colony in the Crimea) is printed in Dittenberger, op. cit., No. 360. Its date is 300–280 B.C. Though it is some four centuries prior to the Borysthenic Oration of Dio of Prusa, delivered to the citizens of a Greek city in the same area, it shows the same apprehensions and general conditions of life as those which Dio records (*Oratis* xxxvi).

'I swear this: I will be in concord with my fellows for the security and liberty of the city and its citizens. I will not betray it [or any of its territories] in any way to any man, Greek or barbarian; and I will keep watch and ward for the people of Chersonesus. I will not subvert democracy, nor will I be a party to, or help to conceal, any man who betrays or subverts it; but I will inform the magistrates in the city. . . . I will serve in office, and on the Council, as well and justly as I can, for the benefit of the city and its citizens. I will keep watch and ward over the safety of the people, and I will not divulge, either to Greek or barbarian [i.e. to the "Scythians" living round the city], any secret which may injure the city. I will not give or receive a gift to the detriment of the city and its citizens. . . . I will not join in any party-club (*synōmosia*) directed against the community of Chersonesus, or against any of the citizens who is not proved to be an enemy of the people; and if I have joined in such a body with any man, or been bound to any man by oath or vow, may it be better for me if I break away from it, but may the contrary befall me if I hold to it. And if I know that any such body exists or is being formed, I will inform the magistrates.'

D. *A Hellenistic Utopia*

Diodorus Siculus, at the end of book II of his *Bibliotheca Historica*, gives an account of a 'Sun-State', or Heliopolis, which had been described in a sort of romance by a certain Iambulus (if that was his name and not a pseudonym), possibly about the middle of the third century B.C. Iambulus set his 'Sun-State' in a group of 'islands of the Sun', which he placed in the Indian Ocean, to the south of Arabia. But his 'Heliopolis' is really a Utopia; and the romance of Iambulus was the first and original precursor of Sir Thomas More's *Utopia* and the Dominican Campanella's *Città del Sole*. The interest of Iambulus is that he represents the stirring of social ideas, and the dream of a social revolution, which may be traced in the Sparta of Agis and Cleomenes and also appears, about the same time (the latter half of the third century B.C.), in the poem of Cercidas on social justice. Sir William W. Tarn, in his *Alexander*

the Great (vol. ii, pp. 413–14) and in his *Hellenistic Civilisation*
(3rd edition, p. 125), suggests that the Sun State of Iambulus was
the inspiration of an attempted revolution at Pergamum a century
later, in 133 B.C. The leader of that revolution, Aristonicus, who
numbered slaves in his following and had pledged himself to their
liberation, called his supporters by the name of 'Heliopolitans'.
He was crushed by the Romans, and his 'Sun-State' set in darkness. But whether it was actually inspired by Iambulus is a matter
as obscure as the identity of Iambulus himself.

c. lvi. Diodorus, following Iambulus, begins by describing the
physical characteristics of the island, or islands, of the Sun, and of
the inhabitants. 'The men were bent in body, had a grip of iron,
and were hairless except on the face. They were good-looking
and had a good carriage; they had wide open ears and exceptionally quick hearing; their tongues were double, down to the root,
which enabled them to imitate every human language and the
notes of all birds—and even to carry on two conversations at
once. Their climate was happily temperate, so that they were
vexed neither by heat nor by cold: their crops grew all the year
round. As Homer said of the garden of Alcinous, day was equal
to night throughout the year, and there was no shadow at midday
because the sun was directly over their heads.

c. lvii, § 1. 'They lived in kin-groups and "systems", with their
relatives gathered round them to a number of not more than 400.
They spent their days in the meadows, since the country offered a
ready abundance for their daily food: the virtue of the soil was
such, and the climate so temperate, that nature supplied them
spontaneously with more sustenance than they needed. § 2. They
made their bread, which was sweet and good, from a plant like
vetch: § 3. they had plenty of springs of water, some hot and good
for baths, and some cold and good for their health. § 4. They paid
attention to every subject of education, but particularly to astrology [which was spreading westward from Babylonia in the third
century B.C.]: the letters of the alphabet which they used were
twenty-eight in regard to the sounds which they expressed, but
only seven in regard to their forms, each of the seven forms being
capable of four modifications. They did not write, as we do, in

transverse lines across the page, but in straight lines going down-wards. The men were exceedingly long-lived, attaining the age of 150, and mostly free from any disease: those who were maimed or had any physical defect were compelled by an inflexible rule to put an end to their lives. § 5. It was their custom to live to their appointed age, and when they had filled their span of life volun-tarily to meet death: there was a peculiar grass in their country, such that any man who rested upon it passed quietly into an un-conscious sleep and never woke again.

c. lviii, § 1. 'They did not marry wives, but had their women in common: the children so born were brought up in common and treated with equal affection by all. While they were infants the women who suckled them often exchanged their charges, so that even the mothers could not recognize their own children: consequently there was no jealousy among them, and they always lived without any quarrels, counting concord (*Homonoia*) the chief of all blessings. §§ 2–4. There were curious animals in their country, small and circular, like tortoises, each marked diagonally with two yellow lines, and each having an eye and a mouth at the end of either line: all of them had a number of feet round the circumference of their bodies, and could move in any direction they pleased: their blood had the quality of congealing at once, and if any part of their body, other than a vital part, were cut off, the wound immediately healed. § 5. Each of the "systems" kept a large bird of a peculiar nature, and they used it to discover the qualities of their children's character in infancy: they placed the children on the backs of the birds, and watching how they be-haved when the birds began to fly they kept and reared the children who stood the trial of the flight, and rejected those who showed themselves squeamish and full of alarm, holding that these were not likely to live long and were disqualified by their mental defects. § 6. The eldest member of each system always exercises authority, as if he were a king, and all the others obey him: when he reaches the age of 150 and departs from life in accordance with custom, the next eldest succeeds to his authority. § 7. The sea round the island is sweet to the taste: of the stars we know in Greece, the greater and the lesser Bear and many others are not visible. There are really seven islands in all, alike and equidistant, and all living by the same customs and rules.'

c. lix. Diodorus proceeds to an account of diet and dress and worship in the Islands of the Sun, mixed up with an account of its fauna and flora. § 1. 'Though they live in the midst of an easy abundance, the islanders do not let themselves go in the enjoyment of pleasures: they make simplicity their aim, and content themselves with satisfying their necessities: they just roast or boil their meat, and know nothing of sauces and garnishes. § 2. The gods they worship are the universe and the sun and the heavenly bodies generally. . . . § 5. All the details of their mode of life are arranged in a definite order: they do not all take their meals at the same time, or all eat the same food: they make their arrangements for each appointed day, now eating fish and now fowls, now the flesh of animals, and now olives and the simplest dishes. § 6. They pursue their occupations in turns: at any given time some will be in attendance on others, some will be fishing, some busied in crafts, some busy about other useful duties, and some engaged in public duties according to a regular round, with the exception of the aged. § 7. At festivals and times of rejoicing they sing or recite hymns and praises in honour of the gods, and especially of the Sun, to whom they ascribe their island and themselves as belonging. § 8. They bury the dead at ebb-tide in the sand, so that the grave is filled up and covered in at high tide. . . .'

c. lx. Iambulus and his companions stayed in the islands of the Sun for seven years, and were then expelled. They put to sea, and were carried to India. Iambulus was separated from his companions, who were drowned, and got to the court of a phil-Hellene king who had a passion for education. Here he found a warm welcome; and hence he made his way first to Persia and finally to Greece, where he wrote an account of his wanderings.[1]

[1] The Cynics—or at any rate one of them, Crates (*floruit circa* 325 B.C.)—had cherished the idea of an island-paradise, styled by the name of Pera (which in Greek means a wallet or scrip, such as the Cynics carried). 'There is a city, Pera', Crates wrote in a poem, 'in the midst of the wine-coloured sea of Illusion: fair and fruitful it is . . . owning naught. Thither sails no fool or parasite . . . but it bears thyme and garlic, figs and loaves . . . they [i.e. its inhabitants] delight in freedom and immortal kingship [i.e. self-mastery]).' (Quoted in D. R. Dudley,

§ IV. FEDERALISM IN GREECE FROM THE DAYS OF THE
MACEDONIAN SUPREMACY (338 B.C.) TO THE ROMAN
SETTLEMENT OF 146 B.C.

Introduction

In the course of the fourth century B.C. there was a general
tendency towards federal or quasi-federal forms in Greece. The
Second Athenian League (instituted in 377 B.C.), seeking to avoid
the centralization and 'imperialism' of the First or Delian League,
made provision for a double parliament, partly composed of
the Athenian Council and Assembly as one element, and partly
of a synod of representatives of the other cities of the League
as the other. The Boeotian League, which was as old as the
fifth century, also entered on a new life during the fourth, with
a federal synod of 660 members elected in equal numbers from
its eleven electoral divisions, and with a strongly *representative*
character. (Indeed it was in the nature of leagues—as groups of
many cities, and as necessarily requiring a central league assembly
with members drawn from each city—to foster the evolution of
central bodies of *representatives*, appointed by election or possibly
by lot. The individual city might be content, and more than
content, with a primary assembly of all its citizens: the group of
cities generally needed something more, or at any rate something
different—though, as will be noticed presently, the later Achaean
League was peculiar in this respect, and attempted something in
the nature of a *primary* central assembly.) Besides the Athenian
and the Boeotian Leagues, the fourth century also produced
northern leagues in the Chalcidic peninsula and in Thessaly, and
southern leagues in Achaea and Arcadia. Macedonia itself, under
Philip, turned to federal forms—which were in the nature, however, of a confederation or *Staatenbund* rather than of a federation
or *Bundesstaat*—when Philip instituted the League of Corinth in
338 B.C. This was an alliance or *symmachy* (and not, as a federation
was, a *sympolity*), the members of which contributed contingents
to a common 'Greek Defence Force' and were represented on a

History of Cynicism, p. 44.) Have 'the islands of the Sun' any connexion with the
Cynic island-paradise?

common council in numbers proportionate to the contribution of each. This League of Corinth served as a basis or background to the Asiatic conquests of Alexander: after serving its temporary purpose it declined (though it was on occasion renewed under Alexander and his successors); and the general policy of Macedonia towards the cities of Greece was, if anything, inimical to federation, and followed the opposite line of *Divide et impera*.

But the troubles and confusion of the third century none the less offered an opportunity for the growth of independent and spontaneous federations. The most notable of these was the Achaean League in the north of the Peloponnese.[1] This was a 'sympolity' of some ten Achaean cities, which from the middle of the third century onwards had a single *stratēgos* (president and commander-in-chief) and a regular organization. The cities of the League kept their own constitutions, with their individual senates and assemblies; they retained their own courts; they even maintained the right of issuing their own coins, which were concurrent with the coinage of the League. On the other hand, there was a regular federal authority—on the executive side the *stratēgos* and the ten *dēmiourgoi* (corresponding to the ten cities of the League) who formed a sort of cabinet; and on the deliberative side a council (*Boulē*) and a general assembly. The affairs which were reserved for this regular federal authority included foreign policy, the army, the finance and taxes which these involved, and a uniform system of weights and measures.

The surviving evidence is not sufficient to enable us to attain any clear or conclusive view of the exact structure and working of the federal council and assembly; but it is possible that by the second century the general assembly of the League, consisting of all the citizens of all the cities who were over the age of 30, met only on extraordinary occasions, under the style and title of *synklētos*, to discuss matters of treaties and alliances and generally of peace or war, and that otherwise the Council (*Boulē*), however its members were appointed (it may have been by lot, and they may have been paid for their services), acted as the ordinary meet-

---

[1] Mention should also be made of the Aetolian League in Northern Greece (see below, p. 78) but we know less of its constitution.

ing or *synodos*.[1] The reader will notice, in the extracts which
follow, references to (1) meetings of the magistrates only (the
Stratēgos and *Dēmiourgoi*), (2) sessions of the *synodos* (in Latin
concilium), which may mean meetings of the *Boulē* acting as the
ordinary deliberative organ of the League, and (3) sessions of all
the citizens over the age of 30, meeting as a *synklētos* on extraordinary occasions. Another feature of the League, which is also
illustrated in the following extracts, was a rule under which the
meetings of the League were held in different cities in turn. This
system of what may be called a movable metropolis was intended
to prevent any one city from acquiring an ascendancy: it may
remind us of a suggestion made by Rousseau in the *Du Contrat
social*, intended to reconcile direct sovereignty of the people with
the existence of the great State, or again of a practice of early
trade unionism by which the local branches of unions in the different areas of England became in turn the 'governing branch'.
Another rule which also protected individual cities was one by
which votes were taken in the *synodos* (and also in the *synklētos*)
by cities and not by heads: this served to prevent the city in which
the meeting was held from acquiring a preponderance. The effect
of these rules, and of the general good sense with which the
League conducted its affairs, was, as Tarn notes (*Hellenistic
Civilisation*, 3rd edition, pp. 75–76), a 'strikingly successful
balance . . . between federal and city interests'. At its zenith, in
the years after 228 B.C., the League included not only the original
cities of Achaea, but also the rest of the Peloponnese with the one
exception of Sparta. But the League was suppressed by Rome in
146 B.C.; like Macedonia before her, she was not friendly to the
principle and practice of federation.

Of the documents which follow, the first two are concerned
with the formation and the constitution of the League or 'confederation' of Corinth. The rest are mainly concerned with the
action and debates of the Achaean League (§§ C, D, and E); and
here the translator desires to thank Professor Larsen, of the University of Chicago, for the references and the help he has given.
An inscription of the year 150 B.C. has been included, on the

[1] See the note below, p. 73.

suggestion of Mr. Peter Fraser, of All Souls College, Oxford; and the translator has ventured to add, *proprio motu*, a final passage from Polybius, which may be called the swan-song of Greek federation—and of any idea of Greek unity.

A. *The peace and league made after the battle of Chaeronea in 338 B.C.*

A document of 338/7 B.C.: 'the peace of the Greeks with Philip of Macedon' (found on the Acropolis at Athens and printed in Tod, *Greek Historical Inscriptions*, ii, No. 177), may be simply a treaty of peace, or it may be a league of alliance (*symmachia*), or short of that (as the concluding words suggest) it may be a preparation for such a league. In any case, it throws light on the general background of the League of Corinth, in which Philip drew together a number of the Greek States under his leadership, after his victory at Chaeronea, by an act which has been called one of 'the great achievements of statesmanship in the world's history'. But while some scholars regard the document as a 'mere peace treaty', others regard it as a constitutional document creating a confederation. The balance seems to incline in favour of the former view: the creation of a confederation was perhaps the result of a later and separate document. And yet the conclusion of the document—with its mention of a common council (*synedrion*) and its specification of the number of votes to be given by each member—suggests some sort of formal organization. But for any full account of that organization we are thrown back on what we can gather from the renewal of the League (for the second time[1]) in 302 B.C. (see B below).

'I swear by . . . all the gods and goddesses: I will abide by the treaty of peace: I will not violate the agreements (*synthecae*) made with Philip of Macedon: I will not bear arms, to their hurt, against any of those who abide by the oaths, whether by land or sea: I will not occupy by measures of war any city or fort or harbour belonging to any of those who participate in the peace, by any art or device: I will not seek to subvert the kingdom of Philip of Macedon and his descendants, or the constitutions existing in any

---

[1] It had been renewed for the first time by Alexander.

of the states at the time when they swore the oaths to the peace: I will not myself do anything contrary to these agreements, or allow others to do so, so far as in me lies. And if any man do anything regarding these agreements in infraction of peace, I will give help according as the injured parties require; and I will go to war with any who contravene the common peace according as the common council and the leader (*hēgemōn*, i.e. Philip) require.'

There follows an imperfect list of members (the pillar on which the inscription was carved is broken), with the number of the votes—from one to ten—to be exercised by each member: the number apparently depended on the strength of the contingent which each furnished. It would appear from this that the document, if it does not itself constitute a confederation, at any rate presupposes such a body.

B. *The provisions of the League of the Greeks, or Hellenic Confederation (originally formed by Philip of Macedon at Corinth in 338 B.C.), as renewed in 302 by Antigonus of Macedonia and his son Demetrius*

From the *Corpus Inscriptionum Graecarum*, iv[1], No. 68.

'The Council (*synedrion*) shall assemble, in time of peace, during the holding of the [four Panhellenic] sacred games: in time of war, it shall assemble as often as, in the view of the members of the Council and of the general left by the king[1] for the common security, it shall seem to be advantageous. The place of the meetings of the Council, until the common war [now being waged] shall be ended, shall be wherever the presidents (the *proedroi* or "bureau"), and the king or the person designated by the king, shall announce: when peace comes, the meetings shall be held wherever the games in which crowns are awarded [i.e. the four Panhellenic games] are appointed to take place.

'The resolutions of the Council are to be final (*kyria*). The members may transact business when over half of them are present: they may not do so if a smaller number is in attendance. Let it

---

[1] This probably refers to the general of the forces left by Demetrius in southern Greece, where he had lately been active.

not be permitted to the member cities to demand an account from the councillors sent by them in regard to the resolutions passed by the Council [i.e. the councillors are to be plenipotentiaries, and not delegates subject to a mandate]. The presidents (*proedroi*), when the war ends, shall be five members of the Council, designated by lot. Let not more than one be so designated from any people (*ethnos*) or city. The presidents shall, by common resolution, assemble the members and the clerks, along with the servitors; they shall bring forward the subjects on which it is necessary to take counsel, and they shall communicate the resolutions taken upon them to the clerks: then, having clear copies, they shall enter all the opinions expressed, taking care in every way for the proper conduct of business, with power to fine any person guilty of disorderly conduct. If any member proposes to introduce any matter which is of advantage to the kings and the Greeks, or wishes to denounce any person as acting to the detriment of the allies or not obeying the agreements made, or desires to bring any other business before the Council, let his name be registered with the presidents, and let them bring the matter before the Council. The presidents are to be responsible [? to the Council] for any action they take. Any indictment against them shall be handed, by any person who so wishes, to the presidents appointed by lot to succeed [the presidents thus indicted]. Let them, when they have received it, bring it before the members of the Council in the first session next ensuing. Until the common war shall be ended, the presidency shall be always vested [not in persons drawn from the Council, but] in those who come from the kings. If any city fails to send a representative to the meeting of the Council according to the covenant of the league, let it pay for each person so absent 2 drachmas in respect of each session, until the councillors disperse, unless any representative depose on oath that he has been ill. And if any city fail to send the force agreed upon, when such force has been announced as due to be sent, it shall pay for each day of a man's absence half a mina for a horseman, 20 drachmas for a heavy infantryman, 20 for a light-armed soldier, and 10 for a sailor, until the time of service for the Greeks is finished.

'The agreements and oaths, and the names of those who are to be members of the Council, shall be recorded in the chief temples. This is the oath.

'I swear by Zeus, Earth, Sun, Poseidon, Athene, Ares, and all the gods and goddesses: I will abide by the alliance with the kings Antigonus and Demetrius and with their issue, and with the other allies who are members of the Council of the League: I will regard as friends or as enemies those whom they regard as such: I will not bear arms for their hurt against any of the allies who abide by the covenant, either by land or sea, nor will I cut off [from supplies] any of the members of the Council, nor will I seek to overturn the rule of Antigonus and Demetrius or their issue. And if any of the other allies do any of these things, acting in any way contrary to what is written in the covenant, I will not, to the best of my power, permit such action to be taken; and I will go to war with those who contravene the common peace based on the alliance.'

Note. The inscription is of importance as giving the terms of the first 'confederation' recorded in an historical document. The terms recorded—especially the insistence that representatives are to be plenipotentiaries, and the attempt to secure the sending of adequate contingents—are notable. Plutarch, in his *Life of Demetrius*, c. 25, records the holding of a general council at Ithome, after the entry of Demetrius with an army into the Peloponnese: he adds that it was largely attended, and that Demetrius was declared *hēgemōn* of Hellas, as Philip, who originally formed the alliance, and Alexander, who afterwards renewed it, had been before him.

c. *A Debate in the Federal Assembly of the Achaean League on Foreign Policy*, 198 B.C.

The issue before the assembly was whether the League should abandon its relations with the kingdom of Macedonia, and enter into alliance with Rome, then engaged in the Second Macedonian War which ended in the Roman victory at Cynoscephalae in 197 B.C. Envoys appeared before the assembly both from Rome, which promised Corinth to the League if it came over to the Roman side, and from the King of Macedonia. The debate and its result is reported by Livy, book XXXII, chapters xix–xxii *passim*.

c. xix. . . . 'A council (a *synodos*[1]) was assembled at Sicyon to give audience to the envoys. The state of mind among the Achaeans was singularly perplexed [they feared Rome, but they had old ties with Macedonia—and yet they distrusted its king]. It was not only that they did not know what line to take publicly, either in the senates of their several cities or in the common council of the federation: they were not even clear in their own minds, when they thought it over, what they wished or preferred.' The first of the three days assigned for the meeting was spent in listening to the speeches of the various envoys.

c. xx–xxi. 'Next day the assembly met again: the magistrates, speaking by a herald, as is the custom of the Greeks, invited any who wished to come forward and express an opinion: there was a long silence, and the members of the assembly sat looking at one another.' The 'praetor' of the League, as Livy calls him—in other words the President and Commander-in-Chief—pressed in vain for some suggestion: he could not elicit a sound or a murmur from that crowded meeting with its members drawn from so many States. He then expressed his own opinion, in favour of entering into alliance with Rome.

c. xxii. 'Following the President's speech a number of voices were heard, some agreeing with the speaker, some attacking those who agreed with him. Presently there arose an altercation which went beyond individual differences and engaged one state in dispute with another; and soon the magistrates of the league (called *Dēmiourgoi*, and ten in number) were involved in the struggle as hotly as the members themselves. Five of them said that they would move in favour of alliance with Rome and would give their votes for it: the other five held that there was a legal provision which made it improper for the magistrates to move any motion, or the council to pass any resolution, that ran counter to the alliance of the League with Macedonia.' The second day thus passed in dispute: on the third and last day, on which feeling ran high, one of the magistrates changed his opinion, under pressure, and a majority of them then moved a resolution in favour of

---

[1] The meeting may possibly have been a *synklētos*, or extraordinary assembly of all citizens over 30: see the extract from Polybius below, p. 76, under § E.

alliance with Rome. The resolution was carried by a large majority, but the representatives of some of the member states which had particular ties with Macedonia withdrew from the meeting; their withdrawal was excused on the ground that they had recently received great favours from Macedonia.

D. *Another Debate in the Achaean Assembly on Foreign Policy,* 187 B.C.

After the war between Rome and Antiochus III of Asia, and following on his defeat at Magnesia in 190 B.C., there was a general settlement. In its course the assembly of the Achaean League met for a discussion of foreign policy, partly to receive and decide upon offers made to it by Eumenes King of Pergamum and Seleucus IV the son and successor of Antiochus, and partly to hear and deal with reports submitted to it by its own envoys who had been sent to negotiate with Rome and with Ptolemy V of Egypt. The discussion and its results are reported by Polybius, book XXII, c. x–xiii *passim*.

c. x. 'Aristaenus was now President of the League. Ambassadors arrived from King Ptolemy while the synod of the League was in session at Megalopolis. King Eumenes had also sent envoys, bringing the offer of a sum of 120 talents, which was to be invested and the interest from it used to pay the expenses of the members of the Council (*Boulē*) in attending the general synods of the League.'[1] The envoys of Seleucus also offered a squadron of ten ships of war. The first business done was to accept, without any debate, the report of the Achaean envoys who had been sent to negotiate with Rome on the relations between the League and its neighbour Sparta. The offer of Eumenes was then debated.

c. xi. One of the representatives of Sicyon opposed the acceptance of the offer. 'That the Council should be maintained

---

[1] Dr. Tarn, in the *Cambridge Ancient History*, vol. vii, p. 737, calculates that the interest on 120 talents would suffice to pay the annual expenses of over 6,000 persons, and he therefore suggests that the Council of the League must have been a very large body. He is also inclined (1) to identify the Council with the synod, and accordingly (2) to conjecture that the synod, originally an assembly or *ecclēsia*, had come in time to absorb what had once been a separate council and to take its place and its name (ibid., p. 738).

year by year at the expense of Eumenes, and should swallow this species of bait before deliberating on matters of general policy, was obviously discreditable and dangerous to the League. It was Eumenes who now offered money: tomorrow it might be Prusias of Bithynia, or it might be Seleucus. The interests of kings and democracies were opposite in their nature: the greatest and most frequent issues of debate always turned on the difference between themselves and kings: it was clear that one of two things was bound to happen—either the interest of kings would prevail at the expense of their own welfare, or if that did not happen, they would show themselves guilty of ingratitude in the sight of all the world by opposing their own wage-payers.' This argument carried the day; and the offer of Eumenes was unanimously rejected, with acclamation.

c. xii. The ambassadors of Ptolemy and the Achaean envoys who had been to Egypt were next given a hearing. The Achaean envoys spoke of having renewed the treaty of alliance with Egypt, upon which Aristaenus, the President of the League, inquired 'which treaty?' The fact was that there was more than one, and the various treaties differed greatly. No answer was given to the President's question: the members of the synod all began to talk, and the chamber was full of confusion. The President refused to allow a vote to be taken, and he had the issue adjourned in view of the confusion in which it was involved. The offer of Seleucus was next discussed, and the assembly, while voting in favour of a renewal of friendly relations with him, refused for the time being to accept the offer of a squadron of ships.

c. xiii. 'After deliberating on these issues the meeting ended its session, and the members all returned to their own cities.' A Roman envoy now appeared, on his way back from a mission to Macedonia, and was given a hearing at a meeting of the magistrates (possibly the ten *Dēmiourgoi*) convened by Aristaenus at Argos. He censured the League for its harsh behaviour to Sparta,[1]

---

[1] The Achaean League was always at outs with Sparta: 'it could neither conquer nor win over Sparta; on this rock it was ultimately to founder' (Tarn, *Hellenistic Civilisation*, 3rd edition, p. 20). At the time of which Polybius is speaking the hand of the League had been laid heavily on Sparta: money had been exacted from her, and the proceeds used to erect a row of columns in one of the cities of the League;

and requested it to correct its policy and amend its ways. Aristaenus was silent, showing thereby that he agreed with the Roman envoy: others defended the action of the League; and it was eventually resolved by the meeting of magistrates to leave things as they were. Thereupon the Roman envoy asked that 'the Many' (i.e. the synod of the members of the League) should be convened in an assembly to meet him. The meeting of magistrates then asked him to produce his instructions from the Senate on the issue which he had raised; and when he did not answer their request they refused to convene an assembly to meet him, arguing that their rules did not permit them to do so unless written instructions were produced from the Senate stating the issues on which the assembly ought to be convened. The Roman envoy, in a rage, refused to accept the answer given him by the magistrates, and then departed unanswered.

E. *A Third Debate in the Achaean Assembly on Foreign Policy: winter of* 169 *and summer of* 168 B.C.

Rome was at this time engaged in the Third Macedonian War, which ended with the battle of Pydna in 168. Antiochus IV of Syria was seeking to take advantage of the preoccupation of Rome, and of troubles in Egypt, to go to war with the two Ptolemies—Ptolemy Philometor and Ptolemy Physcon—who were then reigning jointly.

Polybius, book XXIX, c. xxiii. . . . 'In the winter (end of 169 B.C.) an embassy arrived from both of the Ptolemies to ask for help. There were repeated and heated debates in the League.' One party was averse from giving aid: another—led by Lycortas, the father of Polybius, and Polybius himself—wished to help the kings in accordance with the terms of the existing treaty of alliance. The embassy from Egypt asked for 1,000 foot and 200 horse, with Lycortas as leader of the whole allied force and Polybius in command of the cavalry. The embassy arrived when the synod of the Achaean League was meeting in Corinth. The majority of the members of the League was ready to join forces

and the Spartan walls had been pulled down (Mommsen, *History of Rome*, Eng. trans., vol. ii, p. 280).

with the Ptolemies not merely by sending a detachment, but by raising a general levy, if it were necessary: the opposition argued that on grounds of general policy the League ought not to meddle in foreign affairs, and in the present juncture should certainly take no action, but keep itself free and ready to serve the interests of Rome.

c. xxiv. 'The majority of the assembly became alarmed at the thought of appearing to fail the Romans. [Lycortas and Polybius, however, argued that the Romans needed no help, while Egypt did.] The majority then inclined the other way and were in favour of helping Egypt; but the opponents of that policy prevented any decision from being taken, alarming the magistrates by the contention that it was not legally possible to discuss the giving of aid to a State in an ordinary assembly—that is to say in the regular *synodos* of the League. After a time an extraordinary assembly—the *synklētos*—was convened to meet at Sicyon, at which all citizens who were over 30 attended along with the members of the Council (*Boulē*). Many speeches were made;' and Polybius once more argued, with general approval, the case for sending aid to Egypt, urging that the Romans were not now in need of assistance, and that if they should need it in the future, the League had resources enough to assist them even if aid were now sent to Egypt. Two opposing resolutions were then submitted to the extraordinary assembly—one in favour of sending aid to Egypt, the other in favour of sending a mission to reconcile the two Ptolemies with Antiochus. After a brisk debate there was a considerable majority for the first resolution.

c. xxv. . . . . 'The opponents of the policy of sending aid to Egypt now used a stratagem. A messenger, in the course of his journey, appeared in the theatre with a letter from one of the Roman consuls, in which the Achaeans were recommended to follow the policy of Rome and to attempt to reconcile the Ptolemies with Antiochus. Actually the Romans had made the attempt themselves, and had failed; but this fact was apparently withheld from the assembly, and the effect of the consul's letter was that Polybius and his party, unwilling to oppose the recommendation made in the letter, took no further part in the business.' The resolution in favour of sending aid to Egypt was then dropped, and a resolution in favour of sending a mission of reconciliation was adopted.[1]

F. *An Inscription commemorating the help given by a citizen of the Achaean League to Oropus*, circa 150 B.C.

Oropus, a town on the straits of Euboea, had been sorely vexed by Athens and had appealed for help to the Achaean League. The help was promised, but not actually sent: the mere promise of it was enough to bring the Athenians to reason. One Hiero, of Aegira (a town of Achaea on the Corinthian Gulf), had been of special service and had given special help to Oropus in its troubles. The decree set forth in this inscription, on the motion of Olympichus, a citizen of Oropus, is an expression and permanent memorial of the gratitude of Oropus to him (and to the Achaean League) for help.

'On the motion of Olympichus, the son of Hermodorus [both father and son had held office as priests of Amphiaraus at Oropus];

'Whereas Hiero of Aegira, the son of Telecles, continues to be well disposed to the people of Oropus, at all times speaking and acting on their behalf when the greatest of calamities and breaches of faith befell them; and whereas, at the time when the magistrates and we [i.e. Olympichus] attended the synod of the League in Corinth, he contributed to our maintenance, and by his counsel and advice wrought on the Achaeans to show every manner of forethought on behalf of our city and the temple of Amphiaraus (forasmuch as we also [like the Achaeans] continue to be in the friendship and faith of Rome);

'and whereas, when the Achaean League resolved to convene an extraordinary meeting (*synklētos*) afterwards at Argos on these matters,[2] the aforesaid Hiero, wishing at all times to show his

[1] In the event it was Rome that stopped the war between Antiochus and the two Ptolemies. A Roman envoy, Popilius, met Antiochus when he advanced into Egypt, and, drawing a circle with his staff around the place where he stood, asked him to give an answer to the message sent by the Senate before he stepped out of the circle. The answer of Antiochus was that he would do whatever Rome commanded; and he accordingly withdrew his forces.

[2] This is the same procedure of an ordinary *synodos* followed by an extraordinary *synklētos*, which is recorded by Polybius on a previous occasion (see the previous extract).

goodwill and goodness, received into his house all the envoys of
Oropus who attended that meeting, and offered sacrifice on our
behalf to Zeus the Saviour, and spoke against the Athenians and
others who were members of the mission opposed to us, and
wrought on the Achaeans not to stand idly by while a Greek city
was being enslaved (and that when it was in the friendship and
faith of Rome);

'and whereas by his forethought and goodness it has come to
pass that we have recovered our fatherland and returned to our
city with our children and wives;

'therefore, in order that the people of Oropus may show themselves mindful of the benefits which they have received at any
man's hand, and that others may be led to desire to do likewise
in the knowledge that they will receive the honour due to their
benefactions,

'it has been resolved by the people of Oropus—may the blessing of Fortune be upon it—to confer the honour of a statue of
bronze on Hiero of Aegira, the son of Telecles, for the merits and
the goodness which he continues to show to the people of
Oropus, and to announce the erection of the statue at the athletic
games held at the great festival of Amphiaraus.' (From Dittenberger, *Sylloge Inscr. Graec.*[3], vol. ii, No. 675.)

G. *A Last Appeal to the Greeks for Unity*

A conference was held at Naupactus, in 217 B.C., with a view to
ending the war then being waged by Philip V of Macedon and
the Achaean League against the Aetolian League. (Aetolia too,
like Achaea, was a league, with ambitions as large in northern
Greece as those of Achaea in the south.) During the conference an
Aetolian representative, Agelaus of Naupactus, made a notable
speech which is reported by Polybius (book VI, c. 105), pleading
for unity among the Greeks in face of the danger impending from
the Western Mediterranean. News of the battle of Lake Trasimene
had inclined the belligerents to peace (which was, in the event,
concluded): they were all concerned with the thought of what
might befall them as the result of the Second Punic War.

c. 105. 'Agelaus said that it would be best of all that the Greek should never wage war against one another; they should thank Heaven heartily if they could all speak with one voice and join hands together like men fording a river: then they might get rid of attacks from barbarians and save themselves and their cities in unison. Even if that were not wholly possible, he asked them nevertheless, in view of their present circumstances, to take a sober view and to be on their guard, with a prescient eye for the strength of the forces engaged in the West and the war now being waged there. It was plain, he urged, already, to all who had even an ordinary concern for the state of public affairs, that if either Carthage defeated Rome or Rome defeated Carthage in war, the victor was very unlikely to be content with subjugating the Italian and Sicilian Greeks: he would move farther afield, and extend his designs and forces beyond any proper bounds. He therefore begged them all, and especially Philip, to stand on guard. The proper safeguard, he suggested, was that Philip should abandon any idea of destroying the Greeks and thus making them an easy prey to their assailants: on the contrary he should take counsel for his own safety, and show a general interest in the welfare of all the Greek States, since they were all related to and connexions of Macedonia. If he handled affairs in this sense, the Greeks would be well disposed to him and serve as firm allies against any attack; while foreign powers, dismayed by the trust reposed in him by the Greeks, would be less inclined to plot against his authority. If he was eager for action, he ought to look to the West, and to pay attention to the war which was being waged in Italy; and then, by a politic intervention as a third party in the struggle, he might use the right moment for a policy of attempting to control the whole course of events. The present moment, Agelaus argued, was not amiss for such a policy. He exhorted Philip, accordingly, to put off to a quieter season any differences or hostilities with the Greeks, and to make his main effort in this quarter [i.e. the West], so that he should be in a position to make peace or war when he wished with them [i.e. the powers of the West]. If once Philip waited for the clouds now hovering in the West to move and settle down over the regions of Greece, he was terrified to think "how the truces and the wars, and all the games which we now play with one another, might well be so abruptly cut short for us all that we should be reduced to praying to Heaven for the power we once enjoyed—the power of making peace and war when we liked, and generally of settling for ourselves the issues in dispute among us".'

Peace was made for the moment between the belligerents, but war soon broke out again; and Greece, and Macedonia with her, drifted towards the Roman conquest and subjugation which soon befell them both. Probably it would have befallen them in any case: Rome, victorious in the West by the end of the Second Punic War, was strong enough to subdue the East at her leisure. The next chapter of Polybius' history (c. 106) contains his reflections on the ending of the separate history of the Hellenistic East and on the fusion of West and East in a new Graeco-Roman system.

c. 106, § 4. 'This was the occasion, and these were the counsels, which first involved the affairs of Greece with those of Italy, and also of North Africa. It was no longer with an eye to affairs in Greece that Philip and the authorities at the head of the Greeks now made war, or peace, with one another: the attention of all was already fixed on objects in Italy. A similar fortune soon befell the inhabitants of the Aegean islands and the Greeks of Asia Minor. Those who had differences with Philip of Macedon, and some of those who had quarrels with Attalus the King of Pergamum, no longer turned for help to the Seleucid King Antiochus, or to Ptolemy in Egypt: instead of turning to the East or the South, they looked henceforward to the West, some of them sending envoys to Carthage and others to Rome. In the same way the Romans sent embassies to the Greeks, fearing the ambitious designs of Philip, and anticipating that he would take advantage of the situation in which they were placed. . . .'

A Note on some Federal Tendencies in Roman History

The Roman genius of centralization, which already under the Republic—and even more under the Empire—gathered all threads into the city of Rome, was naturally hostile to the spirit of federalism, as the Greek leagues had found to their cost. But there were some tendencies making for federalism (though they were tendencies quickly arrested) even in the Roman Republic and the early Roman Empire. Two such tendencies deserve some mention.

When the Italian 'Allies' of Rome revolted against her rule in the Social War of 90–89 B.C., the cantons in two of their groups—the Marsic and the Samnite groups—formed a double or 'binary' league of their own. If the authority of Diodorus Siculus (xxxvii. 2) may be trusted, this league had consuls and praetors on the Roman model, and it had also a representative council, acting as a sort of federal Senate and exercising full powers during the course of the war. But this system, if it was ever adopted, was not Roman, but anti-Roman; and scholars have doubted whether the Marsi and the Samnites ever went beyond the appointment of two supreme commanders for their armies and the institution of a council of war to act in conjunction with them.[1]

The second federal tendency—if indeed it may so be called—appeared in Rome itself, and it appeared in the days of Augustus. It showed itself in the shape of an attempt to diminish the monopoly of voting power exercised by the city of Rome in the election of magistrates, and to enlist the members of some of the local government authorities of Italy in the exercise of that power. According to a statement made by Suetonius in his *Life of Augustus* (c. xlvi), Augustus introduced a measure providing that, in the elections of the higher Roman magistrates, the members of the town councils (*decuriones*) of his new colonies[2] in Italy should cast their votes in advance in their different localities, and send them in sealed boxes to Rome—when (one may conjecture) they would be counted along with the votes given in Rome itself by the citizens who resided there and could give their votes in person. There is no evidence that this measure was ever carried into effect; but the statement of Suetonius suggests that Augustus wished to find room for some element of general Italian self-government, and that he was seeking to turn the urban monopoly of Rome into something which might develop into an Italian league. True,

---

[1] H. M. Last, in the *Cambridge Ancient History*, vol. ix, pp. 186–7.

[2] According to the *Monumentum Ancyranum*, cap. iii, Augustus had settled in new colonies, or sent back into their own old towns, more than 300,000 soldiers: see below, p. 225.

the election of magistrates at Rome was already becoming a mere ceremony, and the local governing authorities of Italy were, in effect, only being invited to participate in a form of ritual. Yet even so, and though there is no evidence that the measure proposed by Augustus was ever put into practice, there is something in his plan which may warrant the conjecture that he dreamed of a united Italy (the ideal Italy described by Virgil in the second book of the *Georgics*), developing along federal lines, with the city of Rome reduced to a part instead of continuing to pose as the whole.[1]

§ V. KINGSHIP. (I) THE HELLENISTIC KINGDOMS

Introduction

Three kingdoms eventually established themselves in the area of Alexander's conquests, each ruled by one of his generals or the descendant of a general. One of them was the Macedonian kingdom, in which the greatest figure was Antigonus II, called Gonatas (the grandson of Antigonus I, another of Alexander's generals): he took the title of king about 284 and ruled till 239. A second kingdom was the Seleucid kingdom of Western Asia, established by Seleucus I, called Nicator, another of Alexander's generals, who died in 280 B.C.: this was a composite kingdom, half Oriental and half Western, with two capitals, one on the Tigris and one at Antioch: it was also, in its character, the least regional and the most 'oecumenical' of the Hellenistic kingdoms, and perhaps the closest to Alexander's own ideas. The third kingdom was the Ptolemaic kingdom of Egypt, the descendant of the old kingdom of the Pharaohs in its government, its buildings, and its life: this was a highly regional State, established by another general, Ptolemy I, called Sotēr, who died about 283 B.C.: it was also the longest lived of the three kingdoms, surviving to the days of the Emperor Augustus, while the Macedonian kingdom collapsed, and was annexed by Rome, in the middle of the second century

[1] H. M. Last, in the *Cambridge Ancient History*, vol. x, pp. 461–2; see also Professor J. A. O. Larsen, in the American journal *Classical Philology*, vol. xlix, No. 1 (Jan. 1954), p. 12.

B.C., and the Seleucid kingdom fell into anarchy, and the dynasty came to an end, in the days of Sulla and Pompey.

The Macedonian monarchy was of the nature of a free tribal kingdom, analogous to the early Teutonic kingdoms in England: the army served also as something of a folk-moot, electing the new monarch on a vacancy of the Crown; and Macedonia thus contained the germ of a constitutional monarchy. One of its early kings, Demetrius the Besieger (the son of the first and the father of the second Antigonus), was indeed a flamboyant figure, whose career was dramatic and even meteoric: handsome and dashing, he was ready to play the part of a very god—not indeed in Macedonia, but at any rate among the Athenians—allowing himself to be honoured as a 'saviour deity' by a gilt statue, and to be celebrated in an 'ithyphallic hymn' along with the goddess Demeter (see below, p. 90). But the 'Besieger' flashed across the sky of Greece and disappeared; and it was his son, Antigonus II Gonatas, who set the permanent type of Macedonian monarchy. That type was prosaic, and in some ways Prussian: like Frederick William I or Frederick the Great, Antigonus II was a 'service-king', pledged to work for the State; he spoke of his office as a 'noble servitude', and he could even speak of the diadem which he wore on his head as a 'rag' which meant an infinity of trouble. If Frederick the Great courted French *philosophes*, Antigonus equally cultivated the Stoics of his day, and was surrounded by a sort of Stoic circle. He sought to invite Zeno himself to his court: Zeno sent him instead Persaeus (a native, like himself, of Citium in Cyprus) to act as adviser; and we are told that Persaeus wrote (whether for Antigonus or for the world generally) a treatise 'on Kingship' and another 'on the Spartan constitution'. We also read that Antigonus II was a friend and a generous benefactor to Cleanthes, the successor to Zeno as head of the Stoic school (*supra*, p. 21); and we are naturally led to wonder whether there was a peculiar sympathy between Stoicism and the cause of monarchy. The evidence hardly favours that view: on the one hand, Stoicism, in the course of its development, was allied with different political causes according to the circumstances of the time; on the other hand, Antigonus II, if he was the patron and friend of several of the early Stoics, was also associated with other schools. He invited to his court, for example, the Cynic Bion of Borysthenes (*circa* 330–250 B.C.), and Bion came in spite of an attempt of Persaeus to prevent the visit. He was a curious and dubious visitor, the son of a fishmonger and a courtesan: what he taught Antigonus, if he taught him anything, we do not know: he was essentially a root-less being, a genuine 'citizen of the world' (*cosmopolītēs*), as he called himself—but genuine rather in the negative sense of owing allegiance to no city than in the positive sense of actively belong-ing to the one and only city of God. Perhaps Antigonus II was a dilettante in philosophy, always ready to hear some new thing. In any case the Macedonian monarchy, under his successors, showed little interest in any sort of theory, but persevered in its duty of 'servitude'.

The Seleucid monarchy had no such regional (one may almost say national) character as the Macedonian. Ranging almost from the Indus to the coast of Asia Minor, and down into Syria and Palestine, it was a composite amalgam of East and West, resting on a mixture of ideas which were partly Greek and partly Baby-lonian, with some Persian elements. Unlike the Macedonian kingdom (but like the Ptolemaic), the Seleucid monarchy was an absolutism. The Seleucids were autocrats; but they generally respected the rights of the cities and military colonies scattered up and down their dominions, and they were generally popular. The genius of the monarchy was predominantly Greek; but the Seleucids seem to have fostered the old Babylonian culture in the Eastern part of their realm, possibly as a counterweight to the influence of Persian nationalism. The Greek cities of Asia Minor readily deified their rulers: just as, at a later date, the worship of Julius Caesar and of Augustus can first be traced in Ephesus and other cities of the province of Asia, so, soon after 300 B.C., divine honours began to be paid by these cities to the Seleucid dynasty. It was easy for the Greeks to regard a king as a new form either of deity in general or of some particular god (a *neos theos* or a *neos Dionȳsos*), or again to conceive him as a visible 'manifestation' (*epiphaneia*) of divine intervention in human shape. They were the more ready to do so since kings were justified to them by their works and their fruits (they were 'Saviours', or 'Benefactors', or 'Victors', who ended war, brought peace, and gave men the blessings of quiet); and kings were very ready to receive what their Greek subjects were willing to give, recognizing that deification, as Sir W. W. Tarn writes, 'gave them a footing in Greek cities, and ensured the continuing validity of their acts after death'. Thus we find Antiochus I, about 280 B.C. deifying his father, the founder of the dynasty, as Zeus 'the Conqueror' (*Nīkātōr*): this was a case of deification *after* death, while the Ptolemies in Egypt, inheriting the traditions of the Pharaohs, were already going further and 'assuming the god' even in their lifetime. Whether Oriental ideas (as well as Greek) encouraged the deification of the ruler in the Seleucid kingdom is not clear; it is possible that the Persian idea of the *hvarenô* (the divine grace in the form of a 'glory' or halo which illuminated and indicated the true king) may have been transmitted to the Seleucids along with the dominions of Persia; and it is also possible that old Babylonian ideas, which made the king a vicar of God, or a son of God, or an actual god, may have come to them in the wake of the Babylonian culture which they fostered.[1]

The one Seleucid who pressed the idea of deification to any large consequences was Antiochus Epiphanes (Antiochus IV), about 170 B.C.: he apparently sought to secure a greater unity for his composite kingdom by encouraging a common Greek culture, and he seems to have made the worship of himself as 'Zeus Manifest' (*epiphanēs*) a part of this policy: he was certainly the first of the Seleucids to impress on coins the fact (or idea) of the deification of the ruler. His policy led to a violent clash with Jewish religious and national feeling; and that clash is recorded in the Book of Daniel (see below, p. 124), as also in the First Book (and, in an alternative version, in the Second Book) of the Maccabees (see below, pp. 143–4). (The account of Alexander and his successors in the opening verses of chapter i of the First Book gives the general Jewish view of the policy of the Seleucids; see below, p. 142.)

The Egyptian monarchy was far less composite, and far more

[1] See L. Delatte, *Traités de la Royauté*, 1942, 125–6 and 138–9.

unitary, than the Seleucid: it was regional, local, secluded, and specifically Nilotic. It carried the heavy inheritance of a long past: it preserved the pattern and the general character of the old Pharaonic monarchy which had long ruled the constricted and yet far-stretched Nile valley—a valley some four or five miles wide, but hundreds of miles in length, with the yellow sands of the desert stretching on either side of the long green rope of riverine vegetation. The monarchy of the Ptolemies was essentially Egyptian—alike in its architecture (the Ptolemaic temples, at any rate to an untutored eye, are even more Egyptian than their predecessors); in its system of economy; and in its political structure and methods of administration. A monotony of unity and a tyranny of conformity are its chief characteristics. In the old Pharaonic world of ideas there had been 'an identification of king and gods and land and people': Egypt was a single corporate body, and all Egyptians were members of it, 'from the Pharaoh, causing the sun to rise and the Nile to flood, . . . down to the peasants raising the food, and cutting and carrying the stones of the royal tombs and temples'.[1] The Ptolemies inherited and consolidated the Pharaonic past: they managed (or their officials managed for them) a system of thorough-going 'State socialism' under which the reigning king was *l'état*, in receipt of all the benefits (though he might allocate some of them to the priests and officials and soldier-settlers), and in total control of agriculture, industry, transport, and the movement of commerce. The natural conmitant of such 'State socialism' was a bureaucratic staff and a bureaucratic cobweb of routine which the discovery of papyri[2] (in the dry and tenacious sand which has at once buried and preserved so large a legacy) is now revealing to scholars in its detail and daily operation.

[1] Bradford Welles, in an article on 'Ptolemaic Administration in Egypt', in the *Journal of Juristic Papyrology*, vol. iii, 1949, pp. 21–48.

[2] Perhaps the most remarkable of these papyri is No. 703 (of the third century B.C.) in the *Tebtunis Papyri*, vol. iii, part 1. It runs to 280 lines, and contains instructions for the management, collection, and dispatch of the royal revenues from agriculture, transport, monopolies, and all other sources. It is a civil service document, or précis of rules, rather than a statement of social or political ideas; and it is not translated in this volume. But it is the translator's duty to refer the reader to it, and to Dr. A. S. Hunt's illuminating notes upon it (pp. 66–102 in the volume cited above).

But if Ptolemaic Egypt was fundamentally Egyptian, at any rate in its buildings, its economy, and its administration, Greek elements had already entered Egypt, even before the Ptolemies: the Macedonian conquest had introduced a Macedonian dynasty and Macedonian soldier-settlers or 'cleruchs'; and the foundation of Alexandria had planted on Egyptian soil a great cosmopolitan city, largely Greek in its population, and penetrated by the Greek culture of its 'Museum', its famous library, and its sophisticated and scholarly literature elaborated on Greek patterns. What was the weight and the influence of these elements in the Egypt of the Ptolemies? The dynasty was Macedonian in blood, and the marriage of brother and sister maintained its Macedonian character down to the reign of Cleopatra, a vigorous and daemonic Macedonian[1] of the type of Olympias the mother of Alexander. But the Macedonian kings and queens of Egypt had no Greek bias, any more than they had an Egyptian bias: their only bias ran in their own dynastic interest, and in the direction of their own splendour and the increase of their own wealth and dominions. They maintained, indeed, an army of Macedonian and Greek soldier-settlers or 'cleruchs', planted on the soil, and either drawing rents from the Egyptian fellahin or cultivating farms for themselves; but the 'cleruchs' were not favourites, and the Ptolemies pressed heavily on them as well as on the native Egyptians. If Alexandria had in its composite structure a predominant Greek *politeuma*, which formed a large part of its population of half a million or more inhabitants, it had also a stirring Jewish *politeuma* and other cosmopolitan elements: its culture had a character of syncretism, which could mix the Jewish Scriptures with the dialogues of Plato, as the writings of Philo were to show; and in any case Alexandria was far from being typical of Egypt. It was something peculiar, and conscious of its peculiarity, as a papyrus of the first century B.C. is sufficient to prove (see below, p. 100). Generally, and on the whole, it may be said that while on occasion there were conflicts between the

---

[1] Cleopatra was partly Greek (by way of Syria) in descent, and she had some small Persian ingredient in her stock, but she was mainly Macedonian. Shakespeare makes Antony address her as 'Egypt', and he seems to have thought of her as having 'a brow of Egypt', but there was no Egyptian element in her blood.

native Egyptians and the foreign settlers, and though there were sometimes signs of nationalist feelings and resentments, the general system enforced by the Ptolemies was that of a neutral government and a pure pursuit of dynastic interest: the Egyptians were not humiliated, or the Greeks and other foreign settlers privileged, and the ultimate beneficiary was always the monarchy.[1]

But while Ptolemaic Egypt was thus, in the main, the home of a peculiar regionalism, with its own Nilotic character and its peculiar Pharaonic tradition, and while it neither gave much to the rest of the world nor received much at its hands, it certainly stirred the curiosity of the Greeks, as it afterwards interested also the Romans. Greek writers turned to the theme of Egypt, and attempted Greek interpretations or rationalizations of its system of kingship and its institutions. An Idyll of Theocritus (of the reign of Ptolemy II, *circa* 272 B.C.) draws a flattering picture of Ptolemaic monarchy (see below, p. 93); and a Greek papyrus of the first century B.C. which praises Alexandria also praises, in its disconnected and cryptic argument, the institution of kingship. Some scholars have held that Greek civil servants and administrators improved and clarified the administrative methods of the Ptolemies; they have also argued that the Greeks 'contributed one notion to Ptolemaic Egypt, a rationalization of kingship', as they also contributed 'a second political rationalization' by drawing from, or applying to, Egypt the lesson that the old Greek *polis* must yield to the better and more viable political unit of a large territorial state at once remote from the clash of warfare and self-sufficient in its natural resources.[2] The argument seems conjectural; and the one solid fact which our authorities record is the advice given to Ptolemy I by a Greek politician (a pupil of Aristotle's Lyceum) that he should read 'books on kingship', such as Greek thinkers (the Stoic Persaeus was one) were now beginning to write under the stimulus of the new age of

---

[1] There is a lucid and convincing article on this theme, entitled 'Politique de race ou politique royale', by Claire Préaux, in the *Chronique d'Égypte*, 1936, pp. 111–38.

[2] See Bradford Welles, in the article cited above, p. 37 and pp. 39–40. He suggests that Hecataeus of Teos, in his *Aegyptiaca*, used by Diodorus Siculus in book I, cc. 77–80, of his *Universal History*, produced this 'second political rationalization' for the benefit of the Ptolemies.

Alexander and his successors. This was a matter of the importation of Greek political ideas into Egypt rather than of the export of ideas from Egypt into Greece and the rest of the world; and there is little evidence of such export except for the writings of Philo, in the first half of the first century B.C., when Ptolemaic Egypt had ceased to exist and had become a part of the Roman Empire. In any case the political ideas of Philo (see below, p. 155) are the offspring of the peculiar soil of Alexandria, and the product of a peculiar syncretism of the Pentateuch with Plato and Zeno which was developed in that soil. Egypt itself—the Egyptian Egypt of the Ptolemies—contributed little to the general stock of ideas during the last three centuries B.C. It is true that Ptolemy I introduced the worship of the deified Alexander about 305 B.C.: it is true that his successors deified Ptolemy after his death, and even deified themselves during their own lifetime. But the deification of rulers was common elsewhere than in Egypt, and needed no help from Egypt; it was a general habit of the Greek mind in the Eastern Mediterranean, as it also was, and had long been, a habit of the Babylonians and other peoples of western Asia. A dictum of Professor Breasted may be quoted in conclusion of the matter: 'when the Roman emperor became an Oriental sun-god, *sol invictus*, the process was in large measure due to the influence of the Asiatic Solar religion rather than to the Solar Pharaoh'—or, we may add, to his successor the Solar Ptolemy.[1] It was the Orontes of Syria, rather than the Nile, that flowed into the Tiber.

A. *Hermocles' Ithyphallic Poem sung by the Athenians in honour of Demetrius the Besieger, when he occupied the city*

The Athenians about 500 B.C. had honoured in song, and with statues erected in the agora, the two 'Liberators', Aristogiton and Harmodius, who were held to have been responsible for the overthrow of tyranny and the expulsion of the family of Peisistratus. Two centuries later they changed their tune, and honoured with

[1] Quoted by E. R. Goodenough in *Yale Classical Studies*, vol. i (1928), p. 28. 'The same statement', Goodenough adds, 'may be carried back to the solar aspects of the Hellenistic king.'

a gay song (in a lively metre called 'ithyphallic') the reoccupation
of their city by the Macedonian Demetrius in 290 B.C. They had
already welcomed him on an earlier occasion (307 B.C.), when
they had worshipped him and his father Antigonus as 'Saviour
Gods', and had set up gilt statues to both in the agora by the side
of those of their old 'Liberators'. They now added the adulation
of song, or hymn, to the rest of their rejoicings. The song, which
is preserved in the *Deipnosophistae* of Athenaeus (253 D), shows
the attitude of 'the common man' to ruler-worship at the beginning of the third century B.C.

'How are the greatest and dearest of the gods come to the city!
For the hour has brought here together the goddess Demeter and
Demetrius.[1] She comes to perform the holy mysteries of the
Maiden; but he comes to us merry, as beseems a god, in beauty
and with laughter. It is in majesty that he appears, his friends all
around him in a circle, and he in the midst of them, as if they were
the stars and he the Sun. Hail to thee, son of the mighty Poseidon
and of Aphrodite. For the other gods are either far away, or they
have no ears, or they do not exist, or they pay no heed whatever
to us; but thou art here and we see thee, not in wood, or in stone,
but in very truth. We therefore pray to *thee*. First of all, o most
dear, give us peace, for thou art the Lord. And then there is that
Sphinx, the Aetolian, who lords it not only over Thebes, but also
over all Greece: he sits on his rocks, like the Sphinx of old, and
seizes and carries off all our people. I cannot drive him away (for
it is the way of the Aetolian to seize his neighbour's goods, now
and at all times): punish thou him thyself, if it may be so, we pray
thee; but if thou canst not, find for us some Oedipus to deal with
this Sphinx, and either dash him down from the rocks or turn him
into stone.' (From *Collectanea Alexandrina*, ed. J. U. Powell,
p. 173.)

The Athenians in their decline—and perhaps in consequence of
it—readily mixed frivolity with adulation; at any rate they were
ready to take things lightly. The poem of Hermocles may have

---

[1] The name of Demetrius seems to have suggested his association with the
goddess Demeter and her daughter Persephone (the Maiden, or *Korē*), whose
mysteries were celebrated at Eleusis near Athens.

been composed by command of Demetrius; but we learn from a writer quoted by Athenaeus that the Athenians sang it not only in public but in their homes.

B. Four Documents relating to Kingship in Ptolemaic Egypt

1. *A decree passed by the Council of the islands of the Aegean, c. 280 B.C., in honour of Ptolemy II Philadelphus*

The Aegean islands had been brought into connexion with Egypt by Ptolemy I Sotēr, and had formed a sort of league under his leadership from 308 B.C. onwards. This decree, passed by their Council (*synedrion*) in the reign of his successor Ptolemy II Philadelphus, is evidence of the attitude of the Greeks to Ptolemaic kingship, as the decree (3 below) inscribed on the Rosetta Stone a century later, 196 B.C., is evidence of the attitude of the Egyptians. The text is printed in Dittenberger, *Sylloge* [3], vol. i, No. 396.

'The decree of the Council of the islands of the Aegean. [Having been invited, on his behalf,] to send representatives to Samos to do business concerning a sacrifice and the nomination of envoys for the games which Ptolemy II is instituting in Alexandria, in honour of his father Ptolemy I, to rank with the Olympic games . . . the common body of the councillors have thus resolved:

'Whereas King Ptolemy Sotēr was the cause of many great benefits to the people of the islands and the other Greeks, having liberated their cities, restored their laws, established their ancestral constitutions everywhere, and remitted some of their taxes; and whereas now King Ptolemy [Philadelphus], having inherited the kingdom from his father, continues to show the same good disposition and care for the people of the islands and the other Greeks, and offers sacrifice in his father's honour and institutes games, to rank with the Olympic games, in athletics, music, and horse-racing, maintaining thereby his reverence for the gods and continuing to show his good disposition to his ancestors; and whereas for this purpose he invites the people of the islands and the other Greeks to vote that the games shall rank with the Olympic games;

'accordingly it is proper that all the people of the islands, having before honoured Ptolemy Sotēr with god-like honours both for

his public benefactions and his help to individuals, should likewise, on the invitation of the present King Ptolemy [Philadelphus],
co-operate with him generally, and, in particular, should vote
with all dispatch, in accordance with his desire [here there is a
gap in the inscription] . . . for the giving of proper honours [and
tokens] of their goodwill, and for approving the sacrifice and
sending the envoys at the proper seasons for all time to come, as
the king has enjoined;

'and there should be games to rank with the Olympic, and
the victors in them who come from the islands should have the
same honours as are prescribed in the laws of each people of the
islands for victors in the Olympic games;

'and King Ptolemy, the son of King Ptolemy Sotēr, should have
a golden crown as a memorial, of the worth of 1,000 staters, for
his virtues and his good disposition to the people of the islands;

'and the Council should cause this resolution and decree to be
written on pillars of marble, and set up in Delos by the side of
the altar of Ptolemy Sotēr.

'In the same way let this decree be also passed by the several
cities which belong to the Council, and let them write it on pillars
of marble and set it up in the temples in which other titles of
honour are inscribed in each city.

'The Council shall also choose three envoys, to go to Alexandria
and there to offer sacrifice to Ptolemy Sotēr on behalf of the
common body of the islanders, and to give the crown to the
King. The money for the crown, and for their maintenance and
expenses of travel, shall be provided for the envoys by the cities,
each according to its quota. . . .'

The three envoys came from the islands of Cythnos, Naxos,
and Andros.

Note. A parallel to this decree of the Aegean islanders in honour of
Ptolemy II is furnished by a decree of the League of the Ionians in
honour of Eumenes, King of Pergamum, and the answer of the king
to the decree (printed in C. Bradford Welles, *Royal Correspondence in
the Hellenistic Period*, No. 52, from an inscription discovered at Miletus).
The date is 167/6 B.C.

In the decree, which the king begins his answer by reciting, the

League of the Ionians (1) has voted for Eumenes, as a common benefactor of the Greeks and as their defender against the 'barbarians' [i.e.
the Gauls who had settled in Galatia], a golden crown for valour and a
golden statue, to be erected in any city of his choice, together with a
proclamation of his honours in their common games, and (2) has sent
him, through their ambassadors, their greetings and congratulations,
along with their petition that he would take thought and make provision for the well-being of their league.

In his answer the king accepts the honours decreed by the League,
and promises its members (1) that he will present it with an adequate
income for celebrating a day in his honour at the Pan-Ionian festival,
and (2) that he will himself defray the cost of the making of the golden
statue, which he wishes to have set up in Miletus.

It would thus appear that the League had, if anything, the better of
the bargain.

2. *Theocritus' Encomium on Ptolemy II (Philadelphus)*, c. 272 B.C.

Idyll XVII, v. 13. 'Blessed is Ptolemy in his forefathers. What a
man was Ptolemy the son of Lagus [the father of Ptolemy II and
the founder of the dynasty of the Ptolemies] in accomplishing a
great deed, when once he had formed in his heart a design such as
no other man could have conceived: him the Father raised to
equal honour even with the blessed Immortals; and a golden
throne is set for him in the hall of Zeus. Near him, in friendship,
sits Alexander, the god whose hand was heavy on the gay-
turbaned Persians. Opposite is set the chair of Heracles who slew
the Centaurs: it is wrought of solid adamant, and there Heracles
holds high festival with the other children of the sky-god, rejoicing with exceeding joy in the grandchildren of his grandchildren;
for Zeus the son of Cronus granted to them the gift that their
limbs should never grow old, and they, being his offspring, are
called Immortals. *Both* [of those who sit opposite to him, i.e. both
Ptolemy I and Alexander] had Heracles' mighty son [Caranus,
the legendary founder of the dynasty of Macedonian kings] as
their ancestor, and *both* carry back their line to Heracles as their
beginning . . ..[1]

[1] Ptolemy I, one of Alexander's generals, was supposed to be Alexander's half-
brother, and therefore, like him, to be a descendant of Heracles.

v. 34. 'What a woman, too, was Berenĭcē [wife of the first and mother of the second Ptolemy], who shone among wise women and was a sovereign comfort to her parents. Upon her sweet-scented breasts did Aphrodite, the august daughter of Diana and queen of Cyprus, press her delicate hands; and so, men say, no woman was ever so pleasing in a husband's eye as was Ptolemy's beloved wife—and truly he was loved in return by her even more dearly. . . .

v. 46. 'Thou it was, Aphrodite, thou excellent in beauty and queen of all goddesses, who hadst her in thy care; and through thee it was that the beauteous Berenice crossed not the river of Acheron, with its voices of lamentation, but was caught up by thee before she could go down to the black ferry-boat and its ever-loathed master Charon; and thou didst place her in thy temple and give her a share in the honours paid to thee.[1] . . .'

v. 71. Theocritus here recalls how Ptolemy II was born to Berenĭcē in the island of Cos, one of the islands of the Dodecanese, and saluted at birth by the spirit of the island. Then, he adds, there came a further salute. 'Thrice a great eagle, [the bird of Zeus and] a bird of fate, called from on high in the clouds. That was, I deem, a sign from Zeus. Zeus, the son of Cronus, has all august kings in his care, but eminent above them all is he whomsoever Zeus has loved ever from his birth: prosperity in abundance walks in his company; he rules over broad lands and wide seas. There are a thousand countries, and a thousand nations of men, that grow rich crops with the help of rain sent down by Zeus; but there is no country that grows such a crop as does the level land of Egypt when the flooded Nile sifts the moist clods of its soil, and no country has so many signs of the work done by busy mortals. Three hundred towns stand builded there, and three thousand more are added to thirty thousand, with twice three and thrice nine to complete the tale;[2] and over them all the lord Ptolemy is king. Moreover, he takes to himself and into his kingdom a part of Phoenicia, and parts of Arabia, Syria, Libya, and the country of the dark Ethiopians; and he lays his commands on the

---

[1] Berenĭcē was deified after her death and associated with Aphrodite in temple-worship.　　[2] $300+3,000+30,000+6+27 = 33,333$.

people of Pamphylia, the Cilician spear-men, the Lycians, the war-like Carians, and on the isles of the Cyclades; for the best ships that sail across the sea are his.[1] Yea, all the sea and the land and the echoing rivers have Ptolemy for their king: many are the horsemen, and many the shield-bearing footmen, clad in shining bronze, who gather around him.

v. 95. 'His wealth weighs down in the balance that of all kings: so much is there that comes day by day from every quarter to his rich hall;[2] and his people are busied meanwhile in peace about their works. No enemy, coming by land, has crossed the Nile, that river so rich in fish, to raise the clamour of war in villages that are not his; neither has any enemy, coming by sea, leaped ashore in arms from his swift ship to make spoil of the cattle of Egypt: so mighty is the man who is throned king of these broad domains, the golden-haired Ptolemy, skilled in hurling the spear, whose mind is fixed, as befits a good king, on guarding all his inheritance—yea, and he adds to it also himself. Not unused does the gold which he gathers lie spread in the rich rooms of his palace, like the stores piled up by ever-toiling ants: much goes to the glorious houses of the gods, to which he always offers the first-fruits along with other gifts; much of it he gives to his valiant princes, much to cities, and much to his good comrades. Never, too, does there come to the holy contests of the god Dionysus a minstrel, who knows how to raise the clear notes of song, but he receives a worthy reward; wherefore these interpreters of the Muses sing praises to Ptolemy for all his benefits. . . .

v. 121. 'He only, of all the men of old, and of all who still leave the print of their feet warm in the dust beneath as they walk—he alone has raised temples laden with incense in honour of his beloved father and mother [Ptolemy I and Berenice]; therein he has set them, splendid in gold and ivory statues, to succour[3] all

---

[1] The Egyptian empire, extending north through Syria to the south of Asia Minor, and south down the Red Sea and the Upper Nile to Arabia and the Sudan, was largely a maritime empire, dependent on sea-power.

[2] The papyri discovered in recent years attest the grip of the Ptolemies on the economy of Egypt, and show how they 'nationalized' agriculture, industry, and commerce for the benefit of the Crown.

[3] They were both deified after their death as the 'Saviour Gods' who brought succour to men.

who live upon earth: and when the time comes in the course of
the revolving months he burns on the blood-reddened altars
many fat thighs of oxen—he and his noble wife with him, than
whom a truer bride never clasped her husband to her breast in
their chamber, loving from the depth of her heart, as she did, a
husband who was also a brother.[1] . . .

v. 135. 'Hail and farewell, King Ptolemy: equally with the
other demi-gods will I make mention of thee, and the words
which I utter will not, I deem, be rejected by those that come
after; but thy excellences shall come to thee from Zeus [though
thy praises come from me].'

3. *The inscription on the trilingual Rosetta Stone* (196 B.C.)

The famous Rosetta Stone, the key which unlocked the mystery
of hieroglyphics, is a trilingual inscription in three forms or
versions, one in priestly or hieroglyphic Egyptian, one in the
current Egyptian of the country (the 'demotic'), and one in
Greek. The Greek version here translated is probably based on
the other two, and perhaps primarily on an original 'demotic'
version. The substance of the inscription is a priestly document,
called a decree or *psēphisma*, which commemorates the announce-
ment of the young king Ptolemy V's formal accession to the
throne (*paralēpsis*) some nine years after the death of his father.
The gist of the document is described by Mahaffy in *The Empire
of the Ptolemies*, § 178: 'After . . . enumeration of the king's titles,
and the elaborate dating, the decree says that the Egyptian priesthood, assembled in solemn conclave at Memphis where the king
celebrated his formal accession in the temple of Ptah—in consideration of his benefits to the temples both by donations and
remission of taxes, his benefits to the population in the same
respects, his victorious subjugation of a dangerous rebellion, his
further benevolences to priests and temples—decrees to set up
statues of him in all shrines . . . and to establish special feast-days
in his honour.' The interest of the document, for the present purpose, lies in the swelling titles of the Ptolemaic monarchy; the

---

[1] In the family of the Ptolemies brothers married sisters, according to the old
custom of the Pharaohs.

feeling shown for the linked history of the dynasty; the assimilation of the king to theEgyptian deities and the assertion of his own divinity ('god, born of god and goddess'); and, finally, the suggestion of the close connexion between 'Church and State', or rather between the priesthood and the king.

The text translated is that in Dittenberger's *Orientis Graeci Inscriptiones Selectae*, No. 90, in vol. i, pp. 140–66.

In explanation of the passages which follow, the succession of the first five Ptolemies should first be recorded. Ptolemy I, Sotēr or Saviour, the husband of Berenice I, declared himself king in 304, and ruled to 283/2. Ptolemy II, Philadelphus, the son of Ptolemy I and the husband first of Arsinoë I and afterwards of his sister Arsinoë II, ruled from 283/2 to 246. Ptolemy III, Euergetēs, the son of Ptolemy II and the husband of Berenice II, ruled from 246 to 221. Ptolemy IV, Philopatōr, the son of Ptolemy III and the husband of Arsinoë III (his sister), ruled from 221 to 205. Ptolemy V, Epiphanes, the Ptolemy of the Rosetta Stone, the son of Ptolemy IV, and the husband of the Seleucid princess Cleopatra I, reigned from 205 to 180. Husband and wife were closely associated in the Ptolemaic kingdom—all the more as they were often brother and sister—and this explains the use of the plural in the designations used in the preamble and later in the body of the decree.

Preamble. 'In the reign of the young king, when he had inherited the kingdom from his father [Ptolemy V was only a child when his father died, and was in his thirteenth year at the time of the ceremony of 196]; the lord of kingdoms, great in renown, the restorer of Egypt, reverent in matters pertaining to the gods, victorious over his enemies, who has set straight the life of men; the lord of the thirty-years festival, who is even as Hephaestus the great [the Egyptian Ptah]; a king like the Sun, who is the great king of the places above and those below; the scion of the Kings Philopatores [i.e. Ptolemy IV and Arsinoë III]; whom Hephaestus tested and approved, and to whom the Sun gave the victory; the living image of Zeus [i.e. Amon Ra the god of Thebes], son of the Sun, Ptolemy who lives for ever, the beloved of Ptah:

'in the ninth year [from his father's death]: when Aetus the son

of Aetus was priest of Alexander [the Great], and also of the
Saviour Gods [Ptolemy I and his wife], and of the Gods Brother-
and-Sister [Ptolemy II and his wife], and of the Gods Benefactors
[Ptolemy III and his wife], and of the Gods Philopatores [Ptolemy
IV and his wife], and of the God Manifest and Benevolent
[Ptolemy V, as yet unmarried]; when Pyrrha the daughter of
Philinus was the Prize-bearer for Berenice the Benefactress [the
wife of Ptolemy III], Areia the daughter of Diogenes was the
Basket-bearer for Arsinoë Philadelphus [the wife of Ptolemy II],
and Irene the daughter of Ptolemy the priestess of Arsinoë
Philopatōr [the wife of Ptolemy IV]; in the fourth day of the
[Macedonian] month Xanthus and the eighteenth day of the
Egyptian month Mecheir:

Decree. 'The high-priests and prophets and those who go into
the shrine (*adytum*) for the robing of the gods, and with them the
wearers of the hawk's wing, and the temple-clerks, and all other
priests who have come from the temples in the country-side
(*chōrā*) to Memphis, to meet the king for the ceremony of the
assumption of the crown of kingship inherited from his
father by Ptolemy who lives for ever, the beloved of Ptah,
God Manifest and Beneficent—all these, being gathered in the
temple of Memphis on this day, said:—

'Whereas King Ptolemy who lives for ever, beloved of Ptah,
God Manifest and Beneficent, the son of king Ptolemy and queen
Arsinoë the Gods Philopatores, has in many ways been a benefactor of the temples, and of those who are in them, and of all
those who are subject to his royal rule, being a god born of god
and goddess, even as is Horus, the son of Isis and Osiris, who took
vengeance for his father Osiris; and [whereas], being benevolently
disposed in matters pertaining to the gods, he has offered revenues
in money and kind to the temples, and has borne many expenses
in order to bring Egypt into tranquillity and to restore the
temples; and [whereas], with all the resources at his command,
he has shown himself generous, both [by making grants] from
the revenues accruing to him, and by remitting in full some of
the tributes due to him and reducing others, in order that the
people of Egypt and all others might be in comfort in the days

of his kingship; and [whereas] he has remitted debts, and released prisoners, and conferred benefits on the priests and their temples, and likewise has done justice to all, even as Hermes the twice great [Hermes is the Egyptian Thoth], and has also given orders that those of the [Egyptian] soldiers and the other persons disaffected in the times of trouble [there had recently been civil commotion and war], who are now returning home, should after their return be allowed to remain on their own properties [here the decree goes on to recite the triumphs recently gained by the royal forces over the disaffected, and the other services ascribed by the priests to Ptolemy V—as for instance his 'many gifts to the bull Apis and to Mnevis and to the other sacred animals of Egypt']; . . .

'Therefore this decree—and may good fortune attend it—has been promulgated by the priests of all the temples in the country-side (*chōrā*); that all the honours vested in King Ptolemy who lives for ever, beloved of Ptah, God Manifest and Beneficent, and like-wise those of his parents, the Gods Philopatores, and those of his ancestors, the Gods Benefactors and the Gods Brother-and-Sister and the Saviour Gods, shall for the future be greatly augmented.' Accordingly it is prescribed that an image (*icōn*) of the king should be set up in every temple, with the highest god of the temple by its side in the act of giving him arms for victory, and with the priests offering cult to the images thrice daily and placing sacred robes before them: moreover, there are to be erected statues of the king (*xoana*) and a shrine (*nāos*) of gold in every temple, and there is to be a festival of five days yearly in his honour.

'This decree to be inscribed on pillars of granite in hieroglyphs and demotic script and in Greek letters, and to be set up in each of the first and second and third temples by the side of the image of the king who lives for ever.'

4. *An Egyptian Papyrus of the first century* B.C. *on Constitutions, Alexandria, and Kingship*

It is not clear what the document is intended to be—part of a speech, or of a dialogue, or of a treatise. But there is some sug-gestion of a dialogue form in the fragmentary conclusion of A. III.

A. I. *Three forms of constitution.* '[There is] this difference of opinion. (1) [Many] have preferred [hereditary] *kingship*, and not democracy, praising it [indiscriminately] for being in a position to commit wrong [actually] while committing none [legally]; but while they [i.e. kings of this type] were able to do anything whatever, yet they did not pursue the worse when they failed in the choice of the better. (2) Next I will set beside them the men of *democracy*—Solon, Cleisthenes—and [I will call upon] Zaleucus himself [here there is a gap in the papyrus] . . . but a god according to [some sort of reckoning?] [Here there is a gap in the argument, though not in the papyrus: possibly the mention of democratic 'heroes', and of Zaleucus as a 'god', suggested to the writer the difficulty which he now proceeds to state.] I do not know how I am to seek out, from among all [such] heroes, a hero who is likely [? to perform] the things for which the God once nodded assent to me: such [a search remains] unfinished. (3) The third alternative [? oligarchy] I greet at a distance.' The rest of this first part of the papyrus is fragmentary, and some lines are altogether missing. There is a mention of kings, but the sense is indecipherable.

A. II. *The city of Alexandria.* 'You see with your own eyes the prosperity of the city established at the mouth of the Nile. All other cities are only cities in relation to the territories (*nomes*) attached to them: in relation to Alexandria they are but villages: for Alexandria is a city of the [whole] civilized world. But I [an Alexandrian seems to be speaking] am such as I am because I have political notions [i.e. a notion of what a *polis* means]. . . .

A. III. *The good king.* 'He reverences all [Right]. He maintains a civility of address; rejoices in the Good; adds noble acts to noble acts; fights against foes till he wins the victory: keeps unimpaired his preference even for friends who are altered; and makes immortal the honours he renders to the immortals. . . .' The rest of A. III is fragmentary, and the papyrus is torn. (From *Berliner Klassikertexte*, vii, pp. 16–18.)

(The writer owes his knowledge of this document—and other references to papyri and journals of papyrology—to Mr. C. H. Roberts, the Secretary to the Delegates of the Clarendon Press, to whom, indeed, he is generally indebted.)

c. *The cult of Kingship in the Seleucid realm*

1. *An inscription of the reign of Antiochus II* (261–246 B.C.)

This inscription is evidence of the general official cult offered to the Seleucid kings (and their queens) in each satrapy of their empire. They were regarded as descended from Apollo, and therefore of divine origin. In addition to this general cult there were also local cults in many of the cities of the empire.

'Here is recorded a copy of the King's orders in writing concerning the appointment of Berenice, the daughter of Ptolemy the son of Lysimachus [a Ptolemy who had entered the service of Antiochus I and settled in the Seleucid kingdom], as high-priestess of the queen [the wife of Antiochus II] in the districts of the satrapy. . . .

'In the year . . . in the month of Artemision [April] . . . King Antiochus to Anaximbrotus [the governor of the satrapy in question], greeting. Whereas we desire to augment further the honours of our sister Queen Lāodicē,[1] considering it to be most necessary for us to do so, not only because she shows affection and care for us in our married life, but also because she is reverently disposed to the Deity; and whereas we continue to render her affectionately all other services which it is fitting and right that we should bestow upon her, and, more especially, we think it proper that, in the same way as high-priests are established in all satrapies in connexion with our office of king,[2] so, for her too, high-priestesses should be established in the same centres, who shall wear crowns of gold bearing her [images], and shall have their names enrolled in the title-deeds after those of the high-priests of the gods and of us;

'Therefore, since I have designated as high-priestess, in the regions under your government, Berenice the daughter of Ptolemy the son of Lysimachus, who is connected with us by kinship, let all things be done in accordance with what is herein-

---

[1] Antiochus II and Lāodicē had the same father, but she may have been only a half-sister.

[2] 'The Seleucids had an official dynastic cult covering their whole empire, with a centre in each satrapy, probably early, but reorganized by Antiochus III or possibly Antiochus II' (W. W. Tarn, *Hellenistic Civilisation*, 3rd edition, p. 51).

before written, and let copies of our letter be inscribed on pillars and set up in the most conspicuous places, so that now and for the future our intention in these things for our sister be made plain to all men.' (From Dittenberger, *Orientis Graeci Inscriptiones Selectae*, No. 224: the inscription is also printed in C. B. Welles, *Royal Correspondence*, No. 36.)

2. Not only were the Seleucids themselves the objects of a cult: they also regulated the cults and appointed the priests of the general gods of their empire. An inscription of the reign of Antiochus III (223–187 B.C.), printed in Dittenberger, *O.G.I.S.*, No. 244, may be cited in illustration of this control. Daphnae, to which it relates (and where the inscription was found), is near Antioch.

'Whereas the office of high-priest of Apollo and Artemis at Daphnae, and of the other temples whose shrines are in Daphnae, is in need of a well-disposed person who shall be capable of pre-siding in a way worthy of the zeal for the place which our ancestors and we have cherished, and worthy of the reverence which we have for things divine, we have designated [the name of the person designated is missing] as high-priest thereof, being persuaded that the administration of the temples will best be conducted by him in a proper manner.' The person designated, as the preamble of the inscription goes on to explain, had been in the service of the king and had asked to be allowed to retire from it.

'You are therefore to give instructions that he be recorded in the [temple] deeds as high-priest of the temples aforesaid, and that the man be given the honour which our orders require, and that if, for any business relating to these temples, he summons the assistance of those who attend to the temples and of all such others as ought to obey him, they shall be assembled, by orders duly given, to receive his directions in any matters about which he may write or give instructions.' Dated in the 124th year of the Seleucid era, or 189/8 B.C.

§ VI. GREEK AND HEBREW VIEWS OF THE PROCESS OF HISTORY ABOUT THE MIDDLE OF THE SECOND CENTURY B.C.

Introduction

It is curious and instructive to compare the views of two contemporary writers on the process of history—the Greek historian
and statesman Polybius (*circa* 200–120 B.C.), and the Jewish writer
of the later chapters of the Book of Daniel, who wrote about
166 B.C.

Polybius, a citizen of Megalopolis, one of the cities of the
Achaean League, had accumulated a large and varied experience
of political life when he wrote the forty books of his *Universal
History*. In his early life he had served the Achaean League on
embassies and had held high military office. After the battle of
Pydna, in 168 B.C., in which Rome had defeated Perseus, the last
Macedonian king, he was deported to Italy as one of the 1,000
Achaeans who were made answerable for their supposed sympathy
with Perseus. He lived in Rome down to the year 150 as a member of the Scipionic circle, and it was at this period that he began
his history, which was intended, at any rate originally, to show
that the Roman hegemony was the fulfilment of the cycle of
history. (At a later period, after his return to Greece in 150, he
seems to have experienced some amount of disillusionment; and
there are hints, perhaps added during a revision of what he had
written earlier, that even Rome was imperfect and liable to decay;
see, for example, book VI, c. 57, translated below.) His history,
after a preface dealing with the First Punic War, covers the period
from the beginning of the Second Punic War to the Roman
settlement of Greece in 146 B.C. Only the first five of his forty
books have been preserved in full: the rest survive only in
Byzantine excerpts or in passages of later writers such as Livy,
Appian, and Diodorus Siculus.

Polybius was a reflective historian, with a conscious theory of
historiography and an appreciation of the general problem of
historical causation. He is essentially Greek in his attitude to the
historic process. The unit of life is the *polis*: the essence of the

polis is its *polīteia* or constitution: to understand the process of history you must therefore investigate the nature of political constitutions and the sequence of their changes. Each constitutional type, if left to itself and not mixed with and corrected by elements drawn from other types, tends to corruption and decay: salvation—but it is a secular sort of salvation—depends on the formation of a mixed type, which alone has any prospect of continuing in one stay. Otherwise there is no stability, but a constant cycle of change (*anacyclōsis*) and a recurrence of the revolving wheel. Even the mixed constitution itself is no certain and permanent salvation; for it too may lose its balance, and then it too will decay—as may happen even to Rome.

The writer of the later chapters of the Book of Daniel sees a very different process of history. Living at the time of the Maccabean revolt against the house of Seleucus, he sees history—external history—as a succession of four brute empires. But that is only an external matter, and a mere march on the circumference. Empires come and go: what are they, that they should matter? The essential thing is the religious congregation, 'the people of God'; and the true end and consummation of history is what has been called 'a divine cosmic event'—the coming of the time when God shall inaugurate His own kingdom. The unknown Jew who wrote the later chapters of the Book of Daniel was a very different man from the experienced and reflective Greek who moved in the Scipionic circle. His nerves were taut; his mind was wrung by the oppression and persecution (as he felt it to be) of the Hellenization of his religion by Antiochus Epiphanes; he quivered as he watched and thought; and he burst into an apocalyptic which is poles asunder from the didactic of Polybius. Yet both writers have something of a scheme of world-history: both have a doctrine of change and a succession of epochs. The difference is that the scheme of Polybius has an inner logic, and his doctrine of succession is based on a principle; the scheme of the writer of the later chapters of the Book of Daniel is merely temporal, and the doctrine of succession (possibly borrowed from, or influenced by, the Zoroastrian doctrine of cycles of fixed periods) is a doctrine stamped on to historical vicissitudes rather than elicited from them.

It only remains to add that the Book of Daniel professes itself to be the work of a prophet of the Babylonian captivity of the later sixth century B.C. The earlier part of the book may well belong to a period anterior to the age of the Maccabees; but the later chapters of apocalyptic must, from the nature of their contents, belong to the beginning of that age.

A. *Polybius on Constitutional Change, the Nature of the Mixed Constitution, and the working of Chance in History*[1]

At the beginning of book VI of his *Universal History* Polybius announces his intention of entering upon a disquisition on the Roman constitution. As a preface to that disquisition he gives a summary view of current Greek political theory as it stood about 150 B.C. The importance of this summary view and of the disquisition by which it is followed is that they formed the basis of Roman political theory (for instance in Cicero), and that they were adopted from the Romans by some medieval and modern writers on politics. The praise of the mixed constitution, which is the core of the ideas of Polybius, reappears in Machiavelli's *Discourses on Livy* and in Montesquieu's *Esprit des Lois*.

1. *Constitutional Change*

Book VI, c. 3. 'Of the many Greek constitutions which have prospered, or experienced a complete change of fortune by falling into adversity, it is easy to give some account, whether by way of description of the past or of forecast of the future. There is no difficulty in reporting what is already known; nor is it hard to prophesy the future with the aid of conjectures based on the course of past events. The case is different with Rome. Here it is far from easy, owing to the complexity of her constitution, to describe her present state; and it is equally difficult, owing to our ignorance of the peculiar features of Roman public and private life, to foretell the lines of her future. It thus requires a peculiar degree of observation and study if we are to attain a clear

---

[1] See the article in the *Classical Quarterly* (July-October, 1954) by C. O. Brink and F. W. Walbank on the construction of the Sixth Book of Polybius.

comprehension of the distinctive characteristics of the Roman constitution.

'Most of the writers who seek to give us instruction in the subject of political theory are apt to speak of three different species of constitutions, one of which they call Kingship, another Aristocracy, and a third Democracy. It seems to me, however, that they may very fairly be asked whether they would have us regard these three as the *only* constitutions, or as the *best* among other constitutions. In either case they are, in my view, guilty of ignorance. The *best* constitution is clearly none of the three, but a mixed constitution composed of the characteristic elements of each; and for this part of our argument we can appeal to the evidence not only of theory, but also of practical experience as illustrated by the example of Lycurgus, who built at Sparta the first constitution actually based on this principle. Again, it cannot be admitted that the three constitutions mentioned are the *only* constitutions. We have already seen at work [in the course of the previous narrative] constitutions such as Monarchy,[1] or one-man government, and Tyranny; and both of these differ greatly from Kingship, though they appear to have something in common with it—an appearance which explains why they practise a common deception and unite in using, so far as they can, the title and style of Kingship. Similarly there have been a number of Oligarchical constitutions which seem to have had some elements of kinship with Aristocracies, though the latter are, so to speak, at the antipodes to them; and the same holds good of Democracy.

c. 4. 'The following considerations attest the truth of this point of view. We cannot immediately describe every form of one-man government, or Monarchy, as a case of Kingship: we have to confine that style to a government by one man which receives the voluntary assent of its subjects and acts by persuading the judgement rather than by fear and force. Equally we must not

---

[1] 'Tyranny' explains itself: it is the selfish government of one man by force. 'Kingship', as Polybius proceeds to explain, is a government of one man based on consent and acting by persuasion. 'Monarchy' is a vague residuary term for other forms of government by one man, and would seem to denote the absolute government of one man without consent or persuasion, but also without selfish objects or the use of force.

consider every Oligarchy as an example of Aristocracy: we must limit that style to a constitution which is administered by the justest and wisest on the basis of free election. Similarly, again, we must not extend the name of Democracy to a constitution in which the whole body of the people is at liberty to do whatever it may wish or propose: we must limit our view to a people which has the tradition and habit of showing reverence to the gods, giving support to parents, and paying respect to elders . . .; and we must confine the name of Democracy to the rule of the will of the majority in communities of this order. We must accordingly speak of *six* forms of constitution: the three already mentioned, which are universally . . . recognized, and three others connected with them [but also distinct from them], which are Monarchy, Oligarchy, and Ochlocracy or mob-rule. Historically, the form which first comes into existence, without any effort of construction and by the play of natural forces, is Monarchy. Upon this there follows, and from this there is derived by constructive effort and deliberate arrangement, the form called Kingship. Kingship in turn undergoes a change into the corrupted form connected with it, by which I mean Tyranny; and the dissolution of Tyranny then produces Aristocracy. Next Aristocracy, by a natural process, is perverted into Oligarchy; after that, when the people turns in anger upon the injustice done to it by the notables, Democracy comes into being; and finally the insolence and the lawlessness into which the people falls produce in time Ochlocracy, as the end of the whole process.

'To attain a clear understanding of the truth of this account we must fix our attention on the natural origin, the growth, and the decline of each of these forms. Only those who have learned to know how each form comes into existence will be able also to know its progress, prime, and decline, and thus, in sum, to tell when, and how, and where it will all happen again. This method of explanation I conceive to be peculiarly appropriate to the Roman constitution, in view of the fact that its existence and growth have from the very first followed a natural course.

c. 5. 'Plato and other philosophers have perhaps analysed with a greater accuracy than I can command the course of the natural process by which constitutions pass into one another; but their exposition is so intricate in its argument, and developed at such length, that it is beyond the reach of most readers. I will therefore attempt to treat the matter summarily, so far as it seems to me to come within the scope of a systematic account of history and the compass of ordinary intelligence. If anything appears to be lacking in the course of the general account which I give, the details of the subsequent argument will adequately atone for the difficulties left in the reader's mind at the moment.

'What then are the beginnings, and what is the source, from which constitutions come into existence? We may answer that question by saying that when a deluge, or a failure of crops, or some other similar cause has resulted in the destruction of much of the human race, as the records tell us has already happened and as reason suggests to us may often happen again, all the traditions and arts will simultaneously perish; but when in the course of time a new population has grown up again from the survivors left by the disaster, as a crop grows up from the seed in the ground, a revival of social life will begin. Men will gather together—it is what we should naturally expect of them, as we should of the rest of animal creation—under the impulse of a natural tendency which draws beings of the same stock to herd together; and in the society thus formed it is inevitable that some member who is preeminent in physical strength and moral courage should lead and rule the rest. What we see happening among the species of animal creation which are destitute of reason must be regarded as most truly and certainly produced by nature; and among all animals we see the strongest indisputably acting as leaders—as we do, for example, among bulls, goats, cocks, and animals similar to them. We may thus conclude that human beginnings, and the way of life of primitive men, were of a similar order. Primitive men gathered together like animals and followed the lead of the bravest and strongest; strength would be the standard of authority among them, and the name which one might give to such a government would be Monarchy, or one-man rule. But when, in the process of time, these early communities acquire a basis of common subsistence and common sentiment, the germs of Kingship begin to appear; and men for the first time acquire a notion of the Good and the Just and their opposites.

c. 6. 'The way in which such germs originate and develop is this. The intercourse of the sexes is the result of a natural impulse common to all human beings; and the result of this intercourse is the begetting and rearing of children. When any of the children so reared refuses, on coming to maturity, to show any gratitude or to make any return to those who have given him his upbringing, and when, on the contrary, he sets himself to speak evilly of them or to do them evil, it is obvious that he will be likely to displease and offend his fellows, who have seen the care and trouble given by his parents to the nurture and upbringing of their offspring. Human beings differ from the rest of animal creation in being the only creatures who have a share in intelligence and the power of reasoning, and this being so it is plain that they are not likely to leave such a difference of conduct unnoticed, as other creatures might: on the contrary, they will note such action and be displeased with the agent, foreseeing what may happen in the future and arguing that something similar may be done to one of themselves. Similarly, when one man has been given comfort or help by another in time of trouble, and then, instead of being grateful to his benefactor, actually tries to do him an injury, it is plain that those who know what has happened will be displeased and offended, not only from sympathy with their neighbour, but also from fear of a similar fate befalling themselves. These feelings are the basis of a general notion and conception of the obligation of duty; and that is the beginning and end of justice.

'Similarly, again, when some one man acts in defence of all others in time of trouble, facing and withstanding the attack of the most formidable of wild beasts, he is likely to receive from the people marks of their favour and respect, while a man who does the opposite is likely to meet with censure and disfavour. Such feelings, once more, are likely to produce in the general mind some conception of honour and dishonour, and of the difference between them; and it is further likely that the one line of conduct will win approval and imitation, in virtue of the advantages which it brings, and the other will be shunned. Suppose, accordingly, that in such conditions the leader with the greatest strength, acting in harmony with popular opinion, gives his support to well-doers, and thus comes to be regarded by his subjects as giving each man his due. The result will be that they will no longer obey him, and confirm him in his authority, *merely* from a feeling of fear inspired by his power: they will rather do so from a voluntary approval, based upon their considered judgement; and they will act in this spirit even if he is advanced in years, rallying unanimously to his cause and opposing those who conspire to overthrow his government. In this way he passes insensibly from a position of one-man rule (Monarchy) to that of a true king; and reason herself takes over the lead from mere temper and physical strength.

c. 7. 'This marks the first natural appearance among men of the ideas of goodness and justice, and of their opposites; and here we may see the origin and growth of true kingship. The subjects of such kingship not only support its first holders: they also support their descendants for generation upon generation, in the strength of a conviction that children born of such parents, and educated by them, will follow policies similar to theirs. But if in time they become displeased with the descendants of their original kings, they cease to regard strength of temper and physique as sufficient qualifications for their kings and governors, and they prefer to choose them by the degree of their power of judgement and their capacity for reasoning—practical experience having now taught them the gulf between these two different sorts of qualification.

'[A new age thus began.] In ancient times those who had once distinguished themselves from their fellows, and been vested with royal authority, grew old upon their thrones: they fortified and walled strong places, and extended their territories, partly in order to gain security, and partly to provide their subjects with an abundant supply of commodities; and while they were busy about such matters they escaped all scandal and were free from envy, making no great distinction between themselves and their subjects, either in dress or in food and drink, but enjoying the same sort of subsistence as others and sharing the same general mode of life. But when kings came to their thrones by right of succession and the law of descent, and when they found ready to their hands everything necessary for security and more than everything needed for the supply of their household, they changed their character. Superfluity made them give the rein to appetite: they imagined that rulers ought to wear different clothes from those of their subjects, must have different and more exquisite food and gear for their table, and must even enjoy, without contradiction, satisfaction of their sexual appetites however abnormal they might be. Such conduct produced in some cases jealousy and offence; in others it led to outbreaks of hatred and sullen resentment: kingship changed to tyranny, and with the change there came the beginnings of collapse and the formation of plots against the government—plots which did not proceed from the worst elements in the State, but from its noblest, most magnanimous, and bravest members, who found themselves least able to bear the arrogant insults of their rulers.

c. 8. 'The people at large, when they could find leaders, joined with them in attacking the government, for the reasons already given. Kingship and other forms of one-man rule were then utterly abolished, and the aristocratic form of government took its origin and began to develop—the people feeling an instant gratitude to those who had rid them of their previous rulers, and therefore employing them as their leaders and committing to them the conduct of their affairs. The new leaders at first welcomed their commission, and acted as if they thought nothing of greater consequence than the general welfare—conducting all affairs, private and public alike, with care and circumspection. [But here again time brought a change.] When the children of the original leaders succeeded to the position of their parents, they found themselves without any experience of misfortunes, and wholly without experience of civic equality and freedom of speech; and, trained from their earliest years under the auspices of their fathers' authority and privileges, they plunged into excesses. Some fell victims to avarice and the passion of unlawful gain; some became the prey of drink and the unreined indulgences that go with it; some gave themselves over to the seduction of women and the corruption of boys. They thus turned Aristocracy into Oligarchy, and they aroused in the people once more the same sort of feelings that have already been mentioned, with the result that the end of their history was like the disaster which had previously befallen Tyranny.

c. 9. 'Accordingly, when men saw the envy and hatred which the oligarchs inspired in their fellow citizens, and were encouraged by it to attack them either in word or in deed, they found the whole of the people ripe and ready for action. The issue was easy: some of the oligarchs were put to death, and others sent into exile; but when that had been done the members of the community neither risked the institution of a new king, since they still remembered the fear they had felt of the injustice of previous kings, nor, again, did they feel willing to venture on committing the conduct of public affairs into the hands of a group of rulers, because they had before their eyes the spectacle of the ignorance of governments of that type. The only remaining hope left to them was hope in themselves and in their own powers. They turned to this hope; they changed their constitution from an Oligarchy to a Democracy; they took into their own hands the task and the trust of making provision for public affairs. All now goes well as long as there are men still left who have had experience of the high-handedness and domination of the few; people are ready to give a welcome to the new mode of government, and they count equality and liberty of speech their greatest blessings. But when a new generation grows up, and democracy has descended to the children of those who were children at the time of its institution, custom begins to stale the value which men had previously set on equality and liberty of speech; and each man seeks to get the better of the rest. Those who succumb most to this failing are those who are superior to their fellows in wealth. Ambitious for office, and unable to obtain it of themselves and by their own qualities, they waste their means in angling for popular support and in corrupting the community by every conceivable method. Infatuated by a senseless passion for reputation and glory, they make the masses venal and a ready prey to bribes; and once that is done the democratic form of government collapses, and the rule of force and the strong arm is substituted for popular rule.

The masses become accustomed, under the guidance of a con-fident and daring leader, to eat the bread of idleness at the expense of others, and to pin their hopes of a livelihood on the property of their neighbours; themselves excluded by their poverty from the offices and honours of the constitution, they institute a system of government by force, and gathering in their assemblies they bring about an era of massacres, exile, and the distribution of landed property, which ends by turning them into brute beasts and finally by giving them over again to despotism and a system of one-man government.

'Such is the cyclical recurrence (*anacyclōsis*) of constitutions; and such, in the system of nature's economy, is the way in which constitutional arrangements change and are altered, and in the end return again upon themselves.[1] A man who has gained a clear understanding of these laws may possibly go wrong, when he seeks to forecast the future, about the *time* at which change may be expected; but if he avoids both anger and envy in the course of his argument, he is hardly likely to be deceived about the *stage* of growth or decay at which a given constitution has arrived or the *point* at which it will change.

---

[1] This doctrine of *anacyclōsis* may remind us generally of the Stoic doctrine of recurrence, according to which the *cosmos* was regularly plunged into a con-flagration (*ekpyrōsis*) and regularly underwent reconstruction (*diakosmēsis*). But, even before the Stoics, Plato had already developed a doctrine of constitutional cycles in the later books of the *Republic*. Cicero adopts the doctrine of Polybius, and even its terminology, in his *De Republica* (i. 29. 45), when he speaks of 'miri orbes et quasi circuitus in rebus publicis commutationum et vicissitudinum'.

It may be added that Sallust, in his brief oracular manner, repeats the idea of a cycle of empires (*Catilina*, 2. 1–6). History, h ethinks, began with kings, under whom men lived their lives free from greed, each content with what he had. 'But then Cyrus arose in Asia, and Sparta and Athens came on the scene in Greece: they began to subdue cities and nations, to turn greed for power into a justifica-tion of war, and to regard the height of empire as the height of glory. The risks they ran, and the experience they gained, taught them that arts were what mattered most in war. Human affairs would have followed a more level and steady course, and there would have been less chaos, and less of change and general confusion, if only the mental powers of kings and emperors had found as much scope in peace as they did in war; but an empire is most easily retained by the same methods by which it was originally acquired. With the passage of time, however, sloth began to take the place of industry; lust and pride won the victory over moderation and equity; and when manners change fortune changes with them. It is in this way that empire always passes from the hands of the weak into those of the strong.'

I

'It is when we turn to the Roman constitution that this method of inquiry is most fruitful, and enables us particularly to understand the formation, growth, and prime of that constitution, as well as the change [from growth to decay] which the future is likely to bring. If it may be said of any constitution, it may be certainly said of the Roman, as has already been noticed, that it has owed its original formation and growth to natural processes, and will owe to them also the change which brings about its decline and fall. The truth of this may be tested by the subsequent course of the argument.'

2. *The Mixed Constitution*

We might have expected Polybius, at this point, to pass from his general account of constitutional change to an equally general account of the mixed constitution; examining the principles which underlie it, the nature of its structure, and its power to arrest, or at any rate postpone, the process of change and decay to which, in his view, all other constitutions are liable. Actually he allows himself to run into discursive detail. Instead of attempting a theory of the mixed constitution, as Plato had done in the *Laws* and Aristotle in the *Politics*, he falls into a descriptive vein. He devotes (1) a brief chapter (10) to an account of the Spartan constitution, and then (2) a series of chapters (11–18) to a fuller account of the Roman; he then proceeds (3) to a still fuller account of the Roman army (19–42), followed (4) by a comparison (43–57) of the Roman constitution with other constitutions (mainly the Spartan, Cretan, and Carthaginian),[1] a comparison which ends with some discursive remarks on Roman funerals, Roman patriotism, the Roman attitude to money, and Roman regard for religion. With this he concludes the long essay or digression on constitutional change and the nature of the mixed constitution which forms the bulk of his sixth book; and he then returns to the course of his historical narrative.

The passages which follow are extracts from chapters 10 to 57,

[1] It may be noted that these are the three constitutions which are selected for examination in book II of Aristotle's *Politics*, as constitutions which approach the ideal. Polybius appears to be following the lead of Aristotle in selecting these three.

selected as representing the essence of Polybius' view of the nature of the mixed constitution.

(a) *The Mixed Constitution of Sparta*. Aristotle had already made some brief but pithy remarks on the Spartan constitution, as a good example of the mixed type (*Politics*, IV, c. ix, and also II. vi, § 17); and he had spoken of contemporary thinkers who regarded that constitution as ideal just because it was mixed. The Stoics in the third century B.C. adopted the theory of the mixed constitution (see above, p. 47); but it was the Peripatetics, or followers of Aristotle, who particularly elaborated the theory. Among them Dicaearchus, a pupil of Aristotle who came from Magna Graecia but spent most of his life in the south of Greece and especially at Sparta, is particularly notable. Encyclopaedic like his master, and the author of a *Life of Hellas* which is conjectured to have been the first attempt at a history of culture, he compiled accounts of constitutions, or 'polities', as his master had done (Sparta, Corinth, and Athens are reported to have found a place in these 'polities'); and he also wrote a treatise, styled the *Tripoliticus*, which may have contained a theory of the mixed constitution combining the three constitutional elements (hence the title of his treatise) of monarchy, aristocracy, and democracy. This treatise had some vogue: the mixed type of constitution became known as 'the Dicaearchan type' (*genos Dikaiarchikon*), just as in the eighteenth century of our era the mixed constitution might equally have been described as 'the Montesquieu type'.[1] Possibly Polybius borrowed from the *Tripoliticus*; but he was original in making Rome the chosen example of the mixed or 'Three-Constitution' type. Cicero certainly borrowed from Polybius; and henceforth Rome takes the place of Sparta as the great example of mixture and balance.

c. 10. Premising that Lycurgus of Sparta already understood the whole process of constitutional change, with its stages and its reasons, and interpreting him, in the general fashion of later Greek

---

[1] But it has been suggested that 'the dicaearchan type' (with a small d) is the more proper expression, and that this meant 'the just-rule type'—'dicaearchan' being not a proper name, but an adjectival compound from the Greek words for 'just' and 'rule'. This seems unlikely.

writers, as a political planner and constitution-maker, Polybius briefly describes the main features of his constitution. '. . . Seeing all these perils in advance, Lycurgus did not construct a simple or uniform constitution: he preferred to mix and combine all the excellences and distinctive qualities of the best constitutions. He was anxious that none of the elements—monarchical, aristocratic, or democratic—should grow disproportionately and thus decline into the defects akin to its qualities: he wished each authority to be checked by the others, and none of them to tip the balance or much outweigh the rest. His object was that the constitution should always be kept in a state of equilibrium and poise, like a ship tacking against the wind. Thus the kingship would be saved from arrogance by its fear of the people, which was given an adequate share in the system of the constitution: the people, again, would not venture to neglect and despise the kings,[1] owing to their fear of the Senate; and the members of the Senate, selected by merit, would always be likely to be found on the side of justice, with the result that any element in the State which was placed at a disadvantage by its clinging to tradition would always gain more strength and more weight from being supported by their adhesion and influence. Forming the constitution on these lines, Lycurgus made it possible for Sparta to maintain her liberty during a period unprecedented in any other State.

'Lycurgus, however, formed the Spartan constitution without experience of troubles, and in the strength of an insight, which he owed to the pure light of reason, into the causes and the course of the natural movements of events. The Romans have ended by attaining the same system of government among themselves; but they have done so through many struggles and troubles, and not by the light of reason. It has been the experience won in the course of vicissitudes of fortune which has always enabled them to choose the best policy; and this is the way in which they have arrived at the same goal as Lycurgus and attained the best constitutional system of any State now existing.'[2]

[1] Sparta was peculiar in having two royal families, and two kings ruling together.
[2] It was the boast of Cato and Cicero, perhaps borrowing from Polybius, that Rome had learned her political lessons in the hard school of experience. Cicero

(b) *The Mixed Constitution of Rome*. In the following chapters, 11–18, Polybius proceeds to an account of the Roman constitution as it stood at the time of the battle of Cannae, 216 B.C. Only the more general passages in the account are translated here.

c. 11 *ad finem*. 'There were three dominant parts of the Roman constitution. So evenly, and with such propriety, was everything regulated and arranged in each part, throughout the whole of the State, that no man could say for certain, even if he were a born Roman, whether the constitution as a whole was aristocratic, or democratic, or monarchical. This was only natural. If one looked only at the power of the consuls, the constitution appeared to be altogether monarchical and royal; if one looked at that of the Senate, it appeared in turn aristocratic; if one studied the power of the people, it seemed clearly to be democratic. . . .'

Polybius proceeds, in the three following chapters, to describe in some detail the powers of the Consuls (12), of the Senate (13), and of the People (14). He repeats at the end of each chapter that if one looks only at the list of powers which he has just enumerated, one would speak of simple monarchy or complete aristocracy or pure democracy. In particular he notes, after describing the powers of the Senate, that a man who was resident at Rome in the absence of the Consuls would acquire the idea that the constitution was entirely aristocratic—an idea, he adds, which many of the Greeks, and many foreign rulers too, have been led to adopt through finding that almost all of their business was settled by the Senate (c. 13 *ad finem*). Then, in the next three chapters (15–17), he goes on to describe the system of mutual checks and balances by which each element is at once combined with, and limited by, the other two. 'The consul who, vested with the powers already described, takes the field in force, appears to have the authority of an autocrat for settling the business which he has in hand; but he needs the support both of the people and of the Senate, and without it he is not competent to bring his actions to a conclusion (c. 15 *ad initium*). . . . The Senate again, great as are its powers, is

regards the Roman constitution as the best because, unlike Plato's *Republic*, it is not the work of one man or age, but has been built, as Cato used to say, by the minds of many men and in the course of several generations and ages. See below, p. 189.

compelled in its conduct of public affairs to pay attention to the masses and to have regard to the people; ... moreover, and most important of all, the veto of one of the Tribunes not only deprives the Senate of any power to carry a measure into effect, but will also prevent it from sitting and even from meeting at all; while the Tribunes are always bound to carry out the decisions of the people and to pay primary regard to their wishes (c. 16). . . . Similarly, again, the people are dependent upon the Senate, and are bound both collectively and individually to pay regard to it [here Polybius refers to the Senate's control of public works and property, in which a great number of individuals were interested, and to the senatorial monopoly of membership of all the law-courts which dealt with serious cases and affected individuals by their action]: thus all are bound to rely upon it, and all are troubled by the fear that they may one day need its services, which makes them cautious about opposition or resistance to its will' (c. 17).

Having thus described the powers of each of the three elements in the constitution, and the system of mutual balance by which each is at once united to and checked by the other two, Polybius ends in c. 18 by giving a general picture of the result.

18. 'Such being the power of each of the elements for thwarting or co-operating with the others, the result is a harmony between them so fully adequate to any emergency that it is impossible to find a constitutional system superior to that of Rome. When any common danger menaces the Romans from without, and makes concord and co-operation imperative, the power which the constitution gives is shown in its full strength and quality. Nothing needed for success is left out of account, because all of them always vie with one another in offering suggestions for meeting the contingency of the moment: no decision is taken too late, for all co-operate, in public and private, to ensure the execution of a policy. The consequence is that the genius of the constitution is invincible, and matches any policy on which the State may decide. Even when they are released from external alarms; when their times are times of good fortune, of the abundance that comes from victory, and of the enjoyment of happiness; when, under the influence of flattery and indolence, they suffer the com-

mon fate, and fall into insolence and arrogance—even then, and indeed then most of all, the constitution can be seen at work, busily providing help from its own inner resources. When one of the elements in it tends to be swollen with pride, and becomes contentious and over-masterful, the pride is sure to be reduced, and the conceit cured, by the fact that each element, as has just been explained, is dependent upon the others; and the ambitions of each can thus be counterbalanced and shackled by the rest. In this way all the elements are kept fixed in their position: the aggressive elements have their impulse checked, and the stabler elements show from the first their alarm at the designs of their neighbours.'

Polybius then proceeds, as has already been noted, to a long account of the Roman army, and then turns in conclusion to a comparison of the Roman constitution with a number of Greek constitutions, especially those of Crete, Sparta, and Carthage. In the course of comparing the Roman constitution with the Carthaginian, he makes some notable remarks on the place of religion in the State, and he ends with the suggestion that as all things change, and change for the worse, Rome too will suffer that fate.

c. 56. '. . . To my thinking the greatest difference of the Roman constitution from others—and a difference for the better—is to be found in the sphere of religion. Religious feeling, which is elsewhere regarded as superstition and made a matter of reproach, seems to me to be the cement which binds the Roman State together. This factor is so much dramatized, and is given such a place on the stage, both in private life and in public affairs, that it is impossible to exaggerate its importance. Many people might find this astonishing; but I think it has all been done with a view to impressing the people. If a civic body could be composed entirely of the wise and intelligent, there would perhaps be no need of any such policy; but as the masses are always light-headed, and always full of lawless appetites, unreasoning bursts of anger, and violent fits of temper, the only resource left is to keep them in order by playing on their secret fears and employing dramatic effects. This, in my view, is the reason why the ancients introduced among the masses ideas of the gods and conceptions of the hereafter: they were not acting aimlessly or at random in doing so; indeed, on the contrary, it is the men of today who are acting aimlessly and irrationally in seeking to banish such notions. This is one reason, not to mention others, why Greek politicians, if they are entrusted only with a single talent, cannot be true to their trust in spite of a paraphernalia of ten comptrollers and auditors, backed by as many seals and twice as many witnesses; while Romans who handle large sums of money as magistrates or ambassadors are kept true to the call of duty purely by the pledge of their oath. In other States it is rare to find a man who can refrain from embezzling public funds and is clean of the offence of theft: at Rome it is rare to meet a man who is guilty of such an offence.

c. 57. 'That change and decay is the law of all things is a truth which hardly needs argument: the necessity of the course of nature is sufficient in itself to inspire conviction. But there are two different ways in which all constitutions tend to decay. One of them proceeds from external causes; the other is the result of internal development. Speculation about the former is necessarily uncertain; speculation about the latter leads to definite results. Which kind of constitution develops first, what kinds succeed to it, and how one kind is changed into another, has already been explained; and those who can follow the whole course of the argument from beginning to end will be already in a position to forecast for themselves the future [of the Roman constitution]. That future, I think, is clear. When a constitution has safely emerged from many great dangers and has attained a position of pre-eminence and unchallenged power, the obvious result of a period of established prosperity will be that habits of life will become more extravagant, and that ambition for office and its perquisites will tend to outrun all bounds. As this tendency grows, a change for the worse will begin, produced by the itch for office and the fear of losing face, and accentuated by the growth of ostentation and extravagance in the general habits of social life. Responsibility for the change is then fastened on the people, who are partly stirred by a sense of injury through the oppression of the greedy rich, and partly swollen with conceit through the flattery of ambitious office-seekers. Placed in that position, the people lose their temper: all their ideas are coloured by resentment: they will no longer obey orders, or content themselves with being on equal terms with the magnates: they want all, or at any rate the lion's share, for themselves. When this happens, the constitution will be given the finest of names, and go by the style of Liberty and Democracy; but the fact will be the ugliest of facts—it will be mob-rule or ochlocracy. . . .'

This expectation of decay and this prognostication of the coming of the Gracchi and the later demagogues bring to the mind a story, told in Appian's *Punica* (132), of Scipio and Polybius watching the burning of Carthage in 146 B.C.[1]

'Scipio, seeing the city of Carthage then coming utterly to an end in final and absolute destruction, is reported to have shed tears, and to have been seen weeping for his enemies. At length he came to himself and recovered self-control. He thought to himself how cities and nations and governments must change their lot, just as men do: he thought how this had been the fate of Troy, once a city blessed by fortune, and then the fate of the Assyrian empire and the great empire of the Medes and Persians which succeeded the Assyrian, and after that the fate of the Macedonian empire, which had just been extinguished [168 B.C.]; and as he thought he recited—intentionally, or just that the words came involuntarily from his lips—the verses of Homer

> A day shall be when holy Troy shall be destroyed,
> And Priam of the good ash-spear, and Priam's folk.

Polybius asked him frankly—for he had been his tutor—what he meant by reciting the verses; and it is said that, keeping a guard on himself, he did not name his country expressly—though he had his fears for it, after all, as he looked at the course of human affairs. These things Polybius heard himself and records in his history.'

3. *Polybius' conception of* Tychē, *or Fortune*

In his account of constitutional change Polybius pays homage

---

[1] The translation is from the text printed in J. L. Strachan-Davidson's *Selections from Polybius*, p. 616.

to *Phȳsis*, the natural life-force (which is a force of death and decay as well as of life and growth), by virtue of which constitutions move in their appointed cycles. But if he was a disciple of *Phȳsis*, and if he recognized the regularity—indeed the inevitability—of its cyclical movement, he was also a disciple of *Tychē*, or contingency, and recognized the caprice which it imported into human affairs. In the instability and rapid vicissitudes of the reigns and policies of Alexander's successors (and even in the meteoric career of Alexander himself) men had learned to recognize the play of chance, and Fortune had become 'a thoroughly Hellenistic conception'.[1] Fortune became a city goddess, as at Antioch: she became the genius or *daimon* of princes and rulers. Polybius shares the Hellenistic conception of Fortune, and he shows it when he reflects on the fall of Macedonia after the defeat inflicted upon it by Rome at Pydna in 168 B.C., and again when he reflects on the final collapse of Greece in 146 B.C. (book XXIX, c. 21 and book XXXVIII, cc. 3–6). But he has a balanced mind; and he can put together, and pit against one another, the claims of 'Nature' and the claims of 'Fortune'. The balance of his mind and the breadth of his view are shown in his attitude to Roman success and prosperity, and to the decline and fall of Greece.

(*a*) *The success of Rome.* In the beginning of his *History* (book I, cc. 3–4) he notes that Fortune has never wrought such a marvel, or enacted such a drama, as the establishment of the empire of Rome; but he also notes that the resources of the Romans justified their designs, and were sufficient to explain their success. In a word they deserved what they got, and were not the mere favourites of Fortune. He puts this view clearly when he reflects on the end of the First Punic War (I, c. 63, § 9). 'These facts show clearly', he remarks, 'the truth of the suggestion made in the beginning of this work. It is wrong to think, as some Greeks do, that the success of the Romans was due to Fortune and was a thing that happened of itself. They had every reasonable ground in their favour, and they had practised themselves in affairs of great pith and moment, when they boldly attempted a policy of universal dominion and empire, and carried it to success.' Polybius

---

[1] W. W. Tarn, *Hellenistic Civilisation*, 3rd edition, p. 340.

here challenges the Hellenistic worship of *Tychē*, and opposes himself—so far as Rome is concerned—to a view commonly held in Greece (especially among the Peripatetics) that it was Fortune which had ruined Persia and raised up Macedonia, and which would continue to ruin and raise up empires.

(*b*) *The decline and fall of Greece.* In a notable passage in book XXXVII, c. 8, Polybius deals with the causes of childlessness and depopulation of contemporary Greece, which resulted in its collapse. He begins by saying that 'he is critical of those who make Fortune and Destiny (*Tychē* and *Heimarmenē*) responsible for public events and private vicissitudes'. Divine agencies are not responsible, and are not to be blamed, for things which lie within our own power. 'Take', he continues, 'the following instance. The whole of Greece has been visited in our time by childlessness and a general decline of the population; and this has resulted in the emptying of its cities and the failure of the land to render its produce, though there have been no continuous wars or ravages of plague. If, in this state of affairs, the suggestion were made that recourse should be had to the oracles of the gods, and the question should be put to them, 'What are we to say, or to do, in order to increase our numbers and to improve the population of our cities?', would not the suggestion seem idle, when the cause of the trouble was obvious and the cure of it in our own power? The evil developed rapidly, though we did not notice its growth, for the simple reason that men went out of their way in pursuit of ostentation, avarice, and indolence: they would not marry, or, if they did, they were unwilling to bring up the children born to them, or, [if they *were* willing], most of them would only rear one or two, and that with the object of bringing them up in luxury and leaving them well off. But when there are only one or two sons, and one or other of them dies in war or as the result of some disaster, it is obvious that houses must become empty; and just as, with bees, hives are left desolate, so, too, with men, cities will soon be reduced to poverty and infirmity. When things have come to this pass, there is no need to inquire of oracles how remedies are to be found: any ordinary person will tell you that men have to find the remedy themselves—preferably by changing their hearts and the objects they pursue, or, if they cannot do that, by passing laws to ensure the bringing up of children. Divination and magic are here of no use.'

B. *The Book of Daniel*

1. *The First Vision of the Four Kingdoms, and of the Final Triumph of the People of Israel, in chapter vii*

'In a word, chapter vii is to be understood as a description of the corona-tion feast of Jehovah, expressed in an eschatological form and com-posed under the influence of a theory of successive epochs which attains its consummation in the handing over of the government of the world to the people of Israel, represented in the person of the 'Son of Man'.[1]

(*a*) *The Four Kingdoms*. c. vii, vv. 2–8.[2] 'I saw in my vision by night, and, behold, the four winds of heaven brake forth upon the great sea [the 'sea of chaos' of Babylonian cosmology]. And four great beasts came up from the sea, diverse one from another. The first was like a lion, and had eagle's wings [the Babylonian Empire of Nebuchadnezzar]: I beheld till the wings thereof were plucked, and it was lifted up from the earth, and made to stand upon two feet as a man, and a man's heart was given to it. [This seems to suggest a 'growing humanization' of Nebuchadnezzar's empire.] And behold another beast, a second, like to a bear [a mythical Median Empire[3]], and it was raised up on one side, and three ribs were in his mouth between his teeth; and they said thus unto it, Arise, devour much flesh. [This suggests the 'ravenous nature' of the mythical Median Empire.] And after this I beheld, and lo an-other, like a leopard [the Persian Empire, from Cyrus to Darius III, 540–330 B.C.], which had upon the back of it four wings of a fowl; the beast had also four heads; and dominion was given to it. [The four wings suggest the wide spread of this empire.] After this I saw in the night visions, and behold a fourth beast [the Greek or Macedonian Empire of Alexander and his successors

---

[1] A. Bentzen, in Eissfelt's *Handbuch zum Alten Testament*, No. 19, p. 34.
[2] The text followed in all these passages is that of the Revised Version.
[3] The *actual* Median Empire (660 B.C. onwards) preceded the Babylonian Empire (*circa* 605–540 B.C.).

from 330 B.C. onwards], terrible and powerful, and strong exceedingly; and it had great iron teeth; it devoured and brake in pieces, and stamped the residue with his feet; and it was diverse from all the beasts that were before it; and it had ten horns. [The first three empires had shapes—the lion, the bear, the leopard; the fourth empire has no shape, as being 'too fearful to be likened to any known creature'; it was unique, and uniquely destructive—a testimony to the impression left in the East by Alexander's conquests. The ten horns may be the ten rulers of the Seleucid division of the Macedonian Empire down to 166 B.C.] I considered the horns, and, behold, there came up among them another horn, a little one [Antiochus Epiphanes, the Seleucid ruler from 175 to 163 B.C.], before which three of the first horns [kings who had preceded Antiochus] were plucked up by the roots: and, behold, in this horn were eyes like the eyes of a man, and a mouth speaking great things.' The Septuagint version here adds, 'And he made war with the saints'—i.e. he attacked the religious congregation in Jerusalem in 168 B.C., and sought to introduce a Greek cult, which resulted in the Maccabean revolt and a movement of Jewish independence.

(b) *The Judgement on the Kingdoms in Heaven*. vv. 9–12. On this description of the four empires and of their culmination in Antiochus Epiphanes there follows the Judgement. 'I beheld till thrones were placed, and one that was [like unto an] ancient of days did sit:

His raiment was white as snow, and the hair of his head like
     pure wool;
His throne was fiery flames, and the wheels thereof burning fire.
A fiery stream issued and came forth from before him;
Thousand thousands ministered unto him,
And ten thousand times ten thousand stood before him:
The judgement was set,
And the books were opened.

I beheld at that time because of the voice of the great words which the horn spake; I beheld even till the beast [the fourth beast, or Macedonian Empire] was slain, and his body destroyed, and he was given to be burned with fire. And as for the rest of the beasts [the three first empires], their dominion was taken away; yet their lives were prolonged for a season and a time.' [This may mean that they survived not as empires, but as communities or peoples.]

(c) *The Triumph and Crowning of the People of Israel.* vv. 13–14. 'I saw in the night visions, and, behold, there came with the clouds of heaven one like unto a son of man [i.e. the people of the Saints, the religious congregation of the faithful], and he came even to the ancient of days, and they brought him near before him.' The religious congregation, unlike the kingdoms which are like beasts, has a *human* likeness. But perhaps even more than that is meant; and the religious congregation may not only be 'like unto a son of man', but may be personified and embodied in an actual individual man who is one with it, as it is one with him—this man being its deliverer and king, and as such the anointed one, the Messiah.[1]

> 'And there was given him dominion, and glory, and a kingdom,
> That all the peoples, nations, and languages should serve him:
> His dominion is an everlasting dominion which shall not pass away,
> And his kingdom that which shall not be destroyed.'

(The visions of the first half of chapter vii are followed in the second half by an interpretation which is really a repetition.)

v. 18. 'The saints of the Most High [a phrase intended "to express the divine or supernatural character of God's people as contrasted with the other peoples of the earth"] shall receive the kingdom, and possess the kingdom for ever, even for ever and ever.'

vv. 25–27. 'And he [Antiochus Epiphanes] shall speak words against the Most High, and shall wear out the saints of the Most High: and he shall think to change the times and the law [the times of the Jewish festivals, and the Mosaic law]; and they shall be given into his hand until a time and times and half a time [i.e. for three years and a half, or from the summer of 168 to the winter of 165 B.C.]. But the judgement shall sit, and they shall take away his dominion, to consume and destroy it unto the end. And the kingdom and the dominion, and the greatness of the kingdoms

---

[1] A. Bentzen, op. cit., pp. 33–34.

under the whole heaven, shall be given to the people of the saints of the Most High: his [i.e. its] kingdom is an everlasting kingdom, and all dominions shall serve and obey him [i.e. it]. Here is the end of the matter.'

2. *The Visions in the later chapters of the Book of Daniel*

Two other visions follow, which are partly repetitions, and partly revisions or expansions, of the first vision. The second vision, which occupies chapter viii, is that of the Ram and the He-goat. Here the four kingdoms are reduced to two: Babylonia disappears; Media and Persia become one, and are figured by a two-horned ram; the Greek or Macedonian Empire, which before had no likeness to an animal, becomes a he-goat from the west, with a notable horn between his eyes. An account is given of the defeat of Media–Persia by the 'kingdom of Greece', the notable horn being explained as the first king, Alexander; and this is followed by an account of the dissolution of the kingdom into four parts, or horns, the emergence of the little horn (Antiochus Epiphanes) out of one of these, and the oppression wrought by the little horn for its appointed period, until it is broken. Here the vision ends, with no description of the final Judgement or of the eventual Triumph and Crowning of the people of Israel.

The third and final vision, which occupies the last three chapters (x–xii), begins once more with an account of the Persian and Macedonian empires; but it is mainly occupied with a more or less historical account of struggles between the Seleucid 'Kingdom of the North' and the Ptolemaic 'Kingdom of the South' down to 168 B.C., ending with a prophecy of the final defeat of Antiochus Epiphanes, apparently by an Egyptian army, somewhere in the plain 'between the sea and the glorious holy mountain'. (Actually he died on a campaign in distant Media; but the prophecy is so far correct that the Jewish tribulation ceased with his death, and 'the times and the law' were restored.) This third vision, unlike the second, ends with a judgement (or rather deliverance) and a triumph, which are like, and yet unlike, the judgement and the triumph and crowning which conclude the first vision.

c. xii, vv. 1–3. 'And at that time [when Antiochus has come to his end] Michael shall stand up, the great prince which standeth for the children of thy people [i.e. the angel who is the patron of Israel]: and there shall be a time of trouble, such as never was since there was a nation even to that same time: and at that time thy people [i.e. the true Israel of the righteous or 'saints'] shall be delivered, every one that shall be found written in the book.[1] And many of them that sleep in the dust of the earth shall awake, some to everlasting life, and some to shame and everlasting contempt. [This suggests the idea of a Last Judgement.] And they that be wise [i.e. the godly, or the teachers and leaders of the true Israel which had the virtue of loyalty to the covenant] shall shine as the brightness of the firmament; and they that turn many to righteousness as the stars for ever.'

What is notable here is the clear expression of belief in a future life—or, perhaps more exactly, of belief in the continued existence of the religious congregation as a polity in heaven, with a golden book of membership. This belief in a life after death, coupled with the idea (which forms its prelude) of a divine act of intervention and judgement which is the consummation of the process of history, is what constitutes the importance of the apocalypse of Daniel. 'The Apocalyptists', wrote Dr. Charles, 'were thinkers and *sought to explain all history as a unity.*' The writer of the later chapters of the Book of Daniel, as he is one of the earliest, is also perhaps the greatest of the Jewish Apocalyptists.

Note. One of the books in the Apocrypha—2 Esdras, perhaps written in Rome at the end of the first century A.D.—contains in three of its chapters (cc. xi–xiii) interpretations of the visions of Daniel. These interpretations make the fourth beast of Daniel's first vision typify the Roman Empire. They also give a more individual and personal character to 'the Son of Man', who becomes (c. xiii, v. 3) *'the likeness of a man . . . that . . . flew with the clouds of heaven'.* He is also conceived in an earlier passage (c. xi, v. 37) as 'a lion roused out of the wood roaring', who brings to an end the three-headed eagle which is the Roman Empire.

[1] 'This book of life, which originally was a register of the actual citizens of the theocratic community on earth, has in the present passage become a register of the citizens of the coming kingdom of God, whether living or departed' (R. H. Charles, *Commentary on Daniel*, p. 326). It is thus the book, as St. Augustine might have said, of 'the City of God'.

PART II

HELLENISTIC-JEWISH THOUGHT

(200 B.C.—A.D. 50)

INTRODUCTION

THERE is a period in the history of Judaism, from the composition of the Book of Ecclesiasticus (*circa* 190 B.C.) to the death of Philo Iudaeus of Alexandria (*circa* A.D. 50), which has almost entirely disappeared from the Jewish record. 'Talmudic Jewry', it has been said, 'destroyed its Greek-speaking sister':[1] in other words, a revived Hebraism overwhelmed, during the later centuries of classical antiquity, the Hellenic (or Hellenistic) element which had played so large a part in the history of Judaism during the two centuries before and in the century following the Christian era. At that time, and during that period, Greek thought had been carried by the spread of the Greek language, and by the success of the Jews in attracting proselytes, into the many Jewish congregations, scattered over the Eastern Mediterranean, which had ceased to be specifically Jewish, in any racial sense, and which in blood, if not in belief, were of a mixed and various composition. The dispersion of Jewry in space, and its concomitant increase in numbers as it commended itself by its propaganda to a growing body of new converts, had brought to it, as is recorded in the Acts of the Apostles, 'dwellers . . . in Pontus and Asia, in Phrygia and Pamphylia, in Egypt and the parts of Libya about Cyrene'. Some facts of population and language will illustrate and explain the development of Jewish thought during the period covered by the following documents.

It has been calculated that the Jews were 7 per cent. of the whole population of the Mediterranean area during this period, and that in Egypt they were over 12 per cent., or about 1 million of its 8 million inhabitants. (Egypt, and in Egypt Alexandria, was

---

[1] H. Lietzmann, *The Beginnings of the Christian Church*, Eng. trans., i, p. 75.

peculiarly and particularly Jewish, but Jews were also numerous in Syria: indeed there may have been four times as many Jews in Egypt and Syria, taken together, as there were in Palestine itself.) The language used by this large body of Jews was very largely Greek. Hebrew had gone out of use, except as a religious language known only to scholars; the Aramaic language of Syria, which had become the lingua franca of the Near East and 'the principal speech of traders from Egypt and Asia Minor to India',[1] had then taken its place as 'the vernacular of Israel and . . . a second holy tongue'; but eventually—at any rate in Egypt, to which most of our information relates—it was Greek that had come to be used as the language of the Jewish synagogues. The lessons were read in a Greek translation, which we call the Septuagint;[2] prayers and the confession of faith were recited in Greek, and homilies and sermons were delivered in Greek. The result was what has been called 'the Hellenization of the Jewish religion'—a Hellenization which shows itself in a subtle allegorical interpretation (based upon Stoic methods already current in Greece) of the figures and events recorded in the Old Testament. The *Letter of Aristeas*, of about the year 100 B.C., in which an Egyptian Jew tells the story, or legend, of the origin of the Jewish Septuagint, already suggests (§ 150) that 'the lawgiver has set forth all the rules [i.e. the rules relating to diet in the Mosaic Law] by way of allegory', or, as he says, 'tropologically'; and this allegorical or tropological method is carried to its height in the exposition of the Old Testament by Philo Iudaeus more than a century later (see below, pp. 156 ff.).

These facts of population and language, with their inevitable results, are sufficient to show that in turning from the specifically Greek thought of the period 330–146 B.C. to the Jewish thought of the period 200 B.C.–A.D. 50 we are far from entering into a strange or foreign land. On the one hand, and in general terms, we have to reckon with the fact that in the whole of the Hel-

---

[1] Diringer, *The Alphabet*, p. 254.

[2] The term Septuagint was originally, among the Jews, used only for the translation of the Pentateuch. The other books of the Old Testament were *not* collected *in a canon* among the Jews in Egypt. It was the Christian Church which created what we now call the Septuagint, using for the purpose uncanonical Jewish translations. See A. Bentzen, *Introduction to the Old Testament*, i, p. 37, and H. Lietzmann, op. cit., p. 89.

lenistic period, and throughout all the Hellenistic kingdoms, there was a general fusion and 'conflation' of ideas in the upheaval that followed the conquests of Alexander and the wars of his successors. Babylonian and Egyptian 'wisdom-literature', for example, was brought into contact with the similar literature of the Jews and the Greeks; and Zoroastrian ideas (such as the idea of 'a sequence of ages, numerically determined, leading up to a Kingdom of God in a world transformed'[1]) may have passed into Greek thought, producing, or helping to produce, the theory of cycles of history and their regular recurrence which we find in Polybius, as they would also appear to have helped to produce the Jewish apocalyptic thought of the later chapters of the Book of Daniel.[2] On the other hand, and more particularly, there was a large infusion of Greek methods of thought (such as the Stoic method of allegorical interpretation), Greek ideas of cosmology and metaphysics (Platonic or Stoic or a mixture of both), and even Greek literary forms (such as the form of the dialogue in the *Letter of Aristeas* and the form of hexameter verse in the Jewish sections of the *Sibylline Oracles*[3]), which colours Jewish literature down to the death of Philo Iudaeus—and even later still, as may be seen in the form of prayer of the second century A.D. translated below on p. 164. This infusion of Greek methods of thought, Greek ideas, and Greek literary forms was a natural and inevitable result of the general adoption of the Greek language in the Hellenistic-Jewish synagogues: to adopt the language of Greece was also, in large measure, to accept the thought expressed in its literature.

It is a natural temptation for scholars trained and versed in Greek literature to exaggerate Greek influence in the Jewish literature of the period here under discussion. Some parts of that literature (for example the Psalms of Solomon and the Testaments of the Twelve Patriarchs) would appear to be purely Jewish. Other parts (for instance the Book of Ecclesiasticus) leave room for doubt, though it is possible that when the original Hebrew text was translated into Greek, by the grandson of its author,

---

[1] E. R. Bevan, in the *Cambridge Ancient History*, vol. ix, p. 420.
[2] See above, p. 104. [3] See below, pp. 281, 466.

some Greek ideas were imported (if indeed they were not already present in the Hebrew original), as, for instance, in the passage on 'leisure' translated below. But parts at any rate of the Wisdom of Solomon seem to be indubitably the products of Greek thought, and the whole work would seem to have been written originally in Greek. Professor Lietzmann, writing as a theologian, has noted that 'Hellenistic modes of thought penetrated into Jewish wisdom-literature: the two streams readily mingled, especially as Hellenistic ethics had already absorbed many elements of the "Wisdom" of the Orient'. Similarly Sir W. W. Tarn, writing as a classic and an ancient historian, has observed that 'the learned Alexandrian Jew who at the end of the first century [? B.C.] wrote the beautiful first part of Wisdom had *probably* read Plato'.[1] Perhaps the author of the part of the Book of Wisdom which celebrates the praises of *Sophia* had also read, and used even more, the writings of Posidonius of Apamea, the current teacher both of Romans and Greeks in the first century B.C., who had mingled Platonism with Stoicism in an eclectic philosophy which commanded general vogue (see below, pp. 281 ff.).

Whatever the interaction between Hellenistic thought and Jewish literature, there is certainly a parallel—and also a contrast—between the general trend of Greek speculation and the general trend of Jewish. It has been remarked that both the Greek and the Jew desired liberty, and both of them celebrated the praise of wisdom; but while the Greek sought liberty as an end in itself, the Jew sought it as a means to the observance of the Divine law and the worship of Jehovah; and while the Greek praised wisdom as a participation of human reason in the divine reason which pervaded the cosmos, the Jew praised it as the understanding and fear of the personal God who determined the course of history by His inscrutable will ('for my thoughts are not your thoughts, neither are your ways my ways, saith the Lord').[2] Alike and yet different in their general approach, the Greeks and the Jews were also alike and yet different in the problems which they faced and the solutions which they attempted. Both of them

[1] Lietzmann, op. cit., p. 81; Tarn, *Hellenistic Civilisation*, 3rd edition, p. 230.
[2] Tarn, op. cit., p. 226.

faced an antithesis, and both of them sought to overcome it; but the antithesis of the one was not as that of the other, and the Jewish way of transcending the antithesis was not the same as the Greek way. The antithesis which confronted the Greeks was that of the 'Hellene' and the 'barbarian'; and their Stoic teachers were telling them, by the third century B.C. (perhaps under the influence of the ideas and ideals of Alexander), that all men were brothers—brothers *already*, here on earth, and fellow citizens by the law of nature in the one city of the Universe (see above, p. 40). The antithesis which confronted the Jews was that between the Jew and the Gentile—between the people of God and the 'nations' outside His people; and it was only gradually, and almost reluctantly, that they moved to the idea of some *future* age in which the gulf might one day be bridged. Similarly both the Greeks and the Jews sought a 'better country'—a 'city of God' (*polis Dios*) or 'Kingdom of God'; but while the Greek thought of his city of God as being—at any rate in idea—open to all and a free city of humanity at large, the Jew thought of the Kingdom of God as embracing only the righteous, or rather only the righteous in the one people of the Jews—the righteous who belonged to that people by virtue of belonging, by birth or conversion, to one of its congregations and worshipping in its synagogues. (The great Psalm xvii in the collection called the Psalms of Solomon, noble as it is, stops short at the idea that 'in the reconstituted kingdom only Israel shall dwell':[1] see below, pp. 148 ff.)

While, therefore, there is interaction, and while there are parallels and affinities, between Greek and Jewish thought, there is also a gulf between them. The Book of Wisdom may show us an Alexandrian Jew who is versed in the current philosophy of Greece, and ready to use its terminology: the voluminous writings of Philo Iudaeus may equally, or even more, show us another Alexandrian Jew who draws on Greek philosophy and uses its terms and ideas. But both are fundamentally and essentially Jewish, clinging to the Law and the patriarchs and the tradition of the

---

[1] See H. Lietzmann, *op. cit.*, p. 28: 'In the reconstituted kingdom only Israel shall dwell—no heathen, no Greeks, no Samaritans . . . all shall be pure and holy . . . under the righteous and holy Messianic King . . . in this way, the royal rule of God, the "Kingdom of God", shall be realised in Israel.'

God of Israel. The Jews of Egypt might pray in Greek, and their Greek prayers might contain Stoic phrases (see below, p. 164); but they prayed to the God of Israel, and their thoughts were thoughts of Jerusalem and of the Temple in Jerusalem to which they sent their annual offerings. Some of the Jewish writings of this period are even definitely anti-Greek. This is true of the First Book of the Maccabees, which treats Alexander of Macedon as the beginning of evil, and recounts the story of the revolt of the Jews of Palestine against the hellenizing policy of Antiochus Epiphanes; it is even true of the Second Book, though that is said to have been written in Greek (the First Book may have a Hebrew original) and to have been composed in Alexandria. The Third Book of the Maccabees (which is not concerned with the Maccabees, and records the troubles of the Jews in Egypt) is critical of the Ptolemies and of Hellenistic kingship; and it has been suggested that its author was writing with reference, and in opposition, to the exaltation of monarchy which appears in the *Letter of Aristeas*.[1] It was natural, and indeed inevitable, that Jewish writers should at times show an anti-Greek bias. Anti-Semitism was current in the course of ancient as well as of modern history. There were struggles between Greeks and Jews in Alexandria in the first century A.D., which are recorded by Philo Iudaeus: there were pogroms and massacres: the Jewish historian Josephus records a time at which 50,000 Jews were killed in Alexandria and 60,000 in the rest of Egypt. Tacitus shows (in his *Histories*, book v, c. 5) that Romans as well as Greeks despised and even hated the Jews; and by the reign of Hadrian circumcision was prohibited (see below, p. 271) and conversion to Judaism was forbidden. If the Jews were at times attracted by Greek thought, and could love its sublimities, they lived, none the less, in a hostile world, and they sometimes retorted hate for hate.[2]

[1] The suggestion is made by S. S. Tracy in the final essay of the 1928 volume of *Yale Classical Studies*.
[2] See H. Lietzmann, op. cit., i, pp. 84–87.

§ I. PASSAGES FROM A DIALOGUE ON KINGSHIP, IN THE 'LETTER OF ARISTEAS'

(These passages may be as old as the third century B.C.)

The *Letter of Aristeas* (printed in H. B. Swete's *Introduction to the Old Testament in Greek*, pp. 551–606) is a romance, which may have some kernel of truth, about the translation of the Pentateuch into Greek at Alexandria. The writer was a Jew, and his work is a work of Jewish propaganda; he may have written it about 100 B.C. But inset in it is a long dialogue, mainly on kingship, which depicts Ptolemy II (285–247 B.C.) propounding some 72 questions to the 72 Jewish translators in a series of seven banquets, and receiving their answers to the questions which he propounded about the duties of his office. This inset may be older than the rest of the work, and may belong to the third century. Sir W. W. Tarn, in his work on *The Greeks in Bactria and India*, 2nd edition, pp. 414–36, has drawn attention to a parallel dialogue, preserved in Pali, which records the questions put to some sages by Menander, the ruler of Greek India in the first half of the second century B.C. He suggests that the 'Questions of Ptolemy II' and the 'Questions of Menander' may have a common basis in some sort of tradition of the 'Questions of Alexander'—questions said to have been put by Alexander to Indian pundits during his campaigns, at a place near Taxila, to the east of the river Indus. Whatever the analogies, or the ultimate origins, of the questions and answers in the *Letter of Aristeas*, they throw some light, in themselves, on Hellenistic-Jewish conceptions of kingship in Ptolemaic Egypt.

It may be added that though the 'Questions of Ptolemy II' are largely concerned with the problems of kingship, and though at the end (in § 294) Ptolemy is made to say that 'he has been greatly helped by the doctrine of kingship propounded to him', many of the questions have no connexion with that theme, being more of the nature of a general 'quiz' or of the game which is nowadays called 'any questions?'. (This was a game invented by the Greeks, who loved what they called *aporiai*.) Ptolemy is made, for example, to ask 'how he could be free from disturbance of his mind in sleep' (§ 213), and he is even made to inquire 'How can a man live harmoniously with his wife?'—to which one of the translators is made to answer, 'By remembering that womankind is so made that it is headstrong, hot in pursuit of its wishes, apt to change readily for want of sound reasoning, and naturally weak; so that women must be treated with prudence, and not opposed to the point of quarrel' (§ 250).

§ 211. 'Question of the king: What is the essence of kingship? Answer [of the translator]: It is, if you reason properly, to govern yourself well, and not to be led away, by desire for wealth and fame, into overweening and unseemly desires. You have all that you need; God has no needs, and He judges with equity; do you, too, think such thoughts as are proper for man; desire not many things, but only such things as are enough to ensure your acting as a king should.

§§ 221–3. 'Question: What is the best way of government? Answer: It is to be master of yourself, and not to be led away by impulses. For it is natural to all men that their minds should have a bias towards some particular object: most men are likely to feel an inclination to eating, drinking, and physical pleasure; kings have a bent to the acquisition of territory, according to the magnitude of the renown which it brings; but moderation in all things is good.

§ 249. 'Question: How can a man be a lover of his country (*philopatris*)? Answer: By bearing in mind that it is a good thing to live and die in his own country (*idia*). To live abroad brings contempt on the poor and reproach on the rich, as though they had been banished for wrongdoing. If, then, you are a Benefactor (*Euergetēs*) to all men, as indeed you constantly are since God gives you grace in the sight of all,[1] you will appear to be a lover of your country.

§ 265. 'Question: What is the thing most necessary for a king to possess? Answer: The loyalty (*philanthropia*) and love of his subjects; for these make an unbreakable link of good will. But

---

[1] Clauses such as this—which are partly flattery, and partly invocations of the Divine Name intended to import a flavour of Jewish propaganda into the original source on which the writer probably draws—are common in the answers.

that they should come about, as men would have them come, is the work of God.

§ 267. 'Question: How can a king, when there are mixed multitudes in his realm [as, for example, the Egyptians, Macedonians, Greeks, and Jews of Egypt], keep himself in harmony with them all? Answer: By acting the part proper to each, and by taking justice for his guide, as indeed you do, since God gives you the power of good reasoning.

§ 271. 'Question: What preserves a kingdom? Answer: Care and thought, to ensure that no wrong is done by those who are set in authority over the multitude to make provision for their needs, even as you show care and thought, since God gives you the power of sober reflection.

§ 279. 'Question: What are the guides that kings ought to follow? Answer: The laws, so that they may act justly and bring refreshment to men's lives, even as you do, laying thereby for yourself the foundation of an eternal monument, and following the commandment of God.

§ 280. 'Question: Who should be appointed governors? Answer: Those who have a hatred of wrong, and who do what is right, imitating the ways of their master, to the end that they may always have a good report, even as you do, O mighty king, God having given you a crown of righteousness.

§ 281. 'Question: Who should be made officers over the forces? Answer: Those who excel in courage and righteousness, and who make it their aim to ensure the safety of their troops rather than to win a victory by hazarding men's lives in rash ventures; for even as God does good to all, so you too, imitating Him, are a Benefactor to your subjects.

§ 283. 'Question: On what should kings spend most of their time? Answer: On reading, and on the study of the records of tours [of inspection], such as are written for the rulers of kingdoms to compass the improvement and preservation of man's estate, even as you do, and thereby have won glory unattainable by other men, since God fulfils your wishes.

§§ 288–90. 'Question: Which is best for the multitude—that a man of private station shall be lifted up to be king over them, or

that they should have an hereditary king? Answer: What is
naturally best [is best for the people]. There are kings by inheritance who show themselves cruel and harsh to their subjects; but
it is far oftener the case that men of private station, who have
experienced misfortune and known poverty, show themselves,
on becoming rulers of a people, even sterner than an impious
tyrant [of royal descent]. But as has already been said, a good
disposition which has enjoyed the benefit of education is able to
exercise authority, even as you are a great king, not so much
through the greater glory of your government, or your greater
wealth, as because you have excelled all men in equity and in love
of mankind, God having granted you these gifts.

§ 291. 'Question: What is the greatest duty of kingship?
Answer: To keep one's subjects always in peace, and to see that
justice is speedily done in trials; this comes to pass through the
leader of a people, when he hates evil and loves the good, and
sets great store by saving man's existence (*psȳchē*) . . . .' There
follow the usual flattery and invocation of the Divine Name.

Though the Jewish author of the *Letter of Aristeas* is drawing
on Greek material and following a Greek model, he is convinced
that the tradition of the Jewish Scriptures is greater than the
philosophy of the Greeks. He records how, at the end of the third
banquet, the king congratulated the Jewish translators on their
answers, and how the audience, and especially the philosophers,
joined in applause; for the translators 'were far superior [to the
philosophers] in their ways and their speech, as indeed they needs
must be since they took God for their starting-point' (§ 235).

§ II. THE BOOK OF ECCLESIASTES

The author of the Book of Ecclesiastes (*circa* 200 B.C.) would
appear to have belonged to an aristocratic section of the Jewish
people which was touched by Hellenism. This section inclined to
the Seleucid kings, in preference to the Ptolemies of Egypt who
disputed with them the possession of Palestine and were supported by the common people. Aristocratic and pro-Seleucid,
the author of Ecclesiastes seems to be critical of the Egyptian

monarchy of his age, in the person of Ptolemy IV, Philopator, and to prefer what he regards as the young and rising power of the Seleucid Antiochus III. At the end of chapter iv, verses 13 and 15, he writes: 'Better is a poor and wise youth than an old and foolish king, who knoweth not how to receive admonition any more. . . . I saw all the living which walk under the sun, that they were with the youth, the second, that stood up in his stead.' Similarly, in chapter v, verses 8 and 9, perhaps with reference to Ptolemy IV, he writes: 'If thou seest the oppression of the poor, and the violent taking away of judgement and justice in a province, marvel not at the matter: for one higher than the high regardeth; and there be higher than they. But the profit of a land every way is a king over the cultivated field'.[1] In the same sense, at the end of chapter x (verse 20), he warns his fellow Jews against the royal spies (? of the Ptolemaic king): 'Curse not the king, no, not in thy thought; . . . for a bird of the air shall carry the voice, and that which hath wings shall tell the matter.'

The author of Ecclesiastes, it would thus appear, has no set doctrine of monarchy: he just criticizes one type of monarch, and prefers another, represented for him by the Seleucids. Experience was to prove that he was mistaken in his preference; and within a generation the Jews, under the guidance of the Maccabees, were engaged in a passionate revolt against the Seleucid Antiochus IV and the rigour of his hellenizing policy. If he had written some thirty or forty years later, the writer of Ecclesiastes would have been less of a hellenizer. He might even have omitted his endorsement of the Greek idea of moderation ('nothing in excess') which comes in chapter vii, verses 16 and 17: 'Be not righteous over much; neither make thyself over wise: why shouldest thou destroy thyself? Be not over much wicked, neither be thou foolish: why shouldest thou die before thy time?'[2]

[1] The translation is that of the Revised Version; but an alternative version of the last sentence, suggested in a footnote to it, has been adopted. The implication may be that the rule of a Seleucid king is more favourable than that of a Ptolemy to agriculture and economic prosperity.

[2] On the general relation of the author of Ecclesiastes to the Greek thought of his time see W. W. Tarn, op. cit., pp. 212–13 and pp. 230–1.

§ III. THE WISDOM OF JESUS THE SON OF SIRACH, OR
ECCLESIASTICUS

The book in the Apocrypha which bears this title was originally
written in Hebrew between 200 and 180 B.C., and it is thus a little
anterior to the Maccabean epoch and the visions of the Book of
Daniel. It was afterwards translated into Greek by the grandson
of the author. Along with the Book of Wisdom it is one of the
notable products of the 'wisdom' literature of the Jews. The
greater part of Ecclesiasticus is a series of essays on different
themes, and may consist of notes of the teaching of Jesus the son
of Sirach, analogous to the notes made by Arrian, three centuries
later, of the teaching of Epictetus (*infra*, p. 310). The essays
occasionally begin with a proverb, which serves as a text for the
argument. There is possibly some Greek influence in the first
essay which follows, on the wisdom of the scribe and the opportunity of leisure: the notion of the value of *scholē*, or leisure,
had been developed in the *Politics* of Aristotle, and the idea of the
'wise' man (the *sapiens*) had been expounded in the theory of the
Stoics. But the Jewish thought of the age of the son of Sirach may
well be independent of any external influence; and the priestly
scribe who is versed in the Law is essentially a Jewish figure.[1] The
social theory implied in the essay is a conservative theory of a
fixed and hierarchical class-system, and it is quoted by Burke with
approval in his *Reflections on the French Revolution*.

1. *The Scribe and the Worker*

Ecclesiasticus xxxviii. 24–xxxix. 11. ' "The wisdom of the
scribe cometh by opportunity of leisure; and he that hath little
business shall become wise."[2]

'How shall he become wise that holdeth the plough, that
glorieth in the shaft of the goad, that driveth oxen, and is occupied
in their labours, and whose discourse is of the stock of bulls? He
will set his heart upon turning his furrows; and his wakefulness

---

[1] The 'scribe' (*grammateus* in the Greek of the Septuagint) was a Jewish scholar
who (1) gave lessons in religious schools on the interpretation of the Law, and
(2) preached and interpreted the text of the Old Testament in synagogues.
[2] This is the proverb or text on which the argument of the essay is based.

is to give his heifers their fodder. So is every artificer and work-master . . .; they that cut gravings of signets . . ... So is the smith sitting by the anvil . . ... So is the potter sitting at his work, and turning the wheel about with his feet, who is alway anxiously set at his work, and all his handywork is by number; he will fashion the clay with his arm, and will bend its strength in front of his feet; he will apply his heart to finish the glazing; and he will be wakeful to make clean the furnace.

'All these put their trust in their hands; and each becometh wise in his own work. Without these shall not a city be inhabited, and men shall not sojourn nor walk up and down therein. They shall not be sought for in the council of the people, and in the assembly they shall not mount on high; they shall not sit on the seat of the judge, and they shall not understand the covenant of judgement: neither shall they declare instruction and judgement; and where parables are they shall not be found. But they will maintain the fabric of the world; and in the handywork of their craft is their prayer.

c. xxxix. 'Not so he that hath applied his soul, and meditateth in the law of the Most High; he will seek out the wisdom of all the ancients, and will be occupied in prophecies. He will keep the discourse of the men of renown, and will enter in among the subtilties of parables. He will seek out the hidden meaning of proverbs, and be conversant in the dark sayings of parables. He will serve among great men, and appear before him that ruleth; he will travel through the land of strange nations; for he hath tried good things and evil among men. He will apply his heart to resort early to the Lord that made him, and will make supplica-tion before the Most High. . . . He shall shew forth the instruc-tion which he hath been taught, and shall glory in the law of the covenant of the Lord. . . . Nations shall declare his wisdom, and the congregation shall tell out his praise.' (From the Revised Version.)

2. *The Rich and the Poor*

Chapters xiii and xiv contain several brief essays on riches and poverty. The essay which follows puts the case for the 'man of low degree' and the wisdom which he may utter.

c. xiii. 21–23. 'A rich man when he is shaken is held up of his friends; but one of low degree being down is thrust away also by his friends. When a rich man is fallen, there are many helpers; he speaketh things not to be spoken, and men justify him; a man of low degree falleth, and men rebuke him withal: he uttereth wisdom, and no place is allowed him. A rich man speaketh, and all keep silence; and what he saith they extol to the clouds: a poor man speaketh, and they say, Who is this? and if he stumble they will help to overthrow him.' (From the Revised Version.)

3. *The Government of Wisdom*

c. ix. 17–x. 5. 'As the skill of an artificer is showed by his work, so is the wisdom of a ruler known by his words. A man full of tongue is dangerous in his city; and he that is headlong in speech shall be hated. A wise judge will instruct his people; and the government of a prudent man is well ordered. As is the judge of his people, so are his officers; and as is the ruler of a city, such are all they that dwell therein. An unwise king will destroy his people; but through the prudence of them which are in authority the city will be established. In the hand of the Lord is the authority of the earth; and in due time he will raise up over it one that is profitable. In the hand of the Lord is the prosperity of a man; and on the person of the scribe shall he lay his honour.' (From the version by A. D. Power.)

§ IV. PASSAGES FROM THE FIRST BOOK OF MACCABEES

The composition of this book may perhaps be dated in the period 100–70 B.C. It was written by an orthodox and patriotic Jew, and gives the Jewish account of the struggle in Judaea for religious and national liberty against Antiochus Epiphanes and the Seleucid monarchy, from 167 B.C. onwards.

1. *The Successors of Alexander, and the Accession of Antiochus Epiphanes*

1 Maccabees c. i, verses 1–10 and 41–43. 'And it came to pass, after that Alexander the Macedonian, the son of Philip, who came out of the land of Chittim, and smote Darius king of the Persians

and Medes . . . that he reigned in his stead, in former time, over Greece [i.e., as the note in the Revised Version runs, 'the Greek Empire']. And he fought many battles, and won many strongholds, and slew the kings of the earth, and went through to the ends of the earth, and took spoils of a multitude of nations. And the earth was quiet before him, and he was exalted, and his heart was lifted up, and he gathered together an exceeding strong host, and ruled over countries and nations and principalities, and they became tributary unto him.

'And after these things he fell sick, and perceived that he should die. And he called his servants, which were honourable, which had been brought up with him from his youth, and he divided unto them his kingdom, while he was yet alive. . . . And his servants bare rule, each one in his place. And they did all put diadems upon themselves after that he was dead, and so did their sons after them many years: and they multiplied evils in the earth.

'And there came forth out of them a sinful root, Antiochus Epiphanes, son of Antiochus the king, who had been a hostage at Rome, and he reigned in the hundred and thirty and seventh year of the kingdom of the Greeks' (i.e. *circa* 176 B.C.).

Ibid., verses 41–43. 'And king Antiochus wrote to his whole kingdom, that all should be one people, and that each should forsake his own laws. And all the nations agreed according to the word of the king; and many of Israel consented to his worship, and sacrificed to the idols . . . .' (From the Revised Version, as are also all the other passages.)

2. *Antiochus in Jerusalem, and the Rising of the Maccabees in Revolt*

I Maccabees c. i, verses 54–56. 'And . . . in the hundred and forty and fifth year (*circa* 167 B.C.), they [i.e. the officers of Antiochus] builded an abomination of desolation upon the altar,[1] and in the cities of Judah on every side they builded idol altars. And at the doors of the houses and in the streets they burnt incense. And they rent in pieces the books of the law which they found, and set them on fire.'

[1] The 'abomination' was a Greek altar, placed on the Jewish altar in the Temple court in Jerusalem: the Temple itself was made a temple of Zeus, of whom Antiochus professed to be an 'epiphany'.

Ibid., c. i, verses 62–63. 'Many in Israel were fully resolved and confirmed in themselves not to eat unclean things. And they chose to die, that they might not be defiled with the meats [offered upon the "abomination"], and that they might not profane the holy Covenant: and they died.'

Ibid., c. ii, verses 1–5. 'In those days rose up Mattathias . . . and he had five sons, John . . .; Simon . . .; Judas who was called Maccabaeus; Eleazar . . .; Jonathan . . ..'

Ibid., verses 15–22. 'The king's officers, that were enforcing the apostasy, came into the city Modin to sacrifice; and many of Israel came unto them, and Mattathias and his sons were gathered together. [The royal officers required Mattathias to take the lead in the ceremony of sacrifice to the 'epiphany' of Zeus, and promised rewards to him and his sons if he did so]. Mattathias answered and said with a loud voice, If all the nations that are in the house of the king's dominion hearken unto him, to fall away each one from the worship of his fathers, and have made choice to follow his commandments, yet will I and my sons and my brethren walk in the covenant of our fathers. Heaven forbid that we should forsake the law and the ordinances. We will not hearken to the king's words, to go aside from our worship, on the right hand, or on the left.'

This was the beginning of the Maccabean revolt, which ended in the institution of an independent Maccabean State, with members of the family of Mattathias established as hereditary high-priests and governors, and recognized in that office by Rome.

3. The Glory of the Reign of Simon Maccabaeus (141–135 B.C.)

1 Maccabees c. xiv, verses 4, 9, 12–15. 'And the land had rest all the days of Simon: and he sought the good of his nation; and his authority and his glory was well-pleasing to them all his days. . . . The ancient men sat in the streets, they communed all of them together of good things, and the young men put on glorious and warlike apparel. . . . And they sat each man under his vine and his fig tree, and there was none to make them afraid: and there ceased in the land any that fought against them: and the

kings were discomfited in those days. And he strengthened all
those of his people that were brought low: the law he searched
out, and every lawless and wicked person he took away. He
glorified the sanctuary . . ..

4. *Psalm cx, verses 1–5*

This psalm is held by some scholars to celebrate the acceptance
of Simon Maccabaeus by the people (in what was virtually an act
of popular election) as both prince and high priest in Jerusalem
'after the order of Melchizedek', who was in his day both 'king
of Salem' and 'priest of God' (Genesis, xiv 18).

'The Lord (Jehovah) saith unto my lord [Simon, prince and
High Priest], "Sit thou at my right hand, until I make thine enemies
thy footstool". The Lord shall send forth the rod of thy strength
out of Zion:[1] "Rule thou in the midst of thine enemies." Thy
people offer themselves willingly in the day of thy power: in the
beauties of holiness [i.e. in the vestments of the High Priest], from
the womb of the morning [i.e. in the morning muster of the
army], thou hast the dew of thy youth. The Lord hath sworn,
and will not repent, thou art a priest for ever after the order [i.e.
in the manner] of Melchizedek. The Lord at thy right hand
shall strike through kings in the day of his wrath.'

V. THE TESTAMENTS OF THE TWELVE PATRIARCHS

This is a work, originally written in Hebrew, of about the year
100 B.C. It represents the ideas of a Pharisee devoted to the
Maccabean dynasty as that dynasty stood at its zenith in the reign
of Hyrcanus I (135–104 B.C.). Of the three brief passages here cited
the first is notable as dealing with the problem of the relation between the spiritual and the temporal authority—a problem foreign
to Greek and Roman antiquity (in which there was no distinction
of State and Church), but already present in Jewish thought, and

[1] That is, Jehovah from his throne on the mountain of God summons the
prince and high priest to share His sovereignty, making him a deputy who rules,
in the last resort, by divine appointment, over and above his title derived from
the people's offering of themselves (G. H. Box, *The Clarendon Bible*, O.T.,
vol. v, *Judaism in the Greek Period*, p. 203).

destined to become a problem of the first order in Christian thought from the time of Constantine I onwards. The second passage, on the hope of the Messiah, may be compared with the visions of the Book of Daniel and with some of the Psalms of Solomon (*infra*, p. 149). The last passage, on love of one's neighbour, is notable for its suggestion of the idea of *humanitas* as the bond of community, an idea which was also struggling for expression in Stoicism, but which was particularly developed in the theory of later Christian writers such as Lactantius.

The *Testaments* may be based on synagogue sermons dealing with the lives of the patriarchs.

1. *The superiority of the Sacerdotium to the Regnum—or of Levi to Judah*

Testament of Judah xxi, §§ 1–4. 'And now, my children, I command you, love Levi, that ye may abide, and exalt not yourselves against him, lest ye be utterly destroyed. For to me the Lord gave the kingdom, and to him the priesthood; and He set the kingdom below the priesthood. To me He gave the things upon the earth: to him the things in the heavens. As the heaven is higher than the earth, so is the priesthood of God higher than the earthly kingdom unless it falls away through sin from the Lord and is dominated by the earthly kingdom.'

These words might have been written by one of the medieval popes, such as Innocent III or Boniface VIII. But they are not a pure exaltation of priestly power at the expense of regal. Actually Hyrcanus I was king (in fact though not in name) as well as priest, and he thus combined both offices in his person.[1] But Hyrcanus and the Maccabean dynasty belonged to the priestly tribe of Levi, and not to the royal tribe of Judah; and the writer of the *Testaments* therefore exalts him in his priestly or Levite capacity, and represents Judah as recognizing his superiority.

It is curious to note that the metaphor of the sun and the moon (the priesthood being the sun and kingship the moon), later used

---

[1] Tarn, *Hellenistic Civilisation*, 3rd edition, p. 236. The duplication of offices, and their union in one person, is noted in the *Testament of Levi*, viii, 14: 'a king shall arise in Judah, and shall establish a new priesthood'. See also Psalm CX, quoted above at the end of section C.

by Innocent III, already occurs in the *Testament of Naphthali*, v, § 3: 'Levi laid hold of the sun and Judah . . . seized the moon'.

2. *The Hope of the Messiah*

As Levi had taken the place of Judah in the office of king with the establishment of the Maccabean dynasty, so the tribe of Levi takes the place of the tribe of Judah as the source from which the new Messiah is to come. (Indeed it almost seems at times as if the tribe of Levi were regarded as having already produced the Messiah, in the person of the Maccabean ruler.)

The anticipation of a future Messiah (already present at the beginning of the Maccabean dynasty in the visions of the Book of Daniel, *supra*, p. 126) is expressed in the *Testament of Judah*, xxiv, §§ 1–3: 'And after these things shall a star arise to you from Jacob in peace, and a man shall arise . . . like the sun of righteousness, walking with the sons of men in meekness and righteousness, and no sin shall be found in him. And the heavens shall be opened unto him, to pour out the spirit, [even] the blessing of the Holy Father; and he shall pour out the spirit of grace upon you; and ye shall be unto him sons in truth, and ye shall walk in his commandments first and last.'

Another passage, in which Hyrcanus I seems to be addressed in a Messianic hymn as if he were a present Messiah, is contained in the *Testament of Levi*, c. xviii. The hymn-form and some of the phrases are Messianic: 'Then shall the Lord raise up a new priest, and to him all the words of the Lord shall be revealed; and he shall execute a righteous judgement upon the earth for a multitude of days, and his star shall arise in heaven as of a king. . . . And in his priesthood the Gentiles shall be multiplied in knowledge upon the earth, and enlightened through the grace of the Lord: in his priesthood shall sin come to an end.'

The conception of the Messiah developed and changed in the Jewish literature of the second and first centuries B.C. In the *Testaments of the Twelve Patriarchs*, and also in the Psalms of Solomon (see below, p. 149), the Messiah is a human ruler (if He is also an ideal figure) who will reign on earth and make Jerusalem His capital. But in the *Parables* sections of the Book of Enoch, which

are dated by some scholars as belonging to the same period as the
Psalms of Solomon (i.e. about 60 B.C.), the Messiah who is the
'Son of Man' is regarded as a Being in heaven, 'who even now is
mysteriously manifested to righteous souls and who will be God's
great agent in the final consummation'.[1] There is no fixed picture
of the Messiah, but rather a wavering vision.

3. *Love of the Neighbour*

Some passages in the *Testaments* are the first in recorded literature to enjoin the lesson of Christian love (even before the coming
of Christ) and the duty of forgiveness. They anticipate the Sermon
on the Mount, and they contain, in the germ, teaching similar to
that of Lactantius (below p. 463). One passage is in the *Testament
of Gad*, vi, §§ 3–7: 'Love ye one another from the heart; and if a
man sin against thee, speak peaceably to him, and in thy soul
hold not guile; and if he repent and confess, forgive him. . . . But
if he be shameless and persisteth in his wrong-doing, even so forgive him from the heart, and leave to God the avenging.' Another
passage comes in the *Testament of Dan*, v, §§ 3 ff.: 'Love the Lord
through all your life, and one another with a true heart.' On this
passage Dr R. H. Charles (whose translation has been followed
in the passages here quoted) notes that the text is 'remarkable in
being the first literary authority which conjoins the two great
commandments of love to God and love to our neighbour'.

§ VI. THE PSALMS OF SOLOMON

The Psalms of Solomon mark the end of the century of Jewish
freedom which had begun with the Maccabean revolt about 167
B.C. and had lasted till the Roman conquest of Palestine by
Pompey in 63 B.C. The great dreams of the Maccabean period
had now vanished, but the invincible tenacity of the Jewish mind,
refusing to despair, spun new threads of hope. These threads are
woven together in the Psalms of Solomon. The best introduction
to the passages which follow from these Psalms—passages which

---

[1] E. R. Bevan, in the *Cambridge Ancient History*, vol. ix, p. 418.

recall the theme and repeat the note of the later chapters of the Book of Daniel—is to be found in the first chapter of Hans Lietzmann's *The Beginnings of the Christian Church* (pp. 26–28 of the English translation): 'In the days when Pompey established the Roman authority, new Psalmists arose who gave their people songs in the style and manner of the old 'Davidic' psalm-book. We still have these Psalms under the name of Solomon in a Greek translation, and they are an invaluable record of the faith and hope of that period. . . . In the great Messianic Psalm 17 the lively Messianic hope of the Roman era is clearly and definitely described . . . a divine miracle is expected, which will sweep away the heathen from before the Messiah. . . . Then Jerusalem will rise up anew in its former glory . . . and in the reconstituted kingdom only Israel shall dwell.'

The text followed is that of H. E. Ryle and M. R. James, *Psalms of Solomon*, Cambridge, 1891.

Psalm xvii. *Prayer for the Kingdom of the Messiah*

1. Lord, thou art our King through the ages and evermore;
   For in Thee, our God, our soul shall exult.

2. What is the length of man's life on the earth?
   As is the length of his time, so is the hope set upon him.

3. But as for us, our hope shall be in God, our Saviour;
   For the might of our God is for ever , with mercy,

4. And the kingdom of our God is for ever over the nations in judgement.

5. Thou, Lord, didst choose David to be king over Israel,
   And Thou didst swear to him touching his seed for ever
   That his kingdom should not fail before Thee.

6. But when we sinned, sinners rose up against us,
   They set upon us, and thrust us out:
   Yea, those to whom thou madest no promise took away by force [what was ours] . . . .

The next sixteen verses of the Psalm, 7–22, recite the troubles of the kingdom under the sinful later Asmonean rulers, in the days when the Romans came and Pompey in 63 B.C. stormed the temple hill and entered the inner sanctuary. That recital ended, the writer of the Psalm (which may be dated somewhere about the middle of the first century B.C.) turns to proclaim the hope of the coming of the kingdom of the Messiah—the hope which had already inspired the argument of the later chapters of the Book of Daniel more than a century before. At a time when rulers, judges, and people are sunk in transgression, disobedience, and sin, he prays for the reign of a new 'son of David' and the restoration of the true Israel.

23. Look upon them, O Lord, and raise up unto them their king,
The son of David, at the time which Thou, O God, knowest,
That he may reign over Israel Thy servant;

24. And gird him with strength to break in pieces them that rule unjustly.

25. Cleanse Jerusalem from the nations [? the Romans] that trample her down to destroy her,
[Cleanse her] in wisdom, in righteousness;

26. May he thrust out sinners from the inheritance,
May he root out the arrogance of sinners,
May he break in pieces with a rod of iron all their substance, as it were a potter's vessel,

27. May he destroy the ungodly nations with the word of his mouth,
That the nations may flee at his rebuke before his face,
And that he may convict sinners in the thoughts of their heart.

28. And he shall gather together a holy people, whom he shall lead in righteousness,
And he shall judge the tribes of the people that hath been sanctified by the Lord his God;

29. And he shall not suffer unrighteousness to lodge in their midst,
Nor shall any man that knoweth wickedness dwell with them;

30. For he shall know them, that they are all the sons of their God,
And he shall divide them by their tribes in the land.

31. The sojourner and the alien shall not dwell among them any
    more;
    He shall judge the peoples and nations in the wisdom of his
    righteousness.   . . .

32. He shall have the peoples of the heathen nations to serve him
    under his yoke,
    And he shall glorify the Lord in a place to be seen of all the
    earth;

33. He shall cleanse Jerusalem in holiness as it was in the begin-
    ning,

34. So that the nations shall come from the ends of the earth to
    see his glory,
    Bringing with them as gifts her sons [the sons of Jerusalem]
    that had grown faint,

35. And they shall see the glory of the Lord, wherewith God hath
    glorified her.
    And he shall be a righteous king over them, taught of God,

36. And there shall be no unrighteousness in his days in their
    midst,
    For all shall be holy, and their king shall be the Lord's
    Anointed [the Messiah].[1]

37. For he shall not set his hope in horse and rider and bow,
    Nor multiply to himself gold and silver for war,
    Nor by [ships?] shall he gather hope for the day of battle [as
    Solomon had done of old].

38. The Lord himself is his king, and the Lord is his hope because
    he is strong in his hope of God.
    And he shall have mercy on all the nations [that come] before
    him in fear,

39. For he shall smite the earth with the word of his mouth for
    ever:

40. He shall bless the people of the Lord in wisdom with joy.

41. And he himself is pure from sin, that he may rule over a
    great people,

[1] The Greek text is *Christos Kȳrios*, which would literally mean 'the Anointed
Lord'. But *Kȳrios* represents the name of God, and can hardly be applied to an
earthly king; so that it is better to assume that the word is meant to be in the
genitive, and to translate accordingly.

And judge rulers and blot out sinners by the might of his word.

42. He shall not grow faint in his days [because his trust is] in his God;

For God hath made him strong through a holy spirit,

And wise to give counsels of understanding with power and righteousness.

43. The blessing of the Lord is with him in might,

And his hope in the Lord shall not faint.

44. Who can withstand him?

He is strong in his works, and mighty in the fear of God,

45. Keeping the flock of the Lord in faith and righteousness,

And he shall not suffer any of them to grow faint in their pasture.

46. In holiness he shall lead them all,

And there shall be among them no arrogance that oppression should come upon him.

47. This is the majesty of the King of Israel, the majesty known of God,

To raise him up over Israel, that he may give instruction:

48. His words shall be purified above fine gold, yea even the purest;

In the assemblies he shall judge among the peoples, among the tribes of them that have been sanctified;

49. His words shall be as the words of saints in the midst of the peoples that have been sanctified.

50. Blessed are they that are born in those days,

To behold the good fortune of Israel in the assembling together of the tribes; may God bring it to pass.

51. May God hasten his mercy upon Israel:

May He deliver us from the uncleanness of unhallowed enemies.

52. The Lord Himself is our king through the ages and evermore.

Psalm xviii. 6–10. *Another brief prayer for the Kingdom of the Messiah*

6. May God cleanse Israel for the day of mercy, when he giveth his blessing,

For the day of appointment, when he shall raise up his
    Anointed.
7. Blessed are they that are born in those days,
    To behold the goodness of the Lord—may he bring it to pass
      for the generation that cometh—
8. Under the rod of the guidance of the Lord's Anointed, in
    the fear of his God,
    In wisdom of spirit, and of righteousness, and of might,
9. To direct each in the works of righteousness through the fear
    of God,
    And to establish them all in the fear of the Lord,
10. A good generation, in the fear of God, in the days of mercy.

§ VII. THE WISDOM OF SOLOMON

The book of Wisdom is at once the zenith of the 'wisdom' literature of the Jews and the forerunner of what may be called 'the
philosophy of Alexandria' (an amalgam of Greek thought, first
with the Jewish Scriptures and then with the Christian Gospel)
as it developed during the first, second, and third centuries of our
era, from Philo Iudaeus to Clement of Alexandria and Origen.
The book was written in Alexandria, probably between 100 and
50 B.C. (though some would date it later, in the age of Philo
Iudaeus and the first century A.D.), by an Alexandrine Jew of the
Hellenized congregation, who had studied the 'Law' as recorded
in the Greek Septuagint, and may also have read Plato and the
writings of the Stoics. (There are certainly traces of Greek
influence in his *style*.) His praise of Wisdom, in chapter vii, gives
the essence of the conception of *Sophia* on which the author of
Ecclesiasticus had already based his ideas of social and political
theory, and which was in the future to inspire the theology and
general philosophy of a succession of thinkers. The *Sophia* of
which he speaks, which may also be called *logos* or *pneuma*,[1]
denotes 'a being which is conceived as a property of God, but
which is separated from God Himself when personification is

---

[1] 'There is no recognizable difference between sophia, logos, and pneuma'
(Lietzmann, op. cit. p. 100).

complete'. This conception of *Sophia* as a property inherent in God, or as a distinct and separate accompaniment or companion of God, affected the general conception of the earthly ruler. He too, as the image of God on earth, could be held to have the property of wisdom in himself, and thus be regarded as 'incarnate law' (*nomos empsychos*); or, alternatively, he could be viewed as having wisdom at his side in the shape of a human companion, counsellor, and minister who was versed in 'philosophy'.

In the passage which follows King Solomon is introduced as the speaker, and recites the praise and the glory of wisdom.

c. vii. 7 and 22 ff. '. . . I prayed, and understanding was given me: I called upon God, and there came to me a spirit of wisdom (*pneuma sophias*). . . . She that is the artificer of all things taught me, even wisdom. For there is in her a spirit quick of understanding, holy, . . . all-powerful, all-surveying, and penetrating through all spirits that are quick of understanding, pure, most subtil: for wisdom is more mobile than any motion; yea, she pervadeth and penetrateth all things by reason of her pureness. For she is a breath of the power of God, and a clear effluence of the glory of the Almighty;[1] therefore can nothing defiled find entrance into her. For she is an effulgence[2] from everlasting light, and an unspotted mirror of the working of God, and an image of his goodness. And she, being one, hath power to do all things; and remaining in herself, reneweth all things: and from generation to generation passing into holy souls she maketh men friends of God and prophets. For nothing doth Goth love save him that dwelleth with wisdom. For she is fairer than the sun, and above all the constellations of the stars: being compared with light, she is found to be before it; for to the light of day succeedeth night, but against wisdom evil doth not prevail; but she reacheth from one end of the world to the other with full strength, and ordereth all things graciously' (viii. 1).

---

[1] The word 'effluence' (*aporrhoia*) was a current term of Greek philosophy. In Stoic writers it signified—as did also the word *apospasma* (in the sense of fragment or particle)—the element of reason in man which was a part of the divine reason, and came to him from God to be his 'ruling principle' (*hēgēmonikon*).

[2] The word 'effulgence' is the Greek *apaugasma*, which recalls the Stoic term *apospasma*.

Note. 'The conception of personified Wisdom as closely associated with the chief God [Zeus] belongs to old Greek mythology', as Dr. Edwyn Bevan has noted; and thus we find Greek writers, such as Aelius Aristides (in his oration addressed to Athena), using language which is almost identical with that of the 'wisdom' literature of the Jews. It is easy to conjecture, as some have done, that he borrowed from that literature; but it is perhaps better to conjecture that the writers of the Jewish 'wisdom' literature had themselves borrowed from Greek sources long before the time of Aristides (who wrote in the second century A.D.). Better still, one may conjecture that Jews and Greeks were independent of one another, and that they expressed independently ideas which were in the common air and climate of thought.[1] In any case the similarities of language are striking enough to deserve notice. Just as the Greek Aelius Aristides speaks of Athena (his name for personified *sophia*) as begotten of God the Father in the beginning, 'the Only One of the Only One', and as 'always cleaving to his side and sharing his life', so the Jewish author of the Book of Proverbs, writing many centuries earlier (possibly in the days of the Persian Empire), makes *sophia* say, 'The Lord possessed me in the beginning of his way, before his works of old. . . . I was by him as a master workman . . . rejoicing always before him' (Proverbs viii. 22, 30). See Edwyn Bevan, *Later Greek Religion*, pp. 156–61, and especially 161.

§ VIII. PHILO IUDAEUS

Introduction

Philo (*circa* 30 B.C.–A.D. 45) was a wealthy member of the Jewish community in Alexandria—a community which formed a *politeuma*,[2] by the side of the larger and more powerful Greek *politeuma*, under the general control of the Roman governor. He

---

[1] It has been suggested that 'the leaders of the "Wisdom" literature formed a school which was international in character'. Certainly Egypt and Babylon, as well as Judaea and Greece, developed such a literature (G. H. Box, op. cit., pp. 133–4).

[2] A *politeuma* was a community with some sort of corporate organization which fell short of that of a city. It might be formed on an ethnic or on a religious basis, and might possess a council and magistrates for the management of its own affairs. Its members stood midway between full citizens and mere aliens. Tarn, *Hellenistic Civilisation*, 3rd edition, pp. 147, 220.

took some part in the turbulent politics of Alexandria, at the end
of the reign of Caligula and the beginning of the reign of Claudius;
but he was mainly immersed in scholarship, both Jewish and
Greek, and he left to posterity a large body of writings which
was treasured by Origen (the Christian scholar of Alexandria;
see below, p. 435), and which passed, along with Origen's own
writings, into the library at Caesarea, to be used by Eusebius (see
below, p. 473). At home in the learning of Alexandria and its
great museum and two libraries, he married the tradition of the
Jewish law and the Jewish patriarchs to Greek ideas drawn from
Plato, from Posidonius (see below, p. 281), and possibly also from
the neo-Pythagoreans who had begun to develop their ideas in
the course of the first century B.C.[1] The amalgam is curious;
and the question has been raised whether he owed more to Jewish
tradition or to Greek philosophy, two bodies of thought which
had lived side by side in Alexandria since the translation of the
Hebrew Scriptures into the Greek Septuagint in and after the
third century B.C. The answer would seem to be that Philo was
fundamentally and essentially Jewish in the inner core of his ideas,
but surrounded that inner core with a large and varied shell of
Greek ideas and Greek methods of thought. In particular he used
the Greek method of allegorical interpretation, which the Stoics
had brought into vogue by their interpretation of Homer; and
combining this with the similar method of Rabbinical exegesis,
and both with the subtle ingenuity of a singularly fertile brain,
he produced a library of speculation which is at once a marvel
and a puzzle. His great importance in the history of thought is
that he served to transmit ideas current in the Alexandrian congregation of Hellenistic Jews to the Alexandrian Christianity of

[1] H. Lietzmann (*The Beginnings of the Christian Church*, Eng. trans., p. 93) notes
that Philo regarded Plato as *the* master; 'but he referred frequently to Aristotle . . .,
the Pythagoreans [? the neo-Pythagoreans] . . ., and especially the Stoics, as his
authorities'. Lietzmann adds that, for Philo, 'the genuine Jew corresponded to the
idea of the Stoic sage. . . . He who lived by the Mosaic law determined his actions
according to the will of nature [the Mosaic law being in harmony with that will],
and was therefore the true citizen of the world; he lived by the same standards as
ruled the entire cosmos.'

An account of the general theory of Philo, and of his social and political ideas,
will be found in two works by E. R. Goodenough—*An Introduction to Philo
Judaeus* and *The Politics of Philo Judaeus*.

the third and fourth centuries—and also to the Neoplatonists of Alexandria and Rome.[1]

His voluminous writings include three main works on the Pentateuch. One of these works is the *Systematic Description of Mosaic Legislation*; and one of the sections of this work—the section entitled 'Unwritten Laws'—contains a series of studies of the great figures of the Old Testament, regarded as types or allegories. The *De Iosepho*, which is also entitled *The Statesman*, is one of the parts of this section and a study of one of these figures. It was written, like the other parts of the section, for Gentiles who wished to learn something about the Jewish religion. It presents a view of 'the Statesman' as in the nature of an arbitrator, and thus like Solon of Athens: however powerful the people may be, the statesman must give it no more than its due, just as Solon had done in his day and for his generation. ('I gave the people', so runs a couplet in one of his poems, 'such privileges as suffice, neither diminishing its honour nor giving it any increase.')

The second of Philo's works on the Pentateuch is the *Lēgum Allēgoriae*, intended, it would appear, for the Jews rather than for the Gentiles. These *Allēgoriae* are allegorical comments on passages of Genesis. One of these comments, translated at the end of this section, shows a mysticism which anticipates the teaching of Plotinus (see below, p. 331). The third work written by Philo on the Pentateuch, and the rest of his voluminous writings, need not be mentioned here; but an account of them is given in Professor Kirsopp Lake's introduction to the first volume of the *Historia Ecclesiastica* of Eusebius in the Loeb series.

1. *The career of Joseph as an allegory of the life of the Statesman*

(a) *Cities of Men and their politicians in relation to the 'great city' of the Universe and its life*

De Iosepho vi, §§ 28–31. 'The manner of man under consideration goes by the name of Joseph among the Hebrews, but among

---

[1] Plotinus taught in Rome during the third century A.D. (see below, p. 332); and it was there that Victorinus, in the course of the next century, made a translation of Neoplatonic writings which came into the hands of St. Augustine (while he was living in Italy), and exercised, as he tells us in his *Confessions*, no little influence on the development of his ideas.

the Greeks by that of "addition of a lord".[1] That name is most
exact, and very appropriate to the thing indicated by it. A civic
constitution [i.e. the constitution of a particular city or *polis*]
is an "addition" to nature's universal sovereignty; for this whole
universe is one "megalopolis", with a single constitution and a
single body of law.[2] There is a reason (*Logos*) pervading all nature,
which commands men to do what they ought to do and forbids
them to do what they ought not to do. But the particular cities
which we see about us are unlimited in number, with different
constitutions and dissimilar laws; here you will find one set of
customs and rules, and there you will find another; but they are
all by-products of invention or "additions". The cause of all this
difference is men's aversion from union and combination—not
merely an aversion of the Greeks from the barbarians or of the barbarians from the Greeks, but also an aversion of the men of each
particular stock from their own fellow members. In this mood
they will blame, or so it seems, what is not to blame at all—it may
be bad weather, or failure of crops, or poverty of the soil, or
geographical position (maritime or inland, insular or mainland)—
but they never mention the real cause, which is covetousness and
mutual distrust. *That* is what makes them dissatisfied with the
ordinances of nature: *that* is why they give the name of laws to
measures which commend themselves to the common judgement
of the masses as being in their own interest. It is reasonable, therefore, to regard particular constitutions rather in the light of
"additions" to the one constitution agreeable to nature—just as
civil laws are "additions" to the right reason of nature, and
just as the political man [i.e. the man who goes into politics]

[1] The Hebrew word which we translate as 'Joseph' has the root significance of
'adds' or 'addition'. But there is a fuller form of the word, 'Josephiah' (cf. Ezra
viii. 10), where the root significance of 'God' or 'Lord' is added to that of 'adds'.
In this fuller form the name would presumably mean 'the Lord adds'. But Philo
has inverted the meaning, and made it into 'he adds the Lord' (or 'an addition of
the Lord'); and he has further made 'Lord' a political word instead of the name
of God. He thus suggests that Joseph means a man who has 'added' to himself the
name and position of a secular 'lord' or ruler. (I owe this information to Professor
Winton Thomas.)

[2] Philo's phrase calls to mind the language of Plutarch, a century later, when
he wrote that the polity of Zeno was directed away from life in many city-states
and demes to *one* way of life and *one* system of order. See above, pp. 7–8.

is an "addition" to the man who lives in agreement with nature.'

The doctrine of the 'two States' suggested in this passage—the 'great city' of the Universe, and the limited city, or rather the many limited cities, in which men actually live—is analogous to St. Augustine's doctrine of the two cities, the *Civitas Dei* and the *civitas terrena*; but St. Augustine's view of the *civitas terrena* has a wider scope, and an even more critical tone, than Philo's view of the little municipal states which are 'additions' or accretions to the one great city of the Universe. Indeed Philo, as may be gathered from other passages of his writings, is unwilling to leave a gulf of sheer division between ordinary cities of men and the great city of the Universe. He seeks to bring them into relation; and in the issue his general view appears to be that *kingship* may serve as a bridge of reconciliation between the opposing 'two States', bringing down the irradiation of the Divine Reason, like so many sun-rays, from the 'great city' of the Universe to earthly cities. He even seems to hold that the king, treating all men as equal in the light of Divine Reason, will combine the spirit of democracy with the fact of kingship, and thus enable men to enjoy the sense that they are living under the best of all constitutions, a democracy. (E. R. Goodenough, *Introduction to Philo*, pp. 82 ff.)

(b) The shifts of politicians, and their dependence on many masters

vii, §§ 32–6. Here Philo interprets allegorically Joseph's coat of many colours and the account given in the Bible of his being first cast into a pit for an evil beast to devour and then sold to a company of travelling merchants; and on this basis, with a Rabbinical ingenuity, he finds a political meaning in each element of the story. 'Nor is it without significance that Joseph is said to wear a coat of many colours. Politics (*politeia*) is indeed many-coloured and a thing of many wiles: it admits of innumerable changes due to different characters, actions, motives, peculiarities of conduct, and varieties of time and place. . . . [Like the pilot, changing the course of his ship, or the physician altering his treatment] the politician must be many-sided and versatile; different in peace from what he is in war; one man when his opponents are numerous, and another when they are few—resisting the few energetically, but dealing with the many by way of persuasion. . . . But the story of the man being sold is also to the point; for when the demagogue and tub-thumper mounts the platform, he is like a man sold for a slave at an auction—he becomes bond instead of being free, and is carried off by a thousand masters— loaded and burdened in reality with all the honours and offices which *seem* to be given to him. He is also depicted as being exposed for a prey to wild beasts; and indeed the vanity which lurks in the background to seize and destroy its victims is in the nature of a savage beast. Then, too, in the story the merchants who buy Joseph sell him again. The significance of this is that politicians have not one master, but a multitude of masters, each buying in turn from the one before him and succeeding to his place; and politicians, thus sold and resold, become like bad servants who are always changing their places, driven from one to another by a fitful and inconstant instability of temper which makes them unable to bear any master long.'

(c) *The politician and the people*

After explaining that Joseph's training in the household of Potiphar, before he became Pharaoh's minister, is an allegory of the truth that the future politician must first be trained and practised in household management (*oikonomia*), inasmuch as a *polis* is simply a household 'writ large' (§ 38), Philo proceeds to explain Joseph's relation to Potiphar as an allegory of the relation between politician and people. Potiphar was a eunuch; so, too, is the people; and Philo explains what he means in a passage which seems to be a critique of the Alexandrine *dēmos*. One is reminded of a passage in the *Alexandrine Oration* (Oratio xxxii, §§ 25–31) of Dio of Prusa: see below, pp. 302–3.

xii, §§ 58 ff. 'The purchaser of Joseph is said to be a eunuch, and rightly so, for the mob (*ochlos*) which buys the politician is in truth a eunuch. . . . What, then, is the parallel between eunuchs and the mob? It is this—that the mob, while it seems to follow virtue, is unable to produce wisdom. When a multitude of mixed

and promiscuous persons is assembled, it *says* the right things, but
it *thinks* and *does* the opposite:[1] it accepts the sham in preference
to the genuine, because it is the victim of appearances and does
not pursue the true Good. . . . It is very apposite, too, that the
purchaser and master of Joseph should also be called a head-cook;[2]
for just as a cook is concerned only in providing a constant series
of superfluous pleasures for men's bellies, so the multitude, when
it deals with politics, is concerned only in securing the luxuries
and delights which come by way of the ears [i.e. from oratory]—
delights which merely lower the pitch of the understanding and
slacken the strings of the mind. Cooks, as we all know, are different from physicians: the latter use every effort to produce
nothing but preparations which are wholesome if unpleasant; the
former do the contrary—they prepare nothing but what is pleasant,
with no thought for men's well-being. The parallel to the physician, in a democratic state, is to be found in the laws and in the
councillors and judges who rule in accordance with the laws;
who, regardless of flattery, pay heed only to the security and
safety of the commonwealth. The analogy to the cook, on the
other hand, is to be found in the large crowds of youngsters who
care nothing for men's future well-being, and whose one concern
is how to gain the immediate enjoyment of pleasure.'

(*d*) *The politician as an interpreter of the dream of human life*

Arguing that the true statesman will preserve a manly independence, and refuse to flatter or cringe, Philo ultimately rises, in the
final chapters of the *De Josepho* (cc. xxii–xxiv) to the height of his
argument. Life is a dream: the true statesman, of the type of
Joseph, is the interpreter of the dream.

c. xxii, §§ 125 ff. 'I will venture frankly to say that the statesman is beyond any doubt an interpreter of dreams . . . a man

---

[1] Aristotle, in the *Politics* (III. xi, §§ 2–3, 9, 14), takes a different view. When
the people meet together, they have a collective faculty of judgement which
gives them the palm of superiority; they become a composite person which can
see all sides of a question and come to a just conclusion.
[2] In our Authorized and Revised Versions Potiphar is described as 'captain
of the guard' (Genesis xxxvii. 36 and xxxix. 1); but in the Septuagint version
used by Philo he is called *archimgeiros* or head-cook.

accustomed to estimate at its true worth the common, universal great dream which is dreamed not only by the sleeping, but also by the waking. This [waking] dream, to speak truly, is human life itself. . . . The visions which pass before our waking eyes are like the dreams of our sleep: they come, they go; they appear, they vanish; and before we can grasp them firmly they have already flown away. . . .' Life is a succession of transitory visions; the different ages of life come and go; the external goods of fortune never abide; empires rise and fall like unsubstantial visions. xxiii, § 136. 'Where now is the house of the Ptolemies, or the glory which was manifested by successor upon successor of Alexander, so that it shone to the ends of the earth and the sea? Where are the liberties of the free nations and cities, and where is the allegiance of their subjects? Did not the Persians once rule over the Parthians, and do not the Parthians now rule over the Persians— all through the changes and turns of men's fortunes and their movement upward and downward as if they were pieces in a game?[1] . . . xxiv, § 143. Inasmuch, then, as life is laden with all this confusion and chaos and obscurity, the politician must come forward and like some wise interpreter of dreams he must sit in judgement on the day-dreams and fantasies of his fellows who think that they are awake—using likely conjectures and reasonable persuasions, on each occasion, to show them that this is beautiful and that the reverse; this good and that bad; this just and that unjust. And so, too, with other qualities: he will try to show what is prudent, what courageous, what pious, what sacred, what beneficial, and what profitable, and again what is unprofitable, what unreasonable, what ignoble, what impious, what pro-

---

[1] A passage in a judgement of Chief Justice Crew (1558–1646) is curiously similar. 'Time hath its revolutions: there must be a period and an end to all temporal things. . . . For where is Bohun? Where's Mowbray? Where's Mortimer? Nay, which is more, and most of all, where is Plantagenet? They are entombed in the urns and sepulchres of mortality.' But the origin of the sad lament 'where, where'—which also occurs in Villon's poem with the refrain 'Ou sont les neiges d'antan'—goes back to a passage in the Old Testament, which Philo no doubt had in mind when he wrote. 'Where are the gods of Hamath, and of Arpad? Where are the gods of Sepharvaim, Hena, and Ivah? Have they delivered Samaria . . .?' (2 Kings xix. 34). The mutability and succession of empires was a common theme centuries before Philo. It is as old as Polybius and the Book of Daniel; see above, Part I, ad finem.

fane, what disadvantageous, what injurious and what selfish; and besides these he will also teach other lessons: "This belongs to another: do not covet it", or "This is your own property: use it, but do not abuse it", . . . or "All goes with you as you desire: 'ware change", or "You have often stumbled: hope now for good fortune". For with men things turn to their opposite [and only with God is there no shadow of turning].'

The view of Joseph presented in these passages is a view which seems to be intended for Greek readers, and it is generally favourable to his statesmanship. In another of Philo's writings, intended for Jewish readers—the *Allegories of the Laws*—a very different view is presented, and Joseph appears as a scoundrelly *politicos*, ranged against the virtues of Jacob and Jacob's other sons. E. R. Goodenough, in his *Introduction to Philo Judaeus* (p. 77), suggests that in these *Allegories* Joseph is depicted as the type of the Roman governing classes in Alexandria and the representative of their behaviour as seen by the Jews.

2. *The Vision of God*

The following passage comes from Philo's *Quis Rerum Divinarum Heres*, §§ 69–70. It is of interest not only as an example of Philo's allegorical method of interpretation, but also as anticipating, and perhaps influencing, the ideas of Plotinus: see below, p. 334.

' "Get thee out of thy country, and from thy kindred, and from thy father's house, unto a land that I will shew thee." (Genesis xii. 1.) If any yearning enters into thee, O Soul, for inheriting the good things of God, thou must leave not only thy country (that is, the body), and thy kindred (sense-perception), and the house of thy father (reason), but thou must even run away from thy self, and go out from thy self, inspired by a kind of prophetic afflatus, like those possessed by the . . . Bacchic frenzy [instilled by the god Dionysus]. For the mind, in this state of frenzy—no longer in itself, but exalted and maddened by the heavenly love; led along by the One really Real; pulled upwards towards Him, while Truth goes in advance and removes impediments that it [the mind] may travel along a plain road—behold, this is the "inheritance" '. (Translated by Dr. Edwyn Bevan, *Later Greek Religion*, p. 100.)

Note. The phrase 'Bacchic frenzy' may remind us of the 'sober drunkenness' (*sobria ebrietas*, or, in the Greek, *methē nēphalios*) which was one of Philo's terms of art, and which served to express the sense of possession and of mystic wisdom attainable in moments of ecstasy. It is natural to imagine that these phrases show the influence of Hellenistic mysteries, and especially that of the cult of Dionysus, which was diffused in Asia Minor, sometimes with an admixture of Jewish elements (Lietzmann, *Beginnings of the Christian Church*, Eng. trans., pp. 160–1), and which may well have reached Egypt. Sir W. W. Tarn has noted that the ring worn by Cleopatra—an amethyst, or 'stone of sobriety', with a figure of the goddess *Methē* or Drunkenness engraved upon it—probably means that she was an initiate in the cult of Dionysus.

§ IX. A FORM OF GREEK PRAYER USED IN SYNAGOGUES IN THE SECOND CENTURY A.D.

Included in the *Constitutiones Apostolicae*, a Christian liturgical work of the fourth century A.D., scholars have detected 'a little Greek prayer-book of the Jewish synagogues' from an earlier period. The form of prayer here quoted (which comes from book VII, c. 34 of the *Constitutiones*) has undergone a Christian revision at some later date, if we accept the view that it belongs to a prayer-book originally used in Jewish synagogues. The translator has enclosed in square brackets some insertions which may then have been made. The interest of the document is that it shows the influence of Hellenistic, and especially Stoic, ideas on the Jews of the Dispersion.

§ 1. 'Blessed art Thou, O Lord, everlasting King, who hast [through Christ] made all things, and ordered [through Him] in the beginning the things that were unwrought; who hast separated the waters from the waters by a firmament, and set in them a spirit of life (*pneuma zōtikon*);[1] who hast established the earth and stretched out the heavens, and ordered exactly the arrangement

---

[1] This is a Stoic expression.

of each created thing. For it is by Thy thought, O Master, that
the Universe has been illuminated, and the heavens have been
adorned like a firm arch with stars for comfort against the darkness. . . .' The prayer proceeds with a hymn to Creation, in the
spirit of Psalm 104, but it assumes a different, and definitely Stoic,
tone as it comes to man. § 3. 'Then were made the divers kinds
of living beings, those of the land, the water, and the air, and
those that live both on land and sea; and the cunning wisdom of
Thy providence and forethought gives to each the gift of a corresponding forethought; for as it tired not in producing divers
kinds, so, too, it failed not to make for each its own different way
of forethought.[1] And the end of creation is the rational being
(*logikon zōon*),[2] the citizen of the world (*cosmopolitēs*), whom
Thou hast ordered and wrought by Thy wisdom, saying, "Let
us make man in our image, after our likeness": yea, Thou hast
shown him forth as a world of the world [i.e. as a microcosm].
Thou hast fashioned a body for him from the four substances
[earth, air, fire, and water], and hast wrought for him out of not-
being a soul (*psȳchē*), giving him of Thy grace his five senses and
setting reason (*nous*) over them as the charioteer of his soul.[3]
§ 4. And over and above all these things, O Lord and Master,
who can worthily recount the abundance of Thy rain-bearing
clouds, the flash of Thy lightning, and the roll of Thy thunder,
for the supply of due food to man and the harmonious blending
of the airs he breathes? § 5. And when he went astray Thou didst
deprive man of the life which he drew from Thee, as a workman
his hire, but Thou didst not make him utterly vanish; nay,
putting him to sleep only for a little in time [or, 'at last'], Thou
didst call him to resurrection (*palingenesiā*), and didst loose the

---

[1] The Greek word *pronoia*, here translated as 'providence' and 'forethought',
was a regular Stoic term for the purposive design of reason running through the
universe.

[2] This is a Stoic expression.

[3] In a tower by the road-side at Longthorpe near Peterborough there is an
upper room richly decorated with fourteenth-century frescoes. One of them is
the figure of a wheel, with different animals on it typifying the five senses, and
over them a human face to typify reason controlling the senses. (I learn that the
frescoes are described, with plates and figures, by E. Clive Rouse and Audrey
Baker, in a forthcoming volume of *Archæologia*, 96, pp. 1 ff.)

bonds of death, Thou who art the raiser of the dead [through Jesus Christ our hope].'

Note. The following chapter, 35, continues the prayer, and reinforces it with many quotations all drawn from the Old Testament—the Book of Deuteronomy, the Psalms (including Psalm 104), the prophets Isaiah and Ezekiel, and the Book of Daniel. But c. 34 is sufficient to indicate the mixture of Greek philosophy and the Jewish Scriptures which marks the development of the prayer. 'The difference from Psalm 104 is obvious, and comparison immediately brings the Hellenistic elements into the light of day: (*a*) the Stoic idea of the organized cosmos purposive in all details, and penetrated by the "Spirit of life" of the godhead; (*b*) man as a creature endowed with senses, whom reason rules "as a charioteer"; (*c*) his body consists of four elements; and (*d*) he is "a citizen of the world" ' (H. Lietzmann, *The Beginnings of the Christian Church*, Eng. trans., p. 102—a work from which the translator has derived his knowledge of the matter).

PART III

THE PERIOD OF LATIN THOUGHT

(100 B.C.–A.D. 100)

INTRODUCTION

THE lines of Horace are famous: 'captive Greece took captive her fierce conqueror, and introduced the arts into Italy'. Certainly the Greek culture which was brought to the Scipionic circle, about the middle of the second century B.C., by three Greek visitors— the Stoic Panaetius, the exiled Achaean statesman Polybius, and the sceptical philosopher Carneades—was a leaven and a stimulus to the germination of Latin thought. But it may also be said that the triumphant movement of Roman legions and Roman government into the Eastern Mediterranean, after the defeat of the Seleucid king at Magnesia in 190 and that of King Perseus of Macedonia at Pydna in 168, gave Rome a new self-consciousness and a fresh power of self-expression which were the natural and inherent consequences of her political advance. What Aristotle said of the development of Athens after Marathon and Salamis might almost be said of Rome after Magnesia and Pydna: 'their achievements, in the period of these wars and afterwards, had elated their pride; and anxious to explore fresh fields they took all studies indiscriminately for their province'.[1] In these conditions a Latin literature flowered; beginning with Plautus, and continued by Ennius and Terence during the first half of the second century B.C., it achieved its great glories in the next century with Cicero, Lucretius, and Virgil. For two whole centuries—from the birth of Cicero in 106 B.C. to the death of Trajan in A.D. 117—Latin was the main language of the thought of classical antiquity, and Greek was in temporary abeyance.

Greek returned, as it were, and resumed its ancient dominance, with the accession of Hadrian; but it had not, of course,

[1] *Politics* VIII, c. vi, § 11.

disappeared entirely during the two Latin centuries. The forty books of the 'historical library' of Diodorus Siculus (*circa* 60–30 B.C.), and the voluminous philosophical writings of Philo Iudaeus (in the first half of the first century A.D.), are testimonies to its survival. In much the same way, after the revival of Greek in the reign of Hadrian and the return of its dominance, Latin still survived, and even flourished—particularly, for some reason, in northern Africa, which produced both Fronto and Apuleius, two writers who both attempted to revive the decaying vogue of Latin by archaism of vocabulary and euphuism of style. (But the great glories of African Latinity belong to a later age and a different sphere of thought: they appear in Tertullian (a Christian Tacitus mixed with a Christian Juvenal), in Lactantius (who has been called a Christian Cicero), and above all, in the solemn and subtle beauty of the prose of St. Augustine.) Yet in spite of these survivals (and these later glories) the fact remains that 'with Trajan, the genuine literary tradition of Rome came to an end'.[1]

Even in its hey-day Latin literature drew largely on Greek sources, both for the substance of its ideas and for the form and style of their expression. It was a literature which was at once original and imitative—original in that it showed the engineering skill of the Roman genius by the ordered deployment of its matter, and equally original in its gift (before it succumbed to the 'Asianist' floridity current in the Eastern Mediterranean) of terse marmoreal expression; but also at the same time imitative, both of the forms and genres which the inventive Greeks seemed to have fixed for eternity, and of the general philosophy (and not least the social

[1] H. Lietzmann, *The Founding of the Church Universal*, Eng. trans., p. 25. Lietzmann notes that Africa—that is to say, the Christian congregations in Africa—made Latin the language of the Church even before Rome did. Greek, the original language of Christianity, continued to be the language of church worship at Rome till the middle of the third century A.D.; but Africa, though it probably drew its Christianity from Rome, and though its congregations originally used Greek, had already a Latin Bible by the end of the second century A.D. and used Latin as the language of worship. In Gaul, too, as we know from the records of the Church in Lyons, Christianity was preached in Greek (there were old Greek settlements in the valley of the Rhône). Irenaeus, who came from Smyrna towards A.D. 180, and became the bishop of Lyons, wrote his works in Greek, though he tells us that he often spoke Celtic, perhaps in sermons and on missions.

and political philosophy) which the schools of Greece had bequeathed to the world. It was seldom that Rome spoke with the authentic voice of her own experience: occasionally it may be heard, as when Cicero quotes some pithy remark of the elder Cato; but the voice of Cicero, in his philosophic or semi-philosophic writings (for the most part hurriedly composed towards the end of his life), is a muted and borrowed voice, and though the language may be Latin the substance is generally Greek. Perhaps it was impossible for a new and tentative literature, confronted by great models, to be other than derivative. Lucretius, apologizing for the paucity of the Latin language, none the less turned the philosophy of Epicurus into magnificent verse. Virgil, sensitively and delicately receptive of all the highest culture of his day, imitated and equalled Theocritus in his *Eclogues*, as he imitated and also excelled Hesiod's *Works and Days* and the *Phaenomena* of Aratus in his *Georgics*, and as he also imitated, if he could not excel, the *Iliad* and the *Odyssey* in his epic of the wanderings and triumphs of Aeneas. Cicero, voluminous and hasty, had little time, as he had little gift, for original thought; in the long series of quasi-philosophical works which he composed (all of them, except the fragmentary *De Republica* and the partially preserved *De Legibus*, in the three hectic years between the beginning of 45 and the end of 43 B.C.), he was content to paraphrase and gloss Greek originals in a sort of eclectic amalgam. He professed himself a Platonist of the Academy, but he was almost equally a Stoic of the school of Panaetius (especially in his *De Officiis*); and he was perhaps above all a disciple of the mixed Platonism and Stoicism of Posidonius of Apamea, whose pupil he had been in Rhodes. Seneca, in the next century (5 B.C.–A.D. 65), was also a borrower, and something of an eclectic; but the philosophy which he particularly professed was that of Stoicism. The Latin historians of the two Latin centuries were more independent of the Greeks than the poets and philosophers (if indeed we may properly speak of any Latin philosophy till we come to the days of St. Augustine, the first great thinker who wrote in Latin); but Sallust had studied and imitated Thucydides; Livy, if he had studied Roman annals and was imbued with Roman patriotism and a sense of Roman *gravitas,* was none the less trained in the methods of Hellenistic historiography; and Tacitus is perhaps the one Roman historian who achieved original and independent work in the fine lapidary style which suited the Roman genius.

In the sphere of social and political ideas the greatest original contribution which Rome made to the world was perhaps that of the Roman lawyers. It is possible, indeed, that if the texts of Hellenistic laws had survived, or Hellenistic textbooks on law had come down to us, we might find that Rome was indebted to Greece even in her own sphere of jurisprudence; and it is certain that in the substance of their general education, and in the fund of philosophical ideas (especially the ideas of Stoicism) which they brought to their work and applied—consciously or unconsciously—to the problems they encountered in the course of their legal activity, the Roman jurists had something of a Greek tincture. It is true that some scholars have gone farther, doubting the idea of the native and natural development of Roman law, and seeking to ascribe a large influence to Hellenistic types and models; but they have little if any evidence to support their contention. We know practically nothing of the supposed Hellenistic types and models; we know a great deal about the native Roman jurists; and what we know of them and their methods and of their high standing in Rome (both under the Republic and in the days of the Empire), is sufficient to tell us that they were remarkable men, who made a remarkable and original contribution to the inheritance of Europe. It was law and legal science which were the great gift—a gift as original as it was great—that Rome made to the Middle Ages and to the development of modern Europe. We may even say, without paradox, that the law and legal science of Rome were an even greater contribution than all the speeches of Cicero (certainly a greater contribution than all his philosophical writings) or than all the poems of Ovid—however much these were conned in medieval universities and the schools of the Renaissance.

The Roman jurists—the *iurisconsulti* or *iuris periti*—were indeed a remarkable body of men, to whom it is difficult, if not impossible, to find any parallel in the history of any other State. They

were men versed in public affairs, often the holders of high office
at Rome, who both influenced the development of positive law
and promoted the growth, for the first time in history, of legal
science. They influenced the development of positive law by
serving, in an advisory capacity (which may almost be called
directorial as well as advisory) on the *consilia* of the Republican
magistrates and, in a later age, on the inner councils of the
emperors. They promoted the growth of legal science by the
teaching which they gave to students and by the writings which
they published—writings which might take the form of *Digesta*
or general treatises on law, or again of *Institutiones* or textbooks
for students, but which were also couched in the form of *Responsa*
or answers to particular cases (actual or theoretical) discussed in
the course of their teaching.[1] These writings have no parallel in
Greece or the Hellenistic East: they are an indigenous and original
expression of the Roman genius. They begin before the end of the
Republic, about 100 B.C.; they continue for centuries (though
they began to fail after the middle of the third century) until they
are excerpted, summarized, and, as it were, codified, on the initiative of Justinian, in the first half of the sixth century A.D. The first
systematic treatise on law was that of Q. Mucius Scaevola, who
was consul in 95 B.C.: the heights of development were gradually
reached under Trajan, Hadrian, and the Antonines (A.D. 98–180).
The *Digesta* of Salvius Iulianus, a work often quoted in the *Digest*
of Justinian, was a notable land-mark in this progress.

The second century of our era was indeed a great period in the
growth of the classical jurisprudence of Rome; it produced not
only the *Digesta* of Salvius Iulianus, but also the *Institutiones* of
Gaius, a textbook which is the chief surviving monument of the
legal literature of its period. Gaius, born in the reign of Hadrian,
possibly in a Greek province, lived and worked as a teacher and
writer in Rome; and by an accident of fortune his textbook (long
known, like the writings of other jurists, only from quotations
in the *Digest* of Justinian and in other late works) was discovered
in a palimpsest at Verona in 1816, and has thus survived intact

[1] On the various forms of the writings of the Roman jurists see P. F. Girard,
Manuel de Droit Romain, 8th edition, pp. 71–72.

except for gaps and lost folios. But the tradition of the Roman jurists did not end with the second century: they still played a large part even during the troubled years of the third century. Three famous jurists—Paulus, Papinian, and Ulpian—all held the office of prefect of the guards (*praefectus praetorio*) under the dynasty of the Severi (A.D. 193–235)—that office now being vested with supreme criminal jurisdiction in Italy, and also serving as a court of appeal from the decisions of provincial governors. Paulus was not so famous in antiquity as the other two, but he was repeatedly cited in the *Digest* of Justinian; Papinian, who may have come from the Eastern Mediterranean, and who was executed by Caracalla in A.D. 212, was ranked above all other jurists for his sagacity and authority by the judgement of a later age; Ulpian, who came from Tyre and was murdered in an *émeute* of the praetorian guard in A.D. 228, was so much honoured by the compilers of Justinian's *Digest* that they drew one-third of their material from his writings.[1] The last of the classical jurisconsults, and the end of a line of succession which had lasted for some three centuries and a half, was Modestinus, who held the office of *praefectus vigilum* towards the end of the dynasty of the Severi (about A.D. 235). He deserves to be mentioned, if only for his definition of marriage as 'a companionship (*consortium*) for the whole of life and a sharing together in the law of God and man'.

§ I. LUCRETIUS AND EPICUREAN PHILOSOPHY
A. *Preface on Epicurus*

The memory of the philosophy of Epicurus survives mainly in the *De Rerum Natura* of Lucretius, a poem which in power and passion is perhaps the greatest achievement of the Latin genius. It may therefore be pardonable to give some brief account of the social and political ideas of the Epicurean school in connexion with, and as a preface to, the passages quoted below from the

[1] One treatise of Ulpian has survived in an abridgement (the *Regulae*); and a treatise of Paulus (the *Sententiae*) has also survived in an abridged form by virtue of being included in the *Lex Romana Visigothorum*. But apart from these two abridgements, and the recovered text of the *Institutes* of Gaius, we depend in the main upon the quotations in the *Digest* of Justinian for our knowledge of the writings of the Roman jurisconsults.

fifth book of Lucretius' poem, which was written about the middle
of the first century B.C. In strict chronology an account of
Epicurus and his school should follow upon or even precede any
statement of Stoic views (for Epicurus began to teach in Athens
at an earlier date than Zeno); but in the realm of thought, as
distinct from the realm of time, he is rather to be associated with
the greatest of his disciples, though a disciple of a later date, than
with his contemporary and opponent the founder of the Stoic
school.

For our knowledge of the life and the writings of Epicurus we
are indebted to book x of the work of Diogenes Laertius (written
some time after A.D. 200) on *The Lives and Opinions of Eminent
Philosophers*. This gives us a life of Epicurus, or rather a series of
jottings about his life, along with three letters written by him to
disciples and a statement of his 'main principles' or *Kȳriai Doxai*.
In addition to what is to be found in Diogenes Laertius we have
also a number of 'Fragments', some contained in a 'Vatican Collection' discovered in 1888 and others drawn from quotations in
the works of later writers. (The whole of this material has been
edited by Dr. Cyril Bailey, in the original Greek, with a translation and commentary, under the title of *Epicurus, the Extant
Remains*.)

Epicurus was an Athenian citizen by birth, born in the island of
Samos about 341 B.C., but afterwards domiciled in his mother-
city of Athens until his death about 269 B.C. He first came to
Athens, at the age of 18, in the year before the death of Aristotle,
and more than twenty years after the death of Plato; and here he
eventually set up his school in a garden (*kēpos*). This led to his
school and disciples being called 'the Garden', just as the school
and disciples of Zeno—who taught in a colonnade or porch
adorned with frescoes—came to be called 'the Porch' (*Stoa*). The
aim of Epicurus, as a thinker, was to base his thought on the actual
facts of sensation (not but what he went beyond them in adopting a theory of the origin of the universe as due to atoms falling
in the void and 'swerving' freely as they fell—even if the eye
could not observe their swerving fall—into collocations and combinations); and he taught his pupils to follow his example. This

was perhaps the reason why he thought little of ordinary education, holding, it may be, that it filled the mind with second-hand
ideas instead of first-hand observations; and he is recorded to have
advised one of his disciples to 'hoist sail and fly from all education
(*paideiā*). His reliance on the facts of sensation may also be said
to be the basis of a doctrine of pleasure, and a theory of the value
of pleasurable sensation, which inspired his moral philosophy and
teaching; certainly he taught his disciples to cultivate their sensations, and to cultivate most the finest. He thus preached renunciation (in the sense of abstention from lower pleasures); his followers
were taught to 'form little isles of quietude apart';[1] they lived
'undisturbed' lives, as it were in a garden, saying (we may
imagine), as Marvell afterwards said,

> Dear Quiet, have I found thee here,
> And Innocence, thy sister dear?

Diogenes Laertius recounts (x, § 9) how 'his friends came to him
from every quarter, and lived with him in the garden . . . in a
most frugal and simple style; indeed it is said that they were
content with half a pint of thin wine, and their drink was generally
water'.

Many of the Epicureans came from the west coast of Asia
Minor; Epicurus himself was born in Samos, an island off that
coast; his successor at the head of his school came from the
adjacent island of Lesbos; several of his disciples came from
Lampsacus, the city on the Dardanelles in which the philosopher
Anaxagoras, exiled from Athens about 450 B.C. (and in some ways
a forerunner of Epicureanism), had spent his last days. It is tempt-
ing to think that they brought with them from the west coast of
Asia Minor a joy and grace of life which Zeno, who came from
the south of Asia Minor and had something of a Semitic austerity,
was far from possessing. Zeno, according to Diogenes Laertius,
was gaunt, tall, and swarthy; Epicurus, though he had poor
health, was a man of great personal charm. He had an 'un-
surpassed benevolence to all men'; he 'had friends so many in
number that they could not even be counted by whole cities'

---

[1] Sir W. W. Tarn, *Hellenistic Civilisation*, 3rd edition, p. 329.

(he was indeed the prophet of friendship); 'in a word, he showed a love of man (*philanthrōpiā*) in all his dealings'. One of his last letters, written to a pupil as he lay dying, has a beauty of its own. 'On this day of felicity, which is also the last day of my life, I write these words to you. My illness follows its course, abating none of the excess of its intensity; but to balance all that there is joy in my mind as I remember the talks we have had together. I beg you, as becomes the devotion you have shown to me and philosophy ever since the days of your youth, to take care of the children of Metrodorus' [another of his pupils].

It is easy to understand the feeling which Lucretius had for Epicurus—'the Greek who first dared to lift mortal eyes and look superstition in the face'—even two centuries after his death. There was something fine and cultured and civilized in the teaching of Epicurus, just as there was something raw and wild and even primitive in some elements of the early teaching of Zeno (see above, p. 43). Many of us, if we had lived in Athens among the political perturbations of the years before and after 300 B.C., and if we had had the choice of frequenting the Garden or the Porch, might have been tempted by the Garden. But it would have been the part of wisdom to resist the temptation. There was something of true valour, something of the spirit of the pilgrim, in Zeno; there was simply a love of 'undisturbedness' (*ataraxia*), and a desire to escape to 'isles of quietude'—not alone, but along with friends—in Epicurus and his followers. The 'wise man' of the Stoics fought; the 'wise man' depicted by Epicurus, if he 'would even die for a friend', was 'a lover of the country-side', but not of the bustle of the *polis*, who 'had forethought for his property and the future'; who might even marry—'according to his state of life'—and bring up a family, but 'would take no part in public life'; who, while he 'would discourse rightly on music and poetry, would not actually compose poems'. It is not surprising that Stoicism, in one form or another—either pure or mixed with Platonism—pervaded nearly the whole of the period with which we are concerned, from Zeno to Marcus Aurelius, and nerved some of the finest spirits. Epicureanism charmed; but it began—and ended—in charm.

1. *Epicurus on Pleasure*

(*a*) *The principles of pleasure as stated in the Kȳriai Doxai.* (From Diogenes Laertius, x, §§ 140 and following.)

v. 'It is not possible to live pleasurably without living prudently, honourably, and justly; and the converse of this is true.

vi. 'The end being that you may have confidence about what may befall you at the hands of other men, any means whereby you may, at any time, be able to gain such confidence is good.

xii. 'It is impossible to banish fears about matters of the first importance if you do not know what is the nature of the universe but are subject to suspicions arising from what is contained in myths. Therefore it is impossible to obtain pleasures which are pure without the study of nature (*physiologia*).

xiii. 'There is no profit in having security so far as men are concerned, if things above, and things beneath the earth, and indeed all things in the boundless void, remain matters [merely] of suspicion for you.

xiv. 'The purest source of security against what may befall you at the hands of men[1] . . . is in fact that which comes from tranquillity and retirement from much business.' Hence the Epicurean maxim recorded by Plutarch—*Lathe biōsas*, 'live unnoticed'.

(*b*) *The counsels of pleasure as stated in the letter addressed to a disciple called Menoeceus.* (From Diogenes Laertius, x, §§ 127 and following.)

We must distinguish the different sorts of desire.

§ 128. 'A right view of their difference shows us how to refer all our choosing and rejecting to the standard of health of the body and "undisturbedness" [of the soul], since these are the aim and object of a life of felicity, and it is the end of all our actions to escape from pain and fear. When once this consummation comes to pass in us, all the storm in our soul is ended: the living creature (*zōon*) has no longer to move to and fro as though it were searching for something missing and had to cast about for some other sort of object by which the good of soul and body can

---

[1] The next five or six words in the Greek are a crux which defies translation.

be fully attained. . . . This is the reason why we call pleasure the beginning and the end of a life of felicity. . . .

§ 131. 'When we say that pleasure is the end, we do not mean thereby the pleasures of the profligate, or the pleasures which consist in enjoyment, as is the opinion of those who are ignorant and who do not agree with us or misinterpret our views: what we mean is freedom from bodily suffering and mental disturbance. What makes life pleasurable is not a series of drinkings and revellings, or the enjoyment of sexual intercourse, or the delight we have in ... the dishes of a well-furnished table: it is sober reasoning (*nēphōn logismos*) which searches out the reasons for all acts of choice and rejection, and banishes the opinions [or "fancies"] responsible for most of the disturbance which affects our minds.' This is why, as is stated in one of the *Kyriai doxai* already recorded, 'it is not possible to live pleasurably without living prudently, honourably, and justly'. But in another passage, recorded by Diogenes Laertius in § 6, Epicurus is recorded as saying: 'I do not know how I am to conceive the good if I take away, to begin with, the pleasures derived from taste, and then take away those that come from sexual intercourse, and, after that, take away those that arise from hearing and from shape and form'.

2. *Epicurus (and his School) on the Ways of Wisdom.* (From Diogenes Laertius, x, §§ 117 and following.)

§ 117. '. . . The man who has once become wise is no longer liable to suffer from a contrary tendency, nor does he voluntarily pretend to it. He will be more deeply moved by affections [this is contrary to Stoic doctrine of the wise man's "apathy" or freedom from affections]; but this will not be a hindrance to wisdom. A man cannot become wise with any kind of physical constitution.... § 118. Even if a wise man be put on the rack, he still enjoys felicity. Only a wise man will show gratitude, and he will continue to speak well of his friends when they are absent as well as in their presence. When he is on the rack, he will indeed groan and lament. He will not have intercourse with a woman with whom the law forbids intercourse . . ., nor will he punish the slaves of his household, but he will rather have pity and compassion on any who are good servants. ... § 119. Moreover he will marry and beget children, . . . but he will marry according to his state of life. . . . He will not take part in politics[1] . . . nor be a tyrant, nor live like the Cynics. . . . He will not beg; nor will he, even if he lose his sight, put an end to life itself. . . . [This is a challenge to the Stoic doctrine of suicide as a proper escape, or *exagōgē*, from evil.] He will feel grief. . . . § 120*a*. He will have forethought for his property and for the future; he will be a lover of the country-side; he will look fortune in the face, and never desert a friend. He will take thought for his reputation, so far forth as is necessary to escape from being despised. He will take more pleasure than other men in public shows. ... § 121*a*. . . . He will put up statues to others, but whether or no he has one himself will be a matter of indifference to him. Only the wise man will discourse rightly on music and poetry, but he will not actually compose poems. [But Lucretius, though a 'wise' man, *did*.] . . . He will make money, but only by means of his wisdom and when he is in need. He will pay court to a monarch if occasion so demands. He will have joy in [? the misfortune of] any man if it be for his correction. He will found a school, but not so as to draw a crowd after him; he will lecture in public, but only if asked; he will enunciate doctrines, rather than raise doubts. In his sleep he will still be the same as when he is awake; and he will even die for a friend, if the occasion comes.'

3. *Epicurus on Justice, Friendship, and Property*. (From the *Kȳriai Doxai* as recorded by Diogenes Laertius, x, §§ 150 and following.)

On Justice. XXXI. 'Justice according to nature [or 'as it springs from nature'] is a guarantee of the advantage to be gained in not injuring others or being injured by them.

XXXII. 'Among living beings which are unable to make covenants neither to injure nor to be injured, there is no justice or injustice; similarly, too, [there is no justice or injustice] among nations unable, or unwilling, to make covenants neither to injure nor to be injured.

---

[1] 'Men must release themselves from the prison of daily business and politics' (*The Vatican Collection*, No. lviii).

XXXIII. 'There is no such thing as justice in itself: what there is is a sort of covenant, in the dealings of men with one another, in any given place and at any given period of time, not to do or to suffer injury.

XXXIV. 'Injustice is not an evil in itself: it is an evil only in the fear which attends upon the suspicion that one may not be able to escape the notice of those appointed to punish actions which are counted unjust.

XXXV. 'It is not possible for a man who secretly does anything contrary to the covenant, which men have made with one another not to do or to suffer injustice, to be confident that he will [always] escape notice, even if he escapes it momentarily for ten thousand times; for until he reaches the end of his life he cannot be sure of actually escaping on any given occasion.

XXXVI. 'From a general point of view, justice is identical for all; for it is [always] a sort of advantage which accrues in men's fellowship with one another. But from the particular point of view of a given country, or of any other given agent, justice does not prove itself to be identical for all men.

XXXVII. 'Among actions currently accounted by men as just, any which are attested as being of advantage in the circumstances of men's fellowship with one another have the stamp of justice, whether or no they are the same for all. But if any man lays down a law and it turns out not to tend to the advantage of men's fellowship with one another, it has no longer the nature of justice. . . .

XL. 'All who had the power of acquiring the greatest confidence about what might befall them at the hands of their neighbours have also lived the most pleasurable lives with one another, since they enjoyed the firmest assurance; and because they had had the enjoyment of the fullest intimacy, they did not lament the departure of a friend who died before them, as though it were a matter for pity.'

On Friendship. XXVII. 'Of all the things prepared by wisdom to ensure felicity for the whole of life, the acquisition of friends is by far the greatest. . . . '

Two other notable passages on friendship are (1) Fragment LII in the Vatican Collection: 'Friendship dances round the world proclaiming to us all that we should be awake to the felicitations [we receive from our friends?]', and (2) Fragment LXXXVIII in the same collection: 'The noble mind is most concerned with wisdom and friendship; and of these the one is a mortal good, but the other immortal'.

On Property (Fragment LXVII in the Vatican Collection). 'A life of freedom cannot [be concerned to] acquire many possessions, for it is not easy to do so without flattering mobs or monarchs;[1] yet such a life possesses everything [needful] in continuous abundance, and if by chance it should actually come into many possessions, it will distribute them readily in order to win a neighbour's gratitude.' (Fragment XXV in the same collection). 'Poverty, if it be measured by the end and aim of man's nature, is great wealth; but wealth which has no limit is great poverty.'

4. *Epicurus on the Evolution of Language.* (From the letter to his disciple Herodotus, in Diogenes Laertius, x, §§ 75–76.)

'Moreover, we must suppose that our nature too [like that of animals and plants] was taught and forced to do many things, of every sort and kind, by the mere force of circumstances; that a process of reasoning afterwards refined and increased by new discoveries what had thus been provided by nature; and that this was done rapidly in some matters, and in others more slowly, with large advances at some epochs and times, and less advances at others. This, too, explains why names were not originally attached to objects by a convention or agreement (*thesis*): what happened was rather this—that men's natures of themselves underwent peculiar affections and received peculiar impressions, according to the different nations to which they severally belonged; and they accordingly emitted in a peculiar way the breath that was formed in their mouths under the influence of each of these affections and impressions,[2] as might be determined by the dif-

---

[1] Epicurus, according to Diogenes Laertius, wrote a treatise 'On Kingship', as many writers of the period did. But all we know about his views on kingship is that a wise man will pay court to a king on occasion, and (as is here suggested) that such flattery is an easy way of acquiring wealth.

[2] An instance may be cited which is mentioned by Gomperz in his *Greek*

ferences, whatever they were, in the regions where their nations lived.

'Afterwards, by common action in each nation, peculiar names were attached to objects [by all men alike], to make their meanings less ambiguous to one another, and to ensure that they should be indicated more briefly. Sometimes, too, those who knew about them brought to notice things not hitherto seen and provided sounds to express them, being occasionally impelled [by instinct] to utter such sounds, but at other times choosing them deliberately by a process of reasoning and as the weight of argument determined them in seeking to make their meaning clear.'

B. *Lucretius*

Lucretius (*circa* 94–55 B.C.), at the end of the fifth book of his *De Rerum Natura* (v. 925–1457), draws a picture of the development of human society which is unique in Latin literature for its insight and originality. It is partly based on the ideas and teaching of Epicurus; but its foundation is largely the observation, and the imagination, of Lucretius himself.

1. *State of Nature*

The picture begins with a description of the original state of nature, when men lived in groves and hill-side caves and woods on wild berries and the flesh of wild animals; sleeping at night on the ground, as if they were so many wild boars, with the leaves and branches of trees for their mattress and their coverlet. In this state they could have no idea of a common good or any sense of morals or laws in their behaviour to one another: each man followed the simple rule of taking what he could, instinctively taught by nature to look after, and live for, himself. Their fear was of sudden death from the attack of wild beasts, especially in the night, but by day they hunted them in the woods with missiles of flint and heavy clubs. Animals themselves, they lived the wild wandering life of animals; but if their life was 'poor,

Thinkers. An 'affection' of disgust may be expressed by emitting the breath in the sound 'pooh'. Hence the word 'putrid' may be applied to the thing which causes the affection of disgust, and the word 'puritan' may come to be used of the person who frequently expresses disgust.

solitary, nasty and brutish', it was at any rate no more 'short' than the life of men today, who perish in their thousands in mass warfare by land and sea (925–1010).[1]

2. *Growth of Social Feeling, Friendship, and Compacts*

A second stage came as man emerged from the state of nature into some degree of civilization, and began to be knit by some sort of social contract in a mutual alliance with his neighbours.

'Then, in time, they made for themselves huts, clothing from the skins of beasts, and fires: woman was joined to man, and made one with him: the pure joys and intimacy of marriage came to be known, and parents watched the growth of the children they had begotten. Now it was that mankind began to learn gentle ways: the use of fire meant that men's chilly bodies could no longer bear so readily the cold of life under the open sky; married love broke down the rule of brute force; children, by their wiles, softened easily the stern temper of their parents. Now, too, neighbours began to make treaties of friendship with one another, anxious to do no injury and commit no trespass; they commended their children and womenkind to other men by speech and gesture, seeking to say, with stammering words, that it was right for all to have pity on the weak. Perfect concord could not be gained, but the good and greater part of them kept faith honestly; otherwise the whole of mankind would have been destroyed at once, and the generations of men would not have survived to this day' (1011–27).

3. *Political Development: the rise of monarchy, and the emergence of constitutions and codes*

Lucretius proceeds, after discussing the origin of language (not, he holds (following Epicurus), due to an act of creation by any one man, but rather the result of the instinctive expression of

---

[1] It is perhaps permissible to call Lucretius an early 'pacifist'. His Epicurean principle of the pursuit of tranquillity (*ataraxiā*) made him regard war as being— like *religio*, or superstition—a disturbance and a distraction. In the beginning of his poem he addresses a prayer to Venus for the ending of the 'savage game of war' (*fera munera militiai*).

feeling, in distinctive utterances, by all men equally), to account for the origin and development of states (1107–60).

The way of progress in the use of fire and in general invention was shown by men of superior ability and mental vigour. So, too, was the way of political progress. 'Kings began to found cities and build citadels, as strongholds and refuges for their own protection: they divided up the cattle and the soil, giving each man a share according to his looks, strength, and ability—for at that time looks counted for much, and so did vigour of strength. Later came the invention of permanent property (*res*), and the discovery of gold, which readily deprived the strong and good-looking of the honour they had formerly enjoyed; for any rich man's train will usually be followed by men of physical vigour and fine bodily presence.'

Here Lucretius pauses in his argument, or turns aside, to celebrate the one true happiness of a modest tranquillity ('it is great riches for a man to live sparingly, with a quiet mind'), and to recount the dangers of ambition and the struggle for power and glory. 'Far better', he argues, 'to live in peace as a subject than to long for the sovereign management of affairs (*regere imperio res*) and the possession of kingdoms . . .; for envy, like a thunderbolt, generally strikes the topmost towers and all the outstanding pinnacles.'

'So it was', he continues, turning back from the moral to the political argument, 'with kings. They were slain; the majesty that had once attended their thrones vanished, and their proud sceptres lay in the dust; the honoured sign and symbol of sovereignty, rolling in blood under the feet of the mob, groaned in lament for its old solemn splendour; and what had once been feared beyond its due was now trodden down in fury. So the management of affairs sank down to the lowest dregs of the mob, with every man seeking to get sovereignty and supremacy into his own hands. Then men arose who taught their fellows how to appoint magistrates, and laid down for them rules of conduct to induce them to live by law; for mankind, worn out by spending its days in struggle, was so enfeebled by its constant quarrels that it was ready of its own free will to submit to law and strict rules;

and just because all men then girded themselves up, in their anger, more eagerly for vengeance than they are now allowed to do under a just and fair system of law, they were, for that very reason, all the more tired of spending their days in struggle. Ever since that time the fear of punishment has spoiled men's chance of gaining the prizes of life: force and wrong-doing now entangle their authors in a net, and recoil on the heads of those from whom they had their beginning. It is not easy for a man who so acts as to break the compact, made for the institution of a common peace, to lead a tranquil and peaceable life; he may hide his doings for the moment both from gods and men, but he is bound to have secret misgivings that they cannot be hidden for ever. How many there are of whom it is told that they betrayed themselves by words spoken in dreams, or by ravings in sickness, and so brought to light at long last the crimes they had hidden for years.'

4. *Experience the Teacher of Men*

In a series of passages which follow, Lucretius seeks to explain the rise of religious beliefs and ceremonies, the progress of human invention (for instance in the use of metals), and the development of the arts of civilization (in dress, in the culture of plants, and in the discovery of musical instruments and melodies); and he then suggests, in conclusion, that the cause of all man's progress and development is, in a word, experience—

> Usus, et impigrae simul experientia mentis,
> Paullatim docuit pedetentim progredientis.

'Sea-faring and husbandry, fortifications, laws, weapons, roads, clothing; all other similar prizes of life, all and every delights it can bring; songs, paintings, and statues ingeniously fashioned and polished—all these were taught man by practice and the experience of his own busy mind as he gradually advanced, step by step, along the way of progress. Thus time brings gradually forward each advance of mankind, and thus reason lifts it up into the light of day. Men saw one thing after another come clear in their mind's eye, until they reached by their arts the summit of their endeavour' (1448–57).

§ II. THE THEORY OF THE STATE AND LAW IN THE WRITINGS OF CICERO

Introduction

Cicero (106–43 B.C.) was at once an orator, a man of affairs, and a voluminous writer on philosophy. His philosophical writings belong to the end of his life (52–43 B.C.), and especially to the troubled period after 45 B.C., when he threw himself, in his last years, into a busy fever of thought and composition. In the field of social and political theory his main works are three. (1) The first is the *De Republica*, a work in six books, long lost, and only partially recovered (to the extent of about one-third of the whole) from a Vatican palimpsest in 1820. The model for this work was the *Republic* of Plato, but in writing it Cicero used the Stoic Panaetius (who had taught in Rome a century before) and the historian Polybius as well as Plato; it was published in 51 B.C. (2) Cicero's second main work is the *De Legibus*, begun about 52 B.C. but not published till after his death in 43 B.C. The model for this was Plato's *Laws*. Like the *De Republica*, it is fragmentary; only three books survive out of what may have been originally six. (3) The third main work was the *De Officiis*, a treatise on moral (and also political) duties, which professes to be written for his son, then residing in Athens for his 'university' education. This was finished by the end of 44 B.C.; for its first two books the Stoic Panaetius again served as a guide.

These three works are only a part of the voluminous writings on philosophy which occupied the last ten years of Cicero's life. But they are sufficient to enable us to gain some general idea of his thought. He was not original, for he borrowed very largely from Greek authors; he was not consistent, for he borrowed somewhat indiscriminately. It almost seems as if he threw himself into writing about political theory (and also, for that matter, about moral philosophy and religion) more in order to find distraction from the course of actual politics than in order to express any ordered system of thought. In any case he wrote so much, and he wrote in such haste, that he gave himself little time to think. He seems to have regarded himself as a disciple of the Platonism of the New

Academy; and he can accordingly criticize both the Epicurean and the Stoic schools. But his criticism of the Stoics does not prevent him from borrowing the ideas of the Stoic Panaetius; and indeed he is generally a borrower—a borrower from different and even contradictory sources. Yet he has also been, in the course of history, a lender—or rather a giver. Like Rousseau afterwards he could invest political theory with the charm of style; and his style carried his varied aggregate of ideas through the Middle Ages to the Renaissance, and from the Renaissance to the eighteenth century. Perhaps the ages did not learn much from Cicero that was Cicero's own; but at any rate they learned from him much that he had borrowed, and much that deserved to be known.

A. *Passages from the* De Republica

1. *Definition and origin of the State: its three forms or types*

I, c. xxv. 39. 'A *res publica* [or 'public concern'] is a *res populi* [or 'concern of the people']; and a people is not any and every sort of human association united by any sort of bond, but the association of a multitude in a partnership formed by a common sense of law (*iuris consensus*] and a community of interest. The original cause of such an association is not so much the weakness of its members as a natural human instinct of what may be called gregariousness; for men are not isolated or solitary beings, but are rather so constructed that not even among an abundance of all things . . . [are they without society].

I. xxvi. 41. '. . . These associations, instituted for the reason which I have explained, began by fixing their seat in some definite place where men could build themselves houses; and then, using both natural obstacles and their own handiwork to surround it with defences, they called this assembly of buildings—interspersed with temples and open spaces—by the name of town or city. Now every people which forms an associated multitude such as I have described; every civic organization (*civitas*) which serves as a scheme of order for a people; every "public concern" or *res publica*, which is by definition, as I have said, the "concern of the people" (*res populi*)—every such body must be guided by some sort of direction if it is to be permanent; and the existence of such direction is always to be explained by the same general cause which produced the civic organization itself. 42. This direction must be assigned to one person or one body of selected persons, or else it must be undertaken by the whole body and all its members. When the control of affairs is vested in a single person, we call that person a king and the state of that "public concern" (*rei publicae status*) a kingdom. When it is vested in a body of selected persons, the citizens are said to be governed by the will of an aristocracy. When all power is vested in the people, we have what is called popular government. Each of these three forms, provided that it keeps in being the union which originally joined men together in a political society, is at any rate tolerable, without being perfect or, to my thinking, ideal; and any one of the three may on occasion be better than the other two. It seems possible that a just and wise king, or a body of select and leading citizens, or the people itself (though that alternative is the least to be preferred), may, if no injustice or selfishness intervenes to prevent it, enjoy some sort of security.'

2. *The Value of the Mixed Form of State*

I. xxvii. 43. 'But all three have their defects: in monarchies, persons other than the king have not sufficient rights under the system of civil law, or enough of a voice in deliberation; in an aristocratic system of government, the masses can hardly share in liberty, being destitute of any voice in common counsel and of all power; where everything is managed by the people, the government may indeed be just and moderate, but the uniformity of equality is itself inequitable, since it leaves no room for any grading of degrees of worth.'

I. xxix. 45. There is a gap at this point in the text. When we recover the thread of the argument, Cicero is arguing that 'there are astonishing cycles and revolutions of the wheel of change, and vicissitudes in public affairs:[1] these it is the part of a wise man to recognize, as it is equally the duty of a great statesman and

---

[1] Cicero is here referring to Polybius and to his idea of *anacyclōsis*: see above, p. 113.

inspired leader to foresee them when they are imminent, and meanwhile, in steering the ship of state, to control the course which it takes and to keep a firm hand on the helm. My own feeling[1] therefore is that a fourth type of State ought to be awarded the palm—a type which is a mean and a mixture (*moderatum et permixtum*) between the three types previously mentioned.

i. xlv. 69. 'While, therefore, the monarchical is in my opinion far the best of the three types I have just mentioned, even that type will be inferior to the one which balances and reconciles the three primary types of State. It is good that there should be present in a State one element which is outstanding and royal, and another which represents and is devoted to the authority resident in its leading men; but it is also good that there should also be some matters reserved for the judgement and decision of the mass of citizens. Such an arrangement has two advantages: in the first place it ensures a large degree of equability, a value with which a society of free men cannot long dispense; in the second place it ensures stability, for while the first three types are each liable to have their qualities turned into the opposite defects—with a tyrant taking the place of a king, a clique that of an aristocracy, and tumult and anarchy that of a popular government—and while, again, any one of these types may be frequently changed into a different and new type, such things are hardly likely to happen in a mixed and judiciously tempered constitution, unless its leading members are guilty of serious faults. There is no occasion for change when each man is definitely placed in his proper position, with nothing beneath for him to fall or sink into.'

i. xlvi. 70. Cicero represents Scipio[1] as saying, at this point, that he is afraid of seeming to be giving a lecture on political science. He will therefore turn to something which everybody knows— the theme of Rome and the Roman constitution. 'This is my decision, my opinion, and my assertion: there is no State whatsoever which in its constitution, or its system, or its discipline is

---

[1] The speaker here and in the previous and subsequent extracts (the *De Republica* is written in the form of a dialogue) is Scipio Aemilianus (185–129 B.C.), the Roman statesman of the previous century who inspired Cicero with his political ideas of balance and concord. Polybius belonged to his circle.

comparable with that which our forefathers have left us as a legacy—a legacy which they had themselves received from their ancestors.'

3. *The Praise of the Roman Constitution*

II. i. 2. Deserting theory and Greece, Cicero now turns to history and Rome; and Scipio is accordingly made to describe the Roman constitution as an historic product, built by the co-operation of many minds through time, and consecrated by its antiquity. But it appears, as the argument proceeds, that the historic product to be admired and maintained is *not* Rome as it stood in Cicero's own day (50 B.C.), but Rome as it had stood a century before (150 B.C.) in the ideal Scipionic age. Cicero is, after all, an antiquarian idealist, whose motto is the *renovatio reipublicae Romanae* of pre-Gracchan days.

'[Cato the Elder] used to say that the reason why the condition of our State was superior to that of all others was this: in other States it had, as a rule, been single individuals who had laid down laws and established institutions [a Minos in Crete; a Lycurgus at Sparta; . . . a Solon or a Cleisthenes or, in its last days, a Demetrius of Phalerum at Athens]; whereas our State had been formed, not by the wit of one man, but by the minds of many, and not in a single lifetime, but in the course of many generations and ages. No mind, he said, was ever so great that nothing escaped its notice, nor could all minds put together possess sufficient fore-sight at a given moment to comprehend all issues without the aid of experience and the benefit of time 3. And therefore let me in what I say, following the habit of Cato, "go back to the people's beginnings"—for I like to use his very words as well as his ideas. I shall reach the goal more easily if I depict our State in its birth, growth, and maturity, and if I exhibit it when it is firm and robust, than if I seek to imagine for myself something after the style of Socrates in the *Republic* of Plato.'

II. xxxii. 56. Cicero accordingly represents Scipio as giving, in the course of book II, an account of the growth of the Roman con-stitution. The moral which he draws, towards the end of the account, is once more, as in book I, the moral of mixture and balance. 'The Senate, in those days [he has been speaking of the state of the Roman Republic in the third century B.C.], kept the constitution on this basis: the people was free, but few matters were managed by it, and most of them were settled by the authority, regulation, and tradition of the Senate, while the consuls exercised a power which in point of tenure lasted only a year but in point of scope and legal character was of a monarchical type.' On this basis, Cicero seems to suggest, in § 57, that there was enough *potestas* in the magistrates, enough *auctoritas* in the counsels of the leading men (i.e. the Senate), and enough *libertas* in the people to keep the constitution fixed and firm.

It is difficult, if not impossible, to give a connected account of Cicero's view of the Roman constitution on the basis of the scattered and fragmentary references in the surviving text of the *De Republica*. But two propositions may be hazarded. (1) Though he pays tribute to *libertas*, and therefore to the rights of the people, he assigns little actual power to any form of popular assembly; and he lays it down that a principle which should always be observed in politics is 'that the greatest number should not have most power' (*ne plurimum valeant plurimi*). (2) His bias is in favour of the *potestas* of the consuls and the *auctoritas* of the Senate, and particularly in favour of the latter, which is, for him, the centre of gravity. But the matter does not end there. Cicero finds himself eventually impelled, at the end of the *De Republica*, to a general notion of leadership, which alters the balance and character of his political ideas. Though he has espoused and advocated the idea of the mixed constitution, he none the less feels that such a constitution is not, in itself, enough. It is a mechanism moved by the impulse of weights and counter-weights; what if the machine goes wrong, and its balance becomes so disturbed that it will no longer work? A State—so Cicero now seems to suggest—is more than a mechanism: it is rather of the nature of a living being, and it needs, as such, a directing spirit—a spirit which inspires and regulates its parts and keeps them together in harmony. That spirit is public opinion, a sound and sane public opinion, agreed and expressed in a concord of classes (rather than a balance of powers), or what Cicero himself calls by the name of *concordia ordinum*.[1]

But how was such an opinion to be formed, and how, above all, was it to be maintained, in the conditions of Cicero's time? There was no press in the ancient world to collect and guide opinion; there were no organized churches to help in its formation; there were indeed political parties (the conservative *optimates* and the radical *populares*), on which Cicero had already discoursed in his oration *Pro Sestio* (see below, pp. 202–4), but which exacerbated rather than precipitated opinion, and certainly did not produce that *concordia* (or, as the Greeks called it, *homonoia*) which Cicero desired. He therefore turned to the notion of leadership; he argued for the establishment of some form of light and leading (*gubernatio* or *moderatio*) to inform, to guide, and to maintain the sort of public opinion which would ensure that the Roman constitution worked sweetly and in harmony. The notion was vague; the exact nature of the leadership and the precise constitutional form in which it was to be expressed were never clear to Cicero. But the notion, in itself, had its wisdom—though for the Rome of that age, rent by the ambitions of rival 'war-lords' at the head of their legions, it was chimerical rather than practical. Indeed Cicero himself recognized its weakness. In a letter to his friend Atticus (*Epistulae ad Atticum* VIII. xi. 1–2), written shortly after the appearance of the *De Republica*, and in the year which saw the beginning of civil war between Pompey and Caesar, he confesses that his notion had been only a dream. 'Do you remember', he writes, 'that leader of the commonwealth to whom we would fain have everything referred . . ., the man whose aim is to be the welfare of the commonwealth; . . . the man whom I wish to be the author and perfecter of the greatest and best achievement that can ever be attained among men? Our friend Pompey has never thought, and is very far from thinking now, along those lines. Both of them [i.e. both Pompey and Caesar] aim at power; neither of them makes our welfare his aim; . . . both of them want to be kings.'

[1] This argument is developed in C. N. Cochrane's *Christianity and Classical Culture*, pp. 58–61.

The language which Cicero uses about leadership has led some scholars to the view that he anticipated and even planned—so far as theory could do so—the principate of Augustus and his successors. That he expected something in the nature of the principate is very possible; that he sought to prepare its advent is very unlikely. He looked back to the past rather than forward to the future; what he wanted was a guiding and restraining hand such as he thought that Scipio had once laid gently on Rome a hundred years before. Whether the guiding hand was to be that of a single man, or whether there was to be an imposition of a number of hands, he never clearly indicated. In the passage quoted above from his letter to Atticus he speaks of a single leader. Similarly in book v of the *De Republica* he more than once speaks in the singular; he suggests, for example, the need of a *rector* of the State who has studied law and the statute-book in the same sort of way as the bailiff of an estate studies agriculture (v. iii. 5); or again he refers to a *moderator reipublicae* who will be the author and perfecter of welfare (*beata vita*) for the members of a State, in the same sort of way as a pilot guides the course of a ship or a doctor ensures the health of his patients (v. vi. 8). Elsewhere, however, in the *De Republica*, and in his other writings, he frequently refers to *principes civitatis*, using the plural form. We can only conclude that he had a vague idea of the need of leadership; that sometimes, when he thought of Scipio in the previous century, or, possibly, of Pompey (the earlier Pompey) in his own age, or, it might be, even of himself in the great days of his consulship and the suppression of the Catilinarian conspiracy, the leader became a single man who was *primus inter pares*; but generally, and on the whole, he expected leadership from a sort of informal cabinet or group of *principes* who sat in and guided the policy of the Senate.[1] Cicero had not a prophetic or constructive mind; he was content to sigh for an undefined leadership, and to long for a visionary *concordia* and *consensus* which should be its support and stay.

---

[1] The article by W. W. How in the *Journal of Roman Studies*, vol. xx (for the year 1930), on 'Cicero's Ideal in his *De Republica*', summarizes the whole issue fairly.

4. *The Dream of Scipio*

At the end of the *De Republica* comes the famous *Dream of Scipio*. It was made a subject of two books of 'Commentaries' by the Neoplatonist Macrobius, who flourished about A.D. 400, and it was thus handed down (apart from the rest of the *De Republica*, which was unknown, as has already been noticed, until the Vatican palimpsest was discovered in 1820) to the scholars of the Middle Ages and the Renaissance. Macrobius describes the gist of the dream: 'After discoursing on all matters concerning the commonwealth—both in action and in its leisure—and according the palm to justice, Cicero placed on the pinnacle of his finished work a description of the blessed abode of immortal spirits and the mysteries of the heavenly places; and he showed in his description where men are appointed to go—or rather to return— who have guided the course of a commonwealth with prudence, justice, fortitude, and temperance.' The *Somnium Scipionis* is partly borrowed (indeed in one passage it is translated) from the writings of Plato, and partly drawn from Stoic theory. Some passages are translated here less for their intrinsic value than for the influence they exercised in succeeding centuries. The speaker is the younger Scipio (Scipio Aemilianus, 185–129 B.C.), the adopted son of Publius Cornelius Scipio and thus (by adoption) the grandson of Scipio Africanus Maior (236–184 B.C.) the elder Scipio. The elder Scipio is made to appear to the younger in his sleep, and to tell him, in prophecy, that he 'will one day be the person on whom the safety of the State will depend and . . . who must then reform it in the office of dictator'.[1] He then seeks to encourage his grandson by adoption with promises of a future reward in heaven.

vi, c. 13. 'That you may be more alert in keeping watch and ward on the commonwealth, I would have you believe that all who have saved, or helped, or augmented their fatherland have a certain and fixed abode reserved for them in heaven, where they

---

[1] This may remind us of Cicero's argument for a *rector* or *moderator* of the commonwealth. It suggests that when he was thinking of a statesman who was vested with such an office, he was not looking to Pompey in the present—far less looking forward to some Augustus in the future—but merely looking back to the past.

can enjoy everlasting life in felicity. For there is nothing whatever—so far as concerns what is done on earth—which is more pleasing to that high God who rules all the universe than those assemblies and communities of men, united by a common partnership in law, which are called by the name of States; their rulers and guardians (*rectores et conservatores*) come from heaven, and to heaven they return.'[1]

c. 15. The younger Scipio asks why, if this be so, he must linger on earth, and why he may not join at once the blessed who live in heaven. His father by adoption, the son of the elder Scipio, who now appears to him, replies that he must wait till God has delivered him from the prison of the body. 'This is the condition under which are born the men destined to guard the sphere you now see [in your dream] suspended in the centre of the circuit of heaven—the sphere which is called the earth; and to these men is given a spirit (*animus*) drawn from the eternal fires which you call constellations and stars, those rounded globes which perform their circular orbits with a marvellous rapidity under the inspiration of the divine intelligences by which they are moved. . . .'[2]

c. 16. 'But do you, Scipio—[even if you must remain in the body on earth]—do you, like your grandfather here, and like me your father, follow justice and the path of duty, which is a matter of great moment when parents and kinsmen are concerned, and of even greater moment when the fatherland is in question. Such a life is the way to heaven, and to the company of those who have lived their lives and, freed from the body, now inhabit the place you see [the place which, in the language of the Greeks, is called, as Cicero explains, the Milky Way].'

The younger Scipio's father now disappears, and the elder Scipio, Africanus Maior, resumes his discourse, and explains to his grandson the majesty of the universe, the insignificance of the earth in comparison with it (and the still greater insignificance of the Roman Empire, as merely a small part of the earth), and,

---

[1] Some commentators have seen in this passage an echo of the teaching of Posidonius, whose lectures Cicero is said to have attended in Rhodes. Virgil, in the Sixth *Aeneid* (126–31, 660–5), is inspired by similar ideas.

[2] This again appears to be drawn from the teaching of the Stoics, and it has, once more, a parallel in Virgil's Sixth *Aeneid* (724 ff.).

finally, the pettiness of human fame and earthly renown. The younger Scipio, after listening to the discourse, makes his resolve.

c. 24. 'If those who have deserved well of the fatherland have, as it were, a passage before them that leads to the entrance of heaven, then I—although from my childhood days I have already followed in my father's steps and yours, and have not failed to emulate the glory of you both—will for the future be still more watchful in my endeavours, seeing the greatness of the prize that is set before me.'

c. 26. The elder Scipio tells the younger, at the end of the dream, in a Platonic passage part of which is translated from the *Phaedrus*, that he has a self-moving spirit within him, and that this spirit, in virtue of being self-moving, is subject neither to birth nor to death, but is in its nature eternal. 'Exercise it, therefore, on the highest concerns—concerns that consist in care for the safety of your fatherland—; and then the spirit within you, breathed and exercised by such care, will fly the more speedily to this its abode and home. And it will do so all the more quickly if it already begins to peep abroad, while it is still pent in the body, and withdraws itself from the body, as far as it possibly can, to contemplate the things that are outside and beyond it. . . .'

B. *Passages from the* De Legibus *on the Nature of Law*

Cicero does not draw his conceptions of law from the Roman lawyers of his day: he draws on the volumes of Greek theory, especially Stoic, which he had before him as he wrote. His purpose is to prove, on that basis, that law is not conventional, or of such a nature that men may make it what they will at their pleasure: on the contrary, it is the result of natural reason, and it is therefore both stable and uniform—stable in the sense that it does not alter from time to time, and uniform in the sense that it does not vary from place to place.

In the *De Republica* (III, c. 13, § 23) he had stated the 'conventional' view, which was current among the Epicureans. 'One man fears another, and one class another; nobody trusts his own strength; and a sort of covenant (*pactio*) is accordingly made between the people in general and the powerful members of the community. . . . It is weakness, not nature or will, which is the mother of justice. One of three alternatives has to be adopted— to do injury to others without suffering it oneself; both to do it and suffer it; or neither to do nor to suffer it. The best alternative is to do injury to others with impunity, if possible; the next best neither to do nor to suffer injury; the worst of all is to be engaged in a perpetual warfare of doing and suffering injury.' Here a long lacuna ensues, but we are left with the notion of a pact based on the second alternative, and of law as a convention created by that pact.

But, having stated the conventional view, Cicero soon turns, in the same book of the *De Republica* (III, c. 22, § 33), to the 'natural' view. 'True law is right reason conformable to nature [a Stoic phrase]; it is universally diffused, unchanging, and eternal; it summons men to their duty by its commands, and deters them from crime by its prohibitions; but while it affects the good by its commands and its prohibitions, it fails to move the bad. No rule may be made in substitution for this law, no rule can be made in derogation from it, nor can it be utterly abrogated; we cannot be released from it either by the senate or by the people, nor is any commentator or interpreter of it other than itself to be sought. There will not be one law at Athens and another at Rome, or one law now and another in the future: all nations (*gentes*), at all times, will be bound by the one eternal and immutable law: there will be one God who is common to all men and, as it were, their master and ruler (*imperator*); and He it is who devises, debates, and enacts this law, the which if a man disobey he will be a run-away from himself, and rejecting thereby the nature of man he will pay the utmost penalty by that very act of rejection, even if he escapes other punishments which men believe he will incur.' (This passage is preserved in a quotation made by Lactantius, *Divine Institutes*, vi, c. 8, §§ 6–9.)

In the view of his later work, the *De Legibus*, Cicero espouses the side of nature against convention. He writes at large and in vague general terms; he does not clearly distinguish between *jus* and *lex*, nor again between *jus naturale* and *jus civile*; he simply argues that law in general, by whatever name it be called, is the product of nature and the fruit of the natural reason of man.

I. vi. 18. 'Law (*lex*) is that height of reason inherent in nature which commands the things that are to be done and forbids the things which are not to be done. This same reason, when established and settled in the mind of man, is [human] law. 19. Men therefore think of law as being practical wisdom (*prudentia*) which possesses the power of commanding us to do right and forbidding us to do wrong; and they hold that it is called by its Greek name (*nomos*) from its "assigning" to each his due,[1] just as I, for my part, think that it is called by its Latin name (*lex*) from its "selecting" [what should and should not be done]. The Greeks, in thinking of law, place the emphasis on the notion of equity [in the sense of fair distribution]; we place the emphasis on the notion of selection; but both notions belong to the idea of law. If it is right to use words in this way, as I am generally inclined to believe that it is, the origin of *ius* [i.e. the law actually enforced by the courts] must be traced back to *lex*;[2] for it is that [i.e. *lex*] which is the essence of nature, which is identical with the intelligence and reason of the man of practical wisdom, and which is the rule of right and wrong. But as all our discussion moves in the sphere and on the level of popular opinion, it will sometimes be necessary to use words in their popular sense, and to give the name of *lex*, as popular usage does, to any written enactment which sanctions an expression of will commanding or

[1] *Nomos* is thus regarded as derived from the Greek verb *nemein* in its sense of distributing or assigning. Cicero goes on to connect the word *lex* with the verb *lego*, in its sense of selection; but perhaps it may be connected with the verb *ligo*, in its sense of binding or obliging.

[2] Cicero's use of the terms *jus* and *lex* is perplexing. It seems to be the opposite of the use of the terms by the Roman jurists of the second and third centuries A.D. To them *jus* (i.e. *jus civile*) is the generic term, which embraces both written (i.e. enacted) and unwritten (i.e. customary) law; and *lex* is a specific term, which designates one of the several species of written *jus*, and means a 'statute' duly enacted in the assembly of people (see below, pp. 257, 260). *Lex* was thus, in their view, a part of *jus*. To Cicero, however, *lex* is the whole, and *jus* is a part or product of *lex*, posterior to it and inferior to it.

It should be added that the jurists drew a distinction between different kinds of *jus*. They thought of (1) the *jus civile*, the actual law of Rome, recognized in Roman courts, both written and unwritten; (2) the *jus naturale*, the law of Nature herself, a law of equity or ideal law, which might influence the interpretation of *jus civile* but was none the less distinct from it as the ideal is distinct from the actual. Cicero makes no such distinctions, unless we hold that his *lex* is really *jus naturale* and his *jus* is *jus civile*. His thought, or at least his language, is confusing, if not confused.

forbidding some action. On the other hand, we must ascribe the establishment of *jus* to that supreme *lex* which throughout all time has been in existence, before ever a law was written [in the popular sense of the word law] or ever a State was founded.'

I. xii. 33f. Having argued that all men are brothers, and that there is a remarkable similarity among all men in their notions of right and wrong, Cicero proceeds with the exposition of his theory of law. 'It follows that we are intended by nature to be partners with one another in *jus*[1] and to share it among us all. But I would add that in all this discussion I want it to be understood that there are two considerations to be borne in mind: on the one hand the *jus* of which I am speaking exists by nature; but on the other hand evil habits engender so much corruption that they extinguish the sparks of light which are implanted in us by nature and give birth and encouragement to the contrary vices. If the convictions of men had agreed with the promptings of nature, and if they had really, as the poet says, "thought nothing human alien from themselves', *jus* would have been equally respected by all men. The argument is simple: those who have been given reason by nature have also been given right reason; they have therefore been given *lex* too, which is right reason in the sphere of commanding and forbidding; and if they have been given *lex*, they have also been given *jus*. Now all men have been given reason; all men, therefore, have been given *jus*; and Socrates was right when he used to denounce the man who first divorced utility from *jus*, (34) complaining that that divorce was the origin of all our woes.'

I. xv. 42. Cicero proceeds to argue that law is not enactment—if it were it might be anything, whatever the enacter chose—but rather the dictate of Nature herself, and as such stable in time and uniform in space. 'It is the height of folly to regard as "just" anything and everything that may be decreed by the regulations or laws of States. . . . There is one single *jus*, which binds together human society and which is created by one single *lex*. That *lex* is right reason, as applied to commanding and forbidding; and

---

[1] Cicero seems here to use the words *jus* and *lex* as if they were convertible. But *lex* is still, apparently, the ideal, and *jus* the actual.

the man who does not pay heed to it is unjust, whether it be written somewhere or other, or whether it be written nowhere. If justice consists in obedience to the written laws and regulations of States, and if, as those who hold that view assert, all things are to be measured by the one canon of utility, laws will be neglected and broken by any man—if only he has the power—who thinks that their breach will be to his advantage. And the result of that will be that there is no justice at all—as indeed there cannot be when justice is not based on nature, and when the alternative basis of utility is inherently such that one view of it overturns another.

II. iv, § 8. It is clear to me, therefore, that the wisest of men have been of the opinion that law is neither produced by the thought of individuals nor is it something enacted by the will of a people: it is something eternal in its nature, which governs the whole of the universe by the wisdom of its commands and prohibitions. The wise have accordingly held that the primary and ultimate law was the mind of God, commanding or forbidding all things by virtue of his reason; and because that is its source this law, which was thus the gift of the gods to men, is rightly honoured with praise as being the mind and the reason of a Wise Being, fitted to command and forbid. . . . 9. We learned when we were children to repeat, "If thy neighbour call thee to judgement, [go]", and other rules of that kind. But the right way of looking at the matter is this: the rule I have quoted, and other commands and prohibitions proceeding from the people, have indeed in them a power of summoning men to do right and of warning them not to do wrong, but the power which they have is not only prior in time to the life-span of peoples and states—it is also coeval with the existence of God who guards and governs earth and heaven.'

In his general—and vague—idea of the nature of law Cicero was perhaps following the theory of the Stoics, and especially of Panaetius, who had visited Rome about 150 B.C. and had been conversant with the members of the Scipionic circle. He shows little, if any, acquaintance with the genius and the ideas of Roman law; he does not wrestle with the problem of the relation of positive law (jus civile) to the 'natural' law which he exalts; and indeed he seems to dismiss all positive law as nothing in comparison with a vague and undefined 'law of Nature and of Nature's God'. The one reason for recording his ideas is that they had, as has already been noted, a vogue for many centuries, all through the Middle Ages down to the days of the Italian Renaissance, and even beyond. His treatise transmitted some Greek (and especially Stoic) ideas—if only in a popular and simplified form—to later generations; and his name and style thus preserved some elements of the genuine thought of antiquity.

c. Passages from the De Officiis

(a) *The Basis and Bonds of Human Society* (book I, c. 16, § 50). 'A human society or union of men will best be preserved if most recognition is bestowed on those who are united most closely with their fellows. But a deeper investigation is needed into the natural foundations of men's communities and societies. The first foundation is one which may be traced in the great society constituted by the whole of the human race. The bond of that society consists in reason and speech (*ratio et oratio*). It is a bond which connects men together and joins them with one another in a natural sort of society, by a process of teaching and learning, of communication, discussion (*disceptatio*), and the doing of justice. There is nothing which differentiates us from animals so much as reason and speech do; we often speak of animals—for example, horses and lions—as possessing courage, but we never ascribe to them justice, equity, or goodness, since they have no part in reason and speech.'

Cicero's reference to discussion as a natural basis of society deserves notice. A little earlier in the *De Officiis* (I. xi, § 34) he had remarked that there are two ways of conducting disputes, one by the method of discussion, and the other by means of force; the former is proper to men, as the latter is proper to beasts, and men should turn to force only when discussion is out of the question. His reference to the doing of justice as being, like discussion, a natural basis of society equally deserves notice. Years before, when he wrote the *De Republica*, he had argued (book I, c. 32, § 49) that 'if equality of wealth be out of the question, and if, again, all cannot have an equal degree of mental ability, the rights [*jura*] of all citizens belonging to the same commonwealth ought certainly to be equal—for what is a State but a partnership in a system of Right [*juris societas*]?'

(*b*) *The Law of Nature* (III, c. 5, §§ 22–23). 'Nature does not allow us to increase our means, resources, and wealth by despoiling others. This is not merely a rule of nature—that is of *jus gentium* [which Cicero here seems to identify with the law of nature][1]: provision is also and equally made by the laws based on the will of the people—the laws which uphold the commonwealth in each and every State—that men shall not be allowed to pursue their own advantage at the cost of injuring others. For it is the object and purpose of laws to ensure that the unity of the civic body shall be firm and secure, and that those who seek to diminish that unity shall be restrained by punishment, whether with death, with exile, with prison, or by fine.'

(*c*) *Government a Trust* (I. 25, § 85). 'All who may be in charge of the commonwealth should observe two injunctions of Plato: first, they should protect the welfare of their fellow citizens, making it the object of all their actions to the neglect of their own personal interests; and, secondly, they should look to the whole body of the commonwealth, and should not protect the interest of one section at the cost of neglecting that of the rest. The government of a commonwealth is in the nature of a guardianship or trust (*ut . . . tutela, sic procuratio reipublicae*); it should be conducted with a view to the welfare of those who are entrusted to the care of the governors, and not for the benefit of those to whom the government has been committed. A government which consults the interest of one section and neglects that of another inflicts upon a State the grave disaster of sedition and discord; with the result that one body of the citizens forms a "popular" party, another espouses the cause of "the best" [thus forming a party of the *optimates*], and only a handful devote themselves to the cause of the whole State'.[2]

---

[1] On the relation of *jus naturale* and *jus gentium* see below, pp. 257, 260. But Cicero, at any rate in the *De Legibus* (see above, p. 197, note 2), does not use the term *jus naturale*; he uses instead the term *lex*.

[2] For Cicero's general view of the nature and function of parties see the passage from his speech *Pro Sestio* translated below in D.

(*d*) *Government and the Protection of Property* (II. c. 21, § 73). 'The first object to be pursued in the government of a commonwealth is that all should be secured in their property (*ut suum quisque teneat*), and that private possessions should not be diminished by public action.' Here Cicero pauses to criticize the speech of a radical orator, at the beginning of the first century B.C., who had complained that there were not 2,000 persons in Rome who owned any property. That, he urges, was a criminal speech, tending as it did to the idea of the equal distribution of property. 'There can be no greater disaster than the confiscation and redistribution of wealth. The greatest reason for the founding of States and commonwealths has always been the security of private property; for though men were drawn together by the guidance of nature, it is none the less true that they also sought the help of a civic organization in the hope of finding thereby a safeguard for their possessions.'

(Ibid. II. c. 24, §§ 84–85.) 'The strongest of all the forces which support a commonwealth is the maintenance of good faith (*fides*); and good faith cannot be maintained unless the payment of debts is obligatory. . . . Any statesman who would preserve the commonwealth will stand aloof from the sort of generosity which consists in taking wealth from one class to give it to another; he will make it his first object to see to it that every man is secured in his property by a fair system of law and law-courts, the poor not being distressed because of their humble circumstances, or the rich prevented by jealousy from keeping—or recovering—their property; in addition he will also use whatever means he can, both in war and in peace—for example the extension of empire, the acquisition of territories, and the levying of imposts—to increase the strength of the commonwealth.'

D. *A Passage from the Speech* Pro Sestio (56 B.C.), *on Parties*

Cicero has a brief remark on parties in the *De Officiis* (I. c. 25, § 85; *supra*, p. 201), but he had gone more fully into their nature in a speech delivered in court some twelve years earlier.

Pro Sestio Oratio, cc. 45–46, §§ 96–100. 'There have always been two classes of men in our State who have sought to play a part in the commonwealth and to conduct themselves with credit in its affairs. Of these two classes, one has cherished the design of being the party of "the people" (*popularis*), the other that of being, in estimation and fact, the party of "the best" (*optimates*). Those who wished their actions and words to be acceptable to the masses were reckoned as the *populares*; those who so conducted themselves as to win the approval of the best citizens for their policies were reckoned as the *optimates*. Who, then, in point of fact, are "the best"? The answer is that in number, if that is the gist of the question, they are beyond all reckoning—otherwise we could not continue to exist. They include the leaders of our public counsels, with those who follow their lead; they include the men of the upper classes, to whom the Senate is open; they include the Romans in the municipalities and rural areas of Italy; they include men of business; and there are even freedmen among them. In its numbers this party, as I have said, is widely spread and variously composed; but to prevent any error the whole of its character can be briefly described and defined. All men belong to it who are not guilty of crime, or naturally bad, or frenzied with passion, or involved in private trouble; and this "breed", as you have called it [Cicero is addressing one of the witnesses for the prosecution], consists of those who are honest and sound and free from difficulties in their private affairs. Such of them as are concerned in the government of the commonwealth—those who seek to execute its will, promote its interests, and increase its resources— are called the champions of their party, and are regarded as being personally the weightiest of its members, the most distinguished of citizens, and the leaders of the State (*principes civitatis*). We may therefore ask ourselves: What is the goal set before these governors of the commonwealth; the goal to which they must look and towards which they ought to direct their course? The answer is that it is what is the best and the most to be desired by all men who are sound and good and prosperous: it is leisure accompanied by dignity (*cum dignitate otium*). Those who desire this consummation are all reckoned as "the best", those who achieve it are reckoned as the foremost men and the saviours of the State (*conservatores civitatis*); for just as it is not proper for men to be carried away and swept off their feet by ambition for the dignity of public office, so too it is not proper for them to embrace the enjoyment of leisure when such leisure is inconsistent with dignity.

'This "leisured dignity" has for its foundations, and includes as its essential elements, a number of vital interests which should be observed by the leaders of the State and defended by them even at the risk of death. One of these interests is all public worship, and the system of divination by auspices; another, the powers of the magistrates and the authority of the Senate; another is the body of the law, along with ancestral custom, the courts, and the action of judges; another is the maintenance of credit and good faith; another is the provinces and allies of Rome, and the good name of her empire; another is the army, and another the treasury. To become the advocate and champion of these manifold and great interests demands a high spirit, great ability, and steady perseverance; for in a civic body so large as ours there are always a great number of persons who, with the consciousness upon them of wrongdoing, and in fear of punishment, attempt revolutions and political changes; or who, in a sort of ingrained frenzy of spirit, batten on civil discord and sedition; or who, on account of the involved state of their finances, prefer a general conflagration to their own personal ruin. They are men who, once they have found promoters and leaders of their policies and vices, raise such storms in the commonwealth that all who have taken upon themselves the steering of affairs have to be on their guard, and to strive, with all their skill and energy, to conserve what I have called "the foundations and essential elements" and to hold their course until they attain the port of leisure and dignity of which I have spoken.'

§ III. KINGSHIP (II). THE DEVELOPMENT OF MONARCHICAL IDEAS AT ROME FROM THE FIRST HALF OF THE SECOND CENTURY B.C. TO THE ACCESSION OF CALIGULA (A.D. 37)

When she had finally defeated Carthage and acquired control of the Western Mediterranean, by the end of the third century B.C.,

Rome was naturally drawn towards the Eastern Mediterranean and its Hellenistic kingdoms; and there now began a period of fusion—a 'Graeco-Roman' period—in which the arms, the law, the governing ability, and the general engineering skill of Rome were united with the eager canvassing of ideas and the incessant process of debate which were natural to the Greeks. Stoicism was the strongest of the intellectual forces with which the Romans thus came into contact. In itself it had an inherent *gravitas* and *auctoritas* which naturally appealed to the Romans; but over and above that natural affinity the thinkers of the 'middle Stoa'—the thinkers, that is to say, of the second and first centuries B.C.—were ready to temper and adjust their ethical and political teaching to the standards and postulates of the Roman soldiers and statesmen with whom they were brought into contact. Panaetius of Rhodes (*circa* 185–109 B.C.), the head of the Stoic school for the last twenty years of his life, spent some years in Rome, after the year 150 B.C., as a member of the Scipionic circle; and he modified the rigours of the primitive Stoa by softening its severe cult of the elect *sapiens* with his unshrinking and unbowed wisdom, and by admitting that moral progress (*prokopē*, as the technical term ran) was possible for ordinary men of experience and good sense, if only philosophers lent them their aid. It was in this way that he tempered Stoic ethics to square with the spirit and standards of the Roman aristocratic circle in which he moved and taught.

What were the political ideas which the Stoics of the second century B.C. could offer to Rome? Their political ideas, like their ethical ideas, seem to have differed from the original doctrine of the old Stoa under Zeno. The older Stoics, conceiving monarchy as the absolute and irresponsible rule of a single man (*archē anupeuthȳnos*), had held that only the perfect *sapiens* could carry such a burden (which was, in effect, to condemn any monarchy except in Utopia); or, at the most, and as a concession, they had allowed that a man of ordinary stature might rise to the demands of absolute and irresponsible rule if and provided that he were advised, and guided as well as advised, by the perfect wisdom of a philosopher.[1] In neither of these forms was the political doctrine

---

[1] Aristotle is reported to have argued, in an epistle or exhortation to Alexander

of the early Stoics definitely monarchical; indeed some of them (for instance Persaeus; see above, p. 83) seem to have been votaries not of a monarchical, but of a mixed, constitution, thus lending their aid to a doctrine which belonged to more than one school and was a sort of *koinē*, or lingua franca, of general speculation in the Hellenistic world.[1]

It was thus easy for the thinkers of the middle Stoa, when they came into contact with Rome after 150 B.C., to content themselves with the idea of being the advisers and guides of the existing Roman system of consuls, senate, and people—or rather, and more exactly, of the Roman aristocracy of soldier-statesmen which really dominated the system. Rome had no love of kingship, which she had ejected centuries before; the Stoics, equally, had no love for it, at any rate in itself (though they might be willing to be advisers of kings wherever there were kings to advise); and Rome and the thinkers of the middle Stoa could thus agree on the idea of a prudent government by a 'wise' aristocracy, with no cult or preference of monarchy. True, the idea of 'wisdom' left something of a loophole for the subsequent development of an intelligent (and therefore presumably benevolent) 'leader'— or, it might be, a group of 'leaders'; and the thought of Cicero, in some passages of his writings, seems to run in this direction (see above, pp. 191–2). But until the pressure of events made it necessary to explore the loophole—or, in other words, until the urgent need of ending civil commotions, and the no less urgent need of providing an effective government for a great mass of conquered territories, compelled men to feel their way to some system of leadership—statesmen and philosophers were alike contented with

'On Kingship', that for kings to be philosophers was neither necessary nor even helpful: 'what was really necessary was that they should be willing to hear, and ready to accept, the advice of genuine philosophers' (from Themistius, *Oratio* 8, quoted in V. Rose's *Aristotelis Fragmenta*, No. 647). Musonius Rufus, a Stoic of the first century A.D., used the same argument (see below, pp. 309–10).

[1] Persaeus, it is true, also wrote on Kingship—probably for Antigonus Gonatas. But the Peripatetics, following Aristotle, naturally turned to the mixed constitution; the Peripatetic Dicaearchus wrote about it (see above, p. 50); while the eclectic Polybius carried on the tradition, and handed it on to Cicero. In one way or another, whether through Stoic intermediaries or through the direct influence of the Aristotelian tradition, the mixed constitution had become a general tenet by the middle of the second century B.C.

the historic fact of a *de facto* aristocracy which could be interpreted as being (though it never actually was) a happy mixture
of senatorial aristocracy with an element of consular monarchy
and some elements of popular democracy in the shape of the
double assembly of the *populus* and the *plebs*. Perhaps the conclusion of the matter, so far as the Stoics were concerned, is that
they were opportunists: they trimmed their sails to each wind,
and saluted each rising sun: they could be aristocrats with the
aristocrats; they could be monarchists, playing the part of
éminences grises, when monarchy was in vogue; and when, at
last, the need of leadership, or the ambition of would-be leaders,
produced a system of empire, Seneca showed that a Stoic could
hail the rule of a Nero (see below, p. 236), and Marcus Aurelius
proved that a Stoic could be a sage emperor.

With that we may leave the theories of the Stoics, and turn to
the forces which, from the middle of the second century to the
end of the first century B.C., were actually shaping the movement
of political thought—that general community *thought*, as distinct
from the *theory* of philosophers, which underlies and sustains any
current political order. These forces were two. One, which has
already been suggested, was the actual pressure of the historical
process; the urgency of civil commotions, from the days of
Tiberius Gracchus onwards; the rise of something in the nature
of standing professional armies, with 'war-lords' at their head
either impelling them or impelled by them; the increasing mass
of conquered territories, crying for peace and order and some
settled system of government, but failing to find what they cried
for. All that spelled some form of monarchy: monarchy to end
civil commotion; monarchy in command of armies and master
over 'war-lords'; monarchy as a cement of empire and the builder
of an *ara pacis* for the Mediterranean world. The other force,
which linked itself readily to the pressure of the historical process,
was the force of popular belief; popular hero-worship; the readiness of the masses to look for a *praesens divinus* to be their 'Saviour'
and 'Benefactor'. The Eastern Mediterranean was the home of
this second force; and it readily surged from the East to the West.
We learn from Livy that Scipio Africanus, early in the second

century B.C., had already been affected by the ideas of the Greek East; current report had it that he was of divine stock, and went daily to the Capitol to converse with his divine father; nor did he deny (any more than he confirmed) the report which thus connected his name with the tradition of Alexander of Macedonia.[1]

It was mainly from Asia Minor, and from the Hellenistic kingdom of the Seleucids, that the idea of the deified ruler made its way to Rome. (Egypt, as has already been noted, transmitted little in comparison.) The Greek cities of Asia Minor again led the way, just as they had before been prominent, from the end of the fourth century onwards, in the movement towards the apotheosis of Hellenistic kings. They began by worshipping not a man but a city; Smyrna could worship *Roma Dea* as early as 195 B.C.; and Miletus and other cities eventually followed suit.[2] But men were also soon added to *Roma Dea* in worship; indeed, the people of Chalcis, in metropolitan Greece, dedicated buildings to their 'saviour', Titus Flamininus (the philhellene rival of Scipio Africanus), as early as the first decade of the second century B.C., honouring him along with Hercules and Apollo;[3] and in the course of the next century Roman provincial governors were worshipped willy-nilly in the Eastern provinces of Rome. Eventually the worship of the city and the worship of the man were 'conflated' or confused: *Roma Dea et Caesar* became the order of the day[4]—or *Roma Dea* receded, and *Caesar* alone remained. The worship of Julius Caesar and his eventual successor Augustus is celebrated in inscriptions which are no doubt largely rhetorical (rhetoric dominated education, and thereby dominated style, from the first century B.C. to the age of St. Augustine), but which none the less, with all their turgidity, are expressive of a genuine feeling for the 'superman' (and if a superman, why not a 'god',

---

[1] Livy, book XXVI, c. 19.

[2] W. W. Tarn, *Hellenistic Civilisation*, 3rd edition, p. 55.

[3] Plutarch, *Life of Flamininus*, c. 16.

[4] 'In 29 B.C. permission was given to the Romans in Asia and Bithynia to dedicate temples . . . to *Roma* and *Divus Iulius* jointly, and to the Greeks to do as much . . . for *Roma* and *Augustus*' (*Cambridge Ancient History*, vol. x, p. 483). Similarly, even in the West, an altar was dedicated in 12 B.C. to Rome and Augustus at Lyons.

open and 'manifest'?) who had turned a chaos of civil commotion and provincial misgovernment into peace and order. The ideas of 'Saviour' and 'Benefactor' were indeed old and worn coins, with the superscription rubbed faint; but a new surge of feeling made them fresh and clear when the *Ara Pacis Augustae* arose on the Campus Martius in Rome in the year 9 B.C. Five inscriptions may be cited here, which illustrate, at the least, the language which men used, and may even indicate something of the feelings they actually cherished.

A. *A decree of the cities of the province of Asia, 48 B.C.*
(The inscription comes from Ephesus, and is as early as the beginning of the Civil War which started in 49 B.C.)

'The cities in Asia, and the demes [i.e. the smaller political units outside and independent of the cities] and the tribes [*ethnē*, or groups with no political organization], to Caius Iulius Caesar, the son of Caius, high-priest (*pontifex maximus*?], *autocratōr*, and consul for the second time, descendant of Ares and Aphrodite, God Manifest (*Epiphanes*), and general Saviour (*Sōtēr*) of the life of mankind.'[1]

B. *A decree concerning the honours of Augustus, passed by the Mytilenaeans, at some time between 27 and 11 B.C.*[2]

The whole decree was carved on two sides of a pillar. The part here translated—which comes from one side of the pillar—has been preserved almost intact; the other part, on the other side, is fragmentary. The gist of the inscription is an instruction to an embassy, sent to Rome to offer an expression of gratitude to Augustus.

'For benefactions conferred . . . gratitude. And that he would call to mind, of his own magnanimity, that those who have won heavenly glory, and enjoy the superiority and strength of gods, cannot but be on a different level from what is lowlier than they are in fortune and in nature. But if any of these [i.e. the present

---

[1] From Dittenberger, *Sylloge Inscriptionum Graecarum*, 3rd edition, vol. ii, No. 760. It was the tradition of the Julian family that they were descended from Mars and Venus.
[2] From Dittenberger, *Orientis Graeci Inscriptiones*, No. 456*b* in vol. ii.

offerings] be discovered in a more glorious form in times to come, the zeal and piety of our city will in no wise be lacking in respect of anything that can deify him more [the Greek word is *theopoiein*]. You are to request him to allow a tablet to be placed in his house, and a tablet or column on the Capitol, containing a copy of this decree. The ambassadors are also to offer thanks for him [i.e. for what he has done] to the Senate, the priestesses of Vesta, Iulia his wife, Octavia his sister, and to his children and kinsfolk and friends. There has also been sent a crown made from 2,000 gold pieces, and this too is [to be] presented by the ambassadors. The ambassadors are to offer thanks to the Senate also, as well as to him, for its having dealt with the city very generously, and in accordance with its traditional graciousness.'

c   *A decree of the Greeks of the province of Asia, circa 9 B.C., making the birthday of Augustus (23 September) the beginning of the civil year*[1]

The compliment to Augustus, which turned his birthday into New Year's Day, was not so great as to make a revolution. The civil year had begun since Macedonian times at the autumnal equinox (i.e. about 21 September—when, incidentally, the Jewish New Year and the Moslem New Year still begin), and the change was only a change of two days. The document here translated falls into two parts: (1) an explanatory placard or 'deltogram' by the proconsul of Asia, explaining the reason for the change, and (2) a decree of the provincial synod (the *koinon* or 'common body' of the province), actually effecting the change. There are several copies still extant of the document, which was 'published' on marble in different cities, much as official notices are now published in newspapers. The record is thus a record disseminated through the whole province and brought to the general notice of all its inhabitants.

[1] From Dittenberger, *Orientis Graeci Inscriptiones*, No. 458 in vol. ii. It may be noted that the birthday of Augustus had already begun to be celebrated as a public holiday by 30 B.C. It may also be noted that in 27 B.C. he was given the title of Augustus, a quasi-religious title supposed to be connected with the word 'augury' and also suggesting the notion of 'authority'. The four Latin words *augeo*, *augurium*, *auctoritas*, and *Augustus* thus form a linked chain.

I. The proconsul's preface. 'Whether the birthday of the most divine Caesar be more a matter of pleasure, or more a matter of profit, it is a day which we may justly count as equivalent to the beginning of everything—if not in itself and in its own nature, at any rate in the benefits it brings—inasmuch as it has restored the shape of everything that was failing and turning into misfortune, and has given a new look to the Universe at a time when it would gladly have welcomed destruction if Caesar had not been born to be the common blessing of all men. Wherefore we may each of us justly count this [i.e. the birthday of Caesar] to have been the beginning of our own life and being, as it is also the conclusion and end of our repenting that we were ever born. And whereas there is no day of good fortune for all men, no day whatever other than this, which could give a more auspicious start to each of us, alike for our common advantage and our individual benefit; and whereas this day falls almost at the same time as the entry on office [i.e. the beginning of the civil year] in the cities of the province of Asia (this being clearly a foreshadowing, by some act of divine will, of the system [of dating now introduced], to the end that there should be a basis for doing honour to Augustus); and whereas it is difficult to show any gratitude equivalent to his many benefactions if we do not devise some new method of acknowledgement for each occasion; and inasmuch as men would have more pleasure in celebrating a birthday which is general and common for all if each received some individual and personal pleasure thereby, through its being the day of entry on office;[1] for all these reasons it seems good to me that in all city governments the birthday of the most divine Caesar should be the new First of the Month [and the beginning of the New Year], and that all men should enter on office on that day, which is 23 September.'

The proconsul ends his preface by explaining that a decree will have to be issued by the 'common body' of the province, reciting all the merits of Augustus, in order that *his* idea for doing honour

[1] The suggestion is that if the year begins, and men enter on office, on Caesar's birthday, they (i.e. the new entrants on office) will have a personal pleasure in the day over and above the common pleasure all men draw from its being his birthday.

to Augustus may remain for ever in force; and he promises to have the decree engraved and set in a temple—the temple of Rome and Augustus in Pergamum—with his preface preceding it, both in Greek and Latin.

II. The decree of the *koinon* of the province of Asia. 'Resolved by the Greeks in the province of Asia. . . . Whereas the Providence (*pronoia*) which has ordered the whole of our life,[1] showing concern and zeal, has ordained the most perfect consummation for human life by giving to it Augustus, by filling him with virtue for doing the work of a benefactor among men, and by sending in him, as it were, a saviour for us and those who come after us, to make war to cease, and to create order everywhere; and whereas Caesar, when he was made manifest, has caused the hopes of those who cherished anticipations [to be outstripped by what he has actually done], inasmuch as he has not only gone beyond previous benefactors, but has also left no hope to his successors of going beyond him; and whereas the birthday of the God [Augustus] was the beginning for the world of the glad tidings [in the Greek the 'Evangel'] that have come to men through him;

'And the province of Asia having resolved by vote at Smyrna... to crown with a wreath the man who should discover a way of doing the greatest honours to the God [i.e. to Caesar Augustus]; whereupon Paulus Fabius Maximus, the proconsul of the province despatched for our salvation from *his* right hand and by *his* judgement—having already benefited the province by thousands of benefactions, most of which no man could ever succeed in describing adequately—has devised a way of honouring Augustus hitherto unknown to the Greeks, which is, that the reckoning of time for the course of human life should begin with *his* birth;

'It is therefore resolved—may good fortune and salvation attend upon it—by the Greeks of the province of Asia that the new First of the Month should begin for all our cities on 23 September, which is the birthday of Augustus.'

The rest of the decree regulates the new calendar which is to

---

[1] The phrase suggests the Stoic philosophy, which may well have been present to the mind of the priest Apollonius who is recorded as having moved the decree.

come into force, with the names of the months—the first month of the year is henceforth to be called 'Caesar'—and the number of days in each. It also contains provisions for recording on marble the 'deltogram' of the proconsul (i.e. the preface before translated) and the decree itself, and for placing a copy of that record in the temple of Rome and Augustus at Pergamum (the capital of the province) and other copies in the principal cities of the different districts of the province.

D. *A decree from Halicarnassus, probably dating from the later years of the life of Augustus* (circa I B.C.), *and probably a local copy of a general decree of the* koinon *of the province of Asia*[1]

'Whereas the eternal and immortal nature of the Universe, in its grace to men, has added a thing of the greatest good to the exceeding benefits already given, having brought to us Caesar Augustus, who in the happy life of our time is father of his own country, *dea Roma*, Zeus the Paternal, Saviour (*Sōtēr*) of the whole race of men, and whose providence has not only fulfilled but even exceeded the prayers of all—for there is peace on land and sea; the cities flourish in obedience to law and in concord (*homonoia*) and prosperity; and there is a culmination and abundance of all good, of bright hopes for the future and of joy in the present, with men filled to overflowing with [delight in] games and offerings and sacrifices and hymns. . . .' [The conclusion is missing.]

E. *Decree of the people of Assus, in the Troad, in honour of Caligula, on his accession in* A.D. 37

' Whereas the [accession to the] principate (*hēgēmonia*) of Gaius [Iulius] Caesar Germanicus Augustus, for which all men have hoped in prayer, has been proclaimed, and the world has found no measure of its joy, and every city and every people has

---

[1] From *Ancient Greek Inscriptions in the British Museum*, Part IV, Section I, No. 894. The end of the inscription provides that a copy of the decree is to be placed by the high priest of the province in the temple of Rome and Augustus common to all the province (at Pergamum), and that other copies are to be placed in other cities by their magistrates.

hastened to see the God, as being convinced that an age most welcome to mankind is now at hand;

'It has been resolved by the Council, by the Romans doing business among us and by the people of Assus, that an embassy be appointed from the foremost and best, both Romans and Greeks, to appear before him and offer him congratulation, and to beg him to keep the city in his mind and under his care, according as he himself promised when he first made his entry (*epibasis*[1]) into our city in this province, along with his father Germanicus.'

To this resolution there is appended an oath. 'We swear by Zeus the Saviour and by the God Caesar Augustus and by our ancestral goddess the holy virgin [Athene Polias], that we will show goodwill to Gaius Caesar Augustus and all his house, and that we will count as friends all whom he chooses for friends and as enemies all whom he so regards. May it be well with us if we keep this oath, and may the contrary befall us if we should break it.

'There went as ambassadors at their own charges [four persons, whose names are given], who offered prayers to Iuppiter Capitolinus for the safety of Gaius Caesar Augustus Germanicus and offered sacrifice in the name of the city.' (Dittenberger, *Sylloge*,[3] No. 361).

§ IV. VIRGIL (70–19 B.C.)

1. *Eclogue IV: the Golden Age*

The idea of the coming of a 'golden age' is closely connected with the establishment and maintenance of the Roman Empire. It is expressed in inscriptions as well as in literature; it ultimately became a courtly tradition, repeated in reign after reign, that each emperor was a *restitutor orbis*, who gave the world a *Saeculum Novum* of gold. (This tradition is one explanation of the struggle

---

[1] The *epibasis* was a solemn occasion, marked by the erection of a commemorative statue. The previous visit of Caligula was in A.D. 18, nearly 20 years before, when he was not more than 6 years of age; and the alleged 'promise' is merely a flattering invention. Caligula, it may be added, was the son of Germanicus and Agrippina; and Agrippina was the daughter of Augustus' daughter Iulia. He was thus a great-grandson of Augustus.

of the Roman State against Christianity, which was regarded as impeding, by its refusal to worship Caesar, his task of the restoration and perpetuation of an age of gold.) The Fourth *Eclogue* of Virgil (written about 40 B.C., before the establishment of the Empire, while the Roman world was still engaged in civil strife) is the earliest expression of the idea in literature. There are many problems raised by the *Eclogue*. The most curious and interesting of them is the problem of Virgil's source. Did he draw for his inspiration on the Sibylline Oracles, and were those oracles, in the form in which he possibly knew them, Jewish–Hellenistic compositions, put together on Egyptian soil, possibly in Alexandria? There is a mass of literature on the subject—some of it fascinating; most of it bewildering. It began with the Emperor Constantine's *Oratio ad Sanctos,* in which he sanctioned the Christian interpretation of Virgil as a prophet of the birth of Christ—an interpretation current for a thousand years afterwards, and even now not entirely dead. Recent interpretations of the *Eclogue* may be found in H. Jeanmaire's *Le Messianisme de Virgile* (1930) and in H. J. Rose's *The Eclogues of Virgil,* c. viii (1942).

Lines 4 ff. 'The last age, foretold in the Sibyl's verse, is come, and the great order of the ages begins anew. Now the Virgin [Astraea, or Justice] returns; the reign of Saturn recurs; now from the heights of heaven a new generation descends. Only do thou, pure Lucina [goddess of childbirth], show thy favour to the child that is to be born, the child under whom the race of iron shall at last cease and a race of gold shall arise all over the world. . . . He shall receive divine life; he shall see heroes mingling with gods and himself be seen of them; and he shall rule a world that has been given peace by the virtues of his father.[1]

'But first[2] upon *thee,* child, earth untilled will freely shower her gifts—pouring around thee straying shoots of ivy mixed with

[1] The 'father' may be, and very likely was in Virgil's idea, Octavian, the future Augustus; but some have thought that he was Antony, and that the child to be born was a child of Antony and Cleopatra. The latter view would fit in better with the possible origin of the Sibylline oracles in Egypt; but the former is more intrinsically probable in view of Virgil's later references to Augustus in the *Georgics* and the *Aeneid.*

[2] i.e. already in his cradle, and in his early years, the child will himself enjoy the golden age which he will afterwards give to all mankind.

foxgloves, and bean-flowers by the side of laughing evergreens.[1]
Goats shall come home of themselves with their udders full of
milk; cattle shall not fear the mighty lion; even thy cradle shall
wreathe a garland of gay flowers about thee; the serpent too shall
perish. . . .

'But when [thou art grown; when] thou canst read the praises
of heroes and the story of thy father's deeds, and knowest what
true valour is; then the fields shall slowly yellow with the sway-
ing corn, red grapes shall hang from wild untended thorn-bushes,
and the solid oaks shall drip down honey like the dew. Yet there
shall still survive in men's hearts some few traces of ancient guile,
and these shall bid them to essay the sea in ships, to girdle their
towns for war with walls, and to cut furrows in the earth. Then
there shall rise another Tiphys [the pilot of the ancient Argonauts],
and a second Argo shall carry chosen heroes over sea; then there
shall also be other wars, and once more the great Achilles shall be
sent to the siege of Troy.

'But next,[2] when years of stalwart growth have made thee
already a man [the Age of Gold shall truly begin], the shipman
shall come home from the sea, and there shall be no more vessels
for the exchange of merchandise; then every country shall of
itself produce everything. Earth shall no longer suffer under the
harrow, nor the vine from the pruning-hook; the hardy plough-
man shall now unyoke his oxen; wool shall no more be taught
[by the dyer] to counterfeit many colours, but the sheep in the
fields shall of themselves change the colour of their fleeces—now
to the soft rose-tint of the murex, now to the yellow of saffron—
and of its own motion a vermilion hue shall cover the lambs as
they feed.

' "On this wise run, ye ages to come"—so sang the Fates, in accord, to their spindles, by virtue of the immovable will of Destiny.

'Now do thou (for the time is at hand) enter upon thy great

[1] The words translated by 'bean-flowers' and 'evergreens' both denote plants
peculiar to Egypt—the one a large plant of the lily kind which grows in the
Egyptian marshes, and the other a thorny evergreen. This may conceivably bear
on the sorce of Virgil's inspiration.

[2] There are three stages in the prophecy—infancy, when the child lies in his
cradle; adolescence, when he reads the stories of the past and watches the recurrent
cycle of events; and finally manhood and the true Golden Age.

honours, dear offspring of the Gods, Jove's own great progeny.[1]
See how the universe bows down to thee from its massy vault—
the earth, and the spaces of the sea, and the depths of heaven; behold how everything rejoices in the age which is to come. . . .'

Virgil then prays that he may live to celebrate the glories which
the child will one day win, and ends with a final invocation:
'Begin, thou little child, to smile in recognition on thy mother;
mother has carried thee for ten long months in weariness. Begin
now, little child; he who has no smile for his parent will never be
welcomed by a god to his board or by a goddess to her bed.'

The importance of this Fourth *Eclogue* is not that it anticipates
Christianity (it is essentially 'pagan' in tone), but that Virgil, with
a poet's prescience, has caught the tone and expressed the feelings
of the next three centuries and more (40 B.C.–A.D. 337). His theme
is a united Mediterranean world, living in peace and quiet under
a system of divine kingship which guarantees the renewal of an
age of gold from generation to generation. The nearest parallel
to his theme and his treatment of it may be found in the third
book of the Sibylline Oracles, which may have been mainly composed in the second century B.C. In a passage which may be a later
addition and of Jewish–Hellenistic–Alexandrian origin, the 'Sibyl'
prophesies that Cleopatra will inaugurate a Golden Age of union
between Asia and Europe, when Justice (the Virgin of the Fourth
Eclogue) will reign on earth, with Concord (*Homonoia*) at her
side (356 sqq.). A later passage in the same book (652) foretells
'the sending by God from the sun of a king who will make wars
cease in all the earth' and inaugurate an age of gold. Other
passages in the same book (743–59 and 787–94) depict this golden
age in terms which look back to Jewish prophecy and anticipate
Virgil's *Eclogue*—telling how earth shall yield the gift of an
infinity of crops, and honey shall drop from heaven, and flocks
and herds shall abound; 'there shall be deep peace all over the

---

[1] The word used by Virgil, *incrementum*, means 'increase'. I have translated it
as if it were used in the sense in which we speak of 'earth's increase', and I have
accordingly written 'Jove's progeny'. But the word may mean an increase added
to Jove rather than an increase or progeny proceeding *from* him; and Virgil may
thus be saying that the divine child is a great addition to Jove's divinity, extending
its range and power.

world, . . . wolves and lambs shall eat their meat together on the mountains, . . . the lion shall feed at the stall like the ox, and a little child shall lead him about in bonds'. The parallel with Virgil afterwards (and with the prophecies of Isaiah and Micah in the Old Testament before) is close; and though such analogy is not enough to *prove* affiliation, it is possible that Virgil—skilled, like his contemporary Catullus, in Alexandrine literature—may somehow have drawn light from the East.[1]

Note on the Emperor Constantine's Interpretation of the Fourth Eclogue

The *Oratio ad Sanctos*, which is printed among the works of Eusebius,[2] contains an allegorical interpretation of the Fourth *Eclogue* in the Alexandrine style which Philo Judaeus had applied to the Old Testament. Some passages are here translated to show

[1] The *Sibylline Oracles* are a curiosity of literature. Of Oriental origin, they passed into Greek literature, and came to be written in Greek hexameters. They were composed and re-composed over a period of some 800 years (*circa* 300 B.C.– A.D. 500), and during these eight centuries they passed through three phases. In the first they were Greek; in the second stage, in the course of the second century B.C., they were adopted and made a vehicle of propaganda by the Jews; in the third, about the fourth century A.D., they were taken over by the Christian Church.

Book III, from which the quotations in the text are taken, belongs largely to the Jewish phase. It starts from a prediction of Alexander; it proceeds to the praise of the Jews and to prophecies of the coming of the Messiah. It contains some passages, possibly added at a later date, referring apparently to the Roman triumvirate of 43 B.C. and to Cleopatra. The origin of the whole book has been ascribed to the Jews of Egypt. (See A. Bentzen, *Introduction to the Old Testament,* 2nd edition, vol. ii, pp. 241–2.)

(The Romans counted a number of Sibyls, and gave them the names of different countries and places. Their supposed prophecies were at one time kept on the Capitol. These perished in the burning of the Capitol in 83 B.C., but a new collection was made, and Virgil may have had access to it.)

[2] The oration is printed in the editions of Eusebius' writings (by F. A. Heinichen and I. A. Heikel) immediately after his *Vita Constantini*. It *may* have been delivered by Constantine, perhaps in 323—just before his final war against Licinius, then emperor in the East—and perhaps with the intention of winning the support of the Christians in the East for his cause. If so, it was written for him by some scholar at his court. That scholar may have been Lactantius, and not Eusebius. Eusebius knew little of the Latin West; Lactantius, who came from the province of Africa, was familiar with Virgil and also acquainted with Greek, and he was at the time the tutor of Constantine's eldest son Crispus (see A. Piganiol, *L'Empereur Constantine*, pp. 134–8). But I. A. Heikel in his edition of Eusebius, vol. i, pp. xci–cii, comes to the conclusion that the *Oratio ad Sanctos* is a forgery, possibly belonging to the fifth century.

how Virgil could be interpreted in the fourth century—as indeed he continued to be interpreted for a thousand years afterwards.

c. 19, §§ 5–9. The orator, turning it into a Greek hexameter, quotes the line of Virgil about the return of the virgin (Astraea, the goddess of Justice) and the recurrence of the reign of Saturn. But he quotes it so that it runs, 'The Virgin comes again, bringing the beloved King'; and he interprets it on that basis. 'Who, then, is the Virgin who returns? Is it not she who was filled and made with child by the Holy Ghost? And what was there to prevent her, when she was thus made with child by the Holy Ghost, from still being at all times and remaining a virgin? He too [i.e. the beloved King] will return once more, and by his coming will lighten the burden of the world.' The orator then quotes, in his own paraphrase, the words of Virgil about the descent from heaven of a new progeny, the ending of the iron age, and the beginning of the age of gold; and again he adds an interpretation based on his own paraphrase. 'We understand these words both literally and allegorically. To those who seek more deeply for their sense, they are a guide which brings to our view the divinity of Christ; but in order to prevent any of those who held authority in the imperial city from being able to accuse the poet of writing what was contrary to its traditional laws, and of rejecting the forms of belief in the gods which were held by previous generations, Virgil veils the truth. He knew, I believe, that blessed mystery which receives its name from the Saviour [the mystery of salvation]; but in order to evade the savagery of cruel hearts, he drew the thoughts of his readers to things with which they were acquainted, as he does in saying that altars should be erected, temples raised, and sacrifices offered to the new-born child.'

c. 20. The allegorical method is then applied to other passages in the *Eclogue*. When Virgil says that 'the serpent too shall perish', he is foretelling the bruising of the serpent's head by the Saviour (§§ 3–4). When, again, he speaks of new Argonauts and a new Trojan War, he is announcing a great truth which moves Constantine—or rather the writer who wears the mantle of Constantine —to an exclamation of admiration (§§ 8–9). 'Bravo! thou wisest of poets. Thou hast carried poetic licence, with a wise stewardship,

to a just and proper height. For it was not thy purpose to divine
the future, since thou wert not a prophet; and thou wert also, I
believe, held back by some sense of the danger threatening those
who should seek to dispute the traditions of earlier generations.
It was therefore with cautious steps, and in order to avoid danger
as far as he could, that Virgil presented the truth to those who
could understand it; and while he censures fortifications and war,
which indeed are still, even today, to be found in the life of man,
he depicts the Saviour as advancing to the war against Troy, and
he means by Troy the whole world. For verily the Saviour
waged war against the opposing power of evil, and he was sent to
fight it by the guidance of his own foreknowledge and design,
and by the command of the Supreme Father.'

2. *The Second Book of the* Georgics: *the praises of Italy, land of
Saturn and mother of Caesar*

Virgil, still pursuing, if in a different form, the theme of an age
of gold, sees its dawn in Italy and finds its inspiration in the men
of Italian breed, and among them (but unique among them) in
'greatest Caesar'.

Lines 149 ff. 'Here is perpetual spring, and here summer reigns
even in seasons not her own; here the herds yield their increase
twice in the year, and twice the tree gives its service of fruit. . . .
Add to this all the noble cities, achievements of the hands of man;
all the hill-towns piled by labour on the tops of sheer rocks, and
the rivers gliding on their course under ancient walls. And shall
I tell of the seas that wash our upper and our lower shores? of
our far-spread lakes? . . . of our harbours . . .? This land has also
shown seams of silver and lodes of copper in its veins; and its
rivers have carried abundant gold in their flow. This land is the
mother of a stirring breed of men—the mother of the Marsians,
the mother of Sabine manhood, the mother of Ligurians inured
to evil days, the mother of Volscian spearmen; she has given birth
to a Decius, a Marius, a great Camillus—to the Scipios stern in
battle—and to thee, greatest Caesar, victor at this hour[1] on the

---

[1] Virgil is writing some years after the composition of the Fourth *Eclogue*,
about the year 30, when Augustus was in the East in the course of the war against
Cleopatra and 'Orientalism'.

farthest bounds of Asia, driving the weak-kneed Indians before thee far from our Roman citadel. Hail to thee, land of Saturn, great mother of the harvest of the field, great mother of a harvest of men! . . .'

3. *The* Aeneid: *Roma Dea et Divus Caesar*

The *Aeneid* was written by Virgil, encouraged and perhaps even advised by Augustus, in the last ten years of his life, between 30 and 20 B.C. It thus belongs to the period of comparative repose and restoration which followed the end of the civil wars. It is an epic of Rome; at once a celebration of the past and a proclamation of the new Augustan era in which Rome was to 'rule the peoples by her sovereignty' and to 'impose the law of peace' upon them. Read, remembered, and recited in succeeding centuries, it may be called 'the testament of Rome'.

(*a*) *The promise of Augustus.* Book VI, lines 779 ff. Anchises, in the underworld, shows his son Aeneas the future. He points to Romulus, the legendary founder of Rome, under whose auspices, he prophesies, 'glorious Rome shall spread her empire as wide as the world, and lift her spirit as high as the heavens'; and then from Romulus he turns to Augustus, the founder of the Empire.

Lines 789 ff. 'Behold there Caesar, and with him all the strain sprung from Iulus,[1] destined one day for the high vault of heaven. This, this is he of whose promised coming thou hast heard so often; this is Caesar Augustus, the scion of deity, who shall establish again a golden age (*aurea saecula*) in Latium, among the fields where Saturn once was king, and spread his dominion beyond both Libya and India. . . . Even now, at his coming, the realms of the Caspian and the lands of the Black Sea shudder before the oracles of the gods, and the trembling waters of the Nile's seven branches are hot in tumult. [Hercules himself did not range so widely in his labours; and even Bacchus himself did not carry his triumphs so far.] And can *we* then doubt to spread our valour by our deeds?'

---

[1] Iulus, the grandson of Aeneas according to legend, was the legendary progenitor of the *gens Iulia*, the clan or family to which Julius Caesar, and his successor, Caesar Augustus, belonged.

(b) *The Tradition and Mission of Rome.* Book VI, lines 841–53. 'Who could pass *thee* by in silence, great Cato, or forget *thee*, Cossus? Who could forget the breed of the Gracchi? or the two Scipios, twin thunderbolts of war, the banes of Libya? or Fabricius, powerful in poverty? or Serranus [called to the office of consul from] sowing the seed in his furrows? or the Fabii . . . and among them thee, Maximus, master of caution,[1] who redressed for us the sum of things sole-handed by delay?

'Others, I deem it true, shall mould the breathing bronze more deftly; they shall create living images from blocks of marble; they shall plead causes more eloquently, trace with their measuring-rod the orbits of the heavenly bodies, and tell of the rising of the stars.[2] Thine it is, Rome, ever to remember to rule the peoples in sovereignty, to impose the law of peace, to spare the conquered, and to curb the proud; and it is these that shall be *thy* arts.'

(c) *The Emblems on the Roman Shield.* Book VIII, lines 675 ff. Venus gives to Aeneas the shield on which her husband Vulcan, 'not without knowledge of prophecy, nor ignorant of ages to come', has depicted the fortunes of Italy and the triumphs of Rome.

'There, in the middle of the shield, might be seen the brazen-prowed ships and the battle of Actium.[3] . . . On one side, on a tall poop, stood Caesar Augustus, leading his Italians into battle, with the Senate and people and the gods both of hearth and of heaven on his side; twin flames came forth from the gladness of his brows, and the star of his father was revealed on his crest. . . . On another side was Antony, with his barbarian power and motley arms, coming in victory from the peoples of the dawn and the shores of the Red Sea, bringing with him Egypt, the forces of the East, and men from remotest Bactria; there followed in his train—oh the shame of it!—his Egyptian wife. . . . So

---

[1] Q. Fabius Maximus, called *Cunctator* (the Delayer), was dictator in 217 B.C., and kept Hannibal in check by 'stone-walling'. Virgil quotes here a line of the old Latin poet Ennius in his praise.

[2] In brief, Greece is the greater in the realm of culture and its arts and sciences (sculpture, rhetoric, and astronomy); Rome bears the palm in the management of men and the sphere of government.

[3] The battle of 31 B.C., in which Italy and the West, commanded by Augustus, defeated Egypt and the East under the command of Antony and Cleopatra.

monstrous gods of every shape, and among them the dog-headed Anubis, stood with arms in their hands, face to face with Neptune and Venus and Minerva [the gods on the Western side]. . . . [The battle raged long.] Then Apollo, the god of Actium,[1] gave heed; downward he bent his bow; in terror of his shafts all Egypt, and every Indian, and the Sabaeans and all the Arabs, turned to flight. [Then the shield showed the Queen flying away from the battle; it showed her, pale at the coming of death, by the waters of the Nile; finally, it showed the glory of the victorious Augustus.] Caesar, borne in his chariot through the gates of Rome in a triple triumph,[2] consecrated to the gods of Italy the immortal offering he had vowed, and dedicated through all the length and breadth of the city three hundred lofty temples. . . . [The streets rang with jubilation: there was singing and sacrifice in every shrine]; Caesar himself, seated on the white marble threshold of the shining temple of Apollo, passed in review the gifts of the peoples and caused them to be hung on the resplendent gates; the conquered nations filed before him in long array, various in their arms and the fashion of their dress as well as in their languages.'

(d) *The final reconciliation of East and West under Latin auspices.* Book XII, lines 820 ff. Virgil, following a current legend of the origin of Rome, makes Aeneas sail from fallen Troy with his band of fugitives to start a new life and found a new State on Italian soil; but, himself an Italian to the core, he is clear that the genius of the new State is to be Italian, and that the Trojans of the East are to be absorbed, by marriage and assimilation, into the native stock of Italy and the Western Mediterranean. In the mythological machinery which forms the background of the poem Jupiter has favoured Aeneas and Troy; Juno has been on the other or Italian side, and has sought to thwart Aeneas and his designs in Italy. At the end of the action Jupiter and Juno agree on a reconciliation: Aeneas is to found his State (destined eventually to embrace the whole of the Mediterranean in an *imperium*

---

[1] And also the chosen deity of Caesar Augustus.
[2] He returned to Rome in August 29 B.C., and celebrated a triple triumph for the victories of his arms in Dalmatia, at Actium, and in Egypt.

sine fine), but it is to be an *Italian* State, rooted and grounded in Italian speech and the Italian way of life. This is the gist of Juno's prayer and Jupiter's assent.

Juno's prayer to Jupiter, lines 820–7. 'I ask thee this for the sake of Latium and the glory of thy kindred [Caesar's family, the progeny of Jupiter]. When they shall draw together—so let it be—in peace through a happy marriage, and shall share their laws and knit their covenants, do not command the Latins born of the native soil to change their ancient name, or to become Trojans and be so called. Do not bid them to change their language or to alter their dress; let there be still a Latium, and let there be kings coming from Alba[1] through all the ages; let there be a Roman breed, with strength drawn from Italian valour.'

The assent of Jupiter, lines 833–9. 'I grant thy wish; and moved by thy prayer I yield in willing assent. The men of Ausonia[2] shall keep the language and customs of their ancestors: as their name is, so shall it remain; and the Trojans, mixing only in blood, shall sink themselves in their life. The manner and rites of their worship shall be added to them by me, and I will make them all Latins speaking one language. Hence shall arise a race, mixed with Ausonian blood, which thine eyes shall see surpassing men, yea, and surpassing gods, along the path of duty (*pietas*).'

With this treaty of reconciliation, or 'Act of Union', Virgil brings to an end, just before his death (in 19 B.C.), the prophecy— for so it may be called—which he had begun, twenty one years before, in his Fourth *Eclogue*. He had begun with a sort of 'carol' on the birth of a divine child: he ends with a solemn celebration of the 'Roman breed' and 'Italian valour', on the keynote of *pietas*. The Golden Age, after all, is a return—a return, in dutiful loyalty, to the native original genius of the Italian people.

§ V. AUGUSTUS ON HIS 'RES GESTAE'

Records of their reigns, inscribed on clay or stone, had been set up by Eastern rulers from time immemorial. Augustus set up

---

[1] Alba, now Castel Gandolfo, situated in the Alban Hills S.E. of Rome, was the traditional head of an early Latin league.

[2] An ancient name used by the poets to indicate central (and southern) Italy.

such a record of his principate, towards its close; and this not only in Rome, but also, in copies, throughout the Empire. The great copy which has survived is one which was inscribed on the walls of a temple in Ancyra (the modern Ankara); and it is known accordingly as the *Monumentum Ancyranum*. It is headed, 'A copy of the deeds done by the deified Augustus, whereby he brought the world under the sovereignty of the Roman people, . . . as inscribed on two brazen pillars erected in Rome.' The following extracts (translated from the edition by E. G. Hardy, Oxford, 1923) contain some of the more important passages illustrating the political ideas and social policies of Augustus.

A. *The Early Years and the Establishment of Power*

c. 1. 'At the age of nineteen (in 43 B.C.) on my personal initiative and at my personal expense, I raised the army by means of which I restored the liberty of the commonwealth, suppressed by the tyranny of a faction. For this the Senate enrolled me in its ranks, with votes of congratulation . . . and gave me a command [by the title of pro-praetor]. It ordered me, as pro-praetor, with the co-operation of the consuls, to see to it that the commonwealth suffered no detriment.[1] In the same year, as both the consuls had fallen in battle, the people made me a consul and one of the triumvirs for the settlement of the commonwealth.

c. 2. 'I drove the murderers of my father into exile, punishing their crime through the regular courts, and when afterwards they made war on the commonwealth I defeated them twice in the field.

c. 3. 'I undertook civil wars by land and sea, and foreign wars all over the world, and when victorious I spared all the citizens who survived the wars. The foreign nations which could safely be pardoned I preferred to save rather than to destroy. About 500,000 Roman citizens bound themselves to me by taking the military oath. More than 300,000 of these I settled in colonies, or sent back into their own towns, at the end of their term of

---

[1] This is the famous *Senatus consultum ultimum*, or 'proclamation of a state of emergency'.

service; and I gave them all land, bought by myself, or, in lieu of land, money provided by myself.

c. 4. '. . . Three times I celebrated triumphs; . . . twenty-one times I was acclaimed *imperator* for victories in battle. . . . In my triumphs there were led before my chariot nine kings or sons of kings. . . . When I made this record I had been thirteen times consul, and I had held tribunician power for thirty-seven years.'

B. *Measures of Policy: Food Supply: Census: Benefactions and Entertainments*

c. 5. 'When food was extremely scarce, I did not decline to take charge of the supply of corn, and I managed it to such effect that in a few days I relieved all the people, by the money I spent, from the fear and peril in which they stood.

c. 6. '[On three occasions], when the Senate and people of Rome agreed that I should be elected, without any colleague, to superintend laws and manners in the exercise of supreme authority, I refused to accept the award of any form of office which was not in accordance with the institutions of our ancestors; and it was by virtue of the tribunician power [and not as a dictator] that I executed the measures of policy which the Senate wished to see carried out by my means.[1]

c. 8. 'In my sixth consulship, with Agrippa as my colleague (28 B.C.), I carried out a census of the people, and I held the lustral sacrifice [offered on the completion of the census] after an intermission of forty-two years. On this occasion 4,063,000 Roman citizens were entered on the roll. A second time (8 B.C.) . . . I again carried out a census, without a colleague, but holding consular authority myself; at this census 4,223,000 Roman citizens were entered on the roll. A third time, holding consular office, and having my son Tiberius Caesar as my colleague (A.D. 8), . . . I once more carried out a census; and at it 4,937,000 Roman citizens were entered on the roll. . . .

'By the enactment of new laws I restored many of the traditions of our ancestors which were passing out of use, and in my

---

[1] Augustus adds that he sought and received from the Senate colleagues to aid him in his exercise of tribunician power.

own person I handed down a number of examples for the imitation of posterity.

c. 13. 'The gates of the temple of Ianus—which our ancestors ordered to be shut whenever there was peace, secured by victory, throughout the domain of the Roman people on land and sea, and which, before my birth, are recorded to have been shut only twice since the foundation of the city (753 B.C.)—were shut three times by decree of the Senate while I was First Citizen (*Princeps*).'

In a number of following chapters Augustus records his benefactions and buildings. Among his benefactions he mentions the shows and games and spectacles which went along with them, and which are henceforth one of the bases of the Empire.

c. 22. 'Three times I gave a show of gladiators in my own name, and five times in the names of my sons or grandsons; in these shows there fought about 10,000 men. Twice I gave the people, in my own name, an exhibition of athletes brought together from all quarters, and I gave a third in the name of my grandson. . . . Twenty-six times, in my own name, or in the names of my sons and grandsons, I arranged hunts of African wild beasts for the people, in the circus, or the forum, or the amphitheatres . . ..

c. 23. 'I gave the people the spectacle of a naval battle, on the other side of the Tiber, where the grove of the Caesars now stands, excavating for the purpose a space of 1,800 feet by 1,200. In this spectacle 30 ships with armoured prows, all triremes or biremes, and a larger number of small vessels, were engaged in battle.

c. *The Victories of Augustus by Sea and Land*

c. 25. 'I cleared the sea of pirates. In the course of the war there were captured about 30,000 slaves who had run away from their masters and taken up arms against the commonwealth; these I handed over to their masters for punishment.

'The whole of Italy voluntarily took an oath of allegiance[1] to me, and demanded that I should be its leader in the war in which I won the victory at Actium. The same oath of allegiance was

---

[1] This may be regarded as a basis of the position of the *princeps*; see A. Piganiol, *Histoire de Rome* (1954), p. 202.

taken by the provinces of the Gauls, the Spains, Africa, Sicily, and Sardinia [i.e. the whole of the Western Mediterranean].

c. 26. 'I extended the boundaries of all the provinces of the Roman people which were bordered by nations not in the obedience of the Empire. I restored order in the provinces of the Gauls and the Spains and in Germany—that is to say in the whole of the region bounded by the Ocean from Cadiz to the mouth of the Elbe. I caused order to be restored in the Alps, from the region nearest to the Adriatic westward to the Tyrrhenian Sea, without waging war unjustly on any of the tribes. My fleet sailed along the Ocean from the mouth of the Rhine eastwards as far as the territories of the Cimbri, which no Roman had ever approached before either by land or by sea: the Cimbri, the Charydes, the Semnones, and other German peoples of the same region sent envoys to seek my friendship and that of the Roman people.

c. 27. 'I added Egypt to the empire of the Roman people. . . . I recovered all the provinces which lie to the east of the Adriatic, and also Cyrene . . . and I had previously recovered Sicily and Sardinia, which had been seized in the course of the Servile War [by Sextus Pompeius, 38–36 B.C.].

c. 28. 'I planted colonies of my soldiers in Africa, Sicily, Macedonia, both the Spains, Achaea, the province of Asia, Syria, Southern Gaul, and Pisidia. Italy, in addition, received twenty-eight colonies, planted under my auspices, which in my lifetime were populous and prosperous.

c. 29. 'From Spain and Gaul, and from the Dalmatians, I recovered, after defeating my enemies, many military standards which had been lost by other generals. The Parthians I compelled to restore the spoils and standards of three Roman armies, and to seek the friendship of the Roman people as suppliants.

c. 30. 'The tribes of Pannonia, to which no Roman army had ever penetrated before the time of my principate, were conquered by Tiberius Nero, my stepson who was then my legate, and brought by me under the sovereignty of the Roman people; and the frontier of Illyricum was advanced as far as the bank of the river Danube.

c. 31. 'Embassies of kings were often sent to me from India, a thing never witnessed before in the camp of any Roman general.

'Our friendship was sought through ambassadors by the Bastarnae, the Scythians, and the Kings of the Sarmatians who live on both sides of the river Tanais, and also by the Kings of the Albani, the Iberi, and the Medi.' The first three tribes were nomads in what is now south-west Russia; the other three belonged to the Caucasus and its neighbourhood.

D. *The Constitutional Position of Augustus*

c. 34. 'In my sixth and seventh consulships (28–27 B.C.), when I had extinguished the fires of civil war after receiving by common consent absolute control of affairs, I handed the commonwealth over from my own control to the free disposal[1] of the Senate and the people of Rome. For this service done by me I received the title of Augustus by decree of the Senate, and the door-posts of my house were officially covered with laurels; a civic crown was put up over my door, and a golden shield was placed in the new Senate-house [built by Julius Caesar], with an inscription recording that it was a gift to me from the Senate and people of Rome in recognition of my valour, my clemency, my justice, and my fulfilment of duty (*pietas*). After that time I took precedence of others in dignity, but I enjoyed no greater power than those who were my colleagues in any magistracy.

c. 35. 'While I was holding the consulship for the thirteenth time, the Senate, the order of knights, and the whole of the Roman people gave me the title of Father of my Country (*pater patriae*), and decreed that the title should be inscribed in the porch of my house, in the Senate-house, and in the forum of Augustus, under the chariot erected in my honour by decree of the Senate.'

'When I wrote this record, I was in my seventy-sixth year.'

---

1 'Free disposal' is *arbitrium* in the Latin. Actually the *respublica* was *not* handed over to the free disposal of the Senate and people. Besides these two factors there was a third, the *princeps civitatis*—or Augustus himself—and this third factor had a vaguer and more elastic, and therefore greater, power than the other two. It is the old idea of a mixed constitution (see above, pp. 50, 114–21, 187–9), but without a fixed proportion between its various elements, and with one element in the mixture free to determine its own strength in relation to the other two.

The record was drawn up in the summer of A.D. 14, just before
Augustus died. Born in 63 B.C., he had been immersed in action
ever since the murder of Caesar, in 44 B.C., for a period of nearly
sixty years. Others have reigned longer. Perhaps no other man
has governed, as well as reigned, for so long a time, at any rate
in a period which made such demands on the mind.

E. *The Judgement of Later Historians on the Reign of Augustus*

To the account of his reign given by Augustus himself three
passages may be added from ancient historians.

1. The first passage comes from Velleius Paterculus (19 B.C.–
A.D. *circa* 30), who had served in the army and held office as
quaestor and praetor. His summary, naturally biased in favour of
the Empire, comes in book II, c. 89, of his *Historiae Romanae*.

'There was nothing men might pray for to Heaven, and nothing
Heaven could grant to men—nothing desire could conceive, or
fortune could bestow—which Augustus . . . did not realize for
the commonwealth, the people of Rome, and the world. Civil
war had come to an end after twenty years, and foreign wars
were over; peace was restored, and the fever of armed struggle
had everywhere abated; vigour returned to the laws, authority to
the courts, and prestige to the Senate; the powers of the magistrates were renewed in their pristine strength, with the one change
that two praetors were added to the previous eight. At the recall of the ancient and traditional system of the commonwealth,
the land was once more brought under cultivation, the rites of
religion were once more celebrated, men found themselves once
more in the enjoyment of security, and all alike were assured in
the possession of their property; laws were amended to the public
benefit, and enacted in the interest of the general welfare; the
appointment of senators was made without undue severity, but
not without proper precautions. The leading men in the State,
men who had enjoyed triumphs and a full meed of honour, were
induced by the emperor's encouragement to increase the beauty
of the city. The consulship was continued [for Augustus] only for
eleven successive years: that was the utmost length of tenure
which Caesar, after protesting his reluctance, consented to accept;

the office of dictator, which was again and again offered to him
by the people, he as constantly refused to accept. To recount
the number of wars which he brought to a peaceful conclusion,
his general pacification of the world by his victories, and all the
public works which he caused to be carried out both in Italy
and beyond its borders, would tax the powers of a writer who
was ready to spend a lifetime on that one undertaking; we ourselves, remembering the limits within which we are pledged to
keep, have offered to the eyes and mind only a general picture
of the principate of Augustus.'

2. The second passage comes from the *Annals* of Tacitus (book
III, c. 54), and is concerned with the economic basis and justification of the Roman Empire as it was left by Augustus. Tacitus,
writing some time after A.D. 100, is reporting the gist of a letter
addressed by Tiberius to the Senate in A.D. 22, eight years after
the death of his predecessor. The immediate point of the letter is
the need for economy and the enforcement of sumptuary legislation—but in its course Tiberius proceeds to raise larger issues.

'Why was the virtue of thrift so general in the past? It was because each man kept a grip of himself, and we were all of us
citizens of one city; for when our dominions did not extend beyond Italy, even our temptations were not what they now are.
Since then, our victories abroad have taught us to consume the
goods of others, as our victories at home in our civil wars have
taught us to consume our own. How narrow today is the area in
which the aediles can seek to enforce economy; how small an
extent it covers in comparison with the rest of the field! Yet,
upon my word, there is not one man to warn us that Italy is
dependent on help from abroad [i.e. on a supply of foreign corn],
or that the existence of the Roman people is always at the mercy
of the hazards of sea and storm. Do you think that our own woods
and farms will maintain us, if the resources of the provinces are
not available to aid the work of masters and slaves and to supple-
ment the area of our soil? This . . . is the burden which the prince
has to carry; were it neglected the commonwealth would utterly
collapse. [Austerity is necessary;] the rest of the civic body must
cure itself by a change of heart; we of the Senate must reform

ourselves for very shame; the poor must be changed by the pressure of need and the rich by the effects of surfeit.'

3. A third passage comes from the *Roman History* of Dio Cassius, a Roman official from Asia Minor who wrote his history in the beginning of the third century, some 200 years after the death of Augustus. But he drew on imperialist tradition (and on early memoirs and early histories), and his general verdict on the reign of Augustus may thus be regarded as a statement of that tradition, a statement given in Greek to the Greek world of the Eastern Mediterranean.

Dio Cassius, *Romaica*, book LVI, c. 43, § 4 to c. 44, § 1. 'There were other reasons [besides his courtesy and his clemency] why the Romans sincerely mourned for Augustus. He had mixed monarchy with democracy; he had at once preserved their liberty, and established order and security, with the result that, escaping both the licence of democracy and the arrogance of tyranny, they now lived under a system which combined a moderate and temperate degree of liberty with submission to a monarchy free from any terrors. They were subjects without being slaves, and citizens of a democracy unvexed by faction. If any of them remembered the measures which Augustus had taken in the course of the civil wars, they ascribed them to the pressure of circumstances, and they thought it proper to judge his true temper from the period after his acquisition of undisputed authority, when, indeed, he showed himself very different from what he had been in earlier years. To examine each of his acts in detail would be to confirm the accuracy of this view; but it is a sufficient summary of them all to say that he put an end to all faction, and that he so transformed the government, establishing its authority in full vigour, as to give it the maximum of strength— with the result that even when he had recourse to some more violent line of action, as will often be the case under extra-ordinary conditions, one might lay the blame with justice on the circumstances rather than on the man.'

§ VI. SENECA

Introduction

Seneca the younger, son of the elder Seneca the Rhetor, born about 5 B.C. at Cordova in Spain (a country which afterwards furnished to Rome two emperors, Trajan and Hadrian), was a rhetorician who cultivated a mannered style, wedded that style to a profession of Stoic philosophy, and attempted also, besides being a stylist and a Stoic, to pursue the career of a politician. After holding various offices, he became first tutor and then minister to Nero, by whom he was eventually condemned to death on a charge of treason (A.D. 65), but allowed to face death voluntarily by the method of suicide, or *exagōgē*, which the principles of Stoicism allowed and even encouraged. Besides a number of probably early and certainly pompous tragedies (which nevertheless had a great vogue in the England of Queen Elizabeth I), he wrote a number of short semi-philosophical treatises, such as the *De Otio*, which justifies the action of a Stoic in retiring from public life, and the *De Clementia*, which was addressed to Nero, early in his reign, in praise of the magnanimity which Seneca expected him to show. He also wrote more than 100 letters to a friend called Lucilius, and these are the writings which—like Cicero's letters to Atticus—show the rhetorician and would-be philosopher in undress and at his best.

The contrast between Seneca's philosophy and his practice is striking, but it does not concern us here. His writings had a great vogue in later ages; indeed he came to be hailed as an *anima naturaliter Christiana*; and a supposed correspondence between him and St. Paul was current by the fourth century, and was long accepted as genuine. In fact he would appear to have been a professing but superficial Stoic (very different from Epictetus), who wrote for the sake of writing and more in order to attain rhetorical effects than because he had anything original to say. If 'style is the man', it may also be said that the man Seneca was only style—and style of the rhetorical, antithetical, glittering order which repels rather than attracts the taste of a later age.

1. *The two Commonwealths*

In a chapter of the *De Otio*, iv. 31, Seneca anticipates, though in a different vein, Christian thought on the two commonwealths, the *civitas Dei* and the *civitas humana* (see above, pp. 158–9, and below, pp. 421, 440–3).

'We must embrace in our mind the idea of two different commonwealths. One is the great and truly common society, which contains both gods and men; in it we are not confined to this or that angle of vision, and we measure the bounds of it only by the sun. The other is the society to which we are assigned by the circumstance of our birth: this will be Athens, or Carthage, or some other such city, which does not belong to all men, but only to a certain number. There are some of us who serve both commonwealths simultaneously, both the greater and the less: others serve only the less; others again only the greater. We can serve the greater commonwealth even in our time of leisure; indeed I wonder whether we cannot serve it even better in our leisure, by seeking to discover what virtue is, whether it is one or many, and whether nature or art does more to make men good. Is there only this one universe, embracing sea and land and all that therein is, or has God scattered broadcast many systems of the same order? Is the matter of which everything is made entirely continuous, and without any gap, or is it discrete, and is an empty void mixed with solid substance? Does God rest from His labour and simply contemplate His work, or does He direct it? Is He outside it, and diffused around it, or is He immanent in the whole of it? Is the world immortal, or is it to be counted among the things that are transitory and subject to time? If a man contemplates it, what service does he render to God? Is it the service of ensuring that all His great works are not without a witness?'

2. *On Philosophy and Civilization*

In the ninetieth of his letters to Lucilius, which is a *Protrepticus* or exhortation to philosophy, Seneca deals with the argument of Posidonius of Apamea (who had taught at Rhodes in the first century B.C.) that philosophy was the inventor of the arts of

civilization. He argues that it was mother-wit and chance, and
not philosophy, which found out useful inventions, and in this
he is at one with Lucretius (*supra*, p. 184); but he claims for
philosophy the discovery of true wisdom—wisdom in the sense
of an understanding of nature and human life and a grasp of
ultimate truth.

§ 3. 'Philosophy taught men to worship the divine and love
the human; it taught the sovereignty of the gods and the fellowship of men. That fellowship remained for a while intact, in the
days when avarice had not yet distracted society, or become the
cause of poverty even for those to whom it brought the maximum
of wealth—for men ceased to possess everything when once they
wanted to have private property of their own. § 4. But the earliest
men, and their descendants who, still unspoiled, followed the lead
of nature, had one and the same person both as their leader and
as the law of their life, [acting, as they did,] in obedience to
the will of some one of their betters who was entrusted with that
position; for it is Nature's way to subject the inferior to the
superior. Among animals the largest and strongest lead the rest...;
among men the best takes the place of the largest; a ruler was
accordingly chosen for his intelligence, and the greatest happiness
attended those nations among which a man could only have
power in proportion to his merit. It is safe for a man to have all
the power that he wants when he takes the view that he has only
power to do what he ought. § 5. Posidonius[1] holds that the wise
were kings in the days of what is called the Age of Gold [and that
they then exercised a benevolent sovereignty]. § 6. But when vice
crept in [Posidonius argues] and kingship was turned into tyranny,
laws began to be necessary; and these too were at first laid down
by the wise [such as Solon and Lycurgus, or Zaleucus and
Charondas the disciples of Pythagoras]. § 7. So far I agree with
Posidonius; but I cannot admit that the arts of daily life were
discovered by philosophy, nor would I claim for it the glory of
inventing architecture.' Seneca proceeds, at some length, to
rebuke the arts of luxury, which the true philosopher despises,
and to sing the praises of a simple life. He then puts, and seeks

---

[1] On Posidonius see below, pp. 281 ff.

to answer, the question, what philosophy has really done for man.

§ 34. 'Do you ask, What has the philosopher investigated, and what has he brought to light? I answer, First of all Truth and Nature, which philosophers did not follow, like the rest of animal creation, with eyes that were slow to recognize the essence of what is divine; then, next, the Law of Life, which philosophy made conformable with the order of the universe. The philosopher has taught men not only to know, but also to follow, the gods; he has taught them to accept the accidents of fortune as if they were commands. He has forbidden men to pay heed to false doctrines; he has weighed the worth of each object at its true value. He has condemned the pleasures that are mixed with remorse, and praised the good that will always please; he has made it plain that the happiest man is he who has no need of happiness, and the strongest is he who has himself under control. § 35. I am not speaking of that philosophy [the Epicurean] which would detach a citizen from his country, banish the gods from the world, and make virtue the slave of pleasure: I speak of that [the Stoic] which thinks nothing good but what is honourable, which cannot be tempted by the gifts of man or of fortune, and which has for its reward the gift of not being swayed by reward.'

Seneca ends by saying that philosophy comes late in time; it did not, therefore, exist in the early ages of the world—happy though they were in their simplicity, and good though they were in their ignorance of evil.

3. On Kingship

Seneca's treatise *De Clementia* was addressed to the Emperor Nero early in his reign. The idea of kingship expounded in it may be compared with the ideas of Pliny's *Panegyricus* (pp. 253 ff.) and Dio Chrysostom's *Discourses on Kingship*, both addressed to the Emperor Trajan (*circa* A.D. 100) (pp. 303 ff.).

(a) *The king as the breath* (spiritus) *of the Commonwealth* (*De Clementia* I. iii, § 5). 'Just as the whole of the body is the servant of the mind (*animus*) . . . so this innumerable multitude [of all the human race], which surrounds the life (*anima*) of one man, is ruled by his breath (*spiritus*) and swayed by his reason, and would crush and break itself, by its own force, if it were not sustained by his counsel. I. iv, § 1. . . . He is the bond by which the commonwealth is held together; the breath of life which is drawn upon by thousands and thousands who would be nothing but a burden and a prey if the mind of sovereign authority (*mens imperii*) were withdrawn. . . . § 3. . . . If public interests count more than private for men of good sense, it follows that the person into whose being the commonwealth has passed is also preferable to any other; for Caesar many years ago so cast his mantle over the commonwealth, that the one cannot be separated from the other without the destruction of both: he needs it, for the strength which it gives, and it needs him, to serve as its head.'

(*b*) *The king as a mirror of God* (ibid. I. vii, § 1). 'I have just made mention of the gods; and that reminds me that I shall do well to set up this rule as a standard to which the prince should conform— he should wish so to do to his subjects as he would that the gods should do to him. . . . viii, § 3. Herein consists the servitude of supreme greatness,[1] that it can never become any less; but this inescapable lot is one which you [Nero] share with the gods. The gods, too, are kept in bondage by the heaven which is their abode; and it is no more permitted to them to descend from their height than it is safe for you to descend from yours: you are tied to the pinnacle on which you stand. *Our* motions are noted by few: (§ 40) *we* can go in and out, and change our dress, without public observation; *you* can no more be hidden from view than the sun. There is an abundant light shed about you; the eyes of all are turned on you. Do you think that you can speak of "getting up"? No—you have a levée: you "rise" [like the sun].'

(*c*) *The good king as a father of his people.* Seneca draws a picture of the good king, in I. xiii, § 4, and then proceeds, at the beginning of the next chapter, to characterize him as essentially *paterfamilias*, or rather *pater patriae*. 'What, then, is his office and duty? It is that of the good parent, accustomed generally to admonish his

---

[1] The phrase is reminiscent of the saying of Antigonus Gonatas of Macedonia, a friend of the early Stoics, that kingship was a 'noble servitude' (see above, p. 83).

children—sometimes gently, and sometimes with threats—but
occasionally correcting them by physical punishment. . . . No
parent, however, resorts to the infliction of punishment until he
has employed all possible remedies. § 2. What a parent has to do
is equally the duty of a prince; and therefore we call him, with
genuine feeling and not in empty flattery, by the name of *Pater
patriae*. Other titles are granted merely in the way of honour: we
have called men *Magnus* [like Pompey], or *Felix* [like Sulla], or
Augustus, and by the gift of such names we have heaped every
title we could on greed for authority; but we have given the name
of *Pater patriae* only to those whom we wanted to know that they
were receiving *patria potestas*, which is, of all sorts of power, the
most tempered, directing all its efforts to the well-being of the
children of a family, and postponing its own interests to theirs.'

§ VII. TACITUS

Tacitus was born about A.D. 55, and died some time after 115. He
wrote a *Dialogus de Oratoribus* in his youth, during the reign of
Titus; later, under Nerva, he composed his *Agricola* (a life of his
father-in-law which deals largely with his career in Britain) and
a brief treatise *de Origine et Situ Germanorum*. He also wrote
Annals, from the death of Augustus in A.D. 14 down to the year 66,
and *Histories* (of which the later books are lost) covering the period
from A.D. 69 (the year of the accession of Vespasian) to the death
of Domitian in 96 .He wrote in a terse and brusque style, using,
as a rule, short hammer-like sentences, which have often an epigrammatic sting; he was a master of irony; and though he was
biased against the imperial system, he could also do justice to
its merits, his bias neither deflecting his search for historic truth
nor perverting the general justice of his judgement.

A. *On the State of the Roman Empire at the end of the first
century* A.D.

1. *The Internal Government of the Empire*

(a) *The difference between the history of the Roman Republic and that
of the Empire* (*Annals* iv. 32–34). '[The historians of the Republic]

described freely and discursively great wars, sieges of cities, and the rout and capture of kings; or—when they turned to domestic affairs—they narrated the struggles of consuls with tribunes, or the passage of agrarian and corn laws, or the struggles between the people and the nobility. My story is confined in scope and inglorious in character: the themes of it are peace, undisturbed or but little challenged; the sad fortunes of the capital; and emperors who had no interest in the extension of their empire. But there will, none the less, be some profit in investigating matters which, if at first sight they seem of small moment, are often the source from which movements of great magnitude take their origin.

'All nations and cities are governed by the people, or by an aristocracy, or by individuals: the form of State which is made by picking and choosing among these elements, and mixing them together, is more easily praised than brought into being; and if it comes into being it cannot long endure. At Rome, in the days when the people were in power, or the nobles held sway, it was at one time necessary to study the character of the masses and the methods by which they might be discreetly controlled, and, in much the same way [at another time when the nobles were in power], credit for understanding their age and for wisdom was given to those who had acquainted themselves best with the temper of the Senate and its leading men. Today the situation is changed, and Rome is a virtual monarchy; but it may still be useful to collect and to chronicle facts since it is only a few who can distinguish for themselves what is prudent and honourable from what is discreditable, or again what is useful from what is hurtful, and the majority of men learn only from the experiences of others. But if the record may thus be of service, it can give only a minimum of pleasure. [The themes of the older historians, such as] the geography of different countries, the vicissitudes of battles, or the notable deaths of great men, attract and refresh the mind of the reader; we merely string together a story of savage edicts, perpetual accusations, treacherous friendships, the ruin of the innocent, and other and similar causes resulting in a similar destruction. . . .'

(b) *The loss of freedom of thought under the Empire (Agricola,*

c. 2–c. 3). 'Not only writers, but also their books, were lately
the objects of savage attack; and the police were charged with
the duty of burning the writings of the best minds of the day. Our
rulers thought by that fire to stifle and quench the voice of the
Roman people, the liberty of the Senate, and the moral sense of
mankind; and over and above their proscription of books, they
expelled the teachers of philosophy and drove every liberal art
into exile, so that no vestige of things honourable should be left
for men to see. We certainly gave a great proof of our patience
while this was being done; if a previous age had witnessed how far
liberty could go, *we* learned to know, when legal inquisitions
deprived us of the power of freely exchanging ideas, to what
length servitude could be carried. We might have lost our very
memories along with our voices, if we had been able to forget as
readily as we are able to keep silence. 3. Today [i.e. with the turn
of affairs about A.D. 100] we are recovering at last our old spirit.
But though the Emperor Nerva, in the very beginning of this
most happy age, immediately joined together what had before
been kept asunder, empire and liberty (*imperium et libertas*), and
though his successor Trajan is now daily occupied in augmenting
the felicity of our times, . . . the weakness of human nature is such
that remedies produce their effects more slowly than diseases. As
our bodies are slow to grow, but quick to perish, so it is with our
minds and their interests: you can repress them more easily than
you can renew them; and besides, there is a charm in indolence
itself which soon makes itself felt and turns the doing of nothing,
which we began by loathing, into a state of which we are fond.'

2. *The External Policy of the Empire*

(*a*) *The indictment of Roman imperialism by Calgacus, the Cale-
donian chieftain*. 'Whenever I reflect on the causes of this war and
on our perils, I have high hopes that this hour and your present
unity will be the beginning of liberty for all Britain. We are all
still untouched by slavery; there are no more lands beyond us;
even the sea has ceased to be safe now that we are threatened by
the Roman navy; battle and arms, which bring honour to the
brave, are now also the best way of safety for the coward. Former

battles, in which men fought against Rome with various degrees of success, left hope and the chance of succour still in the grasp of our hands; we were the noblest tribe in all Britain, we lived in its innermost sanctuary, we had no country of slavery present to our view, and we had thus kept even our eyes inviolate and free from contact with tyranny. Standing on the edge of the world and liberty, we have been sheltered till this day by being remote and hidden from notoriety; for the unknown is always exaggerated. But today the utmost extremity of Britain stands revealed to the view: there is no nation beyond us; there is nothing at all but seas and rocks and, what is more deadly still, the Romans, whose arrogance it were in vain to shun by obedience and moderation. They are the world's great robbers; when there is no more land left to devastate, they search the seas; they are greedy for money when their enemy is rich, and avid for glory when he is poor; neither East nor West can glut their appetite; they are unique among all peoples in coveting the goods both of rich and of poor with an equal passion of greed. Plunder, butchery, and theft they miscall by the name of "empire", and where they make a solitude, they give it the name of peace' (*Agricola*, c. 30).

(*b*) *The defence of Rome and her Empire in a speech made to the Gauls by the legate Cerialis at Trier* (*Histories*, iv. 74). 'There were always rival kings and wars in Gaul until you came under our authority. We, though we were often provoked by you, only used the right of victory to put one burden upon you, by which we could maintain peace; there can be no peace among the nations without arms, no arms without pay, and no pay without taxes; but everything else, apart from what you thus pay, belongs to the common stock. You yourselves often command our legions; you yourselves govern these and other provinces; we keep nothing separate or exclusive to ourselves. . . . Suppose, which God forbid, that the Romans were driven out, what would be the result but wars of all nations with one another? This structure has been welded together by the good luck and the experience of eight hundred years; it cannot be pulled down except at the cost of ruin for those who pull it down; and your danger will then be the greatest, because you have gold and wealth, which are the principal causes of war. I would bid you, therefore, to love and cherish peace, and to love and cherish the city to which both of us—vanquished and victors alike—belong on an equal footing. I bid you be warned, by the examples before you of both of these different fortunes, not to prefer defiance, with its attendant destruction, to obedience with its companion security.'

B. *On German Liberty as contrasted with Roman Slavery*

Tacitus gives some account of the character and polity of the Jews (*Histories*, v, cc. 5, 8), and alludes, though only briefly, to the Christians (*Annals*, xv, c. 44). To the Germans he devoted a whole pamphlet, mainly (it would seem) in order to damn Rome by praising her chief enemy in Europe. In it he dwells on the native virtues and unexhausted strength of a people which he depicts as Arcadian in its simplicity and the pastoral purity of its life. He lauds the Teutonic tribes as so many 'nature-peoples', superior, as such, to the sophisticated and degenerate Romans; he regards them as almost invincible (*tam diu Germania vincitur*) and as a pattern of primitive liberty. Some of the characteristics on which he particularly dwells are the following:

(*a*) *Purity of Race* (c. 4). 'I agree with the view of those who hold that the peoples of Germany, unmixed as they are by marriage with any other nation, form a race (*gens*) which is peculiar, pure, and unique. This explains why their physical structure, in spite of their numbers and their diffusion, is everywhere the same.'

(*b*) *Courage* (c. 6, *ad finem*). 'To yield ground for the moment, provided that you return to the attack, is regarded by them as a mark of policy rather than of panic. They bring off the bodies of their comrades even when the fortunes of battle are dubious; they think it the greatest of crimes for a man to throw away his shield; and anyone thus disgraced may not attend a religious rite or be present at a council meeting. Many who have survived a battle have hung themselves to escape the ignominy from which they suffer.'

(*c*) *The position of women*. c. 8. 'Tradition tells how women, who stand behind their menfolk in battle, have restored a broken and wavering line by their perseverance in prayer and by throwing themselves in the path of the enemy. . . . The men believe that there is something holy, and some gift of foresight, in women; they do not despise the counsels they offer or leave unheeded the oracles which they give.' c. 18. When a marriage takes place, the husband gives the wife a horse with bit and bridle, a shield, a spear, and a sword: she, in return, gives him some kind of arms. 'Thus in the very beginning of marriage, and in order to prevent her from thinking herself beyond any idea of military duty or the chances of war, the wife is warned that she comes to share her husband's toils and perils, and to dare and endure the same risks, both in peace and in war. [That is the meaning of the mutual exchange of arms]: these are the terms on which she must live and die. She must hand on what she receives at her marriage untarnished and unblemished to her children, or deliver it to her son's wife to pass on to her grandchildren.'

(d) *Political institutions*, c. 11. 'Less important matters are discussed by their chieftains: issues of importance come before the whole tribe; but the chieftains discuss in advance the questions which are left to the final decision of the people. . . .' It may take two or three days to get an assembly together: that is a defect of their liberty. 'In their assemblies the king, or a chieftain, beigns the discussion; speakers gain a hearing according to their age, rank, military renown, or eloquence; the issue depends on power of persuasion rather than on the right to command. If a motion displeases the meeting, it is greeted with a shout of disapproval; if it is to their liking, the people clash their spears; the applause that carries most honour is the applause by arms.' This picture of pure and primitive liberty is qualified, a little later, by the account which Tacitus gives of a sort of feudal aristocracy, in the shape of the chieftain's following, or 'tail' (*comitatus*). c. 13. 'Young men of family enlist in the company of stalwart and proved warriors, and there is nothing to be ashamed of in being a follower. The following, too, has its own hierarchy, determined by the judgement of its head; there is a keen rivalry among the men, who shall stand first with the chief, as there is also rivalry among the chiefs, which shall have the most and best followers. Dignity and power consist in being always surrounded by a large circle of picked youth; and this brings a chieftain honour in peace as well as a body-guard in war. The name and renown of a chieftain, in neighbouring states as well as in his own tribe, depend on the eminence of his following in point of numbers and valour: those who are outstanding are sought out by embassies and courted with gifts, and they often determine the issue of a war by the simple fact of their reputation.'

(e) *Social life and habits*, c. 16 (*On Housing*). 'It is well known that the peoples of Germany do not live in cities, and will not even tolerate settlements of adjacent houses. They live in scattered and separate habitations, as a spring or field or grove takes their fancy. They do not lay out their villages as we do, in a row of contiguous buildings: each man surrounds his house with some sort of open space, whether as a safeguard against fire or from ignorance of the art of building. c. 26 (*On Agriculture*). They take up land for ploughing in [family or village?] groups, and they take as much of it as they can find labour to cultivate; they then divide it up on the basis of each man's standing, and the amount of ground available makes the division easy. They change their plough-lands every year, and yet there is land left over.' But just as a sort of feudal aristocracy is joined to democracy in the account of political institutions, so a sort of medieval serfdom is united with an economy of free cultivators in the account of social institutions. c. 25. 'The unfree [other than those who are the victims of gambling and who are bought and sold as chattels] are not employed in our fashion as household slaves with different domestic duties: each of them has his own plot and each is master of his own hearth. The master of these serfs requires them, as we do tenant-farmers [*coloni*], to render so much corn or cattle or clothing, and this is the extent of their obligation; whatever else is needed in the master's house is done by his wife and children.'

C. *On the Connexion between Good Oratory and Political Liberty*

The *Dialogus de Oratoribus*, which scholars are now agreed in ascribing to Tacitus, is probably an early work (about A.D. 80), and is notable for its argument that republican liberty was the only nursing-mother of good oratory and literature. The same argument is repeated in c. 44 of the Greek treatise *On the Sublime*, once attributed to a writer called Longinus (the counsellor of Zenobia), of the third century A.D., but now generally ascribed to an unknown author of the same age as Tacitus.

Dialogus de Oratoribus, c. 1. *The question at issue.* 'The question is often asked . . . why former ages were distinguished by the talents and the fame of so many great orators, while our own age is so utterly destitute and empty of all renown for oratory that it has almost ceased to use even the name of orator. Today we give the name only to the ancients; the men of our own time with a gift of speech are called pleaders, barristers, counsellors, or anything else rather than orators.' The same question is raised, almost in the same terms, at the end of the treatise *On the Sublime*; see p. 247 below.

cc. 36–41. *The answer to the question.* 'Great oratory is like a fire: it must have fuel to feed it; it is fanned by motion; and it glows the more brightly the more it burns. The same sort of cause was responsible for the oratory of the past in our country. It is true that the orators of our own time have attained the success which could fairly be expected in a tranquil, placid, and happy state of political life; but it is also true that the men of an earlier generation were stimulated to greater heights by the tumult and licence among which they lived, in days when there was a general jostle of competition with no one man in control, and each orator showed as much judgement as he could persuade a vacillating people to tolerate. . . . Oratory, and oratory only, brought the highest of rewards; [in the popular assembly, the Senate, and the law-courts;] it was also highly necessary and it was then as fine and glorious a thing to be reckoned eloquent as it was a disgrace to show oneself dumb and speechless.

c. 37. '. . . There was a splendour in the very crimes, and a magnitude of the cases tried, which gave a great impetus to eloquence; and indeed it makes a great difference whether the matter in question is merely one of theft or contract or an injunction, or a greater matter such as bribery at an election, or the fleecing of allies of the State and the murder of citizens. True, it is better that such cases should never occur, and the best form of government is one in which none of us suffer any such risks; but it is also true that, when they do occur, they afford a rich material for eloquence. . . . The more frequently that oratory stands, as it were, in the line of battle; the more numerous the blows which it inflicts and receives; the greater the adversaries and the hotter the struggle on which it ventures—the higher and loftier, and the more observed for the risks incurred, is the role which it plays in the public gaze; for it is the nature of us all to enjoy seeing others in peril while we are ourselves in security.

c. 38. '. . . By the middle of the reign of Augustus eloquence itself, like everything else, had been "pacified" by a long period of quiet, by the continuous inaction of the popular assemblies, by the persistent tranquillity of the Senate, and also—and above all else—by the discipline imposed by the prince. c. 39. . . . But spirited horses are tested by the racecourse and long gallops; and similarly there is a field for the orator on which he must have a free and unfettered run if his eloquence is not to be weakened and hampered. . . . Nowadays only one or two persons are present at a speech, and the business is done in a sort of solitude; but an orator needs hubbub and applause, and the presence of some sort of a gallery, which is just what the orators of the past enjoyed every day. . . . c. 40. . . . Eloquence which is great and notable is a pupil of the licence which fools call liberty; it is the companion of civil commotions, and the spur of an unbridled people; it is without deference, and without veracity; it is contumacious, full of temerity, and arrogant; and these are defects which are not to be found in well-ordered states.[1] . . . Our own State, as long as it strayed from the way [in the days of the Republic], and while it ruined itself by the strife of parties and in dissension and discord, with no peace in the forum and no harmony in the Senate, . . . doubtless produced more vigorous eloquence, just as an untilled field produces plants of a richer growth. But the eloquence of the Gracchi [after all] was not of so much value to the State that the

---

[1] It is possible to suspect some irony in the whole of this statement, which seems to damn what it really seeks to praise.

State could tolerate the laws which they advocated; and the fame of Cicero's eloquence was not great enough to compensate him for the death he died.'

c. 41. The conclusion reached by Tacitus is a sort of 'trimmer's' balance between the Republic and the Empire: each has its merits and its defects: 'let each enjoy the benefit of its own age without criticism of the other'. 'There is less scope . . . for medicine in a country whose inhabitants have robust health; and oratory has less honour and a darker prospect of renown in a country where men's dispositions are good and prepared to respect authority. What need is there for long speeches in the Senate, when the best minds in it are quick to agree? What need is there for many orations in popular assemblies, when deliberations on matters of state are conducted not by the ignorant and the crowd, but by perfect wisdom and a single mind?'[1]

The end of the anonymous treatise *On the Sublime* offers a close analogy to the argument of Tacitus, and is probably of the same date, as it certainly shows the same temper.

c. 44, § 1. 'A philosopher has recently raised this question "It astonishes me", he writes, "as no doubt it also does many others, why it is that our age produces a type of men with great powers of persuasion and political gifts, men of keen and eager temper and peculiarly rich in the charms of speech, and yet cannot produce, except very rarely, types of a truly sublime and eminent eloquence: so general, and indeed universal, is the dearth of oratory which marks our age. § 2. Must we", he exclaims, "put our trust in the reason commonly given, that democracy is a good nursing-mother of great men, and that fine oratory has, as a rule, risen and decayed only with its rise and decay?" It is the claim of liberty that, wherever it is given enough scope, it has nourished the spirit of lofty characters, inspired men with hope, and promoted the diffusion of a zest of mutual competition and common ambition for the prizes of public life. § 3. Nor is that all: the rewards open to all in a constitutional system of government give exercise and an edge to the mental qualities of orators;

---

[1] Here again it is possible to suspect some irony in the argument.

they keep them from rusting; they make them, as you would naturally expect, shine out freely in sympathy with the freedom of actual life. Nowadays, however, we seem as if we were children schooled to a just servitude; children (as one may almost say) kept in the swaddling-bands of custom and habit from their tenderest years; children who have never tasted that finest and most fertile source of eloquence, liberty. And what is the result? Why, that we come out at the end of it all as nothing but first-rate flatterers. . . . § 5. 'The day of slavery', as Homer says, 'takes away half of a man's spirit.' Our position today may be compared with that of the pygmies or dwarfs, who, if what I hear is true, are kept in cages that not only stop the growth of the prisoners but even thin them down through the pressure of the bars on their bodies. This is why one of our writers has called any form of servitude, even at its best and justest, 'the cage of the soul and the common gaol'."

In the concluding sections of c. 44 (§§ 6–11) the anonymous author of *On the Sublime* answers, or seeks to answer, the argument of the critical philosopher by turning from politics to morals, and by arguing that it is not the absence of political liberty but the presence of moral defects—the love of money and the love of pleasure—which prevents the rise of great orators and 'sublime' oratory. § 6. 'It is easy [that argument runs] and a natural instinct of us all, to blame the age we live in. But may it not be the case that it is not the peace now enjoyed by the Universe (the *oikoumenē*) which ruins fine characters? Is not their ruin rather the result of the ruthless war that grips our passions? Is it not the fruit of the sinful affections that are like a garrison [of mercenary troops] occupying the society of our days and putting it utterly to plunder? The love of money and the love of pleasure are the tyrants that enslave us . . . . § 10. It may even be better for men such as we are to be governed by others rather to enjoy liberty; for our appetites, if they were let loose, would be just like beasts liberated from their den, and they would set the world on fire with the evils which they caused.'

Here again, as at the close of the *Dialogus* of Tacitus, the end of the argument is a sort of 'trimmer's' balance. But the final remarks of the anonymous author seem like a formal offering on the altar of imperial peace, and perhaps he is not intending any real palinode to his previous hymn of liberty as the mother of true eloquence.

§ VIII. PLINY THE YOUNGER

A. *The Christian Church and the Roman Empire in the Time of the Emperor Trajan* (circa A.D. 112)

The younger Pliny (*circa* A.D. 60–114), as governor of Bithynia, was concerned with the legal problem of the position of Christian 'non-conformists' who dissented from the established system of worship of the Emperor. Was such dissent disloyalty, and as such a crime against the community of the Roman name, which recognized the Emperor as the cement and symbol of its unity and expressed that recognition by 'supplication to his image'?[1] If it was, in its nature, a crime, how was the fact of the crime to be ascertained; what was the general legal procedure to be followed; what, in a word, was to be the legal action of the government in dealing with the Christian dissident? Pliny put these problems to Trajan in a letter (book x of his *Epistles*, 96), and received a brief answer from the Emperor (ibid. 97), which, if it solved some of the problems, still left a large margin of doubt. (See H. Lietzmann, *The Founding of the Church Universal*, Eng. trans., pp. 156–7.)

x. 96. 'It is my habit to refer to you, Sire, all matters on which I am in doubt. Who can better guide my hesitation or instruct my ignorance? I have never been present at the hearing of legal cases concerned with Christians; and I am therefore ignorant of what it is that is usually punished or investigated, and to what extent this is done. I have hesitated greatly about several problems. Is there any distinction to be made on the ground of age, or are

---

[1] It is a question still debated by historians whether the *nomen Christianum* was in itself a crime which involved the legal consequence of punishment. A reference in Tertullian (*Ad Nationes*, I. 7) to an *Institutum Neronianum* has been interpreted to mean that there was a legal rule to this effect from the days of Nero onwards. But the interpretation is dubious; and it is more likely that the *nomen Christianum* created a presumption of guilt, but was not in itself a proof of guilt without further evidence. See the *Journal of Theological Studies*, N.S. iii, 1952, pp. 199–213.

even the youngest to be dealt with in just the same way as the older? Is pardon to be granted to repentance, or does a man who has once been a Christian derive no benefit from having ceased to be one? Is the name of Christian itself to be punished, even if it is not attended by any crime, or is it the crimes that go with the name that are to be punished?

'Meanwhile, and for the time being, this is the line which I have followed in dealing with persons who were brought before me as Christians. I have asked them, "Are you Christians?" If they confessed that they were, I have asked them the question a second and a third time, threatening them as I did so with punishment; and then, if they persisted in their confession, I have ordered them to be taken away [for punishment]. I had no doubt in my mind that—apart from their belief, and whatever it might be—such inflexible pertinacity and obstinacy ought in any case to be punished. There were also others who showed a similar folly, but whom, as they were Roman citizens, I remitted for trial in Rome.

'Eventually, as the proceedings continued, and the range of offences, as usually happens, grew wider, a number of different problems arose. An anonymous list was put before me which contained the names of many persons who denied that they were or had been Christians, and who, repeating the words I dictated to them, invoked the gods, made their supplication . . . to your image (which I had ordered to be brought into court for the purpose along with the statues of the deities), and cursed the name of Christ; none of which things, I am told, any real Christian can be made to do. I therefore thought that these persons ought to be acquitted. Others, who had been named by an informer, first said that they were Christians and then denied that they were; they *had* been, they said, but they had ceased to be—some of them three years back, some of them many years ago, and some even as far back as twenty years. All of them venerated your image and the statues of the gods; and they, too, cursed the name of Christ. They stated that the whole of their fault, or error, had consisted in their habit of meeting before dawn on an appointed day, and singing in turn among themselves a hymn to Christ as their God; they had also bound themselves by oath not to the commission of any crime, but to refrain from theft or larceny or adultery, from any breach of faith, and from refusing to acknowledge a debt to a creditor; after which it was their habit to depart and then to meet again for the purpose of taking food—but food of an ordinary sort and an innocent character;[1] but they had ceased to do even this after the issue of the edict in which, acting under your instructions, I had forbidden the meetings of religious fraternities. This made me think it all the more necessary to discover what truth there was in their statement, and I even used torture for the purpose on two of their serving maids, called deaconesses (*ministrae*), but I found no evidence of anything except a mean and extravagant superstition, and so I postponed the hearing of the case and proceeded at once to consult you.

'The matter seemed to me to be important enough for such consultation, especially in view of the number of the persons who were involved. There are many of all ages and every rank, and also of both sexes, who already are, or will be, implicated. The contagion of the superstition has spread not only in cities, but also through villages and the country-side; and yet it still seems possible to arrest and correct it. Certainly it is a fact that the temples, which had been almost deserted, have begun to be attended again, and that the regular services, which had not been held for a long time, are being revived; animals for sacrifice, which had previously found very few purchasers, are now on sale in abundance. This makes it easy to guess what a number of persons can be brought back to the right path if the way is eased for repentance.'

97. *Trajan to Pliny.* 'You have followed, my dear Pliny, the right line of action in trying the cases of the Christians who had been brought before you. No general rule can be laid down in any definite terms. Christians are not to be sought out; if they are brought into court and found guilty, they are to be punished— but with this reservation, that any person who has denied that he is a Christian, and has given actual proof by making supplication to our gods, should be pardoned as a penitent even if he is under suspicion in regard to the past. Anonymous lists ought not to be

---

[1] The Christians were accused by their enemies of 'Thyestean banquets' and other enormities in their gatherings.

regarded in dealing with any offence: they are the worst of precedents, and they do not agree with the spirit of our age.'

Note. The policy of Rome in dealing with Christians and Christian churches finds some sort of parallel in the Roman attitude to secular associations (*collegia*). They were suspect as leading to faction and involving political consequences. (The cities of the Greek East had long suffered from the action of clubs, or *synōmosiai*, and the factions which they caused—see above, pp. 60, 61—and the Roman emperors had the experience of the past to warn them of the dangers of such combinations.) The correspondence of Pliny and Trajan on the issue of instituting—or forbidding—a fire-brigade in Nicomedia, a city in Pliny's province of Bithynia, is significant of this fear.

Pliny to Trajan (Pliny's *Letters*, x. 33). 'When I was touring another part of the province, a widespread fire destroyed many private houses and two public buildings . . . in Nicomedia. It spread far and wide, mainly owing to the strength of the wind, but also through the indolence of the inhabitants, who, it is plain, remained unconcerned and inactive spectators of the disaster. Apart from that, there were no pumps in any public place, no hooks, nor any other means of keeping fires under. These will now be installed, and I have already given orders to that effect. Will you, Sire, consider whether you think that a union of workers (a *collegium fabrorum* or fire-brigade) should be instituted, with a staff of at least 150? I will see to it that no person other than a fireman (*faber*) should be admitted to the brigade, and that the right [of association] granted to them should not be used for any other purpose. It will not be difficult to supervise so small a body.'

Trajan to Pliny (ibid. 34). 'You have had the idea, for which there are many precedents, that a union of workers could be instituted at Nicomedia. But we have to remember that your province, and especially cities such as Nicomedia, have been troubled by factious societies of this sort. Whatever name we give to a body of persons leagued together as a unit, and on whatever ground we give it, they will become fraternities (*hetaeriae* or clubs), even if their numbers are small. It is enough for your purpose that the materials should be provided which may be of help in keeping fires under; that owners of property should be warned to prevent fires by their own action; and that, if occasion demands, the people at large should be called upon for help.'

B. *The* Panegyric *of Pliny on the Emperor* Trajan (circa A.D. 100)

(a) *The blessings brought to the Provinces by the Emperor's Rule.*
c. 32. 'How good it is that all the provinces should have come into
our custody, and under our sway, after we had been granted a
prince who shifts about the fertility of the soil (now encouraging
it in one place and now in another), as time and its needs demand;
a prince who nourishes and protects a nation cut off from Rome
by the sea as carefully as if it were a part of the Roman people and
the populace (*plebs*) of Rome. The very skies have never before
been so auspicious that they have ripened and blessed the crops of
all countries simultaneously; from all alike the Emperor banishes
at least the evils of sterility, if not sterility itself, and if he does not
bring them fertility, at any rate he brings them its benefits; he
connects East and West so closely by mutual commerce that all
nations can learn from one another what exports each can offer
and what imports each of them needs, and can thus come to
understand how much it is to the advantage of those who have
served the cause of a divided and distracted liberty to have in its
place a single person to whom they can pay their services.[1] When
all men's goods are several, each has his misfortunes visited on his
own head; but when men's goods are pooled and united, the misfortunes of an individual do not fall particularly upon any person,
while the gains of all accrue equally to all. But if there be some
divinity in the soil, and some spirit dwelling in the rivers, I offer
my supplication both to land and to water that they may rest
content with the prince's generosity, and I pray that the land may
lodge in its gentle bosom the seed entrusted to it and give it back
many fold. We do not demand interest; but may the soil feel,
none the less, that interest ought to be paid, and may it make good
the deceitful promise of one year by the performance of all years
and ages to come—the more as we make no demand.'

(b) *The example set by Trajan and the subject's duty of imitation.*
c. 44. 'How good it is that you [our Prince] should have come
through adversity to the enjoyment of prosperity. You have lived

---

[1] The economic argument for empire put forward in this passage is similar to
that which Tacitus reports Tiberius as using in a letter to the Senate (*Annals* III,
c. 54; see above, p. 231).

among us; you have run risks; you have known fear; you have
had the experiences which then fell to the lot of all who were
innocent. You know, and you have felt for yourself, how much
bad rulers are detested even by the very persons who make them
bad. You remember what you used to wish along with the rest
of us, and what complaints you used to make. Now you play
the part of a prince with the mind and judgement of a private
person; and indeed you show yourself better to us than you
prayed that another might be to you. The result of it all upon
our minds is that, from being in a state in which our utmost
prayer was for a prince something better than the worst, we have
swung round to a state in which we can bear only the best; and
so there is now no man so ignorant of what you are, and of what
he is himself, that he desires to have your office after you are gone.
Indeed it is easier for a man to be capable of being your successor
than it is for him to desire to be such. Who would willingly take
on himself the burden of your responsibility? Who would not
shrink from comparison with you? You have experienced in
your own person the difficulty of succeeding to a good prince—
and you had the advantage of being [Nerva's] adopted son. Is it a
small thing, or a thing which is easy of emulation, that nobody
now pays the price of security by the loss of honour, or that life
and its dignity are now everywhere safe, and men need no longer
live in hiding before they can be counted prudent and wise?
Clearly the same rewards attend the virtuous, under the government of a prince, as they enjoyed in the days of republican liberty,
nor is the approval of conscience any longer the one reward of
good service. . . .

c. 45. 'Former princes, with the exception of your father [Nerva]
and one or two others—but here I have said too much—took
more pleasure in the vices of their fellow-citizens than they did
in their virtues; in part because men in general like to see their
own character reflected in others, and in part because these princes
believed that the men who would most readily tolerate servitude
would be those for whom nothing but servitude was proper.
Accordingly they poured all their favours into the lap of men of
this stamp, while good men were left hidden in a tomb of neglect

and retirement, and were only brought into the light of day when informations were laid against them and they had to encounter perils. You [my prince] draw your friends from the best, and indeed it is meet and right that a good prince should hold in the highest regard the men whom a bad prince has most disliked. You know the gulf fixed between a prince and a tyrant, and how, because of that gulf, a prince has no stronger supporters than those who most strongly resent a tyrant. It is men of that stamp whom you promote to honour and exhibit to the world as types and examples of the mode of life and the sort of men that please you; and this is the reason why you have not yet taken upon you the office of censor, or the duty of a control of morals, preferring to test our tempers by the effect of the rewards you give rather than by the results of the remedies you apply.

'Besides, I hardly know whether a prince who permits men to be good does not render a greater service to morals than one who compels them to be so. Malleable as we are, we can be led in any direction by a prince, and we become, so to speak, his shadows. We want him to like us and to approve of us—a favour which those who are unlike him must vainly hope to gain; and we thus arrive by perseverance in doing our duty at a consummation which means that almost all of us live by one man's moral standard. Nor is the world so much out of joint, that we should be able to imitate a bad prince and yet be unable to imitate one who is good. Go forward, then, Caesar; thy purpose and thy deeds will have all the force and effect that the assumption of censorship could possibly have; the way in which a prince lives is itself a censorship, and a standing censorship at that; we are guided by it and converted by it; we need the giving of an example more than the exercise of authority. Fear is a teacher of Right who cannot be trusted: men learn more from examples than they do from terrors; for examples have this merit above all else—they prove that what they command to be done *can* actually be done.[1]

(c) *Trajan's justice, which makes him a Jove upon earth. c. 80.*
'Whenever you sit in judgement, you show a severity which is

---

[1] The whole doctrine of 'imitation of the prince' here set forth finds a parallel in the doctrine of the neo-Pythagorean 'Ecphantus'; see below, pp. 370-1.

yet gentle, and a clemency which is yet free from laxity. You do not make it your business to enrich the treasury; and the one reward of your decisions is the reward of being a good judge. Litigants as they stand before you are less concerned about their own fortune than they are about your opinion of them; and they fear more your view of their character than they do your view of their case. Oh, it is truly the office of a prince, and even of a god, to reconcile jealous states; to keep proud peoples in order, more by the use of reason than by the exercise of authority; to intervene when officials go wrong, and to undo what ought not to have been done; and finally, in a word, to be like the swiftest of stars, seeing all things, hearing all things, and—from whatever quarter the call may come—always ready, like a god, to act as a present help and comforter. Such, I cannot but believe, is the way in which the Father of the world governs it by His nod, when He lowers His gaze to the earth and deigns to number the fortunes of mortal men among the divine works of His hands; but now, in that field of our human fortunes, He is free from care and engagement, ever since He granted you to the world, to be his vicegerent in dealing with all mankind, and could give His time only to heaven. For indeed you are His vicegerent, and a full and complete satisfaction to Him who is your principal, when all your days are spent to our greatest possible benefit and your own greatest possible praise.'

Note. Pliny's *Panegyricus* is one of the first of the 'Mirrors' or 'Dials' of Princes which became common in succeeding generations of classical antiquity and were afterwards to acquire a modern vogue during the revival of classical letters in the sixteenth century of our era. Dio of Prusa was delivering his four discourses on Kingship in honour of Trajan about the time when Pliny was writing (see below, p. 303); neo-Pythagoreans, such as Diotogenes and 'Ecphantus', took up the tale (below, pp. 361 ff.); and Eusebius with the Christian writers of his time echoes the strain in his *Laus Constantini* (below, p. 477). Later, in the sixteenth century, Erasmus, Machiavelli, Sir Thomas Elyot (in his *Book of the Governor*), and the Spaniards Vives and de Guevara (the latter in his 'Dial of Princes') all hail and depict the 'new Prince' of their times.

§ IX. SOCIAL AND POLITICAL IDEAS OF THE ROMAN
JURISTS OF THE SECOND AND THIRD CENTURIES A.D.

(*especially Gaius*, circa A.D. 160, *and Ulpian*, circa A.D. 220)

For some account of the Roman jurists of these centuries see the introduction to this Part, pp. 170–2.

A. *The General View of the Nature of Law* (Jus[1])

1. *The View of Gaius* (*Institutes*, i. 1, §§ 1–7)

§ 1. 'All peoples which are governed by statutes (*leges*) and by customs partly use their own peculiar law, and partly the law which is common to all mankind. The law laid down by each people for its own members is peculiar to itself, and is called "civil law" (*jus civile*), i.e. the law peculiar to a given city; the law laid down by natural reason for all men is observed among all peoples alike and is called *jus gentium* or the law used by all nations.[2] So the Roman people [in common with all other peoples] partly uses its own peculiar law, and partly the law common to all mankind. . . .

§ 2. 'The law of the Roman people consists of the following kinds of rules: statutes; plebiscites; senatusconsults;[3] constitutions of the emperors; the edicts of such magistrates as have authority to issue edicts; and the answers given by jurists to questions submitted to them.

§ 3. 'A statute is a rule issued and laid down by the people (*populus*): a plebiscite is a rule issued and laid down by the *plebs*. The *plebs* differs from the people in the fact that the term "people" signifies *all* citizens, including the patricians, while the term

---

[1] *Jus* is 'law' in the broad sense of *all* the legal rules (however made) which are recognized and enforced by courts of law. *Lex* is one sort of legal rule—a statutory rule made by the people in its capacity of 'legislature' or statute-making authority.

[2] Gaius uses three terms—*populus*, *civitas*, and *gens*. The two former are much the same: a *civitas* is a *populus* organized as a city-state. The term *gens* is wider: it will include kingdoms and tribes as well as city-states.

[3] For the period in which Gaius wrote—the latter half of the second century A.D.—this is a statement of form rather than a record of fact. Statutes and plebiscites ceased from the second half of the reign of Tiberius. The form of senatusconsults was used by the emperors, as a convenient cover for what were really imperial decrees, down to the time at which Gaius wrote; but the form was dropped after the turn of the second century, and the *constitutiones principum* became the one mode of legislation.

plebs signifies the rest of the citizens other than the patricians. The result of this was, in the past, that the patricians held that they were not bound by plebiscites, because these acts had been passed without any authority from them; but a statute called the *Lex Hortensia* was afterwards enacted, which provided that plebiscites should bind the whole people; and thus plebiscites were placed on a level with statutes.

§ 4. 'A senatusconsult is a rule issued and laid down by the senate; and such a rule has the force of a statute, though this point has been disputed.

§ 5. 'A *constitutio principis* is a rule laid down by the Emperor in the form of a decree, an edict, or a letter; and there has never been any doubt that such a rule has the force of law, since it is by virtue of a law [or statute] that the Emperor himself receives his authority (*imperium*).[1]

§ 6. 'Authority to issue edicts is possessed by the magistrates of the Roman people; but the authority attains its highest point, first, in the edicts of the two praetors, the "Home" and the "Foreign", whose jurisdiction in the provinces is exercised by the provincial governors, and secondly, and similarly, in the edicts of the curule aediles, whose jurisdiction in the provinces of the Roman people is exercised by the quaestors. But in the provinces of the Emperor[2] no quaestors at all are sent out, and the edict of the aediles is accordingly not published in these provinces.

§ 7. 'The answers given by jurists are the decisions and opinions of persons permitted to pronounce on the law (*jura condere*). If their opinions agree, the opinion they give has the force of law; if they disagree, the judge who decides the case may follow the opinion which he prefers . . ..'

It is plain from § 1 of the passage translated above that Gaius regards *jus* as twofold, and not, like Ulpian (see below, p. 260), as threefold. In other words, he recognizes only *jus gentium* and *ius civile*, and he has no place, as Ulpian has, for a third sort of

---

[1] See the passage cited from Ulpian below, p. 262.

[2] From the time of Augustus there was a division between imperial provinces, reserved for the emperor, and the senatorial provinces (or 'provinces of the Roman people'), which the Senate was supposed to administer.

jus called *jus naturale*. To Gaius *jus gentium* was not only the law used by all nations, i.e. a universal law; it was also, in the same breath, a law dictated by natural reason, and therefore natural or valid in itself apart from any question of its general use. A quotation from Gaius in the *Digest* of Justinian (xli. 1. 1) suggests that he had the further idea that *jus gentium* was primitive, as well as being universal and the product of natural reason. 'We acquire property in some things by the *jus gentium*, which is observed among all men alike, by virtue of natural reason; and in other things by the *jus civile*, that is to say the law peculiar to our State. Inasmuch, therefore, as the law of nations came into being at an earlier date and is coeval with mankind itself, we must treat of this law first.'

2. *The View of Ulpian* (as recorded in passages of the *Institutes* and the *Digest* of Justinian)[1]

1. 'Justice is a constant and perpetual wish to give each man his due.

2. 'Jurisprudence is knowledge of things divine and human; the science of the just and unjust.

3. 'The man who intends to follow the law (*jus*) should first know the origin of the word. *Jus* is so called from justice; for, as Celsus[2] pithily defines it, it is the art of the Good and the Right. By virtue thereof we [who follow the law] may well be termed priests; for we revere justice and profess knowledge of the Good and the Right—separating the right from the wrong; distinguishing between the lawful and the unlawful; seeking to make men good not only by the fear of punishment, but also by the encouragement of reward; and, unless I am mistaken, making a true—not a sham—philosophy our aim and endeavour.

4. 'The three commandments of law are these: to live decently

---

[1] The Latin text of the passages here translated is that given in the 8th edition of C. A. Pellat's *Manuale Juris*, pp. 6, 8, 10. The text is also given in O. Lenel's *Palingenesia iuris Romani*, under Ulpian (vol. ii, pp. 926–7, Nos. 1908, 1910, 1915).

[2] Celsus was a jurist, born in the last quarter of the first century A.D., who served on the *consilium* of the Emperor Hadrian and wrote *Digesta*, or a treatise on law.

(*honeste*, i.e. as one's position requires); not to injure another in his position; and to give each man his due.

5. 'The study of law has two aspects: it is both public and private. Public law is the law which concerns the position of the Roman State (*res Romana*); private law is the law concerned with the benefit of individuals; for there are some matters which are to the public benefit, and some which are to the benefit of private persons. The public law deals with matters such as public worship, priesthoods, and magistracies. Private law is tripartite: it is made up of natural rules, the rules of [or common to] all nations, and civil rules.

6. 'Natural law (*jus naturale*) is the law which nature has taught all animate beings; for such law is not peculiar to man, but is common to all animals born on earth or in the sea, and also to the birds of the air. From it springs the union of male and female, which we call marriage; from it springs the procreation of children, and from it their education; hence we see that other animals besides man, even those which are wild, are regarded as acquainted with this law.

7. 'The law of nations (*jus gentium*) is the law used by all nations of men. The difference between it and natural law can easily be gathered from the fact that natural law is common to all animate beings, while the law of nations is common only to men in their relations with one another.

8. 'Civil law is a law which is neither altogether different from natural law and the law of nations, nor wholly dependent upon them; accordingly when we add something to or take something away from [these forms of general or] common law, we make a law which is peculiar to us, or civil. This law of ours is composed either of written rules or of unwritten [i.e. customary] rules: as the Greeks have it, some laws are written (*engraphoi*), and some unwritten (*agraphoi*).'

Three notes may be added to this statement of Ulpian's general view of law. The first is a passage from the jurist Hermogenianus (later than Ulpian, and about A.D. 300) on the content of *jus gentium*; the second is a remarkable passage from the jurist Salvius

Iulianus (a contemporary of Gaius) on the nature and basis of customary law; the third is a famous passage from Ulpian on the basis of the Emperor's power of making 'constitutions', which is ascribed by him to a popular (or we might even say democratic) origin.

(*a*) *Jus gentium.* 'It is from this law of nations that there have been introduced among us wars; the separation of nations; the foundation of kingdoms; the distinction of properties; the setting of boundaries to estates; the grouping of buildings together; commerce; buying and selling; letting and hiring; and the creation of obligations—except for some which have been introduced by civil law.'[1] (This statement of the content of *jus gentium* suggests that Hermogenianus, like Ulpian before him, had a separate conception of *jus naturale* as something higher and less conventional than *jus gentium*.)

(*b*) *Unwritten, or customary, law as a part of* jus civile. 'Inveterate custom is not improperly observed as being *lex* [i.e. as having the same authority with a written statute duly passed by the people]; and this is the sort of law (*ius*) which is said to be established by usage (*mores*). For since written laws themselves bind us for no other reason than that they have been approved by the judgement of the people, it follows that those rules which the people has ratified without any writing ought also to bind everybody; for what is the difference whether the people declare their assent by a vote, or by facts and their acts (*rebus et factis*)? For this reason, too, it has very rightly been accepted as a principle that statutes [as they can be made] can also be abolished not only by the vote of the statute-maker, but also by the silent agreement of all men, and through their passing into disuse.'[2] (This remarkable passage

---

[1] From the text in C. A. Pellat, op. cit., p. 10; see also O. Lenel, op. cit., vol. i, p. 206, under Hermogenianus, No. 1.

[2] From the text in C. A. Pellat, op. cit., p. 14. A passage of Hermogenianus (printed on the same page of that work) is somewhat similar to the passage of Salvius Iulianus: 'Unwritten rules which have been approved by long established custom, and observed for a long period of time, are recognized equally with rules which have been committed to writing, as being in the nature of a tacit agreement of the members of the community.' Similarly Ulpian, at the beginning of his *Liber Regularum* (P. F. Girard, *Textes de droit romain*, 1923, p. 463), lays it down that 'usage (*mores*) is the silent consent of the people, rooted in long custom'.

of Salvius Iulianus anticipates Gierke's definition of law as 'the conviction of a human community, either manifested directly by usage or declared by a common organ appointed for that purpose'.)

(c) *The basis of the Emperor's power of making 'constitutions'.* 'The pleasure of the *princeps* [as declared in a *constitutio*] has the force of a *lex*, inasmuch as by the *lex regia*, which is passed [in each reign?] in regard to his sovereign power (*imperium*), the people confers on him and into his hand all its own sovereign power and authority.[1] Whatsoever therefore the Emperor (*imperator*) has (1) determined by the issue and signature of a *letter*, or (2) decided by a *decree* given in the course of a judicial examination, or (3) settled out of court by a *provisional judgement*, or (4) enjoined by the terms of an *edict*—all such pronouncements form what we commonly call constitutions. Obviously some of these acts are personal, and do not constitute a precedent; for example if the prince grants a favour to somebody for his services, or imposes some penalty, or gives some assistance to a man without creating a precedent, he does not go beyond the limits of his own private person.'[2] (The first sentence in this passage of Ulpian, as will be seen from the next section, had a deep and lasting effect on the theory of the origin and the limits of political authority.)

B. *The Views of the Second- and Third-century Lawyers on the Nature of* Dominium

Under the general head of *dominium*, if a loose use of that term is permissible,[3] three things may be included: (1) dominion of the

---

[1] There survives on a bronze tablet, or rather part of a bronze tablet, the *Lex de Imperio Vespasiani*—an enactment, in the regular form of a *lex rogata*, conferring powers on Vespasian. The surviving part of the inscription recites certain specific items of power. We do not know what was mentioned in the lost part. It may have been, as the passage from Ulpian would seem to imply, general sovereign power (*imperium*); it may have been only some further list of items. See below for the text of the *Lex de Imperio*, p. 272.

[2] For the Latin text see C. A. Pellat, op. cit., p. 12, and O. Lenel, op. cit., vol. ii, p. 928 (under Ulpian), No. 1916.

[3] In a strict and accurate use of terms the word *dominium* belongs to the sphere of private right (*res privata*), and the word *imperium* is the word used in the sphere of public right (*res publica*) to designate 'political authority'. But I have ventured to use the word *dominium* as a general word for *all* authority—whether in the sphere of the State, or in that of the household (as shown in the power of a father over his children and servants), or in that of private ownership.

political order, exercised over the members of an organized political community, or in other words 'political authority'; (2) dominion of the social order, exercised by a paterfamilias over children and slaves, or in other words 'household authority'; (3) dominion of the economic order, exercised by an owner of land or other property over the things under his control, or, as we may term it, 'owner's authority'. This general conception of *dominium* (and this distinction of its three forms) does not appear in the Roman lawyers themselves[1] (though it does appear in the early Fathers); but it will serve as a useful scheme for the examination and explanation of their views.

1. *Political Authority*

The Roman lawyers of the second and third centuries A.D. have no philosophy of the nature of political authority, nor do they expound any theory of its origin or its limits. As practical lawyers they are concerned only with the question—'Who is it that makes the law of the State (the *jus civile*), which judges in their courts recognize and enforce?' In other words they are concerned only with that aspect or activity of authority which appears in the making of law. Their answer to the one question with which they are concerned is, in a word, 'the community'. It is true that, according to Gaius, there are six different sorts or parts of *jus civile*, each made and set down in writing by a particular authority— one being made by the whole people, another by the part of the people called the *plebs*, another by the Senate, another by the Emperor, and so on. But two other things are also true. The first is that the most solemn parts of *jus civile*—the *lex* and the *plebiscitum*—proceed from the community. The second is that some at any rate, if not all, of the other parts, which are made immediately by organs other than the community itself, are conceived as being made by those organs (e.g. the *princeps*) in virtue of a law of the community delegating power to them for that purpose. This is suggested by Gaius, in § 5 of the passage translated above; it is expressly stated by Ulpian, in the passage at the end of the

---

[1] But one of the Roman lawyers, Tryphoninus, is reported in the *Digest* of Justinian as having used the term *dominatio* to designate authority in general, and as having held that it was introduced by *jus gentium*, while *libertas* belonged to the system of *jus naturale*.

preceding section. Moreover, the argument of Salvius Iulianus adds the further consideration that over and above the six different parts of *jus* which are to be found in writing there is also an unwritten or customary region of *jus* which is certainly the creation of the community. The general view of the lawyers is thus to the effect that *jus* proceeds from the community, either directly or indirectly through an organ commissioned for the purpose. In a sense this view was a sham, so far as the actual facts of their own time were concerned. There is no record of the people passing a *lex* after the end of the first century A.D.; and legislation had become in form, as well as in fact, a matter of imperial pronouncements by the end of the second century. But it is none the less a matter of the first importance that the jurists of the second and third centuries A.D. preserved in their writings, and transmitted to the age of Justinian for incorporation in his *Institutes* and *Digest*, the tradition of the ancient forms and the ancient theory. It was a republican ghost that spoke in an imperial palace; but it spoke none the less, and its voice continued to be heard in succeeding centuries, all through the Middle Ages and down to the age of the Renaissance.

The Roman lawyers of the second and third centuries A.D. thus gave to later political speculation the bricks with which it could build. When we reflect how sedulously the Roman law-books were conned for century after century, we must ascribe to their scattered hints an importance and an influence which in themselves they did not possess and indeed never claimed. The hints were far from being a philosophy; but they became the parents of philosophy. They gave to the Schoolmen, along with other and similar hints which the Schoolmen drew from the Scriptures and Fathers (who were themselves already indebted to the inheritance of Roman law)—and also, after the middle of the thirteenth century, from a recovered knowledge of Aristotle's *Politics*—the basis of the theory that the people is the source of legal authority, and that all true kings, being entrusted with authority by the people, must use their authority for the good of the people. In a word, they provided the sub-structure of ideas and the foundations of thought for the theory of the Social Contract.

But it was not only the scattered hints of an implied theory of politics in the writings of the Roman lawyers that helped the building and supplied the bricks of a theory of the Social Contract: it was also the actual law of contract which they expounded that supplied the mortar—the cohesive scheme of ideas—to hold the theory together. Not that the Roman lawyers themselves ever applied the idea of contract to politics. They simply dealt with contracts between individuals—private contracts—contracts, for instance, of 'letting and hiring', and not contracts for instituting and obliging kings. It was reserved for a later age to borrow their private-law doctrines and to apply them to public law. But this borrowing and application actually took place; and we may therefore note some of the elements of the Roman law of private contracts as it is stated in book III of the *Institutes* of Gaius.[1]

§ 88. 'Obligations are divided into two main species; for every obligation arises either from contract or delict.

§ 89. 'First let us consider those that arise from contract. Of such there are four *genera*; for an obligation by contract arises either *re* (by delivery of a *res*, which creates a *real* contract), or by words (*verbal* contract), or by writing (*literal* contract), or by consent (*consensual* contract). . . .'

Only the consensual contract comes into consideration when we are concerned with the borrowing of ideas from the law of contract and their application to politics.

§ 135. 'Obligations are created by consent in sale (*emptio venditio*), hire (*locatio conductio*), partnership (*societas*), and mandate (*mandatum*).

§ 136. 'The reason why we say that in these cases the obligations are contracted by consent is that no formality whether of words or writing is required, but it is enough that the persons dealing have consented. . . .

§ 137. 'Further, in these contracts the parties are reciprocally liable for what each is bound in fairness and equity to perform for the other [whereas in other contracts, such as the verbal and the literal, the liability is unilateral].'

[1] The translation followed is that of Professor de Zulueta in his edition of 1946.

Of the four forms of consensual contract only the two last, partnership and mandate, can be applied to politics.

§ 148. 'We enter into a *partnership* either in respect of our entire fortunes, or for some particular business . . ..

§ 154. 'The partnership of which we are speaking, namely that which is formed by simple consent, is *juris gentium*, and thus obtains by natural reason among all men.' By natural reason, it can therefore be argued (as it was by medieval thinkers), men may institute, with 'no formality whether of words or writing', a political society (or *pacte d'association*, as Rousseau calls it) of each with all; and each and all will then be reciprocally liable for what they are bound in fairness and equity to perform for others.

§ 155. 'There is a contract of *mandate* when we give a commission either in our own interest or in that of another. Thus whether I commission you to conduct affairs of my own or those of a third party, a binding contract of mandate is formed, and we shall be liable to one another for whatever each ought as a matter of good faith to perform for the other.' On this basis, therefore, it can be argued that men may, in their own interest, commission a ruler or governor to conduct their common affairs, and the effect of that commission will be a binding contract of mandate (or *pacte de gouvernement*, as Rousseau calls it), between those who give the commission and the man who receives it, which makes both sides liable to one another—the governor to the people, and the people to the governor—for whatever each ought as a matter of good faith to perform for the other.

Such were the materials supplied by the lawyers of the second and third centuries A.D. for the construction of a theory of political association and political authority.[1] They were materials which those lawyers had drawn, in the main, simply and solely from the study of Roman law, public and private. No doubt they had

---

[1] The materials have been presented here in the shorter form which appears in the *Institutes* of Gaius—the only form which belongs to the period covered by this volume. A longer and later form—the only form known to the thinkers of the Middle Ages, and the form which they used in constructing their political theories—appears in the *Institutes* of Justinian, book III, cc. 13 ff., especially c. 25 (*De Societate*) and c. 26 (*De Mandato*).

some general knowledge of the philosophy of the Stoics: it was the generally current philosophy of their time, and it had the sanction of the contemporary philosopher-emperor Marcus Aurelius. Ulpian, in particular, may have been led by Stoicism to his notion of a *jus naturale* distinct from *jus gentium*. But on the whole it may fairly be said that their own law was sufficient to teach the Roman lawyers the general lessons which they in turn transmitted to later generations.

2. *Household Authority, or Masters and Slaves.*

Gaius, who had no theory of *jus naturale* as distinct from *jus gentium*, had consequently no theory (as we shall see that Ulpian had) of a natural condition of men in which all were alike free and equal. His references to slavery in book 1 of his *Institutes* are brief. He simply takes slavery as a universal fact of all nations, warranted by the *jus gentium*, and he contents himself with noting that in *jus civile*, by two constitutions of the Emperor Antoninus Pius, the position of slaves had lately been improved.

Book 1, § 52. 'Slaves are in the *potestas* of their masters. This *potestas* is an element of *jus gentium*, for it is observable that among all nations alike masters have power of life and death over their slaves, and whatever is acquired through a slave is acquired for his master.

§ 53. 'But at the present time neither Roman citizens nor any other persons subject to the rule of the Roman people are allowed to treat their slaves with excessive and causeless harshness. . . . [Gaius then quotes the two constitutions of Antoninus, and adds] Both enactments are just, for we ought not to abuse our lawful rights.'

Ulpian and his contemporaries, able to operate with the conception of *jus naturale* as well as with that of *jus gentium*, take a different line. They regard slavery as unnatural, in the sense that it is not warranted by the law of nature, though they regard it as universal, and as warranted by the law of nations. Two passages of Ulpian bearing on the matter are cited in the *Digest* (l. 17. 32 and i. 1. 4).

1. 'So far as *jus civile* is concerned, slaves are counted as not being persons (*pro nullis*); but this is not so under natural law, because, so far as *jus naturale* is concerned, all men are equal (*omnes homines aequales sunt*).

2. 'Manumissions too belong to *jus gentium*. Manumission is delivery from the hand [of the master]—that is to say, it is the grant of liberty; for as long as any man is in a condition of slavery, he is subject to the hand and *potestas* [of a master], but when he is manumitted he is freed from *potestas*. This institution [i.e. manumission] took its origin from the *jus gentium*, since under *jus naturale* all men were born free, and manumission was not known because slavery was unknown; but after slavery had entered the world in virtue of *jus gentium*, there followed the benefit of manumission [in virtue of the same *jus*]. And whereas before we were all called by the one natural name of men, three sorts and conditions of men began to appear under the rules of *jus gentium*—free men; at the opposite pole from these slaves; and as a third sort or condition freedmen, that is those who had ceased to be slaves.'[1]

Two similar passages are also cited in the *Digest*, one from the jurist Florentinus, and another from the jurist Tryphoninus, both contemporaries of Ulpian.

1. 'Liberty is the natural power of [doing] what each man chooses to do, unless where an act is prevented by duress or by the law. Slavery is an institution of *jus gentium*, whereby a man is subjected to the *dominium* of another in defiance of nature. Slaves (*servi*) are so called because commanders of armies are in the habit of selling their prisoners, thus preserving (*servare*) instead of killing them' (Florentinus in the *Digest*, i. 5. 4).

2. 'Liberty is included in natural law, and *dominatio* was introduced by the *jus gentium*' (Tryphoninus in the *Digest*, xii. 6. 64).

It would thus appear that the jurists of the beginning of the third century A.D., following the trend of imperial legislation (which began to ameliorate the condition of slaves from the time of the Emperor Claudius onwards), had moved to a theory of

---

[1] I owe the references to these passages (and to those which follow) to A. J. Carlyle's *History of Medieval Political Theory in the West*, vol. i, c. 4, p. 47. The text of the second passage quoted from Ulpian is printed in O. Lenel, op. cit., vol. ii, p. 927, under Ulpian, No. 1912.

slavery which made it a conventional and unnatural, if universal, institution. This theory served as an influence making for further amelioration of the conditions of slaves.

3. Owner's Authority, or Property

While the legal theory of A.D. 200 refused to recognize *dominium* over persons as natural, it did not go so far in regard to *dominium* over things, or the right of private property. Whether they distinguish *jus gentium* from *jus naturale*, as Ulpian and his successors did, or identify the two, as Gaius earlier had done, the lawyers of the second and third centuries accept the fact of private property, without any question, as something given in the nature of things.

Gaius, as we may see from a passage already mentioned (at the end of Section A. 1 above), regards property as acquired either by the *jus gentium* or by *jus civile*, and he suggests that property acquired by the former is based on a law (*a*) observed among all men alike by virtue of natural reason and (*b*) coeval with mankind itself. From this it follows that such property is at once naturally reasonable, and also primitive. In a passage of his *Institutes* (ii. 65, 66, 69) he cites as examples of property acquired by *jus naturale* or *naturalis ratio* (by which he means the same as *jus gentium*) three classes of things: (1) things which become ours by *traditio*, or in virtue of their alienation to us by their previous owner; (2) things which become ours by *occupatio*, having previously had no owner, such as beasts, birds, and fishes; and (3) things which become ours by capture from an enemy.

Ulpian and his successors say little about the problem of private property; we can only guess that they regarded it as justified both by *jus naturale* and by *jus gentium*—if indeed they ever used that distinction in treating of the matter. But there is one lawyer, Hermogenianus, who in a passage already mentioned (in the first of the three notes at the end of Section A. 2 above) seems to suggest the view that property which is acquired and justified by *jus gentium* is hardly natural. It is not what he actually says which suggests this view; it is rather the company which he makes property keep, and the institutions with which he connects it. The law of nations, he says, has introduced the distinction of properties, and the setting of boundaries to estates, along with wars and the separation of nations. This seems to imply some previous state of man, before these things were introduced, in which, as there were no wars or nations, so there were also no boundaries or property. But this implication may not have been present to the writer; and we perhaps refine too much if we detect in his words a distinction between the institutions of *jus gentium*, including property, and the institutions (or absence of institutions) of some 'state of nature', prior to the introduction of *jus gentium*, which knew no setting of boundaries or distinction of properties.

c. *Paulus on Offences against Public Manners and the Political Order*

From the *Sententiae* of Iulius Paulus, a jurist of the first part of the third century B.C., on Divination, Sedition, and Treason. (From Girard, *Textes de droit romain*, 6th edition, pp. 445–6, 449.)

1. *Divination, New Forms of Religion, and Astrology*

Book v, c. 21, § 1. 'Diviners, who pretend to be inspired by a god, are to be banished from the city, that public manners may not be corrupted, through human credulity, to cherish any expectation of the future, or the mind of the people be in any way disturbed. Accordingly, for the first offence, they are beaten and driven from the city; if they are obstinate, they are sent to a public prison, or deported to one of the islands, or at the least banished. § 2. Those who introduce new forms of religion, not known in practice or to men's reason, by which men's minds are affected, are deported if they are men of standing (*honestiores*), and punished by death if they belong to the lower classes (*humiliores*). § 3. A man who consults astrologers, soothsayers, prophets, or diviners about the health of the Emperor or the affairs of the State is punished by death, along with the person consulted by him and giving him an answer. § 4. A man will do well to keep aloof not only from the practice of divination, but also from the study of it and from books relating to it.'

2. Sedition—and Circumcision

Book v, c. 22, § 1. 'The authors of sedition and riot, or disturbers of the people, are either crucified, or thrown to wild beasts, or deported to one of the islands, according to the degree of their standing. . . . § 3. Roman citizens, who allow themselves or their slaves to be circumcised in the Jewish fashion, have their property confiscated and are deported for life to one of the islands: the doctors who perform circumcision are punished with death. § 4. If Jews cause slaves of another nation, who have been acquired by them, to be circumcised, they are either deported or punished with death.'[1]

3. On the Lex Iulia of treason

Book v, c. 29, § 1. 'By the Lex Iulia a man is held guilty of treason (maiestas laesa) when by his aid and counsel arms have been levied against the Emperor or the State, or the Emperor's army led into an ambush, or when a man without instructions from the Emperor has waged war or raised troops, gathered or seduced an army, or deserted the emperor. Of old, such men were forbidden the use of fire or water [i.e. they were outlawed]; now, those who are of the lower classes are thrown to wild beasts or burned alive, and those who are men of standing are punished with death. This crime is not only a matter of acts: it is also greatly multiplied by impious words and imprecations. § 2. When a man is accused of treason, inquiry must first be made into the resources, the faction, and the instigators that are behind what he has done. A man accused of so great a crime is not to be punished under colour of some specious plea, but on the ground of the actual crime, and therefore, when such a case is being investigated, men of all ranks are liable to torture.'

[1] Circumcision had been tolerated till the reign of Hadrian, but was prohibited then and afterwards.

D. *Legal Documents of the Reigns of Vespasian, Hadrian, and Caracalla*

1. *The* Lex de Imperio *passed at the accession of Vespasian.* (From Girard, *Textes de droit romain*, 6th edition, pp. 106–8.)

This *lex*, inscribed on a bronze tablet, was found at Rome in the fourteenth century A.D., in the days of Cola di Rienzo. It will be noticed that while Ulpian, writing more than a century later (*circa* A.D. 220), states that the people transferred '*all* its sovereignty and power' to the prince by the *Lex Regia*, this law (which is really a *Senatus Consultum* incorporated, or turned, into a *lex* by popular approval) transfers only (1) specific powers, and (2) such as were warranted by tradition and precedent. It contains eight enacting clauses and a 'sanction'. By the various clauses the princeps is 'permitted' to make treaties (the form is *uti liceat*), to summon and guide the Senate, to recommend candidates for office, to extend the bounds of the empire, and so forth—generally with the appended formula 'as it was permitted to Augustus, Tiberius, and Claudius'; but in three of the clauses—a clause relating to the Emperor's action in the Senate, a clause relating to his recommendation of candidates for office, and a clause about the ratification of imperial acts done before the passing of the *Lex de Imperio*—this formula does not appear. Two important clauses, which contain the formula, are the sixth and seventh:

'that it be his right and power to do whatever he shall think to be for the advantage of the State, and for the greater dignity of affairs—both divine and human and whether they be public or private—as it was for *divus* Augustus, Tiberius, and Claudius;

'that the Emperor Caesar Vespasian shall be exempt (*solutus*) from any laws previously passed by the people, and any enactments made by the *plebs*, which contained a provision that *divus* Augustus, Tiberius, and Claudius should not be bound thereby; and that it be permitted to the Emperor Caesar Vespasian to do any and every act which by any law or enactment it behoved *divus* Augustus, Tiberius, and Claudius to do.'[1]

---

[1] On this *Lex* see A. Piganiol, *Histoire de Rome* (1954), p. 285.

2. *A decree of the Emperor Hadrian* (A.D. 121) *giving greater freedom to the Epicurean School at Athens in the choice of its head.* (From Girard, *Textes de Droit Romain*, 6th edition, p. 197.)

This decree is, in small, a precursor of what the edict of Caracalla (see below, No. 3) was on a far larger scale. Before the decree the head of the Epicurean school must be a Roman citizen. The effect of the decree was to enable aliens to be heads of the school, and generally to increase its liberty in the choice of a head. The first part of the decree recites the petition of Plotina, the widow of Trajan, as a friend of the school, for Hadrian's intervention; the second part shows him intervening according to her desire.

'. . . I ask in the name of Popillius Theotimus, who is now the head [of the school] at Athens, [1] that it be permitted to him by you to make a testamentary disposition in Greek, in regard to the part of his functions which concerns the regulation of the succession, and to have the power of appointing a person of the status of alien as his successor, if the benefit to be derived from such a person suggest that course; and [2] that the grant made by you to Theotimus may be enjoyed after him, on the same terms, by future heads of the Epicurean school—the more as it is the rule, whenever a mistake has been made by the testator in regard to the appointment of his successor, that the best man for the post should be substituted by the students of the school in general assembly, and as this can be done more easily if the field open to choice is wider. . . .'

Hadrian grants the petition: 'Theotimus may make his testamentary disposition in Greek [and not in Latin], and he and his successors in the headship may appoint either an alien or a Roman citizen to take their place.'

3. *Edict of Caracalla* (A.D. 212) *granting citizenship to the inhabitants of the Empire.* (From the text in Girard, op. cit. pp. 204-5.)

'The Emperor Caesar Marcus Aurelius Severus Antoninus Augustus [i.e. Caracalla] proclaims. Now it is necessary . . . to examine how I may show my gratitude to the immortal gods, for the protection given me . . . by such a victory. Wherefore I am of opinion that I can with munificence and piety thus satisfy their majesty—that is to say, by bringing together into the worship of the gods men who are aliens (*peregrini*) whensoever they come under the definition of my men (i.e. when they are my subjects). I grant to all aliens in the inhabited world Roman citizenship, with each form of constitution [in each several city and country] remaining unaltered—except as concerns unfree subjects (*dediticii*). For it is necessary that the generality should not only . . . [a gap in the text], but should also now be included [as partners] in the victory. This edict has [augmented?] the majesty of the Roman people by reason of the same [status] having been accorded thereby in regard to aliens. . . .' The rest of the papyrus which contains a copy of the edict is fragmentary.

Note. This *Constitutio Antoniniana*, according to Dio Cassius, was intended to increase the revenue: only Roman citizens were liable to legacy duty, and Caracalla wished to increase the range of that liability. According to the text here translated, the motive was religious: Caracalla wished to show his gratitude to the gods for his victory (over an alleged conspiracy) by adding a great body of new adherents to the civic worship of the State gods—who (it may be mentioned incidentally) were now solar gods of the Asiatic type. See the *Cambridge Ancient History*, vol. xii, p. 457; and also, on the general problems raised by the *Constitutio,* A. Piganiol, op. cit., pp. 414–15.

PART IV

LATER GREEK THOUGHT
FROM POSIDONIUS TO THEMISTIUS

INTRODUCTION

THE first period of Greek thought in the course of the six centuries from Alexander to Constantine may be said to end with the *Universal History* of Polybius (*circa* 146 B.C.). For two and a half centuries after that first period—from the age of the Gracchi to the reign of the Emperor Hadrian—the development of thought mainly proceeds in the Roman West and the Latin language; and it has been said, with justice, that 'Greek literature in the first century B.C. and the first century A.D. has nothing which can be compared in importance with the work of Latin writers'. Greek thought, indeed, continued to be active during this Latin period. Posidonius of Apamea taught and wrote in Rhodes (100–50 B.C.), though only scattered fragments of his multifarious writings survive. Philo, versed in Greek thought but fundamentally Jewish, wrote voluminously in Greek, in a series of treatises, at once philosophical and theological, on themes and topics drawn from the Old Testament (A.D. 1–45). The Pseudo-Aristotle who wrote the treatise *De Mundo* (*circa* A.D. 50) left a moving legacy of pure Greek thought. Here too may be mentioned Plutarch, of Chaeronea in Boeotia (*circa* A.D. 50–120), who bequeathed to posterity a whole library of moral essays and biographical works. He is a bright and candid spirit, who illuminates the comparative darkness of Greek literature and thought at the end of the Latin period. An eclectic philosopher, mainly Platonic but with Stoic sympathies (see below, pp. 308–9), he wrote for the people rather than for philosophers, always cherishing a warm interest in things human, and always ready to 'condescend upon the particulars' of the character, conduct, personal traits, and recorded sayings of historic figures—as he notably shows in his lives of Agis IV and Cleomenes III (see above, pp. 53–57).

But these are scattered and separate lights; and the continuous succession of Greek thinkers and writers does not begin again till the reign of Hadrian, when under the encouragement of imperial patronage the Greek East emancipates itself from the Latin West, recovers a sense of direction, and discovers for itself a new style and new themes. Yet much of the flow of Greek literature, during the second and third centuries A.D., is thin and often shallow. Greek might be the staple of the day, and a Roman Emperor might write his *Meditations* in the language of Greece; but the bulk of those who wrote in Greek were concerned with style rather than substance, and the polish of their style, in spite of its gloss and for all its decoration, was not enough to conceal the poverty of their thought. This was the result and fruit of what is called 'the Second Sophistic', a movement of education and literary fashion which sacrificed intellectual substance on the altar of literary form. Rhetoric was the reigning mode; schools of rhetoric, which trained men in style and opened the doors to literary success (but not, as the schools of the sophists of the fifth century B.C. had done, to success in the law-courts and politics), were the vogue; and these schools of rhetoric, which were still a power in the days of St. Augustine (himself at one time a professor of rhetoric), were a tyranny as well as a power in the days of the Middle Empire, under the rule of Flavian and Antonine emperors and in the epoch of the Severi.

It was Philostratus (*circa* A.D. 170–250) who in his *Lives of the Sophists* invented the name of 'the Second Sophistic', dating the beginning of the new epoch from the days of Dio of Prusa (*circa* A.D. 100). In fact the 'Second Sophistic' was nothing essentially new; it was only a new and lively expression of an old Greek instinct for using high notes and high-sounding words—an instinct at which Aristophanes had laughed long ago (for instance in the *Clouds*), but which steadily persisted through the centuries because it was in the blood. It was not only—or not so much— the Athenians who spent their time in framing euphemisms and euphonious phrases; indeed the Athenians were singularly restrained for Greeks, and they cultivated a chaste Atticism of expression; it was rather the Greeks of what may be called the colonial lands of western Asia who followed the arts of gloss and decoration. But the inhabitants of Greek lands generally came to fall under the spell, the more as professors of rhetoric, paid from public funds, were there to give regular instruction from the reign of Vespasian onwards, and all the more as the title 'Sophist' now became a title of honour, and not—as it had been in Plato's day and is again in our own time—a term of criticism. The sophists of the second and third centuries A.D. toured cities in triumph and delivered solemn orations to admiring crowds; they graced public festivals and family gatherings with their speeches and addresses; they were the rivals, and often the successful rivals, of Cynic preachers and Stoic philosophers; indeed they often professed to be the true lovers and teachers of *Sophia*. It was the other side of the picture that they vulgarized what they touched, and substituted 'sounding brass' for true education, serious philosophy, and genuine poetry.

Dio, later called Chrysostom, and credited as the first flower and fruit of the new rhetoric, came from Prusa (in Bithynia), and lectured in Rome, the Crimea, and Alexandria. Aelius Aristides (*circa* A.D. 130–90) came from Mysia and was domiciled in Smyrna; with his religious addresses to the goddess Athena (and also to the Egyptian Ptolemy-created god Sarapis), and with his lofty panegyric addressed to Rome, he was ranked as the leading figure in the movement of the Second Sophistic. One of these sophists, who lived in the third century (but there were also others afterwards in the fourth and later centuries), was also the historian, in a rambling and anecdotal style, of the whole movement from Dio of Prusa onwards. This was Philostratus, a member of a Lemnian family. But his chief title to fame is not so much his *Lives of the Sophists* as his *Life of Apollonius of Tyana*, a work, written at the request of the Syrian wife of the Emperor Septimius Severus, which gives an account of a wandering neo-Pythagorean sage and prophet of the first century A.D., in a hagiographical style that mixes wonders worthy of Baron Münchausen with some curious observations on politics professing to be those of the 'prophet' (see below, p. 328). Standing apart from the sophists, though he had begun his career in their ranks, is the Hellenized

Syrian Lucian (*circa* A.D. 125–95), a wit and satirist who developed, and substituted for the set oration, a new and laughing form of dialogue which combines Platonic form with the comic spirit of Menander and his fellows of the Greek New Comedy. But occasionally, in a serious moment, Lucian can flash a beam of light on the social life and ideas of his age, and his essay on 'The Death of Peregrinus' is a testimony of the first order to the nature of the Christian community in the second century A.D. (see below, p. 452).[1]

If the sophists generally were concerned with form and style more than with thought and ideas, the reverse is true of other Greek writers of the period of revival which began with the reign of Hadrian. Epictetus, ex-slave and Stoic philosopher, breathed a spirit of religious conviction into his teaching; and the record of his *Discourses* preserved in the notes made by his pupil Arrian (a soldier and official of the Roman Empire who also wrote the *Anabasis of Alexander* about the middle of the second century A.D.) has been the food of generations. The same may be said, and said even more, of the profound and moving *Meditations* of the Stoic Emperor Marcus Aurelius, who had studied the thought and followed in the track of Epictetus, but went even beyond his predecessor in the power and penetration of his thinking. It may seem curious that a Roman emperor, born in Rome and belonging to the Latin West, should have addressed his meditations 'To Himself' in the language of the Greek East. But Greek was the natural language of any genuine and fresh philosophy, as it was also, during this period (*circa* A.D. 100–270), the current language of the Christian liturgy and Christian apologetics. Indeed we may trace, in this matter of language, a close parallel (as natural as it is close) between the march of Greek philosophy and the progress of Christianity. Both philosophy and Christianity spoke to the world in Greek.

In the realm of philosophy it was not only the Stoics of the

---

[1] One of the sophists of this age wrote a treatise 'On Polity'. This was Herodes Atticus of Marathon, who lived in the second century A.D. But the treatise is only an imitative exercise, or *meletē*, couched in the style of 400 B.C. and based, in point of content, on a speech delivered centuries before by a sophist of the 'first sophistic'.

second century who left their monuments in Greek; the Platonists, or rather the Neoplatonists, of the third century also used the same vehicle of thought. The new Platonism began among the Greeks of Alexandria (always, in antiquity, a vat of fermenting thought); it began early in the third century with the teaching of Ammonius Saccas, the master of Plotinus—and also the master of the Christian theologian Origen; and if Plotinus eventually established himself as a teacher in Rome (245–70), he used the Greek language in his teaching and writings—writings from which his disciple Porphyry, who collected and arranged them for posterity in the six books of the *Enneads*, erected an abiding Greek monument to the memory of his master. In the realm of Christian teaching and writing too, no less than in that of philosophy, Greek was the great vehicle, and here again Alexandria was a lighthouse or beacon, like its own Pharos, for the Mediterranean world. The Old Testament used by Christian preachers and teachers was the Greek Septuagint which had been produced in Alexandria for use in the Jewish-Hellenistic synagogues. The New Testament was written and read in Greek; the language of the Christian liturgy, in Rome itself, as has already been noticed (see above, p. 168, n. 1), was Greek down to the middle of the third century. By the end of the second century there had also arisen—and here, once more, Alexandria was the centre—a school of theology (the 'catechumen school') conducted in Greek for the members of the Christian community. One of its earliest heads was the Greek Clement of Alexandria, probably born in Athens and certainly versed in Greek philosophy (*circa* 150–210); after him came Origen (*circa* 185–255), the son of a Christian family in Alexandria, who along with Plotinus was the greatest thinker of the last Greek age, and who, after teaching for years in his native city, eventually carried his learning and his books to Caesarea in Palestine, and there established a school and a library which made his adopted city a school of Christian scholarship for the Eastern Mediterranean.

In the field of general literature, in the realm of philosophy, and in the Scriptures, liturgy, and theology of the Christian Church, Greek was thus the dominant language—not indeed exclusively, but none the less generally—during the period from

the accession of Hadrian to the death of Plotinus in the year
270. It was not only the language of literature, of learning, and of
liturgy; it was also a language of current speech, freely used at
Rome and in Italy, and even farther afield in the valley of the
Rhône from Marseilles up to Lyons. But it was natural, and indeed
inevitable, that Latin should ultimately offer a challenge in the
lands of the West; and it was in the province of Africa that this
challenge seems first to have been offered. That province was a
lively centre of intellectual activity; but it was only the few members of its more educated classes who had any knowledge of Greek,
and though Punic was still spoken among the common people,
Latin was the general medium of intercourse. The needs of the
Christian Church in Africa became the immediate occasion of a
revival of Latin letters. By the end of the second century Latin
had here become the language of the liturgy, even earlier than it
did in Rome; and, what was more, the Greek Septuagint version
of the Old Testament and the Greek of the New Testament had
both been translated into Latin—possibly at Carthage. Rome, and
with Rome Italy, went the same way, perhaps at the same date
in making an independent 'European' translation of the Bible to
match the 'African' version, but at a slightly later date in adopting
a Latin liturgy. It was in Africa, however, rather than in Italy, that a
Christian Latin literature first arose; and the creator of that literature was Tertullian, the father of ecclesiastical Latin. Already,
therefore, during the years in which he was writing (circa 195–
220), Latin had begun to return, and to return on the plane, and
in the field, of Christian thought. Tertullian was not of the same
intellectual stature as the two great Greek thinkers of his age,
Origen and Plotinus; but he created a Latin style and an instru-
ment of expression which inaugurated a new epoch in the history
of thought. With the appearance of a Latin Bible and liturgy,
and with the writings of Tertullian, the West had begun that
independent development which proceeded on its march first to
Lactantius, the contemporary and counterpart of the Eastern bishop
Eusebius of Caesarea, and then to the great figures of St. Ambrose,
St. Augustine, and their successors through the centuries. Rome and
Carthage could now hold a candle to Alexandria and Caesarea.

§ I. POSIDONIUS

Posidonius (135–50 B.C.) has been called 'the last great Greek, facing the Roman world in independence but with understanding'.[1] His birthplace, however, was Apamea, a town in Syria to the south of Antioch, and he may, like Zeno, have been a Hellenized Semite; but he spent his life mainly in Rhodes, where he held civic office and founded a school. He was in touch with some of the great Romans of his day; he had talked with Marius, he knew Pompey, he corresponded with Cicero, and he was known to Caesar. He travelled all over the Mediterranean; he visited Gaul somewhere about 100 B.C., and studied the Atlantic tides at Cadiz. He was an encyclopaedist after the manner of Aristotle, but he took too much of learning for his province, and his depth was less than his range. He was an historian as well as a philosopher,[2] but he did some of his best work in descriptive geography and oceanography; he calculated the circumference of the earth, was the author of our five zones, studied meteorology, and researched into volcanoes. None of his writings survive, save fragments quoted by later writers; and though German scholars have constructed whole systems of what may be called 'Posidonianism', there is little evidence for any of the systems. We may be tolerably sure that he bequeathed to the world into which Christianity was about to enter a general view of the universe which was the background of most men's thought; but we are not in a position to say exactly what that view was. It has been said of him, for example, that 'he was the mediator not only between Greece and Rome, but also between East and West',[3] and some scholars have accordingly discovered Oriental ideas in his philosophy; but he was a pupil of the Stoic Panaetius of Rhodes, and his actual philosophy would seem to have been a version of the Greek Stoicism of his time, tinged and ennobled by Platonism. (It was from Platonism that he drew his sense of the part played by the passions in

---

[1] P. Wendland, *Die Hellenistisch-Römische Kultur*, p. 61.
[2] He had a theory of the origin and development of civilization, and of the service rendered by philosophy to its growth; Seneca refers to and quarrels with his theory (see above, p. 235).
[3] Wendland, op. cit., p. 134.

spinning the plot of human life: unlike the earlier Stoics, who thought of man as a rational mechanism in which the clock of reason ticked away in superior state above the affections of the body, he held that 'moral experience . . . revealed irrationality and evil as ineradicably rooted in human nature and controllable only by some kind of "catharsis" '.)[1] He would appear to have believed, like Nicolas of Cusa in the later Middle Ages, in a *concordantia catholica* or 'general harmony' uniting heaven and earth, and making earthly government, in its true nature, a copy of heavenly; in this life the wise—the philosopher and the true statesman— were to interpret and copy the true order of the divine commonwealth, and at death (as Cicero, perhaps following Posidonius, tells us in the *Somnium Scipionis*) they were to be translated to it.

The extracts which follow are taken, in the main, from the fragments of the *Histories* of Posidonius quoted by later Greek writers. These *Histories*, in fifty-two books, started where Polybius had ended, in 146 B.C., and went down to the period of the Sullan dictatorship, about 80 B.C. They contained geographical (one may even say sociological) description as well as historical narrative; the passages on the Celts are interesting, if not profound; they may be compared with the *Germania* of Tacitus, which they possibly inspired; they show an interest in, and an observation of, the primitive culture of Gaul which may have affected Caesar, who is said to have taken the *Histories* of Posidonius with him when he set out to conquer Gaul. We may at any rate give Posidonius credit for having studied national characters, in the temper of a philosopher, as expressed in ways of life and affected by conditions of climate. He had some grasp of what is nowadays called 'oecology'; he related men and their ways to the habitat in which they lived. He had enough historic sense to compare the

[1] E. R. Dodds, *The Greeks and the Irrational*, pp. 239–40. Professor Dodds quotes a passage in which Galen says of Posidonius, 'He thought that there was a seed of evil in ourselves, and that what we all need is . . . to go in search of those who will purify us and prevent the increase of the evil in us'. One thinks of St. Paul's cry in the Epistle to the Romans, 'O wretched man that I am, who shall deliver me from the body of this death?' Another passage in Galen (quoted in von Arnim's *Stoic. Vet. Frag.* iii, No. 460) shows how Posidonius was led by his sense of the 'seed of evil' to quarrel with the earlier Stoics: 'they fail to see that the first step on the path to happiness is that we should not be swayed in any of our actions by the irrational, unhappy, godless element in our soul'.

Celts of his day with the early Greeks of Homer; and his account of their life is free from the bias of Tacitus' picture of the Germans.

The last extract can only be connected conjecturally with the name of Posidonius. It comes from the opening of the *Bibliotheca Historica* of Diodorus Siculus, and *may* represent Posidonius' philosophy of history. But this last extract is not, after all, the last word to be said about Posidonius. There is a still further, but still more conjectural, word to be said. There is a remarkable little treatise *De Mundo*, written probably about the time when St. Paul was writing his Epistles (a century, that is to say, after the death of Posidonius), which may conceivably represent, or even reproduce, his general philosophy. Notable scholars have held that view. The reader is accordingly asked to proceed from the study of the historical and historiographical passages translated in the present section to the philosophical passages from the *De Mundo* translated in the next, bearing in mind, as he does so, the possibility (it is only that, and no more than that) that he *may* perhaps be reading something which was inspired by the teaching of Posidonius, but comforting himself by the reflection that he is certainly reading something which is notable in itself, whatever its source or its inspiration.

A. *On the Celts*

From Athenaeus, *Deipnosophistae*, iv. 36, § 1. 'Posidonius the Stoic, in his *Histories*, composed in a manner germane to the philosophy which he professed,[1] describes many of the customs and laws of many different peoples. "The Celts", he writes, "set out their meals on straw-covered floors, putting them on wooden tables raised a little from the ground. The meals consist of a few loaves, with plenty of meat, some boiled and some cooked either on the coals or on spits. They handle their food in a cleanly fashion, but as if they were lions at their prey; they take up whole joints in both their hands and gnaw the meat off; what does not come away easily they cut off with a short knife, which is kept in its own case

[1] The philosophical aspect of Posidonius' *Histories* (and of his geographical descriptions) is also noted by Strabo: 'there is much in Posidonius which deals with causes ('aetiological' is the word used by Strabo) and which has an Aristotelian spirit'. (Quoted in Jacoby, *F. Gr. Hist.* ii, p. 224, No. 15.)

fixed on their sword-scabbards. § 2. Fish is also served at meals by the inhabitants of river-sides and of both the sea-coasts of Gaul; it is eaten with salt and vinegar and spices, which last, by the way, they also put into their drinks. They do not use olive-oil owing to its scarcity; indeed they do not like it, because they are not used to it. § 3. When a number of people are dining together, they sit in a circle; the person of the highest rank, as determined by martial prowess or birth or wealth, sits in the middle like the leader of a chorus. The next in rank sit beside him; the rest are seated, one after another, on either side, according to the degree of their rank. Guards with shields stand behind; the spearmen are seated opposite, in a circle like their masters, and join with them in the banquet. § 4. The servants carry the drink round in vessels like our Greek beakers, made of earthenware or silver; the plates for the food are similar, some of them made of brass, and some of them wooden, or woven, platters. The drink of the wealthy is wine, which they import from Italy or from the country round Marseilles; they generally drink it neat, but they sometimes add a little water. The poor drink beer made from corn; they sometimes mix it in a preparation with honey, but most of them drink it unmixed; they call it *korma* [or *courmi*, the Low Latin *cerevisia*]. They all drink from the same vessel in sips, not more than a ladleful at a time; and they do this repeatedly. The attendant brings it round to the right and the left; and this is the way they are served. § 5. They turn to the right when they salute the Gods." '

Ibid. iv. 40. 'Posidonius writes, in book XXIII of his *Histories:* "The Celts sometimes fight at their meals. Assembled in arms, they start sparring matches and challenge one another at arm's length; sometimes they go to the length of wounding one another, and then, getting excited and angry, they come to a death struggle unless bystanders intervene. Indeed . . . it used to happen that when meat was placed on the table, the strongest would seize the joint; and if another man then claimed it, the two would fight to the death." '

Ibid. vi. 49. 'Posidonius of Apamea in book XXIII of his *Histories* writes: "The Celts take attendants about with them in war, too: they call them followers [or, literally, 'table-companions']. These

men chant the praises of their chief, both to crowded gatherings
and to different listeners in turn. Such recitals are given by men
called 'bards'; these are poets who recite men's praises insong."'[1]

B. *On the Syrians*

From Athenaeus, op. cit., xii. 35. 'Posidonius, speaking of the
luxury of the cities of Syria in book xvi of his *Histories*, writes as
follows: "The inhabitants of these cities, who, owing to the fertility
of the soil of Syria, have no trouble in getting the necessities of life,
would often meet in gatherings which they made into continual
feasts. They used athletic grounds and the equipment of those
grounds as if they were mere public baths, anointing themselves
with costly oils and unguents; they spent their whole time in the
'Schools', as the clubs of these boon-companions were called,
just as if they were their homes, gormandizing for most of the
day on wine and food—set out in such plenty that they would
carry off with them a good deal of it—to the accompaniment of
flutes and the sound of many-stringed lyres, so many and so loud
that a whole city would ring with the din."'

Ibid. xv. 46. 'The best thing about scents, my friends, is a story
which I came across in reading book xxviii of the *Histories* of
Posidonius and have since treasured in my memory. The philosopher writes, "In Syria, at the royal banquets, when wreaths
are distributed among the guests, attendants enter with skins full
of Babylonian scents, and going in procession round the room
they scatter drops of scent from a distance on the wreaths of the
guests as they recline at the tables; and nothing else is brought in
to sprinkle them [e.g. no water is brought to keep the wreaths
fresh?]."'

c. *On the Insurgence of the Eastern Mediterranean against Rome and the Attempted Revolution at Athens*, 87 B.C.

From F. Jacoby, *F. Gr. Hist.*, Part II, pp. 244–6.

(*a*) *The dispatches sent by the 'philosopher' Athenion to the people of
Athens*. 'Appointed by the Athenians as an envoy to the court of

---

[1] An account of the Celts of Galatia in Livy (xxxviii. 17) may be based on
Posidonius.

Mithridates, when the march of events was moving in favour of the king, he went to his camp, and meeting there with great success he became one of "the king's friends". Thereupon he excited the Athenians by the dispatches he sent them; he gave them the impression that he exercised such great influence with Mithridates as would ensure them not only freedom from the burden of debt, but also the chance of regaining their old democratic government, of living in concord, and, over and above that, of receiving generous gifts both personally and collectively.'

Athenion thus encouraged old dreams of a social revolution (see above, p. 60) and the idea of recovering political liberty and escaping the tutelage of Rome. Returning to Athens from his embassy, he was received by the people in state, and addressed them in a solemn oration.

(b) *The speech of Athenion to the people of Athens.* 'I have news to give you which you could never have expected, or even imagined in dreams. King Mithridates now rules in western Asia. . . . The kings of Persia and Armenia are his body-guard; with them are the rulers of all the peoples settled round Lake Maeotis [the Sea of Azov], and on the coast of all the Black Sea, in a circuit of 30,000 stadia [over 3,300 miles]. The Roman governor of Pamphylia . . . has surrendered to him, and follows his camp in chains; the Roman consular commander, . . . tied by a long chain to a Bastarnian over seven feet high, is dragged along on foot after the mounted soldier. Of the other Roman citizens, some lie prostrate before their idols; others have exchanged their square-cut togas [for Eastern dress], and now speak again of their original fatherland. All the cities of Asia greet Mithridates with superhuman honours and address him as their God-King. Oracles from every quarter prophesy for him the sovereignty of all the earth. Great armies are accordingly on the move into Thrace and Macedonia, and all parts of Europe are going over to him *en masse*. Envoys are now at his court not only from the tribes of Italy, but also from Carthage; all of them are anxious to be his allies in the war for the destruction of Rome.'

After announcing this insurgence of the Eastern Mediterranean, accompanied by Italian defection and Carthaginian support,

Athenion went on to advise the Athenians about the course they should follow.

'What do I advise you? I advise you not to tolerate longer the anarchy which the Roman Senate is making you endure till such time as it thinks fit to decide on the kind of constitution we are to have. Let us not tolerate the closing of our temples, the neglect of our gymnasiums, the absence of audiences from our theatres, the silence of our law-courts, and the withholding from our people of the Pnyx [the Athenian place of assembly], which is sanctified for us by divine oracles. Let us not tolerate, citizens of Athens, the muzzling of the holy cry of "Iacchus" [at the feasts of Dionysus], the closing of the solemn shrine of the goddesses [Demeter and Persephone], and the silence of the schools of the philosophers.'

The speech was followed by the election of Athenion to the office of general (*stratēgos*). The 'philosopher' (Athenion professed to be a follower of Aristotle and a member of the Peripatetic school) thanked the Athenians for the honour, and assured them, 'Now you are your own generals, and I am at your head; if you combine your strength, I shall be able to do as much as you all can do when you all pull together.' Brave words! But the end of it all was that Athenion established a temporary tyranny—and then, when the Romans defeated Mithridates, collapsed.

D. *The Conception of History stated by Diodorus Siculus, and possibly borrowed from the* Histories *of Posidonius*

Diodorus Siculus, *Bibliotheca Historica*, i, c. 1, § 1: 'It is right and proper that we should all feel a great debt of gratitude to the writers of *general* histories who have made it their ambition to serve the *general* life of their kind by their personal labours.[1] We gain from them instruction, without running any risks, on what makes for our welfare; for they provide their readers with the best fruits of experience by the works which they write. . . . § 3. In addition, they have also made it their ambition to bring the

---

[1] Diodorus, imbued with Stoic ideas of the one common cosmopolis or 'city of the Universe'—ideas perhaps drawn from Posidonius—attempts in his *Historical Library* to write history in terms of those ideas, and to show how the process of events, culminating in the universal empire of Rome over the whole of the *oikoumenē*, has moved to their realization.

whole of mankind, which is one in mutual affinity if divided in space and time, into a single system and under one comprehensive view. Herein they are acting as if they had been born to be agents of divine Providence; for just as Providence has united in a general sympathy the orderly movement of the visible stars and the natures of men[1]—making them revolve continually in a circle through all eternity,[2] and measuring out its portion to each element from the web of destiny—so it is with the writers who describe the general doings of the Universe as though it were a single city—they too make the work they produce a single "statement of account" (*logos*), or general balance-sheet, of the general course of events....

c. ii, § 2. 'If it be true that the myths of the underworld, however fictitious their basis may be, contribute no little to the encouragement of piety and justice among men, how much more are we bound to believe that history—[no myth, but] the prophetess of truth and the mother-country from which the whole of philosophy springs—can shape the characters of men to virtuous and goodly living.'

Note. Diodorus wrote his Universal History about the middle of the first century B.C. That was the time when the influence of Posidonius, an historian as well as a philosopher, was at its height. The conception of history stated by Diodorus accords closely with what is known of general Stoic ideas and the teaching of Posidonius. We know that Diodorus borrowed much of the material of his history (in its nature a compilation) from earlier and from contemporary writers; and it may very well be that he borrowed his general plan and conception of history from the great and dominant historian and thinker of his age. This is the conjecture of Reinhardt (*Poseidonios*, pp. 32–33); and the translator has followed that conjecture. A sentence in Reinhardt's chapter on Posidonius as an historian may be quoted in conclusion: 'here [in the *Histories* of Posidonius] we have the great representative work of an historian rooted and grounded in Stoic philosophy, as

[1] This notion of sympathy, or 'analogy', between the stars in the sky and men's characters and fortunes (a basis of astrology) was one of the Stoic tenets, and could be, and was, extended to the notion of an all-pervading sympathy which connected plants and animals with the movement of the stars and the fortunes of men.

[2] This phrase suggests the idea of cyclical recurrence (*anacyclōsis*) which we find in Polybius and Cicero (*supra*, pp. 113, 187).

Orosius was in Christianity, Thucydides in Greek Enlightenment, and Taine in Positivism' (op. cit., p. 32).

§ II. THE PSEUDO-ARISTOTELIAN TREATISE 'DE MUNDO' AND ITS CONCEPTION OF THE COSMOS

This treatise may be dated somewhere about the middle of the first century A.D. It professes to be a letter of Aristotle to Alexander, and it contains some Aristotelian elements; but in the view of Wilamowitz-Moellendorff (*Griechisches Lesebuch*, ii. 1, p. 186) 'the best in it is really borrowed from Posidonius, not only in its substance, but also in its style'. In any case, and whether or no it contains elements drawn from Posidonius, the treatise is notable in itself as a lofty expression of paganism at its best, in the form of a pure monotheism, given to the world at the time when St. Paul was teaching and writing (*circa* A.D. 50). It must have had vogue: it was translated into Latin (by Apuleius), and even into Armenian. The argument of the treatise may be compared with the 'arguments for belief in the Divine' stated by Sextus Empiricus (in his *Adversus Mathematicos*, ix, §§ 60–87; see Dr. Edwyn Bevan's *Later Greek Religion*, pp. 79–88)—the more so as Sextus Empiricus is also believed to have drawn on Posidonius. An analysis and appreciation of the *De Mundo* is given by H. Lietzmann in *The Beginnings of the Christian Church*, Eng. trans., pp. 174–6. An account of its philosophy is also given by E. Peterson at the beginning of his remarkable little book on *Der Monotheismus als politisches Problem*.

A. *The Harmony of the Cosmos based on a balance of opposites*

De Mundo, c. 5. 'Some thinkers have wondered how it can possibly be that the Cosmos, composed as it is of opposite elements—the dry and the moist, and the hot and the cold—has not long ago been destroyed and annihilated. But others might equally wonder how a *State* should continue to exist, composed as it is of the most opposite classes of people—poor and rich, young and old, weak and strong, bad and good. Yet to feel such wonder is also to show oneself ignorant of the most astonishing feature of political concord (*homonoia*)—the creation from many heterogeneous elements of one homogeneous disposition which includes every sort of character and fortune.

'Perhaps Nature has a desire for opposites, and perhaps it is from opposites, and not from likes, that she creates harmony; just as she has united the male with the female, but not either of them with its own kind, thereby creating and combining from opposites—and not from likes—the first and original concord. Art too, in imitation of nature, would seem to follow this line; painting mixes white, black, yellow, and green colours to create portraits in harmony with their originals; music blends high, low, long, and short notes to create a harmony of different sounds; literature makes a compound of consonants and vowels to produce thereby the whole art of letters. ... It is exactly as was said by the riddling philosopher Heraclitus: "Combinations—that is, wholes and not wholes; convergent and divergent; concordant and discordant—; one made up of all, and all made up from one." Thus it is that the constitution of all wholes—of heaven, for example, and of earth, and indeed of all the universe—has been disposed in order by the power of a single harmony, acting through the union of the most opposite elements; and thus the mixture of dry and moist, hot and cold, light and heavy, straight and round has disposed in their order all the earth and the sea, the aether and the sun, and the whole of heaven. One and single is the force which pervades all things,[1] and which has created from things separate and different—air and earth and fire and water—all the universe (*cosmos*); comprehending it all within the surface of one sphere, compelling the most opposite natures to agree with one another therein, and contriving from them security for the whole. The cause of this security is the agreement of the elements; and the cause of that agreement is their equilibrium (*isomoiria*) and the inability of any one element to encroach upon another: the heavy is in equipoise with the light, and the hot with its opposite— Nature teaching us in these large letters that equality is somehow the preserver of concord, and concord, in its turn, the preserver

---

[1] So in the Wisdom of Solomon, c. vii. 24, it is said of Wisdom that 'alone in kind . . . she pervadeth and penetrateth all things'.

of the Universe, which is the begetter of all things and itself of excelling beauty. . . .'

B. *The Wonder of the Universe, and of the Earth, and of the Rhythm of Birth and Death*

'Moreover [beyond its beauty], the Universe is in magnitude the all-highest, in motion the swiftest, in its shining the brightest, in its power unageing and unfailing. . . . From it all creatures that are have breath and life.[1] . . . The earth also, which is garlanded with plants of all kinds, bubbling on all sides with springs, and traversed all over by living creatures; which brings forth all things in due season and gives them nourishment and welcome, and bears on her breast innumerable shapes and natures—she, likewise, keeps her unageing nature, although she is shaken by earthquakes, and overwhelmed by floods, and scorched in some of her regions by fires (? volcanoes).[2] . . . So it is too with individual beings [as distinct from the Universe and the earth]: some are in the stage of birth, some in their maturity, and some in decay; the births balance the deaths, and the deaths ease the way for the births; and the total state of security, which is brought about by them all as they are continually being balanced against one another and are now dominant and now again dominated, keeps all unfailing for ever.'

C. *The First Cause which holds all things together, and the distinction between its power and its being*

c. 6. 'It remains to speak summarily of the Cause which keeps wholes together, just as we have spoken summarily of the other topics. In dealing with the theme of the Universe we should go wrong—even though we are not attempting accuracy of detail but only seeking to give a general impression—were we to omit the most sovereign power in its working. There is an old saying, handed down everywhere from father to son, that all things come from God and are held together for us by Him, and that there is

[1] In the Greek *psyche*, or 'life-force' (see below, p. 319, n. 1).
[2] We may remember that Posidonius studied volcanoes. Indeed the whole passage seems to be reminiscent of the cosmology of Posidonius.

nothing of such a nature that it can in itself, and by itself, be self-sufficient if it loses the security which He gives. This is the reason why some of the ancients were led to say that "all these things are full of gods"—all the things which are presented to us by our eyes and ears and the rest of our senses—and their saying is right and proper if it be applied to the *power* of God, though not if it be applied to His *essence*.[1] He is indeed the preserver and begetter of everything brought about in this Universe in any way whatsoever; but He does not take upon Himself the labour of a living creature that uses its own limbs when it acts and puts out its own effort. He applies only the untiring *power* by which He exercises sway over things which seem remote. He Himself has for His portion the first and highest seat, and He is therefore called the Highest, and sits, as the poet says, on "the topmost towers" of the whole heaven; and so it is that the matter which at any moment is near Him profits most, so to say, from His power, and after that the matter next to it, and so on in a succession of descent down to the region in which we live. This is why the earth, and all that is on it, being farthest removed from the benefit of the divine influence, is weak and of a different nature from the rest of the Universe, and is full of much disorder; though, in so far as it is the nature of Godhead to penetrate all things, our world and the worlds above us alike feel its effect, sharing to a greater or less degree, in proportion as they are nearer to God or farther from Him, in the benefits of His influence. It is better therefore to hold, as is proper and suits best the nature of God, that the power which is seated in heaven is, in a word, the [transcendent] cause of security for all things, even those farthest removed from it; better than it is to think that this power penetrates and frequents with its *presence* a region where it is not good or seemly that it should show itself, or to hold that it acts directly on earthly affairs. Why, it is not even fitting for human rulers to address themselves to every chance duty; it would not be right, for example, for the commander of an army, or the head of a state or family, to take

---

[1] The suggestion is that God acts everywhere by His power or *dynamis*, but He is not present everywhere as a Being or *ousia* in actual presence, since He acts in the main at a distance through organs or intermediaries.

on himself the duty of acting when it was necessary to tie up the bedclothes or do any other menial task which any slave could do; on the contrary he would act as we are told the King of Persia did' [i.e. by sending the signal for action down through a graded hierarchy of agents].

D. *How the First Cause exerts its power indirectly, through a series of agents*

'If, therefore, it was improper that Xerxes should appear to be doing things for himself, carrying out his purposes in person and managing matters by his own personal supervision, how much more would it be unseemly for God. It is far more proper, and much more seemly, that He should be seated in His own *being* on the farthest height, while His *power* pervades the whole Universe, moving the sun and moon, making all heaven revolve in its orbit, and being the cause of security to all that is on the earth.' His action is like that of the skilled engineer, who performs a number of different operations by one movement of a cord in a machine; or, again, it is like that of the puppet-show man, who by pulling a string makes all his puppets go through their various motions in a regular rhythm. 'In the same way the Divine Nature, beginning with some simple motion of the first agent, communicates its power to things adjacent to it, and from them again to things at a greater distance, until it passes and goes through all things. Thus one thing, moved itself by another, goes on in its turn to move yet another in due order, all things thus acting in a manner appropriate to their own constitution; yet the way they go is not one and the same for all, and they follow different and various, and sometimes even opposite, ways, albeit the original keynote that led to the whole motion was one and a single note. . . . It is as if one had in one's lap simultaneously a water animal, a land animal, and a creature with wings, and let them all loose in one movement; obviously the one that could swim would leap into its own natural element and swim off, the land animal would creep away to its own habits and haunts, and the creature of the air would rise up from the earth and go off aloft in flight—the one

First Cause having given to each its own proper facility of
motion. . . .'

E. *The Universe singing together as a chorus, and marching as one 'army
of unalterable law'*

'So a single harmony, proceeding from all [the heavenly bodies]
as they sing together and dance through heaven, is born of unity
and ends in unity; and hence the whole has been truly called the
Cosmos (or order), and not chaos (*akosmia*, or disorder). Just as
at a concert, when the leader has given the note, the whole chorus
of men—and sometimes also of women—joins in at once, combining the different voices, both the high and the low, in one
concordant harmony, so it is also with God, who conducts the
whole sum of things; for it is by the keynote given from above by
Him who may be called, in a metaphor, the leader of the world's
chorus that the stars and all heaven for ever move . . .[1].

'The going of the Universe is in truth, and particularly, very
like what happens in times of war, when the trumpet gives the
signal to an army: as each hears the sound, one will shoulder his
shield, another put on his breastplate, another buckle on his
greaves or helmet or baldric; one man will bridle his horse,
another mount his chariot, and a third pass on the watchword:
the captain of a company at once joins his unit and the lieutenant
his men; the horseman gallops to his troop and the light-armed
soldier hurries to his place; all move to a single command according to the instructions given by the officer in charge. We must
think in a similar way about the Universe at large: here, too, each
unit performs its proper function when all are moved by one
impulse; and while the impulse itself is unseen, and indeed
invisible, that fact is in no way an impediment either to its own

[1] The beginning of Goethe's *Faust* naturally springs to the mind
Die Sonne tönt nach alter Weise
In Brudersphären Weltgesang.
But Cicero, in his *De Republica* (book VI, c. xviii), had already discoursed—
perhaps drawing from neo-Pythagorean sources—on the music of the spheres.
'What is that great and sweet sound that fills my ears?' the younger Scipio asks.
'It is' the elder Scipio replies, 'the sound . . . made by the sweep and motion of
the spheres: blending high notes with low, it regularly issues in a variety of
harmonies.'

operation or to our confidence in it. [There is an analogy to this in man]: the life force within ourselves (the *psychē*), by virtue of which we live and have houses and cities, is unseen, and yet visible in its fruits. By it the order of our life has been discovered and disposed, and by it that order is sustained—the irrigation and planting of the soil, the devices of the arts, the uses of law, the order of constitutions, domestic affairs, foreign hostilities, peace. We must think so also of God, who is strongest in power, fairest in beauty, immortal in life, and best in goodness; for though He be invisible to all mortal natures, He is seen and known in His works. . . .'

The translation is made from the text in Wilamowitz-Moellendorff's *Griechisches Lesebuch*, vol. i, part 2, pp. 190–6.

§ III. DIO OF PRUSA

Dio of Prusa, also called Chrysostom, was a Greek rhetorician and writer of the period of 'the Second Sophistic', who lived from about A.D. 40 to some time after 112. Born in Asia Minor, of a good family, he settled first in Rome; but banished by Domitian in A.D. 82, he led for some years a wandering life, which took him as far afield as Olbia, on the Black Sea, and Alexandria in Egypt. He regained favour under Nerva and Trajan, and became a preacher and philosopher of some fame. His philosophy is an ordinary mixture of Stoicism and Cynicism; but his experience of life in exile and his fund of human sympathy give an abiding interest to his writings. Some eighty of his orations survive. Many of them (such as the first four orations, on Kingship) are mainly a matter of well-turned commonplaces; but there are at least three which deserve study—the Euboean oration (6) on the social condition of town and country in Greece; the lively and critical oration delivered to the people of Alexandria (32); and the Borysthenic oration (36), with its vivid description of the plight of the Greek colony of Olbia. Perhaps the best of these, as a document illustrative of the social conditions and ideas current in the Greek world about A.D. 100, is the Euboean oration, and especially the part of it which deals with urban conditions and the reform of urban life. Some of this is so 'modern' that it might have been written by a town-planner of our own days.

A. *From the Euboean Oration (7), on the lines of a proper urban policy for Greece*

The first part of the Euboean oration is largely in the nature of an Arcadian pastoral dealing, in the form of a story, with the delights and opportunities of life in the country; but it sketches, almost incidentally, an agricultural policy designed to bring more land under cultivation and to foster the growth of a peasant population. At present, Dio argues, nearly two-thirds of Euboea is waste, owing partly to neglect and partly to lack of population; why not encourage people to take up and cultivate derelict public land, with freedom from rent for the first ten years, and, after that, on a *métayer* tenancy under which they pay a small part of the produce (§§ 34–37)? From this suggestion of agricultural policy he turns in the second part of his oration to suggest an urban policy (§§ 104–52).

'We must now consider the condition and occupations of the poor who lead an urban life in cities; we must see by what sort of method, and by following what sort of pursuits, they will best be able to achieve a decent standard of life, no worse in its way than that of the money-lender, with his high rates of interest, . . . or of the owner of large blocks of flats. . . .

'There may well be only a few jobs available in cities for poor men of this order, and their remuneration may need to be supplemented by the provision of outside help, considering that there is house-rent to be paid and other things to be bought—not only clothes and furniture and food, but even the wood to keep a fire going. . . . Very possibly it will not be found easy to meet the demands of such a life when men have no capital of their own except their bodies—especially as they will not be willing, if they follow our advice, to accept any and every kind of occupation, or to jump indiscriminately at any means of making money. So perhaps we shall be forced, by the logic of our argument, to remove from our cities the poor who try to keep themselves decent, as the one way of getting in real life Homer's "well-ordered cities", inhabited only by men of substance; and we shall accordingly, it would seem, refuse to allow free labourers to have houses inside the city-walls. But what, in that case, are we to do with all these people? Shall we disperse them in settlements up and down the countryside? That is how the Athenians are said to have been distributed all over Attica in antiquity, and again at a later date when Peisistratus was tyrant of Athens; and this mode of life was not to their disadvantage, nor did it produce an ignoble type of citizens—on the contrary it bred men who were in all respects better and soberer than the later generation which was maintained inside the city by the pay its members received for attending the public assembly, or for acting as jurors in the law-courts, or for serving as clerks in the civil service—a mob at once lazy and vulgar. It would not therefore involve any great danger or difficulty if such people were one and all turned entirely into rustics and country-dwellers. None the less, I am inclined to think that they might manage even if they stayed in the town.'

Dio accordingly proceeds to ask what decent urban occupations can be found, to prevent the poor from being compelled, by the pressure of unemployment, to betake themselves to some low and degrading sort of trade (109). Unfortunately he gives no clear or positive answer to the question. He confines himself to suggesting (1) what is the general nature of a decent urban occupation, and (2) what are the low and degrading forms of employment which ought not to be allowed in a city.

His view of the general nature of a decent urban occupation is that it should not be such as to encourage any immoral tendency in the mind, or to injure the health of the body by making it flabby and feeble for lack of proper exercise. This is a vague definition, and he gives no actual example, contenting himself with the assertion that men who follow a decent occupation will never lack work or a living, or ever give the rich an excuse for calling them, as they now do, a helpless and shiftless lot; on the contrary they will be more productive and make better shift than the rich, and they will never be at a loss for anything needful or useful (112–13). This leads him to protest, as the poor man's advocate, against the social snobbery which, not content with sneering at a man's own occupation, will also sneer at that of his parents, and go out of its way to proclaim, 'Oh, his mother was a domestic servant, or a grape-picker, or a wet-nurse', or 'His father was only a schoolmaster, or merely a private tutor'.

Dio ends his argument by an enumeration of the low and degrading forms of employment which ought not to be allowed in cities. His list is curious and instructive: it includes the arts of cosmetics and the internal decoration of houses; it includes acting and miming and dancing, and also harp- and flute-playing; it includes, in a conjunction which seems strange today, the professions of hawker, town-crier, attorney, and legal advocate ('for if', he argues, 'it is necessary for some men to become handicraftsmen, there is no need for any man to become a tongue-craftsman or a law-craftsman', 124). At this stage of his enumeration he pauses in order to note that he is not attempting to deal with the subject of 'polity' (as Plato and Aristotle had done), or to describe the best form of government; he is simply seeking to deal with the problem of poverty, to show that the poor man's state is not hopeless, and to suggest that it offers those who are willing to do manual work a great number of opportunities for getting a living by means which will neither lower their standing nor injure their bodily health (125). An inquiry such as this (he argues) is of general service in the field of 'polity', and contributes to the adoption of a proper line of policy; and thus the study of occupations and crafts, and of the general way of life which is suitable for ordinary people, proves itself to be intrinsically worthy of prolonged and careful investigation (125, 127).

This last stage of Dio's argument brings him back to the enumeration of low and degrading occupations, and he turns as he ends to what he regards as the worst of them all—the keeping of brothels and the encouragement of prostitution. Here he leaves the theme of social economics for the field of social morality, and he becomes eloquent, and even moving, in his criticism of contemporary Greek practice. He shows a genuine feeling for the dignity of human personality and the rights of women (he speaks of Greek women as 'in former times not utterly subject, but now living in complete and total slavery'); and he would have prostitution legally forbidden. He gives two reasons why this 'outrage' (*hubris*) should not be condoned. The first is that 'all mankind alike has been made for honour, and for an equal measure of honour, by God who gave it its being, and all of it has the same signs and tokens of its just title to honour—reason, and the knowledge of good and evil' (138). The second is that wrong, when it is fostered by licence, can hardly be kept within bounds, and State-permitted vice, instead of acting as a bulwark to domestic virtue, invades and corrupts such virtue by its pernicious example.

It may be said of the whole of this argument that even if it runs at times into vague and facile generalities, it is none the less a sketch of social policy, and a plan of social welfare, which has hardly any parallel in classical literature. Possibly Dio was influenced by some knowledge of the social legislation of Nerva and Trajan (*C.A.H.* vol. xi, pp. 210–3); but the agricultural measures of Hadrian (ibid., p. 317) offer the closest parallel, at any rate to the proposals in §§ 34–37.

B. *From the Borysthenic Oration* (36), *on the Polis and the Cosmos*

In § 20 of this oration, delivered in a Greek colony on the north of the Black Sea about A.D. 95, Dio had defined a *polis* as 'a body of men dwelling in the same place under the government of law'. A little later in the oration he enters upon the question whether or no the whole Cosmos is to be regarded as a *polis*. In dealing with that question he first states the views of his own school of thought, the Stoic, and then expounds, in a curious and notable passage, what he calls a 'myth sung in secret rites by the Magi' of Persia. Modern scholars have traced this myth, and it appears that Dio was actually 'giving the contents of a hymn of the "Magi", i.e. those Persian missionaries who laboured in Asia Minor, who mingled the ancient Persian theology of Mithra with astral elements of Babylonian origin, and who Hellenized the whole by assimilating it to Stoic doctrines' (Lietzmann, *The Beginnings of the Christian Church*, English translation, p. 265).

§ 29. 'Our school [the Stoic] does not regard the Cosmos as literally and actually a *polis*. That would be opposed to their doctrine of the *polis*, which they define, as I have already said, as

an organization ('system') of men. Having laid it down authorita-
tively that the Universe is a living being (*zōon*), they could hardly
go on with any propriety or conviction to say that it is a "system"
or *polis*. § 30. Nobody, I imagine, would readily consent to regard
the same thing as being at once a *polis* and a living being. And yet,
when they consider the existing order of the Universe [divided
into a variety of parts, but united, none the less, in and through
all its parts, and governed by one soul and power], Stoic thinkers
apply to it the metaphor of the *polis*, partly because of the number
of the births and deaths that occur in it [as they do in a *polis*], and
partly because of the similar order and regularity of its government. § 31. Their doctrine, in short, has sought to bring mankind
in general into harmony with the Godhead, and to include, in the
compass of a single term, all that belongs to the sphere of Reason
(*Logos*), since it is in Reason, and therein only, that Stoicism finds
a strong and irrefragable foundation of society and justice. On
this view the term "polis" could not be used of a political association which had mean or small men as its leaders, or which was
always vexed and made a prey to sedition by tyrants at one
extreme and mobs at the other, or, in and between, was troubled
by cliques and oligarchies and other similar defective forms of
government. The word "polis" would, on the contrary, be applied to an association which was graced by the soundest and best
type of kingship, an association really governed by a king, acting
in accordance with law, in a spirit of complete friendship and
concord. § 32. This, indeed, is what the wisest and the most
ancient of all rulers and law-givers [Zeus] ordains for us all,
mortals and immortals alike; it is the will of the leader of all
Heaven and the master of all Being, who thus acts as his own
interpreter and offers his own method of government as an
example of what brings bliss and felicity. He it is whom the poets,
taught to do so by the Muses, laud and call by the name of "father
of Gods and men".'

In the following sections, 33 to 35, Dio celebrates the intuition
and insight of the ancient poets, such as Homer, 'to whose ears
there came some few words from the lips of the Muses, or who
were in some way inspired by a union of divine nature and truth,

coming like the gleam of a fire that shines out of the darkness'. Taught by the poets, he goes on to say (§§ 36–37), men acknowledge Zeus as father and king, thus implying that the universe is in the nature of a family or kingdom. If that is so, we may call the cosmos 'the house of Zeus' (*domus Dei*), on the ground that he is the father of its inhabitants; indeed we may even call it 'the city of Zeus' (*civitas Dei*), on the ground that he is King of us all, thus using the metaphor drawn by the Stoics from the larger association of the *polis* in preference to the metaphor of the house or family. 'This then', Dio concludes in § 35, 'is the theory of the philosophers' [but actually he has been stating it as the inspiration of the poets]; 'it is a theory which attests the existence of a noble and benevolent community in which gods and men are joined; it is a theory which gives a share in law and citizenship not to all living beings of every sort and kind, but only to those who partake of reason (*logos*) and understanding; and it thus introduces a code far better, and far juster, than the Spartan Code which gives the Helots no chance of ever becoming Spartan citizens' [whereas the man who cultivates his faculty of reason, and becomes, in the Stoic phrase, wise or *sapiens*, *can* become thereby a citizen of the *civitas Dei*].

In the rest of his oration, §§ 35–61, Dio recites and explains the cosmological myth of the Magi. It is a mixture of Platonic and Stoic ideas with the ideas of Zoroastrianism and of Babylonian astrology. It begins with a picture of the four horses which draw the chariot of Creation (Zeus being the chief of the four); it includes the element of a world-conflagration (the *ecpyrōsis* of Stoic theory) and the Babylonian element of a deluge; it ends with a consummation in which Zeus absorbs the other three horses and 'attaining the purest nature of uncontaminated light' creates a new and splendid universe in the perfection of which he rejoices. This part of Dio's oration has curious affinities with Gnosticism; and it is, like Gnosticism, a part of that 'orientalization' of thought, often running to wild extremes, from which an organized and disciplined Christianity eventually saved the world.

Note. The pseudo-Aristotelian treatise *De Mundo* (see above, pp. 289–95), which is a little prior to this oration, contains an argument similar to that of Dio. The monotheism of the *De Mundo* is, indeed, purer than that of Dio, and may almost be called the highest expression of 'natural religion' ever attained by pre-Christian thought. But the Pseudo-Aristotle, like Dio, regards the world as being, at any rate metaphorically, a single 'State' or Society embracing both gods and men.

c. *From the Alexandrine Oration* (32)

Dio delivered an oration (somewhere around the year A.D. 100) to the Greek *polīteuma* or civic organization in Alexandria. He gives a vivid picture of its character, and paints the general social background which lay behind the work of Philo in the first century A.D., and that of Clement of Alexandria and Origen in the second and third century.

§ 25. 'I say that the people in a democracy resembles most a potentate (*dynastēs*) with very large powers and possessed of great authority and force—a potentate all the greater, and controlling all the more persons, in proportion as the people is itself more numerous and inhabits a greater city. § 26. [Now potentates in general are of two kinds]: one of the kinds is kings, men who have been deified as a means to the general security, men who are real guardians, gracious and just leaders of their subjects, . . . rejoicing in the good order (*cosmos*) of the cities which they rule; the other kind is harsh and fierce tyrants—men who are under the sway of flattery and deceit. § 27. So, too, the peoples of democracies are also of two kinds: one of the kinds is reasonable, mild, and genuinely calm, with an appetite for freedom of thought and its expression . . . and this kind I reckon as being of the divine and kingly type [i.e. as akin to the good kind of kingship]. . . . § 28. The other kind, which is more common, is rash and over-bearing, hard to please in any way, fastidious, like tyrants—but even worse, because their vice is not a single or simple vice, but a composite vice made up of tens of thousands of vices. . . . § 29. To which of these two kinds are we to assign the people of Alexandria?' Dio does not answer the question directly. He admits that the Alexandrines, when they are listening intently to a speech, are a sight worth seeing; but he then proceeds to depict their behaviour when they are excited—as they often are. § 31. '. . . There is a story current about an old saying in regard to you, 'What can one say of the people of Alexandria? They are people before whom one ought only to cast plenty of bread and a good view of a horse-race, for there is nothing else they care for.' . . . § 41. [So it is still today: visitors to Alexandria say to one another, as they leave it] "We have seen a city which goes mad about songs and horse-races, and in these matters behaves in a way utterly unworthy of itself." ' Mixing the sweet with the bitter, Dio compliments his hearers on the fact that their city is 'at the cross-roads, as it were, of the whole world', and is thus a universal market (§ 36), and again on the wide and cosmopolitan range from which its population is drawn (§ 40); he allows that Alexandria is 'all but the centre of the inhabited globe, as well as the most populous of cities' (§ 47); but he persists in his criticism of the vulgar concerts and the mad horse-races of the city—or at any rate of the Greek *politeuma* in the city. § 62. 'Who among all the artists at your concerts can sing a finished song or produce a fine rhythm? Nothing comes from them but croonings of women and thrummings of dance-tunes and intoxicated extravaganzas, which they mix in a hotch-potch, like bad cooks who are trying to be clever, in order to tickle the appetite of an ignorant and lickerish audience for their music. . . . § 74. So much for what goes on in the theatre. But when it comes to your racecourse, who could describe your behaviour—your bawling and din and anguish, your changes of attitude and colour, and the variety and volume of your curses? . . . Why, if you yourselves [instead of the horses] were being lashed by whips [such as the Furies are represented as using] in tragedies, you would not show such distress.'

D. *From the four Orations on Kingship* (1–4)

Dio delivered four discourses on Kingship (*peri basileias*). They would all appear to have been delivered at different times in the presence of the Emperor Trajan, about the years A.D. 98–104. They are accordingly in the nature of encomia of monarchy, with little if any original thought; but they are of interest as illustrating current views on the matter in the high midsummer of the Empire. (See also p. 300 above for Dio's theory of kingship.)

The First Oration on Kingship

1. *The King a shepherd.* §§ 12–13. 'Only the good king receives his sceptre from Zeus, and he receives it on the one condition that he should direct his counsel and care to the interests of his subjects . . . becoming in fact the herdsman and shepherd of his people, and not a reveller at banquets given at their expense.'

2. *The King as concerned to secure the greatest good of the greatest number.* §§ 22–23. ' "Father" of his fellow-citizens and subjects, he is not only addressed as such in words (*pater patriae*); he is shown to be such by his deeds. As for being "Master" (*despotēs*), he takes no delight in being so called, even as far as concerns slaves, and much less as concerns the free; for he regards himself as holding the office of king not so much for his own benefit— since he is only one person—as for the sake of all. . . . § 65. Zeus saw that his son, Heracles, did not wish to be a ruler from any desire for pleasures and privileges, which is the reason why most men are enamoured of authority, but rather in order that he might be able to do the greatest good to the greatest number (*pleista kai pleistous eu poiein*).' He therefore sent Hermes to guide him in the choice between the Two Ways—the safe and broad way leading upward to the Royal Summit, and the narrow and precipitous way which goes to the other and lower summit, the Summit Tyrannical, named after the giant Typhon.[1]

3. *The King's Friends.* § 32. Aristotle, in the *Politics* (III, c. xi, § 2), had urged that the people, meeting in its assembly, became something in the nature of a composite single person, with many feet, hands, and senses. Dio argues that a king who has friends as his counsellors also becomes, in virtue of their company, a composite person with many organs and faculties. Aristotle, too, had

---

[1] The name Typhon would suggest to a Greek the notion of overweening and violent conceit (for which the Greek word is *typhos*). The idea of the Two Ways is as old as the apologue of 'the Choice of Hercules', ascribed to Prodicus of Ceos (400 B.C.). Dio uses it again in a different form in his Thirtieth Oration, called *Charidemus*, §§ 36–38, where he imagines two cup-bearers, the male Intelligence (*Nous*) and the female Incontinence, the one offering to the choice of the banqueters the cup of sobriety, and the other the cup of mere pleasure.

used much the same argument in the *Politics*, III, c. xvi, § 12. 'The
more companions a king acquires, the more eyes he has to see
what he wishes to see, the more ears to hear what he ought to
hear, and the more brains for the planning of advantageous
policies. It is just as if Heaven had given to a person who had only
one body a number of minds, all of them taking thought on his
behalf.' The argument is repeated, in greater detail, in Dio's Third
Oration on Kingship, §§ 104–7.

4. *The King as a copy of the Heavenly King and a link in the chain
of the Universe*. §§ 37–38. 'After the previous description of the
good king, I wanted to speak next of the first and greatest King
and Ruler, whom mortal men, and those who administer their
affairs, must always copy in the conduct of government, directing
and conforming their own ways, as far as they possibly can, to
the standard of his ways. This is the reason why Homer speaks
of true kings as "Zeus-trained" and "like Zeus in counsel". . . .
In fact almost every king who has ever, either among Greeks or
barbarians, proved himself worthy of his title, is shown by his
record to have been a disciple and follower of Zeus.[1]

§ 42. 'It is a noble theme of discourse to treat of the order of the
Universe—how the whole sum of things, in all its felicity and
wisdom, is ever traversing infinite time without intermission in
infinite cycles, attended on its course by good fortune, by a corresponding genius, by forethought, and by a principle of perfect justice
and goodness; and how, too, it makes us like itself, being as we
are—in virtue of the community between its nature and ours—
arrayed under one and the same ordinance and law with it, and
sharing as we do in the same system of government. . . . §§ 45–46.
So it is with kings also, inasmuch as, I take it, they hold their
powers and commission from Zeus; those who look to him, and
who order and rule their subjects well and justly, according to the
law and ordinance of Zeus, are blessed with a good lot in life and

---

[1] In his Thirtieth Oration, the *Charidemus*, § 26, Dio suggests that the human
world is a colony from heaven, endowed by its founders, as Greek colonies were
by their 'oecists', with the rights and laws of the 'metropolis' or mother-city.
'When the gods acquired control of the universe, they planted mankind on the
earth, which then was void and empty, as a sort of colony of themselves, with
less honour and felicity, but with the same rights and laws—just as great and
prosperous states plant out smaller states.'

a happy end; those who go astray, and dishonour him who entrusted them with their commission and gave them his gift, have no profit of all their great authority and power—unless it be to serve as manifest examples of evil-doing and incontinence to all of their generation and to all that come after them.'

The Second Oration on Kingship

The Second Oration is in the nature of a literary exercise couched in the form of an 'imaginary conversation' between Alexander of Macedon and his father Philip. The one new idea which it adds is that a king who becomes a tyrant will be deposed by Zeus.

The Deposition of Unjust Kings. § 79. Just as herdsmen depose a savage bull from the leadership of the herd, and prefer a stately and magnificent animal which combines a mild temper with a good courage, 'so too the Gods act, and such is the way of Zeus, the great King of kings, according to his nature as the common father and protector of gods and men. If any man proves himself a ruler who relies on force and violates justice and law, using his power against his subjects and friends instead of against his enemies . . . Zeus thrusts him aside and removes him, as a man unworthy to be king or to share in his own honour and title.'

Third Oration on Kingship

The Third Oration, addressed, like the first, to Trajan, is a general statement of the theory of kingship current in the philosophic schools of the day.

Types of Government. § 45. 'Of constitutions which are in accordance with law and justice, and attended by a good genius and corresponding good fortune, there are three forms which are most conspicuous, and three names attached to them. One of these forms is the first to appear and the most practicable: it is the form with which the present discourse is concerned; it is the form in which a city, or a number of peoples, or the whole of mankind, is governed—and governed well—by the discretion and virtue of one good man. § 46. The second form is that which is called aristacracy: it is the government not of one person, nor of a large number of persons, but of an *élite* of the few best who enjoy a position of leadership; it is a form which is already far removed from being practicable or beneficial. Such a view, so it seems to me, is what Homer too had in mind when he said, "It is not good to have many masters; let there be but one master, one king, to whom the Son of Cronus gave the sceptre." § 47. The third form may be said to be the most impracticable of all: it is a form based on the expectation that the moderation and goodness of the people may one day be the means of discovering a constitution which is equitable and based on law; it is called democracy or government of the people, a name which suggests a spirit of equity and consideration—if only the thing were possible. § 48. To these three forms of constitution there stand opposed three perversions which are all without a basis of law. The first of them is tyranny, under which the force and insolence of one man, the worst in the community, brings all the rest to ruin. The second is oligarchy, a harsh and unjust form, which is brought into being by the aggrandizement of a handful of wealthy and wicked men at the expense of the many poor. § 49. The third and last is based on the motley and nondescript flood of the masses, who have no knowledge whatsoever and are excited into confusion and savagery by reckless demagogues, just as a wild and stormy sea is tossed up and down by gales. . . .' § 50. We may dismiss these perversions. 'But we are bound to examine more carefully the happy and heaven-sent system which is now in force [i.e. the imperial system of Trajan's reign]. There are many clear images and striking examples of this form of government to be found in the world around us. Nature shows us, by the evidence of herds of cattle and swarms of bees, how natural it is that the stronger should rule over and care for the weak. But there cannot be found any clearer or better image of kingship than the way in which the whole universe is governed under the sovereignty of Him who is the first and highest of gods. § 51. A ruler after this manner has, to begin with, the enjoyment of the favour of the gods, inasmuch as he receives the highest honour and confidence from them, and he will make the worship of the Deity his first and greatest aim; he will not only profess, but he will also genuinely believe, that there are gods, and he will do so in order that he too [like them] may have men under him who hold their office by the title of merit.'

Fourth Oration on Kingship

This, again, is an address to Trajan, possibly on his birthday; and again, like the Second Oration, it is a literary exercise couched in the form of an imaginary conversation, between Alexander and Diogenes the Cynic. § 13. 'Alexander, when he was in Corinth, left his companions and went to visit Diogenes. This was no going to court, for Diogenes kept no sort of court, either great or small; in fact he had no home or hearth of his own, like those who are blessed with the goods of this world; he treated whole cities as his homes, and spent his time in public buildings and in temples consecrated to the gods; indeed he accounted all mother earth as his hearth, since she is the common hearth and nurse of us all.'

In the conversation which follows Diogenes warns Alexander (§§ 75 ff.) that 'he will never be a king until he propitiates his guardian spirit and treats it with due consideration, proving it a free, governing, and royal spirit, and not—as it is now—an un-free, servile, and evil spirit'. He then proceeds to explain that there are three spirits, or ways of life, which a man may cherish—that of luxury, that of avarice, and that of honour and glory. The moral which he then draws is that all three may lead men astray— even the way of honour and glory, because it breeds contention and encourages instability of purpose; and his final words are an exhortation to Alexander 'to seek a pure and better harmony than he has hitherto had, and to sing praises to the god and to the spirit of temperance and goodness'.

§ IV. PLUTARCH ON KINGSHIP, WITH A PARALLEL PASSAGE FROM MUSONIUS RUFUS

A

Plutarch (*circa* A.D. 50–120) wrote works of popular philosophy in an eclectic vein, following, in the main, the ideas of contemporary Platonism, but adding Stoic and other elements. The famous passage in which he traced a connexion between the ideas of Alexander and the political philosophy of the Stoic Zeno has already been quoted (*supra*, pp. 7–8); and his account of social movements at Sparta under the kings Agis and Cleomenes has also been cited (*supra*, pp. 53–57). There is little else in his voluminous writings which bears on the history of social and political ideas; but one or two passages in a brief allocution addressed *To an Uneducated Ruler* deserve mention for the conception of kingship which they seek to express.

To an Uneducated Ruler, § 3. 'Who, then, shall rule the ruler? We may answer, with Pindar, "Law, the king of us all, both mortals and immortals"—not the external law which is written in books or on tablets of wood, but the law which is Animate Reason (*empsychos logos*) embodied in him [i.e. the ruler]; the law which always lives with him and watches over him, and never leaves his soul destitute of the gift of leadership.'

Ibid., § 5. 'Just as the sun in heaven, the beauteous image of God, appears as a reflection in a glass to those who are able to see it therein, so God has established in States the light of Justice, and the light of the Reason (*Logos*) which is His companion, to serve men as an image of Himself which the blessed and wise among them can copy with the aid of philosophy, thus fashioning themselves in the likeness of the most beauteous of all things; nor is there anything which implants this disposition [to copy God] other than the power of Reason which is drawn from philosophy.'

B

This idea that the Logos of God can be imitated by the logos of man, when man's reason is stirred into action by the study of philosophy, is also expressed, at an earlier date, by Musonius Rufus, a Stoic writer of the latter part of the first century A.D., who is said to have been a counsellor of Vespasian and to have taught Epictetus. Stobaeus in his *Florilegium* (IV. vii, § 67) quotes the following passage from an essay of Musonius which bears the title 'Kings too should study philosophy'.

'In general, it is absolutely necessary for the good king to be free from error, and perfect in word and deed, seeing that he must, as the ancients held, be an Animate Law,[1] devising how his State may become a home of law and concord (*homonoia*), and therefore averting lawlessness and discord from it and acting as a follower of Zeus and a father of his subjects, even as Zeus [is the father of all men]. But how could a man be of this pattern unless he had a surpassing nature, and unless he had received the best education and had all the virtues which become a man?... Now what philosophy always intends and seeks to secure is how a man may escape evil and acquire goodness. If this be so, what could be of more profit to a king who wished to be good than the study of philosophy; or rather, how ... could a man ever be a king or live a good life if he did not study philosophy? I think that a good king should immediately, and necessarily, become a philosopher; yes—and I think that the philosopher should immediately be given the power of a king.'

This, as has already been noticed (*supra*, p. 47), was the Stoic answer to the problem raised by Plato in the *Republic* about the relation of philosophy to kingship.

§ v. *From the* 'DISCOURSES' OF EPICTETUS

Epictetus, born in Phrygia (a region of religious enthusiasm which afterwards produced the 'revivalism', as it may be called, of Montanus and his disciples), lived and taught at the end of the first and the beginning of the second century A.D. He was trained and educated in Rome, to which he had come, by way of the slave-market, as a house-slave of the higher type which provided amanuenses, secretaries, and even teachers; and in this way he became, on being emancipated, a teacher of philosophy. Banished from Rome when Domitian expelled the philosophers, he settled at Nicopolis (in Epirus), and became the master of a school or academy. Among his hearers was a Roman official Arrian (the author of a history of Alexander of Macedon already quoted in

---

[1] This notion of the king as 'Animate Law' is said by Musonius to be ancient, and it may be traced already in the *Politics* of Aristotle (III, c. xiii, § 14). It became a regular commonplace, and is used in the legislation of Justinian, *Nov.* cv. ii, § 4.

Part I), who reported faithfully what he had heard from his master in four books of *Discourses*, which are not so much a planned course of lectures as a series of separate meditations or *pensées*. The basis of the teaching of Epictetus was Stoicism, but he mixed the best of the popular discourses of the Cynics with Stoic doctrine, and he has been called a 'Cynic–Stoic' preacher. He also drew on the Platonic tradition of the teaching of Socrates; and it has been remarked that he refers both to the Cynic Diogenes and to Socrates more frequently than to Zeno. He knew nothing of Christianity, or of the Christian Churches of Asia Minor, or of the teaching of St. Paul; but there is a spirit of religious faith in his *Discourses*, and a moral exaltation, which make one think of Tertullian's phrase *anima naturaliter Christiana*. 'This is no longer the . . . pedantic pantheism of the ancient Stoa. Over that dry landscape the fertilising rain of a genuine religious feeling has fallen, and has caused to spring, from hidden seeds, a real faith in God, which inspired the Stoic preaching of virtue with new power.'[1]

A. *Man and God*

II. viii, §§ 10–12. *Man a particle of God.* 'Are not they too [the animals] God's creatures? They are; but they are not primary creatures, or *parts* of God. You are primary; you are a particle[2] of God; you have within you something which is a part of Him. Why, then, are you ignorant of your kinship? Why do you not know the source from which you have come? . . . When you walk, when you talk, don't you know that you are . . . exercising God? Wretched man that you are, you carry God about with you—and you do not know it!'

I. vi, §§ 19–21. *Man created to be a spectator and interpreter of God.* God created the animals for the service of man. 'But He brought man into the world to be a spectator of Himself and His works —and not only a spectator, but also an interpreter of them. Therefore it is a disgrace to man to begin and end where creatures without reason do; he should rather begin at the same point as

---

[1] Hans Lietzmann, *The Beginnings of the Christian Church*, Eng. trans., p. 174.
[2] *Apospasma*—a technical Stoic term (cf. Horace, *divinae particula aurae*).

they do, but end only when he reaches the point where Nature too has come to an end in her intention for man. Now she has not ended her plan for man till he reaches the stage of contemplation, understanding, and a way of life in harmony with nature.'

I. xvi, §§ 15–18. *The duty of man to sing the praise of God.* 'If we had sense, we ought, above everything else, to sing hymns to the Deity, both in public and in private; to praise His name; and to recount His benefits. When we dig and plough and eat, we ought to sing a thanksgiving: "great is God, that He has given us these tools to till therewith the earth; great is God, that He has given us hands, and has made us to eat and drink, to grow without taking thought, and to go on breathing even in our sleep". That is what we ought to sing at every moment, but the greatest and divinest hymn that we ought to sing to Him is for His having given us the power of understanding these things, and of following the right way.'

II. xiv, §§ 23–28. *On contemplating the 'Fair' of the world, and learning to understand its government by God.* 'It is with us as it is with men at a fair. Cattle and oxen are brought to be sold; most men are there just to buy and sell; . . . there are only a few who come to the fair because they like to watch and think. [But these men say to themselves], "What, then, is the universe (*cosmos*), and who is its governor? No one? But how can it be that a State (*polis*) or a family cannot last for even a moment without a governor and guardian, and yet so great and beautiful a device as the universe itself should be disposed in such good order by accident and the working of chance? There is therefore One who is its Governor. What kind of being is this Governor, and how does He act? And we whom He has made—what are we, and for what are we made? Have we some connexion and relation with Him, or have we none?" That is how the few [who watch and think] are affected, and they give all their time for the future to one thing and one thing only—the study of the fair before they leave it and go hence.'

IV. vii, §§ 6–9. *God's government and man's freedom.* 'Cannot reason and demonstration teach us that God has made all things in the universe; that He has created the whole universe free from any hindrance, and to be an end in itself; and that He has made the parts of it to serve the whole? Other creatures have been shut out from the power of understanding His government; but man, a rational being, has resources for thinking out all these things— for getting to know that he is a part of the universe, what sort of part he is, and how it is well for the parts to yield themselves to the whole. Moreover, man, as a rational animal, and naturally noble, high-souled, and free, sees that some of his surroundings are free from hindrance and under his own control, but others are subject to hindrance and under the control of others. The things free from hindrance are those which are in the area of moral choice; the things subject to hindrance are those which lie outside that area [such as health, wealth, and other 'externals']. Therefore, if he regards his good and his interest as consisting only in the first class of things—those free from hindrance and under his own control—he will be free . . ..'

B. *The City of God and Citizenship of the Universe*

I. ix, §§ 1–6. *The citizen of the Universe.* 'If there be truth in what the philosophers tell us about the kinship of God and men, what is there left for us but to follow the line of Socrates, who never answered the question "Where do you come from?" by saying "I am an Athenian, or, a Corinthian", but always said, "I belong to the universe."[1] . . . Think of a man who has observed the government of the universe and learned that "the greatest and the most sovereign and comprehensive of all communities is that of men and God, and from Him has come the seed of life, not only to our fathers and grandfathers, but also to all things that are begotten and grow upon the earth, and among them primarily to rational beings, inasmuch as these, and these only, walk close with God by virtue of reason, and are thus of a nature to share in a joint abode with Him"[2]—think of such a man, and then ask yourself why he should not speak of himself as belonging to the universe and being a son of God.'

[1] The word used in the Greek is *cosmios*—i.e. belonging to, or a citizen of, the *cosmos*.
[2] The quotation comes from some Stoic source, and possibly from the Stoic-Platonic teacher Posidonius.

II. x, §§ 3-4. *The duty of the citizen of the Universe.* 'You are a citizen of the universe (*politēs tou kosmou*) and a part thereof, and a part, too, which is primary and not [like the animals] auxiliary; for you can understand that it is divinely governed and you can reason out the results of its being so governed. What, then, is the service to which such a citizen is summoned? It is to take no thought for his own private interest, and never to think and plan as an isolated unit, but to act as a hand or a foot would act if they had reason and could understand the material constitution of the body, and were moved by no impulse or appetite which had no reference to the good of the whole.'

III. xxiv, §§ 9-11. '. . . Shall we not now remember what we have been told by the philosophers . . . that this universe is one city (*polis*); that the substance from which it has been created is one; . . . and that all of it is full of friends—first the gods, and then also men, who are naturally made to be of one household with one another.'

c. *The Self and the Community*

I. xix, §§ 11-15. *The end of man's action is his own true interest.* The nature of an animate being is such that it does everything for the sake of itself. Nay, even the sun does everything for his own sake; and so, moreover, does Zeus himself. But yet, when Zeus wishes to be the "Bringer of Rain" and the "Giver of Crops" and the "Father of Men and Gods", it is obvious that he cannot attain these results, or win these titles, without serving the common interest; and, generally, he has so constituted the nature of rational beings that they should be unable to gain any private or personal benefit without making some contribution to the common or social interest. Thus it ceases to be unsocial for such beings to do everything for their own sake. What would you expect from them? That they should give up themselves and their own private advantage? But how, in that case, can there be one and the same principle of action for all—the principle that each should appropriate[1] [what it needs] to itself?'

---

[1] The Greek word is *oikeiōsis*, which suggests the notion of 'taking into the household' and 'making at home', and has thus different associations from our word 'appropriation', which suggests the notion of 'acquisitiveness'.

II. v, §§ 25–26. *Man a part of a community and in its service.* 'You are a man. Now if you look at yourself as an isolated unit, it is your nature as such to live to old age, and to have wealth and health. But if you look at yourself as a man and a part of some whole, it befits you, in virtue of belonging to that whole, at one time to suffer ill health, at another to make a voyage and run a risk, at another to be in want, and at some other time, it may be, to die prematurely. Why, then, should you grumble? Do you not understand that just as a foot [if it were isolated from the body] would no longer be a foot, so you too [if you were an isolated unit] would not be a man? What is a man? A part of a civic community (*polis*); indeed of two communities, first the community of Gods and men, and then the [civic] community which we describe as the nearest possible approach to it—the community which is a small copy of the community of the Universe.'

D. *The Civic Community and its Government*

III. vii, §§ 19–21. *Political Duty.* 'Can you picture to yourself a State composed of followers of Epicurus? "I will not marry", one of them says. "Neither will I", says another: "one ought never to marry." But then one ought not to have children or a family, or to take part in civic life; and what is to happen then?... Your [Epicurean] doctrines are wrong; they are subversive of the State, destructive of families, and not fit even for women. Drop them, man. You live in a State which governs an empire; it is your duty to hold office, to judge with justice, to respect the property of others, to see beauty in no woman but your wife.'

III. xiii, §§ 9–11. *The peace of philosophy greater than the peace of Caesar.* 'You can see that Caesar seems to secure us a world of deep peace, with no more wars or battles or any great bands of brigands or pirates; we can travel by land at any season, and we can sail from the East to the West. But can he, then, give us also peace from fever, or from shipwreck, or from fire, or from earth-quakes or thunder and lightning? From the passion of love? No. From sorrow? No. From envy? No. From none whatsoever of these can he give us peace. But the teaching of the philosophers [i.e. the Cynic–Stoic teaching] promises to give us peace from these troubles too, as well as from the others. "Listen to me, men," it says, "and then, wherever you are and whatever you are doing, you shall know no pain, no anger, no compulsion, no hindrance, and you shall pass your days in calm [the Stoic 'apathy'] and freedom from all troubles."'

III. xxii, §§ 83–84. *The Cynic philosopher-preacher has no part in public life.* 'You may ask me, too, if you will, whether the Cynic will enter public life. Poor fool, are you looking for any finer field of public action than that in which the Cynic will act? Or do you want somebody to step forward in Athens and talk about finance and ways and means, when he ought to be discoursing to all men—Romans and Corinthians equally with Athenians—not about ways and means and finance, nor about peace and war, but about felicity and misery, success and failure, slavery and liberty? When a man is labouring in that great field of public action, do you ask me whether he is to enter public life? Ask me another question, and again I will give you an answer. Will such a man hold office? You silly fellow, what greater office can he hold than what he already has?'

E. *Social Institutions: Marriage and Property*

II. iv, §§ 8–10. *Promiscuity or monogamy?* ' "Are not women by nature common?" I agree.' But, Epictetus goes on to argue, food is common at a feast, yet each has his allotted portion; and a theatre is common to all citizens, yet each has his individual place. 'So, too, women are common by nature; but when the law-giver has allotted them, as a host does the food at a feast, are not you too, like other people, willing to be content with your share, instead of coveting and filching what is another's?'[1]

III. xxii, §§ 68–69. *The Cynic philosopher-preacher may marry, but is best unmarried.* If a man adopts the Cynic's profession 'there will be nothing to prevent him from marrying and having children; for his wife will be another such person as himself, and so will his father-in-law, and his children will be brought up in the same way. But in an order of things such as the present, which is like a

---

[1] The early Stoics had taken the view that any man might take to himself any woman. Epictetus modifies this view.

field of battle with armies facing one another, the Cynic preacher ought perhaps to be free from encumbrances, wholly engaged in the service of God, able to go up and down among men, tied by no bonds of private duty, and entangled in no connexions which he can only shed at the cost of losing his character as a good man and true and can only preserve at the cost of abandoning his mission as messenger, scout, and herald of the gods.'

Encheiridion, 39. *The limit to property.* 'Each man's body [i.e. his bodily needs] is a measure of the amount of his property, as a foot is the measure of the size of a shoe. If you take your stand on this principle, you will keep to the measure; if you go beyond it, you will inevitably end by being swept away like a man falling from a precipice. . . . Once go beyond the measure, and there is no limit.'

§ VI. FROM THE 'MEDITATIONS' OF MARCUS AURELIUS

Marcus Aurelius, born in A.D. 122, was emperor from 161 to 180. During the course of his reign, in the stress of military campaigns and among all the pressure of affairs, he set down 'notes for himself' (that is the Greek title of what he wrote), in the shape of reflections or meditations which might give him comfort and strength. These meditations are in no sense 'discourses' (or lectures) intended for an audience; they are the dialogue of a man talking to himself and his soul, in solitude; and in that respect they differ from the *Discourses* of Epictetus. On the other hand, there are many affinities between the *Discourses* and the *Meditations*. They are both documents of Stoicism, and of Stoicism at its best, though the Stoicism of Marcus is purer and stricter than that of Epictetus, who, as we have seen, mixed elements of Cynicism, and also of Platonism, with his Stoic creed. In a sense Epictetus is more original; Marcus drew freely upon him and often quotes his opinions; but in another sense the emperor, drawing on his own experience and reflection, and thinking out things independently for himself, is more original than the professional teacher who uses in the main the fruits of his reading, and does so in order to produce a concordance or reconciliation of all that he has read. There is, too, in Marcus a poetic power, rising sometimes to a solemn grandeur, which transcends the conversational style and the argumentation of Epictetus. It may be that, even after so many centuries, we still feel something of awe as we read the reflections of the Stoic Emperor who once ruled the whole of the Mediterranean world; and perhaps we feel ourselves more on a level with the lame ex-slave who lectured in Nicopolis than with the majestic and sternly self-disciplined Caesar who ruled in Rome. But it is a tribute to the power of Stoicism that it set them both on the same plane, however different their origins and their position in the world; indeed it could even set Marcus (of whom a scholiast writes, in glossing the heading of book II of his *Meditations*, that 'he openly Epictetizes') in the attitude of a disciple at the feet of his master. Yet the disciple, at the end of the count, is greater than the master.

A. *Man, God, and Nature*

v. 27. *Living with the gods.* 'A man lives with the gods if he always presents to their view a soul that is satisfied with what they give, and that does the will of the genius (*daimōn*) given him by Zeus, as a particle of his own Being, to be his protector and governor. This genius consists in the Mind and Reason of each of us.'

vii. 9. *One Universe, one God, and one Law.* 'All things are twined with one another, and the ties that twine them are sacred; there is scarcely a single thing which is alien from other things; for all things are ranged in order together, and all join together to make a single ordered world (*cosmos*). There is one World composed of all things, one God who pervades all things, one Substance, one Law; a common Reason in all creatures with minds; a single Truth; and there is also one perfection of beings that are akin to one another and share together in the same Reason.'

viii. 34. *Man part of the Unity of Nature.* 'If ever you saw a hand or a foot cut off . . . that is just what a man, so far as he can, inflicts on himself when he will not accept what befalls him, and severs himself from others or does anything unsocial. Somewhere, at some time, you have been torn away from the natural unity of the universe; you were born a part, and now you have cut yourself off. But here there comes in the subtle turn—you can unite yourself again [to the universe]. To no other of its parts has God granted this power of coming together again after severance and divorce. Behold His goodness in doing such honour to man. For He has put it in man's power, first, that he should not at all be rent from the universe, and next that if he should be so rent, he may return again, and grow into union once more, and take up his position again as a part.'

ix. 9. *The Affinities of Nature in their ascending stages.* Among inanimate things there is an attraction of earth to earth, fire to fire, air to air; 'and so all that shares in the common being of *intelligent* nature hastes to join what is akin to it as much as inanimate things do—or even more than they do. For the higher it ranks above these other things, the more ready it is to commingle and coalesce with what belongs to the same family as itself.

'Thus, for a beginning, we find among irrational creatures swarms, herds, colonies of birds' nests, and what we may generally call unions of love; for already at this stage there are animate beings[1] at work, and the bond of affinity in this higher order of being shows itself to be closer than that among plants or stones or blocks of wood. But in the next stage, among rational creatures, we find political communities, friendships, families, assemblies, and—even in times of war—treaties of peace and truces. Finally, at a still higher stage of being, and among things distant from one another, there is still some sort of unity, as for example among the stars; and thus the ascent to the higher stage can still mean the presence of sympathy, even between distant objects.'

B. *The City of God*

iv. 4. *The one State of the Universe.* 'If the capacity for intelligence is common to men, so too is the faculty of Reason, by virtue of which we are rational beings. If that be so, then that part of reason—the practical reason—which tells us what to do and what not to do, is also common. If that be so, so too is

---

[1] The Greek word, *psychē*, though often translated 'soul', means simply 'animate being' (such as all animals have), which lifts its possessor above the inanimate but leaves it below the rational creature, man.

law. If law is common, we are all fellow citizens; and if that be so, the universe (*cosmos*) is, as it were, one State or city. What other political community is there in which all mankind can be said to share jointly? This is the source—this State or city common to all men—from which we draw the capacity of Intelligence, the faculty of Reason, and the gift of Law[1]. . ..'

iv. 23. *The city of Cecrops and the city of Zeus.* 'I say to the universe, All that is in tune with thee is in tune with me; nothing that comes to thee at the right time is too early, or too late, for me. All that the seasons bring, mother Nature, is fruit for me; all things come *from* thee, all things are *in* thee, all things come *to* thee. The poet says, "Dear City of Cecrops"; but thou—wilt thou not say, "Dear City of Zeus"?'

vi. 44. *The two countries—Rome and the Universe.* 'Every man's interest consists in following the lead of his own constitution and nature. Now my nature is a rational and civic nature; my city and my country, so far as I am [Marcus Aurelius] Antoninus, is Rome; but so far as I am a man, it is the universe. Whatever therefore is to the advantage of these two cities, and that only, is good for me.'

x. 15. *Live as on a mountain, and be a citizen of the world.* 'Live your life as if you were on a mountain; it makes no difference where life is spent, be it here or be it there, provided that one lives everywhere as if the whole world were one's city.'

c. *Self-development and Community-service*

i. 16, § 2. *The spirit of fellowship.* 'From my father [Antoninus Pius, who adopted Marcus as his son] I learned the spirit of fellowship—*koinonoēmosynē*.'[2]

x. 6. *Man as part of a Whole.* 'Whether we accept the conception of atoms or that of Nature [i.e. whether we adopt the

---

[1] In iv. 24 Marcus, repeating a phrase of Aristotle, speaks of man as 'an animal intended by nature to live in a *polis*'. But the *polis* of which Marcus is thinking is not a city such as Athens, but the *civitas Dei*. This is 'the greatest *polis* and *polīteia*, whose Reason and Law it is the end of rational beings to follow' (ii. 16); this, again, is 'the highest *polis*, in which all the rest are but households' (iii. 11).

[2] Marcus coins this word. It is as if we said 'communanimity', on the analogy of 'unanimity'. It signifies the spirit which makes men to be of one mind with one another.

materialist view of the Epicureans or the theistic view of the Stoics], let us begin by laying it down that I am part of a Whole which is governed by Nature, and then let us hold that I am somehow akin to the other parts which are of the same order. Remembering this, and in virtue of my being such a part, I shall not quarrel with any dispensation that comes to me from the Whole; for nothing can harm the part which is to the interest of the whole.'

iii. 4. *Self-regard and regard for others.* § 1. 'Waste not the remainder of your life in imagining things about other men, unless you can bring your imaginations into some connexion with the advancement of the common good. You cut yourself off from other work if you keep on trying to imagine what other men are doing or saying, and why they are doing or saying it. § 3. [The wise man is one who is] thoroughly dyed in justice, who welcomes with all his mind every happening and dispensation, but who seldom—and then only under the stress of some great necessity which touches the common interest—concerns himself with imagining what other men say or do or think. It is only by his own affairs that he is moved to activity, and it is the threads spun for himself out of the sum of things which he has constantly in mind. . . . § 4. But he also remembers that he has an affinity with everything that is rational, and that while it is the nature of man to care for the well-being of all men, one ought not to cleave to the opinions held by all, but only to those that are held by such as live rationally in conformity with nature.'

Note. Two later passages put briefly the case for self-regard and the case for regard for others. (1) *For self-regard,* viii. 56. 'However much we have been made for the sake of one another, yet the ruling Reason [the 'genius' or 'particle of God' within us] is in each case its own sovereign'. (2) *For regard for others,* vi. 54. 'That which is not for the advantage of the hive is not for that of the bee either.'

The Value of Co-operation and Fraternity. (*a*) ii. 1. 'We have been made for co-operation,[1] like our feet, hands, eyelids, and the teeth

---

[1] In the Greek the word used is *synergos*, fellow-worker, with its abstract form *synergia*. The Greek word for 'fraternity' (or, as it may also be termed, 'fellowship') is *koinōnia*.

of our upper and lower jaws.' (*b*) vi. 42. 'We all co-operate for the achievement of one single object, some consciously and intelligently, and others ignorantly; as, I think, Heraclitus means by his saying that "even in our sleep we are workers and co-operators".' (*c*) v. 16. 'The good for a rational being is fraternity; for, as has been shown of old, we have been made for fraternity.' v. 30. 'The Mind of the universe is set to fraternity; at any rate it has made lower things for the sake of things higher, and it has made the higher things to work in with one another. You can see how it has subordinated and co-ordinated things, assigned to each the place due to it, and drawn the things that excel into concord (*homonoia*) with one another.' (*d*) vi. 7. 'In this take your delight, and let this be your refreshment—to go on from one fraternal act to another, with God in your mind as you go.' (*e*) vi. 14. 'The man who holds in honour a spirit (*psychē*) which is rational, catholic [i.e. at home in the universe], and civic, pays heed to one thing only: beyond all other things he seeks to keep his spirit in a state of being and motion which is rational and fraternal, and he co-operates to this end with all that is akin to him.'

D. *The State and its Government*

i. 14. *The idea of the State.* 'From my brother Severus I learned the conception of a State based on uniform law and governed on the principles of equality and free speech, and of a monarchy which prized the liberty of the subject above all other things.'

ix. 23. *Political obligation.* 'Even as you are in yourself an element that helps to complete the political structure, so let every act that you do serve to complete the life of that structure. Every act which has not reference to the end of fraternity tears your life asunder, prevents it from having unity, and is of the nature of a rebellion.'

E. *The River of Time and the Cycles of Regeneration*

iv. 43. *The ever-rolling stream.* 'Time is as a river fed from all that comes into being: it is a violent flood. One thing comes into sight and sweeps past you; then another is carried down, and then

another still will be borne away. vi. 15. Flux and change are continually renewing the universe, just as the unceasing current of
time is always making the endless course of the ages new. Is there
anything in this river, of all the things that rush past, which any
of us can prize, when we have no firm footing allowed us? [If
it were so,] it would be as if a man should begin to feel an affection
for a sparrow that flies past him, and is instantly lost to his view.'

xi. 1. *The mind as a spectator of all time and all existence.* 'But [the
rational spirit] goes about the whole of the universe and the void
which encompasses it, and studies its fashion, and comprehends
and considers the cyclical regeneration of all things, and discerns
that the men who come after us shall see no new thing, and that
they who came before us saw nothing beyond what we see; so that
the man who reaches the age of forty and has any sort of wits
about him has seen all that has been, and will be, because all
things are the same.'

xii. 36. *Nunc Dimittis.* 'Man, you have lived as a citizen in this
great city of the universe, and what does it matter whether you
have lived there for five years or for five score? The portion
allotted to each of us under its law is the same. What is the hard-
ship, then, in your being dismissed from the city, not by a tyrant
or unjust judge, but by Nature who brought you into it, even as
the manager who has engaged him might dismiss a comic actor?
"But", [he might say,] "I have not finished the five acts; I have only
had three." "True," [one may answer,] "but in life three acts are
all the play." He who was once the cause of thy being made,
and is now the cause of thy being unmade, determines thy span.
Thou hast not caused thy birth or thy death. Go, then, in peace.
For He who dismisses thee is at peace with thee.'

§ VII. ARISTIDES' PANEGYRIC ON ROME

Aelius Aristides (*circa* A.D. 120–89) was a 'sophist' or rhetorician,
who wrote and delivered a number of declamations in the style
of Dio Chrysostom, but with less originality. Born at Smyrna,
and educated at Pergamum and Athens, he travelled in Egypt and
lectured both in Asia Minor and at Rome. Over fifty of his orations

survive, composed in an Attic style to serve as models of eloquence; they include a eulogy of Athens, as well as the praise of Rome; they deal with religion (one of them, for instance, is addressed to Zeus and another is in praise of Athena) as well as with political and other issues. The passages which follow are taken from the oration 'To Rome', which may have been delivered at Rome about A.D. 150 in the reign of Antoninus Pius.

A. *The Genius of the Roman Empire*

§ 58 (p. 107 of Keil's edition, vol. ii). 'This [the secret of managing an empire], which had eluded, if I may say so, all your predecessors, was reserved for you [the Roman people] to discover and bring to perfection. This is no occasion for surprise. Just as, in other spheres, the arts keep pace with the material on which they work, so it was here: when the largest of empires and the power pre-eminent above all others arose, there also arose, on that basis and as its accompaniment, the art [required for its management], and either was strengthened by the other; experience inevitably accrued from the size of the empire, and conversely the knowledge thus gained of governing with justice and equity resulted in the increase of its size. But what is much the most worthy of study and admiration, in connexion with your constitution and the magnificence of its conception, is that there is nothing like it in the universe. For if one divides all the members of the empire—and when I say that, I mean all the inhabitants of the world—into two parts, then you have made the finer and nobler half of them your fellow citizens, or even kinsmen, and you have kept the other half as your subjects and under your government. Neither the sea, nor the wide space of intervening land, prevents any man from becoming a citizen; with you, there is no division between Asia and Europe, but everything is set out in the open for everyone to enjoy; nobody is a foreigner who is worthy of office or trust; you have established a common democracy of the earth, under the rule and governance of the One Best Man, in which all men come together as if in a common forum, and where each will get his deserts. What an ordinary city is for her own boundaries and territory, this city of yours is for all the inhabited world: she is appointed to be its common capital; and you might say that all the "dwellers round about,"[1] and all folk living in their "demes" at a distance, come to her as their one common citadel. She has never refused any man admission: like the surface of the globe, which is all men's abode, she receives men from all the earth, just as the sea receives the rivers. There is another attribute which she shares with the sea: the sea grows no fuller from the influx of the rivers, as though it were destined to keep the same volume whatever accessions it may receive; and similarly Rome, vast as she is, shows no visible increase [from the influx of new citizens]; like a man who folds a thing in his bosom, she hides everything in her embrace, becoming—and looking—neither larger nor smaller as her members come and go.

'So much of this, in passing, since the argument has led us to mention it. But, as I was saying, you are great, and you have measured the bounds of your city greatly; you have not prided yourselves on making her wonderful by refusing to share her benefits with all other men; you have sought a consummation worthy of her, and you have made "Roman" the name not of a city, but of a whole race, and that race not one among many others, but a match for all the rest. For as things now are you do not divide the races of men into Greeks and Barbarians—that would be a ridiculous division to make when your own city, one may say, is more populous than the whole of Greece—; you divide them instead into Roman and non-Roman; to such a height have you raised the name of your city. And so, that being the distinction which is now to be drawn, there are many men in every city who are your fellow-citizens as much as they are fellow-citizens with their own kinsfolk. There is no need of guards to hold any citadel for you: the great and the influential in each city garrison it themselves for you; and thus you hold the cities with a double hold—the hold from Rome, and the hold from within themselves.'

---

[1] *Perioikoi* in the Greek—a reference to the dependent rural population living round about the city of Sparta; as the following words are a reference to the country folk living scattered in their 'demes' round Athens.

B. *The Roman Constitution*

§ 90 (p. 118 of Keil's edition). 'Within your own city you seem to me to have established a constitution in a different way from any other people. Before your time there seemed to be three types of constitution in the world, two of which had each two different names when regarded from the point of view of the behaviour of the government—the names of tyranny and oligarchy in the one case, and those of monarchy and aristocracy in the other— while the third type was democracy, whether in its good or bad form;[1] and the various cities differed from one another in the type of their constitution, as choice or chance determined in each case. Your constitution is not like that; it is like a mixture of all the types, excluding in each case the worse form of the type [i.e. excluding tyranny, oligarchy, and the worse form of democracy]. That is the alternative, and that is the form of constitution, which has triumphed at Rome. Accordingly, when one looks at the strength of the popular element, and notices how easily the people can attain all its wishes and demands, one will think that the constitution is a democracy, with nothing wanting to it except the errors of popular government; if, on the other hand, one looks at the Senate, which is the deliberative body and has in its hands the office of State, one will think that there cannot be a better form of aristocracy than this; but if, again, one looks at the superintendent and president of all these powers [i.e. the emperor], who makes it possible for the people to attain their wishes and for the few to enjoy office and influence, one sees in him a single person who represents the most perfect form of monarchy—a form at once free from the evils of tyranny and yet greater than the majesty of kingship. There is nothing unreasonable in this distinction between your city and others, or in thinking thus of your city—as one cannot think of any other—in its conduct of external policy and its management of internal affairs. You are the only people who are, so to say, rulers by nature. Other States which had empires before you became in turn masters and slaves of one another; inexperienced in the arts of empire, they came and

---

[1] Aristides thus implies six constitutions, much as Aristotle had done.

went like players who change their positions in a ball-game; the Macedonians became the slaves [? conquerors] of the Persians,[1] the Persians of the Medes, and the Medes of the Assyrians; but all men have known you as rulers as far back as their memory goes. Free as you have been from the first, and born, as it were, to be rulers, you have well and wisely contrived all the means that lead to this goal: you have discovered a form of constitution which no State had ever discovered before,[2] and you have given to all men orders and stations which they cannot but keep.'

c. The Victory of Rome over Chaos compared with the Victory of Zeus over the Titans

§ 102 (p. 121 of Keil's edition). 'There is no need now to write descriptive guides of the world, or to enumerate in treatises the laws in use among different peoples; you have become the common guides of all mankind, by throwing open all the gates of the inhabited world and giving to all who want it the power of seeing everything for themselves; you have appointed a body of common law for all men, and you have put an end to a previous state of things which was interesting enough as a matter of description but intolerable when it was rationally considered; you have fostered intermarriage and drawn all the inhabited world together into a single family.

'The poets tell us that before the reign of Zeus the whole world was full of contention and din and disorder, but when Zeus ascended the throne all was put right; the Titans went away into the lowest depths of the earth, driven there by Zeus and the other gods of his company. Just in the same way one might conclude, on a comparison of the state of affairs before your day and the state which now exists, that before you established your empire the world was tossed up and down in confusion, and swept aimlessly along, but when you took control troubles and contentions ceased, everything was set in order, a bright light began to shine

---

[1] Aristides, if the Greek text is correct, seems to invert what actually happened: the Macedonians, Persians, and Medes all became masters, and not slaves,.

[2] Here Aristides appears to forget Sparta, already depicted by Aristotle in the Politics as having a mixed form of constitution.

on men's life and government, laws began to appear, and the altars of the gods received the devotion of faith.'

§ VIII. PHILOSTRATUS

Philostratus, a rhetorician of the period and style of the 'second sophistic' (to which Dio of Prusa and Aelius Aristides, his predecessors, also belong), was born *circa* A.D. 170 in one of the Aegean islands, studied in Athens, and came eventually to Rome, where he was persuaded by the Syrian wife of the Emperor Septimius Severus to write a biography of Apollonius of Tyana, a neo-Pythagorean sage (and perhaps also something of a charlatan, with an inclination to magic) who had travelled in India, wandered about the Mediterranean, and talked with the Emperor Vespasian, in the course of the first century A.D. The biography (which is perhaps also a romance) was published about A.D. 217, over a century after the death of Apollonius. It is from this biography—or romance—that the following passages are taken. Whether Apollonius ever held or expressed the views here stated, or whether they were simply put into his mouth by Philostratus, hardly matters for the present purpose; they are of interest in themselves as representing views which were current, or at any rate circulated, during the early years of the third century A.D. in cultivated and courtly circles. (Philostratus, it may be added—it is one of the curiosities of literature—was also the author of a collection of 'Love Letters', on which Ben Jonson drew for the ideas, and even the phrases, of the famous poem 'Drink to me only with thine eyes'.)

A. *A State needs Party-spirit as well as the Spirit of Concord*

Life of Apollonius of Tyana, book IV, c. 8. 'Apollonius said that a State, if it was to be well managed, needed the spirit of parties (*stasis*) as well as the temper of concord (*homonoia*). . . . He explained his saying as follows. "Black and white can never be one; the bitter cannot be blended healthily with the sweet; but concord *can* be so mixed with party-spirit as to produce political security. Let us look at my saying in this way. Far be it from any State to indulge in mere party-struggles which lead to the use of the sword and make men throw stones at one another; what all States need is provision for the upbringing of children, a system of laws, and the presence of men who can both speak and act. All the same, when we consider the value of mutual rivalry in the service of the common weal, and how one man may suggest a better view than another, or be a better magistrate or a better ambassador, or manage public works more brilliantly, we find, as I see the matter, a beneficent sort of strife, and a struggle of different sides in the service of the common weal. True, the idea that different persons should follow different ways of contributing to the welfare of the State seemed foolish to the Spartans of old; they cultivated only the arts of war, building themselves up for this one end and attempting nothing else. But to me it seems best that each of us should do only what he knows how to do, and what he is able to do. Where one man is admired for his leadership of the people, another for his wisdom, another for using his wealth to promote the common good, another for his generosity, another for his severity and for having no sympathy with wrongdoers, another for keeping his hands free from any suspicion of uncleanness, there a State will safely lie down—or rather it will stand upright—in prosperity and well-being." '

B. *A Discourse on Empire*

Book v, c. 35. According to Philostratus, Apollonius and two other philosophers discussed the future of Rome in Egypt (A.D. 70) with Vespasian. Should the Republic be restored after Vitellius had been removed, or should Vespasian retain and maintain the imperial system? . . . The debate may remind us of the passage in Herodotus, iii. 80–82, which narrates a discussion among the Persian grandees, after the death of Cambyses, whether the Persian monarchy should be retained or some form of republic substituted. Apollonius gave an opinion in favour of the continuance of the imperial system: 'I have no concern with any particular constitution, for I live my own life in obedience to the gods; but I do not think it right that the flock of mankind should perish for want of a just and temperate shepherd. Just as one man who is pre-eminent in virtue can transform democracy into the likeness of the rule of the one best man, so, conversely, the rule of one man, when it provides everything which tends to the welfare of the community, is really a democracy.'

Apollonius proceeds, in c. 36, on being asked by Vespasian to instruct him in all that a good king should do, to give the future emperor his advice.

'You ask me for something which cannot be taught: kingship is the greatest thing among men, but it is a thing which no man can teach. I will tell you, however, what I believe you would do well to do. Do not think of wealth as consisting in what you have laid by—for is such a store any better than a heap of sand collected at random from any quarter?—or as consisting in what comes to you from men who groan under the burden of taxes[1] (gold is counterfeit and black if it has its source in men's tears); you will make better use of your wealth than any king does if you give assistance to the needy and security to the well-to-do. Tremble at the thought that your will is always law; if you do, you will be all the more temperate in your use of power. Do not lop off the tall and outstanding ears in the cornfield, for that story in Aristotle runs contrary to justice;[2] better root out disaffection from men's minds, as you would weeds out of a field, and inspire fear in revolutionary spirits, not so much by immediate punishment as by the threat of future penalities. Let law, Sire, be *your* sovereign; you will legislate for your people with more moderation if you do not neglect law yourself. . . . Act as a king in what pertains to your office; act as a private person in regard to your bodily wants. . . . It only remains to speak of the governors sent out to the provinces (the *ethnē* or 'nations'). I will not speak of those whom you appoint yourself—you will, I am sure, make those appointments on the basis of merit; I will speak only of those who owe their office to the chance of the lot.[3] So far as they are con-

---

[1] Caracalla (211–17) is reported to have said 'No man except me needs to have money, and I need it in order to pay the soldiers' (Dio Cassius lxxvii. 10. 4).

[2] The story, told in the *Politics*, is that of the tyrant Periander, when asked for advice by the envoy of another tyrant, switching off with his stick the tallest ears of corn in the field in which he was standing at the moment.

[3] Philostratus is here alluding to the senatorial, as distinct from the imperial

cerned, and so far as the lot allows you to do so, you should send men who suit the provinces which have fallen to their share. Only persons who speak Greek should govern Greeks, and only Romans should be set over those who speak that tongue and use that language. I will explain what gave me this idea. When I lived in the Peloponnese, the governor of Greece was a man who did not understand Greek affairs, any more than the Greeks understood him [and his outlook]. He, then, often did wrong, or had wrong done to him; his assessors and partners in judicial hearings drove a traffic in the judgments they gave, and brought the governor into disrepute as a mere tool in their own hands.'

Note. This sense of the rights of the 'nations' to some recognition of their own individuality is notable. It also appears in Celsus (as quoted in Origen) when he champions the rights of the 'nations' to their own gods and form of religion, and criticizes Christianity for its would-be universalism and its engulfing of national cults (see below, p. 433).

§ IX. PLOTINUS

Introduction

Platonism passed through various phases during the 600 years from 300 B.C. to A.D. 300. At one time, during the phase of the Middle Academy, it took over the doctrine of scepticism from the school of Pyrrhon (a contemporary of Alexander); and Carneades, its leader and representative figure in the second century B.C., challenged the Stoic Panaetius and the tenets of his school in a debate in Rome in 156 B.C., when he shocked the Romans by showing himself ready to defend (or challenge) any opinion, and more particularly by defending the opinion that might was right.[1] In a later phase, during the first century B.C., a revived form of Platonism, shedding its scepticism and its opposition to Stoicism, allied itself with Stoic tenets in the teaching of Posidonius of

provinces. For the former, ex-consuls and ex-praetors cast lots to determine which they should have.

[1] The debate left a lasting impression; Cicero mentions it in book III. 9 of the *De Republica*, and Lactantius refers to it, centuries later, in his *Divine Institutes*, book V, c. 14.

Apamea (see above, pp. 281–2). In a final phase, that of Neoplatonism, the great figure was Plotinus (A.D. 205–70), who carried
Platonic doctrines into the heights of mysticism and produced
a philosophy at once analogous and opposed to Christianity, of
which we may trace the influence alike in the *Confessions* of St.
Augustine and in the career of Julian 'the Apostate'.

Where Plotinus was born is uncertain, but possibly it was in
Egypt; his name may be Roman, but his language was almost
certainly Greek, and he spent his early life in Alexandria (always
a lively centre of thought from 300 B.C. to A.D. 400 and even
afterwards), where he attended for some time the school of
Ammonius Saccas, in which the great Christian thinker Origen
was also a pupil. Somewhere about A.D. 240 Plotinus joined the
army of the Emperor Gordian, wishing to acquire some knowledge of Persian ideas and Indian systems of thought, but when
the emperor was assassinated in the course of his Eastern campaign
he escaped with difficulty to the West and settled eventually
(about A.D. 246) in Rome, where he taught till his death in 270.
Here he was closely connected with the Emperor Gallienus
(260–8)[1] and his wife Salonina. Gallienus, it may be noticed, was
remarkable for a spirit and policy of toleration (he published,
about A.D. 260, an early edict of toleration in favour of Christianity
which is an anticipation and harbinger of Constantine's 'Edict of
Milan'); but his own personal belief inclined to Greek philosophy,
and at one time he encouraged Plotinus in the idea of founding a
Platonic city, or 'Platonopolis', on a site in Campania.

The lectures which Plotinus gave in Rome, during a period of
a quarter of a century, were collected and edited by his disciple
Porphyry, a Semite from Tyre, and published under the title of
the *Enneads* (i.e. the 'nine treatises', each composed, on a uniform
plan, of six different chapters). Porphyry, who lived from 232 to
304, also wrote a Life of his master, which is prefixed to the
Enneads. Of the interpretation and development of Plato's philosophy in the *Enneads* nothing need here be said; but the relation
of the Neoplatonism of Plotinus to contemporary Christian theory

---

[1] His sole reign began in 260, but he had already been created Augustus by
the Senate, and associated with his father Valerian, as early as 253.

is a matter of the first importance. That relation has two aspects, which are mutually contradictory. On the one hand, there are analogies between Neoplatonism and Christianity. In both there is the doctrine of a Trinity (though the Plotinian Trinity of the original and transcendent One, the intermediate and mediating *Nous* or Intellectual Principle, and the lower *Psychē* or Vital Principle, is different from the Christian Trinity); and in both there is the ultimate idea of the 'vision' or enjoyment of God, which for Plotinus is *henōsis* or union with the transcendent One. (Porphyry tells us in his Life that Plotinus four times, during the period of their intercourse, passed into this union; and when St. Augustine, who studied Neoplatonism, experienced 'the vision of Ostia', he tells of his experience in terms and phrases which are reminiscent of passages in the *Enneads*.) On the other hand, there is also a deep gulf between Neoplatonism and Christianity. Neoplatonism has a dry and austere intellectualism, without any personal God;[1] Plotinus holds that *knowledge* is religion, and *thought* the Good; and he draws the consequence that in order to get knowledge and to pursue thought, and thereby to find true religion, you must escape from the world of action. The result is that the Neoplatonist—unlike the Christian, with his deep sense of the corporate body of the Church, and with the feeling of obligation to the State which even a Tertullian shows—is non-political, and even non-social. He leaves the world, in the flight of 'the Alone to the Alone'. He has thus no interest in the State; the 'Platonopolis' of which Plotinus dreamed is a hermitage rather than a *polis*. Indeed he has no interest in *any* form of society (unless it be a philosophic conference or circle). He is non-social as well as non-political; he has no feeling for community, and no feeling for any association or voluntary society, any more than for the State and its political organization.

---

[1] It was here that St. Augustine, much as he was influenced by the 'books of the Platonists' (as he calls them) which he had read in a Latin translation, found Neoplatonism arid and unsatisfactory. 'I read there . . . of *God the Word* . . . but that *the Word was made flesh, and dwelt among us*, I read not' (*Confessions*, book VII. 14). 'Somewhat later, I confess, did I learn how in that saying, *The Word was made flesh*, the Catholic Truth is distinguished from the falsehood of Plotinus' (ibid., book VII. 25).

A. *Plotinus and Platonopolis*

From Porphyry's *Life of Plotinus*, 12. 'The Emperor Gallienus and his wife Salonina greatly honoured and venerated Plotinus. He made use of their friendly feeling towards him to beg for the restoration of a city of philosophers which had once stood, as tradition had it, in Campania, but had now fallen into ruins. He also asked that the surrounding country should be granted to the city when it was refounded, that its inhabitants should follow the laws of Plato, and that its name should be Platonopolis; and he promised that, if this were done, he would retire there with his associates. The philosopher's wish could very easily have been carried into execution, if some of the emperor's courtiers, instigated by envy or spite or some such evil passion, had not opposed the scheme.'

Note. The intention of Plotinus was not so much the foundation of a *polis*, in the old Greek style, as the establishment of a 'monastic' retreat, for the purpose of contemplation and study, with an adjacent territory to support its inhabitants, on the lines of the Essenes of Palestine or the Egyptian ascetics. In a sense, therefore, he sought to anticipate St. Benedict rather than to restore the *polis* of Plato. It is not clear what is meant by 'the laws of Plato'. It can hardly be the dialogue called the *Laws*, with its plan for a city of over 5,000 inhabitants; the Platonopolis of Plotinus would have counted its members, at the most, in tens. Probably 'the laws of Plato' simply means the ideals and the educational ideas suggested in the *Republic*.

B. *The Vision and Enjoyment of the Good and Beautiful*[1]

From the First *Ennead*, c. vi, §§ 7–9 (concerning Absolute Beauty and Goodness in its own intrinsic essence). 'What of the man who sees this Beauty, . . . which furnishes all things with ability, and abiding in itself gives out [from itself] to all things and takes nothing into itself? If he abides in the contemplation thereof, and enjoys what he contemplates, and grows into its likeness, what Beauty can he yet lack? For this is itself Beauty absolute in the highest; this is

---

[1] The word translated by 'Beauty', *to kalon*, has in Greek a double sense: it means what is ethically 'fine' or 'good' as well as what is aesthetically 'beautiful'. Plotinus can distinguish the Good and the Beautiful, but he also unites them.

the ultimate ['the First'[1]]; and, being such, it makes beautiful those who love it, and makes them worthy of love. It is for this that the greatest and uttermost struggle is set before the souls of men; it is for this that all their toil is spent—that they may not be left without part in the best and highest vision, which to gain is to have the bliss of beholding that most blissful sight, but if a man gain it not he is unfortunate indeed. For the unfortunate man is not he who fails to find beauty of colour or bodily form, or he who fails to gain power or offices or empire; it is he who fails to find this one and only thing for the winning whereof a man must put aside empires and offices in all the earth, yea and in sea and sky, if only, by leaving aside and looking beyond such things, he can turn to it and behold it.

§ 8. 'What, then, is the way to the vision, and by what means is it won? How shall a man come to see this Beauty beyond compare, which abides, as it were, in the sanctuary of a holy temple, and comes not outside to be seen by the profane? Let him who can do so go forward, and follow on into the sanctuary, putting off and leaving outside the sight of the eyes, and turning not back to the former splendours of bodily forms. When he sees any bodily beauties, he must in no wise hasten towards them; he must recognize that they are but images, traces, and shadows; and he must escape from them to that of which they are but images. If a man runs towards them in eagerness to lay hold of them, he is like one who has seen a fair image borne on the face of the water, and who, in his eagerness to grasp it, acts in the way which I think is fabled in one of the myths; for just as the man in the myth [Narcissus] plunged to the bottom of the river and disappeared, so, and in the same way, the man who clings to bodily beauty, and refuses to let it go, will plunge—not indeed in body but in soul—into dark depths in which there is no pleasure for Intelligent Mind; and there he will sojourn in blindness and in Hades,[2] consorting there, as here, only among shadows.

' "Let us escape to our own dear fatherland"—that would be

[1] The Ultimate (which Plotinus calls 'the First') is the original and transcendent One, standing above *Nous*, or the Intelligent Principle, as that in turn stands above the *Psychē* or Vital Principle.

[2] The Greek word 'Hades' suggests the Unseen, or the place of sightlessness.

truer counsel.[1] What, then, is to be the nature of our escape, and how shall we set sail? We ought, with the poet, to follow the example set by Ulysses in the fable, when he got away from Circe the witch or Calypso, refusing to stay with them longer, despite the pleasure they gave to his eyes and all the visible beauty of their companionship. Our fatherland is the place from which we have come, and it is there that we have our father.

'What, then, is the voyage before us, and the manner of our escape? It must not be sought on foot; our feet at all times bear us only from one place to another. Neither must you prepare a chariot and horses, or any manner of ship:[2] all these things you must abandon, turning your eyes away from them; you must, as it were, close your eyes, change your present vision for another, and quicken the sight of the inward eye which we all of us have but few of us use.

§ 9. 'What, then, does that inward eye behold? It can not, when it has just been quickened, look upon bright objects. The soul itself must therefore be [gradually] trained; first to look upon fine pursuits (*kala*); then upon fine achievements—not indeed those that are wrought by the arts, but such as are done by men who are called "good"; and then I bid you to look into the souls of the men who accomplish fine achievements. How, then, can one look into a good soul, and know what manner of beauty it possesses? Turn to yourself; look at yourself; and if you do not yet find beauty in yourself, then do as a sculptor does when he is carving a statue which is to be a thing of beauty. Part of the marble he

---

[1] Just as Plotinus here quotes a line from the *Iliad* (ii. 140), and then proceeds from that text to speak of the vision of the transcendent One, so Philo, two centuries earlier, had quoted a verse from the book of Genesis, and then gone on from that text to discourse of the vision of God; see above, p. 163.

[2] A curious analogy to the language of Plotinus, in this passage, is to be found in the *Confessions* of St. Augustine, book I, c. xviii. 28: 'It is not on foot or by change of place that men leave Thee or return to Thee, nor did that son of Thine [in the parable of the prodigal son] seek horses and chariots or a ship.' It almost seems as if St. Augustine was so familiar with the language of Plotinus that he repeated his phrases even in a different context. (Since I wrote these words I have noticed that St. Augustine quotes the words of Plotinus again in book VIII, c. viii. 19: speaking of the will and covenant of God, he writes, 'Therein we enter not by ships or chariots or feet, no, nor even move as far as I had come from the house to that place where we were sitting'—the little garden, attached to a house in Milan, where he was talking with his friend.)

cuts away, and part he chisels down; one part he seeks to make smooth, and another clear and bright, until he has brought out at last a face of beauty on his statue. You must do likewise: you must cut away whatever is superfluous, straighten whatever is crooked, and make what is dark clear and bright, working at it until it shines; you must continue to work at your statue till the god-like splendour of goodness shines out on your sight and you can see true Temperance (*Sophrosynē*) standing on her holy pedestal.

'If you have become such as this, and seen this; if you have had pure commerce with yourself, so that you have nothing that hinders you from thus becoming One [i.e. a pure unity], or anything else that adheres internally to yourself; if you are, in yourself, wholly, and only, true light, a light not measured by magnitude, a light neither circumscribed by form and shape into diminution of itself nor again increased into magnitude by having no bounds whatever, a light immeasurable on every side because it is greater than any measure and every quantity—if you see yourself becoming such as this, then you have become pure vision, and you may take heart about yourself; already here, on earth, you have risen upward; you need none to show you the way; so . . . fix your gaze, and *look*. For such, and such only, is the eye which sees beauty in all its greatness.

'But if the eye comes to the seeing all bleared with defects—uncleansed, weak, and unable for want of courage to behold things that are utterly bright—, then it beholds nothing at all, even if another should show it, in actual presence before it, what there is to be seen. That which sees must be made akin to, and like, what is seen, before it seeks to attain vision. The eye could never have seen the sun if it had not become like the sun; nor can the soul see beauty unless it has become beautiful itself. Let every man first become god-like, and every man become beautiful, if he would see god and beauty. As he rises upward, he will come first to Intelligent Mind (*Nous*), and there he will see all the Forms in their beauty, and he will say that beauty is here ⟨in these Forms; for it is in virtue of them, as the offspring and the essence of Intelligent Mind, that all things have their beauty⟩.[1] Beyond this

---

[1] The words in brackets may be a gloss which has crept into the text.

rises next what is called "the nature of the good", which has beauty as a porch before it.

'And so, in the sum of the account, one may say that the Ultimate [the First Principle] is Beauty; but if one seeks to distinguish the thoughts (*ta noēta*) [present in the Intelligent Mind], one may say that the thought or idea of Beauty has its place in the Forms of that Mind, but the Good is what is beyond it and is the source and origin of Beauty. Or, alternatively, one may place the Good and the Beautiful side by side as the Ultimate—except that the former [i.e. the Good] includes the Beautiful.'[1]

c. *The View of the Descent and Ascent of the Soul*

From the Sixth *Ennead*, ix, § 11. 'The nature of the soul will not, as it moves, come down to utter not-being; but it will, in its descent, come to evil, and so far it will come to not-being, yet not to absolute not-being. Then, when it sets out on the opposite course upward, it will not come to anything Other, but only to its own self; and thus, not having its being in anything that is Other, it has its being in nothing but itself. But to have its being only in itself, and not in anything other than itself, is to have its being in the Beyond [i.e. the One Ultimate, or the First and Last]; for one becomes, even in one's self, something that is not in the order of [mere] being, but is above and beyond that order, by virtue of that with which one enters into communication. If, therefore, a man see himself becoming such as this, he has in himself a reflection [of the One Ultimate which is above the order of being]; and if he then departs out of himself, like an image in a glass moving up to its original, he will have come to the end of his journey. If he falls away from the vision, he can quicken again the virtue that is in him; and knowing himself to be once more duly ordered and disposed, he will be lightened of his burden, and move by the virtue that is in him up to Intelligent Mind and so through wisdom to It [the Ultimate, which is not only above the

---

[1] The translation of these last words is based on an emendation proposed by a Dutch scholar. Perhaps the reading of the original manuscript, which may be translated, 'except that the Beautiful is there [? in the Good]', means the same.

order of being, but transcends even Intelligent Mind].[1] This is the life of gods, of men who are god-like, of the blessed; it is release from the things of here and now; it is a life free from the pleasures these give; it is the escape of the Alone to the Alone.'

Note on St. Augustine's debt to Plotinus: The Vision of Ostia

The analogy—and the difference—between St. Augustine and Plotinus is remarkable. St. Augustine had studied Plotinus in the Latin translation of Victorinus, and had learned that 'the Platonists [i.e. Neoplatonists] in many ways led to the belief in God and His Word' (*Confessions*, viii. 3). He had read in 'the books of the Platonists' a doctrine of the Word which was in its measure like that in the Gospel according to St. John; but he had *not* read in those books that 'the Word was made flesh and dwelt among us' (ibid. vii. 13–14). The passage translated here shows, however, how deeply he had been influenced by what he had read in Plotinus. A moving study of that influence will be found in P. Henry's *La Vision d'Ostie*.

Confessions, book IX, c. x. 23–26. '. . . She [my mother] and I were standing alone, leaning against a window from which we could see into the garden of the house in which we were living. It was in Ostia, on the Tiber, and here, far from crowds, we were recruiting our strength, after the fatigue of our long journey, for

---

[1] A poem of Matthew Arnold, *In Utrumque Paratus*, gives a fine expression to the Neoplatonic doctrine of the Descent and Ascent of the soul. The Descent is first suggested in the form of a conditional sentence—

> If, in the silent mind of One all-pure,
> At first imagined lay
> The sacred world: and by procession sure
> From those still deeps, in form and colour drest,
> Seasons alternating, and night and day,
> The long-mused thought to north, south, east, and west,
> Took then its all-seen way;

and then the Ascent comes in the form of an imperative addressed to the quickened soul—

> O waking on a world which thus-wise springs!
> . . . O waking on life's stream!
> By lonely pureness to the all-pure fount
> (Only by this thou canst) the colour'd dream
> Of life remount!

the voyage before us.[1] So we were talking together, very sweetly, by ourselves and, *forgetting those things which are behind, and reaching forth unto those things which are before*, we were inquiring between ourselves—in the presence of the Truth, which is Thee—what the nature of the eternal life of the Saints would be. . . .

'When our talk was brought to a point where any delight whatsoever of our fleshly senses, in any bodily light whatsoever, seemed not only not worthy of comparison, but not even worthy of mention, before the sweetness of eternal life, we lifted ourselves up with a still more burning desire to Him who is the same for ever (*in id ipsum*); and we passed step by step through all bodily things and even the very heavens, from which the sun, moon, and stars *give light upon the earth*. Then we ascended farther, thinking within ourselves, and speaking, and wondering at Thy works; and so we came to our minds,[2] and then we went beyond them, that we might attain to the region of unfailing plenty, where Thou feedest Israel for ever with the food of Truth. There life is wisdom, by which all these things are made—both things that have been, and things that shall be—yet she herself is not made, but she is as she hath been, and so shall she be for ever; or rather "have been" and "shall be" are not in her, but in her is only "being"; for she is eternal, and "have been" and "shall be" are not eternal. So while we were speaking and longing for her, we attained to her in a measure with the whole effort of our hearts. At that we sighed, and there we left, gathered together, the *first fruits of the spirit*, and we returned to the sound of our voices, where words have a beginning and an end. Ah, what is like *Thy Word*, O Lord, which abideth in itself without growing old, and maketh all things new?

'So we were saying: "If for anyone the tumult of the flesh were silent; silent the images on earth, or in the waters, or in the air; silent even the poles of heaven, and the very soul silent to itself, surmounting self by not thinking on self; silent all dreams and imaginary revelations, every tongue and every sign; yea, if all

---

[1] They were about to return to Africa, their home; but Monnica died before the voyage.

[2] The *Nous* of Plotinus, or Intelligent Mind; see the passage translated above, on the ascent of the soul.

that exists only in transition were for anyone altogether silent (since now, if a man but listen, all these things speak and say, *We made not ourselves, but He made us who abides for ever*); if, those words once said, all things then became silent, having their ears lifted up unto Him who made them, and if then He Himself alone spoke to us, and that not through the things of sense, but through His very self, so that we heard His Word through no tongue of flesh, or angel's voice, or sound of thunder, or riddle of any parable, but we heard only Him whom we love as He speaks to us in these things, and we heard him speaking to us as Himself and by Himself apart from these things, even as now we are reaching forth and attaining by the quick wings of thought to the eternal Wisdom which abides above all things; if *this* could go on and on, and other visions of a wholly different kind could be taken away, and this one vision could ravish and engulf us, and hide the beholder away in inward joys, so that eternal life should be always such as this moment of understanding, for which we sighed, now is—would not this be an '*enter thou in the joy of thy Lord*'? And when shall that be? When *we all rise again, but shall not all be changed.*" '

No words need be added, or can be added, to this marvel of vision. St. Augustine lived through what Philo had dreamed and Plotinus had taught.

§ X. ESSAY ON KINGSHIP. III. THE PERIOD FROM THE DEATH OF AUGUSTUS TO THE REIGN OF THE EMPEROR CONSTANTINE

A. *The Development of the Idea of Kingship from the Reign of Augustus to the End of the Reign of Marcus Aurelius*

The record of the conception of monarchy or the 'Principate', at the end of the first century B.C., not only appears in inscriptions (see above, pp. 209–14); it also appears, even more vividly, in the *Res Gestae*, or annals of achievement, left by Augustus himself to posterity (see above, pp. 224–30), and it may also be traced in the poetry of Virgil's Fourth *Eclogue* and in passages of his *Georgics* and *Aeneid* (see above, pp. 214–24). A scholar as well as a poet, and conversant with the literature and ideas of his day, Virgil drew on the thought of the Eastern Mediterranean as well as on native Italian feeling. The Fourth *Eclogue*, as has already been noted, has its parallels, and it may be some of its sources, in the Jewish-Hellenistic third book of the *Sibylline Oracles*; and there are passages in the sixth book of the *Aeneid* which are reminiscent of what is recorded of the teaching of Posidonius of Rhodes.[1]

Meanwhile there had developed in the Eastern Mediterranean, among the Jews, a conception of divine monarchy, Messianic in its nature, which stands by itself and is independent of (and indeed opposed to) the current conception of monarchy, alike in the Seleucid kingdom—to which, in its day, Judaea belonged except for transitory periods of Egyptian conquest—and in the Roman Empire which succeeded to the Seleucid inheritance. This Jewish conception of monarchy appears already in the beginning of the Jewish revolt against the philhellene policy of Antiochus Epiphanes, and it is expressed (about 166 B.C.) in the visions of the seventh chapter of the Book of Daniel (see above, p. 126). Here the process of history is made to culminate in the triumph of a 'son of man', who—beginning as a corporate body, in the sense of the religious congregation composed of the faithful members of the Jewish people—seems eventually to be identified with the individual person of a Messiah who is one with the corporate body, as it is one with him. This culmination of history means the handing over of the government of the world to a monarchy which is at once divinely instituted and democratically approved, as Psalm 110 would appear to suggest (see above, p. 145). The Maccabean monarchy, in which the king or 'prince' was also high priest, is the immediate and initial expression of this conception; and an alternation or oscillation between the fact of that monarchy (which proved more and more a disappointment as the successors to it grew progressively weaker) and the idea and expectation of a coming Messiah may be traced in Jewish literature after the end of the second century B.C. It appears, for example, in the *Testament of the Twelve Patriarchs* (see above, p. 147), of

[1] See above, p. 134, n. 1 and n. 2.

about 100 B.C., and it appears again in the great Messianic 'Psalm of Solomon' (17), some time after 63 B.C. (see above, pp. 149–52).

The last expression of Jewish political thought in antiquity is to be found in the writings of Philo Iudaeus of Alexandria, in the first half of the first century A.D. (see above, pp. 157–63); but the thought of Philo—at any rate in his treatise *De Iosepho* (which also goes by the title of *The Statesman*)—is hardly concerned with monarchy, and is not in the line of that specifically Jewish tradition which runs from the Book of Daniel, through the First Book of the Maccabees, to the Testament of the Twelve Patriarchs and the Psalms of Solomon. The Maccabean kingdom has now gone, and the spirit of Messianism is hardly present in Philo. He is, it is true, essentially Jewish, but his ideas are the ideas of the Hellenistic Jewry of Alexandria rather than the ideas of Jerusalem; and the 'Statesman' depicted in his *De Iosepho* is not a monarch (and certainly not a divinely instituted monarch), but rather a 'politician' of many shifts and wiles who has to trim his sails to a people like that of Alexandria. Philo, however, was a many-hued thinker; if he could picture Joseph as a 'politician', he could also depict Moses as a great legislator and guide; and in some passages of his writings he appears to think of kingship as a link between the ideal *megalopolis* of the whole universe and the actual earthly *polis*, a link which gathers up in itself the light of divine reason and brings down that light to illuminate the work of practical government (see above, p. 159). In a word, Philo lives in the ideal as well as in the actual—in the city of God as well as in the city of Alexandria: he is something of a Platonist (or an Augustinian before St. Augustine) as well as a member of the Jewish *polīteuma* of a very earthly city; and he veers from the one to the other. When he draws on Plato and the reformed Stoicism of Posidonius he has one set of ideas; when he allegorizes the life of Joseph, with reference to the conditions of life in Alexandria, he has another. He is a chameleon who takes his colour from the immediate environment surrounding his thought at each given moment of his thinking. He left much to the later thought of Alexandria, both Christian and Neoplatonist, but he hardly left any clear conception of the scope and function of monarchy, or indeed any clear conception of politics generally.

The Jewish idea of monarchy (and the brief Jewish practice of monarchy in the time of the Maccabees and their successors) ran its independent course, and then—except so far as it left any legacy to the Christian thought which arose on its ashes—it ceased to be. The Hellenistic and Oriental conception of monarchy which had been flowing into Rome from the area of the old Seleucid kingdom ever since the beginning of the second century B.C., and more particularly since the beginning of the Civil Wars in 49 B.C., still continued to flow. But Roman writers themselves added elements to the monarchical tradition and the general mysticism of monarchy during the first century A.D. Seneca, ready to put a rhetorical style at the service of a Nero, celebrated the monarch in his *De Clementia* as the very breath of the commonwealth, the mirror of God, and the father of his people (see above, pp. 236-8). Tacitus had a far more critical spirit; but even Tacitus can state the economic argument in favour of the imperial system of government (see above, p. 231), and he can make a Roman legate in Gaul defend the cause of the Roman Emperor (p. 241). Pliny the Younger, in his *Panegyricus* addressed to Trajan, anticipates the *Laus Constantini* which the Christian bishop Eusebius offered to the first Christian emperor: he notes the blessings brought to the provinces by imperial rule; he lauds the example set by Trajan for the imitation of his subjects; he praises his justice, which makes him a Jove upon earth (see above, pp. 253 ff.).

The great Roman lawyers in their turn take up the tale of monarchy: Gaius, in the second century A.D., and Ulpian, whose writings belong mostly to the years A.D. 211-17, both seek to explain the prince's power of issuing *constitutiones* which have the force of law (see above, pp. 258 ff.); and Ulpian's explanation (p. 262) is of particular importance in the subsequent development of political theory. But the Roman lawyers of the second and the early third century A.D. were not pure or absolute monarchists; they maintained a republican tradition even in asserting a monarchical fact; they set no limits to monarchical authority, but they sought to derive that authority from a grant made by the people in the form of a concessionary law. *Quod principi placuit legis habet vigorem*, Ulpian writes; but he adds at once, in the same sentence, *utpote cum lege regia . . . populus ei et in eum omne suum imperium et potestatem conferat*. 'The pleasure of the prince has the force of law—*because* the people by a *lex regia* confers upon him and into his hands all its sovereignty and authority.' It is true that the act of the people was only a form, and that the people had no choice in the matter. But forms matter; and the form described by Ulpian mattered vitally, for long centuries, in the development of political ideas. The Roman lawyers had no conception of 'divine right'; they were much nearer to the idea of a 'social contract'. But if they were thus democrats in form, it must be confessed that they were monarchists—and absolute monarchists—in fact; and while in the future the element of democratic form preserved in their theories was to be vitally important, in the present and in their own day they helped to consolidate the cause of monarchism.

Latin thought and Latin literature had, on the whole, carried the day over Greek thought and its expression during the two hundred years from 100 B.C. to A.D. 100. From the days of Lucretius and Cicero to the days of Pliny the Younger there is, as has already been noted, an eclipse of Greek literature. A Greek thinker like Posidonius might be the teacher of Roman statesmen in the first century B.C., and a Hellenized Jew such as Philo Iudaeus might write volume on volume in Greek in the first century A.D.; but Posidonius left no abiding memorial, and Philo belongs to the Jewish rather than the Hellenic tradition. From the reign of Hadrian (A.D. 117–38), or even earlier, there begins a revival of Greek thought, Greek literature, and Greek influence. It shows itself in Epictetus and Marcus Aurelius; but it also shows itself, in a more questionable and yet notable form, in the stylized and rhetorical writings of the thinkers (if indeed they can be called thinkers) of the period of the 'Second Sophistic' from Dio of Prusa onwards. Dio, like his successors, makes no qualifications or limitations, such as the Roman lawyers had made, when he treats of monarchy (see above, pp. 303 ff.). He sets a trumpet to his lips in the various discourses on kingship which he addressed to

Trajan about the year A.D. 100; and Aelius Aristides of Smyrna, in his oration 'To Rome', follows the example of Dio in the period of the Antonines (see above, p. 324). Philostratus, in a later age (*circa* A.D. 220), is more original, if less eloquent: in his life of Apollonius of Tyana he can urge the need of mixing the spirit of party with the feeling of concord; and while he argues in favour of imperial rule, he also pleads for some recognition of the rights of the various nations comprised in the Roman Empire (see above, pp. 330–1). Plutarch, writing at an earlier date (about A.D. 100)—not as a rhetorician, but as an eclectic philosopher who mixed Platonism in with elements of Stoicism—drew a famous picture of the 'virtue or fortune' of Alexander the Great, and wrote a stirring account of the efforts of the Spartan kings Agis and Cleomenes to reform the social conditions of their country; he also, in a brief address 'to an uneducated ruler', developed a theme which had occupied the attention of his contemporary, the Stoic philosopher Musonius—the theme that the king should be, or embody, Animate Reason or Animate Law, and should therefore draw on the teachings of philosophy and the philosophers to attain the ideal of kingship (see above, p. 309). But the literature of the second century A.D. has little to add to the store of political ideas; and it is not till we come to the following century that we find new developments in the practice and in the idea of monarchy.

B. *The Development of the Idea of Kingship from the Reign of Septimius Severus to the Reign of Constantine*

In the principate as it stood at the end of the reign of Marcus Aurelius we may trace three different bases or foundations of the authority of the monarch. The first is the legal basis, which consists in the *Lex Regia* enacted by the Roman people for the purpose of conferring sovereignty and authority on the *princeps*; and this basis is already present in the time of Augustus. The second basis has been called the 'Charismatic';[1] it is in its nature religious; it consists in the imperial cult by which the authority of the monarch

[1] Professor Ensslin (following Max Weber) in the *Cambridge Ancient History*, vol. xii, p. 353.

is vested with a sanction of divinity. This second basis is initially personal, but it develops with the passage of time and the succession of rulers into something more than personal, something which we may call traditional, or even institutional; and thus there emerges a third basis, the dynastic basis of continuity and a general tendency to heredity, often indeed interrupted by military *coups* and the play of contingency, but always reasserting itself and ultimately triumphant. The result, it has been said, was 'that spontaneous respect for an outstanding personality gave place to an obligation to respect the idea of a ruler, personified in the holder of the office; an obligation that found justification in philosophy and theology'.[1]

During the second century A.D., from the accession of Trajan to the death of Marcus Aurelius, the justification of monarchy had been mainly philosophic. It was the thought of Greece, and particularly that of the Stoic school, which was generally dominant; and the current idea of monarchy was that which had been expounded by the Stoic philosopher Musonius Rufus (see above, p. 310) and illustrated by the reign of the great Stoic Emperor Aurelius. In an age in which philosophers were attached to families, and stood by the side of the *pater familias* as directors of consciences and virtual confessors, it was natural that they should also be ready to serve by the side of the imperial *pater patriae* in a similar capacity. But the end of the reign of Marcus Aurelius marks a great change, and inaugurates a new epoch. Philosophy yields to theology—theology of a sort, the sort which has been called 'solar theology'. The West, and the Greek thought of the West, gives place to the East and its cults, more especially the cult of the Sun-god. There was a 'triumph of Eastern over Western ideas, which was to transform the world';[2] from the Romanism which 'had triumphed with the victory of Augustus at Actium . . . the pendulum was swinging back once more towards the East'.[3] It is true that there was nothing absolutely new in this surge of the East towards the West. The Seleucid monarchy,

---

[1] Ibid., p. 355.
[2] H. Stuart Jones, *The Roman Empire*, p. 212.
[3] N. H. Baynes in the *Cambridge Ancient History*, vol. xii, p. 704.

long ago, had given to the Roman West several forms or 'hypo-stases' of the Sun-god, and along with them the Iranian cult of Mithras, the god of light—the god of light itself, the diffused celestial light which is prior even to sunrise. But the impact of the East in the third century A.D. had, none the less, a new and far more massive volume.

The reign of Septimius Severus (193–211) is here of the first importance. The emperors of the second century had been either of Spanish origin (Trajan and Hadrian both came from the neighbourhood of Seville), or, like the Antonines, they were of old Italian stock from the south of Etruria. Severus came from the province of Africa[1]—a province of southern sun and heat, fertile in ability, which had produced, even before his accession, the new African Latinity (old and even archaic as well as new) of Apuleius and Fronto, and was producing during his reign the vigorous thought and the remarkable style of Tertullian. But it is not the *Africitas* of Severus himself (he belonged to a family which continued to speak Punic, though he was educated enough to deliver an oration in Greek) that matters so much: it is rather the Syrian origin of his wife, Iulia Domna, one of the most remarkable women in the long history of Rome. She was the daughter of the hereditary priest (a prince as well as a priest) of the *baal* or local Sun-god of Emesa, the modern Homs, a town to the north-east of Beyrout. She was also a woman of vigorous character and a vivid and stirring mind; she impelled Philostratus to write the biography (or romance) of the neo-Pythagorean sage and charlatan, Apollonius of Tyana; and she seems to have impelled her husband to new developments of the imperial cult which made it more and more Oriental. Severus and Iulia Domna are figured on coins together as Sol and Luna; she is also por-trayed, by herself, as the goddess Cybele. The Afro-Syrian house of Severus and his wife, increasingly designated in inscriptions by the style of *domus divina*, is a new portent in the history of the Empire and the theory of monarchy; and the portent grows with the growth of the Syrian element in the amalgam. Iulia Domna had a sister, Iulia Maesa, the second daughter of the prince-priest

[1] His birthplace was Leptis Magna, in the modern Tripoli.

of the *baal* of Homs; that sister had two daughters; each of the daughters had a son by a Syrian husband; and after the death of Caracalla, the son and successor of Septimius (211–17), the son of one of these daughters became the Emperor Heliogabalus or Elagabalus (218–22), and the son of the other became the Emperor Alexander Severus (222–35). The Syrian Orontes was indeed flowing into the Tiber, with a rapid and increasing volume, during the forty years between the accession of Septimus Severus in 193 and the death of Alexander Severus in 235. Nor did this Syrian influence end with the four emperors of the dynasty of the Severi—Septimius, Caracalla (the son of Septimius by Iulia Domna), and the two Syrian grand-nephews of Iulia Domna, Heliogabalus and Alexander Severus. The relics of that influence may still be traced in the days of the later Danubian emperors. They are conspicuous in the reign of Aurelian (270–5) and in the association of the Empire with sun-worship which marks his reign. They are still to be traced even in the reign of Constantine.

Septimius himself, apart from the influence of his Syrian wife, was a military absolutist. The old *Romanitas* of the Empire, and the privileged position of Italy, began to disappear before a levelling cosmopolitanism which treated all parts and provinces alike; and just as local differences were thus ironed out by a uniform pressure, so, too, were social or class differences. Senators were levelled down to the position of knights (*equites*), as knights were levelled up to the position of senators; the edict of Caracalla of the year A.D. 212, which granted an equality of Roman citizenship 'to all aliens in the inhabited world except unfree subjects' (see above, p. 273), and which thus spread through the Roman world a general uniformity of status, may be regarded as the logical outcome of the levelling policy of his father.[1] A policy of this order needed some sanction in a new glorification of the office of the emperor, conceived as the principle of unity and the prime source of all energy; and that new glorification began to

[1] Another outcome of that policy may be traced in the changed attitude of the government to associations or *collegia*, which ceased to be inspired by private initiative and were made State corporations subject to State control. This change seems to have been introduced, or at any rate accelerated, during the reign of Alexander Severus; see H. Stuart Jones, *The Roman Empire*, p. 273.

be provided by ideas derived from a solar theology in the Syrian style. The emperor comes to be regarded as 'illuminating' his empire in the same way as the sun illuminates the world. There were precedents for such a conception. The Emperor Nero, a century and a half before, had erected a colossal image of the Sun with his own features before his Golden House, and had had himself represented on coins with a radiate crown in the image of the Sun; he had been designated in inscriptions as 'the New Sun', and identified with Apollo the Greek god of light.[1] Whether or no these precedents were remembered (they were Greek in inspiration rather than Oriental), it is certain that the new Syrian influence, so potent in the reign of Septimius Severus and his successors, expressed itself in a cult of the Sun. Severus himself is depicted with a *nimbus* or halo of sun-rays, or as wearing a radiate crown; his son Geta is shown on a coin as the offspring of the unconquered Sun-god (*Sol invictus*) and the Sun-emperor.[2] In and after the reign of Caracalla the lion of the Sun is frequent on coins, and serves to indicate the Sun-god as the source of imperial authority. The extravagances of the reign of Elagabalus, so called from his connexion with the *baal* served by his family, are a matter of personal fantasy; if the style of 'priest of the Unconquered Sun-god Elagabalus' was placed by him in the forefront of the imperial titles, and the black stone which was the god's symbol was brought from Homs to be housed for a time in a great temple in Rome, this was not a politic effort to strengthen imperial authority by basing it on solar theology, but rather the expression of a puerile egoism and a parochial pride in the local deity of his own family. The follies of his reign might well have extinguished the whole cult of the Sun-god and the Sun-emperor. That it did not do so, and that the cult survived for nearly a century after his assassination in 222, is a proof of the hold which it had gained on the general thought of the age.

The dynasty of the Severi was followed by a generation of confusion and anarchy which lasted till the accession of Aurelian in A.D. 270. The one notable emperor in the course of that con-

---

[1] A. Momigliano in the *Cambridge Ancient History*, vol. x, pp. 732–3.
[2] Ibid., vol. xii, p. 357.

fused generation was Gallienus, who ruled first as a colleague of Valerian and then as sole emperor, from 253 to 268; he was the first to grant a measure of toleration to the Christian Church, and he and his wife were the patrons of Plotinus and Neo-platonism (see above, p. 332). But he was a dilettante, and a master of pomp and pageantry, rather than a vigorous ruler; and it needed the strong arm of the soldier Aurelian (270–5) to reduce chaos into order and to restore imperial authority. The succession now begins (indeed it had already begun during the brief reign of Claudius Gothicus from 268 to 270) of the line of Danubian emperors. Aurelian himself was the son of a Pannonian peasant who had risen high in the army; Diocletian, his eventual successor (284–305), was a Dalmatian of humble origin who had also risen in the army and, like Aurelian, owed his elevation to the legions; Constantius I, the father of the Emperor Constantine, was an officer of Illyrian extraction and equally humble origin, married to a wife, Helena, who according to tradition had been a maid in a Balkan inn. (Their son, the first Christian emperor, was born in a town on a tributary of the Danube, in the province of Upper Moesia.) The series of the Danubian emperors based on an army career and elevated to their office by military action is readily explained by the fact that the Danubian army was at once the strongest army in the Empire and the nearest to Rome. It does not seem equally clear, or as readily explicable, why they should have inherited, or at any rate continued, the form of imperial cult and the association of the office of emperor with the religion of the Sun, which had arisen and attained such vogue during the period of the dynasty of the Severi. There must have been some basic cause, though that cause can only be conjectured. There was certainly, at any rate in the reign of Aurelian, a definite occasion; and that occasion is recorded in history.

The basic cause of the continuation of a conception of monarchi-cal authority which based it on Sun-worship and solar theology is probably to be found in the army. It was the army which made the Danubian emperors; but what had made them might also unmake them, and they needed some basis of authority more stable and more assured than a military pronunciamento. The old legal basis of the *Lex Regia*, if it still survived, was no more than a form; there was now no traditional or institutional basis of dynastic succession as there had been in the second century; the one basis left, if it could be secured, was the 'charismatic' basis of some form of supernatural grace (*charisma*). The humble origin of several of the emperors possibly made them all the more anxious to find a high and solemn sanction for the great office which they had attained; and the saying with which Aurelian is recorded to have met a mutiny in the army—'the purple was the gift of God, and God alone could limit that gift in time'[1]—attests at once a desire to find something more than a military basis and a wish to transcend his own peasant origin. But there was also a particular occasion, as well as a general cause, which impelled the Emperor Aurelian to continue the cult of the Sun-god and to claim that the grace of the 'Unconquered Sun' was the ground of his authority. In the course of his Eastern campaigns he came under the influence of Syrian sun-worship; and the story was told (but it may be no more than a story) that he ascribed his victory in a battle fought before Homs to the intervention and help of the Sun-god of that city who had been the god of the Severi. Henceforth he exalted *Sol invictus* as 'the lord of the Roman Empire' (*dominus imperii Romani*); and a temple in his honour arose in Rome with its own college of *pontifices dei Solis*. But the *Sol invictus* of Aurelian is not only the Syrian *baal* of Homs: he is a syncretic or synthetic deity, with elements of the Greek Apollo and some features of the Iranian Mithras united to Roman forms. He 'embodied the idea of a unifying deity to correspond to the sole earthly ruler of the world'; he 'was to be the centre of a revived and unified paganism, and the guarantor of loyalty to the Emperor'.[2] Under the influence of this conception the emperor ceases to be *praesens deus* and becomes 'the Vicar of God', holding an authority which is a trust from the Sun-god and an earthly emanation of his effulgence. This idea of the *vicarius dei* is thus

---

[1] Quoted in H. Stuart Jones, *The Roman Empire*, p. 335; cf. also the *Cambridge Ancient History*, vol. xii, p. 360. (The emperor alone had the right to wear the purple *paludamentum* or mantle, the symbol of sovereignty.)

[2] A. Alföldi in the *Cambridge Ancient History*, vol. xii, p. 193: H. Mattingly, ibid., p. 309.

prior to Constantine and the triumph of Christianity; but it readily passed into Christian theory, with God the Word and the *Logos* banishing and displacing the Sun-god, and it is expounded in the writings of Eusebius of Caesarea, the adviser of the Emperor Constantine and the apologist of his ideas.

The theory of 'divine right', and of the emperor as ruling 'by the grace of God' (*Dei gratia*), which thus emerges in the reign of Aurelian, not only passed into Christian theory: it seems also to have found expression in the neo-Pythagorean treatises on monarchy quoted by Stobaeus under the obscure names of Diotogenes and Ecphantus (see below, p. 361), and it appears, or may be held to appear, in an oration on kingship delivered about A.D. 300 which has somehow found a place at the end of the *Corpus Hermeticum* (p. 374). This is no more than conjecture, and perhaps a dubious conjecture. The evidence of the coinage of Aurelian and his immediate successors, and that of the symbols and the titles they used, has the benefit of certainty. Under Aurelian the majesty of the Sun as the source of imperial authority is stamped clear on the coins; at the end of his reign they 'show Sol as bestower of empire through the "loyal" army'.[1] In them we can trace a solar monotheism which sanctions what may be called a solar autocracy: 'one God, one empire, one emperor—that was the goal which Aurelian sought';[2] and his one god the Sun is sometimes figured on his coins as giving him a globe in token of his power over all the world. Another token or symbol, which was part of the imperial insignia, was the sceptre with the eagle; but that is rather to be associated with Jupiter (who holds the sceptre and gives it to kings, and has the king of all birds at his side) than with the Sun-god and his gift of power. The diadem, however—the head-band or fillet originally worn by the Persian kings and then adopted by their Macedonian conquerors—had come to be particularly associated with the Sun-god; and there are coins of the period which show a radiate diadem, indicative of the rays of the Sun.

Diocletian continued the temper and the style of Aurelian's

---

[1] H. Mattingly in the *Cambridge Ancient History*, vol. xii, p. 719.
[2] H. Lietzmann, *From Constantine to Julian*, Eng. trans., p. 20.

absolutism; but he did not inherit or profess his brand of solar monotheism. He was a polytheist in something of the style of Celsus;[1] he recognized a number of cults and a variety of local gods of 'the nations'; and he was even willing, for his own part, to tolerate Christianity as one of the cults, and to recognize the Christian God as one among many others. He had an instinct for administration and a shrewd common sense which made him prefer utility to mysticism; he might indeed feel, or rather suggest, that he had a divine commission, and accordingly assume the name Iovius (as his colleague in the Empire simultaneously assumed that of Herculius); he might even use the *nimbus* or halo which traditionally marked the descent of the deity among men, and served to express the glory of light which shone from the emperor; but his real interest was in an impressive ceremonial, based upon Oriental models, which would inspire a reverent awe and attest the unique majesty of monarchy. This was the inheritance which he bequeathed to his successors, and which was afterwards perpetuated for centuries in the Byzantine Empire. He was not the first to demand *proskynēsis*, but he regulated its form: those who approached his presence must kneel and kiss the hem of his robe. He also laid down the rules of *admissio*, or 'presentation at court'; the ceremonial of the court drew a barrier between the monarch and his subjects and determined degrees of precedence among his ministers and attendants. Synesius, more than a century later, in an address to the Emperor Arcadius, was to rebuke the 'secrecy of seclusion' maintained by the pomp and ceremony surrounding the imperial person (see below, p. 383); but the pomp had its use, as Diocletian had calculated, and it continued to endure for more than a thousand years.

Constantine inherited the legacy of ceremony which had been bequeathed by Diocletian; but in some ways he went back to Aurelian, while in another and greater way he went forward into the future. Like Aurelian, he conceived himself as the vicegerent of God; like Aurelian he adopted, at one period of his career, the Unconquered Sun as his patron deity, and the sun then figured prominently on his coins. This was the period of what has been

[1] On the views of Celsus, as recorded by Origen, see below (p. 430).

called his first conversion (about A.D. 310), when he turned from the Jovian-Herculian cult of Diocletian and his associate emperor to the sun-worship of his Balkan ancestors.[1] His second conversion, which carried him forward from sun-worship on the path that eventually led him to the profession of Christianity, soon followed on his first, with the victory won over his rival Maxentius at the battle of the Milvian Bridge (A.D. 312) and the vision of the Cross in the afternoon sky which he had seen before the battle and of which he afterwards told his adviser and historian Eusebius. But the conversion of Constantine to Christianity was gradual; and perhaps it was also, to the very last, partial and incomplete. His policy was never a policy of pure Christian monotheism; it was rather a policy of parity, *un système paritaire*, which gave an equal status and a common toleration to different creeds; and this is the gist of the so-called 'Edict of Milan' of A.D. 313 (see below, p. 466). Nor was his personal belief, any more than his policy, ever purely and only Christian; he was rather a syncretist, with a wavering and hospitable mind which could simultaneously house the teachings of his Christian advisers, the Danubian traditions of his youth (especially the tradition of sun-worship), and the lessons of Greek philosophy. He seems to have followed the same general line as two of his predecessors— Gallienus the would-be philosopher who trusted in the ultimate victory of one commonly accepted philosophy after the manner of Plotinus, and Aurelian the solar monotheist who put his faith in the triumph of the one god of the Sun; like them he sought a single philosophy of one *Summus Deus* and a faith common to all the 'nations'.[2] True, he had a sense of mission, a mission of which he had already been aware in his British days (*circa* 306); but the mission of which he thought was a personal inspiration rather than a mission imposed or suggested by the Christian Church and its Gospel (see below, p. 480).

The change in the conception and character of the Empire which came with the victory of Constantine, and with his gradual and partial conversion to Christianity, was not a total or

---

[1] N. H. Baynes in the *Cambridge Ancient History*, vol. xii, p. 680.
[2] André Piganiol in *Historia*, i (1950), pp. 94–95.

fundamental change. Already, in the third century, the Empire had acquired a religious basis; indeed, as has been suggested, it may have been compelled to adopt such a basis, as a safeguard against the domination of the army and the subjection of imperial authority to the reign of military pronunciamentos. Once the Empire was thus based on religion, it must either persecute Christianity, as a rival and a danger to the different religion which for the time being it preferred to profess, or it must accept and profess Christianity as the *vera religio* which was henceforth to be its permanent basis. If Aurelian had claimed that a solar monotheism was the proper religious basis of empire, 'a dangerous rival to this claim was the equally monarchical and universal idea of the God of the Christians';[1] and the movement of Constantine's mind, along with the movement of events, led him ultimately to acknowledge, and to prefer, the claim of that idea. It has accordingly been argued, with justice, that the change which began in 312–13 was due not so much to the personal views and opinion of any statesman or individual as to the logic of the Empire itself (*die Reichsideologie*).[2] There was indeed a change, or even a revolution, but there was also continuity; and we can trace the logic of the line of thought along which imperial theory moved from an attack on Christianity to a recognition of its claim. Monotheism of one form or another—the solar monotheism of a supreme Sun-god uniting all local cults, or the Christian monotheism of the one God who is the Word of Creation—was the dominant idea of the age; and the logic of empire ultimately demanded the triumph of that idea in its higher and stronger form.

From this point of view, and remembering the continuity of the general idea of monotheism which went along with a revolution in the conception of the one true God, we can understand how the Christian Church, on its side, took over much of the legacy of the pagan past for incorporation into its own theory of empire.[3] It continued to think of the emperor as the vicegerent

[1] A. Alföldi, in the *Cambridge Ancient History*, vol. xii, p. 194.
[2] H. Berkhof, *Kirche und Kaiser* (translated from the Dutch), pp. 41 ff.
[3] 'The theory of Christian sovereignty, as Eusebius set it forth, is itself a symbol of the way in which the past of the ancient world was carried over into the

of God; it ascribed to him all the majesty, and the radiance of illumination, which had been ascribed to him before in the pre-Christian theory of empire. This was not servility; it was hardly even policy; it was simply a matter of inheritance. When the emperor had become, or professed to have become, a Christian, how could the Christian Church possibly diminish his power, either by the theory it professed or by the action it took? Were not Christians rather impelled to magnify his power to a higher degree, now that he had added to his greatness the great and supreme service of turning to their own faith? Not that, indeed, he had made the Empire Christian, or even that he had himself become fully and utterly Christian: the Empire was relatively neutral, and wedded to a system of parity, just as the emperor himself kept his own mind, if not neutral, at any rate still 'indeterminate'; but even if his Christian subjects were only on a basis of parity, they had still to preach the majesty of the emperor—indeed they had to preach it all the more—in order not to be left behind by other creeds and bodies of opinion with which they were put on a level. They even augmented his majesty, in comparison with other creeds, by professing and acknowledging the right of the emperor to summon councils of the Church and to sanction their deci-sions. . . . Yet this, after all, was but the short-time result of the revolution (for it *was* a revolution, in spite of the continuity which it preserved with the past) which began in the reign of Con-stantine. There were also to be long-time results. And one of those long-time results was the claim of the Church to a sphere of its own, separate and independent from the sphere of the State, even when 'the State' was represented by an emperor who was the vicar of God. The Christian Church cherished a great text about the claims of Caesar and the claims of God. That text rendered Caesar his due; but it claimed for God the things that were God's. That claim was destined to be pressed more and more in the course of the generations. It is already being pressed by a bishop of Cordova in the reign of Constantine's successor (see below, p. 396, n. 1). The long-time results of the Constantinian revolution

Christian Empire' (N. H. Baynes in the *Cambridge Ancient History*, vol. xii, p. 699; see also his *Byzantine Studies* (1955), pp. 168–72).

are different, after all, from the short-time results as they were seen by Constantine himself and by the Christian thinkers of his reign.

The theme 'of Kingship' (*peri basileias*) had been treated by many writers during the six centuries that lie between the career of Alexander and the conversion of Constantine. Some final reflections occur to the mind in reviewing the lessons of those six centuries. By the end of the fourth century B.C. monarchy had become inevitable in the Eastern Mediterranean, partly in consequence of the increased size of States, now far transcending the dimensions of a self-governing republican city-state, and partly as the result of the fusion and intermixture of peoples, produced by the conquests and struggles of Alexander and his successors, which made impossible the formation of any homogeneous body of public opinion such as a city-state needed for its basis. By the end of the first century monarchy had become equally inevitable in the Western Mediterranean, where Rome had come to transcend the measure of a city-state and had grown into a great empire. The one conceivable alternative to monarchy was federalism, and federalism was impracticable under the conditions and in the temper of the ancient world. It had indeed been attempted, but only in the Eastern Mediterranean and among the Greeks of Achaea and Aetolia; and even there it had failed. Perhaps the fundamental reason of its failure was military; no league could assemble or train a standing army which could cope with the disciplined phalanx of the Macedonian monarch or the legions of the Roman Senate. But there were also political reasons for its failure. A federation could not coexist with a primary assembly (though the Achaean League seems to have attempted the impossible); and a primary assembly was the breath of life for the Greek city-states. Nor was it only the popular feeling in favour of direct democracy which militated against federalism. Local feeling was equally offended by the existence and the claims of a central system which cut across an ingrained instinct of civic autonomy.

Winning its way under Alexander and his successors in the East, and ultimately victorious with Augustus in the West, the cause of monarchism attached itself to religious feeling, and acquired in the course of its history various forms of religious sanction. It might indeed have other bases: the legal, when some measure of popular approval, in the shape of a *lex de imperio*, was attempted; the dynastic or institutional, when the process of time had given a line of monarchs some continuity of history and policy; or even the military, when the legions (and especially those of the Danubian area) sought to play the dangerous role of king-makers. But these other bases either faded, as did the legal and the dynastic bases, or, like the military basis, they did more harm than good to the cause which they seemed to support. The religious basis and sanction was at once more permanent and less dangerous; and from the beginning of the third century to the reign of Constantine it continued to grow in strength. By its nature monarchy could now tbe regarded as a service to humanity. It not only benefited the monarch, but it also benefited his subjects and promoted the general welfare of the whole community; it attracted loyalty; it civilized and sublimated the rude fact of power; it provided, in the person of an idealized monarch, conceived as the image and vicar of God, a substance and a model for the imitative instinct of man.

The great and general service of monarchy, in the later ages of antiquity, may best be expressed in the one word 'harmony'. This is the note which is constantly struck, in the philosophies, or would-be philosophies, of monarchy which are current about the year A.D. 300. It appears in the neo-Pythagorean treatises of the *Florilegium* of Stobaeus (if this is the date of those treatises); it appears in the oration appended to the *Corpus Hermeticum*; it appears in the various writings of the Christian bishop Eusebius. This 'harmony', or, as the neo-Pythagoreans call it, *synarmogā*, may be said, on a general view of the whole development of monarchy, to be triple. First, there is the racial harmony of different stocks and peoples in a common concord or *homonoia*—the harmony which had been conceived by the imagination of Alexander. Next, there is the political harmony of different constitutions under a monarchy which mixes with itself both the aristocracy of merit and the democracy of the masses in a

reconciling polity which, in the view of Philostratus,[1] is really a
true democracy. Finally, there is the social harmony of different
interests, professions, and occupations, under a monarch who
represents no class, or rather represents all, standing above their
play in a majestic impartiality. Here we almost touch Hegel and
the high Germanic theory, current in a modern age and country
of monarchism, which held that the unity of the State must be
incorporated 'in an actual individual, in the will of a decreeing
individual, in monarchy'.

When we reflect on the services rendered by monarchy to the
ancient world, we may well regard it as a stage in the education
of humanity. Loyalty; the consecration of power; the presentation of an ideal for imitation; the creation of harmony among the
tumult of human wills—these are all precious things. But there
is also another precious thing, which indeed is the one thing needful; and this one thing was not there. This is the free will of man,
elicited and enlisted by a free system of government for participation in the high privilege, which is also an arduous duty, of
common deliberation and common decision of common affairs.
The monarchism of the ancient world was a degradation as well
as an elevation. If it set the monarch in a blaze of light, it left his
subjects in darkness. One of the great discoveries of the modern
world, made almost accidentally and more than half-uncon-
sciously, is the discovery of constitutional monarchy—the
monarchy which reigns but does not govern (that is a matter for
the people, acting through its elected representatives); the
monarchy which, by the fact of reigning, attracts loyalty, con-
secrates power, presents an ideal, and helps to create harmony,
but which also, by the fact of *not* governing, leaves it to the people,
and demands it of the people, that they should govern themselves.
One may still be a monarchist today—but not a monarchist after
the pattern of Eusebius. Synesius is a better guide.[2] But better
than Synesius is St. Thomas Aquinas—the first theorist in Europe
of constitutional monarchy.

[1] See above, p. 330.
[2] See below, pp. 380 ff.

§ XI. THE NEO-PYTHAGOREAN WRITERS ON KINGSHIP

Introduction

Stobaeus, who compiled (probably in the fifth century A.D.) a collection of excerpts as an *Anthologion* or *Florilegium* arranged under a variety of headings, has a number of such excerpts with the heading of 'Counsels on Kingship'. Among these are passages, written in a Doric form of Greek which seems to be artificially archaic, from two authors, both described as 'Pythagoreans', who go by the names of Diotogenes and Ecphantus. These passages are curious, and even mysterious. Their authors are unknown; we know nothing of Diotogenes, a name which never occurs in any connexion in the rest of Greek literature; and though there was an actual Ecphantus, who *was* a Pythagorean, he belonged to the fourth century B.C. and wrote in Attic Greek, and he must thus be a different person from the 'Pseudo-Ecphantus' (as he is perhaps better called) who wrote in Doric Greek. Even the dates at which the two so-called 'Pythagoreans' wrote are uncertain and disputed among scholars; some regard them as exponents of Hellenistic ideas of Kingship, and assign them to the third century B.C.; others assign them to the second or third century A.D., and regard them as exponents of the ideas of Kingship current in the Roman Empire before the triumph of Christianity.

There would seem to be good reason for adopting the latter view. In the first place the two authors, described by Stobaeus as 'Pythagoreans', are almost certainly neo-Pythagorean; and neo-Pythagoreanism, a revival and extension of the original Pythagorean doctrines of the fifth century B.C., only began to appear in the first century B.C., and only attained a general vogue in the days of the Roman Empire.[1] (The original Pythagoreans of an

---

[1] Pseudonymous 'Pythagorean' writings were a common phenomenon of the age. W. Scott, in the introduction to his edition of *Hermetica* (vol. i, pp. 3–4), gives a brief but clear account of their origin. 'Plato was commonly held to have learned from Pythagoras; . . . in Plato one got the wisdom of Pythagoras at second hand; it would be still better if one could get it at first hand. It must have been chiefly in response to this demand that there were produced (mostly between 100 B.C. and 100 A.D.) large numbers of pseudonymous writings ascribed to this or that early Pythagorean—or in some cases even to Pythagoras himself, in spite of the recorded fact that Pythagoras himself had left nothing in writing.' Scott adds in a footnote (p. 4, note 1) that 'the author of each of them put forth under

earlier date, such as Alcmaeon and Archytas, had preached the doctrine of a mixed constitution, combining their conception of the value of a political mixture of different constitutions with parallel and connected ideas of the value of a medical mixture of the different humours of the body and a musical mixture of the different notes of the scale; and, differing entirely from the 'royalism' of the two authors cited by Stobaeus, they had rejected the notion of the rule of any one element in each and all of these spheres, whether it were in politics or in medicine or in music.) In the second place there are definite and specific elements in the argument of 'Ecphantus'—if not in the briefer and more pedestrian argument of Diotogenes—which suggest and seem to repeat ideas about the position and nature of the emperor (in Greek termed *basileus*) which had become current during the third century A.D., and especially in the reign of Aurelian (270–5). Aurelian, ascribing a victory in battle to the aid of the Sun-god, who had acquired a general vogue in the period of the Severi (193–235), had dedicated a temple in Rome to the 'unconquered Sun' who illuminated all peoples with his rays, and he had conceived his own position, in the office of emperor or *basileus*, as that of the vicegerent of *Sol Invictus*. The language of 'Ecphantus' (see below, p. 367) reproduces these ideas; and it is possible to suspect that his Doric treatise 'On Kingship' is a sort of neo-Pythagorean literary exercise, deliberately written in an archaic style, and deliberately borrowing the name of the Pythagorean Ecphantus of the fourth century B.C., with the intention of giving a venerable flavour of 'Pythagorean' antiquity to the position of the Roman emperor as that position had come to be conceived by the reign of Aurelian.[1]

If 'Ecphantus' is to be explained and dated in this way, he probably carries with him Diotogenes, who is linked with him by

a feigned name, and usually in a would-be Doric dialect, his own version of the syncretic Platonism that was current in his time, and sought to make it appear that this was the sort of thing Pythagoras had taught.'

[1] On the system of ideas which links the emperor to the Sun-god, and makes him a second sun shining on the human world, see Lietzmann, *From Constantine to Julian* (Eng. trans.), p. 20, and the *Cambridge Ancient History*, vol. xii, p. 699. Besides the vogue of the Sun-god, which was Syrian in origin and imported from Syria to Rome, we have also to remember the general vogue in the third century of the cult of Mithras, the Iranian God of Light.

Stobaeus and who also writes in an archaizing form of Doric Greek. It would follow that both of these writers, with their exalted ideas of the sacred nature of kingship, belong to the later days of the Roman Empire, and are long posterior to the period of the Hellenistic kingship of the third century B.C. They are panegyrists of Empire in the style of the younger Pliny, or in that of Dio of Prusa; but they are even more—and still more mystically—'royalists' to the very core.

Attention was first drawn to the theories expounded by these two writers by Professor E. R. Goodenough, in an essay entitled 'The Political Philosophy of Hellenistic Kingship', published in volume i of *Yale Classical Studies* (1928). The fullest treatment of the whole matter is now to be found in L. Delatte's *Les Traités de la Royauté* (1942), which contains the Greek text, with a translation and commentary, as well as essays on the language used and the ideas expressed by Diotogenes and 'Ecphantus'. On grounds of language, syntax, and style, as well as on grounds of substance, Delatte makes out a good case for assigning a late date to the composition of these 'treatises' (op. cit., pp. 284–5).

A. *From the treatise on Kingship by Diotogenes 'the Pythagorean'*

1. Stobaeus, *Florilegium* (ed. Hense), iv, c. vii, § 61. *The functions of a king.* 'The man who is most just would be king, and the most just man is he who is the most law-abiding; for no man could ever be king without justice, and there is no justice without law. Justice consists in law, and law is the cause of justice; the king may be defined either as "animate law" or as "a law-abiding ruler"; and therefore he is the most just and the most law-abiding of men.

'The functions of the king are threefold—military command, the dispensation of justice, and the cult of the gods.[1] He will be able to discharge well the function of military command if he knows how to fight well; he will be able to dispense justice and to hear the pleas of his subjects, if he has learned well the nature of justice and law; and he will be able to observe the cult of the gods

---

[1] This is borrowed from, or based upon, Aristotle's account of the kingships of the heroic age (*Politics*, iii, c. xiv, § 12).

with piety and reverence, if he has studied the nature and excellence of God. It is therefore necessary that the perfect king should be a good general, judge, and priest, because these gifts are consequent upon and proper to the pre-eminence and excellence of a king.

'It is the function of a pilot to preserve his ship, of a charioteer to preserve his chariot, and of a physician to preserve his patients; in the same way it is the function of a king to preserve his subjects who risk their lives in battle, since the man who is the leader of an organization [*systēma*, a technical term in Pythagorean and neo-Pythagorean philosophy] is also its director and controller.[1] Again it is the property of a king—as it is the property of God in the universe of which He is the Leader and President—to distribute and dispense justice, both to the whole commonwealth at large and to each of its members individually. To dispense justice at large, a king must join the whole commonwealth together in one harmony and under one leadership [thus creating a *synarmogā*]: to dispense it individually, and for each member, he must join the parts together in the same harmony and under the same leadership. Moreover, the king is concerned in doing good, and in being a benefactor [*euergetēs*], to his subjects; and this cannot be done without justice and law. The third function, that of the cult of the gods, is one that befits a king; for the Best must be honoured by the best, and the Leader by one who leads. Now of things that are most honourable in nature at large, God is the best; of things that are most honourable on earth, and among men, the king is the best; as God is to the universe, so is the king to the State (*polis*), and as the State is to the universe, so is the king to God. For the State, which is a body joined together in harmony from many different parts, imitates the system and harmony of the universe; and the king, who exercises an authority which is not responsible

---

[1] The idea of a *systēma* was based upon and borrowed from musical theory. It was used to mean an organized unit, of different and even opposed elements, which were none the less united together in a concordance, or, as it was technically called, a *synarmogā*. The idea was applied to a variety of units—the *cosmos*, the *polis*, the family. A definition of a *systēma*, quoted by Delatte, op. cit., p. 209, is that 'it is "compounded" out of opposite and different elements; that it is "composed", or brought into concord, under some one element which is the best; and that it makes for the common benefit of all the elements'.

[to any earthly superior], and who is in himself Animate Law, thus becomes the figure of a God among men.'[1]

2. Stobaeus, ibid., § 62. The previous extract has been concerned with the office of the king; this is concerned with his *personal character*. The author lays it down generally that the good king must have the three qualities of (1) self-control in the matter of pleasures, (2) readiness to share his possessions, and (3) moral wisdom and a general pre-eminence in moral endowment. He then proceeds, in greater detail, to sketch particular attributes of the good king's personal character. It is not clear that he had any particular king in mind; he *may* have been thinking, if his date is in the third century A.D., of a Roman emperor such as Aurelian; but his sketch is essentially academic in its nature. 'The king should tune a well-ordered State into harmony (*synarmogā*) as a musician does his lyre; he should, first and foremost, lay down for himself the most just of standards and a fixed rule of law, in the knowledge that the harmony among the peoples over whom God has given him leadership should also be brought into harmony with himself. In addition to the qualities mentioned, a good king should cultivate proper attitudes and dispositions, and shape himself into a statesmanlike and businesslike figure, so that he will not appear to his people as either harsh or contemptible, but rather as at once attractive and on the alert.' To this end, Diotogenes proceeds to say, he must cultivate the three attributes of (1) a solemn majesty, (2) a gracious behaviour, and (3) a capacity to inspire awe by his severity in punishing wrong and by his rapidity in action.[2] The first and second of these attributes are then examined in some detail. So far as concerns the first, which is 'solemn majesty', the argument runs as follows: 'He must remove himself from the passions

---

[1] The 'God among men' is an old Greek phrase which is used by Aristotle in the *Politics* (III. xiii, § 13) and is even earlier than Aristotle. He uses it of the man so superior in character and political ability that he must needs be an absolute king, since he is 'a law in himself' (or 'animate law').

[2] Diotogenes abounds in 'triads'. The king has three functions: he must show three qualities: in showing the second of these three qualities (graciousness) he must cultivate the three attributes of justice, equity, and mercy. This academic system of 'triads' suggests that he had no actual example of a real person before him, but was spinning an ideal out of his inner consciousness—and perhaps also from a memory of Aristotle's suggestions for the preservation of absolute monarchies in the *Politics* (v, c. xi, §§ 18–34).

of men and seek to come near the gods, not in a temper of arrogance but in a spirit of magnanimity and an insurpassable greatness of excellence. He must so indue himself with propriety and pre-eminence in all ways—in his appearance; his reflections, his arguments, and the character of his soul; the actions, the movements, and the attributes of his body—that all who look upon him are amazed by his modesty, his temperance, and his disposition towards propriety of demeanour, and are thus brought into due order. For merely to look upon a good king ought to affect the souls of those who watch him no less than a flute or harmony could do.[1]

'So far of the quality of majesty; I will now attempt to speak of the quality of graciousness (chrēstotēs). Every king will be gracious if he is, in general, just, equitable, and merciful. Justice is the bringing and stringing together of a community; and it is only such a state of the soul [as justice gives] that keeps men in harmony with their neighbours; for justice has the same relation to community as rhythm has to movement, or harmony to sound;[2] it is a good which is common to rulers and ruled, if it be, as it is, the factor that makes a political community harmonious. And equity and mercy are, so to say, the coadjutors of justice . . . .'

After this account of the royal qualities of majesty and graciousness, and of the attributes, especially justice, which go with graciousness, Diotogenes concludes his argument by urging that the conclusion of the whole matter is that kingship is an 'imitation' of divinity, just as ordinary men, in their turn, are imitators of kingship. 'Qualities such as these belong to the gods, and above all to Zeus the ruler of all. He too has majesty, and is honoured for his excellence and the greatness of his goodness; he too is gracious, because he is a benefactor and a giver of good things, even as it is said of him by the Ionic poet that he is "the Father

[1] The contention of Diotogenes about imitation (already advanced by Pliny and Dio of Prusa; see above, p. 253 and p. 305) is carried farther, and made clearer, by the Pseudo-Ecphantus, who argues that kingship supplies something higher than compulsion (anankē), and better even than the persuasion which produces obedience (peithō); he supplies an example which stimulates men to imitation in a spirit of spontaneous loyalty (§ 65).

[2] The use of the argument from music is a Pythagorean—or neo-Pythagorean—touch.

of gods and men"; he too is an inspirer of awe, because he punishes wrongdoers and rules and controls all things; and he has a thunderbolt in his hand as a symbol of awe. Now for all these reasons we ought to remember that kingship is a thing which imitates divinity.'

B. *From the Treatise on Kingship by Ecphantus the Pythagorean*

1. Stobaeus, IV. vii, § 64. *The Universe and its Ruler: the king as a reflection of the Ruler of the Universe and a light to his people.* 'That the nature of all living beings is attuned in harmony with the universe and all that is in it seems to me to be proved by many sorts of evidence. Being in sympathy with the universe, and having a connexion with it which is at once inevitable and ideal, the nature of living beings follows the sweep of the whole, and is carried round in it to participation in the general system of good order, as well as into the particular station appropriate to each unit.[1] This is the reason why the universe as a whole is called the Cosmos [a word which in Greek means 'order' as well as 'universe'], and why it is the most perfect of living beings.[2]

'In the parts of the universe, which are many and different in their nature, some one living being has rule over others in virtue of its innate capacity and its greater share in divinity.' The sentences which follow appear to distinguish three parts of the universe— the heavenly, the lunar, and the terrestrial—each with a different ruling element. 'In the terrestrial part, where we are ourselves concerned, man is the best endowed by nature, but among men the king is the most divine, having more of the better elements in our common nature; for while in body he is like the rest of us, being made of the same substance, he has none the less been created by the best of Artificers, who shaped him with Himself as the model.

'The king is therefore a being who is sole and unique, as being the reflection of the Higher King; he is always known to his

---

[1] The idea is similar to that of Dio of Prusa; see above, p. 305.
[2] The universe, on this view, not only contains all living beings: it is also itself a living being (*zōon*). Dio of Prusa had already expounded this view as being a part of Stoic doctrine; see above, p. 300.

Creator [as he is in himself]; but by his subjects he is seen in his office of king, as it were in a blaze of light. For by his office he is judged and tested, being thereby as an eagle—the mightiest creature among all birds—when it faces the sun. The like holds good of the office of kingship [i.e. *it* is as the sun]; it is divine, and difficult to behold owing to excess of light, except for those who are of the true breed. False claimants to kingship, who are of bastard stock, are convicted and condemned, like men who have ascended to a height beyond their real powers, by the many flashes of light about them and the dizziness that comes upon them; but such as have come properly to kingship, by reason of their fitness for it, find it a safe habitation, because they are able to make good use of their office.[1]

'So kingship in itself is a pure and incorruptible thing, and hard for men to attain through the exceeding greatness of its divinity. The man who is established in it must be most pure and transparent in nature, so that he may not darken the greatness of its light by any spots and stains in his nature, as some have defiled even the most holy places, or, again, as some evil persons, when they encounter others, defile those who encounter them. The man who would be associated with kingship must partake in its undefiled nature; he must understand how much more divine than other men he himself is—and also how much more divine than he are those others [i.e. the gods] whom he must make himself reasonably like if he would do the best by himself and his subjects. . . .

'The prevalence of good order [in the universe], and the fact that nothing can be found in it which is not under rule and government, instructs a king in the way that his government should be conducted. Beauty at once shines out of his government; and the king who has copied beauty[2] by virtue of his excellence is beloved both by Him whom he has copied and, even more, by his own subjects. For no one beloved by God would

---

[1] This is the passage which suggests the reign of Aurelian, with its Sun-worship and its doctrine of the emperor as vicegerent of the Sun. The 'radiate' crown used in his reign, which combines the 'diadem' or fillet with the nimbus, suggests the descent of the sun's rays on the wearer.

[2] There is something reminiscent of Plotinus in this phrase; see above, pp. 336-7.

be hated by men—any more than the stars and the whole universe hate God; for if *they* had hated their Leader, they would not have followed Him in obedience—as now they do because the goodness of His government is the cause of their being well governed. So I hold that the earthly king too cannot fall short of the Heavenly in any of the virtues; but since he is, as it were, a being from another country, and a stranger who has come to men from it, one may hold that his virtues are the work of God Himself, and belong to him by the grace of God.

'If one seeks to pursue truth to its foundation the argument runs as follows. The primary and most necessary community for the human race is that in which the king set over us is one partner, and the other is He who orders all things in the whole of the universe. This community cannot cohere without friendship and a common mind. Again [on a lower level], one might study what happens in the range of *political* associations, leaving out of the argument the [primary and most necessary] community based on *social* habit and instinct.[1] Political association falls short of the nature of God and the king; for God and the king have not the mutual need which leads the members of such an association to render common aid to one another by supplying one another's defects. God and the king are perfect in virtue; but friendship as it exists in a State, clinging, as it does, to *some* sort of common purpose, is just an imitation of the concord [*homonoia*] of the universe. No State could ever survive without an ordered system of offices, and for such a system there is needed—both by the ruling element and the ruled—a body of laws and some sort of political authority. The common good thereby sought will best be preserved by a certain harmony and a concord of the masses, with obedience joining itself in unison therewith. But he who rules by reason of his excellence is called, and is, a king; for he has such friendship, and such communion, with those who are subject

---

[1] This study of the lower range of political association leads to the same conclusion: just as the 'primary' community needs, for its coherence, 'friendship and a common mind', so the community consisting in political association needs, for its preservation, 'a certain harmony and concord of the masses, with obedience'. But the friendship and common mind of the one are higher than the 'concord of the masses, with obedience', which is the mark of the other.

to him, as God has with the world and all that is in it. The perfection of goodwill must be shown [under such a system], first by the king to his subjects, and next by his subjects to the king—goodwill such as a father shows to his son, or a shepherd to his flock, or the law to those who follow its precepts.'

2. Ibid. § 65. *The quality and property of kingship: its influence on the obligation of subjects, which it turns into a spontaneous loyalty, transcending compulsion and mere obedience.* 'The king will show the same sort of virtue in ruling over others as he shows in his private life. He will not acquire any property as being in need of it, or as for his own personal service; he will rather acquire it as a man who naturally co-operates with others. For though there is a community [and all belong to it], each member of a State will none the less live a life of self-sufficiency so far as he is personally concerned. The man who is self-sufficient appears to be a man who would not need the help of others, at any rate in following his own way of life; but if a man is to live a life of *full* activity, it is plain that he may acquire other things [besides what he needs for his own way of life] without ceasing in any way to remain self-sufficient. For instance, he will have friends in consequence of his virtue; and when he uses them will not be doing so in virtue of any other quality than what he shows in dealing with his own private life. It is inevitable that such other things [e.g. friends] should follow the same line [i.e. should require the same quality for their acquisition and use as his own private resources require], there being no other separate quality at hand for dealing with them.

'God—who has neither ministers nor servants; who issues no commands; who does not crown or publicly honour the obedient, or inflict dishonour on the disobedient—God rules of, and by, Himself, to all the great height of His authority; but He does so, I take it, simply by making Himself worthy of imitation, and then implanting in all men a longing to attain His own nature. He is of Himself, and in Himself, good; to be good is His only and readily discharged function; and those who imitate Him do all things thereby better than others. In each of us, too, the act of becoming like Him (*homoiōsis*) is an act proceeding from our own self-sufficiency; for there is not one virtue that does the things that are pleasing to God, and another that imitates Him. Is it not so with our earthly king, and is he not also, and as much, self-sufficient? For if he made himself like any one being he would make himself like the Greatest, and every man who seeks to make himself like the Greatest will be God-like.

'But the acts of force and compulsion, which subjects undergo, sometimes do away with the desire of imitation which each of them will feel. It is impossible to become like [a king] without feeling goodwill towards him, and nothing puts an end to goodwill so quickly as fear. Would that it had been possible to banish from human nature even the need of obedience.[1] For that is a relic of our earthly shortcoming, in consequence of which the living being, perishable as he is, is not exempt from the need of obedience. For obedience is a duty which is a near neighbour of compulsion; and the acts that have escaped the net of compulsion are produced in the first instance [i.e. before the stage of spontaneous loyalty is reached] by dint of obedience. But all who spontaneously follow the beauty of the Good have no awe of the duty of obedience, as they have also no fear of the stress of compulsion. Only the king can bring about this blessing [of spontaneous loyalty] in men's nature, and make them able—through imitation of himself, their superior—to follow in the path of duty. His guiding Reason (*logos*), once it is received, strengthens those who have been degraded as if by intoxication, and have fallen into forgetfulness in consequence of being ill-nurtured; it heals them in their sickness; it expels the forgetfulness which has lodged itself in their minds in consequence of their evil-doing, and plants memory in its place—a memory from which is born the thing that is called obedience. And this obedience, taking its beginning from poor and weak seeds, grows up into something fine and strong from its root [i.e. spontaneous loyalty] in that earthly ground on which the guiding Reason does the work entailed upon it by the weakness of our nature—the work of consorting with men, and of

[1] It is interesting to note that the writer can long for the 'withering away of the State', and dream (as Lenin did) of a state of pure society, with men 'observing the elementary conditions of social existence without force and without subjection'.

making good the defects of such as lag behind in consequence of their evil-doing.

3. Ibid. § 66. *The wisdom of the king and its fruits—justice (with equality and fellowship) and temperance.* 'If he has such a sacred and divine intelligence, a man will be truly a king. Being obedient to that intelligence, he will be the cause of all that is good, and of nothing whatever that is evil. But [over and above that] it is evident to all that he will be *just*, and that because he has a spirit of fellowship. For fellowship comes through equality; and while justice takes the lead in the distribution of equality, fellowship has also a share in it. It is impossible to be unjust when you are distributing equal rights, or to distribute equal rights without having a spirit of fellowship.

'Again it is impossible to conceive that a man who is self-sufficient [as a king is] will not be *temperate* and master of himself. Extravagance is the nursing-mother of intemperance, as that is, in turn, of arrogance (*hubris*), which is the source of most of men's woes. Self-sufficiency cannot fall into extravagance or any of its fruits; on the contrary, being a governing principle, it will always be a leader itself and never be led by anything. This is the nature of God, as it is also that of the king; either of them is master of himself and self-ruling (this is how self-sufficiency gets its name),[1] and neither of them is mastered or ruled by anything.

'Now it is clear that this could not be the case in the absence of *wisdom* (*phronēsis*), and it is also manifest that God is the Wisdom of the universe; for the universe (*cosmos*) is bound together by virtue of a right order (*eucosmia*) and a proper discipline, and these could not exist in the absence of intelligence (*nous*). So is it, too, with a king; he cannot have, in the absence of wisdom, the virtues that have been mentioned—justice, temperance, the spirit of fellowship, and whatever else is akin to these.'

---

[1] This is a false etymology. The Greek word for self-sufficiency (*autarkeia*) has the same sort of sound as the Greek word for self-rule (*autarchia*)—though the two words are spelt differently and come from different roots—; and the writer accordingly seeks to argue that the one is derived from the other. (It is curious to reflect that a similar error is often made by modern journalists, who use the Greek word for self-sufficiency, which should be 'autarky', and misspell it as 'autarchy'.)

Note on the General Theory of the two Treatises

The views of Diotogenes and 'Ecphantus' are neither of them expressed in such lucid Greek that it is easy to state them clearly, or to distinguish them readily from one another. Briefly, it may be said that Diotogenes is the more pedestrian, and 'Ecphantus' the more mystical and suggestive. Diotogenes dwells on the function of the king rather than on his nature; he thinks that he is god-like in what he does, rather than in what he is; and he regards him as copying God in his action, rather than as being in himself a god or akin to God. In a word his king is human rather than divine, but a human copy of the divine. 'Ecphantus' goes farther. To him the king is unique; 'a being, as it were, from another country, and a stranger who has come to men from it' ..., 'created by the best of Artificers, who shaped him with Himself as model'. His is the unique office and privilege of direct contemplation and imitation of God, from whom he receives illumination; his subjects, who see God as it were at second-hand, in and through him, have the duty of seeking and gaining salvation by contemplating and imitating him, even as he contemplates and imitates God. 'Ecphantus' thus goes beyond Diotogenes in regarding the king as rather divine than human, and as god-like in his nature as well as in his function. In a word, he is the mystic of monarchy: he shows, as Delatte says, 'how Caesarism waged its struggle against doctrines of religious salvation by borrowing the armoury of theosophy' and then offering, in lieu of those doctrines, its own system of political salvation. The curious thing is that Eusebius, in the beginning of the fourth century, seems to have borrowed the mysticism of 'Ecphantus', and, applying it to Constantine, to have made it part of Christian doctrine. It thus became, in and through his writings, a part of the general social theory of the Church of the fourth century (see below, p. 478).

§ XII. AN ENCOMIUM ON KINGSHIP FROM THE 'CORPUS HERMETICUM' (? circa A.D. 300)

The *Corpus Hermeticum* is a body of writings, in Greek, which profess to record the religious or philosophic teachings of Hermes

Trismegistus—a pseudonym used to 'grace the measure' of a number of would-be philosophers with an itch for writing esoteric treatises, some time about the third century A.D., and probably somewhere in Egypt. (It has been edited, along with some cognate writings, under the general title of *Hermetica*, by W. Scott, Oxford, 1924, 1925.) There is no need to speak here of the nature and contents of this body of writings; for the passages here quoted, from book XVIII of the *Corpus*, have nothing whatever to do with the collection in which they have been somehow included. They are parts of an oration 'on kingship'—analogous to the *Panegyricus* of the younger Pliny or the four orations on the same theme by Dio of Prusa—which is entirely different in style and matter from the other seventeen books of the *Corpus*. The date of the oration may be about A.D. 300; the 'kings' celebrated in it (for the author uses the plural, and refers to more than one king) may be Diocletian and his colleagues; the place in which the oration was written, for delivery at a festival, may possibly be Alexandria (W. Scott, op. cit., vol. ii, pp. 461–4).

If the neo-Pythagorean documents cited by Stobaeus, and translated in the previous section, belong to the third century A.D., and if they may be referred to the reign of Aurelian (A.D. 270–5), this oration would be only a little later in date, and would thus connect itself with them in time. But there is also a further connexion beyond this possible connexion in time. The use of musical analogy, and the application of musical terms, which runs through the neo-Pythagorean documents (as indeed it was always a feature of Pythagorean ideas), recurs in this oration; and one is led to wonder whether its author belonged to the same school of thought as the writers cited by Stobaeus. But this is a matter of conjecture, or even of guess-work; and the passages of the oration (which, incidentally, is fragmentary and imperfect) may be left to speak for themselves. The translation of the crabbed and difficult text is that of the editor of *Hermetica*, W. Scott.

Book XVIII. 3. 'Let no man who is present at this festival find fault with my art by reason of my personal defects; but be it known that the spirit which God breathes into men of my sort is unfailing. For God, who is by nature a musician, and not only works harmony in the universe at large but also transmits to individuals the rhythm of his own music—God, I say, can never fail.

7*b*. 'The aim of my endeavour is the glory of kings; and it is the trophies which our kings [Diocletian and his colleagues] have won that make me eager to speak. Onward then! for so God wills; and the melody that the musician makes will sound the sweeter by reason of the greatness of his theme.

8. 'Since then his lyre is tuned to treat of kings, and is set to the right pitch for songs of praise, he first uplifts his voice to laud the supreme king of the universe, and comes down thereafter to those who hold their sovereignty after His likeness. For this our kings themselves would wish, that the song should come down step by step from heaven above, and that our praise of them should be derived in due succession from the Power that has conferred on them their victories.

9. 'Let the musician then address his song to that Most Mighty King, who is immortal and reigns from all eternity; that primal Victor, from whom all victories come to those who follow after. 15.[1] Thus let us praise God; but from Him we will pass down to those who have received the sceptre from His hand. For we must practise ourselves by praising earthly kings, and so habituate and train ourselves for adoration of the Deity.

10. 'My discourse comes down to the praise of those who rule on earth, and hastens on to these our kings, whose rule provides safety and peace for all; those to whom God has given the topmost height of sovereignty, and on whom victory has been conferred by God's right hand; for whom the prizes have been made ready even before they win them by their prowess in the wars; whose trophies are set up even before the armies meet in battle; who strike terror into the barbarians even before the troops march forth to fight. 16. For we must make requital to our kings, for that they have spread abroad among us the prosperity which comes of this great peace. The virtue of a king is shown in making peace; nay, the very name of *king* confers peace; for the king is so

---

[1] The numbering of the sections here (and elsewhere) is irregular, as the editor has transposed some sections of the text from their position in the manuscripts.

called for this cause, that *with smooth tread*[1] he plants his feet upon the topmost heights, and prevails by means of reason; so that this name is in itself a token of peace. Moreover, even the statues of the king serve as havens to men tossed by the fiercest storms; and it has come to pass ere now that the sight of a mere image of the king has given protection from all fears. . . .

14*b*. 'Among those, then, who dwell in the world above [the gods in heaven] there is no disagreement; all have one purpose; there is one mind, one feeling in them all; for the spell which binds them one to another is Love [Eros], the same in all, and by it all are wrought together into one harmonious whole (*harmonia tōn pantōn*).'

Here the Greek text ends, but, as Scott suggests, the implied conclusion is that 'in like manner there is concord among our kings'.

§ XIII. PASSAGES ON KINGSHIP IN SUIDAS

'Suidas' was not an author: the word is a fanciful name, meaning 'stronghold', for a Byzantine lexicon of the tenth century A.D. But late as it is, the lexicon contains definitions and quotations, some of which may go back as far as the second century of our era. It may therefore be worth while to quote what 'Suidas' has to say on kings and kingship.

1. Under the word *basileus* the entry in the lexicon is: 'A king is one who receives from his ancestors, by right of succession, an authority with fixed bounds;[2] a tyrant is one who usurps authority by force. But writers use either term indiscriminately.'

2. Under the word *basileia* the first entry is: 'Kingship is irresponsible authority.' To this the compiler adds a gloss which is apparently drawn from a Stoic source: 'It is said that not only the good, but also kings, enjoy liberty; for kingship is irresponsible

[1] This is an etymology which is also a pun. The writer takes the Greek word for kingship (*basileia*), splits it into two (so that it runs *basi leia*), and then translates the split word to mean 'with tread' (*basi* or *basei*) 'smooth-going' (*leia*).
[2] Thucydides, who is perhaps the basis of this definition, speaks of 'ancestral (or hereditary) kingships with fixed privileges' (i. 13. 1). The lexicographer substitutes 'bounds' (*perasi*) for Thucydides' 'privileges' (*gerasi*).

authority, which can exist only for the good', i.e. for the wise, and therefore good, man of Stoic theory. A further gloss is then added by the compiler, which is drawn from the *Lexicon Ambrosianum*, a work which goes back ultimately to an epitome, or 'concise dictionary', put together by a certain Diogenianus in the reign of Hadrian. This further gloss is: 'Neither nature nor justice gives kingship to men; but [it belongs] to those who have the capacity to command an army or to handle affairs wisely. Such were Philip and the successors of Alexander. For his son was not helped in any way by heredity, owing to the incapacity of his mind.[1] And [it is said] that those who were in no way related [? to Alexander] became kings of all the earth.'

3. Under the same word *basileia* there is another and separate entry. It appears to be a quotation, but there is no indication of its source. '[It is stated] that kingship is a thing belonging to the common stock [i.e. the community], but the property of the public is not a thing belonging to kingship. Accordingly one ought to hate exactions which come from compulsion, and are accompanied by arrogance (*hubris*), as being acts of tyrannical licence; but one ought to honour requests for contributions which are made with good reason and in a spirit of human kindness (*philanthrōpia*), as being a matter of care and solicitude [for the public weal].'

§ XIV. TWO LAST GREEK VOICES[2]

A. *The Speech of Themistius to the Emperor Jovian* (A.D. 364)
on Kingship and Toleration

The Emperor Jovian, on succeeding to Julian 'the Apostate', had issued an edict of toleration for all forms of religion. Pagan thinkers feared that the edict might be disregarded by the Christians, and

[1] This entry seems to be based on a mistake. The posthumous son of Alexander, also called Alexander, plays no part in history and soon disappears. It was the illegitimate half-brother of Alexander, Philip III, who was made his nominal successor, but failed (and was eventually murdered) owing to his mental deficiency.

[2] In strict chronology both Themistius and Synesius are beyond the scope of this volume, which ends with the reign of the Emperor Constantine. But these last voices of the Greek tradition are so much in harmony with its previous tenor, and so notable in themselves, that their inclusion may be forgiven.

that the emperor might be induced by them to prohibit other forms of belief. (St. Augustine himself, at a later date, could use the text *Compelle intrare*—'compel them to come in, that my house may be filled'—in a way that suggested the compulsory imposition. of the Christian faith.) Themistius, an Aristotelian scholar as well as an orator and a dignitary of the Empire, appealed to the emperor for freedom of thought and its expression, and for the diversity of opinion which is the fruit of that freedom, in an oration which has something of the spirit of J. S. Mill's *Essay on Liberty*. But he begins his oration with a profession of belief in kingship which recalls the flights of Pseudo-Ecphantus (see above, p. 367) and of Eusebius of Caesarea (see below, p. 478).

1. *On Kingship*

Oratio V *ad Iovianum*, 64 B–C. From the text of W. Dindorf. 'Would you know the contribution which philosophy makes [to the idea of kingship]? It tells us that the King is Animate Law; a divine law coming from above in the course of time . . .; an efflux of that [i.e. the divine] nature; a providence nearer to this earth; one who looks at all points to Him, one who is at all points and in all ways directed to imitation [of Him], one who, as Homer says, is wholly "born of God" and "bred by God", and who shares with God in the other appellations given to Him—kind to strangers, protector of suppliants, friendly, ripener of harvests, giver of good things, leader in justice, steward of leisure, prince of felicity. These are the offerings made to kings by philosophers who are truly so called. But the fallacious and the brazen, who raise pretensions to our mistress philosophy when she is left desolate—these were never held by Plato to be the authors of human felicity.'

2. *On Tolerance*

Ibid. 67 B–D. 'You, and you only, as it appears, are aware that a king is not able to apply compulsion to his subjects in all things. There are some things which have escaped the yoke of necessity— things which are stronger than threats or commands; and among them are all the virtues, and especially the virtue of reverence for the Divine. *You* have recognized in your wisdom that a man in whom the movement of the mind is to be really and truly unforced, self-governing, and voluntary must be a leader in these good things. If it is not possible even for you, Sire, to bring it about that a man should be kind by rule and prescription without choosing internally to be so, how much more is it impossible to make a man reverent and dear to heaven by inspiring him with fear of transitory necessities and poor weak bugbears, which time has often brought in its course and as often carried away? We stand most foolishly convicted if we do honour to the purple instead of to God, and change our worship as easily and as often as the tide veers in the Euboean channel. . . . 68*a*. Not such are you, most godlike of kings. You, "autocrat" and self-governor in all things, as you are and will be to the end, assign by law to all men their share in the rights of worship; and in this, too, you emulate God, who has made it a common attribute of the nature of men that they should be duly disposed to piety, but has made the mode of their worship depend on the will of each. To apply the compulsion of necessity is to deprive man of a power which has been granted to him by God. This is the reason why the laws of Cheops and Cambyses hardly lasted as long as their makers, but the law of God and *your* law remains unchanged for ever— that the mind of each and every man should be free to follow the way of worship which it thinks [to be best]. This is a law against which no confiscation, no crucifixion, no death at the stake has ever yet availed; you may hale and kill the body, if so be that this comes to pass; but the mind will escape you, taking with it freedom of thought and the right of the law as it goes, even if it is subjected to force in the language used by the tongue.'

3. *On Diversity of Belief*

Ibid. 69C–70A. 'Nor is your army, Sire, all ordered on one and the same scheme. Some are infantry and some cavalry; some bear arms, and some carry slings; some have their station by your person, some near it, others far away from it; some are content if they are known to the bodyguard, and some cannot get so far. But all depend, none the less, on you and on your judgement; and this is true not only of the men in the army but also of all other men—all who serve you otherwise than in war—farmers, orators, administrators, philosophers, and all the rest. Bethink you, Sire, that the Author of the universe rejoices in this diversity. It is His will that Syria should have one sort of polity, Greece another, and Egypt another; nay, Syria itself is not all alike, but divided into small parts. No man conceives things in exactly the same way as his neighbour; one has this opinion, and another that. Why, then, attempt to force men to the impossible?'

Note. This argument of Themistius recalls that which Celsus had already advanced in the second century (see below, pp. 431, 433). But it goes beyond Celsus in its sweep and range.

B. *Synesius on Kingship and the Duty of National Service:*
An address to the Emperor Arcadius (circa A.D. *400)*

Synesius (*circa* 373–414) was the son of a family in Cyrene which claimed to be descended from the kings of Sparta. He studied the philosophy of Neoplatonism under Hypatia at Alexandria, and then served on an embassy sent by the cities of his province to Arcadius in Constantinople, delivering an address 'on kingship' to the emperor during his stay in the city. Returning to Cyrene, he spent the next ten years (*circa* 400–10) partly in civic affairs, but mainly in his library and in hunting, to both of which he was devoted. Towards the end of his life he was called by popular acclamation to be bishop of Ptolemais, a town on the sea-coast of the province of Cyrenaica. As a bishop he mixed philosophy with a liberal or modernist form of theology; he also acted vigorously as a sort of *defensor civitatis* (an office which bishops often held), raising a military force to repel nomadic attacks. He is one of the most stirring and lively figures of his generation— orator, sportsman, philosopher, soldier, hymnodist, and a great letter-writer. The forty years of his life were crowded with activity; and his youthful oration on kingship, while it contains some commonplaces on a subject which had become trite by continual repetition, is also fresh and original in a characteristic plea for the institution of a system of national service.

1. *Kingship and Tyranny*

From the text of J. G. Krabinger, 6 C–D. 'Tyranny is a neighbour, and a very near neighbour, of kingship, just as foolhardiness is a neighbour of courage and licence of liberty. Unless he is kept by philosophy within the bounds of virtue, the high-minded man will stoop and become a braggart; and instead of being high-minded he will be feeble in judgement. I would bid you therefore fear tyranny, as being nothing other than a disease of kingship; and I would have you distinguish it from kingship by the characteristics I have set before you in my discourse, and by this especially—the greatest of them all—that law is the way for a king to follow and his own way is the law for a tyrant. But authority is a sort of substance which is common to both, although their ways of using it are opposed to one another.'

Synesius, writing seven hundred years after Aristotle, here follows the lines of Aristotelian thought, as he also does in the beginning of the following passage.

2. *The King a copy of God*

Ibid. 8 A–C. Starting from Aristotle's conception of external goods as 'instruments' (*organa*), which are a necessary equipment or *chorēgia* for a life of goodness, but only to be used as means to the attainment of such a life and not as ends in themselves, Synesius begs Arcadius to be true to the teaching of his master. 'Use in this way the goods which lie ready to your hand, I beg you; it is only in this way that you can use them well. Let families, cities, peoples, nations, and continents enjoy the blessings of the wise care and royal providence which God, who has set Himself as the pattern to be followed by you in the realm of intelligible things [*noēta*, a Neoplatonic term], has given to you as an image of His providence, wishing things here below to be ordered in imitation of the world above. Dear to the Great King in heaven is he who is named after Him here, if he does not belie his name; and he does not belie it if only some one or other of the titles by which God is called can be applied to him.'

3. *The Duties of a King*

(*a*) *Self-mastery* (ibid. 10 A–B). 'First and foremost, let piety be established as a sure pedestal on which the statue of kingship shall securely rise; and then no storm will ever overturn it from the pedestal on which it stands. . . . Taking my start from this truth, I say that the king, with God for his guide, should first and foremost be king of himself, and should establish a monarchy in his own soul. Be sure of this: man is not a simple entity, made after a single pattern; God has settled together, in the constitution of one being, a multiple and multilingual crowd of different forces. We are, I believe, a far stranger and far more many-headed beast than the hydra. It is not with the same part of our being that we think, desire, and feel pain or feel indignation; nor do our fears flow from the same source as our pleasures. No; you can see that there is both a male and a female element present in these affections; there is courage as well as cowardice; there is the presence of things opposed to one another in all sorts of ways. But there is also present a mean or middle nature which pervades them all; and this we call Mind (*Nous*). This is what I would have enthroned as sovereign in the soul of a king, when once it has overcome the mob-rule and democracy of the passions.'

(b) *The duty of a King to bind friends to himself* (ibid. 11 D–12 A). 'The friendship of tyrants is treacherous; but the true king knows that while in God there is the quality of being sufficient to Himself, and while He is a Being of endless age, transcending all who are under His government, the nature of a man who governs many men of the same substance as himself is not in itself sufficient for the comprehension of every duty. To remedy, therefore, the defects of his nature he holds communion with friends, thus multiplying for himself the force he possesses. So he will see with the eyes of them all; hear with the ears of them all; and come to conclusions aided by the judgements of them all as they move together towards one result.' (Cf. Dio of Prusa, *supra*, p. 304.)

(c) *The King's duty to his army* (ibid. 13 B–14 B). 'Our argument proceeds in its course to bring the king out of his palace; and, next after his friends, it gives him to his soldiers, who are his second friends. . . . He will profit by close intercourse with his army, not only in having it about his person as a single body congruous with him in its nature, but also for another reason. Much of what is done on such occasions [i.e. occasions in which the army is involved] is either an exercise in military duties [tactics], or in the nature of preludes and preparations for military operations [strategy], and this serves as a stimulus to greater and serious duties.'

(*d*) *The King and his court: his duty of appearing in public* (ibid. 15 C). From his suggestion of the duty owed by the king to the army, Synesius naturally turns to a criticism of the policy of secluding the *basileus* in a 'Byzantine' secrecy. 'I contend that nothing in the past has had a worse influence on Roman affairs than the pomp and ceremony surrounding the person of the King, a ceremony conducted for you in a secrecy of seclusion by your attendants, as if they were celebrating a ritual, with all the "barbarian" [i.e. Persian] apparatus used in your court. Appearance and reality do not usually go together. Do not be angry with me for saying this; it is not your fault; it is the fault of those who started this mischief and transmitted to the present an evil which is accentuated by the passage of time. The result is that this majesty—this fear of your being brought down to the level of ordinary men by becoming a common sight—makes you a recluse; you are besieged, as it were, by your own self; you see very little, and hear very little, of the experiences that produce a stock of practical wisdom; your only delight is in the pleasures of the body, and in the most material of those pleasures, such as come from touch and taste; you live, in a word, the life of an anemone in the sea.'

Ibid. 16 D. Synesius presses his argument home by a personal appeal to Arcadius. 'Do you fare any better since this mystery surrounding kings was instituted, and now that you are kept in your chamber like a lizard that hardly ever puts out its head into the sunlight—all in order that you should not be detected by men as being but a man yourself? Or did you fare better in the days of old, when kings lived like men in the centre of the armies they commanded; when they were sunburnt, and lived generally a plain and simple life, with none of the pomp attending a concert of music or the performance of a tragedy?'

(*e*) *The duty of the King to encourage national military service* (ibid.

22 C–23 A). From criticism of the seclusion of the emperor in his palace, and following on his plea for the king's duty to his army, Synesius advances to an argument for national service in lieu of the use of 'Scythian' mercenaries. 'To fail to prepare a force which can counterbalance these mercenaries, and to act instead as though their ranks were native-born, by giving exemption from military service to the many who ask for it, and by letting off the inhabitants of the country-side to attend to other pursuits—what is this but the act of men who are rushing to their doom? Instead of tolerating the coming of Scythians into the Empire to bear arms, we ought to ask for men to come from the agriculture they love to fight on its behalf; we ought to enlist a force so all-embracing that it includes philosophers from their studies,[1] craftsmen from the meaner occupations, and salesmen from their shops; we ought to persuade the population of drones, which lives in the theatres for want of anything whatever to do, to bestir itself, for once, before it has to turn from laughter to tears—and we ought to do this for the simple reason that there is no motive of shame, whether of the better or the worse sort, that stands in the way of making the Roman army native and national. The proper system in the State is the same as that in the family: it is the part of the male to bear arms, as it is that of the female to pay attention to domestic matters. How, then, is it possible to endure that the male element in our country should be a foreign element? How can it be other than a disgrace that the most populous of States should relinquish to others any ambition to win honour in war?'

4. *An appeal for true Kingship*

Ibid. 28 D–29 B. 'Somebody has said that it is a disgrace that there should be public contests in throwing the javelin and boxing, and crowns awarded to those who win, while there are no awards for those who show temperance and practise virtue. I think it is likely, and more than likely—indeed altogether inevitable—that if States followed their kings in a policy such as this [i.e. in giving

---

[1] Synesius, himself a philosopher (and in his later life also a bishop), acted up to his own teaching when he organized a military force to repel the attacks of nomads on the people of his diocese in the Libyan Pentapolis.

awards for temperance and virtue], they would live the life of the days of old, the life of the Golden Age, the life men celebrate in odes; they would have no time for evil, and they would have leisure for all good things, and especially for true religion; to which true religion the king will himself be their guide, seeking from the hands of God the inspiration of all achievements whether small or great. For here, I deem, is something more solemn to see and to hear than any other thing whatever—a king who stands in the midst of his people, lifting up his hands and bowing down his head to the King who is King both of himself and his people. And it is reasonable to believe that there will be joy in the heart of the Deity when He is glorified by the worship of a pious king, and that such a king will be made one with Him by ineffable bonds. So it comes to pass that, besides being beloved of God, he is above all else a lover of men, appearing to his subjects in the likeness of the King above. . . .

'We have made benevolence a mark of kingship; and, again, we have counted as royal titles names such as "the giver of good things", "the gracious", and other like names such as God also bears. Let us suppose that these attributes, and the rest that were mentioned along with them before I made my promise to paint the picture of a king in my discourse, are now assembled in all their forms, and the picture will then be completed. The chief of these attributes is, I take it, that a king, as being a doer of good works, will not grow weary of welldoing, any more than the sun grows weary of shedding his rays on plants and animals; for it is no trouble for the sun to shine, having brightness in his very being and serving as a fountain of light.'

Ibid. 31B. 'God has granted many gifts to the office of kingship which are enviable and happy gifts. None is greater than this— that men should, above all else, admire and celebrate in that office the influence which it carries over the minds of subjects, and the power which it gives to its holder to change their opinion of his character—though that opinion be ingrained in them by his early training and previous habits—as he can do by showing that he honours the opposite qualities [to those they suppose him to show] and holds them in the highest regard. For the thing, whatever it be, in which the king rejoices, must immediately have vogue and be imitated by the majority.'

Ibid. 31C–32A. 'This is my prayer for you. May you, Sire, set your heart on philosophy and true education. . . . According as philosophy is present or absent, human affairs are better or worse; utterly blessed or entirely miserable. It is for the blessings she brings, and not for philosophy herself, that I have made my prayer. May it be my lot to have granted to me the prayer which Plato offered but was not granted [the prayer that kings should become philosophers or philosophers kings]. May I live to see you adding philosophy to kingship—and then nobody shall ever hereafter hear me saying a word on the theme of kingship.'

APPENDIX

A BYZANTINE PARALLEL TO THE ADDRESS OF SYNESIUS

The Logos Nouthetētikos *of Niculitzas to the Emperor*
(*Alexius Comnenus?*)

Nearly seven centuries after Synesius delivered his address to Arcadius (*circa* A.D. 400), a Byzantine soldier and officer, who seems from internal evidence to have been called Niculitzas, addressed another emperor in Constantinople with a speech of 'admonition' and counsel on the nature and duties of kingship. He dealt with two matters which Synesius had already handled in his day—the matter of the use of foreign troops (but where Synesius had spoken of 'Scythians', or Goths, he speaks of 'Varangians' from Norway and from Norman England), and the matter of the emperor's duty not to hide in what Synesius had called a 'lizard-like' seclusion, but to show himself actively in the themes (or provinces) and the subject nations of his empire. The speech is notable not only as illustrating the *living* continuity of the classical tradition in Byzantium (the author can even speak of Augustus with a familiarity which suggests that the founder of the Empire was still in living memory, after more than a thousand years), but also, and almost conversely, as illustrating the *static* permanence of the Eastern Empire—so different from our contemporary age of change and vicissitude, which we call, or rather used to call (for we are now more dubious), by the name of 'progress'. There is something which today is attractive, as well as tragic, about the permanence of Byzantium—

> Hades' bobbin bound in mummy-cloth . . ..

The little treatise of Niculitzas is printed in the *Notes* of the Historico-Philological Faculty of the University of St. Petersburg for the year 1896 (pp. 93–104), under the title of *De Officiis Regis Libellus*. The Russian editors justly describe it in their preface (p. 4) as 'sermonem minime servilem, sed satis liberalem . . . neque dignitate quadam carentem'. Niculitzas had served, along with Harold Hardrada and his Varangians, in a campaign against a Bulgarian rising in the year 1040. The mention in his treatise of Varangians from England (*Angelē*) suggests that he was writing after the Norman Conquest, which resulted in the emigration of a number of Anglo-Saxon soldiers for service in the 'foreign legion' at Constantinople; and the editors conjecture that this mention may warrant the conclusion that the treatise was written about the year 1080, and was intended for Alexius Comnenus, who ascended the throne in 1081. The writer of the treatise may possibly have known the writings of Synesius, which were known and studied by Byzantine writers; indeed he is said to have been the favourite author of the scholar and statesman Theodore Metochita (*circa* 1300).

(*a*) *The King and the Law* (p. 93). 'Some say that the emperor (*basileus*) is not subject to law, but *is* law. I agree. But there is this qualification. When he acts and legislates [duly], he does well and we obey him. If, however, he should say, "Drink poison", you will in no case do so. And if he should say, "Go to the sea and cross it [like?] a diver", you cannot do this either. From this you may know that the *basileus*, since he is a man, is subject to the laws of piety. This is the reason why we write this treatise for pious and Christian kings hereafter.

'God has raised you, our revered lord, to the throne of kingship and made you by His grace, as you are called, a terrestrial god, to do and to act as you will; therefore let your acts and deeds be full of understanding and truth, and let justice be in your heart. Look therefore—and act—with eyes of equality upon all men, both upon those who are in authority and upon all others; do not evilly entreat some of your subjects, at your will, and confer benefits on others against all right reason. Let there be equality for all; let him who offends receive his deserts according to his offence; but if you feel sympathy for him and pardon his offence, that too is a god-like and kingly act. Grieve not those who offend not, but rather, if you will, do them good. He who offends not against you is better than he who offends; and if you confer benefits on the offender . . . [lacuna] . . . you will appear as one who has done good to the evil and evil to the good.'

(b) *The use of foreign troops* (p. 95). 'Foreigners who are not of royal descent in their own country I would not have you advance to great honours, nor would I have you entrust them with great offices; for if you do so you will do no good at all to yourself or to your officers who are of Roman [i.e. Byzantine] origin. When you honour a foreigner who has come to you from England with the dignity of colonel or general, how can it be an honour to make a Roman a general? You will make him wholly an enemy. That is not all; in the foreigner's own country, when men hear that he has come to such honour, they will laugh and say, "Here we hold the man for naught and lo, when he has gone away to Romania, he has gained great honour; it would seem that in Romania there is no man to be found who is fit for the position, and that is why our countryman has been exalted; if the Romans had been efficient, they would not have raised this man to such a height." Let not Your Majesty answer, "I conferred this benefit upon him in order that others might join my service when they saw what I had done." That is not a good policy. If you wish, you can have as many men as you would like me to bring to your banners, merely for food and clothing. It means much to the Romans, Sire, that you should not bestow great honours on foreigners; for if foreigners serve you merely in return for their uniform and rations, you may be assured that they will none the less serve you faithfully and whole-heartedly, looking to you only for the gift of a trifle of money and rations.'

(c) *The value of equality* (pp. 98–99). 'Let me tell you, Sire, how the beginning of the reign of Michael the Paphlagonian[1034–41] came about. That monarch of blessed memory had no famous ancestors; he came of a stock that was undistinguished and altogether humble; but he had great merits. Some ignorant persons report that he was noble and of good birth; but he was meanly born and of lowly origin. For myself I say that all men, kings and rulers and bread-winners alike, are the children of one man, Adam; and I have seen those who were puffed up in their own conceit turning to robbery and divination and the practice of magical arts. *Those* are the people I call ignoble. For man, who is a rational being, becomes, if he so will, a god by the grace of God. Such was that king of blessed memory, Michael IV. He was rich, as I have said, in great merits; but he had many kinsmen by blood who were poor men and for whom provision was made by public charity.'

(d) *The King as a model for imitation* (pp. 99–100). 'The king is a model and example for all men, and all look to him and imitate his ways. If his ways are good, they are eager to follow them speedily; if they are bad and blameworthy, men still do the same. I bid you, therefore, lay hold on the four virtues, and make them all yours: courage—by which I mean courage of the soul—justice, temperance, and wisdom (*phronēsis*). There is a wisdom that acts for good, and a wisdom that acts for evil; the same is true of courage; but you will never find temperance or justice active for evil. Lay hold, as I have said, on these four virtues, and you will be raised from earth to the heavens; your power will be great; the Lord will give you length of days; and justice and truth will abound on your countenance and in your heart.'

The writer then recalls how Augustus was aided and admonished first by Athenodorus, a philosopher from Alexandria, and then by Abgar the prince of Edessa.[1] He draws the following moral

---

[1] Edessa, one of the earliest homes of Christianity in the region of Syria, had a prince called Abgar who according to tradition corresponded with Jesus. This may be the basis of the idea that an Abgar of Edessa was the adviser of Augustus. It is a matter of historical record that Arius of Alexandria and Athenagoras of Tarsus were the instructors of Augustus in philosophy (Piganiol, *Histoire de Rome*, 4th edition, p. 230): and 'Athenodorus of Alexandria' would seem to be a combination or confusion of the two.

from the record. 'Take to yourself such a man, and give him leave to admonish you at all times for what you have said and done that is contrary to reason. Do not say, "I am wise and know all things": there are many things you know, but there are more of which you are ignorant. God alone has all truth: man, of whatever rank he may be, has deficiencies; as the angel said to St. Zosimas, "No man has perfection." '[1]

(e) *The duty of the King to show himself in all his dominions* (pp. 103–4). 'I know, Your Majesty, that the nature of man desires relaxation. But there has come into vogue a fashion which is not helpful, but rather the reverse: that the emperor should not go out into the countries which are in his obedience, on the east and on the west, but should spend his time in Constantinople as if he were imprisoned there. Now if some other person had fixed you in one city, you would in that case have had to make an effort and to go abroad. But as it is, you have inflicted this on yourself. What is one to say? I bid you go out into the countries which are in your obedience and among your provinces: see for yourself the injustices suffered by the poor, and the doings of the tax-gatherers whom you send out; see if the poor have been wronged, and set all things to rights. Then the provinces of your Roman subjects and the countries of the nations in your allegiance will have a king, and a real person who looks after their welfare; you will know the capacity of each province and fortress and country; you will know how each is situated, what injuries it suffers, and what benefits it receives; there will be no rebellion, nor any revolt against your tax-gatherers, but all your dominions will be in peace. I know that your ministers, in order to save you from trouble, will advise you that this is not a good policy and tell you that you will oppress your countries and provinces by making a progress through them with an army and a royal escort. They may also say that if you leave Byzantium, another man will make himself emperor in your place. I have thought of this and laughed at it. For the person left by you in the palace, and charged with

---

[1] Compare the idea of Musonius Rufus (and other Stoics) that the king, if not himself a philosopher like Marcus Aurelius, should have a philosophic adviser; *supra*, p. 310.

the direction of matters that come to your notice there from the nations and the Romans, will be wholly effective and adequate, and he will be likely to keep on the watch and to do what is proper to be done. May I also tell you another thing? The emperors and those who bore the title of Augustus among the Romans always followed the policy which I am now proposing to you. This was not only done by those who ruled in Rome: it was also done by those who ruled in Byzantium—the great Constantine and his son Constantius, and the emperors Julian, Jovian, and Theodosius. Sometimes they went east and sometimes west, but they spent little of their time in Byzantium. All countries [in the Empire] were then at peace: all Europe and Africa, and the finest part of Asia up to the Euphrates valley and Adiabene—Armenia and Syria, Phoenicia, Palestine, Egypt, and the great and celebrated Babylon itself—all these were subject to the Romans. . . .'

THE SOCIAL AND POLITICAL IDEAS OF THE CHRISTIAN CHURCH DOWN TO THE AGE OF CONSTANTINE

INTRODUCTION

In this last part an attempt has been made to collect some of the main passages in Christian literature concerned with social and political ideas, from the days of the beginnings of the Christian Church down to the age of Eusebius of Caesarea, the contemporary and adviser of the Emperor Constantine. The Christian literature which expresses these ideas is mainly written in Greek: the writings of Tertullian and Lactantius are almost the only exceptions. The basis and foundation of that literature is to be found in the first section, which gives an account of the principles of social and political life laid down, or suggested, in the Gospels and the Epistles of the New Testament. Here are collected the original and primary passages that illustrate the notion of law, the conception of society, the theory of government, and the ideas about property and the institution of slavery, which the Christian thought of the first century had already attained.

These are the basic foundations. Upon them, in the second century A.D., there was built, as a superstructure, the organization of regular churches, conceiving themselves as united in a single Church universal. It was an organization of which the human bond was the episcopate, and the bonding elements were the canon of the Scriptures, as it was gradually established, and the creed contained in the tradition developed and cherished in the memory of the churches from days of the Apostles onwards. This organization is expressed or implied in the *Teaching of the Apostles* (the *Didachē*) and in the *First Epistle to the Corinthians* assigned by tradition to Clement the Bishop of Rome (both of the early years of the second century); it is definitely described and defended in the *Epistles* of Ignatius, the Bishop of Antioch, written about A.D. 100, and in the *Adversus Haereses* (written about A.D. 180) of Irenaeus the Bishop of Lyons, a Greek whose life had carried him from Asia Minor to Gaul, and whose book has been called 'the first comprehensive work belonging purely to the literature of the Church itself'.[1] These writings of the second century were of profound importance in the history of the organization of the Christian churches; but they were not so much concerned with the general theory of Christian society, or with the principles on which that society should act, as they were with the particular problems of the internal structure of government to be followed in each local church, and of the establishment of a tradition to be carried in, and maintained by, all the churches alike.

The next story to be added to the building—and it was added at the end of the second and the beginning of the third century—was the philosophical theology of Alexandria. This was the achievement, or at any rate the endeavour, of the Christian scholars of the Church in Egypt, and especially of Clement of Alexandria and Origen, who sought to bring Christian theology into relation with Greek philosophy, and to establish a bridge of connexion between the ancient *ratio* of the Greek past and the 'new creation' of the Christian *fides*. To the passages, all too brief, which are here translated from their writings, there is also added, in the sixth section, some account of the pagan theory of society and religion—a theory of polytheism, and a defence of the different historical cults based on the soil and tradition of the different historical nations—as that theory was expounded, towards the end of the second century, by a Platonist called Celsus. Celsus is only a name (we know nothing of his life), and the polemic which he directed against the Christian Church survives only in the quotations made from it by Origen in the eight books of his *Contra Celsum*; but his work was a notable attempt to stem the advance of Christian universalism, with all its new world of ideas, and to pit against it the 'True Reason' (the *Alēthēs Logos*, as he called it) of the ancient thought and philosophy of Greece. In a

---

[1] Lietzmann, *The Founding of the Church Universal*, Eng. trans., p. 207.

word, he challenged in advance the possibility of any eirenicon such as Clement of Alexandria and his successor Origen were afterwards to attempt.

A further stage in the building of the tradition of Christian thought is marked by the Latin phase of Tertullian and Lactantius. They are separated from one another by a whole century (Tertullian wrote about A.D. 200 and Lactantius about 300); but they both had their roots in the province of Africa, with its vigour and passion of thought and its zest for its own new style of Latinity. Their writings mark the beginnings of Latin Christianity (before Tertullian, Christian literature is almost entirely Greek); and they have a Latin touch which is notable. In particular they show the Latin sense of order and of an engineered march of thought (a *via munita* built for the going of the mind, parallel to the roads which Rome had built for the going of her legions); they are instinct with the Latin feeling for the drill of a disciplined society (so vividly described by Tertullian), and they breathe the passion for justice and *humanitas* (notably in the *Divine Institutes* of Lactantius) which the Roman lawyers had cherished down to the days of the Antonines and even under the Severi. The Greek Christian writers of Alexandria, in the beginning of the third century, were more concerned with being than with doing; with problems of metaphysics and the high philosophic inheritance of the schools, rather than with problems of social order and the rich legal legacy of the courts. The Latin writers of the province of Africa, during the whole course of the third century (from Tertullian, through Cyprian of Carthage, down to Lactantius), are more concerned with the fact of the Roman Empire and the system of its law, the duty of Christians in the face of that fact and under that system, and the distinction to be drawn between the things of Caesar and the things of God. Yet the contrast is not absolute. Tertullian belongs to the Latin world of the West; but he can think highly about the conception of the Logos, and he can write finely on the relation between Christian belief and pagan philosophy. Clement of Alexandria and Origen both belong to the Greek world of the East; but Clement can handle the practical problem of the right use of wealth with a discretion and a gravity not unworthy of the practical genius of Rome, and Origen, in commenting on the Epistle to the Romans and its theory of government, can show a Roman power of judgement as well as a Greek gift of subtlety.

The end of the development of Christian thought on social and political questions, so far as this work is concerned, comes with the reception of Christianity as a *religio licita*; and the main issue which was henceforth debated—an issue destined to be raised by that reception—is the issue of the relation between the Christian Church and the State. The 'Edict of Milan' of A.D. 313 is a landmark in the history of religious toleration. Christianity had now finally gained recognition for itself; but the question would arise in the future (it is already raised by implication in the oration delivered by the philosopher Themistius as early as 364) whether Christianity would give to others, in its hour of recognition, what it had gained for itself, and would allow the old cults of the nations, which Celsus had defended against it, still to survive by its side. Meanwhile, in its hour of triumph, and in the state of its life and thought during the reign of Constantine, Christianity found an exponent in Eusebius of Caesarea. He ends the general 'statement of account' which is rendered in this last Part. Greater thinkers than he were to arise in later years, but in his day, and for his generation, he was the spokesman of the Christian Church (at any rate as it stood in the East—for he shows little knowledge of the West and little interest in its doings); and we may learn from him what the Church felt, and how it attempted to act, in the days when its protracted struggle for existence had at last ended in triumph. The Church of God now stood by the side of the empire of Caesar, not yet asking in so many words, but destined to ask, and to ask insistently, in the future, the momentous question, 'What are the things which belong to God, and what are the things which belong to Caesar?' Any solution of that question was still in the future when Eusebius wrote; he assumed a happy and spontaneous harmony of Caesar and the Church, with Caesar presiding in synods of the Church (not without a bishop—Eusebius himself—to advise him), and with no hint as yet of division. But the great saying of Jesus had still to be interpreted;[1] and that, as history has shown us, is a matter not for one age or for a single generation, but for long and slow time.

§ I. THE SOCIAL AND POLITICAL IDEAS OF THE NEW TESTAMENT

No introduction is needed to the passages which follow: a chapter of Dr. A. J. Carlyle's *History of Medieval Political Theory in the West* (vol. i, part iii, c. viii) is a sufficient commentary upon them, and also a mine of reference. Some of the passages are quoted in the Latin of the Vulgate as well as in English, on the ground, and for the reason, that the Latin of the Vulgate was the one text which affected Western thought for over a thousand years, from the time of St. Jerome down to the appearance of vernacular versions, English and German, in the course of the sixteenth century.

A. *The Nature of Law*

The law which occupied the thought of St. Paul was the law of Moses, the written law of the Jews—the *nomos*, in his own Greek; the *lex*, in the version of the Vulgate. But he was also an apostle to the Gentiles; and he felt his way towards the notion of a universal law which had no single legislator, such as Moses had been for the Jews, and was not written in any visible document, but was still, none the less, a law. The words in which he describes this law became the basis of a Christian conception of Natural Law which was expounded in later ages by St. Thomas Aquinas and is still expounded today by the Papacy in encyclicals.

From Romans ii, vv. 11–15 (in the Revised Version). 'There is no respect of persons with God. For as many as have sinned with-

---

[1] Ossius, the bishop of Cordova, was already confronting the Emperor Constantius with an interpretation that anticipates Gelasius I and the medieval Papacy, as early as A.D. 355. 'God has put into your hands the Kingdom; to us [the bishops] He has entrusted the affairs of His Church; and as he who would steal the empire from you would resist the ordinance of God, so likewise fear on your part lest, by taking upon yourself the government of the Church, you become a great offence.' Ossius then quotes the saying of Jesus, and concludes, 'Neither therefore is it permitted unto us to exercise an earthly rule, nor have you, Sire, any authority to burn incense.' (Quoted by S. L. Greenslade, in *Church and State from Constantine to Theodosius*, 1954, p. 45.)

out law [the Greeks or Gentiles] shall also perish without law: and as many as have sinned under law [the Jews] shall be judged by law; for not the hearers of a law are just before God, but the doers of a law shall be justified: for when Gentiles [*ethnē*, in the Greek, and *gentes* in the Latin] which have no law do *by nature* the things of the law, these, having no law, are a law unto themselves;[1] in that they show the work of the law written in their hearts, their conscience bearing witness therewith, and their thoughts [or, 'reasonings'] one with another accusing or else excusing them.'

This runs in the Vulgate: 'Non est . . . personarum acceptio apud Deum. Quicunque enim sine lege peccaverunt, sine lege et peribunt: et quicunque in lege peccaverunt, per legem iudicabuntur: non enim auditores legis iusti sunt apud Deum, sed factores legis iustificabuntur. Cum enim gentes quae legem non habent, *naturaliter* quae legis sunt faciunt, eiusmodi legem non habentes, ipsi sibi sunt lex: qui ostendunt opus legis scriptum in cordibus suis, testimonium reddente illis conscientia ipsorum, et inter se invicem cogitationum accusantium, aut etiam defendentium.'

On this basis the Church of Rome has built the theory of a natural law side by side with, or rather superior to (and therefore in some sense controlling), all enacted or positive law. This theory is expressed, for example, in Pope Pius XI's Encyclical *Mit brennender Sorge* of March 1937. 'We have in mind particularly the so-called natural law, that is written by the finger of the Creator Himself in the tables of the hearts of men (cf. Rom. ii. 15), and which can be read on these tables by sound reason not darkened by sin and passion. Every positive law, from whatever law-giver it may come, can be examined as to its moral implications, and consequently as to its moral authority to bind in conscience, in the light of the commandments of the natural law. The laws of man that are in direct contradiction with the natural law bear an

---

[1] Not, of course, in the sense in which these words are generally now used, of men doing what they like, but in the sense that men are, or make, a law for themselves which prescribes what is right and just, by virtue of the operation of their own sense of what is right and just.

initial defect, that no violent means, no outward display of power, can remedy.' (The translation is that of the Catholic Truth Society, London, and the passage quoted comes on p. 35 of that translation.)

B. *The Conception of Society*

It has already been seen that the apocalyptical chapters of the Book of Daniel, written about 160 B.C., set the religious congregation of Israel, or people of the saints, over against the kingdoms of the world, and anticipate the coming of a time when the congregation shall be given 'the kingdom and the dominion and the greatness of the kingdoms under the whole heaven'. The conception of a 'kingdom of God' or 'kingdom of heaven' recurs in the Gospels. The content of the conception varies in different passages of the Gospels; now it is something spiritual and inward—a state of mind or condition of the soul, uniting all in whom it is present, but uniting them invisibly; now it is something outward—a visible society which men shall see coming, and coming 'with power'. It is not till the days of St. Paul, and the formation of a Christian Church (or churches) among the Gentiles by regular preaching and missionary effort, that the conception which is struggling to birth in the teaching of the Gospels begins to appear more clearly. Any idea of a 'kingdom', set over against other kingdoms, and asserting its own independence of them or even its superiority to them, begins to fade. The idea emerges of a society totally new in its kind, of a different order from all kingdoms and from the Empire which has come to embrace them all— a society spiritual and yet, in view of a definite membership, visible—which just because it is new in kind, and of a different order, can exist in peace by the side of kingdoms and the Empire.[1] For this society St. Paul uses the Greek term *polis* or derivatives

[1] 'A new people were coming forward who could no longer be called Jewish, Greek, Scythian, or barbarian; . . . "an elect race, a royal priesthood, a holy nation, a people for God's own possession" (1 Peter ii. 9, quoting the Septuagint version of Exodus xix. 6 and xxiii. 22). All the peoples who had appeared in the world hitherto were conditioned by flesh and blood. . . . Christian people alone were born of the spirit, by the sacrament of baptism in particular. This sacrament united Christians chosen out of all nations, and made them into a new, supramundane organism which Paul described as the body of Christ...' (H. Lietzmann, *The Founding of the Church Universal*, Eng. trans., pp. 51–52).

of that word: he thus sheds the associations, mainly Jewish, of the word 'kingdom', and adopts the associations of the word 'city' or 'commonwealth'. He accordingly speaks of it (Philippians iii. 20) as a *polīteuma* or civic community existing 'in the heavens' and yet including Christian believers on earth who have attained, or rather received by grace, the gift of righteousness. Once they are members of that *polīteuma*, he argues, believers are 'fellow citizens' (*sympolītai*) 'with the saints' in heaven. But during their life on earth, and at the same time that they belong to the *polīteuma* existing in heaven, they also belong to another and earthly polity, and they have thus a double citizenship. They are members of the earthly polity, and they owe obedience, like all other members, to its law and its government; and yet, because they have the other citizenship in the heavenly polity, they are but 'sojourners and pilgrims'[1] in the earthly polity, living there for a season, but having their true and 'continuing city' elsewhere. Here, in this Pauline conception of the double citizenship of the Christian believer, we have in the germ already the teaching and the philosophy of St. Augustine's *City of God*.

But we have also something more—indeed something very much more. We have the beginning of a great revolution in human thought and life. The thought of pre-Christian antiquity assumed a close and all-inclusive society (whether it were a small *polis* or a great *imperium*) which controlled the whole of life, both secular and religious. Indeed there was no distinction, in that system of thought, between the secular and the religious, the temporal and the spiritual; the one society was both, and the government of the one society—without making any distinction, or, indeed, being aware of any distinction, between the temporal and the spiritual—was also, and equally, both. This idea of the close and all-inclusive society, already present in antiquity before the Hellenistic age of Alexander and his successors, had been

---

[1] The words come in the First Epistle of St. Peter (ii. 11); but this epistle, as Lietzmann notes (*The Beginnings of the Christian Church*, Eng. trans., pp. 213–14), though it bears the name of Peter, and professes to come from Rome, breathes the Pauline atmosphere, and was probably written by a member of some Pauline circle, possibly 'in one of the original Pauline churches in the province of Asia'.

strengthened by the developments of that age. The deification of rulers had established itself as an institution: kings had come to be acknowledged as being, by virtue of their office, 'gods manifest' as well as men. This system of deification had rooted itself in opinion, and it had been reinforced by a feeling of gratitude just at the time when Christianity was born and was beginning to grow. Augustus and his successors had ended the horrors of nearly a century of civil war; they were hailed as 'benefactors', 'saviours', 'fathers of mankind', by the acclamations of their subjects; and if formal deification came only with their death, they were already, during their lives, the object of a cult. It was into this world of ideas that the teaching of Christianity came, and it came as the blowing of a wind which opened the shut doors of the old close and all-inclusive society. The great word which is the text of the revolution was spoken by Jesus Himself. 'Render . . . unto Caesar the things that are Caesar's; and unto God the things that are God's' (Matthew xxii. 21).[1] (The Latin of the Vulgate runs, 'Reddite . . . quae sunt Caesaris, Caesari: et quae sunt Dei, Deo'.) This saying was the great word of liberation, which prepared the way for the development of a *society* (and ultimately of *societies*) other than the political State—first, of religious society, and then, upon its analogy, of other free societies in other spheres of man's thought and activity. 'However limited', Professor Whitehead writes, 'may be the original intention of the saying, very quickly God was conceived as a principle of organization in complete disjunction from Caesar.' That principle of organization issued in St. Paul's conception of the *polīteuma* existing 'in the heavens', above Caesar and all the dominions of Caesar; and it has continued to move through time ever since, at once liberating and creating.[2]

A further note remains to be added in regard to the conception of society which appears, or is suggested, in the New Testament.

---

[1] Tertullian's exposition of this text is notable; see below, p. 456.

[2] It may be contended that Stoicism had already a conception of a World-State, or city of Zeus, distinct and disjoined from all actual States and cities of men. But the Stoic World-State was a tenuous conception, which never came down from the clouds; and the idea of obedience to its higher law (which always remained a mere idea) never produced the liberation, or resulted in the creation, which came from the Christian idea and *practice* of obedience to the law and government of the heavenly polity.

The commonwealth of which St. Paul spoke, a commonwealth in which Christian believers on earth were fellow citizens with the saints above, was a society which knew no respect of persons. It transcended all the old distinctions—of Greek and barbarian, of Jew and Gentile, of freeman and slave; it was a universal society, composed of members who, within its bounds and so far as concerned its life, were equal to one another, knowing no distinctions either of race or of class. Here the teaching of the New Testament continues, but also elevates, the teaching of the Stoic philosophers. The Stoics too had thought of a universal fraternity and a general equality; but they had also distinguished the 'foolish' (*stultus*) from the 'wise' (*sapiens*), and they had left the foolish to his folly. St. Paul may seem to be speaking as a Stoic in some passages of his Epistles. A Stoic might have said, as he says in the Epistle to the Galatians (iii. 28), 'There can be neither Jew nor Greek, there can be neither bond nor free'; a Stoic might also have said, as he says in the Epistle to the Colossians (iii. 11), 'There cannot be Greek and Jew . . ., barbarian, Scythian, bondman, freeman.' But no Stoic could ever have said what he says at the beginning of the First Epistle to the Corinthians (i. 20–27):

'Where is the wise? where is the scribe? where is the disputer of this world? hath not God made foolish the wisdom of the world? For seeing that in the wisdom of God the world through its wisdom knew not God, it was God's good pleasure through the foolishness of the preaching to save them that believe. Seeing that Jews ask for signs, and Greeks seek after wisdom: but we preach Christ crucified, unto Jews a stumbling-block, and unto Gentiles foolishness; but unto them that are called, both Jews and Greeks, Christ the power of God, and the wisdom of God. . . . For behold your calling, brethren, how that not many wise after the flesh . . . are called: but God chose the foolish things of the world, that he might put to shame them that are wise.'

c. The Theory of Government

Though St. Paul has a conception of the double citizenship of the Christian, he does not seek to challenge—on the contrary he seeks to defend—the obligation which Christians owe, as citizens of the earthly city, to its law and its government. God has permitted, and even instituted, the governments of this world; the Christian citizen, in obeying them, is rendering obedience to the God who made them.

There are two main passages of the New Testament in which the defence and justification of the States of this world and their governments are set forth, one of them written by St. Paul himself and the other by a follower of his line of thought. The first passage comes in the Epistle to the Romans (xiii. 1–7), and it may almost be said, particularly towards its close, to be a commentary on the saying of Jesus about what is to be rendered to Caesar and what is to be rendered to God.

'Let every soul be in subjection to the higher powers[1] [i.e. the sovereign authorities of the earthly State]: for there is no power but of God; and the powers that be are ordained of God. Therefore he that resisteth the power, withstandeth the ordinance of God: and they that withstand shall receive to themselves judgement. For rulers are not a terror to the good work, but to the evil. And wouldest thou have no fear of the power? do that which is good, and thou shalt have praise from the same: for he is a minister of God to thee for good. But if thou do that which is evil, be afraid; for he beareth not the sword in vain: for he is a minister of God, an avenger for wrath to him that doeth evil. Wherefore ye must needs be in subjection, not only because of the wrath, but also for conscience sake. For this cause ye pay tribute also; for they are ministers of God's service, attending continually upon this very thing. Render to all their dues: tribute to whom tribute is due; custom to whom custom; fear to whom fear; honour to whom honour.'

The first two verses of this passage run in the Vulgate: 'Omnis anima potestatibus sublimioribus subdita sit: non est enim potestas nisi a Deo: quae autem sunt a Deo, ordinatae sunt.[2] Itaque qui

[1] The word 'power' is perhaps misleading, because it may suggest to English readers the idea of the rule and right of might. The word used in the original Greek means 'authority' or 'magistracy'; it denotes, in its personal sense, the man or body of men duly entitled, by virtue of the custom or written rule of a political society, to conduct the government of that society.

[2] This punctuation implies the meaning, 'the powers that are of God are ordained powers'. (It is the punctuation in the text of Wordsworth and White.)

resistit potestati, Dei ordinationi resistit: qui autem resistunt, ipsi sibi damnationem adquirunt.'[1]

The second passage in the New Testament in which the higher authorities are defended and justified comes in the First Epistle ascribed to St. Peter (1 Peter ii. 13–17)—an epistle probably written, as has already been noted, by a member of some Pauline circle, perhaps in the province of Asia.

'Be subject to every ordinance of man [in the Greek 'creation' or 'institution'] for the Lord's sake: whether it be to the king, as supreme; or unto governors, as sent by him for vengeance on evil-doers and for praise to them that do well. For so is the will of God, that by well-doing ye should put to silence the ignorance of foolish men: as free, and not using your freedom for a cloke of wickedness, but as bondservants of God. Honour all men. Love the brotherhood. Fear God. Honour the king.'[2]

The latter part of the passage just quoted may explain why Pauline teaching is directed to the vindication of the authority of government. *Potestas* had to be set over against a misconception and exaggeration of *libertas*. The Christian converts of the Gentile churches, intoxicated by a sense of the liberty of the Christian man, were sometimes carried into a 'libertarianism', or even an antinomianism, in which they claimed freedom not only from the rules of the Mosaic law but also from the rules of all law and the control of all authority. In this way they might be guilty of 'using . . . freedom as a cloke of wickedness'. In more than one of his Epistles St. Paul protests against this false interpretation of liberty: he protests against it to the people of Galatia, to the citizens of Thessalonica, and above all to the Corinthians. His vindication of the authority of government is the positive side of these protests.

The Pauline teaching on government, and on its claim to obedience in virtue of its being ordained of God, became, in the

---

[1] Origen's commentary on the teaching of St. Paul in this passage is notable; see below, p. 441.

[2] The teaching of this passage, and of the passage in the Epistle to the Romans, is reinforced at the beginning of the second chapter of the First Epistle to Timothy, where St. Paul exhorts 'that supplications, prayers, intercessions, and thanksgivings be made for all men: for kings and all that are in high place; that we may lead a tranquil and quiet life in all godliness and gravity'.

course of the centuries, the teaching of St. Thomas Aquinas. But the Pauline teaching is modified and qualified in the theory of St. Thomas.[1] St. Thomas, with his encyclopaedic range of knowledge, and with that broad temper of mind which made him seek to reconcile the *fides* of the Christian Scriptures with the *ratio* of the legal and philosophical thought of antiquity, sought to bring together what he had learned from St. Paul about the institution of government with what he had also learned from Aristotle and Ulpian. St. Paul had said, 'Non est . . . potestas nisi a Deo.' But Ulpian had laid it down that it was the *people* which, by the *Lex Regia*, conferred *imperium et potestas* on the prince; and Aristotle, in the *Politics*, had laid it down, even earlier, that the rights of the people might be held to include the election of their magistrates and the calling of them to account. How were the three to be brought together and reconciled? The answer of St. Thomas, in his Commentary on the Epistle to the Romans, was to distinguish three different senses of *potestas*. There was *ipsa potestas*—the inward essence or *principium* of authority—and that came from God; but there was also the *modus* of acquiring authority, or in other words the form of the constitution; and there was also, in addition, the *usus* or exercise of authority. Now both of the latter—both *modus* and *usus*—might come from the people, since the people might both fix the permanent form of the constitution (monarchical, aristocratic, democratic, or mixed), and confer the exercise of authority on a given person or body of persons from time to time. St. Thomas could thus combine the idea of the divine right of kings (and of governments generally) with a conception of the rights of the people; and this mixed doctrine—half theocratic, we may almost say, and half democratic—became the general doctrine of the Church of Rome.[2]

[1] It may be said to be modified already in Origen's commentary on the Epistle to the Romans; see below, p. 443.

[2] St. Thomas does not expressly mention the people in the text of his commentary on Romans xiii. His words are: 'Potestas potest considerari quantum ad tria: 1. Quantum ad ipsam potestatem, et sic est a Deo: 2. Quantum ad modum adipiscendi potestatem, et sic quandoque potestas est a Deo, quandoque vero non est a Deo: 3. Quantum ad usum ipsius, et sic quandoque est a Deo, quandoque non est.' But though he does not expressly mention the people in this passage, we learn from his other writings that the people may, and does, act in determining

D. *The Conception of Slavery*

The Pauline conception of the relation of master and slave is parallel to, and may be said to follow on, the Pauline conception of the relation of government and subject. As Christian liberty does not abolish, or diminish, civic duty, so it does not abolish, or diminish, the household duty of the bondservant. (St. Paul is concerned only with the domestic slave; he is not thinking of the plantation slave on the great estate, or the industrial slave in the mine or in the factory.) The institution of domestic slavery, which might well be compatible with mutual respect and even affection, is simply accepted as a given fact; the Gospel does not 'turn the world upside down'. This attitude was not one of cowardice, afraid to risk a revolution, or, again, of calculation, anxious to respect opinion and prejudice: it was simply an attitude of acceptance—acceptance of what at the time, and for centuries to come, was unquestioned. Slavery was there, a given fact, accepted, as well as given; slaves might be skilled copyists, students of philosophy (such as Epictetus), secretaries, or confidants, if they might also be hewers of wood and drawers of water; the right course for the Christian was to 'adorn Sparta' and to make the best of the institution. This is the spirit shown in the Pauline Epistles.

Colossians iii. 22–25 and iv. 1. 'Servants, obey in all things them that are your masters according to the flesh; not with eye-service, as men-pleasers, but in singleness of heart, fearing the Lord: whatsoever ye do, work heartily, as unto the Lord, and not unto men; knowing that from the Lord ye shall receive the recompense of the inheritance: ye serve [literally, ye are slaves to] the Lord Christ. For he that doeth wrong shall receive again for the wrong that he hath done: and there is no respect of persons. Masters, render unto your servants that which is just and equal;[1] knowing that ye also have a Master in heaven.'

The Epistle to the Ephesians, which is held by Lietzmann (*The Beginnings of the Christian Church*, Eng. trans., p. 215) to be

the *modus* and conferring the *usus* of political authority when they are not (as in the case of Saul) determined and conferred directly by God.

[1] More exactly, 'Render to your slaves what is just, and [render to them] equality'.

written by some unknown writer at a later date but to be based on St. Paul's Epistle to the Colossians, repeats the same thought almost in the same words (vi. 5–9).

There are a number of other passages in the Pauline Epistles (including the First Epistle of St. Peter) which deal with the problem of the relation of slavery to Christian liberty. One of the most conservative is the passage in the First Epistle to the Corinthians (vii. 20–23), in which the slave is exhorted to remain in his position, and to be content with his status, even if he has the power and the opportunity of becoming free.

'Let each man abide in that calling wherein he was called. Wast thou called being a bondservant? care not for it: nay, even if thou canst become free, use it rather [i.e. remain in the position of slave]. For he that was called in the Lord, being a bondservant, is the Lord's freedman: likewise he that was called, being free, is Christ's bondservant.'

The same cautious, or conservative, attitude is shown in the first of the Epistles ascribed to St. Peter (ii. 18), in which slaves are exhorted to be subject to their masters in fear, 'not only to the good and gentle, but also the froward'; and it appears in the First Epistle to Timothy (vi. 2), which advises slaves to count their masters worthy of all honour, and urges those whose masters are Christians not to 'despise them because they are brethren, but . . . serve them the rather, because they that partake of the benefit [of the service of slaves] are believing and beloved'. The brief Pauline epistle to Philemon, which is unique in dealing with a personal and particular slave, is generous in its reference to the runaway slave Onesimus, whom Paul sends back to his master in terms of warm affection, suggesting that he might henceforth be regarded by him 'no longer as a servant, but more than a servant, a brother beloved' (16), a brother both of St. Paul who sends him and of his master who receives him back.

Ignatius, the Bishop of Antioch, writing about A.D. 100, or some forty or fifty years after St. Paul, shows a similar balance of view. 'Despise not men or women slaves. Yet let them not be puffed up, but rather bear their slavery to the glory of God, that they may win from Him thereby a better liberty. Let them not seek to be emancipated at the expense of the common fund [belonging to the congregation], that they may not be found the slaves of desire' (*Epistle to Polycarp*, c. iv, § 3).

E. *The Conception of Property*

There is little on the theme of property in the Pauline Epistles. St. Paul exhorts to alms-giving, both in aid of the ministers of the Gospel and in support of the poor; and at the end of the First Epistle to Timothy (vi. 17–19) he asks that the rich should be charged 'to do good, to become rich in good works, to be ready to distribute, to be willing to communicate'. But it is in the Gospels and the Acts of the Apostles, rather than in the Epistles of St. Paul, that we have to look for the view of the early Christian Church on the nature and limits of property.

The Gospels record the counsel of perfection given by Jesus to the young man who had great possessions: 'If thou wouldst be perfect, go, sell that thou hast, and give to the poor, and thou shalt have treasure in heaven' (Matthew xix. 21; Mark x. 21; Luke xviii. 22);[1] they record grave doubts about the effect of riches on the spirit of man: 'How hardly shall they that have riches enter into the kingdom of God' (Mark x. 23); and St. Luke records the beatitude of poverty: 'Blessed are ye poor; for yours is the kingdom of God' (Luke vi. 20, differing from Matthew v. 3, where the beatitude pronounced is on 'the poor *in spirit*') There are also the words of the Magnificat 'The hungry he hath filled with good things. And the rich he hath sent empty away' (Luke i. 53); and in the same Gospel which records the Magnificat there is also the great parable of Dives and Lazarus which has impressed itself deeply on Christian thought through all the ages (Luke xvi. 19–31).[2]

[1] The treatise, or sermon, of Clement of Alexandria on this text is notable; see below, p. 426.

[2] It is perhaps hardly fanciful to suggest that Luke (with his record of the beatitude of the poor, the verses of the Magnificat, and the parable of Dives and Lazarus, which he alone records) shows a special interest in the problem of poverty and property, and illustrates what may be called the 'social-revolutionary' trend in the Christian gospel, a trend always present by the side of the more conservative teaching which appears in the epistles of Paul and the First Epistle of

The record in the Acts of the Apostles is the story of the early and burning enthusiasm of the mission stage of the first Christian Church, when the members, seeking perfection, followed with a prompt and literal obedience the advice which Jesus had given to the rich young ruler. 'All that believed were together, and had all things common; and they sold their possessions and goods, and parted them to all, according as any man had need' (Acts ii. 44–45). 'And the multitude of them that believed were of one heart and soul: and not one of them said that aught of the things which he possessed was his own; but they had all things common. . . . Neither was there among them any that lacked: for as many as were possessors of lands or houses sold them, and brought the prices of the things that were sold, and laid them at the apostles' feet: and distribution was made unto each, according as any one had need' (Acts iv. 32, 34–35). But this early passion for perfection, natural to a group newly knit, newly filled with a sense of spiritual unity, and eager to 'have all things common' just as the hearts and souls of its members were all of one accord—this was the passion of an exalted mood which faded as the mood abated. The early Church in Jerusalem was not a model for the Jerusalem Church of later days, and still less for the churches of the Gentiles. Not communism, but alms-giving, became the doctrine and practice of the Christian Church, as it had always been the doctrine and practice of the religious congregation of Israel, and as it had been commended by the teaching of Jesus (Matthew vi. 2–4). Not the surrender of all, in a moment, and in a flood of abnegation, but the giving of some part (the greater the better), in the course of long years and by the steady exercise of a regular self-discipline—such is the philosophy of St. Paul and the practice of the churches which he founded.

It may thus be said that the New Testament accepts property, just as it accepts slavery, but that it accepts both on conditions— the condition that the master should render to the slave that which is just and equal; the condition that the owner of property should be 'ready to distribute and willing to communicate' some part of

Peter. It is a trend which shows itself markedly in the Epistle of James; see below, pp. 409–11.

his possessions, showing thereby the grace which St. Paul calls *haplotēs*, the grace of a Christian 'simplicity'. And yet this is not the whole of the matter. The acceptance of the institution of property, subject to the condition of some measure of its common use, is only one side of the teaching of the New Testament. There is the other, or 'social-revolutionary' side, which appears in the record of the saying of Jesus to the young man of great possessions (a record common to the first three Gospels); which appears particularly in several passages of Luke's Gospel; and which may be said to appear with a special vehemence and passion in the Epistle of James. Here, in the writer's denunciation of the rich and his trust in the poor, there is a fervour which is akin to that of the prophets of the Old Testament.

James ii. 2–9. 'If there come into your synagogue a man with a gold ring, in fine clothing, and there come in also a poor man in vile clothing; and ye have regard to him that weareth the fine clothing, and say, Sit thou here in a good place; and ye say to the poor man, Stand thou there, or sit under my footstool; are ye not divided in your own mind, and become judges with evil thoughts? Hearken, my beloved brethren; did not God choose them that are poor as to the world to be rich in faith, and heirs of the kingdom which he promised to them that love him? But ye have dishonoured the poor man. Do not the rich oppress you, and themselves drag you before the judgement-seats? Do they not blaspheme the honourable name by which ye are called? Howbeit if ye fulfil the royal law, according to the scripture, Thou shalt love thy neighbour as thyself, ye do well: but if ye have respect of persons, ye commit sin, being convicted by the law as transgressors.'

Ibid. iv. 13–v. 8. 'Go to now, ye that say, today or tomorrow we will go into this city, and spend a year there, and trade, and get gain: whereas ye know not what shall be on the morrow. What is your life? For ye are a vapour, that appeareth for a little time, and then vanisheth away. For that ye ought to say, If the Lord will, we shall both live, and do this or that. But now ye glory in your vauntings: all such glorying is evil. To him therefore that knoweth to do good, and doeth it not, to him it is sin.

'Go to now, ye rich, weep and howl for your miseries that are coming upon you. Your riches are corrupted, and your garments are moth-eaten. Your gold and your silver are rusted; and their rust shall be for a testimony against you, and shall eat your flesh as fire. Ye have laid up your treasure in the last days. Behold, the hire of the labourers who mowed your fields, which is of you kept back by fraud, crieth out, and the cries of them that reaped have entered into the ears of the Lord of Sabaoth. Ye have lived delicately on the earth, and taken your pleasure; ye have nourished your hearts in a day of slaughter. Ye have condemned, ye have killed the righteous one; he doth not resist you.

'Be patient therefore, brethren, until the coming of the Lord. Behold, the husbandman waiteth for the precious fruit of the earth, being patient over it, until it receive the early and the latter rain. Be ye also patient; stablish your hearts: for the coming of the Lord is at hand. Murmur not, brethren, against one another, that ye be not judged: behold, the judge standeth before the doors.'

These passages, with what may be called their 'class-consciousness', depart from, or go beyond, what may be called the main line of early Christian thought. Indeed the whole epistle, with its rigid insistence on 'works', is not only non-Pauline (and a definite polemic against Paul's teaching of justification by faith): it has even been said to be also non-Christian. Lietzmann has suggested that it is possibly 'a product of the Greek synagogue'—that is to say of a congregation of Hellenized Jews—'made Christian by a few additions' and then commended to all who might read it by an ascription of its authorship to James the brother of Jesus (*The Beginnings of the Christian Church*, Eng. trans., pp. 202–3). If this be the case, the epistle cannot be used as evidence of the *Christian* view of property. But Lietzmann's view is perhaps extreme; and other scholars are far from convinced that the epistle represents an essentially Jewish basis of thought which has been but superficially christianized. They hold that the echoes of the teaching of Jesus ring too clearly, and are too much the ground-theme of the whole argument, for that to be possible; and they suggest that the epistle is really a series of reflections, cast in the form of a homily, by a Hellenistic Jew who was fundamentally Christian. In that case it *can* be used as evidence of Christian thought (or at any rate of one trend of Christian thought) on the problem of poverty and property; and it may be held to show that 'social-revolutionary' element which has always been present in Christianity, though qualified by other elements and different ideas, and which may break out in a one-sided way when conditions suggest or favour its emergence.

§ II. THREE DOCUMENTS OF THE EARLY CHRISTIAN CHURCH, *circa* A.D. 100

A. *The* Didachē, *or Teaching of the Apostles, on the ritual and organization of the Christian Church*

The *Didachē*—or, as its full title runs, 'The teaching of the Lord through the twelve Apostles to the Gentiles'—was discovered in a manuscript at Jerusalem towards the end of last century. It gives an account, written from within the Church, of the services (baptism, fasts, and especially the Eucharist) of the Christian communities at the beginning of the second century A.D.: it also attests, and here its testimony is of particular value, the transition from an earlier 'pneumatic' or spiritual stage, when 'apostles' and 'prophets' and 'teachers' preached and taught as the spirit impelled them, to the stage of organization in which an appointed 'bishop' and official 'deacons' became the essence of each Christian community. The nature of this transition is explained in H. Lietzmann's *The Founding of the Church Universal*, c. ii. Briefly, we may say that the early 'pneumatic' Christian community, with its sense of the immanence of the divine *pneuma* and with enthusiastic prophets as its guides, was in 'danger of dissolution into conventicles of a more or less syncretistic character'—each in some measure permeated by some form of gnosticism, or in other words by some esoteric belief in a peculiar subjective 'knowledge' (*gnōsis*) of God and the spiritual world. Christianity, if it was not to become a fluid play of subjectivity, had to defend itself 'against the pneumatic and gnostic danger'; and the defence which it found for itself was a triple defence—the fixing of a *canon* of the

Scriptures; the formulation of a *creed*; and especially the erection of 'the *ecclesiastical office of the bishop* as a higher authority than that due to the unbridled exercise of pneumatic gifts' (Lietzmann, op. cit., p. 57). We may trace in the argument of the *Didachē* the beginnings of this defence.

In chapters 9 and 10 the writer of the *Didachē* gives the earliest form of the liturgy of the Eucharist. Here he lays a firm basis for the life of the Christian community. He turns, in three following chapters (11, 12, 13), to deal on this basis with the position of the prophets—the wandering 'apostles' (or missionaries) and teachers who went from church to church. They are to be received, if and provided that they teach what has been set forth in the previous chapters. They are to stay for one day, or if need be for a second; but if they stay three days, they are false prophets. If, again, they ask for money, they are false prophets. 'Not all who speak in the spirit (*pneuma*) are prophets: they are only so if they have the ways of the Lord. By their ways, therefore, the prophet and the false prophet shall be known' (11, § 8).

The kernel of the *Didachē* may be said to come in chapters 14 and 15. 'Gather together on the Lord's Day, and break bread and hold the Thanksgiving (*eucharistia*), having first made confession of your sins, that your sacrifice may be pure. Let no man who has a dispute with his neighbour join with you until reconciliation be made, that your sacrifice be not profaned. For this is what was said by the Lord, "In all places and at all times bring Me a pure sacrifice; for I am a great King, saith the Lord, and My name is wonderful among the nations".

(15) 'Choose therefore for yourselves bishops and deacons worthy of the Lord, men who are merciful, not covetous of money, true, and proved. For they too render you the service of prophets and of teachers. Do not, therefore, disdain them. For they it is who are honoured among you, with the prophets and teachers. Reprove one another in peace, not in anger, as you have it [enjoined upon you] in the Gospel. Let no man speak to any man who errs against another, and let not that man be heard by you until he repent. Make your prayers and your alms, and do all your actions, as you have it [enjoined upon you] in the Gospel of our Lord.'

Thus the canon of the Scripture ('the Gospel of our Lord'); the creed, already beginning to be formulated in the Eucharist; and the erection of the ecclesiastical office of the bishop—these three defences of a stable Christian community may all be traced in the *Didachē*.

B. *The First Epistle of Clement to the Corinthians*

The ideas of the *Didachē* find a parallel in the First Epistle of Clement of Rome to the Corinthians. The date of the epistle is somewhere around the year A.D. 100; it was addressed by, or on behalf of, the Roman Church to the Church in Corinth, which had lately been vexed by the problem whether bishops were 'business', or secular, officers, with an authority delegated by the congregation, and as such (like the officers of Greek cities) elected only for a limited period, or whether they were 'charismatic' officers, possessing an intrinsic grace and an authority derived from the Apostles, and whether, as such, they were irrevocable by the congregation or any other body. It is notable that the Church in Rome should already, by this early date, be making a pronouncement as a judge, or at any rate an adviser, on the affairs of the Church in Corinth. It is also notable that the letter sent by the Roman Church should already show a spirit of order and law which reflects the genius of secular Rome (as, for instance, in the first passage (c. 37) here quoted). It has been said that the canon law of the Roman Church was born in some of the passages of this letter (c. 42 and c. 44); and along with the contemporary Epistles of Ignatius of Antioch (see below, p. 416) Clement's letter contains the earliest statement of the divine ordination of the clergy, through apostolic succession, and the consequent indelibility of their orders. It is thus a witness to the growth of an organized Christian society, with its own inherent government, side by side with the State. Who Clement was, and whether he was the actual writer of the epistle which bears his name, is not certain. But there was, according to the list of Roman bishops given by Irenaeus of Lyons (about A.D. 180), a Clement who was the third to hold the office of bishop of Rome.

c. 37. 'Brethren, let us serve in the army [of our Master]

with all earnestness, abiding under His blameless commandments. Let us think of the soldiers who serve our generals; of the good order, the deference, and the discipline with which they carry out their instructions. Not all are prefects, or tribunes, or centurions, or commanders of a troop, or holders of any other rank; but each in his place carries out the instructions of the emperor and his generals. The great cannot exist apart from the small, nor the small apart from the great; there is a spirit of unity among all, and in this there is an advantage. Let us take, again, the example of our body: the head is nothing apart from the feet, or the feet apart from the head, and the smallest members of our body are necessary and useful to the whole; but all the members cooperate, and obey a single direction, unto the preservation of the whole.

c. 42. 'The Apostles had the Gospel preached to them for our benefit from the Lord Jesus Christ; and Jesus the Christ was sent from God. The Christ therefore was from God, and the Apostles from the Christ; and both He and they come, in due order, from the will of God. Having therefore received their instructions, being assured by the resurrection of our Lord Jesus Christ, and having confidence in the word of God, they went forth in the assurance of the Holy Spirit, preaching the gospel that the Kingdom of God was about to come. They proclaimed it from one land and city to another, and they appointed those who were the firstfruits of their labours, after they had tested them by the Spirit, to be bishops and deacons of those who should come to believe in the Gospel. And this was not a new thing; for mention had been made many years before of bishops and deacons, as the Scripture says in one passage, "I will establish their bishops in righteousness and their deacons in faith."[1]

c. 44. 'Our Apostles knew, through our Lord Jesus Christ, that there would be strife over the title of bishop. Accordingly, since they had received full foreknowledge, they appointed those who have been mentioned before [their first-fruits], and then

[1] The reference appears to be to Isaiah lx. 17. In the Septuagint version this runs, 'I will give thee thy rulers in peace, and thy bishops in righteousness'. In the English Revised Version the translation is, 'I will make thy officers peace, and thine exactors righteousness'.

afterwards gave the injunction that, whenever these should fall asleep, others of approved standing should succeed to their ministry. Such persons, therefore, as were appointed by them, or have afterwards been appointed by other men of repute with the assent of the whole Church, and then have served the flock of Christ blamelessly, in humbleness of heart, peaceably and liberally, and have time and again received the testimony of all men— these, in our opinion, cannot justly be cast out of their ministry. It were no small sin in us if we cast out from the office of bishop men who have blamelessly and holily brought their gifts to it. . . . For we see that you have removed some who were good governors[1] from the ministry which they performed blamelessly.'

c. 61. On the authority of secular rulers. 'Thou, our Master, hast given them the authority of empire (*basileia*) by Thy great and ineffable power, to the end that we, knowing that glory and honour is given to them by Thee, may be subject to them, in nothing resisting Thy will. To whom, o Lord, give health, peace, concord and stability, that they may exercise without offence the government given to them by Thee. For Thou, our heavenly Master, the King eternal, givest glory and honour to the sons of men over the things that are on the earth; do thou, o Lord, direct their counsels to what is good and pleasing before thee, that they, exercising with due reverence the authority given to them by Thee in peace and gentleness, may find favour in Thy eyes.'

c. *The Epistles of Ignatius*

Ignatius, Bishop of Antioch and a contemporary of Clement of Rome, wrote a number of letters to the Churches of Asia Minor (*circa* A.D. 100) while he was on his way to martyrdom in Rome. He expounds for the Eastern Mediterranean, but even more firmly and fully, the same views of apostolic succession and the indelibility of orders which are set forth for the West in the First Epistle

---

[1] The Greek word here used (Clement was writing in Greek, the language used by the Church in Rome down to the middle of the third century) is connected with the idea of a *polīteuma*. A *polīteuma*, in the sense in which the term was used after the time of Alexander, was a civic corporation, quasi-autonomous, falling short of a *polis* or city-state, but, like a *polis*, having a religious centre and possibly also a council and magistrates (Tarn, *Hellenic Civilisation*, 3rd ed., p. 147). The Christian churches of A.D. 100 may be regarded as societies organized on this basis.

of Clement to the Corinthians. 'In Ignatius', it has been said, 'we find the completed monarchical episcopate'; and he may thus be regarded as 'the classical authority for the Roman Catholic doctrine of bishops' (Lietzmann, *The Beginnings of the Christian Church*, Eng. trans., p. 248).

Epistle to the Smyrnaeans, c. 8. 'Follow ye one and all the bishop, as Jesus Christ follows the Father; follow the presbytery [the body or college of priests], as if it were the Apostles; have regard to the deacons as the command of God.[1] Apart from the bishop let no man do any of the things pertaining to the Church. Let that be held to be a true Eucharist which is celebrated by the bishop, or by any to whom he entrusts it. Wherever the bishop appears, there let the congregation (*plēthos*) be; even as wherever Jesus Christ is, there the Catholic Church is.[2] It is not permitted either to baptize or to hold a 'love-feast' (*agapē*) without the bishop; but whatever *he* approves is well-pleasing also to God. c. ix. . . . It is good to know God and the bishop. He who knows the bishop has received honour from God; he who does anything without the knowledge of the bishop is serving the devil.'

Epistle to the Magnesians, c. 6. '. . . Be ye zealous to do all things in concord with God, with the bishop presiding in the likeness of God, and with the presbyters in the likeness of the council of the Apostles, and with the deacons, who are most dear to me, entrusted with the service (*diākonia*) of Jesus Christ . . . .'

The same lesson of obedience to the bishop is enforced by Ignatius in a number of other passages: indeed it runs as a common note through most of his epistles. There is one notable chapter in the epistle to Polycarp, the bishop of Smyrna, which at once exalts the bishop and uses the military analogy which is also used in the First Epistle of Clement to the Corinthians.

Epistle to Polycarp, c. 6. 'Give heed to the bishop, that God may also heed you. My heart is with those who are subject to the

---

[1] Each church thus appears as an organized society governed by a threefold order of clergy—bishop, priests, and deacons.

[2] Just as each particular church is gathered round the bishop, so the Church Catholic or Universal, which embraces all particular churches, is gathered round Jesus Christ; for, in the view of Ignatius, 'those who had been redeemed by Christ constituted a *single* great spiritual unity of saints' (Lietzmann, op. cit., p. 247).

bishop, presbyters, and deacons; and may it be given to me to have my lot with them in God. . . . Be pleasing to Him in whose army you serve, from whom you receive your pay: let none of you be found a deserter.[1] Let your baptism abide as your weapons of war, your faith as your helmet, your love as your spear, your patience as your whole armour; let your works be your deposits[1] that you may receive the credits[1] due to you. . . .'

§ III. IRENAEUS OF LYONS ON THE APOSTOLIC TRADITION AND THE FUNCTION OF THE EPISCOPATE

Irenaeus was born in Asia Minor, probably at Smyrna, about the middle of the second century A.D. Perhaps in consequence of a connexion between Asia Minor and southern Gaul, in which from early times Greek colonies had been planted, he became a priest at Lyons, and afterwards (about A.D. 180) 'bishop of Gaul', with his seat in the city. As bishop he was concerned in the contemporary controversy about the date of Easter, trying to make peace between the East and the West; but his main achievement was a work in five books, which has been called the first systematic exposition of Catholic belief, and which was intended as 'a refutation and overthrow of *Gnōsis*, falsely so called'. It was written in Greek; but it only survives, except for some few scattered fragments, in a Latin translation, generally cited by the title of *Adversus Haereses*. The first two books contain an account of various Gnostic heresies; the last three seek to expound the doctrine of the Catholic Church, as contained in its tradition, to which he attaches primary importance. In keeping with his emphasis on tradition is his conception of what has been called 'the monarchical episcopate'. His system of thought thus sprang from, and was based upon, the religious life of the Christian community under the shelter and with the guidance of its bishop.

Irenaeus records that he had often to speak Celtic. A Greek from Asia Minor, living in Gaul, writing in Greek, mixing with

---

[1] In all these instances Ignatius transliterates into Greek letters the Latin terms *desertores*, *deposita*, and *accepta*. This seems to suggest that he was drawing on a Latin original, or at any rate consciously using Roman terms acquired from contact with Roman officers.

Italians, and speaking Celtic—he is a notable link between the Hellenistic East and the Romano–Celtic West.

A. *The Source of Christian Knowledge and the Foundation of Christian Faith*

Adversus Haereses, IV. lii, § 2. 'True knowledge [in the Greek *Gnōsis alēthēs*; in the Latin *Agnitio vera*] consists in (1) the teaching of the Apostles, (2) the ancient constitution of the Church all over the world, and (3) the nature (*charactēr*) of the body of Christ, as manifested according to the successions of bishops [in each particular church], whereby they have handed down [*tradiderunt*] the Church Universal—the Church which has come to us guarded by the fullest statement of its belief without the fabrication of writings,[1] admitting neither addition to that belief nor subtraction therefrom. It is to study without falsification, and to expound lawfully and diligently according to the Scriptures, without either causing danger or being guilty of blasphemy; it is, above all else, to have the gift of love (*dilectionis munus*), which is more precious than knowledge, more glorious than prophecy, and more excellent than all other gifts of grace (*charismata*).'

B. *The Office and Function of Presbyters and Bishops in the Church*

Ibid. IV. xl, § 2. 'Therefore it is necessary to obey the presbyters who are in the Church—those who, as I have shown, are in succession from the Apostles, and who, together with succession to the office of bishop,[2] have received the sure gift of truth according to the pleasure of God. As for the rest—those who are not in the original succession, wherever it be that they are gathered to-

[1] Irenaeus is possibly alluding in this phrase [*fictio scripturarum*] to Gnostic 'gospels' professing to be esoteric revelations. In opposition to such writings he insists on the supremacy of the oral *tradition*, or rule of faith, preserved in and by the Church.

[2] Irenaeus here makes little distinction between 'presbyter' and 'bishop'. Down to the middle of the second century A.D. the government of the Christian churches generally rested with a college of presbyters, one of whom, the presbyter in charge of the worship, was called the *episcopus* or overseer. But by the time of Irenaeus (*circa* A.D. 180) the 'monarchical episcopate', of which he is the first exponent, was establishing itself in lieu of the older collegiate system (Lietzmann, *The Founding of the Church Universal*, Eng. trans., pp. 58–60).

gether—it is necessary to hold them suspect, either as being heretics and holding false doctrines, or as being schismatics puffed up in their own conceit and seeking to please themselves, or again as being hypocrites who do what they do for gain and vain glory.'

c. *The Apostolic Tradition: the Succession of Bishops in the Churches from the Time of the Apostles*

Ibid. IV. iii, § 1. 'All men, in all the churches, who wish to see the truth can look to the tradition of the Apostles as it is manifested in all the world; and to them we can add those who were ordained by the Apostles as bishops in the churches, and the line of their successors down to the present time, who taught no such things [as the Gnostics do] and knew not any such things as *they* proclaim in their ravings. If the Apostles had known hidden mysteries, which they taught the perfect in secrecy and separately from other disciples, they would most certainly have handed those mysteries down to those into whose care they committed the churches themselves; for they wanted their successors, to whom they handed on their own position as pastors and masters, to be altogether perfect and blameless in every respect. Now since it would be a very lengthy business to enumerate, in a book such as this, the lines of succession in all the churches, I will treat only of the succession in the greatest, the oldest, and the universally known church, that founded and established in Rome by the two glorious apostles Peter and Paul; indicating the tradition received by it from the Apostles, and the faith announced to mankind, as they have been transmitted down to our time by the succession of bishops; and thus confounding all who in any way, whether by their own evil self-will, or from vainglory, or from blindness and wrong views, congregate improperly together. For it is with this church that, by reason of the greater weight belonging to its primacy (*potentior principalitas*), all the Church must of necessity be in agreement (*convenire*) . . . I mean the faithful everywhere . . . wherein there has been preserved, by the faithful in all places, the tradition which comes from the Apostles.'[1]

[1] The translation of this last crucial sentence is far from being easy or certain. (*a*) The meaning of *principalitas* may be disputed: does it mean 'priority' in time

Note on the view of Tertullian in regard to the Tradition of the Church

The view developed by Irenaeus in the fourth book of his *Adversus Haereses* is again stated, more than a century later, by Tertullian in his *De Praescriptione Haereticorum* (c. 20): 'In like manner . . . they [the Apostles] founded churches in every city, from which the rest of the churches hereafter have derived the grafting of their faith and the seeds of their doctrine, and are daily deriving them in order to become churches. Thus these churches themselves are also reckoned as Apostolic, because they are the shoot of Apostolic churches. Every kind of thing must necessarily be classed according to its origin. Consequently these churches, numerous and important as they are, form but the one primitive Church founded by the Apostles, from which source they all derive. So that all are primitive and all are Apostolic; whilst that all are in one unity is proved by the fellowship of peace and title of brotherhood and common token of unity— privileges which nothing governs but the one tradition of the self-same bond of faith.'[1]

§ IV. FROM THE EPISTLE TO DIOGNETUS (*date uncertain*) *A Description of the Christian Faith and Society*

The *Epistle to Diognetus* is the work of an unknown Christian apologist. The Diognetus to whom it is addressed may perhaps be identified with the tutor of Marcus Aurelius, and it may there-

(which would be to assume the greater *antiquity* of the Church of Rome, which cannot be proved), or does it mean 'primacy' in order of importance (a primacy presumably due to the fact that Rome was the seat of imperial government)? (*b*) The meaning of the last clause may be equally disputed: does the clause 'wherein there has been preserved . . . the tradition' refer to 'all the Church' (*omnis ecclesia*), or is it to be interpreted as referring to 'this Church', i.e. the particular Church in Rome? Grammatically, either is possible, though the former seems to be preferable, because the words 'all the Church' come immediately before the clause, while the words 'this Church' stand farther back in the sentence. In addition it may be asked, as one of the editors of Irenaeus asks, 'How was the Apostolic tradition preserved in the Church of Rome by the members of foreign churches ('the faithful in *all* places')'?

[1] Quoted in *Documents illustrative of the History of the Church*, edited by B. J. Kidd, vol. i, pp. 146–7. (A few changes are made on the version there given.)

fore have been composed about the middle of the second century A.D. On the other hand, it has been argued that the picture of Christianity as spread throughout the whole of the Roman Empire could only have been painted about a century later (A.D. 250), when the Christian religion, though vexed by persecution, was attracting more and more adherents. In any case the letter is an 'apology' for, or rather a commendation of, the Christian faith to a friendly pagan. The argument is that Christ, the Logos through whom God created the world and through whose incarnation a new knowledge of God came into the world, has made all those who believe in Him members of a new and wonderful polity. The Greek style of the author is notable; he is a master of epigrammatic phrases in the style of 'the Second Sophistic'.

c. 5. 'Christians are not distinguished from the rest of mankind by a particular country, or language, or set of habits; they have no cities of their own for their dwelling-place, nor do they use a particular form of speech or follow a peculiar way of life. Their knowledge has not been found by the reasoning and reflection of curiously inquisitive men; nor are they, as some others are, the champions of a man-made doctrine. They dwell in cities both Greek and barbarian, according as the lot of each has been cast, and they follow the local habits in the matter of dress and food and their general mode of life; but they have none the less a polity of their own, and its constitution is wonderful and admittedly peculiar. They live in their own home-cities (*patrides*), but they live there as sojourners; they take their part in all things, like citizens, but they suffer all things, like foreigners; every foreign city is to them a home-city, and every home-city is to them foreign. Like all men they marry, and have children; but they do not [as others do] expose their offspring. They meet at a common table, but not in a common bed [i.e. they have no community of wives]; they exist in the flesh, but they do not live after it; they spend their time on earth, but their citizenship is in heaven.[1] They obey the established laws, but they go beyond them in their own

---

[1] Compare the language of St. Paul: see above, p. 399.

lives. They love all men, and they are persecuted by all. They are unknown, and yet they are condemned; they are put to death, and yet they are made alive; they are poor, and yet they enrich many; they lack everything, and yet they abound in everything. They are dishonoured, and yet glorified in their dishonour; they are slandered, and yet they are justified; they are abused, and yet they bless; they are insulted, and they repay insult with honour. They do good, and they are punished like evil-doers; and when they are punished they rejoice, as being thereby made alive. They are attacked by the Jews as foreigners, and they are persecuted by the Greeks; but those who hate them cannot give a reason for their enmity.

c. 6. 'In a word, what the Soul is in the body, Christians are in the world. The Soul is dispersed through all the members of the body; so are Christians through all the cities of the world.[1] The Soul dwells in the body, but is not of the body; Christians dwell in the world, but are not of the world. The Soul, itself invisible, is imprisoned in a visible body; and so Christians are known to be in the world, but their faith in God remains invisible. The flesh hates the Soul, and fights against it though it suffers no wrong, because it is prevented by it from indulging in pleasure; so the world hates Christians, though it suffers no wrong, because they set themselves against its pleasures. The Soul loves the flesh that hates it, and it loves the members of the flesh; so Christians love those that hate them. The Soul is imprisoned in the body, but itself holds the body together; so Christians are shut up in the world as in a prison, but themselves hold the world together. The

---

[1] Whether this is a rhetorical flourish, or Christians were actually spread at this time (somewhere between A.D. 150 and 250) through all the cities of the world, it is impossible to say. Harnack, in *Texte und Untersuchungen* (vol. lii, heft iv, pp. 109–10), quotes passages from Origen (writing in the first half of the third century A.D.) which look both ways, some speaking of Christ as named *in universa terra*, and some, on the other hand, speaking of the Gospel as still unknown to the dwellers in many lands (including Britain). One notable passage quoted by Harnack, from a Homily on Psalm xxxvii, may be translated here. 'We Christians are a no-nation [*non-gens*]; some few of us, from this city (? Alexandria), are believers, and there are others from others, but nowhere does a whole *nation* seem to have been brought [into the Christian faith] since the beginning of belief. Unlike the nation of the Jews, and unlike that of the Egyptians, the Christians are not a single whole nation; they are gathered in dispersed bodies (*sparsim*) from each separate nation.'

Soul, itself immortal, dwells in a mortal tenement; so Christians dwell among corruptible things, waiting for incorruption in heaven. The Soul, when it is chastened in food and drink, grows better; so Christians, when punished, increase all the more daily.

'So great is the station to which God has appointed them, and it is not permitted to them to refuse it.

c. vii. 'For this, as I have said, is no earthly invention which was committed to their charge; it is not a mortal idea which they think themselves bound to guard so diligently; it is no stewardship of human mysteries with which they have been entrusted. But God Himself in very truth—God the Almighty, the All-creating, the Invisible—God Himself from heaven planted among men the Truth, the holy incomprehensible Word (*Logos*), and established it in their hearts. He did not, as a man might imagine, send a minister, or angel, or ruler, or one of those who administer earthly things or of those who have been entrusted with the ordering of things in heaven; He sent the very artificer and creator of the Universe, by whom He made the heavens and enclosed the sea in its proper bounds; whose mysteries all the elements faithfully guard; from whom the sun has received the measure of his daily courses to keep; whom the moon obeys when He bids her shine by night; whom the stars obey while they follow the course of the moon; by whom all things are ordered and defined and set in their due place—the heavens and the things in the heavens, the earth and the things in the earth, the sea and the things in the sea, fire, air, the great deep, things in the height above, things in the depths beneath, and things in the space between.[1] This was He whom God sent to men. [Was He sent,] as a man might think that He would be, for domination, or to inspire fear or amazement? No. He was sent in equity and mercy, as if a king were sending a son to be king; He was sent as a man to men; He was sent as by God sending God; He was sent as by a saviour and persuader, and not as by one using force—for there is no force in God. God sent Him as one who called men, and not as one who pursued them:

[1] This passage has some affinities with the pseudo-Aristotelian *De Mundo* (see above, pp. 290–4), but even more with Psalm 104 and the prayer quoted on p. 164 above.

He sent Him as one who loved them, and not as one who judged. For He *shall* yet send Him to be our judge, and who shall abide His coming? . . .' (From the text in Wilamowitz-Moellendorff, *Griechisches Lesebuch*, I. II, pp. 359 ff.)

§ V. CLEMENT OF ALEXANDRIA

Introduction

Clement of Alexandria, possibly an Athenian, and almost certainly born and bred in Greece or in the Greek parts of western Asia, belongs to the latter half of the second century A.D. and to the city of Alexandria, where he became the head of the Alexandrian school of Christian students (catechumens), in which Origen was one of his pupils. There were two great reconciliations which he attempted, one of which sadly failed in the issue, and the other of which—perhaps no less sadly—succeeded. The first reconciliation which he attempted, especially in his *Protrepticus*, was that of 'the new creation', as he calls it, or in other words the Christian faith, with the ancient spiritual inheritance of Greek philosophy. Both were to him, in their different degrees, expressions of the truth of God, which he sought to blend (as Philo, more than a century before, had sought to fuse Stoic and Platonic philosophy with the tradition of Judaism); but the later development of the Christian Church, which rejected Origen, rejected also the reconciliation which Origen's master had attempted.[1] The second reconciliation which Clement attempted, in a long sermon or pamphlet entitled 'Who is the Rich Man that may be saved', is a reconciliation of the social views stated or implied in the New Testament—views apparently radical or revolutionary—with the economic inheritance of the past and its accumulated social system. Here Clement sought so to interpret the New Testament (and especially the passage in St. Mark's Gospel, x. 17–31, which he quotes at the beginning of his sermon or pamphlet) that it could be made to square with the general system of economics developed during the centuries in the richest of all the cities of the Eastern Mediterranean. He only succeeded in his attempt, if indeed he succeeded, by a method of allegorical interpretation,

[1] On this issue of the reconciliation of the Christian faith with Greek philosophy see below, under Origen, pp. 436–8.

indigenous indeed in Alexandria (it had been used abundantly by Philo), but too subtle and too sophisticated to satisfy Christian conscience. This is the reverse side of his influence; and his success in this field is almost as sad as his ultimate failure in the other.

Yet there had to be some accommodation between the 'new creation' and the old class-structure of society if Christianity were to become a general and generally held faith, and were not to sink into a poverty which would have meant a dearth of range and experience as well as literal poverty. There is point, and a measure of wisdom, in Clement's treatment of the problem of wealth, no less than there is in his treatment of the problem of the relation between *fides* and *ratio*. In any case it was impossible for a man of so rich and original an intelligence as Clement's to live in Alexandria, in the second half of the second century A.D., without thinking and writing as he did. To live in Alexandria was to live by the side of a rich commercial community, both Greek and Jewish; it was also to live by the side of a new and rising school of Greek philosophy, that of the Neoplatonists. To live in the second half of the second century A.D. was to live at a time when the Christian community was ceasing to think that the end of the world was at hand and time was ceasing to be, as it had done during the first century (and even the first half of the second), and when it was beginning to feel that it must draw the actual world of time to itself and make some eirenicon with it. Clement speaks, and speaks nobly, on behalf of the place and the time in which he lived and worked.[1]

The following extracts are taken from the sermon or pamphlet on the Salvation of the Rich Man (often called by the Latin title *Quis Dives Salvetur*). The text of the sermon is the passage about riches and the rich young man who was advised by Jesus to sell all that he had and give it to the poor, which comes in St. Mark's Gospel.[2] Clement's interpretation of the passage may be compared with Philo's interpretation of the passage in Genesis about Joseph; but if it is similar, it is also finer and less fantastic.

[1] A full account of the writings and ideas of Clement is given by H. Lietzmann, *The Founding of the Church Universal*, Eng. trans., pp. 276–94.
[2] It also comes in Matthew xix. 16–22 and Luke xviii. 18–25.

A. *Preface, on the Duty of the Christian in regard to the Rich*

§ 3. 'It is the duty of those who are disposed towards love of the truth and the brethren—and who are neither presumptuously harsh to the rich who have been called [to the Christian faith], nor toadies to rich men through their own love of money—first, to free the minds of their rich brethren from vain despair by rational argument, and to show them, by a proper explanation of the sayings of our Lord, that the inheritance of the Kingdom of Heaven is not denied to them if they obey the commandments; and secondly—when they have been taught that their fears are empty, and that the Saviour gladly receives them if they are willing to be saved—to set before them, and to lead them to follow, the ways, and the works and intentions, by which they may attain their hope; the which, as it is not impossible of attainment, so too it cannot be gained without some plan and purpose.'

B. *The Method of interpreting the New Testament and the Sayings of Jesus*

§ 5. After citing the passage in chapter x of St. Mark's Gospel which records the sayings of Jesus, 'Sell whatever thou hast, and give to the poor', and 'How hardly shall they that have riches enter into the Kingdom of God', Clement proposes a general view of their proper interpretation: 'Knowing clearly that the Saviour teaches His followers nothing in a merely human sense, but that all His teaching is inspired by a divine and mystical wisdom, we must not receive His words in their fleshly significance: we must search and learn their hidden meaning (*nous*) with due inquiry and comprehension.' Clement repeats this warning of the need of a spiritual rather than a fleshly interpretation—in other words of an allegorical rather than a literal explanation—in a later passage in § 18. 'So with regard to the saying that the rich shall hardly enter into the kingdom of heaven we must understand its meaning in the spirit of learners, and not in any clumsy, boorish, or fleshly sense; for it was not thus that it was uttered.'

C. *The True Sense of the Saying, 'Sell whatever thou hast'*

§ 11. ' "Sell thy belongings." What does this mean? It is not, as some too readily interpret it, a command to get rid of what belongs to you, and to abandon your property: it is a command to banish from your mind the opinions you have held about property, your feeling for it, your excess of desire, your feverish and diseased worries about it, all the cares and thorns of human existence which choke the seed of life.[1] There is nothing great or enviable in merely being without property, regarded in itself and apart from any consideration of finding life. If there were, then those who have nothing of any sort—those who are helpless and beg for their daily bread; the paupers thrown on the roads, ignorant of God and the righteousness of God—would, merely by being absolutely destitute and in want of the most elementary necessities, be more blessed and dearer to God than all others, and would alone have hold on eternal life.

Nor, again, is it anything new[2] that a man should renounce his wealth and bestow it on the poor or on his country; many have done that before the days of the coming of the Saviour, some to gain leisure for speeches[3] and to acquire dead wisdom, and others for empty reputation and vainglory—men such as Anaxagoras, Democritus, and the Cynic Crates. . . .

§ 12. 'If the "new creation", the Son of God, reveals and teaches something peculiar and special, the commandment given is not the doing of an external act [the word used in the Greek is the philosophical term *phainomenon*], such as others have already done: it is a commandment to do something different which is symbolized by this act—something greater, more divine, and more perfect—and that is to empty the soul and the spirit of the passions that lie in their recesses, and to cut out by the roots and cast away all alien elements from the mind. This is the lesson peculiar to the faithful, and the teaching worthy of the Saviour.[4] . . .'

[1] By life (*zoē*) Clement may be taken to mean true life—spiritual life—life eternal.

[2] New, in the sense of belonging to the 'new creation' of which Clement speaks.

[3] Perhaps Clement means by this word (*logoi*) the orations of the period of the Second Sophistic, or the preachings of the Cynics.

[4] The 'lesson' is stated succinctly by Clement in a later passage: 'it is no gain to a man to be poor in possessions when he is rich in passions' (§ 15).

D. *The Uses of Wealth*

§ 13. 'How much more useful [than the renunciation of wealth] is the opposite line of action—that a man should have a sufficiency of acquired property, and thus at once be free from the effort and distress of acquisition and able to help those whom it is meet that he should? What sharing would be left in the world if nobody had anything,[1] and how could this doctrine be regarded as other than clearly opposed to, and even at war with, other fine doctrines of our Lord? . . . How could a man feed the hungry, give drink to the thirsty, clothe the naked, and take in the homeless . . . if all were themselves, to begin with, in want of all these things?

§ 14. 'We must not, therefore, renounce the wealth which benefits our neighbours too, as well as ourselves. . . . Acquisitions are things which have been acquired [by some effort]; wealth is what promotes well-being and is furnished by God for the welfare of man. It is the setting aside, and the laying down as a foundation, of something which is in the nature of a material to be handled, or of tools to be employed, for good uses by those who have knowledge. A tool, if you use it in a workmanlike manner, is something workmanlike: if you are a poor workman, it suffers from your clumsiness; but it is not to be blamed for that. Wealth, too, is just such a tool. You can use it rightly, and then it ministers to the cause of what is right; or you can use it wrongly, and then it is found to be a minister of wrong.'[2]

E. *On Having and Giving*

§ 26. 'What wrong does a man do if, by taking thought and by saving, he has gathered enough to live upon before becoming a believer? Or what again are we to say if—and this is even more irreproachable—he was placed from the first by God, who is the

---

[1] Aristotle, in criticizing Plato's scheme for the abolition of private property among the guardians of his ideal State, raises the same difficulty: under it 'no man can show himself liberal, or indeed do a liberal act; for the function of liberality consists in the proper use which is made of property' (*Politics*, II. v, § 10).

[2] Here again Clement agrees with, and almost seems to follow, Aristotle. In book I of the *Politics*, c. viii, § 15, Aristotle argues that all arts need tools, and goes on to state that 'wealth may be defined as a number of instruments used in a household or state' and needed for the arts they practise.

Giver of all good things, in a household of men of substance, and born as the member of a family blessed with an abundance of property and all the influence of wealth? If a man is banished from the life to come by the mere fact of being born willy-nilly in wealth, he suffers wrong, rather than does it, at the hands of God who made him, by being held worthy of temporary pleasures but deprived of eternal life. Why should wealth ever have sprung from the earth, if it be but the provider and patron of death?'

§ 31. But if it be right to possess private property, it is also right, and indeed a duty, to use it for the common benefit. 'When Jesus said, "Make to yourselves friends from the mammon of unrighteousness, that when it shall fail they may receive you into the eternal habitations", he taught two lessons. On the one hand He showed that all property is "unrighteous" when a man keeps it to himself as his own private possession, and does not bring it into a common fund for those who are in need; on the other hand he also showed that from this very "unrighteousness" it was also possible to do a righteous and saving act—the giving of relief to one of those who have an "eternal habitation" with the Father. Mark—He does not command you to wait to be asked or solicited: he bids you seek out for yourselves those who are to be helped and who are worthy followers of the Saviour.

§ 34. 'Do therefore the opposite of the rest of mankind: enlist [by your charity] an army of your own which bears no arms and wages no war—an army free from bloodshed, or anger, or any stain—an army of God-fearing old men, of orphans dear to God, of widows whose arms are gentle thoughts, of men whose equipment is love of their brethren. Use your wealth to acquire, for your body and your soul, guards of this order with God for their captain. So your ship, though it be buffeted, will none the less ride lightly, steered upon its way only by the prayers of saints.'

§ 41. To this end the rich need a guide or confessor to aid the distribution of their charity. 'It is therefore in every way necessary that you, with your magnificence and power and wealth, should set over yourself some man of God to be your trainer and pilot. If it be only one man, do him reverence none the less; fear him; practise yourself in giving heed to him when he speaks to you boldly and deals with you harshly even in the act of serving you.'

Note 1. The last two paragraphs point the way forward to the policy and action of the later Church (especially the Church of the Middle Ages) in its organization of a system of charity and its encouragement of ecclesiastical endowments (ensuring the 'prayers of saints'), and again in its clerical guidance of the benefactions of kings and nobles.

Note 2. Clement not only dealt in his writings with the general problems of the acquisition and use of wealth: he also handled, in his *Paidagōgos*, the problems of social behaviour in ordinary daily life—clothes and furniture, feasts and dances, table manners, and the general decencies. Here again, as in his pamphlet on riches, he is writing 'for the wealthy and educated', accustomed to 'the style of living of the upper ten thousand in the rich commercial city of Alexandria' (Lietzmann, *The Founding of the Church Universal*, Eng. trans., p. 286).

§ VI. CELSUS: ON POLYTHEISM VERSUS MONOTHEISM

Passages from the 'True Reason' (Alēthēs Logos), *a defence of the diversity of many 'national' religious societies, as against the Jewish and Christian belief in one universal religious society*

The passages are quoted by Origen, the Christian Father and philosopher of the first half of the third century A.D., in his *Contra Celsum*, a work of Christian apology which cites and answers the arguments of Celsus at length in its eight books. Celsus himself, who is only known from the quotations of Origen, is an obscure but notable figure. He may have lived and written about A.D. 180; he may possibly have lived in Rome, as is suggested by his final appeal to Christians for co-operation with the Roman Empire (see p. 434 below), or—more probably—he may have lived in Alexandria, the home of Origen, as is suggested by his knowledge of Egypt and of the theology both of the Hellenistic Judaism and the Christianity of that country. In any case he was a thinker of cogency and power, who states the case for polytheism in terms of a reasoned philosophy. Origen seems to suggest that he was an Epicurean, but the quotations which he gives from the

True Reason show no trace of Epicureanism, and it has been suggested that he was an eclectic Platonist of the type of the middle Academy (H. M. Chadwick's Introduction to his translation of Origen's *Contra Celsum*).[1] In any case he was a worthy foe of Origen, who—writing some seventy years after the publication of his *True Reason*—treats his arguments with courtesy and respect.

A. *The Jews, professing Monotheism, are really a 'nation'*
(ethnos) like other nations, and their God is one of the national
gods in a world of polytheism[2]

1. *The claim of the Jews* (quoted in *Contra Celsum*, I. 24). 'The goatherds and shepherds [who followed their leader Moses] thought of [only] *one* God, whether he was called the Highest, or Adonai, or the Heavenly One, or Sabaoth, or however and in whatever way they liked to name [the creator of] this universe *(cosmos)*; and they knew nothing more.'

2. *The fact about the Jews* (ibid. v. 25). 'The Jews became a distinctive nation *(ethnos idion)* and enacted laws to suit the character of their country; they still, down to the present day, observe these laws among themselves; and they preserve a form of worship which, whatever else it may be, is at any rate traditional. In this they act just like the rest of mankind; for each and every group follows its own traditional ways, whatever may be the kind of ways that may happen to be established in it. This, it would seem, comes about for two reasons: first, because it occurred to the minds of different peoples to entertain different thoughts, and because men ought to preserve the ways established and sanctioned for their community; and secondly, because it is reasonable to believe that the different parts of the earth were assigned from the beginning to different "overseers" *(epoptai)*, and because, being thus distributed in distinct provinces, they are accordingly governed on that basis. Indeed the management of the affairs of each nation will be right and proper if it is conducted on that

---

[1] It has been suggested that Celsus copied, or followed, a Platonic textbook of the period: Gercke–Norden, *Einleitung in die Altertumswissenschaft*, vol. i. 3, p. 118.
[2] This and the following passages are translated from Lommatzsch's edition of the works of Origen.

basis, as they [i.e. the 'overseers'] would like it to be done; and it is an act of impiety to neglect the ways which have been observed from the first in each locality.' To this Origen replies, ibid. VII. lxix, that the gods or 'overseers' of the nations are daemons, evil daemons, who have fallen away from God and keep the law of sin.

> B. *The Christians, also professing Monotheism and basing themselves on the principle that it is impossible for the same man to serve more than one master, (a) misinterpret that principle, (b) produce a division, a state of sedition or stasis, by setting themselves up against the order and system of different 'national' religious societies under different 'overseers', and (c) are inconsistent with themselves in worshipping more than one God and acknowledging a Trinity*

1. *The Christian misinterpretation of the principle that the same man cannot serve more than one master* (quoted in *Contra Celsum*, VIII. 2). 'The Christians argue that it is not possible for the same man to "serve" more than one "Lord". This . . . is the voice of sedition, of men who . . . wall themselves up and cut themselves off from the rest of mankind. Those who say this are transferring and attaching, so far as they can, their own feeling to God [by making Him as limited as themselves]. It is indeed true that *in the sphere of human affairs* the man who serves one person cannot reasonably serve another man too, since the first person served is injured by the service done to the other; nor could a man who had first pledged himself to one person [in *that* sphere] pledge himself also to another, because he would injure by doing so the person to whom he first pledged himself; and it is thus reasonable that service should not be simultaneously rendered to different "heroes" and other such "daemons".[1] But *so far as concerns God*, who cannot be directly affected by any injury or pain, it is irrational . . . to be so much on one's guard against worshipping more than one God, as one ought to be against serving more than one man, or "hero" or other such "daemon". The man who

---

[1] The assumption seems to be made that 'heroes' and other such 'daemons' belong to the 'sphere of human affairs'.

worships more than one god is worshipping thereby [on each particular occasion] some one particular attribute of the great God, and therefore he does that which is dear to Him even in the very act [of worshipping many gods]. Nor . . . is it possible for any being to be so honoured, to whom this right has not been granted by Him; and therefore a person who knows and worships *all* forms of being that belong to Him does no injury to the God to whom they all belong.'

2. *The Christian guilty of causing sedition or schism in the comity of the system of different 'natural' religious societies* (ibid. VIII. 11). 'Moreover, the man who asserts, when he is speaking of God, that one only has been called the Lord, is guilty of impiety in dividing the Kingdom of God against itself, and thus stirring up sedition; for this is a heresy,[1] and it implies the existence of some other person who stands in opposition to the man who makes the assertion.' Here Celsus implies that the 'Kingdom of God' is a system of the peaceful coexistence of many 'ethnic' or national gods, each traditional and each suiting the character of a country, but all equally forms, or 'attributes', 'of the one great God'.[2]

3. *The inconsistency of the Christians* (ibid. VIII. 12). 'If these [the Christians] had worshipped no other God but one, they would perhaps have had a valid argument against the rest of the world. But as it is they pay an excess of worship to this man [Jesus] who has recently appeared, and yet they think that they do no wrong to God if His servant also be worshipped by them.' To this Origen replies by quoting the text, 'I and my Father are one'.

c. *Christianity and the Roman Empire*

1. *The duty of obedience to the Emperor* (*Contra Celsum*, VIII. 68). 'One ought not to disbelieve the poet of old [Homer] who

---

[1] A 'heresy' is a *hairesis*, a 'choice' of a particular and partial view. In the view of Celsus it is a 'heresy' to assert that only your own particular God is the Lord, because thereby you set your own particular 'choice' in opposition to the gods of others, and thus divide the Kingdom of God (which has many 'mansions' or aspects of deity) against itself.

[2] In the same way Porphyry, the disciple of Plotinus, in a work *Against the Christians*, attacked them for despising 'ancestral traditions' and choosing 'a new and unique way which had no national basis' (Lietzmann, *From Constantine to Julian*, Eng. trans., p. 44).

proclaimed long ago the maxim, "Let there be one master, one king." . . . If you Christians reject this maxim, the emperor may reasonably punish you. For if all of us were to act as you do, there would be nothing to prevent him from being left solitary and desolate; nothing to prevent the affairs of this world from falling into the hands of the most lawless and savage barbarians; nothing to prevent the memory both of your worship and of our "true reason" from disappearing from men's ken.'

2. *The Christian dream of a concord of all men under one law impossible* (ibid. VIII. lxxii). 'Would that it were possible for the inhabitants of Asia, Europe, and Africa, both Greek and barbarian, to be united in the concord of one law. . . . But the man who thinks this has no knowledge.' The wish expressed by Celsus may be his own wish, which he at once confesses to be impossible; but it seems more likely that it is a wish which he attributes to the Christians and proceeds to reject as the fruit of pure ignorance. Origen, in reply to Celsus, argues (1) that the Roman Empire, by uniting the world in peace from the days of Augustus onward, had made it ready for the coming of Christ[1] and for the universal diffusion of Christianity (II. xxx. 1, quoted below on p. 439), and (2) that Christianity is already winning its way to universal acceptance. But on this latter point he wavers, sometimes saying that 'communities of Christians are congregated in all the world' and sometimes confessing that Christians are only 'gathered in scattered bodies out of each of the nations'; see above, p. 422 note.

3. *An appeal to Christians to serve the Empire.* At the end of the 'True Reason' Celsus seeks to enlist the Christians in the service of the Roman Empire. He exhorts them (*Contra Celsum*, VIII. lxxiii) 'to help the emperor with all their strength; to labour with him to do what is right; to fight on his behalf, to be fellow-soldiers with him if he so desire, and to be his fellow-generals'. He encourages them also (ibid. lxxv) 'to take part in the government of their fatherland, if that should be their duty in order to ensure the keeping of the laws and the observance of piety'. Origen's reply to this exhortation and encouragement is quoted below, p. 442.

---

[1] This is an argument developed at length by Eusebius; see below, pp. 475-7.

§ VII. ORIGEN

Introduction

Origen, the greatest of the Greek apologists for the Christian religion, was born in Egypt of Christian parents about the year 180. Educated in Alexandria, he was fortunate in his studies: on the one hand he attended (as did also Plotinus) the lectures of Ammonius Saccas, the nursing father of Neoplatonism, and he thus became the first Christian thinker and writer to enter into the genuine tradition of the Platonic school;[1] on the other hand, he was also, according to the account given by Eusebius, a pupil of Clement of Alexandria, the leader of the Christian school for catechumens in Egypt, and he quickly became first a teacher, and then (by A.D. 203) the leader, of that school. He was thus, as Clement had been before him, a bridge of connexion between Greek philosophy and Christian theology; but he was even more of a bridge than his master. For a dozen years, and down to the age of 30, he taught and wrote in Alexandria; but after the massacres perpetrated in that city on the orders of the emperor (the 'fury of Caracalla'), he withdrew to Caesarea, the political capital of Palestine, where he mainly lived[2] and worked until his death, at the age of over 70, about the year 255.

He was the most remarkable figure, and the greatest thinker and scholar, in the Church of the East. One of his most famous works, preserved in the original Greek, is the eight books of the *Contra Celsum*, an answer (written about 248) to the attack made on Christianity by the Platonist Celsus, some eighty years before, in his *Alēthēs Logos*. Most of his writings, however, and among them his many commentaries on the books of the Old and the New Testament, are preserved only in Latin translations. In addition to his *Contra Celsum* and his commentaries (which alone are represented in the passages that follow), two other achievements of Origen deserve, or rather demand, some mention. The

---

[1] Lietzmann, *The Foundation of the Church Universal*, Eng. trans., p. 298. Lietzmann's general account of Origen (pp. 295–317) is full and sympathetic.

[2] He returned to Alexandria, at the request of its bishop, some time after 215; but he was forced to leave it again—by the bishop's orders and on a point of ecclesiastical discipline—in 231, when he settled once more in Caesarea to teach and write, and to collect a library, during the next quarter of a century.

first is the *Hexapla*, the first and one of the greatest of all works of Biblical criticism, setting out in six parallel columns (whence its name) six different texts of the Old Testament, of which two were in Hebrew (but the second of these in Hebrew transliterated into Greek characters), and the remaining four (including the text of the Septuagint) in Greek. This took some fifteen years of his life (from about 230 to 245), and it was, in itself, a work of scholarship and research sufficient for a lifetime. But Origen also achieved a second and even more remarkable work—a statement of Christian doctrine (written before he finally left Alexandria in 231, and therefore prior to the *Hexapla*) entitled *Peri Archōn* or *De Principiis*. This is a remarkable, indeed an astonishing, attempt to construct the foundations of a system of thought which united the philosophy of Platonism with the revelation of God in the Scriptures as allegorically interpreted on the method already followed by Philo—and indeed followed even before Philo by Greek philosophers (and especially the Stoics) in their interpretation of Homer. Unfortunately this work of Origen, though fragments of the original Greek survive, is only preserved in its full form in Rufinus' translation (made about A.D. 400) which sought to adjust the argument to the demands of orthodoxy. We have lost much of the original version, and we can only deplore our loss.[1]

Something has already been said, in the introduction to a previous section, about the work of Clement of Alexandria in building a bridge between Greek *ratio* and Christian *fides*. But Clement was not the first, as he was not the last, to set his hand to this work; and it may be permissible here, in connexion with the greatest of all the thinkers who attempted to be bridge-builders between ancient Greece and the 'New Creation', to look back to the beginning of the attempt and forward to its close. Justin Martyr was one of the earliest of the 'apologists' who sought to commend the *philosophia Christi* to the disciples of Greek philosophy. 'A genuine lover of true philosophy' (the phrase is that of Eusebius[2]), he had spent his time in the arduous

---

[1] Lietzmann, op. cit., pp. 305–12, summarizes the argument of the *De Principiis*.
[2] *Historia Ecclesiastica*, IV. viii. 3.

study of the thought of Greece until he was converted to the Christian faith (*circa* A.D. 135). Settling in Rome—he had been born in Samaria—he addressed an apology for the faith which he had adopted to the Emperor Antoninus Pius (138–61). He admits, in the course of his argument,[1] that the thinkers of Greece (he refers particularly to Plato and the Stoics) had seen, 'through a part of the seminal divine Word', something akin to the Christian doctrine, and so far had discoursed rightly; he goes on to claim that 'whatever all men have uttered aright belongs to us Christians', in virtue of each Christian's worship and love of the Word incarnate in Christ; and thus he reaches the balanced conclusion that 'all writers, through the seed of the Word which was planted in them, were able to see the truth [though they could see it but] darkly; for the seed and imitation of a thing, which is given according to [man's] capability, is one thing, and the thing itself, of which the communication and imitation are given according to His grace, is another'.

In a similar sense, Clement of Alexandria (who, like Justin, had learned much at the feet of Greek teachers before he settled in Alexandria and joined the Catechumen School) also regarded the philosophy of Greece as a preparation for the Christian gospel. In his *Stromateis*, or 'Miscellanies' (*circa* A.D. 200), he admits—much as Justin had done half a century before—that 'philosophy was necessary to the Greeks for righteousness'. In comparison with the Scriptures and the sovereign revelation which they give, it is only a secondary gift; but 'perchance philosophy was given to the Greeks directly, and primarily, till the Lord should call the Greeks; for this was "a schoolmaster to bring" the Hellenic mind, as the Law was to bring the Hebrew, "to Christ" '. Philosophy, therefore, was a preparation, paving the way for him who is 'perfect in Christ'.[2]

Origen, whether or no he was actually a pupil of Clement (the statement of Eusebius has been doubted), followed and carried farther the line of Clement's teaching. In a homily on the Book

[1] *Apology*, II. xiii. 2–6 (quoted in *Documents illustrative of the History of the Church*, edited by B. J. Kidd, vol. i, p. 79).
[2] *Stromateis*, I. v, § 28, quoted in the *Documents* cited above, p. 159.

of Genesis he seeks to explain the relation of philosophy and Christianity. 'Philosophy is neither at variance with the law of God at all points, nor in harmony with it at all. Many philosophers write of the one God as having created all things. On this point they are at one with the law of God. Some go so far as to add that God made and rules all things by His Word, and that it is the Word of God by whom all things are ordered. In this they write what is agreeable not only to the law but to the Gospel as well. Moral and, as it is called, physical philosophy take the same view as we do, at most points.' But Origen notes four points on which philosophers differ from Christians—in their view of matter as co-eternal with God; in affirming that God takes no interest in the affairs of mortal men; in making the lives of men dependent on the stars in their courses (i.e. believing in astrology, as the Stoics tended to do); and in asserting that this world is eternal.[1]

It is curious to note that Tertullian, writing in the West and in Latin at the same time that Origen was writing in Greek for the East (A.D. 200), takes a very different view. In his *De Praescriptione Haereticorum* he treats philosophy as the mother of heresy, and traces the various heresies of his age to their origin in this or that school of philosophy—Platonism, Stoicism, or Epicureanism. He even apostrophizes the 'wretched Aristotle, who established . . . the dialectic art so ingenious in the construction and refutation [of propositions]'.[2] But Tertullian was a spasmodic and volcanic thinker, not greatly troubled by the need of consistency; and in his *Apologeticus* addressed to the magistrates of the Roman Empire he can argue that the doctrine of the *Logos* taught by the philosophers has its affinities with the Christian doctrine of the Word (see below, p. 446). Yet on the whole his main feeling is expressed in the question he raises, 'What has Jerusalem to do with Athens?'; and generally the Latin West (except for St. Augustine, who had studied Neoplatonism) eschewed the tradition which had begun with Justin Martyr and culminated in Origen.

[1] Homily on Genesis, xiv, § 3, quoted in the *Documents* cited above, p. 182.
[2] *De praescriptione haereticorum*, c. 7, quoted in the *Documents* cited above, p. 145.

A. *On Christianity and the Unity of the Roman Empire*

From the *Contra Celsum* (as edited by Lommatzsch), ii. 30. 'Celsus writes, "As the sun, which illuminates all other things, begins by revealing itself, so should the Son of God also have revealed Himself." We should say in answer, This is what He has actually done. In His days righteousness arose and shone, and there came about an abundance of peace, beginning from the time of His birth, when God was making the nations ready for His teaching; for then He so ordered the world that the nations should all be under the one emperor (*basileūs*) of Rome, and thus He prevented it from coming to pass—through the nations not mingling with one another by reason of the existence of many different kingdoms—that the apostles should find it more difficult to do what Jesus commanded them, saying, "Go ye, therefore, and teach all nations." It is manifest that Jesus was born in the reign of Augustus, the ruler who, if I may use the phrase, levelled together under His one kingship the many inhabitants of the earth. Now it would have been a hindrance to the spread of the teaching of Jesus through all the world if there had been many kingdoms, and this not only for the reason already given, but also because men everywhere would have been compelled to do military service and to fight for their different countries. That was what actually happened, just before the days of Augustus, and had happened even earlier still, when occasions arose for hostilities between Sparta and Athens, or between other contending powers. How, then, could it have been possible for this peaceable teaching, which does not even allow men to take vengeance on their enemies, ever to win the day, unless the whole of the world had been everywhere changed for the better and gentler by the sojourning of Jesus in it?'

The argument here advanced by Origen was an argument which had already been used by an earlier Christian writer. Melito, Bishop of Sardis in Asia Minor, had addressed an *Apology* to Marcus Aurelius, about the year 170, which is quoted by Eusebius in his *Ecclesiastical History*.[1] 'Our philosophy', he had argued, 'first flourished among the barbarians [? the Jews], but

---

[1] *Hist. Eccl.* IV. xxvi, §§ 7–8.

it reached its flower for your peoples in the great reign of your ancestor, Augustus, and it became a blessing of good omen to your empire in a special degree; for it is from that time that the power of Rome has grown in magnitude and splendour. You are the happy successor of Augustus, and will continue so to be . . . if you protect the philosophy which was nourished along with the Empire and began its life with Augustus. Your ancestors honoured it in addition to other forms of worship; and the strongest proof that our doctrine has flourished, for the good of mankind, along with the empire thus happily begun, is to be found in the fact that no misfortune has happened ever since the days of Augustus.' The argument of Melito is adopted and continued by Origen; and in the form in which it is expounded by Origen it passes in turn to Eusebius (see below, pp. 474-6). The view thus comes to be cherished that 'Church and Empire were in the providence of God ordained . . . to co-operate: Augustus and Christ were both the bringers of peace to a disturbed world.'[1]

B. *The Two Commonwealths: the Assembly of the Faithful and the Assemblies of the World*

iii. 30. 'The church (*ecclēsia*) of God, let us say in Athens, is quiet and steadfast, as wishing to please God who is over all things; but the assembly—also called an *ecclēsia*—of the *people* of Athens is full of discord, and in no way comparable to the Church of God in Athens.[2] The same is true of the church of God in Corinth and the assembly of the people of Corinth; and it is also true, we may say, of the church of God in Alexandria and the assembly of the people of Alexandria. If the man who listens to these words is reasonable, and will examine the facts in the spirit of a lover of truth, he will marvel at those who planned, and were able to bring to pass, the establishment everywhere of churches of God, living side by side with assemblies of the people in each city. Similarly, if you compared the Council [i.e. the college of presbyters] of

[1] N. H. Baynes in the *Cambridge Ancient History*, vol. xii, p. 661.

[2] The word *ecclēsia*, used by Christian writers to denote the religious assembly or congregation of the faithful, had been used long before to denote the political assembly of the citizens of a Greek *polis*. Origen, noting the identity of the word, seeks to explain the difference of the things denoted by it.

the church of God with the Council [i.e. the *Boulē* or Senate] of any city, you would find that some of the councillors of the church are worthy, if there be such a thing as a city of God for the whole of the world, to join in the government of that city; but the councillors of the people, in all the cities of men, have nothing in their behaviour or manners worthy of the superior position which they seem to hold among their fellows. In the same way, again, you have only to compare the ruler of the church [i.e. the bishop] in each city with the ruler [i.e., the body of magistrates] of the people inhabiting the city, in order to see that—even among the councillors and rulers of the church of God who fall far short of the mark, and live a life of indolence in comparison with the truly zealous—there can none the less be traced, on the whole and in the main, a real superiority, a superiority in progress towards the attainment of virtue, when they are measured against the behaviour and manners of the councillors and rulers who are to be found in these cities.'

The notion of the two different commonwealths (the *ecclesia Dei* and the *civitas mundi*) recurs in a later passage of Origen's work which comes in the eighth book. After defending the Christian objection to the duty of military service (cc. 73–74), and pleading that 'Christians do more good to their fatherland than other men, by educating their fellow citizens, and teaching them to do honour to the God of the Universe, thus raising up those who have lived a good life in the least of cities into a divine city in the heavens', he turns to the contention of Celsus that men owe a political as well as a military duty to the State (viii. c. 75). 'Celsus also exhorts us "to take part in the government of our fatherland, if it should be our duty to do so in order to ensure the keeping of the laws and the observance of piety".[1] But we Christians, knowing that in every city there is another order of fatherland (*systēma patridos*), founded by the Word of God, summon to the government of our churches those who are strong in judgement and lead a healthy life, not accepting those who are ambitious for office, but compelling those to serve who, owing to the moderation of their

[1] See above, p. 434.

temper, are reluctant to take on hastily the duty of sharing in the common care for the Church of God. So those of us who make good governors of the Church are governors perforce, compelled thereto by the great King, whom we believe to be the Son of God, God the [incarnate] Word. And if the rulers in the Church are good rulers, bearing the name of leaders of the fatherland that is after the order of God—by which I mean the Church; if, in other words, they rule according to the commandments of God, they suffer no molestation for that reason from the positive law [i.e. the law of the State]. It is not because they wish to escape the common duties of life that Christians avoid things of that order; it is because they seek to reserve themselves for the most divine and most necessary duty of the service (liturgy) of the Church, to the end of men's salvation.'

c. The Two Laws

v. 37. 'There are therefore two types of law set before us: one of them being the law of nature, which is such as God would enact, and the other the written law of cities. Where the written law is not opposed to the law of God, it is good that citizens should not forsake it on the plea that such written rules are foreign to them. But where the law of nature, that is to say God's law, ordains what is opposed to the written law, look and see if the Word will not say to thee, "Bid farewell to what is written and to the will of law-givers; give thyself to God the law-giver, and choose to live according to His Word, even if it be necessary to do so at the price of danger and countless troubles and ill-repute." For when the things which are pleasing to God differ from the things which satisfy some of the laws of the State, and when it is impossible to please both God and the men who reverence such laws, it would be a strange thing if we despised the actions by which men please the Creator of the Universe and chose instead the actions by which we are displeasing to God and pleasing only to laws which are no laws and to the friends of those laws. But if in things generally it is right to prefer the law of nature, which is the law of God, to written laws enacted by men contrary to the law of God, is not this all the more a duty in the matter of laws concerned with the worship of God?'

Origen proceeds to give examples, drawn from Egypt and Arabia and Ethiopia, of laws or customs concerned with religious worship which Christians will not accept. They will not, as all the Egyptians do, recognize Osiris and Isis as gods; they will not follow the younger generation of the people of Naucratis, and adore the newfangled god Sarapis, who had been invented by one of the early Ptolemies. This mention of the new god Sarapis reminds Origen that Jesus Himself was in one sense 'new'—and yet also the 'ancient of days'. He therefore concludes the chapter at a tangent, forgetting his theme of the two laws. 'The Son of God,' he writes, 'the first-born of all creatures, even if He seemed to have been newly made man, is in no wise therefore new. The Holy Scriptures know that He is the oldest of all creation, and that God said to Him, speaking of the creation of man, "Let Us make man in Our image, after Our likeness." '

D. Origen's Commentary on St. Paul's View of Secular Government

(*Commentarii in Epistulam ad Romanos*, book IX, cc. 26–27)

c. 26. 'Let us now see what the Apostle adds next: "Let every soul be in subjection to the higher powers." Here St. Paul seems to me most praiseworthy in speaking of the soul (Latin *anima* and Greek *psychē*) as the element which he would have in subjection to the powers.[1] He would never have said, "Let every *spirit* be in subjection to power', but only "every *soul*". Of this difference I have often spoken before, explaining that man is sometimes named by the word "soul", sometimes by the word "flesh" (the Greek *sarx* and the Latin *caro*), and sometimes by the word "spirit". When he is to be named from his better part, and to be understood as a being of a spiritual order, he is called

---

[1] In the common usage of Christian writers (as of Stoic writers before them) the 'soul' or *psychē* is the power of life in all 'animate' things (animals as well as man), and is, as such, lower than the 'spirit' or *pneuma* which is the breath of God in man, and, as such, is often regarded (for instance in the Book of Wisdom), as synonymous with Wisdom (*Sophia*) or the Word (*Logos*).

"spirit"; when he is to be named from his lower part, he is called "soul"; when he is to be named from his worse, he is called "flesh"; and we have often produced proofs of this from the Scriptures. In the present passage the Apostle, since he is concerned to lay down rules for believers, wishes us to preserve, so far as in us lies, quiet and peace in the course of our present life on earth. Now if we are such as to be united with God, and thereby to be one *spirit* with Him, we are said to be in subjection to God. But if we are not yet such, and if there is that common element of *soul* still present in us which has in it something of this world and is bound thereto by some tie of business, the Apostle lays down rules for it and says that it should be subject to the powers of the world; because the Lord also said that those who have in themselves the superscription of Caesar should render unto Caesar the things that are Caesar's (Matthew xxii. 21). Peter and John had nothing to render to Caesar; for Peter says, "Silver and gold have I none". He who has no silver or gold has nothing to render to Caesar, nor any cause for being in subjection to the higher powers. But as for those who have money or possessions, or anything set in the world of business, let *them* listen to the saying, "Let every soul be in subjection to the higher powers".

c. 26. ' "For there is", he says, "no power but of God." Some man may rejoin, "What follows? Can even a power which persecutes the servants of God, attacks the faith, and overturns religion, be a power that comes from God?' We will answer the objection briefly. There is no man but knows that sight and hearing and sense are given to us by God. But having these things from God, we have it in our power, none the less, to use the gift of sight for good or for evil; and the same is true of hearing, and of the movement of our hands, and of the thought of our mind; and herein we give cause for the just judgement of God, when we abuse the gifts which He gave us for good uses and employ them instead for impious and wicked purposes. In the same way all power is likewise given by God "for vengeance on evil-doers, and for praise to them that do well" (1 Peter ii. 14), as the same Apostle, St. Paul, also says in the words that follow (Romans xiii. 3–4). But there will be a just judgement of God upon those who exercise the power which they have received from Him according to their own impious purposes, and not according to the divine law.

c. 27. 'That is why St. Paul says, "Therefore he that resisteth the power withstandeth the ordinance of God; and they that withstand shall receive to themselves judgement." He does not speak here of the powers which inflict persecution on the faith, for of them we must say to ourselves, "We must obey God rather than men" (Acts v. 29); but he speaks of the ordinary powers, "which are not a terror to the good work, but to the evil" (Romans xiii. 3); for if men resist *those* powers, they receive to themselves judgement according to the nature of their deeds.'

c. 28. Origen then comments on the saying of St. Paul (Romans xiii. 4) that a ruler is 'a minister of God, an avenger for wrath to him that doeth evil'. He is moved, he says, by this saying; and he accordingly seeks to explain how 'judges of this world' can be called 'ministers of God'. He argues that the Church deals only by its rules with matters of its own discipline and order; and he cites as an example the 'Apostolic Decree' set forth in Acts xv. 23–29, charging the Christians to whom it is directed to 'abstain from things sacrificed to idols, and from blood, and from things strangled, and from fornication'. 'Note herein', he comments, 'the method of ordaining by the Holy Spirit; for since offences other than these are punished by the laws of this world, and it seemed a matter of superfluity that acts already sufficiently punished by human law should now be prohibited by divine law, the decree touches only those acts on which human law had made no pronouncement, and which seemed to belong to the sphere of religion. Hereby it is plain that the judge of this world executes most of the law of God; for God hath willed that all the offences which by His will are subject to punishment should be punished by the judge of this world, and not by the heads and leaders of churches; and Paul, being aware of this, rightly calls him the "minister of God, and an avenger . . . to him that doeth evil".'

§ VIII. TERTULLIAN

Introduction

Tertullian was born at Carthage *circa* A.D. 160. Trained in rhetoric and in law, he became a vehement apologist and protagonist of Christianity, and helped to give the Christianity of the West the distinctive form which separated it from the Greek Christianity of Alexandria and the East. He was a vivid writer, of African ardour, and, though he was often carried away by his rhetoric and satirical power, he founded the tradition of the African Church which was afterwards continued by Lactantius (*circa* 250–320) and culminated in the life and writings of St. Augustine (354–430). He has even been called the founder of the theology and the language of Western Christianity; but he has also been given such diverse titles as 'a barbarizing Tacitus' and a 'Christian Juvenal'. He was certainly the master of a remarkable, if difficult, Latinity; and if he was not a philosopher he was certainly a thinker. He had an independent and original spirit of vigorous enthusiasm, which carried him eventually into a spiritual 'nonconformity' or 'methodism' of the Montanist order. The same vehemence led him to discard the Roman *toga* for the *pallium* worn by Greek philosophers (though he held the *pallium* to be the national garb of Carthage before her surrender to Rome); and his lively *De Pallio* is a vigorous defence of that garb. His chief work is the *Apologeticus*, a defence of Christianity addressed to the provincial magistrates who tried cases against Christians (written in A.D. 197); but his *De Spectaculis* (an attack on the theatre, or rather the amphitheatre), and especially its final chapter on the 'spectacle' of the last judgement, is also notable.

A. *On Christianity and Stoicism: the conception of the Logos*

Apologeticus, c. 21, § 10. 'We have already said that God created the whole of this universe by His Word, His Reason, and His Power. Your own philosophers [Tertullian is addressing the magistrates of the Roman Empire] are also agreed that the Logos— that is to say the Word and Reason [of God]—may be regarded as the artificer of the universe. It is defined by Zeno as the Creator, which has formed all things in their order; and he holds that it is also called "fate", and "God", and "the mind of Jove", and "the necessity which runs through all things" (the Greek *Heimarmenē*). Cleanthes gathers up all these designations in the conception of "spirit",[1] and he lays it down that this spirit pervades the Universal.

§ 11. 'But we Christians, too, in our view of the Word, the Reason, and the Power, by which we have said that God created all things—we, too, regard Spirit as being the true and proper foundation. In it, when it speaks to us, we find the Word; by its side, as it orders things, we feel Reason present; over it, as it achieves its purposes, we see Power enthroned. All this, we have been taught, proceeds from God; it is begotten, by the act of proceeding; and it is therefore [being begotten] called the "Son of God", as it is also called "God" by reason of being of the same substance with Him—for God too is spirit. § 12. When a ray comes forth from the sun, it is a part of the whole; but the sun will be in the ray, because it is a ray of the sun, and there is no separation of substance [when the ray comes forth from the sun] but rather an extension. So spirit, too, proceeds from spirit, and God from God, just as light is lit from light. The parent-stem of substance remains whole and undiminished, even if you borrow many properties or offshoots from it; (§ 13) so also what has proceeded from God is God and the Son of God, and both are one. So spirit proceeding from spirit, and God from God, the result is a double number, in point of measurement; but if there are two in degree or quantity, there are not two in condition or quality, and what has proceeded from the parent-stem, even if it has gone forth *from* it, has not gone *out* of it. This ray of God, as was always foretold in former times, entered into a certain virgin, and was made flesh in her womb, and was born a man mixed with God. That flesh, taught by the spirit, is nursed, grows up, speaks, teaches, acts . . . and is Christ.'

---

[1] *Spiritus*, the Greek *pneuma*, means literally 'breath'; it was the term used by philosophers (as it was also used by St. Paul) to denote the Breath or Spirit of God. On Cleanthes see above, pp. 36–38. On the conception of *pneuma*, and its relation to the conception of *psychē*, see above, p. 443, n.

B. *On* Fides *and* Ratio, *or Christian Belief and Pagan Philosophy*

De Praescriptione Haereticorum, c. 7. 'St. Paul had been at Athens, and he knew, from the intercourse he had there, the human wisdom which pretends to be truth but is only a gloss, and which, moreover, is itself divided into heresies of its own by the multiplicity of its rival schools. What has Jerusalem to do with Athens (*Quid ergo Athenis et Hierosolymis?*), or the Church with the Academy; and what have Christians to do with heretics? *Our* instruction comes from the porch of Solomon,[1] who himself taught that "the Lord should be sought in simplicity of heart" (*Wisdom*, i. 1). So let those who have produced a Stoic or Platonic or dialectical form of Christianity look to it! We have no need of such painful inquiry, since the coming of Christ; no need of any researches, once the gospel has been preached.'

Apologeticus, c. 46. 'The truth to which the philosophers pretend in their enmity to us—though in fact they are mockers and corrupters who debase truth by their pretences, as being men who care but for glory—this truth we Christians seek under the stress of necessity, and show forth in its purity, as being concerned for our own salvation. . . . Our God is one whom every Christian workman finds and shows to others; and hence he assigns to Him, in fact as well [as in words], the whole sum of the attributes demanded by thought for the being of God—though Plato asserts [*Timaeus* 28c] that the maker of the universe is hard to find, and difficult, when he is found, to explain to others.'

De Testimonio Animae, c. 1. 'I call in a new testimony: . . . I call the soul of man. Stand thou, then, Soul, in the midst of us. . . . But I call thee not as thou art when thou hast been fashioned in schools, trained in libraries, and fed in the Attic "Academies" and "Porches" [i.e. in the tenets of Platonism and Stoicism], and when, so fed, thou art venting out to the world thy gathered wisdom. I summon thee as thou art when thou art simple and natural, unpolished, in thy native grain; I summon thee as thou art in the minds of

---

[1] The 'porch', or *stoa*, was the place in Athens in which Zeno the founder of Stoicism taught. Tertullian would substitute for it the porch of the Temple at Jerusalem, in which the Apostles of the early Church taught the people (Acts v. 12). But he seems here to contradict his own argument on pp. 446–7.

those who have only thee; [I summon thee, Soul,] in thy very self, from the cross-roads, the street, and the mill, in all the fullness of thy being. I need thy *inexperience*, for no man puts his trust in thy small store of experience. I demand from thee the knowledge thou bringest with thee to man—the notions thou hast learnt, either from thyself or from the author of thy being whoever he may be. Thou art not, to my knowledge, thyself a Christian; a Christian soul is not born, it is made. But Christians now implore thee to give thy witness—stranger to them though thou art—against thy friends [the philosophers], so that even in thy presence they may blush at their hatred of us, and their mockery of us, for believing things which *thou* art now convicted of having upon *thy* conscience.'

Ibid., c.5. 'He who does not regard these outpourings of the soul as Nature's own teaching—the silent treasuries of a consciousness coeval with the soul and inborn in it—will argue that the habit and, so to say, vice of speaking after this manner is [not an innate attribute, but] something caused and confirmed by the general dissemination, among the masses, of opinions drawn from published works. But the soul is undoubtedly prior to any written work; speech is prior to all books; sense is prior to the pen; and man himself is prior to the philosopher and the poet.'

c. *Christian Society in Tertullian's Time* (circa A.D. 200)

Apologeticus, c. 38, § 1. 'Ought not this society (*secta*) to be reckoned among legal associations (*licitae factiones*)? It attempts no such actions as those of which illegal associations are commonly suspected. § 2. If I am not mistaken, the reason for the prohibition of associations is concern for the maintenance of public order and a desire to prevent the State from being split into parties. That is a danger which might easily [if unchecked] have vexed public meetings of all sorts, and even public games, making them a prey to the rivalry and contention of party passions; and this all the more as men had already begun to turn the violence of such passions into a lucrative and mercenary business, and to make party a source of profit.[1] § 3. But we Christians are cold to all

---

[1] i.e. by selling its influence to the highest bidder who sought office or some other public emolument.

G g

such fiery passions for glory and renown; we have no need to combine; no concern is more foreign to us than public affairs and the State; we acknowledge one State only, in which all men are included, and that State is the Universe. . . .

c. 39, § 1. 'I will now set forth in my own words what our Christian society does. I have proved that it does no wrong: I will now show that it does good. We are a body (*corpus*) united by community of religious feeling, by unity of discipline, and by the bond of a common hope. § 2. We assemble in our meetings and gatherings with the object of approaching God as a single massed company; of encompassing Him in prayer with the petitions we offer. The violence which we do Him is pleasing to God. We pray for emperors, for their ministers, and for those who are set in authority; for the state of the world, for peace in our time, and for delaying of the latter end. § 3. We assemble in order to call the Holy Scriptures to remembrance, if so be that the nature of the present time compels us to warn men of the future, or to recall anything of the past to their minds; in any case we feed our faith by these holy words; we lift up our hope; we confirm our confidence, and yet, at the same time, we tighten our discipline by inculcating precepts of conduct upon our minds. In our meetings, too, we also gain by exhortations, rebukes, and godly censure. § 4. For the judgements here passed have all the greater weight, because they are made among men who are certain that God sees them; and it is a lively anticipation of the judgement to come when any man has so offended as to be put out of communion in prayer, in the congregation, and in all holy fellowship. Our presidents are the approved elders (*seniores*), who have attained this honour not for a price, but by their character; for nothing pertaining to God is bought for a price.

§ 5. 'Even if we have a treasury, of a kind, it is not made up of moneys paid in entrance-fees, as though religion were a matter of contract. Each member brings some modest contribution on a fixed day in the month, or on any day he chooses—but only if he wishes, and is able, to do so; for no man is constrained, but each man gives freely. These contributions are, as it were, the funds of a bank of piety; (§ 6) they are not spent on dinners and wine-parties, or at thankless eating-houses, but on feeding and burying the poor, on boys and girls who have no money and no relatives, on servants in their old age and shipwrecked sailors; so, too, men condemned to the mines or the islands,[1] or to prison, become the pensioners of their confession, provided that [they have been so condemned] for belonging to the company of God. . . .

§ 11. 'So we, who are united with one another in our minds and our lives (*animo animaque*), have no doubts about sharing *things* with one another. All things are in common among us, save that we have no community of wives. . . . § 14. What wonder, then, if our mutual charity expresses itself in a common meal? . . . § 16. Our meal shows its nature in its very name: it is called by the Greek name for love [*agapē*]. Whatever it may cost, we gain by incurring the cost in the cause of piety; for we help the poor man [and not, as the world does, the parasite] with the refreshment we give.

c. 42, § 1. 'We are said to be useless to the community in the affairs of daily life (*in negotiis*). How can that be the case with men who live by your side, eat the same food, wear the same dress, use the same furniture, and have all the same necessities of life? We are not Brahmins or Indian fakirs (*gymnosophistae*) or men of the woods or exiles from life. § 2. We remember that we owe thanks to God, the Lord, the Creator; we reject none of the fruits of His works: we simply school ourselves not to use them in excess, or in the wrong way. We do not renounce your forum, your meat-market, your baths, your shops, your factories, your taverns, your weekly markets, or any part of your trade and commerce: on the contrary, we share your lives—so far as this world is concerned. § 3. We too sail the seas, along with you; we too serve in the army[2] (*militamus*), spend holidays in the country, and go shopping, like you; our arts are united with yours, and we offer our services for your use. How you can think us of no use for

---

[1] The small islands off the coast of Italy, to which in classical times (and again in our own times) criminals, or men held to be guilty of crime, were deported.

[2] Tertullian was correct: Christians *were* serving in the army in his time. But military service was forbidden to Christians in the *Church Order* of Hippolytus of Rome, a contemporary of Tertullian; and Origen has no place for it (see above, pp. 441–2). Actually Christians were already serving in the army under Marcus Aurelius (*Cambridge Ancient History*, vol. xii, p. 659).

the affairs of your daily life, when we make our living among them and from them, is something I cannot understand.'

Note on Lucian's Account of Christian Society (circa A.D. 170)

Tertullian's account of Christian society at the end of the second century has a parallel in an essay of the Greek satirist Lucian, *On the end of Peregrinus*, written a generation earlier. It is an essay satirizing, somewhat cruelly, a certain Peregrinus (nicknamed Proteus for his many shifts and changes), who from being a wandering Cynic had become a Christian and then reverted to Cynicism. He ended by cremating himself solemnly on a pyre, in the Indian manner, before a crowd of spectators assembled for the Olympic games. The sections in which Lucian describes the Christian period of his life are an unintended tribute to the virtues of Christian society.

§ 11. 'It was then that he also learned the wonderful wisdom of the Christians, after associating with their priests and scribes in Palestine. . . . They enrolled him as one of their leaders, next in order to him whom they still revere—the man who was crucified in Palestine because he introduced this new mystery into the life of man. § 12. He was then arrested for this [i.e. for his profession of Christianity] and thrown into prison. . . . So while he lay there the Christians, counting it as a misfortune to their cause, did everything they could in their efforts to get him released. When their efforts proved vain, they paid him all the attention they could; and this in no casual manner, but with a steady zeal. From the very break of day old women, widows, and orphans might be seen waiting at the prison doors, and some of those in authority among them [? deacons or priests] even slept by his side in his cell by dint of bribing the jailers. Elaborate meals were brought into prison; their sacred books were read aloud to him; and . . . he was called by them "a new Socrates". § 13. There were even people who came from some of the cities of the province of Asia, sent by the Christians, with their expenses paid from the common fund, to aid and comfort and defend the fellow. The Christians show an astonishing alacrity in any common action of this sort: they lavish in a moment all they have. . . . The unfortunate creatures have persuaded themselves generally that they will be immortal and live for ever, which leads the run of them to despise death and surrender themselves willingly to punishment. Moreover, their original law-giver [Christ] persuaded them into the belief that they all became one another's brethren as soon as they had once transgressed the law by refusing to acknowledge the gods of Greece, by doing reverence (*proskynēsis*) to that crucified sage of theirs, and by living in obedience to his laws. They therefore despise all things alike, and regard them as common property, receiving such ideas on trust with no sure ground for their belief.'

Lucian proceeds to tell, in §§ 14–15, that Peregrinus was eventually released by the governor of Syria, and returned for a time to his native town of Parium on the Hellespont. But, the story continues (§ 16), 'He went abroad on his wanderings again, having sufficient funds for his travels from the Christians; and he was maintained in this way for some time. Eventually, however, he transgressed their rules in some point—he was seen, I fancy, eating some food that is forbidden them—and they refused to accept him any longer.' After that he went first to Egypt, then to Rome (from which he was banished), and finally to Greece, where he ended his life, like another Empedocles, by committing himself to the flames.

D. *Tertullian's View of the Foundation of the Roman Empire and of the Duty owed to the Emperor by Christians*

1. *The Foundation of the Empire*

Apologeticus, c. 25, § 2. 'I will not shirk the challenge offered to us by the idea that Rome has been lifted so high, and made mistress of the world, because of her scrupulous regard for religion; the idea, in other words, that her gods are so much gods that those who offer them pre-eminent service enjoy a pre-eminent prosperity as a result. . . . § 12. How idle it is to ascribe the exaltation of the Roman name to the merits of Roman religiosity, when, as a matter of fact, it was *after* the establishment of the Empire that religion flourished in Rome.' The early religion of Rome, Tertullian argues, was a poor thing: a frugal country

religion, with chance altars of turf—and with God himself nowhere (*deus ipse nusquam*). 'The Romans were not religious *before*
they were great, and therefore they were not great *because* they
were religious. § 14. How, indeed, could they be great because
of their religion, when their greatness actually sprang from irreli-
gion? If I am not mistaken, kingship or empire is always sought
by wars and increased by victories; wars and victories mean the
taking of cities and, generally, their destruction; and that cannot
be done without injury to the gods [of the captured cities]. [The
result of wars and victories is that] towers and temples both come
to the ground; laymen and priests are murdered alike; sacred and
profane property is equally plundered. § 15. The sacrileges committed by the Romans are therefore as many as their trophies;
their triumphs over gods are as many as their triumphs over
nations; the spoils they have won in war are no more in number
than the images of captured gods which are still to be seen in their
city. . . . § 17. Surely it passes belief that a people who, as I have
just suggested, grew by injuring religion—or injured religion by
growing—should be supposed to have grown in consequence of
their regard for religion. We must also remember that those whose
kingdoms were melted together to form the mass of the Roman
Empire had religions of their own at the time when their kingdoms went under.

c. 26, § 1. 'Look ye, therefore, and see whether the awarding
of kingdoms be not in the hands of Him who is Lord of the world
that is ruled [by Caesar] and Lord of the ruler of that world;
whether the ordaining of the cycles of empires (*vices domina-
tionum*),[1] each for its appointed time in the world's movement, be
not a matter for Him who was before there was any time, and who
made the world a succession of times (*corpus temporum*); whether
the exalting and casting down of cities be not the work of Him
under whom mankind once lived before there were any States.'

2. *The Duty of Christians to the Emperor*

Apologeticus, c. 30, § 1. 'On behalf of the safety of the emperors
we invoke the one everlasting, true, and living God, whose

---

[1] See above, pp. 113, 187, 288.

favour the emperors themselves desire more than that of all other gods. *They* know who has given them empire; they know, because they are men, who has given them life; they feel that He only is God in whose power only they stand—He to whom they come next, He after whom they come first, He who is before and above all gods. . . . § 3. So the emperor is great because he is less than Heaven; and he is less than Heaven because he belongs himself to God, to whom Heaven and all creation belong. What made him emperor is what also made him man, before ever he became emperor; and what gives him his power is what also gave him the breath of life. § 4. And so we Christians, with our eyes upturned to Heaven—with our hands outspread because they are clean—with our heads uncovered, because we have nothing to hide or to blush for—without any prompter, because we make our supplications from our own hearts—we Christians are always offering our prayers for all emperors. We pray that they may have long life and a quiet government; that their palaces may be peaceable, their armies strong, their council loyal, their people true, the whole world at rest; that they may be granted everything which a man and a Caesar may desire.

c. 31, § 3. 'The command is given us [by the Apostle] explicitly and clearly, "Pray for kings . . . and all that are in high place, that ye may lead a tranquil and quiet life".[1] [We must therefore pray for the emperor in the interest of our own peace.] For when the Empire is troubled we too are sure to be involved in the trouble which besets the other parts; and though we are counted aliens by the masses, we are none the less to be found in some corner of the calamity.

c. 32, § 1. 'There is also another and greater reason why we needs must pray for the emperors and the whole state of the Empire and all things Roman. We know that the great danger which hangs over all the globe—I mean the end of the world, and all the fearful sufferings with which it threatens us—is postponed by virtue of the respite brought us by the Roman Empire. We do not wish to suffer such a fate, and in praying for its postponement we help to ensure the survival of Rome.

[1] 1 Timothy ii. 2. See above, p. 403, n. 2.

c. xxxiii, § 1. 'But why should I say more of the reverence and the loyalty of Christians in their attitude to the emperor? We must needs do him honour as the chosen of our Lord, so that I may justly say, "Caesar is more particularly ours, because he is appointed by our God". § 2. And therefore, since he is mine, I do even more for his safety than you, not only because I ask it of Him who alone can give it, or because I ask it as one who deserves to receive, but also because I make the majesty of Caesar lower than that of God and thus commend him the more to God under whom, and whom only, I set him.'

3. The Things of God and the Things of Caesar

De Idololatria, c. 15. ' "The things that are Caesar's must be rendered to Caesar." But the words which follow are true—"and unto God the things that are God's". What, then, are the things that are Caesar's? They are the things about which the question was then being raised: whether tribute should or should not be paid to Caesar. That was why our Lord said, "Show me the tribute money", and asked "Whose is this image?", and when—He had heard that it was Caesar's, said, "Render therefore unto Caesar the things that are Caesar's, and unto God the things that are God's". He meant thereby that the image of Caesar, which was on the money, should be rendered to Caesar, and the image of God, which was on man, should be rendered to God, so that men should indeed render money to Caesar, but should render their very selves to God. Otherwise what will be God's, if all things are Caesar's? . . . Therefore, so far as the honours due to kings and emperors are concerned, we have a rule which is sufficient for us: that we ought to be subject to magistrates and princes and powers in all obedience according to the rule laid down by the Apostle; but this within the limits of discipline, and so long as we keep ourselves free from idolatry.'

Ibid., c. xix. 'The issue now arises whether a believer may take to military service, and whether a member of the armed forces may be admitted to the Church. We may even ask whether the Church should admit a private or any of the inferior ranks who are under no necessity of joining in sacrifices or in trials which involve the punishment of death. There is no agreement between God's sacrament and the sacrament of man [i.e. the oath of service to God and the oath of service to Caesar]; between Christ's standard and the Devil's; between the camp of light and the camp of darkness. One soul cannot be bound over to two masters (*non potest una anima duobus deberi*)—God and Caesar.'

De Pallio, c. 5. Tertullian had changed the ordinary Roman *toga* for the *pallium* or cloak worn by Greek philosophers. Born himself at Carthage, he even ventured to plead that the *pallium* was the ancestral garb of his country. He was criticized for changing his dress; and his *De Pallio* is an answer, half apologetic and half satirical, to the criticism. In the following passage he personifies the *pallium*, which he represents as speaking in its own person.

'I, says [the cloak], owe nothing to the forum, or the campus, or the senate-house; I do not rise up early to offer my salutation to a patron; I do not hasten to mount the *rostrum*; I pay no homage to army headquarters; the odour of the canals [in the forum] is not in my nostrils; I offer no worship at the bench of the judge, and wear out no seat in the courts; I do not trouble the law, or shout myself hoarse in pleading cases; I am not a judge, I am not a soldier, I am not a ruler; I have seceded from the company of the people. The only business I have is business with myself—unless it be that [in regard to others] I take care that I should not need to care. One can enjoy a better life by seceding into solitude than if one is at the beck and call of others. "But you will make your life discredited for its indolence; surely one should live for one's country and State?" That is an opinion which used to be held. But no man lives for another when he has to die for himself. Anyhow, when you come to your Epicuruses and Zenos, you yourselves give the name of "sages" to all these prophets of peace who have blessed inaction with the appellation of "the supreme and unique pleasure".[1] But I too, after all, shall have licence given me to serve the public in some measure. I am accustomed [to do like the Cynic preachers in *their* cloaks,] to advertise, from the height of a boundary-wall or an altar, medicines for morals which have a

---

[1] Tertullian is thinking of the Stoic 'apathy' and the Epicurean 'ataraxy'—but especially of the latter; see above, p. 31 (foot) and p. 175.

happier effect, in the way of bringing public affairs and cities and empires back to good health, than all your [i.e. the toga's] efforts. Indeed, if I come to close quarters with you, togas have done more harm to the commonwealth than the soldier's cuirass. [If I am but a cloak], at any rate I flatter no vices; I condone no sloth and am subject to no scab.'

E. *Tertullian on the Growth of the Christian Church and its Causes*

Apologeticus, c. 37, § 4. 'We are but of yesterday, and yet we have filled all places belonging to you—your cities and your blocks of buildings, your fortresses and your towns, your markets and your very camps, your tribes and your companies, your palace and senate and forum. The one thing we have left you is your temples. § 5. . . . There is no war for which we would not have been fit and ready, even though we were unequal in numbers— you know how willing we are to face death—if it were not that by our doctrine it is more lawful to be killed than to kill. § 6. Even if we were unarmed, and even without rebellion, we could have defeated you, simply by disagreeing with you, and merely by incurring the odium of desertion. For if so large a body as we are had broken away from you, and gone off into some remote corner of the earth, the mere loss of so many citizens, of whatever sort they might be, would have put your government to shame; and indeed it would actually have punished you by leaving you desolate.'

c. 50, § 13 (end of the *Apologeticus*). 'We are multiplied by all your mowing us down; the blood of Christians is like seed. § 14. There are many among you who exhort men to the endurance of pain and death: [there is Cicero, Seneca, Diogenes (the Cynic), Pyrrho (the Sceptic), and others]. Their writings have never made as many disciples as the Christians have made by the teaching of their deeds. § 15. That very obstinacy for which you reproach us is itself a lesson. Who is not moved, as he notes it at work, to inquire what there really is in it? Who is there who does not join us after he has made his inquiry? And who does not, when he has joined us, wish to suffer [with us], that he may win the whole grace of

God and full pardon from Him by the payment of his own blood? For all sins are forgiven to the man who does *that*. § 16. And this is why we give thanks instantly for the sentences you pass upon us. There is a contention between the things of God and the things of man; and to be condemned by you is to be acquitted by God.'

F. *On Religious Liberty and the Priesthood of the Christian Man*

Tertullian had always believed in a secular system of political order, with a voluntary Christian society standing by its side in the enjoyment of a religious liberty which, while it was compatible with the payment of taxes and the offering of prayers for the emperor as the head of the secular system, nevertheless excluded the rendering of military service or the holding of civil office. Inspired in his later days by the enthusiasm of the Montanists, and by their insistence on the 'spiritual' liberty of the believer, he came at length to set limits even to the clerical *potestas ordinis* within the Christian society itself, and to profess something of a 'Lutheran' doctrine of 'the priesthood of the Christian man'. In discussing marriage in one of his treatises, he lays down a rule which equally binds the clergy and the laity, and during the course of his argument he contends that the layman can upon occasion exercise the powers and fulfil the duties of the priest.

De Exhortatione Castitatis, c. 7. 'Are not we of the laity also priests (*Nonne et laici sacerdotes sumus*)? It is written: "Christ has made us kings and priests unto God and the Father." It is therefore not Christ but the authority of the Church which has constituted the difference between the order [i.e. the clergy] and the people; that, and with it the distinction given to the clergy and consecrated for them by the joint sessions of their order, insomuch that where there is no joint session of the ecclesiastical order, you [the layman] make offering [in the Eucharist] yourself, you baptize persons yourself, and you are by yourself a priest unto yourself. Wherever there are three [gathered together], there is a Church, even if they are laymen; for each man lives by his own faith, and there is no acceptance of persons with God; inasmuch as it is not the hearers of the law who are justified by God, but the doers, as the Apostle also says. Therefore, if you have the *right* of a priest in yourself whenever it is necessary, you must also have [i.e. you must undergo] the *discipline* of a priest whenever it is necessary that you should have the priest's right.'

Note. Tertullian thus puts layman and priest on the same level, not so much because he would exalt the layman to the level of the priest, as because he wishes to subject the layman to the same rule of discipline as the priest, in the matter of contracting a second marriage [or, as he expresses it, becoming 'digamous']. He argues that 'digamy' is not permitted to priests, and therefore it is not lawful for the layman who is—or in the absence of an ecclesiastical 'order' may act as—a priest.

§ IX. LACTANTIUS ON JUSTICE AND 'HUMANITAS', AND ON THE ULTIMATE DECLINE AND FALL OF THE ROMAN EMPIRE

Introduction

Lactantius (*circa* A.D. 250–317), a native of the province of Africa, continued at once the African tradition of scholarship, which goes back to Apuleius and Fronto (the tutor of Marcus Aurelius), and the African tradition of Christian thought and theology which begins with Tertullian (A.D. 160–225). Like St. Augustine after him, he had been trained in the methods of classical rhetoric; during the reign of Diocletian he became a professor of rhetoric in Asia Minor; and he was eventually appointed by the Emperor Constantine as tutor to his son Crispus. Along with Eusebius of Caesarea (see below, p. 473), he became the apologist and prophet of the new Christian Empire; and it has been said that the two were the Virgil and Horace of Constantine, founding a political ideology in support of his government as their predecessors had done for the government of Augustus. He has also been called the 'Christian Cicero', mainly on the ground of his style, but also because he followed the lines of Cicero's thought in the *De Republica*, the *De Legibus*, and the *De Officiis*. (In his Ciceronianism he is similar to his predecessor Minucius Felix, also an African, who early in the third century B.C. had copied in his *Octavius*, a work of Christian apologetics, the style and even the ideas of Cicero, and who has been accordingly called 'the first in the line of Christian

Ciceros'.) The chief work of Lactantius is his *Divine Institutions,* intended as a Christian parallel to the earlier *Institutes* of the Roman lawyers. He was a humanist as well as a Christian apologist: he knew the *Sibylline Oracles,* and he also knew and treated with respect the *De Rerum Natura* of Lucretius, a poem which his teacher Arnobius seems to have known by heart. One of his leading ideas is his idea of *humanitas,* which he interprets in a broad and generous sense (see below, p. 464).

A. *The Conception of Justice in Lactantius'* Divine Institutions

1. *Justice as a relation to God, with* pietas *and* aequitas *as its two fountain-heads*

The fifth book bears the general title *De Iustitia.* At the beginning of c. 7 of the book Lactantius defines justice as one and the same with religion: 'justice is nothing else but the pious and religious worship of the one God' (§ 2).[1] In a later chapter the definition is carried farther.

c. 14, § 9. 'Justice embraces all the virtues together; but there are two of the virtues, and these the chief, which are utterly inseparable from it. These virtues are piety and equity [*aequitas,* a word derived from a root which means 'even' or 'even-handed']. Faith, temperance, honesty, innocence, integrity, and other qualities of the same order, may exist by natural endowment, or through the training of parents, in men who are ignorant of justice, as indeed they have always existed; (§ 10) for the ancient Romans, who used to take pride in justice, took pride particularly in these virtues which (as I have just implied) may be said to come from justice but are also separable from their origin. § 11. Piety and equity are, however, the very veins, as it were, of justice, and the two fountains which constitute the whole of its being; but [though they are thus fundamentally alike] piety is the very source and spring which gives rise to justice, while equity provides it with the weight it carries and the method it uses. Now

---

[1] St. Augustine, in the *De Civitate Dei,* follows the line of Lactantius. He argues that justice consists in giving to each his due. It must therefore include, and include particularly, the giving of His due to God; and it must therefore signify, above all else, 'the pious and religious worship of the one God'.

piety is nothing but the conception of God. . . . § 12. If, then, piety consists in knowing God, and worship is the essence of that knowledge, we may be sure that a man who has no reverence for God is ignorant of justice; for how can a man know justice itself when he does not know the source from which it comes? . . . § 15. The other part of justice is equity; and by 'equity' I do not mean the possession of good judgement—though that too is a praiseworthy quality in a good man—but a capacity for putting oneself on the same level with others, which Cicero calls by the name of *aequabilitas*. § 16. God, who has created men and given them the breath of life, has willed that they should all be equal— that is to say, on a level. He laid down the same conditions of life for all; He made them all for wisdom, and promised them all immortality; not one of us is cut off from His heavenly benefits. § 17. He gives us all equally the blessings of light, drink, food, and sleep; and in the same way He bestows on us all the gifts of equity and virtue. No man is a slave, and no man a master, before Him; if He is the father of us all alike, we are all by an equal title his children. § 18. No man is poor in the sight of God but he who is without justice; no man is rich but he who is full of virtue; no man can be called by the name of 'excellent', unless he is good and innocent, or by that of 'honourable', unless he has done works of mercy in abundance, or by that of 'most reverend', unless he has risen through all the stages of virtue. § 19. This is the reason why neither the Greeks nor the Romans could keep a hold on justice: they had men in their States who were separated from one another in a number of different classes (*gradus*), ranging from the poor to the rich, from the humble to the mighty, and from the private citizen to the exalted authority of the monarch. § 20. But where all are not on a level, there is no equity; and inequality of itself excludes justice, the whole essence of which is to put and keep on a level men who come into this life on an equal footing.'

2. *Justice as a relation between man and man, with* humanitas *and* societas *as its offices and results*

Book VI, c. x, § 1. 'I have said what is owed to God: I will now say what ought to be rendered to man—though what you render to man is itself really rendered to God, whose image man is. § 2. However, [we may make a distinction, and thus we may hold that] the first office of justice is to be united with God, and the second to be united with man. This first office is called religion; the second has the name of loving-kindness, or *humanitas*. The office of "humanity" is an office proper to the just and the worshippers of God, because it, and it only, has within it the motive that impels men towards a community life. § 3. God, who did not give wisdom to any beings other than man, made animals the more safe from danger of attack by arming them with natural defences; but as He made man naked and frail, that He might arm him rather with wisdom, He gave him, besides other gifts, this feeling of piety towards others, to the end that men should protect, love, and cherish one another, and should give and receive help from one another in all their dangers. § 4. "Humanity", therefore, is the great bond which unites men to one another; he who breaks this bond must be counted a criminal and a parricide; for if we all come from the one man made in the beginning by God, we are certainly of one blood, and it must therefore be regarded as the worst of offences to hate any man, however guilty. . . .'

§ 8. 'On account of this connexion of fraternity between us all, we are taught by God to do good, and never to do evil. § 9. What is meant by doing good is also laid down by God: it is to give help to those who are toiling and heavy laden, and to share food with those who have none. § 10. For God, since He is merciful (*pius*), wished man to be a social being (*animal sociale*[1]); and we must therefore think ourselves into the position of other men. We do not deserve to be delivered in time of danger if we do not succour others; we do not deserve help ourselves if we deny it to others.'

In the following sections, §§ 11–17, Lactantius summarizes the views of Lucretius on the origin of society.[2] He then turns, in §§ 18–19, from Lucretius to Cicero's *De Republica* I. xxv. 39 (see

[1] Aristotle had used the phrase 'political animal' (or, more exactly, an animal intended for life in a *polis*); Seneca, *De Beneficiis*, VII. i. 7, had used the same phrase as Lactantius.

[2] Lactantius was a pupil of Arnobius, the author of a work *Adversus Nationes* in which the fifth book of Lucretius' *De Rerum Natura* is quoted and used.

above, p. 186), and states the case for the natural—as opposed to the contractual—origin of society.

§ 18. 'Others [i.e. Cicero] have said that the cause of men's coming together was the simple feeling of common humanity (*ipsa humanitas*), and that they gathered together because the very nature of man is averse from solitude and anxious for company and society. There is no great quarrel between their views [i.e. the view of Lucretius and that of Cicero]: the causes they suggest are different; the fact they describe [i.e. society] is the same. § 19. Either alternative [i.e. either the contractual or the natural theory of the formation of society] could have been followed, because they are not mutually exclusive; but none the less neither of them is true.' Lactantius proceeds to argue that the true origin of society is to be found in the Christian belief that all men form one family because they are all descendants of one father Adam—i.e. he states a sort of patriarchal theory. 'Men were not born from the ground all over the world . . . *one* man was created by God, and from that one man the whole earth was filled with the race of men.'

Note on the conception of humanitas

Aulus Gellius, in the second century A.D., had already treated of *humanitas* in his *Noctes Atticae* (xiii. 17). But it was Cicero who had first given the term the wide and comprehensive sense which it bears in Lactantius.[1] A stimulating essay on the theme appears in Bruno Kern's *The Discovery of the Mind*, Eng. trans., pp. 247 ff., and especially pp. 254–5. Kern notes that there are two senses implied in the idea of *humanitas*: (1) the sense equivalent to the Greek *paideia*, as when we speak of 'the humanities' or of 'humanism' (this sense is as old as the age of Isocrates); and (2) the sense equivalent to the Greek *philanthrōpia*, as when we speak of 'the Humane Society' or of 'humanity' in warfare. He suggests that Cicero combined the two senses in his own notion of

---

[1] Cicero may have drawn on Panaetius of Rhodes and his treatise *peri kathēkontos*, which was a basis of his own work *De Officiis*. It has been said of Panaetius that he sought to present a picture of true *humanitas* by uniting Roman *virtus* to the *paideia* of the Greeks; Gercke–Norden, *Einleitung in die Altertumswissenschaft*, vol. i. 3, p. 134.

humanitas, and that this set the tone and the standard for the future use of the word. (Kern also notes that Aristippus, the founder of the Cyrenaic school of philosophy, had used the word *anthrōpismos* in this broad sense—a word which corresponds even more closely to the Latin *humanitas* than does the word *philanthrōpia*.)

B. *The Prophecy of the Fall of Rome in the* Divine Institutions

From book VII, c. xv, §§ 7 sqq. 'As the end of this world approaches, the state of human affairs is bound to change for the worse, owing to the growth of wickedness. . . . All justice will be confounded and all laws will perish. . . . All the earth will be in tumult; wars will rage everywhere; all peoples will be in arms, and will invade one another; neighbouring states will ravage each other; and, first of all, Egypt will pay the penalty for its foolish superstitions and be covered with blood as with a river. Then shall the sword traverse the earth, mowing all down and levelling everything as a crop is levelled before the reaper. The cause of this devastation and confusion will be—I shudder to tell it, but tell it I must, for it will surely come to pass—the blotting out of the name of Rome, by which the world is now governed, and the return of empire to Asia, so that the East shall again be mistress and the West her slave. Let no man think it strange that a realm founded by so much effort, augmented so long by so many and such great men, and consolidated by resources so vast, should nevertheless one day collapse. There is nothing built up by human effort which cannot equally be pulled down by that effort: all the works of mortal men are mortal too. The other empires of old, after a long period of prosperity, fell in their day; it is recorded that the Egyptians, Persians, Greeks, and Assyrians had empires in their day; they were all destroyed, and the sum of things then passed to the Romans; but the more the Romans excel all other empires in greatness, the greater will be their fall, for the taller a building is, the more is its momentum in falling. . . . The prophets darkly announce the fall of Rome; the Sibyls openly announce her destruction, and that by the judgement of God, because she has held His name in abhorrence, and in her enmity to justice has persecuted and killed the people who are the children of Truth.'

The reference to the *Sibylline Oracles* may seem curious in a Christian writer, but it was natural enough at the time when Lactantius wrote, about A.D. 300. These *Oracles*, a voluminous compilation in Greek hexameters, have, as has already been noted, three successive strata—an early Greek stratum; a considerable Jewish stratum, partly based on the prophets of the Old Testament and probably emanating from Alexandria; and a final Christian stratum. They were a sort of *Old Moore's Almanac*, and as such they underwent a process of revision and alteration from their beginning in the third century B.C. to their conclusion and disappearance in the sixth century A.D. It has already been noticed (p. 217) that the Fourth *Eclogue* of Virgil is parallel, and may be indebted, to some passages in the third book of the *Sibylline Oracles*. Lactantius alludes to, and practically translates, a passage in the same book (iii. 350 ff.). His argument here supports the conjecture that he may have written the *Oratio ad Sanctos* (supra, p. 218, note 2).

§ x. the 'edict of milan' (a.d. 313)

Introduction

During the two centuries that lie between the reign of Trajan (see above, p. 249, for his correspondence with Pliny) and the 'Edict of Milan' in 313, the persistent profession of Christianity had been a capital offence, and there had been no express recognition of the Church as a permitted religion (*religio licita*). The Emperor Gallienus, the friend of Plotinus, and a lover of Greek philosophy who trusted that it would win by the inherent power of its own light and leading, had indeed called a temporary halt to the persecution of Christians in the year 261. In a rescript of that year, addressed to Christian bishops and reported by Eusebius (*Historia Ecclesiastica* vii, c. xiii, § 2), he granted the ministers of the Church liberty to perform their duties, and ordered Christian places of worship and cemeteries to be left free for Christian use; he added, moreover, that what Churches were now lawfully, by this rescript, enabled to do had already been allowed by him for some time. Christianity thus became, for the moment, a lawful and permitted body. But his rescript perished in the reaction after his death; and it was not until fifty years later, in 311, that another emperor, Galerius, the colleague of Constantine, issued a new edict which inaugurated a permanent and effective policy of toleration. His edict (reported by Lactantius in the *De Mortibus Persecutorum*) permits those who have relapsed under stress of persecution 'to be Christians' again and to re-establish their assemblies—provided that they do nothing contrary to public order; and it ends with the suggestion, or command, that 'it will therefore be the duty of the Christians, in consequence of this our command, to pray to their God for our welfare and that of the public'. This edict stopped persecution and granted legal recognition. It was a positive gift of toleration, but it had its negative side. In the act of permitting Christians to be themselves again, the edict criticizes them for having in the past assembled in divers places people of different nations (thus, it is implied, breaking down the natural separation between different national religions— the charge which Celsus had brought against Christianity); and, moreover, it imposes a limit—the limit of public order or 'discipline'. Nor is there any provision in the Edict of 311, as there is in the later measure of 313, for the restitution of church property.

The measure of 313, a document granting (or rather confirming) the right of freedom of religious belief and its expression, is generally called the Edict of Milan; but it was not an 'edict' (in the strict sense of the word) nor was it issued at Milan. It was a 'rescript' addressed to a provincial governor, authorizing, or instructing, him to promulgate an edict to his province establishing the principle of toleration; and this rescript was issued, not at Milan, but at Nicomedia, in Asia Minor, by Licinius, the colleague of the Emperor Constantine I. The rescript of Nicomedia (as it may more properly be called) was based, however, in all probability, on an agreement previously made between Constantine and Licinius at Milan early in the year 313; and it was in execution of this agreement that in June of that year Licinius issued the document which has, in consequence, come to be known as the Edict of Milan. The text translated here survives in a Greek translation from the Latin (in the *Ecclesiastical History* of Eusebius, book x, c. 5): it may also be found in a transcription by Lactantius (*De Mortibus Persecutorum*, c. 48). The rescript is addressed to the governor of a province.

A. *The Text of the Rescript of* 313

'We have long considered that freedom of worship should not be denied, but that every man's thought and will should be granted the right to take care for spiritual things according as each man may personally choose; and therefore we have already issued orders that both Christians [and others][1] should hold and maintain the faith of their own confession and worship. But inasmuch as in those orders, by which that right was conceded to the persons aforesaid, many and divers conditions clearly appeared to have been added, it may perhaps be the case that some of these persons in a little while became reluctant to practise their religious observances.

'[Accordingly] when I, Constantine Augustus, and I, Licinius Augustus, by good fortune met one another at Milan, and there took occasion to review all matters tending to the advantage and welfare of the commonwealth, we came to the resolution that—with other matters which seemed to us to be beneficial to the great majority, and indeed as the first and foremost among such matters—we ought to regulate the conditions on which respect and reverence for the Deity depend; our purpose, to wit, being this, that we should grant both to Christians and to all men freedom of choice in following such form of worship as they wish, to the end that whatever there be of divinity and heavenly things[2] may be able to show favour to us and to all persons living under our authority. Wherefore by sound and strictest reasoning we resolved upon this policy: that to no man whatsoever should there be denied the right to follow and choose the observance or form of worship which the Christians use, but that every man be given the right to give his own mind to that form of worship which he himself thinks suitable to himself; to the end that the

---

[1] These words appear to have dropped out of the text of Eusebius.
[2] This is a literal translation of the Greek version of Eusebius. In the Latin of Lactantius the phrase runs 'whatever there be of divinity in the heavenly seat'.

divinity [to whose worship we freely pay our service[1]] may be able to afford us his wonted care and goodness in all things.

'It was proper to signify by a rescript that this was our pleasure, so that, with the complete removal of all the conditions which were contained in our former letters sent to Your Excellency concerning the Christians, there should also be removed whatever seemed to be entirely amiss and alien from our clemency, and in order that now and henceforth, freely and unconditionally, all who have been of one mind and purpose—to keep the Christians' form of worship—should do so without any let or hindrance. Which things we have resolved to signify as fully as possibly to you our trusty servant [literally, 'Your Carefulness'], in order that you might know that we have given to these same Christians the full and absolute right to take care for their own form of worship. Further, when you see that this grant has been made to them unconditionally by us, Your Excellency will understand that the same right has also been granted to others who wish to follow their own form of observance and worship—such grant being clearly fitting to the peace of our times—so that all alike may have the right to choose and cherish such forms as they please. This has been done by us to the end that no rite or form of worship should seem to have suffered any diminution at our hands.

'This too, in addition, we also resolve in regard to the Christians, and as concerning the places [buildings] in which it was formerly their wont to meet. These places were the subject of a different rule[2] laid down in the former letter sent to Your Excellency on a previous occasion; but we now lay it down that if any persons should appear to have purchased such places, either from our treasury or from elsewhere, these persons shall restore them to the aforesaid Christians without receiving payment or making any demand for compensation, putting away all negligence and quibbles. Moreover, if any persons have chanced to come into possession of such places by gift, they shall restore them as speedily as possible to the aforesaid Christians; with this proviso [in both

---

[1] These words are not in the Greek version: they come from the Latin text of Lactantius.

[2] This seems to be the sense of Eusebius's Greek, but the Latin form of the rescript has the words *certa forma*, which would mean 'a definite ordinance'.

the cases aforesaid] that if either the purchasers of these same places, or those who have received them by gift, proffer any petition to our generosity, they shall approach the prefect of the district in which the places lie, so that through our kindness they too may receive consideration. All which properties must be handed over immediately to the body concerned [the *corpus*, or corporation?] by your efforts, with no delay.

'Moreover, since these same Christians not only possessed the places in which it was their wont to meet, but are also known to have had other places, not belonging to individuals among them, but forming part of the rights of their—that is to say the Christian— body corporate [in the Latin of Lactantius, *ad ius corporis eorum, id est ecclesiarum . . . pertinentia*], you are to give orders, in execution of the law which we have set forth above, that all such places should be restored without any question whatsoever to these same Christians—that is to say to their body corporate and congregation; provided, of course, that the method heretofore mentioned be here again observed, and that accordingly those who restore these same places without receiving payment may, as we have heretofore mentioned, hope for indemnification to be given them by our liberality.

'In all which things you must use your efforts, to the best of your power, for the aforesaid body corporate of the Christians, that our orders may be executed as quickly as possible, to the end that here also [as well as in other matters] consideration may be given to keeping the common and public peace. . . . For by this policy, as indeed we have said before, the divine favour towards us, of which we have already had experience in many matters, may remain with us no less steadfastly at all times. Wherefore, in order that the form of our enactment and its liberality may be brought to the notice of all, it is proper that what we have written should be set forth by your edict, and published everywhere and brought to the notice of all, to the end that the enactment which proceeds from our liberality may not go unnoticed by any.'

B. *Two other documents on the relation of Church and Empire*

In later chapters of the same book of his *Ecclesiastical History* in which he quotes the 'Edict of Milan' Eusebius cites two other imperial documents which are of some importance as illustrating the relations between Church and State during the reign of Constantine I. The first of these documents (book x, c. 6) relates to a grant of money made by the Emperor to Christian churches in Africa, and is thus a record of State endowment; the second (book x, c. 7) is a grant of exemption to clergy in Africa from 'political liturgies', i.e. from the duty of undertaking unpaid public offices in the service of the State, and it is thus a record of State recognition of *clerici* as a peculiar and privileged order or 'estate'.[1]

1. *Grants of money to churches by the State*

'Constantine Augustus to Caecilian, bishop of Carthage, Greeting. Whereas it has pleased us that in all the provinces of Africa, Numidia, and Mauretania[2] some contribution should be made to certain specified ministers of the lawful and most holy Catholic form of worship for the meeting of their expenses, I have sent a letter to Ursus, the most eminent comptroller of the province of Africa, and I have signified to him that he should take measures to pay to Your grace [literally, 'stability'] the sum of 3,000 "purses".[3] Do you, therefore, when you obtain delivery of the aforesaid sum of money, give orders for its distribution to all the persons aforesaid in accordance with the terms of the list sent you by Hosius.[4] But if you should find that there is any deficiency in the fulfilment of my purpose herein for the benefit of all these ministers, you are to request, without hesitation, whatever you find to be necessary from our finance minister Heraclides, to

---

[1] It should be noted that both of these grants were limited to the Catholic Church under Caecilian, bishop of Carthage. There was a schism in Africa (Donatism, as it was called, was the cause); and the church under the rival bishop Maiorinus was not included in the grants (S. L. Greenslade, *Church and State from Constantine to Theodosius*, 1954, p. 14).

[2] The modern Tunis, Algeria, and Morocco. Carthage, to the bishop of which this letter is addressed, lay in the province of Africa.

[3] A 'purse', or *follis*, was a bag of coins, the value of which might be about one shilling. (In the time of the Emperor Julian, with further depreciation, it is said that one pound of pork cost 6 *folles*.) But Lietzmann, in his *From Constantine to Julian* (Eng. trans., p. 83), writes of a sum of £15,000.

[4] This 'Hosius' was Bishop Ossius of Cordova, who was well known to Constantine and later present as papal legate at the Council of Nicaea, A.D. 325.

whom I gave orders, when he was here, that if Your Grace should request any money from him, he should take measures to pay you such money instantly.'

2. *Exemption of clergy from political 'liturgies'*

'To the most honourable Anulinus [proconsul of the province of Africa], Greeting. Whereas it appears, from many evidences, that the neglect of that religious worship by which a sovereign reverence is maintained for the Most Holy in the heavens has brought great dangers into public affairs, and that a proper restoration and maintenance of such worship have resulted, by God's gift of His benefits, in the greatest good fortune for the Roman name and singular prosperity for all the doings of men, it has seemed good to us, most honourable Anulinus, that those persons who, with due holiness and attention to this principle, minister in the observance of divine worship, should receive the reward of the labours which they undertake in their persons. Wherefore I desire that those persons, usually called by the name of clergy (*clerici*), who live in the province entrusted to thee and belong to the Catholic church of which Caecilian is bishop [i.e. the church in Carthage], and minister personally there in this holy worship, should in all things and without exception be kept immune, once and for all, from the burden of public offices, so that they be not drawn away, by any error or sacrilegious back-sliding, from the ministry due to the Deity, but may rather, without any hindrance, serve to the utmost their own law [the *idios nomos* of the Church, as distinct from the *koinos nomos* of the whole community]. For when they offer the greatest service to things divine, it seems that they bring most benefit to the common-weal. . . .'

§ XI. EUSEBIUS

Introduction

Eusebius (*circa* A.D. 260–340) was closely connected, as a protégé or possibly a relative, with a rich Phoenician, called Pamphilos, who had studied in Alexandria and afterwards collected at Caesarea (in Palestine) a valuable library which contained many of the works of Origen. (Origen had lived in that city, teaching and writing, during the last twenty years of his life.) This library was the training-ground and treasure-house of Eusebius, who thus continued the tradition of the Christian scholarship of Alexandria. He became bishop of Caesarea about 315, was present at the Council of Nicaea in 325, and eventually became the adviser of the Emperor Constantine. (Indeed it may be said, as has already been noted, that he and his contemporary the African Lactantius served Constantine in the same sort of way, in their different spheres, as Virgil and Horace had served Augustus: they helped to create a political ideology for the new empire pivoted on Byzantium, just as the two Latin poets of an earlier age had helped to create the legend and the tradition of the old Empire based on Rome and Italy.)[1]

Eusebius was a voluminous writer, both in the field of history and in that of theology. In the historical field he not only rendered a great service to chronology: he also wrote a valuable *Historia Ecclesiastica* which traces the history of the Christian Church and of its officers and doctors. In the field of theology he wrote a *Praeparatio Evangelica*, which is a study and refutation of paganism, and a *Demonstratio Evangelica*, which is a similar study of the general legacy of Jewish thought. (He was also the author of a *Life of Constantine*,[2] and of a *Tricennial Oration*, or *Laus Constantini*, composed in honour of the thirtieth year of the Emperor's reign.) Inspired by the tradition and memory of Origen, he made his knowledge of history an ally and support of his general philosophy. He is at once the master of a chronological framework, which includes in its range the development of the Christian Church and relates it to the general course of history, and the exponent of a general theory of reasoned theology, which seeks to draw together Greek and Jewish tradition with Christian revelation in a common synthesis. He has his defects. The historical views which he expounds are not always true to

---

[1] It is a curious fact, noted above (p. 218), that Constantine, or Lactantius on his behalf, had sought in the *Oratio ad Sanctos* to enlist Virgil himself as a prophet of the new Christian Empire, on the strength of his Fourth *Eclogue*.

[2] The authenticity of the *Vita Constantini* has been disputed; but see the Appendix to this section.

the facts of history; and his philosophy of history (which made all things work together, since the Augustan creation of the *pax Romana*, for the triumph of Christianity) was repudiated by later Christian thought, as when St. Augustine, for instance, showed that the establishment of the Empire of Rome had *not* meant peace. He is also limited in the width of his view: he thinks almost exclusively of the Eastern Mediterranean, and has little knowledge or understanding of the Latin West. But it has justly been said of him that as a faithful disciple of Origen he used his scholarship to fashion the political theory which was to inspire the Byzantine world—a theory which, if it dismisses the old pagan idea of the emperor as a *praesens deus*, still elevates Constantine and his successors to the rank of vicegerents of God.

A. *The Coincidence of Universal Empire and the Church Universal*

Praeparatio Evangelica, I, c. 4 (edited by F. A. Heinichen). 'It was the work of divine and ineffable power that at the same time with His Word, and side by side with His teaching of the monarchy of the One God who is over all, He should have freed mankind at one stroke both from the polytheism of the influence of daemons and from the polyarchy of different nations.[1] Of old there existed among the nations a multitude of kings and local rulers who bore sway in different cities and countries; some of these cities and countries were democratically governed, some tyrannically, and some by a mixture of governments; there were, as was natural, wars of all sorts in consequence; nations clashed with nations and continually attacked their neighbours; they ravaged and were ravaged; they fought and besieged one another's cities, with the result that the inhabitants of cities and the labourers in the country-side were one and all trained to war from their childhood upward, and always carried arms on the roads and in their villages and fields. But when Christ came, of whom it was said of old by

---

[1] The argument which Eusebius repeatedly urges, and which he had learned from Origen, is that the coming of Christ was attended by two related consequences—the religious consequence of the end of polytheism, and the political consequence of the end of what he calls 'polyarchy', or the system of different nations (or *ethnē*) and different states.

the prophets, "There shall arise in His days righteousness and full-ness of peace, and they shall beat their swords into ploughshares...',[1] there followed upon His coming works according to what they foretold: all the polyarchy in the Roman world was ended, and Augustus became the sole ruler at the same moment that our Saviour was manifested. Thenceforth, and to this day, you would no longer see, as before, city at war with city, or nation fighting against nation, or life being wasted and spent in all manner of confusion. Yet one cannot but pause and wonder why it was that of old, in the days when the daemons tyrannized over all the nations and there was much worship of them among men, man-kind should have allowed itself to be goaded by its gods to rush madly into mutual slaughter—Greeks, at one time, fighting Greeks, then Egyptians fighting Egyptians, then Syrians fighting Syrians, and then Romans fighting Romans, all enslaving one another and wasting one another's cities with sieges, as is shown by the records left by old writers about these matters—why, I say, this should have happened of old, and then abatement should have come to all this straying in the paths of polytheism at the moment of, and along with, our Saviour's most holy and peaceful teach-ing, when the state of dissension among the nations instantly found rest and respite from its ancient miseries. Indeed I hold this to be far and away the greatest proof of the God-given and ineffable power of our Saviour.'

B. *Eusebius' Philosophy of History*

(*a*) *The ending of the Jewish kingdom, the establishment of the Roman Empire, and the coming of Christ* (*Demonstratio Evangelica*, III, c. 2). Eusebius quotes and glosses a passage from the Septuagint version of Genesis (xlix. 10). 'There shall not fail a ruler from Judah, and a leader from his loins, until *he* come for whom it [? the kingdom] is laid up in store; and he is the expectation of the nations.'[2] His gloss upon it is that rulers and leaders will not fail from the Jewish

---

[1] Eusebius here quotes the gist of Isaiah ii. 4.
[2] Eusebius alters some words in the Septuagint version, which in any case is different from the Hebrew original as rendered in the Authorized and Revised Versions.

nation till the Prophesied One appears, and when He comes the kingdom of the Jews will be instantly dissolved, and He will be the expectation not of the Jews, but of the 'nations', i.e. the Gentiles. 'Now you could not interpret these words as referring to the prophets; you can apply them only to our Lord and Saviour; for it was at the same time as He appeared among men that the kingdom of the Jews was taken away from them, and it was at that moment that there ceased to be a ruler among them reigning by title of descent from his ancestors, or a leader guiding the people according to laws of their own; it was then, too, that Augustus first became Emperor of Rome'. Eusebius, in his philosophy of history, thus connects with one another—temporally, and also, by implication, causally—the disappearance of the Jewish State, the emergence of the Roman Empire, and the birth of Christ. The first two dispensations prepare the way—the one negatively and the other positively—for the third.

(b) *How the ending of national States ('ethnarchies') in Egypt and elsewhere made possible the preaching of the Gospel (Dem. Evang. III, c. 7).* 'Any man who thinks the thing over in his mind, and recognizes that it was not of men's doing, must needs wonder at the fact that most of the nations of the world were never brought under the one authority of the Roman Empire until the days of Jesus. For it was at the very same time with His marvellous appearance among men that the fortunes of Rome reached their zenith: then it was that Augustus, in whose reign the line of the Ptolemies of Egypt came to an end with the capture of Cleopatra, first became emperor of most of the nations; and from that day to the present the realm of Egypt, which had stood firm through the ages and indeed, if I may say so, from the very beginnings of man, has ceased to be. From that day, too, the nation of the Jews has become subject to the Romans, as also have the nations of Syria, Cappadocia, Macedonia, Bithynia, Greece, and in a word all other countries which are under Roman rule. That it was by the providence of God that these events should have coincided with the teaching of the Gospel of our Saviour will be admitted by all who reflect how difficult it would have been for His disciples to make their journeys in foreign countries if the nations had been at variance with one another,[1] and if there had been no intercourse between them, in consequence of their being under a number of different national governments (*ethnarchiai*). But as these governments had been abolished, the disciples accomplished their task with impunity and without fear, the God of all men making a way smooth for them, and subduing the spirit of the superstitious, in the cities which they visited, by fear of the superior authority of Rome. For consider how, if there had been no power to hinder those who were led astray by the errors of polytheism into opposing the teaching of Christ, you would long ago have been witnessing civil broils in town and country and persecutions and savage wars.'

(c) *The general ending of political pluralism and the new era of imperial unity* (*Dem. Evang.* VII, c. 2). 'There was a multitude of rulers before the coming of Christ; all the nations were governed by different tyrannies or democracies, and men had no intercourse with one another; Egypt, for instance, was a kingdom apart under its own ruler, and so were the Arabs, the Idumaeans, the Phoenicians, the Syrians, and the other countries; nation rose up against nation, and city against city; thousands of towns were besieged, and thousands of men made captives, in every region and country. But then our Lord and Saviour appeared, and then—simultaneously with His appearance to men, and at the time that Augustus, the first Roman Emperor, obtained mastery over the nations—the multitude of rulers for the most part disappeared, and peace covered all the earth according to the prophecy whereof we are speaking, which says expressly of the disciples of Christ, "Now shall he be great unto the ends of the earth. And this . . . shall be our peace".' (Micah, v. 4–5).

c. *Eusebius on the Emperor as ruling by the grace and in the image of God*

(From the *Tricennial Oration*, or *De Laudibus Constantini*, of A.D. 336)

c. 1, § 6. 'He it is—the Word of God proceeding above all things, and through all things, and in all things, both visible and

---

[1] This is an argument which had been used before by Origen, *supra*, p. 439.

invisible—who is the Lord of all the Universe; from whom and through whom the king (*basileus*), the beloved of God, receives and bears the image of His Supreme Kingship, and so steers and directs, in imitation of his Superior, the helm of all the affairs of this world.'

c. 3, §§ 4–5. 'Constantine—like the light of the sun, with the flashes[1] that shine from his sons the Caesars—illuminates those who are farthest removed from him in space with the rays that are projected far afield from him; . . . and thereupon, yoking the four Caesars, like highly spirited steeds, under the one yoke of his four-horsed royal chariot[2] by his own spontaneous motion, he schools them into harmony with the reins of inspired unison and concord, driving his team like a charioteer who stands on high above it, and coursing over the whole of the earth that the sun shines upon while yet at the same time he is present among all men and watching over all their affairs. So, crowned in the image of heavenly kingship, he steers and guides men on earth according to the pattern of his prototype, confirmed by that example of monarchical authority. It is only to man, among all beings that move on the earth, that God the Great King has given this honour. *He* is the standard of kingly power; and it is He who determines the establishment of a single authority for all men. Monarchy transcends as a system and method of government for all states: polyarchy, which stands opposed to it, on the ground of equality of status, is anarchy and dissension rather than a form of government. So there is one God—not two or three or more, for polytheism is in reality atheism—and there is one King; and the Word and the law that proceed from Him are one, expressed not in letters and syllables, or in inscriptions and on pillars that perish with the passage of time, but living and subsisting as the Word

[1] Eusebius here uses words which are the same as those used by 'Ecphantus' (see above, p. 368). This, as well as the similarity of the ideas which he expresses, suggests that he knew the treatise of 'Ecphantus'; and that in turn suggests that the treatise was a *recent* treatise (and not an old treatise of the third century B.C., which would not be likely to be known to Eusebius).

[2] This metaphor of the four-horsed chariot is parallel to a passage in the Borysthenic Oration of Dio Chrysostom (see above, p. 301). But there is no need to assume that it was borrowed from Dio: four-horsed chariots were common enough in the games of antiquity—and not least in Constantinople.

that is God, and governing the Kingdom of the Father for all who are under Him and next after Him.

c. 5, § 1. 'The king, beloved of God, will already be a partaker in the heavenly kingdom; for he is crowned with the virtues which are inherent in God, and he has received in his soul the emanations[1] that come from God; he has become rational from the Universal Reason, wise by participation in Wisdom, good by fellowship with the Good. . . . § 4. The king, and the king only, is truly a philosopher: he "knows himself", and he understands the supplies of all good things which flow to him in their channels from outside him (or rather down from heaven); he shows forth the august style of his monarchical authority by the choice covering of his robe, and he is rightly and duly clad in the royal purple that becomes him.'

In other passages Eusebius speaks of the king as 'being, as it were, a lieutenant of the Great King', or, in other words, His vicegerent or *hyparchos*, a Greek word which designates the governor of a province (c. 7, § 13); and again he describes him as 'being, as it were, an interpreter—*hypophētēs*—of the Word which is God' (c. 2, § 4), and, as such, summoning all mankind to knowledge of the Higher Wisdom.[2]

An Appendix on the authenticity of a document quoted by Eusebius in the Vita Constantini

In the *Vita Constantini*, c. 2, §§ 24–42, there is quoted a long proclamation addressed by Constantine to his subjects in the Eastern provinces—a proclamation restoring to Christians their losses, and dilating on the bankruptcy of paganism. The authenticity of this

---

[1] The word which Eusebius uses may perhaps be better translated as 'efflux'. He thinks of an 'efflux' or effulgence of divine grace as descending upon the king, and thereby constituting him *rex Dei gratia*.

[2] Erik Peterson, in his valuable little book, *Der Monotheismus als politisches Problem*, p. 78, refers to this passage, and adds in a footnote that 'this was the fulfilment of an old Stoic ideal, expressed by Plutarch in a passage of his *De Alexandri fortuna* (i. 329 *a* and 330 *d*) where he speaks of Alexander as "wishing to make the earth obedient to one Logos and to show that all men are one people under one polity" '(cf. *supra*, p.8). He ends his footnote with the remark, 'Constantine thus realizes the aim that hovered before Alexander the Great'. This book of documents, which begins with Alexander, may thus fitly end with Constantine.

document has recently been proved in a conclusive manner.[1] Professor A. H. M. Jones has identified a contemporary copy of part of the proclamation in a papyrus fragment belonging to the British Museum. The fragment, which tallies with the version quoted in the *Vita* (c. 2, § 28), contains the passage in which Constantine speaks of the British origin of his divine mission. 'It is not vainglorious for one who acknowledges the beneficence of the Almighty to make boast thereof. It was He who sought out my service, and judged it fitting for the achievement of His own purpose. Starting from the British sea and the lands where the sun is ordained to set, He[2] repulsed and scattered by His divine might the encompassing powers of evil, to the end that the human race might be recalled to the worship of the supreme law, schooled by my helping hand, and that the most blessed faith might be increased with the Almighty as guide.' (From an article by T. C. Skeat, in the *British Museum Quarterly*, xviii, No. 3, September 1953, to which my attention was drawn by Mr. C. H. Roberts.)

[1] As already noted above, doubt has been cast on the authenticity of the *Vita Constantini*: see H. Grégoire, in *Historia*, i, 1950, p. 96. But at any rate the document quoted by the author of the *Vita* is authentic.

[2] In the version quoted by Eusebius the word used is 'I' and not 'He'.

ANNALS OF POLITICS AND CULTURE,
338 B.C.–A.D. 337

(*Entries relating to the history of culture are printed in italics*)

THE FOURTH CENTURY B.C.

338.	Battle of Chaeronea; Macedonian Supremacy.
	League of Corinth, with Philip of Macedon as *Hēgemōn*.
336.	Accession of Alexander; Renewal of the League of Corinth.
334.	Alexander's Invasion of the Persian Empire.
332.	Alexander's decree for the return of the exiled democrats of Chios.
331.	Foundation of Alexandria in Egypt.
	Alexander's visit to the shrine of Ammon in the oasis of Siwah.
328.	Alexander in Bactria; the issue of *proskynēsis*.
325.	*Death of Diogenes of Sinope, founder of the Cynic School.*
324.	Mutiny at Opis; the reconciliation; Alexander's dream of *Homonoia*. His supposed decree requesting recognition of his divinity from the Greeks; his actual decree for the return of exiles to their cities in Greece.
323.	Death of Alexander at Babylon.
322.	*Death of Aristotle.*
317–307.	Demetrius of Phalerum, a disciple of Aristotle, governor in Athens for Cassander of Macedonia.
316 (*circa*).	Cassander establishes his brother Alexarchus in Uranopolis, 'the city of Heaven', where he creates a little world-state with its own language.
315.	Foundation of the League of the 'Islanders' of the Aegean.
314.	*Zeno comes to Athens.*
306.	*Epicurus opens a school at Athens.* Antigonus I of Macedonia and his son Demetrius assume the title of king.
305.	The title of king assumed by Ptolemy I in Egypt and Seleucus I in Asia.
	The deification of Alexander in Egypt by Ptolemy I.
302.	The League of Corinth renewed by Demetrius and his father Antigonus of Macedonia.
301.	*Zeno begins to teach in the Stoa at Athens.*

I i

THE THIRD CENTURY B.C.

300–290.   *Foundation of the Museum and Library at Alexandria by Ptolemy I; Demetrius of Phalerum his adviser and librarian.*

290.   Demetrius, son of Antigonus of Macedonia, in Athens; addressed as a god by the Athenians in an Ithyphallic poem.

283.   Death of Ptolemy I; deified as *Theos Sōtēr* after his death by Ptolemy II.
(Later Ptolemy II had himself and his wife deified as *Theoi Adelphoi* during their life.)

283–239.   Reign of Antigonus Gonatas in Macedonia; *his patronage of philosophers, Stoic and Cynic.*

280.   Foundation of the Achaean League.

279.   The Celts invade Macedonia and Greece, and in the next year cross the Hellespont into Asia Minor.

271–270.   Festival of triumph in Alexandria; *Theocritus composes for it an Encomium of the* Theoi Adelphoi *(Idyll XVII).*

270.   *Death of Epicurus.*

263.   *Death of Zeno. Cleanthes his successor as head of the Stoic school.*

251.   Aratus of Sicyon at the head of the Achaean League.

250 (*circa*).   *Cercidas of Megalopolis; his plea for social justice.*

241.   Death of Agis IV of Sparta; failure of his attempted reforms. End of the First Punic War.
Livius Andronicus produces at Rome a tragedy and a comedy based on Greek models.

233.   *Death of Cleanthes; Chrysippus succeeds him as head of the Stoic school.*

228.   Zenith of the influence of the Achaean League.

224.   Antigonus Doson renews the League of Corinth.

222.   Cleomenes III of Sparta takes refuge in Egypt; failure of his reform policy.

218–201.   Second Punic War. During its course Rome fights the First Macedonian War (214–205).
[*To some date in the third century belongs the 'Sun-State' of Iambulus. To the same century also belong the 'Questions of Ptolemy II', recorded in the* 'Letter of Aristeas'.]

THE SECOND CENTURY B.C.

From the beginning of this century Rome moves into the Eastern Mediterranean, and eventually absorbs the Hellenistic kingdoms, first the Macedonian (168), then the Seleucid (by 64 B.C.), and then the Egyptian (30 B.C.).

200 (*circa*).	*Book of Ecclesiastes.*
197.	Second Macedonian War. Defeat of Macedonia at Cynoscephalae.
196.	Flamininus proclaims 'the liberty of Greece'; a pan-Hellenic congress at Corinth renews the old Greek League. *The trilingual inscription on the Rosetta Stone.*
190 (*circa*).	*Book of Ecclesiasticus.* Defeat of the Seleucid Antiochus III by Rome at the battle of Magnesia.
185–50.	*Period of the Middle Stoa.*
184 onwards.	Establishment of a Graeco-Bactrian kingdom in North West India ('*Questions of Menander*', *attributed to one of its kings*).
183.	Death of Philopoemen, general of the Achaean League, 'the last of the Greeks'.
175–163.	Reign of Antiochus IV Epiphanes.
168.	Defeat of Macedonia at Pydna in the Third Macedonian War; Macedonia split by Rome into four dependent Leagues.
167.	Hellenizing policy of Antiochus in Jerusalem.
166.	Rise of the Maccabees. *Visions of the Book of Daniel.*
165–150.	*Polybius in Rome as hostage; a member of the Scipionic circle.*
155.	*Embassy of philosophers from Athens in Rome (Carneades of the Academy, Critolaus the Peripatetic, and Diogenes the Cynic).*
148.	Macedonia made a Roman province.
146.	Achaean League defeated by Rome, and Greek confederacies dissolved; Greece subordinated to the governor of Macedonia.
145.	*Expulsion of Greek scholars and artists from Alexandria by Ptolemy VIII, to win native Egyptian support, with the result that Rhodes and Pergamum become centres of Greek culture.*
144.	*Panaetius the Stoic (185–109) comes to Rome, and is associated with the Scipionic circle.*
141–135.	Reign of Simon Maccabaeus in Jerusalem.

133–129.	The Attalid kingdom of Pergamum bequeathed by its last ruler to Rome. Rising against Rome under Aristonicus; his attempt to found a 'Sun-State'.
129.	*Panaetius head of the Stoic School (down to 109).*
121–63.	Reign of Mithridates VI Eupator, King of Pontus.
106.	*Birth of Cicero.*
100 (*circa*).	*Posidonius of Apamea (135–50), after studying under Panaetius at Athens, travels in Gaul and the Western Mediterranean.*

THE FIRST CENTURY B.C.

100 (*circa*).	*The Testament of the Twelve Patriarchs.*
90–88.	The 'Social' War in Italy; attempt of the Italian *Socii* to found a 'confederation' (?)
88.	Athenion (or Aristion) and the attempted revolution at Athens against Rome and in support of Mithridates VI of Pontus.
86.	Sulla captures and sacks Athens and destroys the Peiraeus.
66–63.	Pompey organizes the East; new Roman provinces in Asia Minor and Syria.
64.	End of the Seleucid dynasty.
63 (*circa*).	*The Psalms of Solomon.*
56.	*Cicero's speech* Pro Sestio.
55 (*circa*).	*The* De Rerum Natura *of Lucretius.*
53.	The Parthian horsed archers defeat the legions under Crassus at Carrhae.
51.	*The* De Republica *of Cicero.*
50.	*Death of Posidonius, who had taught in Rhodes for some 40 years; Cicero had attended his school in 78, and Pompey had visited him twice, in 67 and 63.*
50 (*circa*).	*Book of Wisdom (but its date is perhaps later).*
44.	*The* De Officiis *and the* De Legibus *of Cicero (the latter begun earlier).*
42 (*circa*).	*The Eclogues of Virgil.*
37–30.	*The Georgics of Virgil.*
36–30.	The schemes of Cleopatra and Antony for an Eastern Empire.
31.	Battle of Actium.
30.	Death of Cleopatra and Antony; end of the Kingdom of Egypt.
27.	Augustus organizes the Principate. *Composition of the* Aeneid *of Virgil; his death in* 19 B.C.
13.	The *Ara Pacis Augustae* established at Rome.
12.	The *Ara Augusti* dedicated at Lyons.
9.	Decree of the Greeks of the province of Asia making September 23 (the birthday of Augustus) New Year's Day. [At some time during his principate Augustus planned that the *decuriones* of his colonies in Italy should vote at home for the election of Roman magistrates, and have their votes sent in sealed boxes to Rome (an 'Italian' policy adverse to the monopoly of the *Urbs Romana*).]

THE FIRST CENTURY A.D.

9.	Defeat and annihilation of a Roman army under Varus by Arminius in Germany.
14.	The record of his *Res Gestae* compiled by Augustus (preserved in the *Monumentum Ancyranum*). Death of Augustus.
35 (*circa*).	*Beginning of the missionary work of St. Paul, which lasted for the thirty years down to his death about 64 A.D.; composition of his Epistles during these years.*
45.	*Death of Philo Iudaeus of Alexandria (born 30 B.C.).*
50.	*The Pseudo-Aristotelian treatise* De Mundo.
54–68.	Reign of Nero; persecution of Christians (64); *writings of the younger Seneca, tutor and afterwards minister to Nero.*
69.	Vespasian proclaimed Emperor at Alexandria (July 69); *Lex de Imperio* in his favour enacted later in the year at Rome.
70.	Titus, his son, captures Jerusalem and destroys the Temple. *Some time after this date the three synoptic Gospels were written.*
74.	*Vespasian banishes philosophers from Rome (they were associated with some of the aristocracy in a* Fronde *against the principate which had begun in the reign of Nero and continued till the death of Domitian in 96). In the same year, however, Vespasian also issued a decree, which has been called 'the Charter of ancient Universities', conferring on rhetoricians and grammarians (paideutai) the right to form associations, along with exemption from a number of State obligations.*
82.	*Dio of Prusa banished by Domitian; Epictetus also banished about the same time.*
97 (*circa*).	*Tacitus writes the* Agricola *and the* Germania.

THE SECOND CENTURY A.D.

100 (*circa*).	Dio of Prusa; orations on kingship during the reign of Trajan (98–117).
100 (*circa*).	The Panegyricus of the younger Pliny, addressed to Trajan.
100 (*circa*).	The Epistle of Clement of Rome to the Corinthians, the Didachē (or Teaching of the Twelve Apostles), and the letters of Ignatius of Antioch.
100.	Epictetus teaches at Nicopolis (in Epirus) down to 135; Arrian records his Discourses (and also writes the Anabasis of Alexander) about the middle of the second century.
112.	Pliny in Bithynia as legatus pro praetore; his correspondence with Trajan.
117–38.	Reign of Hadrian; his phil-Hellene policy; development of Athens as a centre of Greek culture; foundation of the Panhellenion, with regular meetings in Athens. Death of Plutarch in Hadrian's reign.
150 (*circa*).	Eulogy of Rome by the Sophist Aelius Aristides; the Digesta of the jurist Salvius Iulianus, who had also revised (circa 130) the praetorian edict.
160 (*circa*).	The Institutes of Gaius. The Epistle to Diognetus may belong to this date, but it is possibly nearly a century later.
161–80.	Reign of Marcus Aurelius; his Meditations (170–80).
180 (*circa*).	Irenaeus of Lyons writes his Adversus Haereses, and Celsus his Alēthēs Logos.
197.	Tertullian (160–225) writes his Apologeticus.

THE THIRD CENTURY A.D.

193–235. Dynasty of the Severi; Syrian influence; the Empire and Sun-worship.

211–17. *The writings of the jurist Ulpian, who (like Papinian before him and like his contemporary Paulus) held the high judicial office of praefectus praetorio.*

212. The edict of Caracalla, or *Constitutio Antoniniana.*

217. *Philostratus writes the* Life of Apollonius of Tyana, *on the suggestion of Iulia Domna, the Syrian wife of the Emperor Septimius Severus. About this time died the theologian Clement of Alexandria (born circa 150), sometime head of the catechetical school at Alexandria.*

231. *Origen (185–255), the greatest thinker of the early Church, who had previously taught in the catechetical school at Alexandria, settles in Caesarea (Palestine), where he wrote the* Contra Celsum, *and left behind him a library used afterwards by Eusebius.*

250 (*circa*). *Greek, hitherto the language of the church in Rome, gives place to Latin.*

245–70. *Plotinus the neo-Platonist teaches in Rome.*

253–68. *Gallienus, joint-emperor for the first part of his reign with his father Valerian, was with his wife Salonina a patron of Plotinus and philosophy, and a phil-Hellene. He issued the first edict of toleration for Christians.*

270–5. Reign of the Emperor Aurelian; his cult of *Sol Invictus.*

270 onwards. *The writings of the neo-Pythagoreans Diotogenes and 'Ecphantus' may belong to this period (but they may conceivably be much earlier).*

284–305. Reign of the Emperor Diocletian.

THE FOURTH CENTURY A.D.

300 (*circa*). The *encomium on monarchy in the* Corpus Hermeticum (*Book XVIII*).

304 onwards. *Lactantius (circa 250–323?) writes his* Divine Institutes. *He may have drafted in 323 Constantine's* Oratio ad Sanctos.

306–37. Reign of the Emperor Constantine.

313. The 'Edict of Milan'; general toleration.

323. *This may be the year of the* Oratio ad Sanctos (*ascribed to Constantine*). *About this time (321) his coins cease to show the sign of* Sol Invictus, *which had been used from 310 onwards in his period of sun-worship.*

324. *Foundation of Constantinople. The Philosopher Sōpatros presides at the ceremony of foundation; in 326 a temple is dedicated in the city to Sophia.*

330 (*circa*). *Eusebius (260–340), after working in the library left by Origen at Caesarea, becomes bishop of Caesarea and acts afterwards as adviser to Constantine. Writer of a* Historia Ecclesiastica, *of a* Vita Constantini, *of a panegyric on Constantine, a chronology, and theological works.*

[364. *The address of the philosopher Themistius to the Emperor Jovian: A plea for freedom of belief.*

393. The year of the last Olympic games in antiquity.

394. *The address of Synesius to the Emperor Arcadius: a plea for national service.*]

For the general history of the whole period 338 B.C.–A.D. 337 the reader is referred to:

H. Bengston, *Griechische Geschichte* (Munich, 1950), pp. 306–591.

A. Piganiol, *Histoire de Rome* (4th edition, 1954), Part II, chap. 3 to the end (valuable for bibliography and notes).

The *Cambridge Ancient History* in the relevant Chapters of Vols. VI–XII (1927–39).

INDEX OF AUTHORS

FROM WHOM PASSAGES ARE TRANSLATED OR QUOTED

(Where no edition is mentioned, the text followed is that of an edition in one of the current Classical series—Budé, Loeb, Oxford, Teubner)

INDEX OF PERSONS AND SUBJECTS

PRINTED IN
GREAT BRITAIN
AT THE
UNIVERSITY PRESS
OXFORD
BY
CHARLES BATEY
PRINTER
TO THE
UNIVERSITY